An Anthology of Christian Mysticism

Harvey Egan, S.J.

An Anthology
of
Christian Mysticism

A PUEBLO BOOK

The Liturgical Press   Collegeville, Minnesota

Design by Frank Kacmarcik

The author and publisher are grateful to the publishers listed in the acknowledgement section for permission to reproduce extracts from copyrighted material in their publications.

A Pueblo Book published by The Liturgical Press

Library of Congress Cataloging-in-Publication Data
An Anthology of Christian Mysticism
p. cm.
"A Pueblo book."
Includes bibliographical references and index.
ISBN 0-8146-6012-6
1. Mysticism. I. Egan, Harvey D.
BV5082.2.C46 1991
248.2'2—dc20   91-17671
                                              CIP

To my mother and in memory of my father

CONTENTS

PREFACE

A 30-year love affair with the Christian mystics has led to the birth of this book. I was an electrical engineer who had read almost nothing religious since my grammar school catechisms, but in 1959 I read my first mystical text, St. John of the Cross's *Dark Night of the Soul*. The book stirred me deeply and I sensed how important it could be for authentic Christian living. I have never lost my initial conviction that John of the Cross and the other mystics of the Christian tradition are of immense importance to anyone interested in Christian living. I half-saw then what I see clearly now: the Church's pastoral life suffers much from its benign neglect of the enormously rich Christian mystical heritage.

My love for the mystics deepened in 1960, when I entered the Society of Jesus. Within two months, I completed Ignatius' 30-day retreat and experienced firsthand the healing and transforming power of his famous *Spiritual Exercises*. Despite my enthusiasm for the *Exercises*, my reading list did not include anything by or about St. Ignatius of Loyola. My master of novices, Father Thomas G. O'Callaghan, S.J., asked: "What do you have against Ignatius?" His ironic question was one of the great graces of my life: I had nothing against St. Ignatius; I simply needed direction.

Undoubtedly, Joseph de Guibert's *The Jesuits. Their Spiritual Doctrine and Practice*[1] was the most important book about Ignatius I read as a Jesuit novice too. De Guibert introduced me, as no other author has, to Ignatius' extraordinary mysticism and to the fecund spiritual and humanistic tradition of the Society of Jesus.

During my final year of formal philosophical studies in 1965, I read Elmer O'Brien's *The Varieties of Mystic Experience*.[2] Since I had read relatively few mystical texts, his excellent anthology introduced me to other titans of Christian living and broadened my appreciation of the riches of the Christian tradition. The anthology revealed how similar—despite their differences—the mystics are as pioneers of a transformed and totally authentic humanity. It also disclosed them as powerful amplifiers of the experience of God; of the faith, hope, and love in every human heart; and, as the full flowering of Christian life. Although I did not understand some texts until after years of study, spiritual experience, teaching, and priestly activity, O'Brien's book taught me the value of a good anthology. It also intensified my already deep interest in the Christian mystics.

I went to Germany in 1969 to begin doctoral studies in theology as a student of Karl Rahner. His theological approach had long attracted me because he anchored it solidly to reflection upon a central, though often hidden mystical experience that takes place in every human heart. He was also one of the few contemporary theologians with an unabashed interest in the mystics and their writings as a theological source.

My doctoral dissertation, *The Spiritual Exercises and the Ignatian Mystical Horizon*,[3] attempted to translate the mystical wisdom of St. Ignatius of Loyola into a modern framework by using Rahner's theological method. The fascination with Ignatius Loyola as mystic culminated in a 1987 book, *Ignatius Loyola the Mystic*,[4] in which I argued that Ignatius' pragmatic successes in asceticism, spirituality, and humanism have obscured Ignatius the mystic.

During my work with Rahner, a close friend urged me to study Eastern mysticisms. He argued that they had much to offer Christianity, noting that I would be forced eventually to take them seriously because Eastern religions had become such a fad in the United States. My study of contemporary theology and of Eastern mysticisms changed the way I approached the classical Christian mystics. Contemporary theological questions and the challenge from Eastern religions uncovered some of the profound wealth in the Christian mystical tradition. I became convinced of the need to retrieve these riches for Christian theology, spirituality, and mysticism.

In 1973, I began teaching courses in eastern and western mysticism at Santa Clara University in California. I used Walter T. Stace's anthology,[5] which gives short shrift to the Christian mystics and mistakenly asserts that all mysticisms are essentially the same. During this period, I was invited to give a series of talks on Christian spirituality and mysticism to an American Buddhist community. To my astonishment, I discovered that most of the membership were former Christians. As the talks went on it became apparent that they knew little about their own Christian mystical heritage.

I also conducted several Ignatian retreats and met an impressive community of Carmelite nuns. These experiences forced me to study the Christian mystics more extensively. Unless I knew my own mystical tradition well, I could not do justice to my courses, retreats, spiritual direction, and other pastoral activities. Most significantly, I realized that as important as the study of Eastern religions is and as necessary as it is for some Christians to study them, my vocation called me to give undivided attention to the Christian mystical tradition.

In 1975, I began teaching at Boston College. For my mysticism course, I used the excellent, but now out-of-print Capps and Wright anthology[6] to counterbalance Stace's excesses. In time, I turned my attention totally to Christian mysticism, wrote *What Are They Saying About Mysticism?*[7] to deepen the context for my courses and pastoral work, and *Christian Mysticism: The Future of a Tradition*,[8] strengthening my theoretical grasp of key Christian mystics and mystical theologians.

My teaching and priestly experiences, as well as the writing and results of the *Christian Mysticism* book, led to a strong desire to put together my own anthology. I wanted to stress how solidly biblical the Christian mystical tradition is and to treat a large number of Christian mystics, even if some selected texts are only snippets.

So this anthology begins with an explanation of Christian mysticism. It proceeds to show its continuity with biblical mysticism and underscores Jesus' trinitarian mysticism as the prime example of all genuine Christian mysticism. It moves on to a biographical and historical introduction to 55 mystics and/or mystical theologians from Origen to Karl Rahner.

I selected these individuals for several reasons: 1) Any anthology must contain titans such as Augustine, Ruusbroec, and John of the Cross; 2) Thirty years of reading the mystics and almost 20 in theology have taught me that some mystics are undeservedly neglected, including Angela of Foligno, Hadewijch, and Ramon Lull; 3) A comprehensive anthology must present a broad cross-section of mystical themes, such as the anonymous author of the *Cloud of Unknowing's* teaching on pseudo-contemplatives, St. John of the

Cross's description of the dark night of the soul, Faustina Kowalska's experience as a "victim" of divine mercy, Rahner's views on the mysticism of everyday life, and Gemma Galgani's experience of the complete stigmata.

I have stayed with the mainstream Christian mystics, deliberately avoiding Jacob Boehme and others who dabbled in alchemy. Simone Weil, Dag Hammarskjöld, and others were not selected because I do not consider them to be mystics of the authentic tradition. Though persons of unusual—and often attractive—spirituality, they lack the purgative, illuminative, and transformative depths attained by the mystics in the anthology. The interpretation of their own loneliness as an experience of God may be an attractive form of contemporary spirituality, but it is not Christian mysticism.

Meister Eckhart, Thomas Merton, Pierre Teilhard de Chardin, and Karl Rahner, though not mystics, were chosen because they are mystical theologians whose trenchant reflections and linguistic creativity have contributed significantly to the Christian spiritual and mystical tradition.

There may be no substitute for reading primary texts, but few people have the time and the resources to do so. I chose longer selections but did not shy away from short ones. Everyone should read Pascal's experience of God as fire, Francis of Assisi's "Canticle of Brother Sun" and prayer, Julian of Norwich's hazelnut vision, and Merton's remarks about "masked contemplatives." This may make Pascal seem more important than he is for mystical studies, but his text is important nonetheless.

In some cases, the texts were selected more for completeness than conviction. For example, commentators have long considered Hilton's parable of the pilgrim and Pascal's "Mystery of Christ" to be Christian classics. Though I disagree, I included these passages.

Pragmatic considerations also entered my decisions so that I refrained from selecting certain Eckhart masterpieces because I know from personal experience that students with considerable philosophical and theological sophistication could not comprehend them.

Finally, I attempted to keep footnotes to a minimum and eliminated the translators' and editors' footnotes in the selected texts.

I am especially grateful to Paulist Press for allowing me to use so much material from its Classics of Western Spirituality series. I also appreciate the permissions received from Cistercian Publications of Kalamazoo, Mich.; The Institute of Carmelite Studies, Washington, D.C.; and Bantam Doubleday Dell, New York, N.Y.

Other publishers and institutions that permitted reprinting are the Abhishiktananda Society, Delhi, India; Alba House, Staten Island, N.Y.; Cassell PLC, London; Curtis Brown LTD, New York, N.Y.; The Catholic University of American Press, Washington, D.C.; Cistercian Studies, the Abbey of Gethsemani, Ken.; Christian Classics, Westminster, Md.; Confraternity of the Precious Blood, Brooklyn, N.Y.; Crossroad/Continuum, New York, N.Y.; Dimension Books Inc., Denville, N.J.; Faber and Faber, London; Éditions Grasset, Paris; Michael Glazier, Inc., Wilmington, Del.; Gordon Press, New York, N.Y.; Iñigo Enterprises, London; Iona Community, Pearce Institute, Glasgow; Harper & Row, New York, N.Y.; Loyola University Press of Chicago, Ill.; The Marian Press, Stockbridge, Mass.; Medieval & Renaissance Texts & Studies, State University of New York at Binghamton; New American Library, New York, N.Y.; New Directions Publishing Company, New York, N.Y.; Pantheon Books, New York, N.Y.; Priory Press, Dominican Province of St. Albert the Great, River Forest, Ill.; Society for Promoting Christian Knowledge, London; Charles Scribner's Sons, New York, N.Y.; Tan Books and Publishers, Rockford, Ill.; Holy Transfiguration Monastery, Brookline, Mass.; and Penguin Books LTD, London.

Time to complete a project is one of the most precious gifts a person can receive. Thus I am deeply grateful to Santa Clara University for the Bannan Professorship for the 1987-1988 academic year and to Boston College for the 1989-1990 sabbatical year.

Special thanks to individuals who gave me so much help. I am sincerely grateful to Sr. Elizabeth of the Trinity, O.C.D., Santa Clara Carmel; to Sister Mary Magdelen, O.C.D., Darlington Carmel; to Sister Suzanne Noffke, O.P., visting professor, University of Chicago; to Professor Bernard McGinn, University of Chicago; to Fr. William

Harmless, S.J., Boston College; to Mary Luti, Andover Newton Theological School; to Alexander Wirth-Cauchon, Boston College's Computing Services; to Riasse-Phou Monk Paisius, St. Herman Brotherhood, Patina, Calif.; and to Fr. Charles Healey, S.J., Pope John XXIII Seminary, Weston, Mass. But very special thanks to Sr. Jo-Ann Veillette, S.A.S.V., for reading and rereading the entire manuscript, for the red ink marks, and for the encouragement.

The Christian mystic awakens to, is purified and illuminated by, and is eventually united with the God of love. As an icon of agapic love, the mystic both amplifies every person's more hidden life of faith, hope, and love and points the way to full human authenticity.

INTRODUCTION

A) WHAT IS CHRISTIAN MYSTICISM?

Christian mysticism is a way of life that involves the perfect fulfillment of loving God, neighbor, all God's creation, and oneself. It is the fundamental human process through which one becomes fully authentic by responding throughout life to a God who gives himself unconditionally as love and as the ultimate destiny of every person. It is an ordered movement toward ever higher levels of reality by which the self awakens to, is purified and illuminated by, and is eventually fully united with, the God of love.

Under God's palpable initiative and direction, mystics fall in love with God—at times abruptly, at times gradually. Through God's special activity, they realize that God is in love with them, and therefore we are all, at least secretly, in love with God and each other. The explicit awareness of God's burning love at the very roots of their being causes mystics an immense longing that allows them no peace until they are irrevocably united to God and transformed into God's very own life.

Awakened by God to holiness, mystics are sensitized to their own sinfulness and vileness. Past sins arise and torture them in a purifying way. Like the physical eye, their spirit's eye becomes extremely sensitive to a speck of dust. They may even experience themselves as a "lump of sin," wholly undeserving of God's mercy, forgiveness, and love (*The Cloud of Unknowing*, chapter 40). Yet this holy love purifies them by removing almost all traces of disorder and sin.

Mystics also experience the vast distance between themselves and their Creator. Steeped in their own terrifying nothingness, they wonder why they are not simply annihilated in the presence of this all-powerful and all-consuming God. Perhaps such experiences gave rise to Meister Eckhart's unorthodox statement: "All creatures are a pure nothing: I do not say they are a bit or that they are something but that they are a pure nothing."[1]

At this stage, mystics love God to some degree, but their quest is more self-seeking than God-seeking. They taste something of God's goodness and love, but their own sinfulness, creaturehood, and seemingly unbridgeable separation from God predominates. Hence, authentic mystics feel a deep need of penance and purification. In addition to long hours of prayer, one finds in the lives of most great mystics "holy follies," or great penances to atone for the sins of their past lives or for the sins of the world.

As they are purged of sensuality and self-love, mystics grow in virtue and in ability to surrender to healing and transforming love. Having stilled the surface mind, they are better able to turn inward, find interior stillness, forget the self, and attend to God's loving self-communication. A deep, joyful sense of being united with God permeates their consciousness.

Gradually, the living flame of God's love is experienced more as illumination than as purgation. It instills a sacramental expansion of consciousness, that is, a loving knowledge that enables mystics to find God in all things and all things in God. Now they have less need to forsake the world to find God. Yet no matter how intimate the mystics' relationship to God may seem, the concomitant experience of separation remains. They may be betrothed to God, but they are not yet married.

When the illuminative aspect of mysticism dominates, mystics discover a deeper sense of their enhanced, transformed self and God's intimacy. Visions, locutions, and a variety of secondary phenomena often occur. Some phenomena come from psychological dysfunction or even the demonic. Others, however, are the psychosomatic reverberations of God's self-communication taking hold of the entire person. God communicates himself to the mystic's spirit, soul, psyche, emotions, and body through these well-known mystical experiences to enhance the mystic's life and encourage even deeper surrender to and communion with God.

The illuminative aspect of God's mystical self-communication has its dark and purgative side, too. During the "dark night of the soul," emotional boredom, aridity, ennui, even near-despair are common. The mystic has an acute sense of sin. God's absence predominates, having, it seems, justifiably abandoned the contemplative. Immense longing for God, incredible loneliness, the feeling of utter impotence and isolation take over. Exterior trials in social, political, and ecclesiastical situations often accompany great interior trials.

Finally, the mystic realizes that the earlier phases of ascent were trite. The haunting presence of past sins, of the distance from God, being unable to love as much as one is loved are concerns that become almost overpowering. Mystics speak of this phase as a cruel spiritual death, like "going down to hell alive" (St. John of the Cross). Nonetheless, mystical death is God's gift to the mystic, the dark side of God's loving, transforming self-communication. Mystical purgation, especially in this radical form, is totally God's doing. Human efforts cannot bring it about.

Although God, through great consolations, prepares the mystic beforehand for this mystical death, the mystic must possess the requisite psychological makeup to endure this stage. Mysticism in the strict sense requires extraordinary moral and psychological tenacity, as well as heroic concentration. The authentic mystics are definitely the pioneers, heroes, and geniuses of the spiritual life. There may be something in common between a Bach, Beethoven, or Mozart and any lover of music, but few music aficionados are musical geniuses. This analogy likewise holds in the spiritual life.

The unitive life is the last stage of mystical ascent. The mystic becomes as closely united to God through God's love as God is united to his own being by nature. Mystically married to God, the mystic becomes "God by participation." Nonetheless, this union remains differentiated, that is, God and the mystic become one while remaining distinctly two. The mystic's person does not dissolve into God. In fact, the more deeply united to God the mystic becomes, the more the mystic's individuality is confirmed and enhanced.

Mystical marriage bestows the conscious sharing in God's own life and power and almost complete self-forgetfulness. The mystic now seeks only God's will and honor and desires to serve God totally. Although external trials may continue, absolutely nothing can touch the peace and freedom at the deepest core of the mystic's being. The transformed mystic desires greatly to suffer, but in no way does this suffering disturb the peace that flows from the ever present, explicit awareness of living God's very own life. In fact, the only thing separating the mystic from the beatific vision is this life itself.

The mystic is experientially united to a love that communicates itself to all persons and to all things. Therefore, the more deeply the mystic experiences union with God, the more deeply union with God's creation is experienced. Transformed by and into Love itself, the mystic becomes creative, totally self-giving, radically concerned about others—in short, spiritually fecund.

Hence, mystics heal in their own persons and through apostolic service the fragmentation found in so much of human life. They become an even deeper part of the great process of life. Wholly in God, yet totally in the world, they experience both absolute peace and a holy anxiety to serve God and God's world.

The mystics insist, however, that the mystical life is more than heroic virtue or service to the world. These are the outward expressions of their union with God, the sacramental expression of their mystical lives. They are socially and often politically active because they seek God and God alone. Only this—not "experiences," not a transformed personality, not serving the world—gives the mystical life its ultimate value.

Nonetheless, the mystics are the most impressive servants of humanity the world has ever seen. These deified, christified, spirit-filled persons are the amplifiers of every person's more hidden life of faith, hope, and love. Their lives help us hear the interior whispers and see the faint flickers of divine truth and love in ourselves and others. The Christian mystics point the way to fully authentic human life by illustrating what it means to be a human being, what life means: eternal union (which begins here) with the God of love.

B) A BRIEF HISTORY OF THE WORD "MYSTICISM"

The word "mysticism" is not found in the Bible. Historically, the word is associated with the Hellenistic mystery religions and cults of the pre-Christian and early Christian era. The "mystical ones" (Greek: *hoi mystai*, occasionally: *hoi mystikoi*), were those who had been initiated into the secret rites (*ta mystika*) of the mystery religions and cults. Moreover, the mystics were required to keep secret the rituals into which they had been initiated. The word "mystical," therefore, originally referred to the cultic or ritual secrets revealed only to the initiated, the mystics. The mystical secret was only a secret about the purely material aspects of the rites and rituals of the Greek mystery religions.

Neoplatonic philosophers may have applied the word "mystical" to some of their speculative doctrines because they found certain aspects of these mystery religions conducive to their way of life and thinking. The Greek verb *myo* means to close the eyes, and some of these philosophers urged a deliberate shutting of the eyes to all external reality in order to obtain a secret, or mystical knowledge fostered by introverted contemplation. Withdrawing from everything external to enter fully into oneself allowed a person to receive inner, divine illuminations.

The great Jewish religious thinker Philo of Alexandria (20 B.C.- 50 A.D.) welded Jewish beliefs and spirituality with Greek thought. He focused sharply on the "mystical," or allegorical, interpretation of scripture. To him, "mystical" did not refer to the secret details of a ritual but to the secret and hidden meaning of God's word. Thus, he was probably the bridge between the Jewish and Greek worlds for the transposed meaning of the word "mystical" as the later Church Fathers used it with respect to scripture.

To many Alexandrian Christians and the early Greek Fathers, "mystical" signified the allegorical interpretation of scripture, especially the disclosing of Christ as the key in unlocking the secrets of the

Old Testament. Origen (185-254) is an example of those Christians who considered exegesis as "mystical and ineffable contemplation" that must combine both scholarly erudition and experiential knowledge of God. The divine reality ushered in by Jesus Christ, the knowledge of divine things, and the spiritual reality present in all genuine worship were likewise considered "mystical." Eventually, Christians used the word "mystical" with respect to the sacraments, especially the eucharist. By the time of Roman Emperor Constantine, the word "mystical" had biblical, liturgical, and sacramental connotations and often denoted the hidden presence of Christ in the scriptures, the liturgy, and the sacraments. It often meant his "spiritual" presence.

The word "mystical" entered definitively into Christian vocabulary, however, through the influential writings of Pseudo-Dionysius, a sixth-century Syrian monk. Although he still used the word "mystical" in discussing problems of the interpretation of scripture, his treatise, the *Mystica Theologia,* taught a mystical contemplation that permitted a person to know God as the "Divine Darkness" by way of unknowing.

However, the phrase "mystical theology" gradually came to mean the knowledge of God attained by direct, immediate, and ineffable contemplation. It was distinguished from both "natural theology" (knowledge of God obtained from creatures) and "dogmatic theology" (knowledge of God received from revelation). St. John of the Cross (1542-1591), for example, spoke of mystical theology as a secret wisdom infused by God into the soul through love. Therefore, the term "mystical theology" originally referred to mystical experience. Contemporary usage, on the other hand, equates mystical theology with the doctrines and theories of mystical experience.

The noun "mysticism" came into common parlance in the 17th century dispute about the place of human effort in contemplative prayer. Mysticism denoted "infused contemplation" in contrast to "acquired contemplation." One attains the latter through "ordinary" grace, asceticism, and psychological concentration. In the former, God makes himself known to the individual through a special grace beyond all human effort.

Some contemporary commentators define mysticism as the implicit or explicit faith, hope, and love that arise in anyone fully faithful to the demands of daily life. Self-surrender—even if only through hidden faith, hope, and love—to the mystery that haunts and graces one's life forms what these commentators refer to as "the mysticism of everyday life."[2]

For example, utter loneliness may contain a silent but sustaining presence. A person may forgive without expecting reward or feeling good about being selfless. The mysticism of everyday life occurs in the selfless love of others or in the radical fidelity to conscience—even if one looks like a fool to others. It also takes place when one is faithful, hopeful, and loving without apparent reasons for so being. To experience immense longing, that is, the wide gulf between what one truly desires and what life actually gives—yet to continue "hoping against hope"—is to experience the mysticism of everyday life.

Even the atheist who lives moderately, selflessly, and courageously experiences the mysticism of daily life. A total acceptance of life and of oneself, despite the collapse of all tangible supports, is perhaps the secular mystical experience. Anyone who does this accepts the holy mystery that fills the emptiness of oneself and life. Because Christ's grace supports the selflessness required for the total acceptance of life, oneself, and the mystery that sustains both, the mysticism of daily life is, at least anonymously, Christian, that is, Christian in fact but not in name.

To speak of a mysticism of everyday life calls attention to the astonishing fact that:

In every human being . . . there is something like an anonymous, unthematic, perhaps repressed, basic experience of God, which is constitutive of man in his concrete makeup (of nature and grace), which can be repressed but not destroyed, which is "mystical" or (if you prefer a more cautious terminology) has its climax in what the older teachers called infused contemplation.[3]

This means that everyone experiences, if only vaguely, a holy, loving mystery. God's self-communication—grace—does not invade the human situation and person extrinsically, but it is intrinsic to human nature itself. One can talk but abstractly about being human without mentioning God's self-communication.

This means, too, that mystical experience does not differ from the ordinary life of grace. No intermediate stage exists between the everyday life of Christian faith, hope, and love and the beatific, or direct, vision of God. Even the extraordinary mystical experiences of the saints never surpass God-given faith, hope, and love. Yet, to speak of a mysticism of everyday life can be misleading because so speaking seems to equate piety, spirituality, and mysticism. More to the point, most mystics acknowledged by the Christian tradition would agree that mysticism in the strict sense is wholly God's gift in a way extraordinarily different from the mysticism of everyday life and from genuine Christian piety and spirituality.

Moreover, to many contemporary commentators, mysticism in the strict sense involves an experience of God that is somehow direct, immediate, intuitive, and beyond the normal workings of the senses and intellect. The mystic is absolutely certain of God's presence and speaks about a particular type of spiritual sensation. The Christian mystical tradition attests to a spiritual, or mystical, form of touching, hearing, tasting, smelling, and seeing God.

The genuine mystic is purified and illuminated by, and eventually united to, a personal God. From this loving union flows a loving knowledge, a "secret wisdom" that short-circuits the memory and stupefies the intellect because it surpasses abstract, conceptual knowledge. Although we can dispose ourselves to receive it, human effort alone cannot bring it about because it is strictly God's gift.

It must be emphasized, however, that the best of the Christian tradition never reduced mysticism to the psychological level nor dissociated it from its biblical, liturgical, and sacramental level. As Louis Bouyer writes, Christian mysticism "is always the experience of an invisible objective world: the world whose coming the Scriptures reveal to us in Jesus Christ, the world into which we enter, ontologically, through the liturgy, through this same Jesus Christ ever present in the Church."[4]

C) COMMON MISCONCEPTIONS

Unfortunately, some contemporary commentators often equate mysticism with irrationalism or impracticality in dealing with daily living. Still others associate it with parapsychological phenomena, the occult, and demonology.

Another common line of current opinion reduces mysticism to moments of ecstatic rapture triggered by anything from artistic inspiration to psychedelic drugs. One school of thought falsely equates mysticism with repressed eroticism, madness, or a variety of "altered states of consciousness," usually engendered by sensory deprivation. A few of the more extreme theories hold that mysticism is a form of "remembrance" of biological conception, life in the womb, or early nursing experiences.

Some commentators attempt to dilute mysticism by identifying it with Christian religious experience in general. Another opinion explains mysticism as a form of experience and life diametrically opposed to an ecclesiastical life of the sacraments, dogma, and authority. According to this view, the mystic is inherently individualistic, iconoclastic, and heretical.

English philosopher Walter T. Stace's influence on contemporary thinking about mysticism has been enormous but pernicious. Writes Stace: "The core of the [mystical] experience is thus an undifferentiated unity—a oneness or unity in which there is no internal division, no multiplicity."[5] Undifferentiated unity signifies that the mystic experiences a total fusion with or dissolution into the Absolute. Mystics, seeing no difference between themselves and the Absolute, claim to be it. This view—actually a philosophical abstraction—rules out the possibility of an authentic Christian mysticism.

One more common mistake is to equate mysticism with the supernatural suspension of the laws of nature. To many, mysticism denotes the miraculous. This line of thought sees the mystic as someone invaded by God's grace that produces a host of extraordinary psychosomatic phenomena, such as the stigmata and visions. With the widespread growth of various neo-Pentecostal movements, charismatic phenomena such as prophecy, speaking in tongues (glossolalia), faith healing, and so on, may be erroneously identified with mysticism.

Influential theologians, including Karl Barth, Emil Brunner, Friedrich Heiler, Albrecht Ritschl, Nathan Söderblom, Ernst Troeltsch, and Adolf Harnack, have also contributed to current misunderstandings. They sharply distinguish biblical, prophetic religions from Oriental mystical religions, claiming that the two are mutually exclusive. Moreover, these authors reject the longstanding Christian mystical tradition as a pagan, neo-Platonic infection and deformation of Christianity, or as Roman Catholic piety in an extreme form.

From this perspective, Christian mysticism is a contradiction in terms. According to these thinkers, genuine Christian faith should reject mysticism as a "work," "law," or "religion" in the most pejorative sense. Barth typifies this view when he considers mysticism as more pernicious than even self-righteous Pharisaism "because it lies so near to the righteousness of God, and it, too, is excluded—at the last moment."[6]

However, other commentators correctly reject the views that mysticism cannot be reconciled with biblical, prophetic religion and that Christian mysticism is a neo-Platonic distortion of genuine biblical Christianity.[7] The writings of the Christian mystics do abound with references to the scriptures because they found in them paradigms and exemplars of their own lives and experiences, as well as suitable imagery, language, and symbolism to express these. To be sure, the word "mysticism" is not found in the Bible. Still, the reality is there and not merely by way of exception. Mysticism, as we shall see in the next chapter, is a reality connected intimately with the very essence of revealed, biblical religions.

Authentic Christian mysticism is founded upon the
solidly mystical spirituality of the Old Testament, of
the New Testament, and Jesus' trinitarian mystical
consciousness that reached its high point in his
salvific death and resurrection.

BIBLICAL MYSTICISM

A) MYSTICISM IN THE OLD TESTAMENT

The scriptures record God's "mighty deeds," or what he did for his
people and how they responded. The Jewish religious consciousness was especially sensitive to history as a sacred, saving sign that
revealed God's plan for and to Israel. In a sense, history was the sacrament of Israel's religion. The particular, contingent course of historical events revealed to her the reality of the interaction between
the divine and the human.

Therefore, the scriptures are not an historical tract in the contemporary sense. The sacred writers grasped the deeper meaning, the
salvific significance, the mystical dimension of the events of history.
In this sense, Church Fathers justifiably searched for the spiritual or
mystical sense of the Jewish scriptures. That the books of the Old
Testament "acquire and show forth their full meaning in the New
Testament . . . and in turn shed light on it and explain it"[1] highlights their mystical quality.

It is within this context that one can understand what St. Thomas
Aquinas meant when he wrote, "Holy Scripture is called the Heart
of Christ, because it reveals his Heart."[2] It likewise explains the conviction of the Church Fathers that the mystical sense of Scripture is
the cornerstone of orthodoxy and authentic Christian living.

The God "who dwells in unapproachable light, whom no man has ever seen or can see" (1 Tm 6:16), created humanity in his very image and likeness. By way of God's self-communication, he united humanity with himself through a variety of special covenants. For example, before their sin, Adam and Eve enjoyed God's intimate presence without interruption. Many theologians contend that Adam and Eve loved all creatures in God and God in all creatures. Their graced condition endowed them with a mystical faith far beyond "ordinary" faith, but still short of the beatific vision. Thus, they possessed a mystical knowledge and love of God almost beyond description.

Abraham, Jacob, Moses, Samuel, and other patriarchs of the Old Testament experienced God's intimate call, had their faith tested, wrestled with and were blessed by God, and spoke to him as a personal friend. Often they were afraid and speechless in his presence. Nonetheless, they were visibly transformed by their encounters, drawn to him as their greatest good, and convinced that he was with his people in all they did and underwent.

Moses and Jacob claimed face-to-face meetings with God—with some qualifications as to how directly they gazed into his face (Gn 32:30; Ex 33:11,23; Nm 12:7; Dt 34:10). Jacob boasted that he had wrestled with God and survived—an experience that left him with an overwhelming sense of God's awesome holiness (Gn 32:24f.). When Job could say to God, "Now my eyes see thee" (Jb 42:5), his agonizing questions ceased and he repented "in dust and ashes."

With some qualifications, the same can be said of the great Old Testament prophets. For example, Elijah, Isaiah, Jeremiah, Ezekiel, Hosea, and Amos were called in a most intimate way to be God's spokesmen. They experienced God as overwhelmingly holy and as "living water," the source of all authentic life, one upon whom they could always count because of his "everlasting love" (Jer 31:3). God's presence, they believed, rendered them invincible in Holy War, if they obeyed his commands.

But God always left his word burning in their hearts, rendering them both powerful to speak it and incapable of holding it in. Their authentication to speak God's word often came because they had "stood in the council of the Lord" (Jer 23:18). Their felt knowledge of God resulted in their invincible trust in God's faithfulness, tenderness, compassion, love, and wrath.

Having received God's Spirit into their hearts, some prophesied a time when all God's people would definitely receive the Holy Spirit. Other prophets called their people to conversion and insisted upon a mystical sabbath rest (Is 30:15), that is, resting in the presence of God. Others prophesied about a coming "son of man" (Dn 7), and established the foundations for a messianic mysticism by engendering an intense desire for the "one who is to come" to establish God's dominion and power over everything.

Many Old Testament prophets were essentially mystics in action.[3] Their profound experience of God in the present sensitized them both to what God had done for his people in the past and to the contemporary social, political, and economic scene. By virtue of their mystical experience of God in the core of their being, they comprehended the incongruence of their times with God's will for his people. In this way they addressed the burning questions of their day. In view of how God had acted in the past when his people obeyed or disobeyed, the prophets did not hesitate to say what God would do for or to them in the future.

The Old Testament patriarchs and prophets are Jewish examples of those who experienced God as the Holy, the tremendous and fascinating mystery.[4] Although absolutely transcendent, wholly other, and darkness itself, he was intimately near and the very light of their lives. His awesome presence evoked feelings of fear, dread, powerlessness, openness to annihilation, creaturely nothingness, and sinfulness.

Nevertheless, this totally good God also attracted, charmed, intoxicated, ravished, and fascinated those exposed to his presence. The holy One awakened radical and transformative feelings of gratitude, dedication, praise, trust, submission, and love. He was experienced as the object of the deepest human desires, searchings, and yearnings. To be united with this living, vital God was the end and goal of all living. It was life itself. This is authentic mysticism.

The patriarchs and the prophets taught the Israelites to expect the same gift of faith as they themselves had received. Israel's faithful certainly experienced communion with God, his saving presence, his protecting hand, and his steadfast love—and some in such a radically purifying, illuminating, and unitive way that it totally transformed their lives.

The Old Testament texts indicate a difference of intensity between the mystical experience of the patriarchs and prophets and the living faith of the average Israelite, but they say nothing about a qualitative difference. The whole context of salvation history and the general laws of God's self-communication—grace—point in fact to faith as the theological locus of mystical experience.

The psalms attest in a special way to Israel's mystical faith. One finds there the mystic's sense of God's infinity, nearness, and joys of communion with him. The hunger and thirst for the God who is light, love, living water, and life itself permeate the psalms. "Be still and know that I am the Lord" (Ps 46:10) is a profound call to mystical faith. The frequency of the words "love" (*ahabah*) and "loving kindness" (*hesed*) underscores the intense intimacy that existed between God and his people. The psalms attest that because we live, move, and have our being in God, no one can escape God's loving presence (Ps 139:7-18).

The felt presence of God that permeated Israel's life completed itself in the blessings and praises found throughout the psalms. They attest that the believer is unconquerable because of God's steadfast love. God can be trusted and must be praised in *all* circumstances.[5] He is praised not only for what he does, but especially for what he is. His beauty, goodness, holiness, and love fill both the created universe and the depths of the human heart. So unselfish is the praise expressed in the psalms that the psalmist wishes to escape death only because in Sheol praise of God is no longer possible. To praise God, according to the psalmist, is life itself.

The Old Testament cries out with intense longings and contains a promise directed toward the future. As Jesus said: ". . . many prophets and righteous men longed to see what you see, and did not see it, and to hear what you hear, and did not hear it" (Mt 13:17). Although God partially satisfied the desires of his people, Israel experienced that it "did not receive what was promised, since God had foreseen something better for us . . ." (Heb 11:39b-40). That "something better" is, of course, Jesus Christ, who proclaimed to the Jews: "Your father Abraham rejoiced that he was to see my day" (Jn 8:56).

Old Testament mysticism remains a preliminary stage to God's new covenant, which would "give the light of the knowledge of the glory of God in the face of Christ" (2 Cor 4:6). Humanity would be able to gaze upon the human face of God and live. The crucified and risen Christ highlights that God is definitively and irreversibly united with his people. "The mediator of a new covenant" (Heb 9:15) established, revealed, and made mysticism accessible in its purest and unsurpassable forms.

B) MYSTICISM IN THE NEW TESTAMENT

a) THE MYSTICISM OF JESUS CHRIST

Jesus Christ is the foundation of all Christian mysticism. Because of the permanent union of a human nature with the divine Person of the Word, Jesus Christ possessed not only a divine knowledge, but also an immediate, direct, and unique human knowledge of the Father, of himself as the Son, and of the Holy Spirit.[6] Jesus' trinitarian consciousness can be called a mystical consciousness in the highest sense. Moreover, the hypostatic union of Jesus' human and divine natures is the ground and goal of the mystical life: the ability for perfect, total surrender in love to the God who wishes us to be fully united with him.

Jesus claimed that "no one knows the Son except the Father, and no one knows the Father except the Son, and anyone to whom the Son chooses to reveal him" (Mt 11:27). In this and other places in the New Testament (Jn 7:29; 8:55), Jesus spoke of his intimate, full, personal, filial loving knowledge of his Father. He knew that he had come from the Father (Jn 5:23) and would return to him (Jn 8:14). The oneness he enjoyed with his Father dominated his consciousness. He heard his Father's word (Jn 8:26), knew his will (Jn 5:30), and saw him working (Jn 5:19). So intimate was Jesus' relationship with his Father that the Father showed him everything he did (Jn 5:20).

In short, Jesus "knew" the Father in the fully biblical sense of the word: experiential loving knowledge. Not only did he lovingly know the Father at a level never known before; he could also enable others to share in his experience of the Father (Mt 11:27; Jn 1:18). Because he was God's Word, light, and life in the absolute sense, he could instill wisdom, light, and life in the heart of those who loved him (Eph 3:17).

To see Christ, moreover, is to see the Father (Jn 14:19). To hear him is to hear the Father (Lk 10:16). To know Christ is to know the Father, and this mystical knowledge of the Father and the Son is eternal life itself (Jn 17:3). To love Christ is to be loved by the Father, a God revealed by Jesus as Love itself (Jn 14:21; 1 Jn 4:8). Jesus promised that those who believed would become one with him and the Father. They would experience the divine Love that existed between him and the Father, that that they, too, could be one, just as Jesus and the Father were one (Jn 17:20).

As the visibility and tangibility of the Father's unconditional love for humanity, Christ is the visible sign that contains what it signifies, or the sacrament of what mysticism is all about: total union and oneness with the God of love. It must be emphasized, however, that the union and oneness proclaimed by Jesus are not fusion with or dissolution into God, but abiding in and indwelling with him. This is the mystery of mystical love: two or more become one, but never lose their individual identities.

Several commentators have underscored Jesus' use of the word "Abba" ("beloved Father," "Daddy") when he spoke to God.[7] Because of the intimacy of this word, no Jew of Jesus' day would ever address God in this way. To pray to God with such filial affection shocked Jewish religious sensibilities.

Jesus' use of "Abba" when he turned to God was unique. Confidently, reverently, obediently, but with full intimacy and familiarity, Jesus called God his "Daddy." This word captures the mystery of Jesus' identity and mission: a full, filial relationship with God. Because of the depths at which he and the Father were one, Jesus experienced himself as *the* Son, as the authenticated revelation of the Father and his will. Jesus' filial consciousness is the exemplar of the perfect mystic's intimate relationship with the Father, God above us, loving Transcendence.

During Jesus' time, the Jews were convinced that with the death of the last writing prophets, the Spirit had been quenched because of Israel's sins. Only in the last days would God's Spirit come to satisfy definitively Israel's great longings for God's presence.

In this context, it is significant that Jesus made the unusual and explicit claim that he himself possessed the Holy Spirit. The gospels portray Jesus both as driven by the Spirit, doing what he does through the Spirit's power, and as its definitive bearer who would give this Spirit at his death. The gospels depict Jesus as the eschatological prophet who brought final revelation and demanded absolute obedience, because in him the eschatological age had dawned.

John's gospel describes the Holy Spirit less as the impetus behind Jesus' ministry than as the "Counselor" to continue and complete it. To John, the Holy Spirit is another Jesus (Jn 14:16), or simply Jesus' Spirit, the Spirit of truth (Jn 14:17). Jesus proclaimed that only in and through his redemptive death would the Holy Spirit be definitively given (Jn 7:39). Moreover, the Holy Spirit is the "living water" promised by Jesus and which flowed from his pierced heart (Jn 7:38; 19:34).

This Spirit would lead Christians into all truth (Jn 16:13) and enable Jesus always to be present to his people (Mt 28:20). Because the Spirit, as "another Counselor" (Jn 14:16), is also Jesus' permanent presence to his followers after the Easter appearances ceased, the Spirit would have the same relationship to Christians throughout the ages that Jesus had to the disciples during his ministry.

Jesus was intimately aware of the presence of the Holy Spirit, God in us, loving Immanence. Therefore, Jesus' mystical consciousness is essentially trinitarian. He knew himself to be uniquely Son because of his relationship to his Father and to the Spirit of their love. Jesus experienced the Father *ec*statically as God above us, the Holy Spirit *en*statically as God within us, and himself as the Son, or God with us. Because of Jesus' essentially trinitarian consciousness, all authentic Christian mysticism must also be trinitarian.

Jesus' trinitarian consciousness manifested itself indirectly in a number of ways. First, he did not hesitate to forgive sins, an activity that scandalized and astonished his contemporaries. What Jewish leader, king, priest, or prophet had ever dared to forgive sins? What religious founder of any of the world's great religions had ever done so?

Second, Jesus used the word "amen" in an unprecedented way, not to endorse or accept another's words, but to introduce his own words, and thereby place them in a divine context. In a way that parallels the Old Testament prophets' utterance, "Thus says the Lord," Jesus did not hesitate to say, "Amen I say to you."

Third, Jesus spoke with unprecedented confidence and authority. Unlike the religious authorities of his day who gathered together as many proof texts and precedents as possible, Jesus spoke with authority (Mk 1:22). He even claimed to be greater than the Temple (Mt 12:6), Jonah (Mt 12:41), and Solomon (Mt 12:42), placing himself above the best in the Old Testament tradition. This is especially clear with respect to his position toward Jewish law on murder, divorce, adultery, retaliation, and the taking of oaths. On these matters he claimed more authority than Moses and implicitly set himself up as God's equal when he said: "You have heard that it was said . . . But I say to you" (Mt 5:27f.).

Like many religious founders, Jesus offered counsel on how to live, preaching that God's reign was present because he was present. His hearers stood before God's definitive offer of salvation, the eruption of his reign into human history, because Jesus himself was present. He called people to faith, discipleship, and a final decision concerning God's reign in such a way that these decisions could not be separated from their fundamental decision toward him. "I tell you, every one who acknowledges me before men, the Son of man also will acknowledge before the angels of God; but he who denies me before men will be denied before the angels of God" (Lk 12: 8-9). Christ expected his disciples to take up their cross daily, to deny their very self, and to lose their lives for his sake. No Old Testament figure had ever spoken like that.

It must be emphasized, however, that Jesus did not "come to abolish the law and the prophets . . .but to fulfill them" (Mt 5:17). Jesus was thoroughly the son of a people who lived from the Old Testament. Accepting the social and religious milieu from which he came, he preached in the language, concepts, and imagery of his day. For the most part, he even interpreted himself and his mission in terms of the Old Testament, in which almost everything he said had already been said.

Even though there is an essential continuity in Jesus from the Old to the New Testaments, there is also discontinuity. He transcended his Jewish milieu, the wise men, religious founders, and philosophers of all ages.[8] Jesus' certainty about his relationship to his Father and to the Holy Spirit did not come from philosophical argumentation or a retelling of the ancient traditions of his people or by meditation. A unique experience of the Father and the Holy Spirit permeated everything he did and was. What other religious founder has been raised from the dead as God's confirmation of his identity and mission, or given his followers a *new* commandment, to love others as he had loved them (Jn 15:12f.)? It is no wonder that Jesus' disciples came to realize that they were in the presence of much more than another prophet or rabbi and adored him as "my Lord and my God" (Jn 20:28).

Through his ministry, passion, death, surrender of his Spirit, and resurrection appearances, Jesus' disciples underwent their own mystical purgation, illumination, and transformation. When they experientially received Jesus' Spirit on Pentecost Sunday (Acts 2:1f.), their mystical transformation deepened. From then on, with the Spirit's own power, they could and would preach about what God in Christ had done for his people. The Spirit had transformed them from a small band of disciples into the mystical Body of Christ, a Church with a powerful missionary impetus.

b) PAULINE MYSTICISM
The phrase, "in Christ," is a summary of Pauline mysticism, initiated by his encounter with the risen Christ on the road to Damascus (Acts 9:1-19; 22:3-16; 26:12-18; Gal 1:12). This event transformed the Jesus and Christian-hating Saul into Paul. This Paul denounced his prestigious past as so much "rubbish," willingly sacrificed everything, and would do anything so as to "gain Christ" (Phil 3:2-11).

Not only did Paul claim that this encounter was the last of the risen

Christ's appearances (1 Cor 15:8); but he also maintained that it established his claim to be a full apostle of Christ Jesus. "Have I not seen Jesus our Lord?" (I Cor 9:1), Paul said in defense of his "apostleship in the Lord," an apostleship to the Gentiles (Rom 11:13).

Moreover, Paul preached "not man's gospel," but a gospel that "came through a revelation of Jesus Christ" (Gal 1: 12). It must be emphasized that precisely as a "man *in Christ*" Paul was ecstatically taken up into the "third heaven," uncertain of being in or out of the body, and "heard things that cannot be told" (2 Cor 12:2).

Paul clearly experienced a God-given purgation that left him "utterly, unbearably crushed" and feeling that he "had received the sentence of death" (2 Cor 1:8-9). The God-given thorn in Paul's flesh and the "messenger" of Satan's harrassment caused him such acute suffering that he implored God to remove them. But only through suffering did he learn that only Christ Jesus could and had rescued him "from this body of death" (Rom 7:24).

Indeed, Paul's experience led him to boast about the insults, hardships, persecutions, and calamities he suffered in Christ's service (2 Cor 11: 21f.). Although "always carrying in the body the death of Jesus" (2 Cor 4:10), he experienced Christ's power working through his weakness (2 Cor 12:9-10). Thus, he wished to glory only "in the cross of our Lord Jesus Christ" (Gal 6:14),[9] "to know nothing among you except Jesus Christ and him crucified (1 Cor 2:2), and to "fill up what is lacking in Christ's afflictions for the sake of his body, that is the church" (Col 1:24). Paul's sole desire was to know Christ "and the power of his resurrection," and to "share his sufferings, becoming like him in his death, that if possible I may attain the resurrection from the dead" (Phil 3:11).

God mystically illuminated Paul and filled him with "all the riches of assured understanding and the knowledge of God's mystery, of Christ, in whom are hidden all the treasures of wisdom and knowledge" (Col 2:2-4). For Paul, the mystery that was made known to him "by revelation," "the mystery hidden for ages," was nothing less than "the mystery of Christ" (Eph 3:1f.), "in whom are hid all the treasures of wisdom and knowledge" (Col 2:3), "Christ the power of God and the wisdom of God" (1 Cor 1:24). In a beautiful statement on mystical illumination, Paul wrote: "For it is God who said, 'Let light shine out of darkness,' who has shone in our hearts to give the light of the knowledge of the glory of God in the face of Christ" (2 Cor 4:6).

God also mystically transformed Paul "into [Christ's] likeness from one degree of glory to another" (2 Cor 3:18). "Predestined to be conformed to the image of his Son" (Rom 8:29), Paul experienced that for him "to live is Christ, and to die is gain" (Phil 1:21). Because Paul found himself "in Christ" as the mystical ambience in which he lived, moved, and had his being, he experienced that to be "in Christ . . .is [to be] a new creation" (2 Cor 5:17; Gal 5:15).

So radically was Paul transformed into Christ, he experienced that it was no longer he who lived, but Christ living in him (Gal 2:20). Therefore, Paul was certain "that neither death, nor life, nor angels, nor principalities, nor things present, nor things to come, nor powers, nor height, nor depth, nor anything else in all creation, will be able to separate us from the love of God in Christ Jesus our Lord" (Rom 8:38-39).

For Paul, the Lord is the Spirit (2 Cor 3:17) through which "God's love has been poured into our hearts" (Rom 5:5). It is this Spirit who led Paul to experience the God of the Old Testament primarily as "the God and Father of our Lord Jesus Christ" (Eph 1:3; 2 Cor 1:3; 11:31). Jesus' Spirit taught Paul the same loving confidence and intimacy that Jesus himself enjoyed with his Father.

Paul considered it almost self-evident that all Christians, especially through baptism and the eucharist, had relatively easy access in their lives to an experience of the Father, the Son, and the Spirit.[10] Although he spoke of the "mature" in faith (1 Cor 2:6) and the "spiritual" (1 Cor 2:15), he expected mature, trinitarian faith of all Christians. For Paul, Christians received not a spirit of slavery but the very Spirit of God, the Spirit of sonship (Rom 8:14-15). Thus, "when we cry, 'Abba, Father!' it is the Spirit himself bearing witness with our spirit that we are children of God" (Rom 8:15-16). "With sighs too deep for words" (Rom 8:26), Christ's Spirit prays in us, even when our weakness prevents us from praying as we ought.

Thus, another significant aspect of Paul's "in Christ" mysticism is its trinitarianism. Paul's trinitarian mysticism prompted him to pray: "For this reason I bow my knees before the *Father*, from whom every family in heaven and on earth is named, that according to the riches of his glory he may grant you to be strengthened with might through his *Spirit* in the inner man, and that *Christ* may dwell in your hearts through faith; that you, being rooted and grounded in love, may have power to comprehend with all the saints what is the breadth and length and height and depth, and to know the love of Christ which surpasses knowledge, that you may be filled with all the fullness of God" (Eph 3:14-19, my emphasis).

So rooted and grounded, Christians experience a richer way of life (Eph 1:8-9) filled with love, joy, peace, self-control, gentleness, patience, and kindness (Gal 5:22) that enables them to bear each other's burden (Gal 6:2). As Paul says: "What no eye has seen, nor ear heard, nor the heart of man conceived, what God has prepared for those who love him, God has revealed to us through the Spirit" (1 Cor 2:9-10).

c) JOHANNINE MYSTICISM
If the phase "in Christ" is a summary phrase of Paul's trinitarian mysticism, Johannine mysticism can be summed up by the phrase, "Abide in me." John teaches that "if what you heard from the beginning abides in you, then you will abide in the Son and in the Father" (1 Jn 2:24). Of course, this is the "word of life" (1 Jn 1:1-3), the Word made flesh, "the eternal life which was with the Father and was made manifest to us." For John, not only the Father and the Son abide in the Christian, but also "the anointing which you have received from him abides in you" (1 Jn 2:27), that is, Jesus' own Spirit, the Spirit of Truth (Jn 14:14- 17). And we know that Christ abides in us "by the Spirit which he has given us" (1 Jn 3:24).

To John, God is love. Therefore, "he who abides in love abides in God, and God abides in him" (1 Jn 4:16). Only on the condition that we love one another will God abide in us and bring his love to perfection in us (1 Jn 4:12). God is love, and we know what love is because Christ willingly died for us (1 Jn 3:16). In fact, we can love only because God first loved us (1 Jn 4:19). Therefore, we, too, ought to be willing to die for others (1 Jn 3:16). This is the foundation of Jesus' *new* commandment, "that you love one another; even as I have loved you that you also love one another. By this all men will know that you are my disciples, if you have love for one another" (Jn 13:34-35).

Because Jesus and the Father are one (Jn 10:30), Johannine mysticism experiences that all Christians should be one, and that eternal life itself is to "know thee the only true God, and Jesus Christ whom thou hast sent" (Jn 17:3). This is the reason Jesus prayed that "they may all be one; even as thou, Father, art in me, and I in thee, that they also may be in us, so that the world may believe that thou hast sent me" (Jn 17:20). If the love with which the Father loved Jesus is in Jesus' disciples, then Jesus himself is in them (Jn 17:26).

As the true vine which the Father dresses, one must abide in Christ to bear any fruit (Jn 15:1-10). Jesus is the genuine light that enlightens everyone (Jn 1:9), because as the Word made flesh, Christ is everything that is knowable about God. Jesus is the true temple (Jn 2:21), the true abode of the Father's presence. Because Jesus is in the Father and the Father is in him, he who sees Christ has seen the Father (Jn 14:9-10). For this reason, John has his reader ponder the divine-human qualities manifested in Jesus' earthly life.

To John, Christ lifted up will draw everything to him once he is lifted up (Jn 12:32). The Spirit could be given only when Jesus was crucified, for out of his pierced heart would flow both blood and living water (Jn 7:38-39; 19:34). Hence, only Jesus, as the living bread and the giver of living water, can quench the mystical hunger and thirst. Christians abide mystically in Christ especially through baptism and the eucharist. Only someone "born of water and the Spirit" (Jn 3:5) can enter the kingdom of God. And only someone who "eats my flesh and drinks my blood abides in me and I in him" (Jn 6:56).

d) CONCLUDING SUMMARY

Therefore, the real ancestry of Christian mysticism is not to be found in the influence of Greek philosophy, but in the Bible. The "origins of the Christian mystical tradition"[11] are first and foremost in Scripture, not in neo-Platonism. Although the Christian mystical tradition was enriched by neo-Platonism and is being enriched in our time by Eastern religions, authentic Christian mysticism looks to the solidly mystical spirituality of the New Testament and Jesus' trinitarian mystical consciousness that reached its high point in his salvific death and resurrection. And both Jesus' mystical consciousness and New Testament mysticism in general cannot be understood without a knowledge of Old Testament mysticism.

The Christian sees in Jesus' death and resurrection the very cause and exemplar of the mystical life in all its purity. Jesus' saving death on the cross exemplifies the mystical letting go of everything consoling, tangible, and finite to surrender totally to the mystery of the Father's unconditional love. Jesus' cross reminds Christians that they can and must love to the end, for the Spirit is born in blood. By contemplating the cross one comprehends Jesus' *new* commandment: not only are we to love God with our whole being, not only are we to love our neighbor as ourselves, but that we are also called to love as *Christ* himself loved us (Jn 13:34; 15:12).

Jesus' bodily resurrection is the ultimate revelation of the Father's acceptance and confirmation of this act of loving surrender to unconditional love. Moreover, it is the seed of the new creation, the sacramental visibility of God's definitive mystical marriage with all creation. Jesus' risen, glorified body is what mysticism is all about: the loving union and transformation of all creation with and into the God of love, that in Christ one can truly be a "new creation" (2 Cor 5:17). Karl Rahner wrote: "Because Jesus Christ redeemed all creation in his love, along with mankind, Christian mysticism is neither a denial of the world nor a meeting with the infinite All, but a taking of the world with one to a loving encounter with the personal God."[12]

In addition to a trinitarian mysticism and one that centers on the crucified and risen Christ, the New Testament also teaches the ecclesiastical, social, and sacramental aspects of authentic Christian mysticism. These aspects show themselves especially in the New Testament's focus upon the mystical Body of Christ and on the liturgy, especially baptism and the eucharist. It is not surprising, therefore, that the original Christian use of the word "mystical" referred to liturgical experience of Jesus Christ always present in the Church. In summary, therefore, Christian mystical life must be emphatically trinitarian, ecclesiastical, sacramental, and inextricably bound to the crucified and risen Christ.

It is now time to allow 55 significant figures in the Christian mystical tradition—from Origen to Karl Rahner—to speak for themselves. Within this tradition, we shall find mystics who emphasize the intellectual side of mysticism and explain it according to the philosophy of their times. Others emphasize the ascetical, light, visionary, or love quality of the mystical life. The anthology also contains examples of bridal, spousal, trinitarian, service, and victim-soul mysticisms. In other words, God's purgative, illuminative, and transformative action—the individual mystic's participation in Christ's death and resurrection—manifests itself in a great variety of ways.

However, this anthology contains mystical *theologians*, as well as mystics. For example, Meister Eckhart, Thomas Merton, and Karl Rahner are not examples of mystics, but of mystical theologians. These persons of deep Christian spirituality did not travel the mystical path. And yet, their reflections upon and linguistic expressions of mystical experience significantly influenced the mystical tradition.

In order to guide the reader through this anthology, it might be helpful to keep the following questions in mind:
1) What is Christian mysticism?
2) Is it a psychological abnormality or does it lead to human authenticity?
3) Is Christian mysticism meant for everyone, or is it reserved for an elite?
4) How does the biblical foundation of Christian mysticism manifest itself throughout the tradition?
5) What is the relationship between asceticism and mysticism?
6) What relationship does Christian mysticism have to the occult?
7) What relationship does Christian mysticism have to secondary phenomena, such as, visions, locutions, ecstasies, levitation, and the like?
8) Does the Christian mystic's union with God dissolve or strengthen his or her identity?
9) Is Christian mysticism truly a way of life involving purgation, il-

lumination, union, and transformation?

10) Does the Christian mystic reject or enhance the religious tradition out of which he or she comes?

11) How do mystical experiences and their interpretations interact?

12) Is the mystic a selfish recluse or a powerful, pragmatic social force?

13) What do all Christian mystics have in common?

Origen conceived the mystical life as the full flowering and the explicit realization of Christ's union with the soul caused by baptism. He also viewed martyrdom as the apex of the Christian life, the perfect imitation of Christ, and a mysticism through which one is definitely purged by, illuminated by, and united to God in Christ.

ORIGEN

The oldest of seven children of fervent Christian parents, Origen was probably born in Alexandria, Egypt, at the height of the Roman persecutions. Leonides, his father, educated him and was martyred for the faith by the Roman Emperor Severus in 202, when Origen was in his teens. Only his mother's ingenuity in hiding his clothing prevented Origen from impulsively following his father to martyrdom. Origen expressed his constant desire for martyrdom in a letter to his father which became the first draft of one of his best works, *An Exhortation to Martyrdom.*[1]

Spared his father's fate, he proceeded to satisfy his own unquenchable thirst for martyrdom by a life of extraordinary asceticism. For example, he took literally the biblical text of Matthew 19:12 ("and there are eunuchs who have made themselves eunuchs for the sake of the kingdom of heaven") and castrated himself. This act would provide much fodder for his future enemies.

After their possessions were confiscated, Origen supported himself and his family by starting a school for grammar. Soon thereafter, the persecutions ended temporarily, and peace between Church and State was restored for a time. Undoubtedly, his exceptional brilliance and heroic witness, as well as the scarcity of skilled catechists, prompted Bishop Demetrius of Alexandria to place the

18-year-old Origen in charge of a large school for catechumens.

His reputation for learning and holiness attracted the attention of Church leaders in many countries, though not always favorably. Thus, while in Palestine in 230, Origen was ordained. However, an Alexandrian synod under Bishop Demetrius, who obviously had second thoughts about his onetime protégé, declared his ordination illicit, proclaimed him unfit for catechetical work, and banished him. Hence, he went to Caesarea to continue his life of Christian intellectualism. Under Emperor Decius, in 249-50, he was imprisoned, tortured, and cruelly kept alive in an attempt to make him apostasize. But he never succumbed. Released from prison when the emperor died, Origen lived only a few more years in broken health.

Within two centuries of his death, many Church officials and theologians denounced him—both for the daring of some of his ideas and because of the excesses of some of his disciples. The Second Council of Constantinople in 553 formally condemned several of his views. For many Eastern Christians, this condemnation earned him the epithet, "heretic of the heretics." Origen is best known as an exponent of the heretical theory of apocatastasis, that in the end, all—even the devils—will be saved. He also taught the preexistence of the human soul.

Origen's Christian genius was recognized during the Renaissance, and interest in his theological genius revived in the 20th century. He is widely recognized now as the first Christian exegetical giant, the first "systematic" theologian, and the first ascetical-mystical theologian.

Perhaps too much emphasis has been placed upon the intellectual achievements of this deeply spiritual man. Origen was a Christian humanist who blended great intellectual ability and a universal openness to all currents of thought with a passionate search for total truth that, for him, was to be found only in Christ crucified. Only because of his profound love of Christ crucified, the heart of, and the key to, Scripture, was Origen ready to "despoil the Egyptians," that is, to bring all the resources of his secular culture to bear on unlocking the mysteries of the Sacred Page.

Origen directed his ravenous intellectualism and passionate temperament to answering learned pagans' objections to Christianity. To do so, he mastered the secular sciences of his day, especially philology and philosophy. He excelled as a Master of the Sacred Page, that is, one who focused his universal intellectual interests upon the scholarly contemplation of Scripture. He bequeathed critical texts, scientific commentaries, learned homilies, and scholia (short, exegetical notes) as his patrimony to the Christian tradition.

Origen is mistakenly known as the father of allegorical interpretation. His exegesis is mystical, not allegorical, because he sought out the deepest meaning of Scripture with all the tools at his disposal. Origen viewed the divine-human drama—salvation history—not as the Platonic shadows of unchanging spiritual realities but as real history. Because the incarnate Word had been sought in the Old Testament, given in the New, and is fully assimilated only in the Church's total experience, Origen contended that Scripture's literal sense must flower into its mystical one.

The first selection is taken from Origen's masterpiece, *An Exhortation to Martyrdom*. The early Christians understood martyrdom as the apex of the Christian life and as perfect imitation of Christ. Through martyrdom, one also attained the full flowering of one's baptism into Christ crucified, total union with God, and the face-to-face vision of God.

In addition to understanding martyrdom in this way, Origen emphasized it as the perfection of Christian wisdom, the loving knowledge of the Unoriginated God revealed through his incarnate Word—a knowledge developed in contemplation that has transformed one's entire life at the price of a crucifying asceticism. Only when one is freed from everything corporeal, follows Christ into the depths and beyond the heavens, and attains God through Christ does the Christian know the greatest mysteries. These mysteries are attainable only by "friends of the Father and Teacher in heaven" and in "face-to-face" vision of God. Thus, for Origen, martyrdom is mysticism through which one is definitively purged by, illuminated by, and united to God in Christ.

It is important to note that Origen spoke not only of an "outward martyrdom" but also of a "martyrdom that is in secret." Origen contended that Christian faith itself is a martyrdom because of the combat one must do against the world, the flesh, and the devil. This theme runs through the entire corpus of his writings and provides the proper context for understanding his moral-ascetical doctrine that would play an important role in the monastic tradition.

Origen conceived the mystical life as the full flowering of and the explicit realization of Christ's union with the soul effected through baptism. It is the full flowering of Christian life, the life of one baptized in the Church and nourished by the Church's sacramental Word and Bread. But he understood martyrdom in this way, too. Both martyrdom and contemplation transform the soul into something "better than a soul," that is, into what it originally was, a mind (*nous*) made in God's image and likeness.

The second selection is taken from Origen's monumental *Commentary on the Song of Songs.* Origen was the first in the Christian tradition to interpret the Song of Songs as the intimate relationship between the Word and the soul, but he never dissociated it from the traditional interpretation that viewed it as the relationship between Christ and the Church. To Origen, this was the book for understanding the union of the bridal soul with the bridegroom Word, the ultimate book about the soul's intimate intercourse with God in Christ at the summit of the mystical life.

One sees in this selection Origen's greatest contribution to the Christian mystical tradition: the view of the mystical life as successive stages of purgation, illumination, and unification. He compares these stages to the contents of three books of Scripture. The book of Proverbs teaches morals, or virtue, and prepares the way for the assimilation of Ecclesiastes. That book teaches natural contemplation by which the correct attitude toward this world—a world both transient and yet holding together in Christ— is attained. Only then can one deal with the "enoptics," or contemplation, found in the Song of Songs.

Contemplation, to Origen, is both knowing God and being known by God; it is union with God and the vision by which the image of God, that we are, is reformed. By contemplation, one becomes divinized—a favorite theme of the Greek Fathers. As the founder of intellectual mysticism, Origen sees contemplation as the process by which the soul's highest point, the mind (*nous*), rediscovers its true nature. Hence, in Origen's view, ecstasy plays no role in contemplation, for it is the nature of *nous* to be united with God.

Moreover, Origen understands contemplation as the discovery of the deepest meaning of Sacred Scripture. Only by sudden awakenings, inspirations, and illuminations received from the Word does the Sacred Page reveal its secrets to the Christian exegete. Origen's Christ-mysticism and Word-mysticism are inextricably bound to his Scripture-mysticism, and vice versa.

Origen depicts the purgative, illuminative, and unitive stages as the seven songs sung by the soul that correspond to seven books of Scripture. The soul sings of its escape from Egypt (conversion), its crossing the Red Sea (baptism), its desert wanderings (asceticism, aridity), its wars against its enemies (moral struggle), the quenching of its thirst at the wells of living water (consolations), and the like. Origen, the optimist, emphasizes that the soul sings and rejoices at every stage of its journey until, graced by divine love and mercy, it is ready to sing the most sublime song of all, the Song of Songs.

The third series of texts were selected because Origen's views on the mystical senses profoundly influenced Christian mysticism. Because of the fall, not all Christians have the mystical senses. Some have only one or two. Still, they can be regained as a person passes through the purgative, illuminative, and unitive stages of mystical ascent. Under grace, the soul becomes spiritually sensitive and discerning. The mystical senses also represent, to Origen, the richness and variety of the soul's experiences in contemplation of the Spirit, the incarnate Word, and the Father. When the mystical senses become Christ, the Scriptures reveal their hidden meaning.

The three selections underscore Origen's conviction that darkness is only one stage of the mystical journey that ends in light through seeing and knowing God. Origen's light mysticism stands in sharp contrast to the views of some other mystics in this anthology (for example, Gregory of Nyssa and St. John of the Cross), who stress unceasing darkness and the total incomprehensibility of God.

These selections also highlight Origen's Christian Platonism. Before one ascends with Christ, one must first descend by imitating and participating in his entire history. Like Christ, the soul must progressively uproot itself from the world by detachment and stripping. Like Christ, it must also do battle against the demons. In this way the soul participates in Christ's "double-cross," that is, both the royal throne from which Christ exercised his universal kingship and the instrument by which the principalities and powers of this world were crucified and defeated.

But as Christ ascended to the Father, so also must the Christian. The selections indicate that Origen held the Greek view on the Trinity: There is one God because there is one Father, the Unoriginated God. The Word is the Father's image, contains the intelligible world that was created through and for the Word, and contemplates the Father unceasingly. One ascends to the Father through the Son in the Spirit.

Origen taught that a Christian possessed mystical as well as bodily senses. These would lead a person to a more profound understanding of Scripture. That knowledge, in turn, would lead to a deeper love of the incarnate Word, and then to a richer knowledge of the Father who is "all in all." The apex of Origen's Scripture-, Christ-, and Word-mysticism is his God (Father)-mysticism.[2]

THE TEXTS

AN EXHORTATION TO MARTYRDOM

XII. We must also understand that we have accepted what are called the covenants of God as agreements we have made with Him when we undertook to live the Christian life. And among our agreements with God was the entire citizenship of the Gospel, which says, "If any one would come after me, let him deny himself and take up his cross and follow me. For whoever would save his soul would lose it, and whoever loses his soul for my sake will save it" (Mt. 16:24-25). And we have often come more alive when we hear, "For what will it profit a man if he gains the whole world and forfeits his soul? Or what ransom shall a man give in return for his soul? For the Son of Man is to come with His angels in the glory of His Father, and then He will repay every one for what he had done" (Mt. 16:26-27).

That one must deny himself and take up his cross and follow Jesus is not only written in Matthew, the text of which we cited, but also in Luke and Mark. . . .

Long ago, therefore, we ought to have denied ourselves and said, "It is no longer I who live" (Gal. 2:20). Now let it be seen whether we have taken up our own crosses and followed Jesus; this happens if Christ lives in us. If we wish to save our soul in order to get it back better than a soul, let us lose it by our martyrdom. For if we lose it for Christ's sake, casting it at His feet in a death for Him, we shall gain possession of true salvation for it. . .

XIII. And according to some deeper insights Isaiah says, "I gave Egypt as your ransom, Ethiopia and Syene in exchange for you, because you were precious in my sight" (Is. 43:3-4). You will know the accurate interpretation of this passage and others if you desire in Christ to learn and to go beyond instruction in an enigma and so hasten to Him who calls you. Then you will know as friends of the Father and Teacher in heaven, since you have never before known face to face (cf. 1 Cor. 13:12). For friends learn not by enigmas, but by a form that is seen or by wisdom bare of words, symbols, and types; this will be possible when they attain to the nature of intelligible things and to the beauty of truth. If, then, you believe that Paul was caught up to the third heaven and was caught up into Paradise and heard things that cannot be told, which man may not utter (2 Cor. 12:2,4), you will consequently realize that you will presently know more and greater things than the unspeakable words uttered to Paul, after which he came down from the third heaven. But you will not come down if you take up the cross and follow Jesus, whom we have as a great High Priest who has passed through the heavens (cf. Heb. 4:14). And if you do not shrink from what following Him means, you will pass through the heavens, climbing above not only earth and earth's mysteries but also above the heavens and their mysteries. For in God there are treasured up much greater visions than these, which no bodily nature can comprehend, if it is not first delivered from everything corporeal. And I am convinced that God stores up and keeps by Himself much greater visions than the sun, the moon, and the chorus of the stars have seen, indeed than the holy angels have seen, whom God made wind and a flame of fire (cf. Ps. 104:4; Heb. 1:7). His purpose is to reveal them when the whole creation is set free from its bondage to the Enemy for the glorious liberty of the children of God (cf. Rom. 8:21).

XIV. Therefore, one of those already martyred and who possessed something more than many of the martyrs in their Christian love of learning will ascend quite swiftly to those heights. And you, holy Ambrose, by examining the saying of the Gospel with great care, are able to see that perhaps none or only a few will attain some special and greater flood of blessings. May such a lot be yours, if you get safely through the contest without flinching. . . .[3]

XXI. Let us enter the contest to win perfectly not only outward martyrdom, but also the martyrdom that is in secret, so that we too may utter the apostolic cry "For this is our boast, the martyrdom of our conscience that we have believed in the world . . .with holiness and godly sincerity" (2 Cor. 1:12). And let us join to the apostolic cry the prophetic one, "He knows the secrets of our hearts," especially if we are led away to death. Then we shall say to God what can be said only by martyrs, "For your sake we are slain all the day long; we are accounted as sheep for the slaughter" (Ps. 44:21-22). And if fear of the judges who threaten us with death should ever try to undermine us with the mind of the flesh (cf. Rom. 8:6f.), let us then say to them the verse from Proverbs, "My son, honor the Lord, and you will prevail. Fear no one else but Him" (Prov. 7:1 LXX).

XXII. . . . I pray that when you are at the gates of death, or rather freedom, especially if tortures are brought (for it is impossible to hope you will not suffer this from the will of the opposing powers), you will use such words as these, "It is clear to the Lord in His holy knowledge that though I might have been saved from death, I am enduring sufferings in my body, but in my soul I am glad to suffer these things because I fear Him" (2 Macc. 6:30). Such was the death of Eleazar, as it was said of him, "He left in his death an example of nobility and a memorial of courage, not only to the young but to the great body of his nation" (2 Macc. 6:31).[4]

This book seems to me an epithalamium, that is, a wedding song, written by Solomon in the form of a play, when he recited in the character of a bride who was being married and burned with a heavenly love for her bridegroom, who is the Word of God. For whether she is the soul made after His image or the Church, she has fallen deeply in love with Him. Moreover, this book of Scripture instructs us in the words this marvellous and perfect bridegroom uses toward the soul or the Church that has been united with Him. . . .

But if any one approaches who is a grown man according to the flesh, no little risk and danger arises for such a person from this book of Scripture. For if he does not know how to listen to the names of love purely and with chaste ears, he may twist everything he has heard from the inner man to the outer and fleshly man and be turned away from the Spirit to the flesh. Then he will nourish in himself fleshly desires, and it will seem because of the divine Scriptures that he is impelled and moved to the lusts of the flesh. For this reason I give warning and advice to everyone who is not yet free of the vexations of flesh and blood and who has not withdrawn from the desire for corporeal nature that he completely abstain from reading this book and what is said about it. Indeed, they say that the Hebrews observe the rule that unless some one has attained a perfect and mature age, he is not even permitted to hold this book in his hands. . . .

With all this in mind it seems necessary before we begin our discussion of what is written in this book to discuss briefly, first, love itself, which is the chief subject of the book, and next, the order of Solomon's books, among which this book is apparently in third place. . . .[5]

And to speak more plainly, if there is someone who still bears the image of the earthly according to the outer man, he is led by an earthly desire and love. But the person who bears the image of the heavenly according to the inner man is led by a heavenly desire and love (cf. 1 Cor. 15:49). Indeed, the soul is led by a heavenly love and desire when once the beauty and glory of the Word of God has been perceived, he falls in love with His splendor and by this receives from Him some dart and wound of love. For this Word is the image and brightness of the invisible God, the First Born of all creation, in whom all things were created, in heaven and on earth, visible and invisible (cf. Col. 1:15f.; Heb. 1:3). Therefore, if anyone has been able to hold in the breadth of his mind and to consider the glory and splendor of all those things created in Him, he will be struck by their very beauty and transfixed by the magnificence of their brilliance or, as the prophet says, "by the chosen arrow" (Is. 49:2). And he will receive from Him the saving wound and will burn with the blessed fire of His love. . . .[6]

For the time being these are the thoughts that have been able to come our way concerning love or loving affection, which is the theme of this epithalamium, the Song of Songs. But we must know how much ought to be said about this loving affection and how much God, if He is indeed loving Affection. For just as no one knows the Father except the Son and anyone to whom the Son chooses to reveal Him (Mt. 11:27), so no one knows loving affection except the Son. And likewise no one knows the Son, since He is also loving Affection, except the Father. And according to what is called loving affection it is only the Holy Spirit, who proceeds from the Father who, therefore, comprehends the thoughts of God as the spirit of a man knows a man's thoughts (cf. Jn. 15:26; 1 Cor. 2:11). Thus, this Paraclete, the Spirit of truth, who proceeds from the Father, goes about seeking if He may find any worthy and fit souls to whom He may reveal the excellence of that loving affection which is from God. Now therefore, by calling upon God the Father, who is loving Affection, through that loving Affection which is from Him, let us turn to the other subjects for discussion.

First, let us examine why it is, since the churches of God acknowledge three books written by Solomon, that of them the book of Proverbs is put first, the one called Ecclesiastes second, and the book Song of Songs has third place. . . There are three general disciplines by which one attains knowledge of the universe. The Greeks call them ethics, physics, and enoptics; and we give them the terms moral, natural, and contemplative. . . . Then the moral discipline is defined as the one by which an honorable manner of life is equipped and habits conducive to virtue are prepared. The natural discipline is defined as the consideration of the nature of each individual thing, according to which nothing in life happens contrary to nature, but each individual thing is assigned those uses for which it has been brought forth by the Creator. The contemplative discipline is defined as that by which we transcend visible things and contemplate something of divine and heavenly things and gaze at them with the mind alone, since they transcend corporeal appearance. . . .[7]

Thus, Solomon, since he wished to distinguish from one another and to separate what we have called earlier the three general disciplines, that is, moral, natural, and contemplative, set them forth in three books, each one in its own logical order.

Thus, he first taught in Proverbs the subject of morals, settings regulations for life together, as was fitting, in concise and brief maxims. And he included the second subject, which is called the natural discipline, in Ecclesiastes, in which he discusses many natural things. And by distinguishing them as empty and vain from what is useful and necessary, he warns that vanity must be abandoned and what is useful and right must be pursued. He also handed down the subject of contemplation in the book we have in hand, that is, the Song of Songs, in which he urges upon the soul the love of the heavenly and divine under the form of the bride and the bridegroom, teaching us that we must attain fellowship with God by the paths of loving affection and love. . . .[8]

But now let us ask first what the songs are of which this is said to be the Song of Songs. I think, then, that they are those that were sung of old by the prophets or by the angels. For the Law is said to have been "ordained by angels by the hand of an intermediary" (Gal. 3:19). Thus, all the proclamations made by them were songs that went before, sung by the friends of the bridegroom; but this is the one song that was to be sung in the form of an epithalamium to the bridegroom when He is about to take His bride. In it the bride does not want the song sung to her by the friends of the bridegroom right away, but she longs to hear the words of the bridegroom now present. She says, "Let Him kiss me with the kisses of His mouth" (Song 1:2). That is why it deserves to be placed before all the other songs. . . Thus, as the perfect bride of the perfect husband she received the words of the perfect teaching.

Now the first song is the one Moses and the children of Israel sang to God when they saw the Egyptians dead upon the seashore and when they saw the mighty hand and the stretched-out arm of the Lord and believed in God and in His servant Moses (Ex. 14. 14:30f, 6:6). Then they sang saying, "We will sing to the Lord, for He has triumphed gloriously" (Ex. 15:1). Now I think that no one can attain that perfect and mystical song and that perfection of the bride who is found in this book of Scripture unless he first walks on dry ground in the midst of the sea, the waters being a wall to him on the right hand and on the left, and thus escapes from the hands of the Egyptians so as to see them dead upon the seashore and unless, seeing the strong hand of the Lord, which He brought against the Egyptians, he believes in the Lord and in His servant Moses (Ex. 14:29-31). And by Moses I mean the Law and the Gospels and all the divine Scriptures; for then he will deservedly sing. . . .

And after that, when he has passed through all the events described in Exodus and in Leviticus and has come to the point when he is taken up into the divine Numbers, then he will sing the second song. . . "And the Lord said to Moses, 'Gather the people together, and I will give them water to drink from the well'" (Num. 21:16). For there he will sing and say, "Consecrate the well. The princes dug it; the kings of the nations prepared it in their reign, when they held dominion over them" (Num. 21:17-18 LXX). . . .

After this song he comes to the song of Deuteronomy, about which the Lord said, "And now write for yourselves the words of this song, and teach it to the children of Israel; put it in their mouths, that this song may be a witness for me against the children of Israel" (Deut. 31:19). . . .

The forth song is in the book of Judges. . . . And this song is sung after a victory, because no one can sing of what is perfect unless he had conquered his adversaries. . . .

Next, the fifth song is in Second Samuel, when "David spoke to the Lord the words of this song on the day when the Lord delivered him from the hands of all his enemies and from the hand of Saul. He said, 'The Lord is my rock, and my fortress, and my deliverer;

my God will be my protector'" (2 Sam. 22:1-2). . . .

The sixth song is in First Chronicles where David first established Asaph and his brothers for praising the Lord. The beginning of the song is as follows, "Praise the Lord, give thanks to Him, and call upon His name; make known His purposes among the peoples! Sing to Him, sing praises to Him, tell of His wonderful works, which the Lord has done, and so forth" (1 Chron. 16:8-9). . . .

If, therefore, the number of songs should be brought to a close with these, then this book, Song of Songs, must evidently be put in seventh place. . . .[9]

THE MYSTICAL SENSES[10]
540 Since Christ is a "fountain" and "rivers of living water flow from him" (cf. Jn 7:38), and since he is "bread" and gives "life," it should not seem strange that he is also "nard" and "gives forth fragrance" and is the "ointment" (cf. Cant 1:12) by which those who are anointed themselves become Christ, as it says in the Psalm: "Touch not my anointed ones" [literally: "my Christs"] (Ps 105:15). And perhaps, according to what the Apostle says, in those "who have their faculties trained by practice to distinguish good from evil (cf. Heb 5:14), each one of the senses of the soul becomes Christ. For that is why he is called the "true light" (cf. 1 Jn 2:8) so that the souls might have eyes with which to be illuminated; and why he is called the "Word" (cf. Jn 1:1), that they might have ears with which to hear; and why he is called "bread of life" (cf. Jn 6:35), that the souls might have a sense of taste with which to taste. So too is he called "ointment" or "nard" so that the soul's sense of smell might receive the fragrance of the Word. And so too is he called perceivable, and touchable by hand, and the "Word became flesh" (cf. Jn 1:14), so that the inner hand of the soul might be able to make contact with the Word of life. But all this is one and the same Word of God which, in each of these, is adapted to the movements of prayer and leaves no sense of the soul untouched by his grace.

541 "We hurry after you, after the fragrance of your ointments" (cf. Cant 1:3, 4). And this happens, as we said, only when his fragrance has been perceived. What do you think they will do when the Word of God takes over their hearing and sight and touch and taste?—

and when he gives to each of their senses the powers of which they are naturally capable?—so that the eye, once able to see "his glory, glory as of the only Son from the Father" (Jn 1:14), no longer wants to see anything else, nor the hearing want to hear anything other than the "Word of life" (1 Jn 1:1) will not touch anything else which is material, fragile, and subject to decay, nor will the taste, once it has "tasted the goodness of the Word of God" (Heb 6:5) and his flesh and the "bread which has come down from heaven" (Jn 6:33, 52-58), be willing to taste anything else after this.

542   There are the more divine senses which Solomon calls divine (cf. Prov 2:3, 5) and which Jeremiah says are the "senses of the heart" (cf. Jer 4:19) and which are called by Paul writing to the Hebrews: "faculties trained by practice to distinguish good from evil" (Heb 5:14).

543   The holy prophets discovered this divine faculty of sensing and seeing and hearing in a divine manner, and of tasting and of smelling in the same way they touched the Word with faith in a way that was, so to speak, simultaneously sensing and non-sensing, so that it poured over them like a healing rain.

544   For just as in the body there are different senses of tasting and seeing, so are there, as Solomon says, divine faculties of perception. One of them is the seeing and contemplating power of the soul, the other, a faculty of taste for receiving spiritual food. And since the Lord, as the bread come down from heaven (cf. Jn 6:51), can be tasted and is food for the soul, and since, as wisdom, he is visible, of whose beauty Solomon confesses to be a lover when he says: "I became a lover of her beauty" (cf. Wis 8:2),. . . the Psalm accordingly says: "O taste and see that the Lord is good" (Ps 34:8).

As a proponent of apophatic mysticism (the negative way), Gregory insists that God transcends all images, concepts, and ideas. His most significant contribution may be the notion that the experience of God is inexhaustible, a movement from "glory to glory," even in heaven.

GREGORY OF NYSSA

One of the four great fathers of the Eastern Church, St. Gregory of Nyssa was born into an illustrious Christian family in Caesarea, Cappadocia, around 335 during the Diocletian persecution. His father was St. Basil, the elder; his sister, St. Macrina; his brothers, St. Basil the Great and St. Peter of Sebate. Ordained as lector and destined for the priesthood, Gregory soon left this course to embrace the ideals of pagan humanism revived by Roman Emperor Julian the Apostate. He married and pursued his father's career as a rhetorician.

Around 358, Basil the Great tried but failed to persuade his brother to go to Pontus where Gregory of Nazianzus had settled at the Annesis monastery. In 372, two years after he became bishop of Caesarea, Basil had Gregory appointed bishop of Nyssa to help him in his disputes with the anti-Nicene emperor Valens.

In 374, the emperor banished Gregory from Nyssa. During this period, Gregory seems to have undergone a powerful religious conversion, helped Basil with his monastic foundations in Cappadocia, and written the *Treatise on Virginity*.

The death of Emperor Valens around 377 enabled Gregory to return as bishop of Nyssa. After his brother's death in 379, Gregory assumed and completed Basil's far-ranging theological, monastic, and ecclesiastical activities.

St. Gregory of Nyssa became prominent at the Council of Constantinople (381), where he received the acceptance of his brother's and his own theological and ecclesiastical views and became a leader in the Eastern Church. For the next five years, he played an important role in the ecclesiastical affairs of Asia Minor through his theological publications and his resolving of many christological, trinitarian, and ecclesiastical controversies.

Toward the end of his life, free of administrative obligations and theological controversies, Gregory turned to the spiritual life and wrote his well-known classics, *Commentary on the Song of Songs* and *The Life of Moses*. These works demonstrate Gregory's awesome mastery of the Scriptures, his penetrating originality, and his desire to give a more mystical orientation to the monastic movement initiated by Basil.

Gregory remains indebted to Philo, the Jewish mystical philosopher; Plotinus, the Greek mystic; and the controversial Christian mystical theologian, Origen. One of Gregory's accomplishments was to transpose their thinking for later ages, while maintaining his full commitment to the Church, to Scripture, and to the Hellenistic tradition—without compromise. Indeed, many commentators see Gregory as the founder of Christian mystical theology.

Greek philosophy in the Hellenistic age was first religious, then ascetical and contemplative, so that Christianity assimilated certain Greek ideas and values for its own. Moreover, the atmosphere that influenced Origen—the prospect of martyrdom—vanished with the Edict of Milan (313). The "white," bloodless martyrdom preferred by the monastic movement was fully underway and functioned as a cooperative laboratory for the ascetical and mystical life.

Gregory read the Bible as an Alexandrian, not as one interested in salvation history as such, but as one who valued it for its ability to lift the human spirit to God. In so doing, he sought the mystical sense (*theoria*) in Scriptures' literal sense (*historia*), and his writings refer frequently to the mystical senses, which are distinct from the bodily senses.

The selections from the *Commentary on the Song of Songs* show that Gregory's mysticism of darkness emphasizes God's unknowability. Through the Incarnation, God made it possible to experience his immediacy in love and in ever-deeper levels of darkness that transcend all knowledge.

In Moses' life, Gregory saw a paradigm of the spiritual journey to God. Moses' threefold experience in light, in the cloud, and in darkness represents human growth from spiritual infancy to youth to full maturity. Unlike Origen, Gregory sees this journey as three overlapping stages, or three aspects of the person's approach to God.

The way of light purifies the person, restores the divine image to the soul, and bestows serenity (*apatheia*) and boldness in the quest for God. Origen viewed the purgative stage as preparation for contemplation, while Gregory stresses that the way of light contains a contemplative aspect through which the person learns that God alone truly exists.

For Gregory, contemplation in the strict sense belongs to the way of the cloud wherein one discovers the emptiness of all created things and God's glory manifested throughout creation. He writes: "For the wonderful harmony of the heavens proclaims the wisdom which shines forth in the creation and sets forth the great glory of God through the things which are seen, in keeping with the statement, the heavens declare the glory of God."[1] Yet, the proper object for contemplation is not only the world created in, through, and for the Word, but it is also the incarnate Word himself.

However, contemplation must be abandoned in the way of darkness. The deeper the darkness, the more is one aware of God's incomprehensibility. In "sober intoxication," "watchful sleep," "passionless passion," and "dazzling darkness," one sees God by not seeing and knows God by not knowing. These oxymorons reveal Gregory as a proponent of the negative way, of apophatic (Greek: *apophatikos*=negative) mysticism, which transcends all images, concepts, and ideas of God. The true vision of God, says Gregory, is "never to be satisfied in the desire to see him" and "the unending journey accomplished by following directly behind the Word."[2]

His view of *epiktasis,* a graced straining toward God (Phil 3:13), may be Gregory's most significant contribution. The "wound of love" bestows a heightened sense of self-possession in the possession of God in the interior of one's spirit and the sense of transcending self into God's luminous darkness. This mystical movement results in an ongoing discovery of the divine essence, a movement from "glory to glory" (2 Cor 3:18). Gregory describes this process as a "satisfied dissatisfaction" of the experience of God.

The soul's experience of God is inexhaustible because God himself is present. Because the soul mirrors the divine nature, self-knowledge is a way of knowing God. But unlike Origen, Gregory emphasizes both the similarity and the greater dissimilarity reflected.

The Word awakens the mystical senses so that the soul's core can smell, taste, touch, and feel God's presence in darkness beyond bodily senses and intellect. A "passionless passion" is enkindled and draws the soul out of itself, forcing it to center on God in an act of total detachment. In contrast to the more intellectual approach of Origen and Evagrius, Gregory stresses that the soul learns that "the true satisfaction of her desire consists in constantly going on with her quest and never ceasing in her ascent, seeing that every fulfillment of her desire continually generates a further desire for the Transcendent." To Gregory, knowledge becomes love.[3]

THE TEXTS

COMMENTARY ON THE SONG OF SONGS
"The Nocturnal Dew"[4]

Open to me, my sister, my love, my dove, my perfect one: for my head is full of dew, and my locks with the drops of night (Cant. 5.2). Our interpretation will help you to grasp the meaning of this text. Moses' vision of God began with light (Exod. 19.18); afterwards God spoke to him in a cloud (Exod. 20.21). But when Moses rose higher and became more perfect, he saw God in the darkness (Exod. 24.15-18).

Now the doctrine we are taught here is as follows. Our initial withdrawal from wrong and erroneous ideas of God is a transition from darkness to light. Next comes a closer awareness of hidden things, and by this the soul is guided through sense phenomena to the world of the invisible. And this awareness is a kind of cloud, which overshadows all appearances, and slowly guides and accustoms the soul to look towards what is hidden. Next the soul makes progress through all these stages and goes on higher, and as she leaves below all that human nature can attain, she enters within the secret chamber of divine knowledge, and here she is cut off on all sides by the divine darkness. Now she leaves outside all that can be grasped by sense or by reason, and the only thing left for her contemplation is the invisible and the incomprehensible. And here God is, as the Scriptures tell us in connection with Moses: *But Moses went into the dark cloud wherein God was* (Exod. 20.21).

Now that we have considered this, we must examine how our text is connected with what we have said. The bride used to be *black* (Cant. 1.4), when she was darkened with obscure doctrines. And then the sun shone, the sun that warms the seeds cast rootless upon the rocks by temptation. She has been overcome by the powers that war within her; she has not kept her vineyard (Cant. 1.5); and because she did not understand herself, she has led herds of goats to pasture instead of sheep. But when she has torn herself from her attachment to sin, and by that mystic kiss she yearns to bring her mouth close to the fountain of light (Cant. 4.15), then does she become beautiful, radiant with the light of truth, having washed away the dark stain of ignorance.

She is compared to a steed (Cant. 1.8) because of the speed of her progress, to a dove (Cant. 2.10) because of the agility of her mind. Like a steed she races through all she perceives by sense or by reason; and she soars like a dove until she comes to rest with longing under the shadow of the apple tree (Cant. 2.3). That which overshadows her the text calls an apple tree instead of a cloud. But then she is encompassed by a divine night (Cant. 3.1), during which her Spouse approaches but does not reveal Himself.

But how can that which is invisible reveal itself in the night? By the fact that He gives the soul some sense of His presence, even while He eludes her clear apprehension, concealed as He is by the invisibility of His nature. What then is the mystic initiation which the soul experiences during that night? The Word touches the door (Cant. 5.2); and by the door here we may understand man's reason in its search for what is hidden; it is through reason that what we seek can make its entrance. Truth, then, stands outside the door of our souls, because we merely know *in part*, as the Apostle says (1 Cor. 13.12), and knocks at the door or reason with symbols and mysteries, saying: *Open.* And by His urgent message He suggests how we must open the door, by handing us certain keys, that is, the beautiful words of our text, by which we may open the locks. . . .

Further you must come close to Truth and become its love, so that nothing separates you from it; you must achieve perfection in the guise of a *dove,* that is, you must never fail or be deficient in all innocence and purity. . . .

But the *drops of the night* are connected with an idea we have considered earlier. When a man enters into the precinct of the hidden and invisible, it is impossible that he should encounter a storm or a torrent of illumination. Rather, it is sufficient if Truth merely whets our knowledge with some meagre and obscure ideas; and these spiritual *drops* flow through the saints and God's representatives.

The *locks,* in my view, are those which hang from the head of the evangelist, and they refer, in allegory, to the Prophets, the Evangelists, and the Apostles. For all these have become rivers for us, drawing their water so far as they could from dark, hidden, and invisible treasures. Even though everyone of these is full to overflowing with the vastness and depth of doctrine, they are merely *drops* of dew in comparison with the actual Truth. . . .

. . . . Even if the dew drop were sufficient to produce great rivers, how could we ever conceive of the very river of the Godhead merely from this little drop?

"The Bubbling Spring"[5]

The path of those who rise to God is, as you see, unlimited. But how does the grace that the soul continually achieves become in turn the principle of a higher good? From the words spoken to the bride, we should have supposed that there would be a halt in her progress towards the heights. For after such an assurance of perfection, what more could anyone hope for? But then we realize that she is still inside (Cant. 5.3) and has not yet gone out of doors; she does not yet enjoy that vision *face to face*, but is still making progress in her participation in good merely by the sounds she hears. . . .

It is the same with one who fixes his gaze on the infinite beauty of God. It is constantly being discovered anew, and it is always seen as something new and strange in comparison with what the mind has already understood. And as God continues to reveal Himself, man continues to wonder; and he never exhausts his desire to see more, since what he is waiting for is always more magnificent, more divine, than all that he has already seen. So too in our text the bride is in wonder and amazement at what she is beginning to see, yet she never, for all that, puts an end to her yearning for further vision. . . .

"The Successive Purifications"[6]

The soul, having gone out at the word of her Beloved, looks for Him but does not find Him. She calls on Him, though He cannot be reached by any verbal symbol, and she is told by the watchmen that she is in love with the unattainable, and that the object of her longing cannot be apprehended. In this way she is, in a certain sense, wounded and beaten because of the frustration of what she desires, now that she thinks that her yearning for the Other cannot be fulfilled or satisfied. But the veil of grief is removed when she learns that the true satisfaction of her desire consists of constantly going on with her quest and never ceasing in her ascent, seeing that every fulfillment of her desire continually generates a further desire for the Transcendent.

Thus the veil of her despair is torn away and the bride realizes that she will always discover more and more of the incomprehensible and unhoped for beauty of her Spouse throughout all eternity. Then she is torn by an even more urgent longing, and through the daughters of Jerusalem she communicates to her Beloved the dispositions of her heart. For she has received within her God's special dart, she has been mortally wounded by the arrow of love. And *God is love.*

"The Odor of Spikenard"[7]

There are many different perfumes, not all equally fragrant, from which a certain harmonious and artistic blend produces a very special kind of unguent called spikenard, taking its name from one of the fragrant herbs that are compounded in it. It is the result of many different perfumes coalescing into a single fragrance; and this is the sweet scent which the Bridegroom perceives with pure senses. In this text I think that the Word teaches us that by His very nature He transcends the entire order and structure of the created universe, that He is inaccessible, intangible, and incomprehensible. But in His stead we have this perfume within us distilled from the perfection of our virtues; and this imitates in its purity His essential incorruptibility, in its goodness His goodness, in its immortality His immortality, in its stability His immutability, and in all the virtues we possess we represent His true virtue, which as the prophet Habacuc says, covers all the heavens (Hab. 3.3).

And so when the bride says to the friends of the Bridegroom, *My spikenard sent forth the odor of him* (Cant. 1.11), this is the profound lesson I think she is teaching us. It is that even though one may gather from all the different meadows of virtue every flower of fragrance, and should make his whole life fragrant with the good odor of all these virtuous actions, and become perfect in this way, even then he would not be able to look steadily upon the Word of God, no more than he could the sun. But he can look upon this Sun within himself as in a mirror. For the all perfect virtue of God sends forth rays of sinlessness to illuminate the lives of those who are pure; and these rays make the invisible visible, and allow us to comprehend the inaccessible by impressing an image of the Sun upon the mirror of our souls. Now as far as our interpretation goes, it is much the same thing to speak of the sun's rays, or the emanations of virtue, or the fragrance of perfume. For no matter which of these analogies we use for the purpose of our discourse, the underlying idea is one and the same: that it is through our virtues that we derive a knowledge of the Good that surpasses all understanding, in the same way that we may infer the beauty of an archetype from its image.

"The Spiritual Senses"[8]

There is another lesson that we are incidentally taught by the deeper study of this book: it is that we have two sets of senses, one corporeal and the other spiritual, as the Word tells us in the book of Proverbs: *Thou shalt find the sense of God.* There is a correspondence between the motions and movements of the soul and the sense organs of the body, as we learn from the words of the Spirit given in our text. Wine and milk, it is true, are distinguished by the taste; but the spiritual realities which they signify are grasped rather by the intellectual power of the soul. A kiss is an operation of the sense of touch: in a kiss two pairs of lips touch. There is, however, a spiritual faculty of touch, which comes in contact with the Word, and this is actuated by a spiritual and immaterial sense of touch, as it is said: *Our hands have handled of the word of life* (1 John 1.1). So too the smell of the divine perfumes does not proceed from the smell of our nostrils but from a spiritual faculty which draws in the sweet odor of Christ by an inhalation of the spirit. And this is the tenor of the text of the maiden's prayer as we have it in the opening section: *Thy breasts are sweeter than wine and the odor of thy ointments above all ointments* (Cant 1.1-2). Here is revealed a notion which is not at all insignificant, I think, nor to be despised. For in this comparison which shows how far superior is the milk we draw from the divine breast to the joy we derive from wine, we learn that all human wisdom or the exercise of the imagination cannot at all be compared with the simple nourishment we derive from divine revelation. For milk comes from the breast and it is the food of infants. But wine is more perfect, because of the warmth and strength which it brings. And yet what is superior in the wisdom of the world is far inferior to the childlike instruction we receive from the divine Word. Hence, it is that the divine breasts are better than human wine, and the smell of the divine ointments is sweeter than all other perfumes. . . .

"The Fruit of the Apple Tree"[9]

The soul has now become a flower and has not been hurt by the thorns of temptation in her transformation into a lily. She now forgets her people and the home of her father and mother, and looks towards her true Father. Thus she is called the *sister* of the Lord (Cant. 4.9), being brought into this relationship by the *spirit of adop-*

tion (Rom. 8.15), and removed from any contact with that pretended father. She then rises higher and higher again and gazes upon the mystery with the eyes of the Dove, that is, with the spirit of prophecy. And this is what she says: *As the apple tree among the trees of the woods, so is my beloved among the sons* (Cant. 2.3). . . .

That is why the apple tree grows in the woods, and being of wood, it is similar to man's nature, tested in all things like ourselves *without sin* (Heb. 4.15). But because this tree bears fruit to charm the senses of the soul, there is a greater difference between the apple tree and the woods than there is between the lily and the thorns. The lily gives pleasure to sight and to smell; but the charm of the apple tree is harmoniously proportioned to three senses: it gives pleasure to the eye by its beauty, to the sense of smell by its fragrance, but also the sense of taste by its nourishment.

The bride then rightly recognizes the difference between herself and her Lord. As Light, He is the object of beauty for our eyes; He is a sweet odor for our sense of smell; and Life for those who partake of Him. *He that eateth Him,* as the Gospel says, *shall live* (John 6.58). Our human nature, nourished by virtue, becomes a flower—but it does not offer nourishment to the Husbandman but simply adorns itself. For He has no need of our goods. . . .

"Sober Intoxication"[10]

Eat, my friends, and drink, and be inebriated, my brothers (Cant. 5.1). For one familiar with the mysteries of the Gospel there will appear no difference between this text and the words used in the mystic initiation of the Apostles. For there too does He say: *Eat and drink.* Now the exhortation to the brethren in the present text to become *inebriated* might seem to go further than the Gospel. But anyone who examines both texts carefully will find that this text is quite in harmony with that of the Gospel. For the command that is here given to the brethren in words is, in the Gospel, transformed into deed. All intoxication causes the mind, overwhelmed with wine, to go into an ecstasy. Hence what is urged in our text actually is realized in the Gospel through the divine food and drink. And this constantly recurs insofar as there is a continual ecstasy in this food and drink, that is, there is a transformation from a worse to a better condition.

Thus do they become *inebriated*, as the Prophet tells us, *with the plenty of God's house*, they *who drink of the torrent of His pleasure* (Ps. 35.9). In this way the mighty David became intoxicated and went out of himself: he saw, while in ecstasy, that divine beauty which no mortal can behold, and cried out in those famous words: *Every man is a liar* (Ps. 115.11), thus giving us some hint of that ineffable treasure.

So too Paul, the new *Benjamin* (Ps. 67.28), while in ecstasy, said: *Whether we be transported in mind, it is to God*, for this ecstasy was a movement toward the Godhead; *or whether we be sober, it is for you* (2 Cor. 5.13). Similarly in his words to Festus he showed that he was *not mad*, but spoke *words of truth and soberness* (Acts 26.25).

I am aware also that the blessed Peter experienced this sort of intoxication, hungry and drunk as he was at the same time. For even before real food was brought to him, *being hungry* and *desirous to taste*, while his household *was preparing it* (Acts 10.10), he experienced that divine and sober inebriation. And he went out of himself and beheld that symbol of the Gospel, the *linen sheet let down by the four corners*, wherein were all manner of men in innumerable forms of birds, *four-footed beasts and creeping things*, and beasts of different shapes, according to various kinds of cults. Of these the Word orders Peter. . . And this message is given three times, that we might learn that in the first voice God the Father purifies, in the second it is God the Son, and similarly in the third it is He Who purifies all that is unclean, God the Holy Spirit.

This then is the inebriation to which the Lord exhorts His table companions, and it is through this that the soul's divine ecstasy takes place. . . .

"Watchful Sleep"[11]

Sleep usually follows drinking, and in this way the banqueters can promote their good health by allowing time for digestion. Thus after her banquet the bride, too, is overcome with sleep. But this is a strange sleep and foreign to nature's custom. In natural sleep the sleeper is not wide awake, and he who is wide awake is not sleeping. . . . But in this case there is strange and contradictory fusion of opposites in the same state. For I *sleep,* she says, and *my heart watcheth* (Cant. 5.2). . . .

From what we have said, then, when the bride proudly declares, I *sleep and my heart watcheth* (Cant. 5.2), we learn that she has risen higher than ever before. . . .

The contemplation of the good makes us despise all these [created] things; and so the eye of the body sleeps. Anything that the eye reveals does not attract the perfect soul, because by reason it looks only to those things which transcend the visible universe. . . .

Thus the soul, enjoying the contemplation of Being, will not awake for anything that arouses sensual pleasure. After lulling to sleep every bodily motion, it receives the vision of God in a divine wakefulness with pure and naked intuition.

Evagrius synthesized Hellenistic intellectualism and the Desert Fathers' mysticism of the heart. To him, the "white" martyrdom of the monastic life provides the ascetical foundation of mysticism and the mystical basis of asceticism.

EVAGRIUS PONTICUS

It is astonishing that someone as remarkable and influential in the history of Christian spirituality and mysticism has remained almost unknown to all but specialists. Evagrius was the first to organize in a concise, nuanced, and precise way the writings of the desert fathers. His lapidary, gnomic, highly polished sentences were easily memorized capsule meditations. Moreover, he may well have been the first to give a complete and coherent monastic, ascetical, and mystical theology to the Christian world. As Origen's intellectual heir and disciple of the desert fathers, he synthesized in his person and writings Hellenistic intellectualism and the Desert Fathers' spirituality and mysticism of the heart that is solidly anchored to the triune and living One and to Jesus Christ.

This complex person went from the highest social, cultural, and intellectual circles to a most austere way of life in the Egyptian wilderness. Evagrius Ponticus is one of the most important names in Christian spirituality and mysticism. With him, its history reached a decisive turning point, for through his *Praktikos* and *Chapters on Prayer* he influenced the entire Christian monastic tradition after him—despite the Church's condemnation of some of his infelicitous speculative views contained in his "Origenist" *Kephalaia Gnostica*.

Evagrius was born in Ibora, Pontos, or modern-day Iverönü, Turkey. His father was a "chorbishop"—a country bishop of somewhat restricted powers who traveled about to minister to the various churches under his jurisdiction. Evagrius came to enjoy the company and the esteem of the great Cappadocian fathers. St. Basil, the Great, ordained him lector; St. Gregory of Nazianzus ordained him deacon.

Constantinople naturally attracted the brilliant, urbane, and cultured Evagrius. There he attained great social prominence, especially as the "destroyer of the twaddle of the [anti-Nicene] heretics." But he gradually lost his religious fervor and fell in love with the wife of a prominent member of society. Warned in a dream about the danger to his soul, he left promptly for Jerusalem where he became the disciple of Melania, the Elder. She was an ascetic Roman woman, well-read in Origen, who ran a hospice for Christian pilgrims on the Mount of Olives. After an illness, he went to live with a community of Origenist monks in Nitria, Egypt.

The texts were selected to illustrate Evagrius' love of the monastic life, especially in its eremetical form. Constantine the Great (d.337), because he bestowed imperial favors upon the Christian faith, unwittingly eliminated the opportunity for the ideal following of Christ, namely, martyrdom. Thus, many Christians now sought the "white," or bloodless, martyrdom of the monastic life. The monks replaced the martyrs as the athletes of the Christian life.

At Nitria, Evagrius became a severe ascetic, though his intellectual life continued, resulting in a body of writings. In addition to this work, he became widely known for his prudent and loving spiritual direction. Occasionally, he went to Alexandria where he used his penetrating mind and oratorical skills against the heretics. His reputation for holiness, learning, and eloquence attracted the attention of Theophilus of Alexandria, the Patriarch of Egypt, who wished to make Evagrius a bishop. Following the maxim of the Desert Fathers, "avoid women and bishops," Evagrius refused this honor and continued to live as a desert father.

His last years were spent in contemplation and peace. So great was his spiritual reputation that he was considered a Church Father in his own time. On the Feast of the Epiphany in 399, he asked to be taken to church where he received Holy Communion and died shortly thereafter.

The texts selected indicate that Evagrius distinguished, but never separated, two stages of spiritual progress in a monk's ascent to God. In the ascetical stage (*praktike*), right ordering of the emotions and liberating the soul from inordinate passions are sought. The monk must also rid the intellect of sense reactions and remove obstacles to contemplation by observing the commandments and practicing virtue. Before ascending to God, he must follow the way of the incarnation: descent into the sinful world to do battle with the demons.

Because of his distinction between asceticism, natural contemplation, and *theologia*, Evagrius has been accused by some commentators of dividing the path of mystical ascent into three distinct stages. However, for him, these three stages—roughly parallel to the later classical purgative, illuminative, and unitive ways—are inextricably connected. Each stage contains aspects of the other two stages. Thus, Evagrius stressed the ascetical foundation of mysticism and the mystical basis of asceticism.

Evagrius is best known for his meticulous, experiential, concise description and analysis of the eight passions and the accompanying passionate thoughts (*logismoi*), which the demons use in their war against us: acedia, anger, avarice, gluttony, impurity, pride, sadness, and vainglory. The selected texts illustrate Evagrius' perceptive observation of the connection between the demons and the passions, and between moods and thoughts. His insights in this matter would continue to play a significant role in the Christian mystical tradition's teaching on the discernment of spirits.

Evagrius was not immediately concerned with sinful acts. The demons attack the monk by stirring up the passions and the imagination which induce passionate thoughts and lines of thought incongruous with the Christian life. So, for Evagrius, the monk's chief battle is against sins of the heart. The number of times the selected texts mention thoughts and the need for continual recollection exemplifies the Desert Fathers' conviction that thoughts were sometimes the monk's chief opponents.

The long text on *acedia*, or monastic boredom, was selected because

of Evagrius' compelling description of the "fiercest demon of all."
Again, Evagrius urges the monk to pay attention to the thoughts
and the line of thinking suggested by the devil. Other texts reveal
that fasting, vigils, the singing of psalms, confessing of one's sins,
tears, works of mercy, and the like, often rout the demons. Angels
aid in the warfare against the demons by bestowing peace upon the
monk. Defeating *acedia* also means the monk's easy victory over the
other demons.

The selected texts often mention *apatheia*, often rendered in English
as "passionlessness," "impassibility," "serenity," "indifference," or
"abnegation." Evagrius views it as the health of the soul, the flowering of asceticism, and as the art of attaining discreet charity. However, *apatheia* can be attained only through effort, grace, and a total
love of Christ and the Trinity. The monk labors to remove all passionate disorders in order to attain the integration of emotional love
and the deeper passions, but for the sake of increased charity.

Apatheia is the relatively permanent state of deep calm that results
from the purification, integration, and transformation of all levels
of psychic life. Not even the stirring of passionate memories, or
vivid dreams, or external events can ruffle this integrative calm. As
apatheia deepens, the human spirit (*nous*) sees its own light and enables the monk to pray without distractions.

Even though Evagrius emphasizes that *agape* is *apatheia*'s daughter,
he also sees it as the mother of *apatheia*. The selected texts teach this
paradox: the monk flees from the world to the desert to battle the
demons and to attain an angelic state, which in fact brings about a
deeper compassion for all humanity.

Following Origen, Evagrius speaks of a "natural" contemplation
(*theoria physike*). For example, by meditating upon the Scriptures
and the universe in the light of the incarnate Logos, one attains
knowledge of God's universe and attributes. Comprehending the
logoi, or "reasons" for all things as they exist in the eternal Logos results in a knowledge that resembles divine reason and replaces
knowledge distorted by passion and desire.

However, during "first contemplation" (*theologia*), Evagrius writes,
"the contemplative soul resembles the heavens where the light of

the Holy Trinity shines."[1] The intellect (*nous*) becomes a place of ineffable peace, receiving a simple, intuitive, loving knowledge of the Trinity. Says Evagrius: "When the spirit has put off the old man to replace him with the new man, created by charity, then he will see that his own state at the time of prayer resembles that of a sapphire; it is as clear and bright as the very sky. The Scriptures refer to this experience as the place of God which was seen by our ancestors, the elders, at Mount Sinai."[2]

Evagrius' light mysticism is apophatic. Unlike Gregory of Nyssa, he contends that contemplation without distraction results in deeper knowledge of God. He inherited the view from Origen that God is knowable, though beyond images, thoughts, concepts, and forms. To Evagrius, knowledge of God is a wholly luminous "infinite ignorance," perfect "*amorphia*," perfect "*anaesthesia*." One attains to a "complete unconsciousness" during prayer when one is not even aware of praying. The Trinity is best known in simple, unselfconscious, loving knowledge beyond all clearly defined images, thoughts, and knowledge.

For Evagrius, prayer and contemplation are monastic life. As the texts here show, one must "renounce all things" to pray without distractions. Prayer without distraction, "pure prayer," results in the final routing of the demons and restores the human spirit (*nous*) to its true nature. In this way is one divinized.

Questionable, however, is Evagrius' Origenistic metaphysics for which he was condemned at the Second Council of Constantinople in 553. He contended that *nous*, or pure intellect, was naturally divine and had originally existed without matter. The present material world is a consequence of the fall. Through contemplation *nous* recovers and discovers its true nature: contemplation of the divine. No. 119 of the *Praktikos* states, "happy is the spirit that becomes free of all matter." The selected texts illustrate Evagrius' unease with matter.

Also questionable is Evagrius' distinction between "the kingdom of Christ" and the "kingdom of God, the Father." The former involves natural contemplation, the latter, *theologia*. Although he writes that perfection is "hidden in the breast of Christ," this mystic was one of the first in the Christian tradition to recognize that contemplation of the divinity seems to require going beyond Christ's humanity. He asks a difficult question: How does one reconcile an apophatic mysticism with a Christianity inextricably linked to Christ's humanity? Origen had adverted to a Logos mysticism that paradoxically transcends an incarnate Logos mysticism, but must never forget the incarnation. This issue troubled Teresa of Avila and to some extent the author of the *Cloud of Unknowing*.[3]

THE TEXTS

THE PRAKTIKOS[4]

INTRODUCTORY LETTER TO ANATOLIUS
(Whenever they confer this [monk's] habit) the Fathers speak the following words to the young monks: "The fear of God strengthens faith, my son, and continence in turn strengthens this fear. Patience and hope make this latter virtue solid beyond all shaking and they also give birth to *apatheia*. Now this *apatheia* has a child called *agape* who keeps the door to deep knowledge of the created universe. Finally, to this knowledge succeeds theology [experiential, mystical, knowledge of God] and the supreme beatitude.

THE HUNDRED CHAPTERS
1. Christianity is the dogma of Christ our Saviour. It is composed of *praktike*, of the contemplation of the physical world and of the contemplation of God.

2. The Kingdom of Heaven is *apatheia* of the soul along with true knowledge of existing things.

3. The Kingdom of God is knowledge of the Holy Trinity coextensive with the capacity of the intelligence and giving it a surpassing incorruptibility.

5. The demons fight openly against the solitaries, but they arm the more careless of the brethren against the cenobites, or those who practice virtue in the company of others. Now this second form of combat is much lighter than the first, for there is not to be found on

earth any men more fierce than the demons, none who support at the same time all their evil deeds.

12. The demon of *acedia*—also called the noonday demon—is the one that causes the most serious trouble of all. He presses his attack upon the monk about the fourth hour [10 a.m.] and besieges the soul until the eighth hour. First of all he makes it seem that the sun barely moves, if at all, and that the day is fifty hours long. Then he constrains the monk to look constantly out the windows, to walk outside the cell, to gaze carefully at the sun to determine how far it stands from the ninth hour [dinner time], to look now this way and now that to see if perhaps one of the brethren appears from his cell. Then too he instills in the heart of the monk a hatred for the place, a hatred for his very life itself, a hatred for manual labor. He leads him to reflect that charity has departed from among the brethren, that there is no one to give encouragement. Should there be someone at this period who happens to offend him in some way or other, this too the demon uses to contribute further to his hatred. The demon drives him along to desire other sites where he can more easily procure life's necessities, more readily find work and make a real success of himself. He goes on to suggest that, after all, it is not the place that is the basis of pleasing the Lord. God is to be adored everywhere. He joins to these reflections the memory of his dear ones and of his former way of life. He depicts life stretching out for a long period of time, and brings before the mind's eye the toil of the ascetic struggle and, as the saying has it, leaves no leaf unturned to induce the monk to forsake his cell and drop out of the fight. No other demon follows close upon the heels of this one (when he is defeated) but only a state of deep peace and inexpressible joy arise out of this struggle.

15. Readings, vigils, and prayer—these are the things that lend stability to the wandering mind. Hunger, toil, and solitude are the means of extinguishing the flames of desire. Turbid anger is calmed by the singing of Psalms, by patience and almsgiving. But all these practices are to be engaged in according to due measure and at the appropriate times. What is untimely done, or done without measure, endures but a short time. And what is short-lived is more harmful than profitable.

49. We have received no command to work and to pass the night in vigils and to fast constantly. However, we do have the obligation to pray without ceasing. Although the body, due to its weakness, does not suffice for such labors as these, which are calculated to restore health to the passionate part of the soul, these practices do require the body for their performance. But prayer makes the spirit strong and pure for combat since by its very nature the spirit is made to pray. Moreover, prayer even fights without the aid of the body on behalf of the other powers of the soul.

50. If there is any monk who wishes to take the measure of the more fierce demons so as to gain experience in his monastic art, then let him keep careful watch over his thoughts. Let him observe their intensity, their periods of decline and follow them as they rise and fall. Let him note well the complexity of his thoughts, their periodicity, the demons which cause them, with the order of their succession and the nature of their associations. Then let him ask from Christ the explanations of these data he has observed. For the demons become thoroughly infuriated with those who practice active virtue in a manner that is increasingly contemplative. They are even of a mind to "pierce the upright of heart through, under cover of darkness" [Ps 10:3].

56. We recognize the indications of *apatheia* by our thoughts during the day, but we recognize it by our dreams during the night. We call *apatheia* the health of the soul. The food of the soul can be said to be contemplative knowledge since it alone is able to unite us with the holy powers. This holds true since union between incorporeal beings follows quite naturally from their sharing the same deep attitudes.

64. The proof of *apatheia* is had when the spirit begins to see its own light, when it remains in a state of tranquillity in the presence of the images it has during sleep and when it maintains its calm as it beholds the affairs of life.

66. The spirit that is actively leading the ascetic life with God's help and which draws near to contemplative knowledge ceases to perceive the irrational part of the soul almost completely, perhaps altogether. For this knowledge bears it aloft and separates it from the senses.

78. The ascetic life is the spiritual method for cleansing the affective part of the soul.

79. The effects of keeping the commandments do not suffice to heal the powers of the soul completely. They must be complemented by a contemplative activity appropriate to these faculties and this activity must penetrate the spirit.

80. It is not possible to resist all the thoughts inspired in us by the angels, though we can indeed overthrow all those inspired by the demons. A peaceful state follows the first kind of thoughts; turbulence of mind attends the second type.

81. *Agape* is the progeny of *apatheia*. *Apatheia* is the very flower of *ascesis*. *Ascesis* consists in keeping the commandments. The custodian of these commandments is the fear of God which is in turn the offspring of true faith. Now faith is an interior good, one which is to be found even in those who do not yet believe in God.

84. The goal of the ascetic life is charity; the goal of contemplative knowledge is theology [experiential, mystical knowledge of God]. The beginnings of each are faith and contemplation of nature respectively. Such of the demons as fall upon the affective part of the soul are said to be the opponents of the ascetic life. Those again who disturb the rational part are the enemies of all truth and the adversaries of contemplation.

91. . . .A dry and regular diet joined with charity leads the monk more quickly into the harbor of purity of heart. This same man delivered a certain brother from the disquieting specters by which he was visited in the night by ordering him to minister to the sick and to fast while he did it. When asked about his rationale for employing this procedure, he replied: "Such afflictions are extinguished by no other remedy so well as by mercy."

THE 153 CHAPTERS ON PRAYER[5]
3. Prayer is the continual intercourse of the spirit with God. What state of soul then is required that the spirit might thus strain after its Master without wavering, living constantly with him without intermediary?

4. If Moses, when he attempted to draw near the burning bush, was

prohibited until he should remove the shoes from his feet, how should you not free yourself of every thought that is colored by passion seeing that you wish to see One who is beyond every thought and perception.

7. Though fountains of tears flow during your prayer do not begin to consider yourself better than others. For your prayers have merely obtained the help you need to confess your sins with readiness and to conciliate the favor of the Lord.

9. Stand resolute, fully intent on your prayer. Pay no heed to the concerns and thoughts that might arise the while. They do nothing better than disturb and upset you so as to dissolve the fixity on your purpose.

15. Prayer is the fruit of joy and thanksgiving.

16. Prayer is the exclusion of sadness and despondency.

17. Go, sell your possessions and give to the poor, and take up your cross so that you can pray without distraction.

18. If you wish to pray worthily, deny yourself every hour. Playing the part of a wise man, study and work very hard to learn to endure much for the sake of prayer.

20. If you desire to pray as you ought do not sadden anyone. Otherwise you run in vain.

30. When an angel makes his presence felt by us, all disturbing thoughts immediately disappear. The spirit finds itself clothed in great tranquility. It prays purely. At other times, though, we are beset with the customary struggle and then the spirit joins the fight. It cannot so much as raise its eyes for it is overtaken by diverse passions. Yet if only the spirit goes on striving it will achieve its purpose. When it knocks on the door hard enough it will be opened.

31. Pray not to this end, that your own desires be fulfilled. You can be sure they do not fully accord with the will of God. Once you have learned to accept this point, pray instead that "thy will be done" in me. In every matter ask him in this way for what is good and for what confers profit on your soul, for you yourself do not seek this as completely as he does.

34. . . . For what greater thing is there than to converse intimately with God and to be preoccupied with his company? Undistracted prayer is the greatest act of the intellect.

35. Prayer is an ascent of the spirit to God.

36. Do you long to pray? Renounce all things. You then become heir to all.

44. When you pray keep your memory under close custody. Do not let it suggest your own fancies to you, but rather have it convey the awareness of your reaching out to God. Remember this—the memory has a powerful proclivity for causing detriment to the spirit at the time of prayer.

52. The state of prayer can be aptly described as a habitual state of imperturbable calm (*apatheia*). It snatches to the heights of intelligible reality the spirit which loves wisdom and which is truly spiritualized by the most intense love.

55. One who has become free of disturbing passion does not necessarily truly pray. It is quite possible for a man to have none but the purest thoughts and yet be so distracted mulling over them that he remains the while far removed from God.

56. Even when the spirit does avoid getting involved with these simple thoughts of things, it does not by that fact alone attain to the place of prayer. It may get involved in the contemplation of objects and waste time in considering their inner nature. For even though these concepts be simple, considerations of real things that they are, they do impress a certain form on the spirit and draw one far away from God.

57. Even if the spirit should rise above the contemplation of corporeal nature, still it does not as yet see the perfect place of God. For it might well be engaged in the contemplation of intelligible things and partake of their multiplicity.

58. If you wish to pray then it is God whom you need. He it is who gives prayer to the man who prays. On that account call upon him saying: "Hallowed be thy Name, thy Kingdom come," that is, the Holy Spirit and your Only-Begotten Son. This is what our Lord taught us when he said: "The Father is adored in Spirit and in

Truth."

60. If you are a theologian [one who has experiential knowledge of God] you truly pray. If you truly pray you are a theologian.

66. When you are praying do not fancy the Divinity like some image formed within yourself. Avoid also allowing your spirit to be impressed with the seal of some particular shape, but rather, free from all matter, draw near the immaterial Being and you will attain to understanding.

69. Stand guard over your spirit, keeping it free of concepts at the time of prayer so that it may remain in its own deep calm. Thus he who has compassion on the ignorant will come to visit even such an insignificant person as yourself. That is when you will receive the most glorious gift of prayer.

70. You will not be able to pray purely if you are all involved with material affairs and agitated with unremitting concerns. For prayer is the rejection of concepts.

97. Crashing sounds and roars and voices and beatings—all of these, coming from the devil—are heard by the man who pursues the practice of pure prayer. Yet he does not lose courage nor his presence of mind. He calls out to God: "I shall fear no evils for you are with me." And he adds other similar prayers.

113. By true prayer a monk becomes another angel, for he ardently longs to see the face of the Father in heaven.

117. Let me repeat this saying of mine that I once expressed on some other occasions: Happy is the spirit that attains to perfect formlessness at the time of prayer.

119. Happy is the spirit that becomes free of all matter and is stripped of all at the time of prayer.

120. Happy is the spirit that attains to complete unconsciousness of all sensible experience at the time of prayer.

122. Happy is the monk who views the welfare and progress of all men with as much joy as if it were his own.

123. Happy is the monk who considers all men as god—after God.

125. A monk is a man who considers himself one with all men because he seems constantly to see himself in every man.

150. Just as sight is the most worthy of the senses, so also is prayer the most divine of the virtues.

153. When you give yourself to prayer, rise above every other joy—then you will find true prayer.

*"Our heart is restless unless it rests in You (God)"
sums up Augustine's entire teaching on our relationship to God and is one of the most quoted lines in the
Christian mystical tradition. He also taught that the
soul's mystical senses perceive God as Light, Song,
Perfume, Food, Body, Love, Beauty, and Wisdom.*

AUGUSTINE OF HIPPO

Augustine is the most significant formative personality in the history of the Western Christian tradition. His 113 books, 800 sermons,
and 250 letters left an indelible mark on the shape, scope, direction,
range, and development of that tradition. Describing both his exterior and interior journey, Augustine's *Confessions* gave the West its
first autobiography. The highly sophisticated way in which he described the interaction between God's action at the depths of the
human soul and a person's psychological makeup may explain
why *Confessions* has been one of the most widely read books in the
Christian West.

Augustine was born in Thagaste, a small town in the Souk-Ahras region of Algeria near the Tunisian border, of a pagan father (baptized on his death bed) and a zealous Christian mother. Educated in
the classics at Madaura and trained as a professional rhetorician at
Carthage, he eventually went to Rome and then to Milan to further
his career as a rhetorician.

Even as a teenager and as a young man, Augustine had been attracted to wisdom and the search for truth. But he also experienced
that his self-love and his strong sensuality conflicted with his ardent desire to seek eternal Beauty and to live accordingly. The
Manichees' uncompromising dualism, their claim to possess hidden truths of universal validity and to be able to prove Christian

truths from reason, and their praise of Christ claimed Augustine's allegiance for about nine years. Augustine also gave his loyalty to his mistress of 15 years and his illegitimate son, Adeodatus.

Although Neo-Platonic philosophy freed Augustine from his material notions of God and his heretical Manichaeism, he realized instinctively that Neo-Platonism knew only the goal, not the way, to true wisdom. Augustine was to learn from the erudite, urbane, and politically astute St. Ambrose, then bishop of Milan, that the true wisdom of the Scriptures is none other than Christ crucified, that genuine ascent to God comes by imitating the humble Christ.

Shortly after the Easter of 387 when Ambrose baptized him, Augustine left for his native Africa. While at the Roman port of Ostia, Augustine and his mother had the conversation that led to a mystical vision of the divine "Wisdom" that transcends all things, even the soul itself. After Monica's death at Ostia, Augustine returned to Thagaste for many happy years of monastic living. The desire to live a monastic life inspired by the Gospels goes back to his youth when he undoubtedly came into contact with Athanasius's Life of Anthony.

However, in 391, Bishop Valerius of Hippo forced Augustine to accept ordination, and to become his assistant. After Valerius's death, Augustine became bishop of Hippo for 35 years. He died at the age of 76 when the invading Vandals besieged his city.

The first selection, Homily on Psalm 41, was chosen because Dom Cuthbert Butler correctly assessed this text as a "masterpiece" and the "most considerable and complete of Augustine's descriptions of the process and nature of the mystic experience."[1] This text, as well as the other selected texts, indicate clearly that, for Augustine, mysticism is the desire and immense longing of the entire Church because Augustinian mysticism is essentially the longing to assimilate and to interiorize everything given in baptism. Thus, his conversion and light mysticism are placed squarely in the context of the Church.

This text also underscores his love for the psalms through which he had experienced the emotions they express. For him, the psalms are expressions of the immensely rich deposit of the emotions of Christ and of his members.

354-430   AUGUSTINE OF HIPPO 57

Moreover, for Augustine, contemplation of the holiness of the saints provided the impetus for experiencing the ineffable, sweet, heavenly music that brings such joy and refreshment. He stressed that one cannot recognize grace in oneself unless one can recognize it in others. The person's social nature, love of neighbor, and the Church as Christ's community are definitely important factors in Augustinian mysticism.

Augustine speaks of a vague, yet ardent, yearning for something only obscurely known. Light and desire provide the motivation for the mystical ascent. However, Augustine insists upon the ascetical foundation requisite for this ascent. Only the clean of heart will see God with their inner eyes. Cleansing the heart demands both waging war against the demons, controlling passions, striving for virtue, and rooting out sins, vices, and imperfections. Although Augustine is known for saying, "Love, and do what you will," he also said, "Love, and be careful what you love."

Although "faith," not vision, is the "normal" Christian state, Augustine maintains what all Christian mystics have averred: God can be seen in some way in this life. By a process of recollection that unifies the person's scattered powers and by plunging into the soul's depths through introversion, Augustine discovers that unchangeable Truth is found only when one transcends both creation and the soul itself.

Some Augustinian scholars underscore the "intellectualism" of Augustine's mysticism, because he does say on occasion: "And then in a flash of a trembling glance, my mind arrived at That Which is."[2] But the selected texts show definitely that Augustine experienced God not only through the intellect's dynamism for truth, but also through the will's insatiable desire for love. Augustine's views on the mystical senses in the human spirit bring out dramatically that he experienced God not only as unchanging Truth, but also as Love, Beauty, Wisdom, Food, Perfume, Light, Song, and Embracement that nourish the inner person in manifold ways.

The texts also indicate that Augustine experienced mystical ecstasy, raptures that suddenly and violently draw the soul away from the senses and itself to bestow a foretaste of the joys of heaven. Without claiming the same for himself, Augustine contended that both Moses and St. Paul had a foretaste of the beatific vision in this life. In mystical ecstasy they saw, without intermediary, God, and lived. In answer to the question, how can one see God and live, Augustine explained that mystical ecstasy is a temporary death, because a person is removed from the senses.

However, in contrast to the Neo-Platonic chimera that eternal Beauty can be contemplated without interruption, Augustine underscores the transient nature of his experience. The deep realization of human frailty, the acute experience of always being "beaten back," and the profound sense of the pure gift, grace-quality of this experience are all features of his and all genuine Christian mysticism.

The selections also illustrate the need for contemplation of God's creation, then for entering the soul's deepest depths through introversion, and finally for the soul's eye to look to the Light above and beyond all created things, even beyond the soul itself. With love and dread, Augustine experienced the paradox of the awesome difference between God and all created things—even the infinitely mysterious depths of the self. In the act of transcending all creatures, he heard the call to be transformed into God. God's very Word had pierced his heart, taught him that nothing created is God—not even the soul. But all creation, especially the soul, calls him to love God and to be one with God. Because God is the Life of the soul's life, Augustine experienced God as more interior to himself than he was to himself.

Augustine is well known for his emphasis on finding God in the soul, on Christ as the "inner teacher," a "psychocentrism," and introspection. A dimension of inwardness and psychological self-probing penetrates all his works, so that his "voice" is more personal than the "objective" mystical exegesis of the Eastern Fathers. One does not find in their writings an account of their personal experiences. Their mystical exegesis of Scripture never swerved from knowing the mystery of God in Christ and from examining the soul's quest for God in that light. However, Augustine uses Scripture primarily to discover the true nature of the human person. Thus, his emphasis is anthropocentric.

The selection from *On the Trinity* underscores Augustine's image-mysticism. For the Greek Fathers, the human soul is the image of the eternal Logos; for Augustine, the soul is made in God's *trinitarian* image. The mind's ability to know and to love itself parallels God's inner-trinitarian life. The soul's ability to cleave to the Trinity by remembering, knowing, and loving the Trinity reforms it as God's image.

Commentators disagree about whether Augustine was a mystic or someone of very deep piety. It may be true that Augustine did not reach the summit of transforming union with God in which the mystic experiences *habitually* the Trinity's presence in the soul. However, his acute sense of sin, human frailty, the infinite distance between the Creator and creatures, God's wonderful condescension in the Incarnation, his haunting restlessness for God, his painful awareness of being unable to love as much as he was loved by God, and his grasp of God's Wisdom, Light, and Beauty contain a mystical maturity that surpasses deep piety. For Augustine, "my Love is my weight." He knew that his heart was restless until it rested in God, but there it rested, even if for only short periods of time. Even his restlessness may be called mystical.

THE TEXTS

HOMILY ON PSALM 41[3]
Like as the hart desireth the water brooks, so longeth my soul after Thee, O God.
1.... "As the deer longs for the watersprings, so, O my God, my soul longs for You." Who is it then, who speaks in this way? If we wish it, it is we ourselves who speak this language. And what need have you to ask who is speaking, when it is within your power to be him whom you ask about? Yet it is not one man alone: it is the body, the body of Christ, the Church. Now, the holy desire is not found in all who enter into the Church; yet, let those who have tasted the sweetness of God and who, in this chant, recognize this sweetness that they love—let them not believe themselves alone in tasting it, and let them be persuaded that a like seed is spread

throughout the field of the Lord, through the whole world, and that this word: "As the deer longs for the watersprings, so, O my God, my soul longs for you" is that of a certain Christian unity. . . .

And indeed it is not ill understood as the cry of those, who being as yet catechumens, are hastening to the grace of the holy font. On which occasion too this psalm is ordinarily chanted on those occasions, that they may long for the fountain of remissions of sins, even as the hart for the water-brooks. Let this be allowed; and this meaning retain its place in the Church; a place both truthful and sanctioned by usage. Nevertheless, it appears to me, my brethren, that such a longing is not fully satisfied even in the faithful in baptism; but that haply, if they know where they are sojourning, and to where they have to remove from hence, their longing is kindled in even greater intensity. . . .

2. This psalm is sung as 'a Psalm of Understanding' (title). For what understanding is it sung? Come, my brethren, catch my eagerness; share with me in this my longing: let us both love, let us both be influenced with this thirst, let us both hasten to the well of understanding. Let us then long for it as the hart for the brook; let us long for that fountain whereof another Scripture saith, *For with Thee is the fountain of life*. For He is both the Fountain and the Light; for it is *In Thy Light that we shall see light*. If He is both the Fountain and the Light, with good reason is He the Understanding also, because He both filleth the soul that thirsteth for knowledge, and every one who hath 'understanding' is enlightened by a certain light; not a corporeal, not a carnal one, not an outward, but an inward light! There is, then, a certain light within, not possessed by those who understand not. Run to the brooks; long after the water brooks, *With God is the fountain of Life*; a fountain that shall never be dried up: in His light is a light that shall never be darkened. Long thou for this light: for a certain fountain, a certain light, such as thy bodily eyes know not; a light, to see which the inward eye must be prepared; a fountain, to drink of which the inward thirst is to be kindled. Run to the fountain; long for the fountain; but do it not anyhow, be not satisfied with running like any ordinary animal; run thou like the hart.

3. But perhaps Scripture meant us to consider in the hart another

point also. The hart destroys serpents, and after the killing of serpents, it is inflamed with thirst yet more violent. The serpents are thy vices; destroy the serpents of iniquity, then wilt thou long yet more for the Fountain of Truth. Whilst thou art yet indulgent to thy vices, thy covetousness or thy appetite, when am I to find in thee a longing such as this, that might make thee run to the water brooks? When art thou to desire the Fountain of Wisdom, whilst thou art yet laboring in the venom of iniquity? Destroy in thyself whatever is contrary to the truth, and when thou has seen thyself to be comparatively free from irrational passions, be not contented to stay where thou art, as if there was nothing further for thee to long for. For there is yet something to which thou mayest raise thyself, even if thou hast already achieved that triumph within, that there is no longer within thee a foe to hinder and to thwart thee. For perhaps if thou art the hart, thou wilt already say to me: 'God knows that I am no longer covetous, that I no longer set my heart on the property of any man; that I am not inflamed by the passion of unlawful love; that I do not pine away with hatred or ill-will against any man'; and as to all other things of this description, thou wilt say: 'I am free from them'; and perhaps thou wouldest fain know wherein thou mayest find pleasure. Long for the water brooks; God hath wherewith to refresh thee, and to satisfy thee when thou comest to Him, athirst, like the swift-footed hart, after the destruction of the serpents.

5. Such a hart, then, being yet in a state of 'faith' only, not yet in 'sight' of what he believes, has to bear with adversaries, who mock the man who believes, and cannot show them that in which he believes, saying, Where is thy God?

7. Meditating day and night on this taunt, I have myself sought to find my God, that if I could I might not believe only, but might see also somewhat. For I see the things which my God hath made, but my God Himself I do not see. . . . Is God, then, anything of the same nature as the soul? This mind of ours seeks to find something that is God. It seeks a Truth not subject to change, a Substance not capable of failings. The mind itself is not of this nature; it is capable of progress and decay, of knowledge and ignorance, of remembering or of forgetting. That mutability is not incident to God.

8. Having therefore sought to find my God in visible and corporeal things, and found Him not; having sought to find His Substance in myself, and found Him not, I perceive my God to be something higher than my soul. Therefore that I might attain unto Him *I thought on these things, and poured out my soul above myself.* When would my soul attain to that object of its search, which is 'above my soul,' if my soul were not to pour itself out above itself? For were it to rest in itself, it would not see anything else beyond itself; and in seeing itself, would not, for all that, see God. Let then my insulting enemies now say, *Where is thy God?* Aye, let them say it! I, so long as I do not see, so long as my happiness is postponed, *Make my tears my bread day and night.* I seek my God in every corporeal nature, terrestrial or celestial, and find Him not; I seek His Substance in my own soul, and I find it not; yet still have I thought on these things, and wishing to see *the invisible things of my God being understood by the things made,* I have poured forth my soul above myself, and there remains no longer any being for me to attain to (*tangam*), save my God. For there is the 'house of my God.' His dwelling place is above my soul; from thence He beholds me; from thence He governs me and provides for me; from thence He appeals to me, and calls me, and directs me; leads me in the way, and to the end of my way.

9. But He Who has His house very high in a secret place, hath also on earth a tabernacle. His tabernacle on earth is the Church. It is here that He is to be sought, for it is in the tabernacle that is found the way by which we arrive at the house. *For I will go into the place of Thy admirable tabernacle, even unto the house of God.* God's tabernacle on earth is the Faithful. How much is there I admire in this tabernacle—the self-conquest and the virtues of God's servants. I admire the presence of those virtues in the soul; but I am still walking in *the place of the tabernacle.* I pass beyond these also; and admirable though the tabernacle be, yet when I come *to the house of God,* I am even struck dumb with astonishment. It is there, in the sanctuary of God, in the house of God, is the fountain of understanding. It was going up to the tabernacle that the Psalmist arrived at the house of God. It was thus, that whilst admiring the members of the tabernacle, he was led on to the house of God: by following the leadings of a certain delight, an inward mysterious and hidden pleasure, as if

from the house of God there sounded sweetly some instrument; and he, whilst walking in the tabernacle, hearing a certain inward sound, led on by its sweetness, and following the guidance of the sound, withdrawing himself from all noise of flesh and blood, made his way on even to the house of God. For he tells us of his progress and of his guidance thither; as if we had been saying, 'You are admiring the tabernacle here on earth; how came you to the sanctuary of the house of God? And he says, '*In the voice of joy and praise, the sound of keeping holiday.*' In the house of God there is a never-ending festival; the angelic choir makes an eternal holiday, the presence of God's face, joy that never fails. From that everlasting, perpetual festivity there sounds in the ears of the heart a mysterious strain, melodious and sweet, provided only the world does not drown the sounds. As he walks in this tabernacle, and considers God's wonderful works for the redemption of the faithful, the sound of that festivity charms his ears and bears the *hart* away to *the water brooks*.

10. But seeing that 'the corruptible body presseth down the soul,' even though we have in some way dispersed the clouds by walking as longing leads us on, and for a brief while have come within reach of that sound, so that by an effort we may catch something from the house of God; yet through the burden, so to speak, of our infirmity, we sink back to our usual level and relapse to our ordinary state (*consueta*). And just as there we found cause for rejoicing, so here there will not be wanting an occasion for sorrow. For that hart that *made tears its bread day and night*, borne along *by longing to the water-brooks* (that is, to the inward sweetness of God), *pouring forth his soul above himself*, that he may attain to what is above his own soul, walking *unto the place of the admirable tabernacle, even unto the house of God*, and led on by the delight of that inward spiritual sound to feel contempt for exterior things and be ravished by things interior, is but a mortal man still; is still groaning here, still bearing about the frailty of the flesh, still in peril in the midst of the offences of this world. He therefore gazes on himself, as if he were coming from that other world; and says to himself, now placed in the midst of these sorrows, comparing these with the things to see which he had entered in there, and after seeing which he had come forth from thence, '*Why are thou cast down, O my soul, and why dost*

thou disquiet me?' Lo, we have just now been gladdened by certain inward delights; with the mind's eye we have been able to behold, though but with a momentary glance, something not susceptible of change: why dost thou still disquiet me, why art thou still cast down? For thou dost not doubt of thy God. For now thou art not without something to say to thyself in answer to those who say, *Where is thy God?* I have now had the perception of something that is unchangeable: 'why dost thou disquiet me still?' And as, if his soul was silently replying to him, 'Why do I disquiet thee, but because I am not yet there, where that delight is, to which I was rapt in passing. Am I already drinking from this fountain with nothing to fear? Have I no longer anything to be anxious about, as if all my passions were conquered and thoroughly subdued? Is not my foe, the devil, on the watch against me? Wouldst thou have me not disquiet thee, placed as I am yet in the world, and on pilgrimage from the house of God?' Still *Hope in God* is his answer to the soul that disquiets him, . . .

THE CONFESSIONS

BOOK NINE[4]

10. The day was now approaching when she [Augustine's mother, Monica] was to depart this life—the day you knew though we did not—it came about, as, I believe, by your secret arrangement that she and I stood alone leaning in a window which looked onto the garden inside the house where we were staying, at Ostia on the Tiber where, apart from the group, we were resting for the sea voyage after the weariness of our long journey by land. There we conversed, she and I alone, very sweetly, and "forgetting the things that were behind and straining forward to those ahead" (Phil 3:13), we were discussing in the presence of Truth, which you are, what the eternal life of the saints would be like, "which eye has not seen nor ear heard, nor has it entered into the heart of man" (1 Cor 2:9). But with the mouth of our heart we also panted for the supernal streams from your fountain, the fountain of life which is with you (Ps 35:10) so that if some drops of that fountain, according to our capacity, were to be sprinkled over us, we might somehow be able to think of such high matters.

And our discourse arrived at this point, that the greatest pleasure of the bodily senses, in the brightest corporeal light whatsoever, seemed to us not worthy of comparison with the joy of that eternal life, unworthy of being even mentioned. Then with our affections burning still more strongly toward the Selfsame we advanced step by step through the various levels of bodily things, up to the sky itself from which the sun and moon and stars shine upon this earth. And higher still we ascended by thinking inwardly and speaking and marveling at your works, and we came to our own minds and transcended them to reach that region of unfailing abundance where you feed Israel forever on the food of truth (Ez.34:13). There, life is wisdom by whom all these things come into being, both those which have been and those which will be. And wisdom itself is not made; it is as it has ever been, and so it shall be forever. Indeed, "has ever been" and "shall be forever" do not pertain to it, but it simply is, for it is eternal. And while we were speaking and panting for wisdom, we did with the whole impulse of the heart slightly touch it. We sighed and left behind "the first fruits of the Spirit" (Rom 8:23) which were bound there, and returned to the sound of our own tongue where the spoken word has both beginning and ending. How is it like your word, our Lord, "remaining ageless in Itself and renewing all things" (Wis 7:27)? We said therefore: If to any man the uproar of the flesh grew silent, silent the images of earth and sea and air, and if the heavens also grew silent and the very soul grew silent, and by not thinking of self ascended beyond self; if all dreams and imagined revelations grew silent, and every tongue and every sign and if everything created to pass away were completely silent—since if one hears them, they all say this: We did not make ourselves, but He who abides forever made us. Suppose that having said this and directed our attention to Him who made them, they also were to become hushed and He Himself alone were to speak, not by their voice but in His own, and we were to hear His Word, not through any tongue of flesh or voice of an angel or sound of thunder or involved allegory, but that we might hear Him whom in all these things we love, might hear Him in Himself without them, just as a moment ago we two, as it were, rose beyond ourselves and in a flash of thought touched the Eternal Wisdom abiding over all. If this were to continue and other quite different visions disappear, leaving only this one to ravish and absorb and enclose its beholder in inward joys so that life might forever be such as that one moment of understanding for which we had been sighing, would not this surely be: "Enter into the joy of Your Lord" (Mt 25:21)? But when shall it be? Perhaps when "we shall all rise again" and "shall not all be changed" (1 Cor 15)?

BOOK TEN[5]

6. It is not with doubtful but with assured awareness, O Lord, that I love you. You pierced my heart with your Word and I loved you. But also heaven and earth and all within them, behold, they bid me on every side to love you, nor do they cease telling this to all, "that they may be without excuse" (Rom 1:20). But more deeply "will you have mercy on whom you will have mercy, and will show compassion to whom you will show compassion" (Rom 9:15); otherwise, heaven and earth proclaim your praises to deaf ears. But what do I love when I love you? Not the beauty of body nor the gracefulness of temporal rhythm, not the brightness of light so friendly to the eyes, not the sweet and various melodies of songs, not the fragrance of flowers and ointments and spices, not manna and honey; not limbs receptive to fleshly embraces: I love not these when I love my God. And yet I do love a kind of light, melody, fragrance, food, embracement when I love my God; for He is the light, the melody, the fragrance, the food, the embracement of my inner self; Where that light shines into my soul which no place can contain, and where that voice sounds which time does not take away, and where that fragrance smells which no wind scatters, and where there is that flavor which eating does not diminish, and where there is that clinging that no satiety will separate. This is what I love when I love my God.

And what is this? I asked the earth and it said: "I am not He," and all things in it made the same confession. I asked the sea and the deep and the creeping things and they answered: "We are not your god; seek above us." I asked the blowing breezes, and the entire air with its inhabitants said: "Anaximenes was deceived; I am not god." I questioned the sky, the sun, the moon, the stars: "Nor are we the god whom you seek," they said. And I said to all these that surround the doors of my flesh: "Tell me about my God, since you are not He, tell me something about Him." And they exclaimed in a loud voice: "He made us." My question was in my contemplation of them; and their answer was in their beauty. And I turned attention upon myself and said: "Who are you?" and I answered: "A man." Now I find in myself a soul and body, one exterior, the one interior. Which of these should I have used in seeking for my God? I had already searched for Him by means of the body, searching from earth to sky, as far as I could direct the beams of my eyes as messengers. But the interior part of me is the better. To this part all my bodily messengers gave in their reports and this inner reality sat in judgment weighing the replies of heaven and earth and all things within them when they said: "We are not God," and when they said, "He made us." The inner man knew these things through the ministry of the outer man; I, the inner man, knew all this; I, the soul, through my bodily senses; I asked the whole mass of the world about my God, and it answered me: "I am not He, but He made me". . .

For truth says to me: "Your God is not sky or earth, or any body." Their own nature declares this. They recognize that there is less bulk in a part than in a whole. Now, my soul, I tell you that you are my better part, since you animate the whole bulk of the body, giving life to it, which no body confers on a body. But God, however, is even for you the Life of your life. . .

27. Late have I loved you, O Beauty, so ancient and so new, late have I loved you! And behold, you were within me and I was outside, and there I sought for you, and in my deformity I rushed headlong into the well formed things that you have made. You were with me, and I was not with you. Those outer beauties held me far from you, yet if they had not been in you, they would not have existed at all. You called, and cried out to me and broke open my deafness; you shone forth upon me and you scattered my blindness; You breathed fragrance, and I drew in my breath and I now pant for you: I tasted and I hunger and thirst; you touched me, and I burned for Your peace.

ON THE TRINITY

Chapter Eight

11. We have now arrived at that point in our discussion where we begin to consider that highest part of the human mind by which it knows or can know God, in order to discover therein an image of God. Although the human mind is not of God's own nature, yet the image of that nature which transcends in excellence every other nature is to be sought and discovered in the most excellent part of our own nature.

But primarily we have to consider the mind in itself, before it participates in God, and there discover His image. We have asserted that it still remains the image of God, although an image obscured and defaced by the loss of its participation in God. This is His image because it has a capacity for God and can participate in God: It has this high destiny only because it is His image.

Chapter Twelve

15. Now this trinity of the mind is the image of God, not because the mind remembers, understands, and loves itself, but because it also has the power to remember, understand, and love its Maker. And in doing this it attains wisdom. If it does not do this, the memory, understanding, and love of itself is no more than an act of folly. Therefore, let the mind remember its God, to whose image it was made, let it understand and love him.

In brief, let it worship the uncreated God who created it with the capacity for Himself, and in whom it can be made partaker. Hence it is written: "Behold, the worship of God is wisdom" (Jb 28:28). By participating in that supreme Light wisdom will belong to the mind not by its own light, and it will reign in bliss only where the eternal Light is. The wisdom is so called the wisdom of man as to be also that of God. If wisdom were only human it would be vain, for only God's wisdom is true wisdom.

Cassian saw the goal of the monastic life as entrance into eternal life that could be experienced here in some way. Through the perfect assimilation of psalmody, the mystical "prayer of fire" is born, transforms the person, and illuminates the Bible's whole meaning.

JOHN CASSIAN

At a time when the Mediterranean area was experiencing the breakdown of Roman rule, civil unrest, theological controversies, and varied, sometimes fanatical, monastic movements, there arose a man who was to write the most interesting documents of 5th century monasticism, give the West its first summa of Christian spirituality, state the problems of this spirituality in a way that has remained largely unchanged to the present day, and become the guide of Western monasticism. Such was his stature that even the great St. Benedict stated in his famous Rule for monks that John Cassian's *Institutes* and *Conferences* should be read regularly.

John Cassian was born in Scythia Minor (present-day Romania), travelled in his youth to a monastery in Bethlehem to live an ascetic life, went to Egypt around 386 with his friend Germanicus to sit at the feet of the great Egyptian monastic masters for seven years, then lived the monastic life in Palestine, the Nile region, and Constantinople where he was ordained a deacon by St. John Chrysostom. In 404, he went to Rome for 10 years, was ordained a priest, and finally went to Marseilles, where he founded two monasteries, and died with the reputation of a saint.

The selected texts bring out clearly that the entire thrust of Cassian's thought was toward the private, mystical experience of God, but always fused with and interpenetrated by private and corporate psalmody and worship. His great heroes were the Egyptian desert fathers who favored the eremetic, anchoritic, hermit way of life as the best means to complete solitude with God. Nonetheless, his austere ascetic ideal remains always firmly anchored to an attractive, realistic humaneness. For example, Cassian forbade anchoritic living, or solitary living, before having passed through a lengthy and fruitful cenobitic life, that is, monastic life in a community.

It was likewise Cassian's genius to interpret and blend perspicaciously the best of Egyptian monasticism, of Origen, and of Evagrius with his own deeply Christian common sense, moderation, and discretion for cenobitic monks. Furthermore, with Cassian, monasticism never lost sight of its graced, mystical, agapic, eschatological orientation.

As the selected texts illustrate, Cassian saw the goal of the monastic life as entrance into the Kingdom of God, into eternal life, which could be experienced here in some way. The monk must have the "passion for the unseen," and must tend to union with God through loving attention to him alone. For Cassian, contemplation—as with perfection—admitted of many degrees and forms. However, the good Origenist that he was emphasized the necessity of reading, pondering, understanding, and assimilating Scripture in order that God's light may impregnate, illuminate, absorb, and establish itself in the soul. Cassian was also a proponent of an apophatic light mysticism, a prayer full of limitless, unbounded light totally beyond concepts, visions, and forms.

The selected texts also illustrate that Cassian had undoubtedly experienced the seamless bond between the "simple" scriptural knowledge of God and the heights of mysticism. For him, through the perfect assimilation of psalmody, the "prayer of fire" is born. Even the most mystical of prayer should begin its ascent from psalmody. But only mystical prayer is capable of revealing Scriptures' whole meaning. And because the human mind can come to authentic truth only if it is transformed through virtue, meditation, and mystical contemplation, even illiterate monks may attain to Scriptures' deepest truths. Moreover, by emphasizing the monk's entire communal, liturgical, and scriptural life, the context of "pure prayer" was less likely to be overlooked and to become the angelism of *misunderstood* Pseudo-Macarian and Evagrian prayer.

The texts were also selected to show that like Pseudo-Macarius, Evagrius, and the best of the Desert Fathers, Cassian saw contemplation as the fruit of, or at least as made possible by, asceticism. Cassian condemned asceticism as an end in itself. Christian asceticism must aspire to contemplative union with God. The monk renounces comfort, sin, and everything but God alone for the sake of Christian love of God and neighbor. The monk undertakes the spiritual combat against the self and the demons in order to attain "purity of heart," the loving purity that borders on contemplative union with God. "Purity of heart" is the equivalent of Evagrian *apatheia*, a term Cassian avoided because of the controversies of his day.

Cassian appreciated deeply both the ascetical foundation of mysticism and the mystical basis of asceticism. Asceticism prepares the soul for contemplative union with God. Contemplative union with God not only nourishes and animates the spiritual ascent; it also completes the first two stages of renunciation. Like Evagrius, the threefold aspects of the ascent to God are actually concomitant, not consecutive. But like Origen, Cassian compares these aspects to the books of Proverbs, Ecclesiastes, and Song of Songs.

"The long section of chapter 10 of the tenth Conference," writes one commentator, "is one of the most beautiful passages of all Christian writing during more than a thousand years of religious devotion."[1] This section, given in the selections below, also illustrates the Eastern monastic practice of *monologistos* prayer, that is, prayer in one formula. Although the Jesus prayer is perhaps the most famous, Cassian may well be the first to give full articulation to the continuous repetition of an evocative verse, in his case, Ps 69:2, "O God, come to my assistance, Lord make haste to help me."[2]

THE TEXTS

6. "Something must now be said about the renunciations. The tradition of the fathers and the authority of the Scriptures put them at three and it is right that we should strive with maximum zeal to achieve them.

"The first renunciation has to do with the body. We come to despise all the riches and all goods of the world. With the second renunciation we repel our past, our vices, the passions governing spirit and flesh. And in the third renunciation we draw our spirit away from the here and the visible and we do so in order solely to contemplate the things of the future. Our passion is for the unseen.

"We read that the Lord instructed Abraham to achieve all three together. He said to him: 'Come away from you native land and from your family and from the house of your father' (Gn 12:1). He said first 'from your native land,' that is, from the riches of this world and from the goods of the earth. Second, 'from your family,' that is, from one's past way of life, character, and faults, which cling to us from birth and are linked to us by a sort of close relationship and blood. He said, thirdly, 'from the house of your father,' that is, from all worldly memory arising before our eyes.

"God in the person of David sings of two fathers, the one to be left and the one to be sought: 'My daughter, hear and see and incline your ear. Forget your people and the house of your father' (Ps 44:11). Now whoever said 'My daughter' is certainly a father and, equally, a father is he who instructed his daughter to forget home and people.

"All this happens when, dead with Christ to all that is in this world, our gaze, as the apostle proclaims, is 'not upon those things which are seen but on the unseen; for the things which are seen belong to time and the things which are not seen are everlasting' (2

Cor 4:18). In our hearts we leave this time-ridden, visible house and we firmly turn our eyes and mind to where we will remain forever. And we will achieve this when, still in the flesh, we begin to soldier in the Lord, not as flesh would have it, but when our deeds and our virtues join the apostle in crying out, 'Our homeland is in heaven' (Phil 3:20).

"The three books of Solomon accord with these three renunciations. Corresponding to the first renunciation is Proverbs, in which the desire for the things of the flesh and for earthly sin are excoriated. Corresponding to the second renunciation is Ecclesiasticus, where the vanity of everything under the sun is proclaimed. And applicable to the third is the Song of Songs, in which the mind, rising beyond all things visible, contemplates all that is of heaven and is brought into union with the Word of God."

CONFERENCE TEN[4]

ON PRAYER
10. "You were quite right to make the comparison between training in continuous prayer and the teaching of children who at first do not know the alphabet, do not recognize letters, and are unable to write with a sure and firm hand. Models are put before them, carefully drawn in wax. By continually studying them, by practicing every day to reproduce them, they learn at least to write.

"The same happens with contemplation. You need a model and you keep it constantly before your eyes. You learn either to turn it in a salutary way over and over in your spirit or else, as you use it and meditate upon it, you lift yourself upward to the most sublime sights.

"And what follows now is the model to teach you, the prayer formula for which you are searching. Every monk who wants to think continuously about God should get accustomed to meditating endlessly on it and to banishing all other thoughts for its sake. But he will not hold on to it unless he breaks completely free from all bodily concerns and cares.

"This is something which has been handed on to us by some of the oldest of the Fathers and it is something which we hand on to only a very small number of the souls eager to know it:

"To keep the thought of God always in your mind you must cling totally to this formula for piety: 'Come to my help, O God; Lord, hurry to my rescue' (Ps 69:2).

"It is not without good reason that this verse has been chosen from the whole of Scripture as a device. It carries within it all the feelings of which human nature is capable. It can be adapted to every condition and can be usefully deployed against every temptation. It carries within it a cry of help to God in the face of every danger. It expresses the humility of a pious confession. It conveys the watchfulness born of unending worry and fear. It conveys a sense of our frailty, the assurance of being heard, the confidence in help that is always and everywhere present. Someone forever calling out to his protector is indeed very sure of having him close by. This is the voice filled with the ardor of love and of charity. This is the terrified cry of someone who see the snares of the enemy, the cry to someone besieged day and night and exclaiming that he cannot escape unless his protector come to the rescue.

"This short verse is an indomitable wall for all those struggling against the onslaught of demons. It is an impenetrable breastplate and the sturdiest of shields. Whatever the disgust, the anguish, or the gloom in our thoughts, this verse keeps us from despairing of our salvation since it reveals to us the One to whom we call, the One who sees our struggles and who is never far from those who pray to Him. If things go well for us in spirit, if there is joy in our hearts, this verse is a warning to us not to grow proud, not to get puffed up at being in a good condition which, as it demonstrates, cannot be retained without the protection of God for whose continuous and speedy help it prays. This little verse, I am saying, proves to be necessary and useful to each one of us and in all circumstances. For someone who needs help in all things is making clear that he requires the help of God not simply in hard and sad situations but equally and amid fortunate and joyful conditions. He knows that God saves us from adversity and makes our joys linger and that in neither situation can human frailty survive without His help.

"I am assailed by a passion for good eating. I am on the watch for food of which the desert knows nothing. Into the drabness of my solitary life come the fragrances of royal dishes and I feel myself dragged unwillingly down by my longing for them. And so I must say 'Come to my help, O God; Lord, hurry to my rescue.'

. . . "The flesh attacks me, and I should fast more strictly. But weariness, or my parched, closed-in appetite keeps me back. And if my hopes are to be fulfilled, if the fevered stirrings of fleshly desire are to be quieted down, then I must pray 'Come to my help, O God; Lord, hurry to my rescue.'

. . . "I want to read, so as to keep my thoughts in order. A headache keeps me from it. Or, at the third hour, sleepiness inclines my face onto the sacred page and I have an urge either to skip the appointed time for rest or to anticipate it. During assembly sleep weighs so much on me that I am forced to interrupt the canonical recitation of the psalms. And so too I must cry 'Come to my help, O God; Lord, hurry to my rescue.'

. . . "I am troubled by the pangs of rage, of greed, of gloom. I am drawn to scatter that gentleness which I had embraced as my own. And so if I am not to be carried off by turbulent rage into bitterness I must groan mightily and call out 'Come to my help, O God; Lord, hurry to my rescue.'

. . . "In my soul are countless and varied distractions. I am in a fever as my heart moves this way and that. I have no strength to hold in check the scatterings of my thoughts. I cannot utter my prayer without interruption, without being visited by empty images and by the memory of words and doings. I feel myself bound in by such sterility that I cannot bring to birth any spiritual feelings within me. And so if I am to deserve liberation from this bleakness of spirit from which my groans and sighs have been unable to save me I shall be obliged to cry out 'Come to my help, O God; Lord, hurry to my rescue.'

"I feel that my spirit has once more found a sense of direction, that my thinking has grown purposeful, that because of a visit of the Holy Spirit my heart is unspeakably glad and my mind ecstatic. Here is a great overflow of spiritual thoughts, thanks to a sudden illumination and to the coming of the Savior. The holiest ideas, hitherto concealed from me, have been revealed to me. And so if I am to deserve to remain for much longer, I must anxiously and regularly cry 'Come to my help, O God; Lord, hurry to my rescue.'

... "Again, when I have been made whole by the consolation of the Lord, when I have been encouraged by His coming, when I feel myself guarded by countless thousands of angels, when I have the daring to seek out and call to battle those whom I once feared more than death, those whose mere touch or presence filled me, mind and body, with terror, then indeed if I am to hold on to this strength of purpose I must, with all my strength, cry 'Come to my help, O God; Lord, hurry to my rescue.'

"Our prayer for rescue in bad times and for protection against pride in good times should be founded on this verse. The thought of this verse should be turning unceasingly in your heart. Never cease to recite it in whatever task or service or journey you find yourself. Think upon it as you sleep, as you eat, as you submit to the most basic demands of nature. This heartfelt thought will prove to be a formula of salvation for you. Not only will it protect you against all devilish attack, but it will purify you from the stain of all earthly sin and will lead you on to the contemplation of the unseen and the heavenly and to that fiery urgency of prayer which is indescribable and which is experienced by very few. Sleep should come upon you as you meditate on this verse until as a result of your habit of resorting to its words you get in the habit of repeating them even in your slumbers.

"This verse should be the first thing to occur to you when you wake up. It should precede all your thoughts as you keep vigil. It should take you over as you rise from your bed and go to kneel. After this it should accompany you in all your works and deeds. It should be at your side at all times. Following the precept of Moses, you will think upon it 'as you sit at home or walk along your way' (Dt 6:7), as you sleep or when you get up. You will write it upon the threshold and gateway of your mouth, you will place it on the walls of your house and in the inner sanctum of your heart. It will be a continuous prayer, an endless refrain when you bow down in prostration and when you rise up to do all the necessary things of life.

11. "Someone like this, someone who has not only reached the state of having the simplicity of the innocent but who is fortified by the virtue of discernment, becomes the exterminator of the most vicious serpents and he keeps Satan under foot. The zeal of his soul makes him like a spiritual deer who feeds on the high mountains of the prophets and the apostles, that is, on their most high and most exalted teachings. Nourished by this food, which he continually eats, he penetrates so deeply into the thinking of the psalms that he sings them not as though they had been composed by the prophet but as if he himself had written them, as if this were his own private prayer uttered amid the deepest compunction of heart. Certainly he thinks of them as having been specially composed for him and he recognizes that what they express was made real not simply once upon a time in the person of the prophet but that now, every day, they are being fulfilled in himself.

"Then indeed the Scriptures lie ever more clearly open to us. They are revealed, heart and sinew. Our experience not only brings us to know them but actually anticipates what they convey. The meaning of the words comes through to us not just by way of commentaries but by what we ourselves have gone through. Seized of the identical feelings in which the psalm was composed or sung we become, as it were, its author. We anticipate its idea instead of following it. We have a sense of it even before we make out the meaning of the words. The sacred words stir memories within us, memories of the daily attacks which we have endured and are enduring, the cost of our negligence or the profits of our zeal, the good things of providence and the deceits of the enemy, the slippery subtle tricks of memory, the blemishes of human frailty, the improvidence of ignorance. As we sing we are reminded of all this.

"We find all these sentiments expressed in the psalms. We see very clearly, as in a mirror, what is being said to us and we have a deeper understanding of it. Instructed by our own experiences we are not really learning through hearsay but have a feeling for these sentiments as things that we have already seen. They are not like things confided to our capacity for remembrance but, rather, we bring them to birth in the depths of our hearts as if they were feelings naturally there and part of our being. We enter into their meaning not because of what we read but because of what we have experienced earlier.

"This prayer centers on no contemplation of some image or other. It is masked by no attendant sounds or words. It is a fiery outbreak, an indescribable exaltation, an insatiable thrust of the soul. Free of what is sensed and seen, ineffable in its groans and sighs, the soul pours itself out to God."

CONFERENCE NINE[5]
ON PRAYER
25. "It would seem, then, that this prayer, the Our Father, contains the fullness of perfection. It was the Lord Himself who gave it to us as both an example and a rule. It raises up those making use of it to that preeminent situation of which I spoke earlier. It lifts them up to that prayer of fire known to so few. It lifts them up, rather, to that ineffable prayer which rises above all human consciousness, with no voice sounding, no tongue moving, no words uttered. The soul lights up with heavenly illumination and no longer employs constricted, human speech. All sensibility is gathered together and, as though from some very abundant source, the soul breaks forth richly, burst out unspeakably to God, and in the tiniest instant it pours out so much more than the soul can either describe or remember when it returns again to itself.

"Our Lord, with this formula of pleading, passed through this same condition or situation. He withdrew to the solitude of the mountain, and in the silent prayer of His agony He gave with his bloody sweat an inimitable example of ardor."

The Fifty Homilies *of the cenobitic monk, Pseudo-*
Macarius, express the immense longing for God in
the soul's mysterious depths. Their central theme is
the soul's transformation into light when the divine
light that permeated Christ on Mount Tabor enters.

PSEUDO-MACARIUS

Because of their penetrating ascetical and mystical insights, the so-
called *Fifty Homilies* of Macarius had a tremendous influence in fur-
thering the monastic movements initiated by Gregory of Nyssa and
Basil the Great. By making the ideas of Basil, but especially of Gregory, more available to a "popular" audience, these homilies played
a significant role in integrating the burgeoning monastic movements into the wider Church life. So far ranging was their influence
that these homilies eventually found their way into Jesuit spirituality, Lutheran pietism, John Wesley's spirituality, and the beginnings
of the Catholic Pentecostal movement in the United States.

These homilies are actually monastic conferences and spiritual conversations, laced with biblical quotations and allusions. They express the immense longing for God that has penetrated the soul's
mysterious depths. Highly dependent upon Gregory of Nyssa, but
devoid of Gregory's darkness imagery, their central theme is the
soul's transformation into light when the divine light enters.

The true author of these homilies was not Macarius the Egyptian
(also known as "the Elder" and "the Great") who was born around
300 and died approximately 389, with a reputation as a miracle-
worker and a genius of spiritual direction, but a Mesopotamian
Macarius born approximately a century later.

These homilies were written when sects of heretical Messalians, also called "Euchites," or "Bogomils" ("Cathars" in the West), with their dualistic conceptions rooted in Manichaeism were becoming wide-spread in Asia Minor. These so-called "praying people" believed that because of Adam's sin, a demon united itself substantially to every human soul and is not expelled even through baptism.

However, the Messalians maintained that severe ascetical practices, especially concentrated, ceaseless prayer will eradicate all passion and desire, and exorcise the demon. The perfect can receive the beatific, immediate vision of the Trinity in this life, even to the point of seeing God with their physical eyes. They emphasized also that one should abstain from all forms of work and the Church's sacraments because these were of no use to obtain the highly-desired experience of God.

However, these homilies are free of Messalianism's misguided emphasis upon angelic "pure prayer," as well as its grosser errors. In fact, Pseudo-Macarius considered the heart, not the Greek mind (*nous*), to be the center of human consciousness. Christ descended into the unfathomable depths of the "hell-heart"[1] so all could ascend with him to the Father. Thus, Macarius sought not a disincarnation of the mind, but the transfiguration of the entire person through union with God. Moreover, his christocentric and sacramental emphases stand as a strong counterpoint to Messalianism. In addition, these emphases were also to give a new orientation to Evagrian-type prayer in later monastic movements. For Macarius, if baptism and the eucharist sanctify the whole person, then pure prayer must likewise involve the body.

Pseudo-Macarius taught a cenobitic form of monasticism. Urging a radical separation from the world by joining a desert community that practiced strict poverty and a total separation even from one's own self through total obedience, he exhorted his monks to live in harmony and to serve each other for the love of God. If his first commandment is to love God totally, he considered zealous, unceasing prayer to be the primary monastic virtue.

He viewed the fallen human person as free, but pulled by two powers: the Holy Spirit and the devil. Christian life on earth is a never-ending spiritual combat between the forces of good and evil, with the human soul as the battlefield and the booty. The monk must do battle against himself, his passions, the various demons that stir up these passions, and his own propensity toward presumption and pride.

To win this battle, the monk must expect nothing from himself, but constantly cry out and ask for God's grace. Through prayer the monk cooperates actively with grace and opens himself to the Holy Spirit's further work in the soul. For those not proficient in this combat, he taught an ascetical, "natural" prayer. By declaring war on oneself, by practicing the virtues, by the ruthless elimination of all distracting thoughts, one constrains and forces oneself to pray by concentrating one's thoughts heavenward. Thus, one should force oneself to do what God will eventually grant.

In fact, Pseudo-Macarius seemed to view thoughts as the devil's chief weapon in the spiritual combat. Because the devil proposes evil thoughts or even seemingly good thoughts—but distracting ones—the monk must learn the source of his thoughts: God, the good angels, the devil, or the self.

One is baptized in the Holy Spirit when one attains deep compunction for sins and a vivid awareness of Jesus Christ as Lord and Savior. The Holy Spirit burns out evil thoughts, teaches discernment, instills calm in the soul, and may lead the monk eventually to "true," or "pure" prayer.

True prayer is experiential, a true sensing of the Holy Spirit working in the soul that bestows interior tasting, various joys, and even different kinds of ecstasies. Because ineffable light often accompanied pure prayer, it is clear that Pseudo-Macarius is an early proponent of "Tabor," or "light" mysticism.

Paradoxically, the monk of true prayer experiences total dependence and total liberty. He is like a poor man befriended by a rich man who has given the poor man total access to his house and wealth. Pure prayer gives true repose and freedom from all evil thoughts that assail the soul. However, the monk should not presume that this state of ineffable peace and perfect joy in which he is a "body-bearing spirit" (*pneuma sarkophoron*) will last. He must invoke continually the Holy Spirit and Jesus, for the spiritual combat never ends in this life.

The following selections give a good insight into Pseudo- Macarius' light and heart mysticism; his emphasis upon continual custody of the heart by unceasing concentration upon Christ, the divine artist, who implants his own image upon the soul; his focus upon the person as a redeemed sinner always threatened by sin but always empowered by grace to make continual progress in the spiritual life, a theme he inherited from Gregory of Nyssa; and how the longing in the soul for God is often rewarded by an awakening of the spiritual senses, raptures, miracles, freedom from sin, profound peace, charity toward all, and becoming one spirit with God, deification itself.[2]

THE TEXTS

HOMILY I[3]

An allegorical interpretation of the vision described in the prophet Ezekiel

1. The blessed prophet Ezekiel relates a glorious and inspired vision or apparition which he saw, and his description is that of a vision full of mysteries unspeakable.

2. And this that the prophet saw was in substance true and certain, but it signified something else, mysterious and divine—a *mystery hidden* verily *from ages and from generations,* but *in the last times made manifest* at the appearing of Christ. The mystery which he beheld was that of the soul, that was to receive her Lord, and to become a *throne of glory* for Him. For the soul that is privileged to be in communion with the Spirit of His light, and is irradiated by the beauty of the unspeakable glory of Him who has prepared her to be a seat and a dwelling for Himself, becomes all light, all face, all eye; and there is no part of her that is not full of the spiritual eyes of light. That is to say, there is no part of her darkened, but she is all throughout wrought into light and spirit, and is full of eyes all over, and has no such thing as a back part, but in every direction is face forward, with the unspeakable beauty of the glory of the light of Christ mounted and riding upon her. As the sun is of one likeness

all over, without any part behind or inferior, but is all glorified with light throughout, and is, indeed, all light, with no difference between the parts,—or as fire, the very light of the fire, is alike all over, having in it no first or last, or greater or less,—so also the soul that is perfectly irradiated by the unspeakable beauty of the glory of the light of the face of Christ, and is perfectly in communion with the Holy Ghost, and is privileged to be the dwelling place and throne of God, becomes all eye, all light, all face, all glory, all spirit, being made so by Christ who drives, and guides, and carries, and bears her about and graces and adorns her thus with spiritual beauty.

12. If then thou art become a throne of God, and the heavenly Charioteer has mounted thee, and thy whole soul has become a spiritual eye, and thy whole soul light; and if thou has been nourished with that nourishment of the Spirit, and if thou hast been made to drink of the Living Water, and if thou hast put on the garments of the ineffable light; if thine inward man is established in the experience of full assurance of all these things, behold, thou livest, thou livest the eternal life indeed, and thy soul from henceforth is at rest with the Lord.

HOMILY VIII[4]

1. A man goes in to bend the knee, and his heart is filled with the divine influence, and his soul rejoices with the Lord, like bride with bridegroom, according to that word of the prophet Elijah which says, *As the bridegroom rejoiceth over the bride, so shall the Lord rejoice over thee* (Is 62:5); and it comes to pass that being all day engaged he gives himself to prayer for an hour, and the inward man is rapt in prayer unto the unfathomable deep of that other world in great sweetness, so that his whole mind is up aloft, rapt away thither, and estranged from things below. For the time being forgetfulness comes into him with regard to the interests of the earthly mind, because his thoughts are filled and taken captive to divine and heavenly things, to things infinite and past comprehension, to wonderful things which no human lips can express, so that for that hour he prays and says, "Would God that my soul might pass along with my prayer!"

2. *Question.* Can any one enter into these things at all times?

Answer. Grace is constantly present, and is rooted in us, and worked into us like leaven, from our earliest years, until the thing thus present becomes fixed in a man like a natural endowment, as if it were one substance with him. But, for the man's own good, it manages him in many different ways, after its own pleasure. Sometimes the fire flames out and kindles more vehemently; at other times more gently and mildly. The light that it gives kindles up at times and shines with unusual brightness; at others it abates and burns low. The lamp is always burning and shining, but when it is specially trimmed, it kindles up with intoxication of the love of God; and then again by God's dispensation it gives in, and though the light is always there, it is comparatively dull.

3. To some, however, the sign of the cross has appeared in light and fastened itself upon the inward man. At another time a man at his prayers has fallen into a kind of trance, and found himself standing in the altar-space in church, and three loaves were offered to such a one, leavened with oil, and the more he ate of them, the more they increased and grew. At another time there was brought as it were a shining garment, such as there is none on earth in the course of this world, nor is it possible for human hands to make the like; for as when the Lord went up into the mountain with Peter and John, He changed the fashion of His raiment and made it to flash with light, so was it with this garment, and the man who was clothed with it wondered and was amazed. Another while, the light shining in the heart disclosed the inner, deeper, hidden light, so that the man, swallowed up in the sweetness of the contemplation, was no longer master of himself, but was like a fool or a barbarian to this world by reason of the surpassing love and sweetness, by reason of the hidden mysteries; so that the man for that season was set at liberty, and came to perfect measures, and was set free from sin.

6. . . . . After the sign of the cross, grace now acts thus. It calms all the members of the heart, so that the soul, for much joy, appears like an innocent child, and the man no longer condemns Greek or Jew, sinner or worldling. The inner man regards all men with a pure eye, and the man rejoices over all the world, and desires that all should worship and love, Greeks and Jews . . . .

13. . . . As the serpent spoke to Eve, and because of her compliance gained admission within, so to this day sin, which is without, gains admission through man's compliance. Sin has the power and liberty to enter into the heart. For our thoughts are not external to us, but from within, out of the heart. The apostle says, *I will that men pray, without wrath and evil disputations.* For there are *thoughts proceeding out of the heart,* as the Gospel says. Go to prayer and observe thy heart and mind, and determine to send up thy prayer to God pure, and look well there, whether there be nothing to hinder it, whether the prayer be pure, whether thy mind is wholly occupied with the Lord, as the husbandman's with his husbandry, the married man's with his wife, the merchant's with his merchandise; or whether thou bendest thy knees to prayer, while others pluck thy thoughts asunder.

20. . . . In Christianity, to taste of the grace of God is like that. *Taste,* it says, *and see how gracious the Lord is.* This tasting is an effectual power of the Spirit in full certainty, ministering in the heart. As many as are the sons of light, and of the ministry of the New Covenant in the Holy Ghost, these have nothing to learn from men; they are *taught of God.* Grace itself writes upon their hearts the laws of the Spirit. They ought not therefore to rest their assurance only upon the scriptures that are written in ink; the grace of God writes the laws of the Spirit and the mysteries of heaven upon the *tablets of the heart as well.* For the heart governs and reigns over the whole bodily organism; and when grace possesses the ranges of the heart, it reigns over all the members and the thoughts. For there, in the heart, is the mind, and all the faculties of the soul, and its expectation; therefore grace penetrates also to all the members of the body.

1. Those who draw near to the Lord ought to make their prayers in quietness and peace and great composure, and to fix their minds upon the Lord not with unseemly and confused outcries, but with effort of heart and vigilant thoughts. If someone suffering from a malady needs to be cauterized or to undergo a surgical operation, one man will bear the pain of it with courage and patience, self-possessed, and making no noise or disturbance, while others undergo-

ing the same affliction give way under the fire or the knife to un-seemly outcries, and yet the pain of the man who calls out is ex-actly the same as that of the man who does not—of him who makes a disturbance as of him who makes none. So are there some who under affliction and travail of the soul submit to it with dignity and make no disturbance, controlling themselves by mental reflexion, while others under the same affliction lose their power of endur-ance, and make their prayers with disorderly noise, so as to give of-fence to those who hear them. There are others again who are under no real concern, but for ostentation or singularity make use of undisciplined outcries, as if by these they could please God.

3. The true foundation of prayer is this, to concentrate attention, and to pray in great quietness and peace, so as to give no offence to those outside. Such a man, if he receives the grace of God upon his prayer, and continues to the last in his quietness, will edify other people more.

HOMILY XXVIII[7]

5. This is a thing which every one ought to know, that there are eyes deeper within than the eyes, and a hearing deeper within this hear-ing. As these eyes sensibly behold and recognize the face of a friend or beloved one, so the eyes of the worthy and faithful soul, being spiritually enlightened with the light of God, behold and recognize the true Friend, the sweetest and greatly longed for Bridegroom, the Lord, while the soul is shone upon by the adorable Spirit; and thus beholding with the mind the desirable and only inexpressible beauty, it is smitten with passionate love of God, and is directed to all virtues of the Spirit, and thus possesses an unbounded, unfail-ing love for the Lord it longs for.

HOMILY XXX[8]

4. As the portrait painter keeps an eye upon the king's face and draws, and when the king's face is towards him, attending to him at his painting, he draws the portrait easily and well, but when he turns his face away, he cannot draw, because the face is not gazing at the painter; in like manner Christ, the good artist, for those who believe Him and gaze continually at Him, straightway portrays after His own image a heavenly man. Out of His own Spirit, out of the substance of light itself, the ineffable light, He paints a heavenly

image, and bestows upon it its good and gracious Spouse. If a man does not gaze constantly at Him, overlooking everything else, the Lord will not paint His image with His own light. We must therefore gaze upon Him, believing and loving Him, throwing away all else, and attending to Him, in order that He may paint His own heavenly image and send it into our souls, and thus, wearing Christ, we may receive eternal rest, and even here may have full assurance and be at rest.

HOMILY XXXIII[9]

1. It behooves us to pray, not by bodily habit, nor with a habit of crying, nor by a custom of silence, or of bending the knees, but soberly, taking heed to our minds, to wait upon God, until He shall come to us and visit the soul through all its modes of egress and its paths and senses, and so to be silent when we ought, and to cry out when we ought, and to pray with loud crying, so long as the mind is strong towards God. As the body, when at work, is entirely occupied with the work on which it is engaged, and all the members of it help one another, so let the soul be entirely given up to asking and love towards the Lord, not wandering and carried about with thoughts, but with all its might endeavouring and gathering itself up with all its thoughts, and bend upon waiting for Christ.

HOMILY XL[10]

2. But the chief of all good endeavor, the topmost of right actions, is perseverance in prayer. From it we may daily gain increasingly the rest of the virtues through asking them of God. By it is formed, in those to whom it is vouchsafed, the fellowship of the holiness of God and of spiritual energy, and the attachment of the disposition of the mind to the Lord in love unspeakable. The man who compels himself to persevere in prayer is enflamed with divine affection and fiery longing by spiritual love towards God, and receives the grace of the sanctifying perfection of the Spirit.

HOMILY XLI[11]

1. The precious vessel of the soul is of great depth, as it says in a certain place, *He seeketh out of the deep, and the heart.* When man swerved from the commandment, and came under the sentence of wrath, sin took him for her subject; and being herself like a great

deep of bitterness in subtlety and depth, she entered within and took possession of the ranges of the soul, even to the deepest inner chambers of it. In such a fashion as this let us liken the soul and sin when mixed with it, as if there should be a great big tree with many branches and it has its roots in the deepest parts of the earth. So the sin which had come in, taking possession of the ranges of the deepest chambers of the soul, came to be customary and to have the first say, growing up with each man from infancy, and going up and down with him, and instructing him in evil things.

2. When therefore the influence of divine grace has overshadowed the soul according to the measure of each man's faith, and he receives help from on high, still grace has overshadowed him only in part. Let not a man imagine that his whole soul has been enlightened. There is still a large range of wickedness within, and the man has need of such labor and pains, corresponding to the grace given him. That is the reason why divine grace began to visit the soul only in part, though it had the power to cleanse and perfect the man in the turn of an hour, in order to test man's purpose, whether he preserves his love towards God entire, not complying with the evil one in anything, but lending himself wholly to grace. In this way the soul, approving itself time after time, and grieving grace in nothing, nor using it spitefully, is helped by this method of little by little; and grace itself finds range in the soul, and strikes root even to the deepest parts and reasonings of it, when the soul on many occasions approves itself and corresponds with grace, which henceforth reigns in the vessel itself.

HOMILY XLVI[12]

3. A babe has no force to accomplish anything, and is unable to go on its own feet to its mother; but yet it rolls itself, and makes a noise, and cries, seeking after its mother. The mother meanwhile pities it, and rejoices that the little one seeks after her with pains and crying; and though the babe cannot come to her, yet because of the child's much seeking the mother comes to it herself, all overmastered by love for her babe, and takes it up, and cherishes it, and nurses it with great affection. This is what God does, in His kindness towards man, with the soul that comes to Him and longs for Him. Nay, much more, impelled by charity, He of His own accord,

in the goodness which is inherent in Him and is all His own, cleaves to the intention of that soul, and becomes *one spirit* with it, according to the apostolic saying (1 Cor 6:17). When the soul cleaves to the Lord, and the Lord pities and loves, coming to it and cleaving to it, and the intention from that time remains continually faithful to the grace of the Lord, they become *one spirit*, one composite thing, one intention, the soul and the Lord.

Because of his alleged apostolic connections and his profoundly cosmic and mystical vision, especially his emphasis upon God as the divine Darkness experienced in an ecstasy of pure love that takes the mystic beyond everything (even knowing and unknowing), Pseudo-Dionysius has been the most influential person in the Christian mystical tradition.

PSEUDO-DIONYSIUS

The most influential person in the Eastern and Western Christian mystical tradition is in many ways the most enigmatic. Scholars have discovered neither his identity nor the exact dates in which he lived and wrote. Furthermore, his relatively brief corpus of writings seems impenetrable, mystifying, and open to diverse—and sometimes contradictory—interpretations.

By claiming to be the Dionysius the Areopagite mentioned in Acts 17:34, this fascinating figure demands apostolic sanction for his writings: four Greek treatises on liturgy and mystical theology and 10 letters. This benign imposter avers to have been converted by St. Paul, to have been his disciple, to have witnessed the eclipse when Christ was crucified, to have been with the apostles Peter and James when the Virgin died, and to have corresponded with John the Evangelist. The later tradition also identified Pseudo-Dionysius with the first bishop of Athens (2nd century) and the martyred first bishop of Paris (3rd century).

It is perhaps because of his alleged apostolic connections, his profoundly mystical and cosmic vision, and his creation of an almost perfect system that his writings attained almost canonical status— at least in the Western medieval world—and that his credentials were never seriously questioned until the 19th century. Scholars un-

5th or 6th century

masked him incorrectly as Dionysius of Alexandria, a 3rd century saint; as an unknown disciple of St. Basil the Great who lived in the second half of the 4th century; and also as Severus of Antioch, a 6th-century heretic. Contemporary scholarship conjectures that he was a 6th-century Syrian monk.

Some Dionysian experts contend that the Areopagite depended heavily upon Proclus, a 5th-century Neo-Platonic philosopher who systematized the 3rd-century Neo-Platonic philosopher Plotinus. Therefore, the Dionysian mystical vision and system can be reduced to a Christian-veneered paganism. For these scholars, Pseudo-Dionysius allegedly transposed the asceticism of the Desert Fathers (the purification of the passions and the achievement of virtue) to the intellectual order. Thus, instead of self-denial and self-emptying in imitation of Christ, one empties the *mind* of all concepts and ideas of God. Even God-language is emptied, for nothing can ever be affirmed of God because he is always "not this, not that."

More importantly, these scholars argue that for "Dionysius" the purifying and unifying factor in the mystical ascent to God is not love. Rather, it is only the stripping away of all thoughts in the mind that creates a state of nescience as the prelude to *intellectual* ecstasy into God. In other words, voiding the mind, nescience, and intellectual fainting are the mystical steps in the ascent to God— not moral purification and personal transformation initiated by and culminating in love.

While admitting Pseudo-Dionysius' clear dependence on Neo-Platonism, especially Proclus, other experts correctly point out that "Neo" already means a Platonism transformed radically by Christianity. These scholars further maintain that the Areopagite profoundly recast Proclus to suit his own *Christian* interest. Finally, these commentators emphasize that if the four treatises are read in the order in which "Dionysius" wrote them, it is beyond a doubt that he must be interpreted and appreciated as a fully *Christian*, patristic theologian and spiritual writer with solid roots in Gregory of Nyssa and Evagrius Ponticus.

Although "Dionysius" made use of Greek philosophy, his mysticism flows from a cosmic and ecclesiastical perspective drawn from Scripture and the liturgy. *The Celestial Hierarchy* depicts a God of love who creates so that creation may share in the trinitarian life. Creation results from a divine love-ecstasy that implants in every creature the desire for the ecstatic movement back to God. The love that moves all creatures is *agape,* pure gift and generosity, the love that is proper to the *Christian* God. Moreover, the heavenly hierarchy of nine choirs of angels grouped in three triads is modeled after the trinitarian thearchy.

In the *Ecclesiastical Hierarchy*, the Areopagite indicates how the heavenly hierarchy is manifested on earth. Love's self-communication takes place in the Logos' incarnation and its consequences: Church, Scripture, liturgy, and sacraments. In the process of the creatures' reascent to the source of love, "Dionysius" depicts the deacons as purifying, the priests as enlightening, the bishops as consummating; the catechumens, energumens (those thought possessed), and penitents as being purified, the faithful as being illuminated, and the monks as surrendering to consummating love and knowledge. Thus, the Dionysian steps of purification, illumination, and union correspond to Evagrian asceticism (*praktike*), natural contemplation of God in creation (*theoria physike*), and loving knowledge (*gnosis*) of the Trinity—not to Plotinian mystical *intellectualism.*

Christ is the one behind all hierarchies and the content of the Church's preaching in word and sacrament. In fact, as one rung in the triad in the ecclesiastical hierarchy, the Church's liturgy and sacraments are especially efficacious in effecting that "sacred uplifting to the divine."[1] Pseudo-Dionysius views them as part of "symbolic theology" that likewise purify, illuminate, and perfect the Christian. In fact, everything culminates in the Eucharist as "'Communion' and 'gathering' [*synaxis*]. Every sacredly initiating operation draws our fragmented lives together in one-like divinization. It forges a divine unity with the One."[2] Through the Eucharist, all is reunited in God, through Christ.

Therefore, Pseudo-Dionysius' last and most well-known treatise, *The Mystical Theology,* must be read in the fully Christian, scriptural, sacramental, and liturgical context of the above two treatises. Like the Fathers of the Church before him, the Areopagite uses the word "mystical" to denote the experience of God's loving self-communication through Christ. This is precisely what Scripture reveals, what gives the Bible its full meaning, and what the liturgy and the sacraments—especially the Eucharist—contain.

The radically "negative" (apophatic) mysticism of *The Mystical Theology* culminates in "the divine Dark [that] is the inaccessible light where God is said to dwell." Although the experience of the divine Darkness is beyond both knowing and unknowing, it is inextricably linked to the experience of the divine self-communication in the ecclesiastical hierarchy as the reflection and earthly extension of the heavenly hierarchy.

In addition, one must read *The Divine Names* as an introduction to *The Mystical Theology*. The former treatise on "affirmative" (kataphatic) theology is imbued with a stirring conviction that God really is manifested in the world. Because of God's immanence, Christian life should be the breaking open and rendering transparent of the theophany which is God's creation.

This treatise explains the truths of the faith as proclaimed by the Church, and emphasizes that the concepts and images used by Scripture to describe God are at most analogical. Thus, everything positive in these expressions can and must be applied to God. Nevertheless, they must always be united with a negative theology that proclaims the inadequacy of all God-language. For example, God can be called "spirit," but God is ultimately beyond what we mean by "spirit." In other words, when one truly perceives God's manifestations in the world, one also realizes that the Trinity thus manifested transcends any and all manifestations. As the Areopagite says, "God is therefore known in all things and as distinct from all things."[3]

Because apophatic theology affirms God's incomprehensibility, the Areopagite maintains that it is more fitting God-language than kataphatic theology. Nevertheless, to sever the link between apophatic and kataphatic theology is to render the former empty. Pseudo-Dionysius teaches implicitly that a purely apophatic theology is a contradiction, for if nothing can be affirmed about God, then theology should be absolutely silent. As he says, "every attribute may be predicated of him and yet he is not any one thing."[4] But, for "Dionysius," apophatic theology's emptiness does prepare the person for "mystical theology" wherein God's loving self-communication and presence are experienced in an ecstasy of pure love through which one goes beyond all things and out of oneself—in a way beyond analogies, beyond supereminent negations, beyond knowing, *and* beyond unknowing. But his sharp distinction between apophatic and kataphatic theology paved the way for the later split between mystical experience of God and faith seeking understanding.

The key to the Dionysian cosmic vision is "hierarchy." For Proclus, hierarchy meant an unchanging order of degraded forms of the perfect One. For the Areopagite, on the other hand, "a hierarchy is a sacred order, a state of understanding and an activity approximating as closely as possible to the divine. . . . *The goal of a hierarchy, then, is to enable beings to be as like as possible to God and to be at one with him.*"[5] Thus, hierarchy is the principle of the radiation of the trinitarian life throughout creation and the principle of divinization.

Therefore, this quotation indicates that Pseudo-Dionysius is in the tradition of the great Christian Fathers who emphasized life's goal as ascending for full union with God, that is, divinization. Unlike Plotinus, who emphasized the withdrawal from all multiplicity to unify oneself and to discover the soul's own divinity, "Dionysius" teaches a unification with God through a God-given loving and ecstatic self-transcendence. For Plotinus, the self must be extinguished to regain itself as the One of undifferentiated unity. For "Dionysius," the self is united to God who transcends the soul and all else, and becomes God while remaining itself. Thus, Dionysian divinization is one of differentiated unity—of two becoming one, while remaining two—of genuinely becoming the other, while remaining oneself, of becoming God by participation.

In summary, "divinization consists of being as much as possible like and in union with God. The common goal of every hierarchy consists of the continuous love of God and of things divine, a love which is sacredly worked out in an inspired and unique way, and, before this, the complete and unswerving avoidance of everything contrary to it. It consists of a knowledge of beings as they really are. It consists of both the seeing and the understanding of sacred truth. It consists of an inspired participation in the one-like perfection and in the one itself, as far as possible. It consists of a feast upon that sacred vision which nourishes the intellect and which divinizes everything rising up to it."[6]

The selected text from *The Mystical Theology* must be read with the above mentioned comments in mind. The text illustrates the Areopagite's three theologies: affirmative (kataphatic), symbolic, and negative (apophatic). The first two theologies focus on what we can affirm about God; the last, about the radical failure of all speech and thought in God's presence. The first two also focus upon God's manifestation in creation; the last, about the secret God-soul relationship discovered only through the soul's inward movement. The deepest knowledge of God occurs when one "suffers" God in total passivity through loving union with the unknowable God in the unknowable way of deep darkness.

But his three theologies all center on mystical, loving knowledge of God attained through contemplation and communion. All three theologies underscore that the creature's response to God's love must be praise and worship, that mystical loving knowledge is liturgy, and that the soul in ecstasy meets God's ecstatic love for it and becomes one with the Good and the Beautiful in a dazzling darkness.[7]

THE TEXTS

THE MYSTICAL THEOLOGY[8]
I. The Divine Dark

1
O Trinity
beyond essence and
beyond divinity and
beyond goodness
guide of Christians in divine wisdom,
direct us towards mysticism's heights

beyond unknowing
beyond light
beyond limit,
there where the
unmixed and
unfettered and
unchangeable
mysteries of theology
in the dazzling dark of the welcoming silence
lie hidden, in the intensity of their darkness
all brilliance outshining,
our intellects, blinded—overwhelming,
with the intangible and
with the invisible and
with the illimitable,
Such is my prayer.
And you, beloved Timothy,
in the earnest exercise of mystical contemplation abandon
all sensation and
all intellection and
all objects or sensed
or seen and
all being and
all nonbeing and
in unknowing, as much as may be, be
one with the beyond being and knowing. By the ceaseless and limitless going out of yourself and
out of all things else you will be led in utter pureness,
rejecting all and
released from all,
aloft to the flashing forth,
beyond all being, of the divine dark.

2
Disclose not this
to the uninitiated
to those, I say, who
clutch at essences and
fancy beyond essences nothing is and

dream they know by ordinary knowing
"Him that has made the dark His hiding place."
If the unveiling of the divine mystery is beyond their ken
what is to be said of those
yet more profane who
to denote the loftiest Cause of all,
define It by the lowest of all and
deny It to be more lofty than the phantasies
various and
profane
they have formed of It,
the while to It must one,
as to the Cause of all,
all modes of being
attribute and ascribe and,
more full still,
to It,
as above them all,
deny them all.
Think not
that the assertion and denial are here opposed
but rather
that beyond the Yeas and Nays of modes, It
is beyond all deprivations.

3
Thus the blessed Bartholomew says
the theology is ample and yet small
the gospel is broad and long and yet narrow,
sublimely, I think, perceiving that one can be
saying much of the Good, the Cause of all,
and yet
saying little
and even
saying nothing
since for It nor word nor wit suffices, because
beyond essence and transcendent,
beyond seeing, truly hidden
except for those alone who

beyond foul and fair,
beyond the holy heights,
have made their way and
left behind all divine
illuminations and
voices and words from heaven and have entered the dark where, as
Scripture tells, He is who is
beyond all. For not without cause was blessed Moses told first to
cleanse himself, then himself withdraw
from those unclean,
to hear, wholly cleansed, the many-tongued trumpets,
to see the myriad lightnings—pure—diverse—
flashing forth,
Then, from the throng withdrawn,
he comes,
the chosen priests his entourage,
to the topmost peak of the divine ascent.
Yet he encounters God not,
he sees God not
(for God cannot be seen),
but sees alone the place on which He dwells. This is the sign, I
think, that
the most divine the most sublime
one can see or know
are symbols only,
subordinate to Him
who is Himself
transcendent to them all; that
they are pointers to His presence
who is beyond comprehending,
who walks the holy heights the mind descries. Moses then,
going beyond where one sees and is seen,
enters the Dark—mystery wholly—of unknowing,
there stills all trying to understand and achieves entire Him that is
all-transcending and he belongs himself no longer to himself nor
any other and, the more excellent way, is joined
to Him all-unknowable
in the stilling of all knowing. By knowing naught, he —beyond
knowing— knows.

II. How One Must Be United to Him and Praise
Him Who Is The Cause of All and Above All
Into this Dark beyond all light, we pray to come and,
unseeing and unknowing,
to see and to know
Him that is
beyond seeing and
beyond knowing
precisely by not seeing,
by not knowing. For that is truly to see and
to know and
to hymn transcendently
Him that transcends all. That is, negating, to do as sculptors do,
drawing [from marble]
the statue latent there,
removing all that
hinders or
hides
the pure spectacle of the hidden form and
displaying, with this mere removal,
the beauty hidden there.
One must, I think, hymn in
negating and
affirming
for affirmations proceed
from the topmost
through the middlemost
to the lowest.
But here, from the lowest
to the topmost,
one denies them all, thus
to lay bare the Unknowable who is
by all known beings veiled,
to see the transcendent Dark that is
by the light of beings hid.

III. *The Negative and Affirmative Theologies*
In our *Outlines of Theology* we have treated what is of the greatest
importance in the theology of affirmation; that is, how God's holy
nature is called both one and three; what, in this nature is fatherhood and filiation and what is the theology of the Spirit; and how
from immaterial and invisible Good have flowed the illuminations
that have their source itself in Goodness and have abided there, in
It and in themselves, existing co-eternally with their act of origin;
how Jesus, beyond essence, took on essence among human realities.
These and all other mysteries are celebrat- ed in accord with Scripture in our *Outlines*.

In *The Divine Names* [we have treated] of the meaning of the Divine
titles: Good, Being, Life, Wisdom, Power, and all other titles the intelligence applies to Him.

In *The Symbolic Theology* [we have discussed] the metaphors which,
drawn from the world of sense, are applied to God: what, in God, is
"form" and "figures" mean; what are His "parts," "organs," the
"places where He dwells," His "adornments"; what, in Him, is the
meaning of "anger," "sorrow," "indignation,"; His "intoxication,"
His "wrath," His "oath" and "curse"; His "sleeping" and "waking"—all the inspired symbolism in which the holiness of God is
figuratively clad.

You will have noticed how more wordy are the latter than the former. Necessarily the *Outlines of Theology* and the explanations of the
Divine Names use less words than *The Symbolic Theology* because the
higher we soar aloft the more our language becomes restricted by
that more synthesizing view we have of the intelligibles.

Now, however, that we are on the point of entering the Dark that is
beyond intelligence, rational discourse will not merely become
more brief; it will disappear in the total cessation of word and
thought. In the theology of affirmation discourse descends by degrees from the highest beings to lowest, embracing as it goes an
ever-widening number of concepts. But here, as we ascend from the
lowest to the Highest, discourse diminishes as it goes, and at the
end of the ascent it will be totally silent, because totally united to
Him that no words can describe.

But why, you will ask, do we make our start from the lowest with the negative theology after having begun from the highest in the affirmative theology? The reason is this: in affirming the existence of what transcends all affirmation, we were obliged to begin from what is most akin to It and then make the affirmation up on which all the rest depended; but to attain in the theology of negation what is beyond all negation we are obliged to begin by denying what are most disparate from It. For is not God "Life" or "Good" more than He is "air" or "stone"? And is it not truer to deny that drunkenness or rage pertain to Him than to deny that He speaks or that He thinks?

IV. The Pre-eminent Cause of All That Is Perceived by Sense Is Not Perceived by Sense

This, then, we say of the Cause,
beyond all things,
of all things: He is
not essence-less,
not life-less,
not reason or unreason,
not body,
not figure or form,
nor possessor of quality or quantity or mass,
not in space,
not visible,
not to be felt,
not sense-endowed or by sense perceived,
not prey to disorder and confusion
as if subject to sense passions,
not powerless
as if subject to the stresses of the world of sense,
not light-less
not changing or failing or divisible or capable of ebb and
    flow,
not "this" or "that" of anything of sense.

V. The Pre-eminent Cause of All That Is Perceived by the Intelligence Is Not Anything Perceived by the Intelligence

Ascending higher, we say
He is
not soul or intelligence,
not imagination or conjecture or reason or understanding
not word, not intellection,
not said, not thought,
not number, not order
not magnitude, not littleness,
not likeness, not unlikeness,
not similarity, not dissimilarity,
not unmoving, not moved,
not powerful, not power,
not light,
not living, not life,
not essence,
not eon, not time
not understandable,
not knowledge, not truth,
not kingship, not wisdom,
not one, not unity
not deity,
not goodness,
not spirit (as we know spirit),
not filiation,
not paternity,
not anything known by us or by anyone among us,
not a nonbeing,
not a being,
not known, as He is, by beings,
not knower of beings as they are,
not definable,
not nameable,
not knowable,
not dark, not light,
not untrue, not true,
not affirmable, not deniable,
for
while we affirm or deny of those orders of beings
that are kin to Him

we neither affirm nor deny Him
that is beyond
all affirmation as unique universal Cause and
all negation as simple pre-eminent Cause,
free of all and
to all transcendent.

Gregory the Great's light mysticism involves a three-fold process of getting oneself together (recollection), entering into one's soul (introversion), and contemplation. The soul uses itself as a ladder to see, hear, taste, smell, and feel something of the totally incomprehensible God.

GREGORY THE GREAT

Born of a Roman senator and a pious mother, Gregory received an excellent education, especially in law, to prepare him for a political and governmental career. He became prefect of Rome and presided over the senate at the young age of 30. However, soon after his father's death, he entered a monastery to follow the "grace of conversion," which he said he had ignored for too long. As a monk, he became a profound contemplative, undermining his health somewhat by rigorous asceticism, and devoting much time to the study of Scripture and the Latin Fathers.

Pope Pelagius II interrupted Gregory's monastic life by ordaining him deacon, then making him the papal representative at the Byzantine court in Constantinople. About 585, Gregory returned to Rome and became abbot of his former monastery, St. Andrew's, and also became the pope's own personal counselor.

Although his past life underscored his skills as a politician, statesman, and administrator capable of accepting responsibility and using authority well, it was only after an intense interior struggle that Gregory, the joyful *monk*, agreed to become pope. Moreover, because of floods, famine, disease, the invasion of the Lombards, and the Church's precarious position vis-à-vis the Imperial power at Constantinople, Italy was in a dreadful state. Gregory's firmness, strength, gentleness, and charity overcame many of these obstacles, however. With almost no help from the Emperor, he personally saved Rome from the Lombards by establishing a separate peace with them. Thus, he earned the great respect of the Roman people.

In addition, he eliminated much of the corruption in the Church's administration of wealth and used its vast resources to help the poor, the destitute, the sick, and to ransom captives. In his frequently strained relations with the churches of the East, Gregory reasserted Rome's universal jurisdiction, but defended the legitimate rights of individual churches. He meant it sincerely when he called himself "servant of the servants of God." Moreover, under his skillful direction, England was converted and the Church was strengthened in Gaul, Northern Italy, and Spain.

Gregory was a prolific writer with a practical, not a speculative, bent. His *Liber Regulae Pastoralis* set forth directives for a bishop's pastoral life, underscored the bishop as the "shepherd of souls," and served as the textbook of the medieval episcopate. His *Dialogues* recount for popular piety the life and miracles of St. Benedict and other Latin saints. It became the model for medieval hagiographers. His 40 homilies on the Gospels, 22 homilies on Ezekiel, 14 volumes of letters, and the 35-volume *Expositio in Librum Iob* (also called *Moralium Libri XXV*) are a summa of dogma, theology, moral teaching, and ascetical and mystical theology that became a storehouse of theology for later centuries. By setting forth a profound view of the Christian life that could reach the heights of contemplation and mysticism, Gregory earned the title, "Doctor of the Desire for God."

He also put an indelible stamp on the Church's liturgy, and was an ardent promoter of monasticism. By giving the monks privileges that exempted them partially from the authority of their local bishop, he laid the foundation for the future exemption of religious orders that were to come directly under papal control.

Hence, in a period of decline, he served as a bridge over which the wisdom and culture of the past would be passed on to the medieval world. In fact, the writers in the Middle Ages saw him as the equal of Ambrose, Jerome, and Augustine, and considered him one of the four doctors of the Latin Church. Contemporary commentators view him as a great stabilizer of the Western world in a period of tremendous political, religious, and ecclesiastical turmoil.

Because of his ecclesiastical and theological accomplishments, scholars have tended to overlook Gregory the *mystic* and the teacher of the mystical life. It may be true that he lacks Augustine's sublimity and Bernard's eloquence, but he should be appreciated as a pivotal figure between the two.

The first selection is taken from Gregory's *Homilies on Ezekiel*, mainly the section dealing with his allegorical interpretation of the doors and windows of Ezekiel's temple, as found in the prophet Ezekiel, chapter 40, and from his *Moralia on Job*. Like others in the mystical tradition before him, Gregory emphasizes the need for purification, the serious acquisition of virtue, and the necessity of love as a prerequisite to mystical ascent. Because the self is fragmented, "recollection"—or gathering oneself together— is also required. Then, by "introversion," the soul contemplates itself, strives to discover its true nature, and grasps itself as a "ladder of ascent . . . whereby in ascending from outward things it may pass into itself, and from itself may tend unto its Maker."

For Gregory, mystical ascent is actually an apophatic process of voiding the mind of all images, and then using the soul's naked knowledge of itself as a springboard to "contemplate" what is beyond itself, namely, God. Paradoxically, for Gregory, both the soul and God are ultimately incomprehensible.

Nevertheless, as the selected texts indicate, the mystical senses do apprehend something of God, but only for a brief time before the soul experiences itself "beaten back." The experience of being beaten back, of the self as a cross to itself, and of strong temptations keeps the person humble.

Like many before him in the Christian mystical tradition, Gregory claims that no one in this life can see God as he is. But unlike the mystics previously discussed, Gregory's language is uncolored by neo-Platonic philosophy. He attempts to describe his experiences in straight forward religious language, although it is clear that Augustine had some influence on Gregory's formulations.

Because his favorite image is the divine Light that one can behold only through a "chink" or through "fog," Gregory is a proponent of light-mysticism. This light purifies, illuminates, transforms, and unites the person to God; moreover, it reveals that only God can fully satisfy the person.

To summarize: the texts were selected to illustrate Gregory's light-mysticism and the three-fold process of "recollection," "introversion," and "contemplation" by which the soul uses itself as a ladder to taste, feel, smell, and touch "something" of the divine Wisdom. Although God is totally incomprehensible, God does becomes "transparent" through the contemplation of his divine Image, the Son.

The selected texts from the *Dialogues* illustrate that, for Gregory, one can be outside of oneself both through sin and through contemplation. In the former, one is lower than oneself; in the latter, one is "transported" above oneself. Moreover, because God's light enlarges the soul, the whole world appears illuminated, and its littleness in comparison to God is confirmed.[1]

THE TEXTS

HOMILIES ON EZEKIEL
The greatness of contemplation can be given to none but them that love (*Hom. in Ezech.* II. V. 17).[2]

8. In the cognition of the Almighty God our first door is faith, and our second is sight (species) to which, walking by faith, we arrive. For in this life we enter the door of faith, that afterwards we may be led to the other. And the door is opposite the door, because by the entrance of faith is opened the entrance of the vision of God. But if anyone wishes to understand both these doors as of this life, this by no means runs counter to a sound meaning. For often we desire to contemplate (considerare) the invisible nature of Almighty God, but we are by no means able; the soul, wearied by these difficulties, returns to itself and uses itself as a ladder by which it may mount up, that first it may consider itself, if it is able, and then may explore, as far as it can, that Nature which is above it. But if our mind

be distracted (sparsa) by earthly images, it can in no way consider either itself or the nature of the soul, because by how many thoughts it is led about, by so many obstacles is it blinded.

9. And so the first step is that it collect itself within itself (recollection); the second, that it consider what its nature is so collected (introversion); the third, that it rise above itself and yield itself to the intent contemplation of its invisible Maker (contemplation). But the mind cannot recollect itself unless it has first learned to repress all phantasmata of earthly and heavenly images, and to reject and spurn whatever sense impressions present themselves to its thoughts, in order that it may seek itself within as it is without these sensations. So they are all to be driven away from the mind's eye, in order that the soul may see itself as it was made, beneath God and above the body, that receiving life from What is above, it may impart life to that which it governs beneath.

When the soul, stripped of bodily images, is the object of its own thought, it has passed through the first door. But the way leads from this door to the other, that somewhat of the nature of the Almighty God may be contemplated. And so, the soul in the body is the life of the flesh; but God, who gives life to all, is the life of souls. And if life that is communicated (vita vivificata) is of such greatness that it cannot be comprehended, who will be able to comprehend by his intellect of how great majesty is the Life that gives life (vita vivificans)? But to consider and to grasp this fact is already in some measure to enter the second door; because the soul from its estimate of itself gathers what it should think concerning the unencompassed Spirit, who incomprehensibly governs what He has incomprehensibly created.

11. When the soul raised up to itself understands its own measure, and recognizes that it transcends all bodily things, and from the knowledge of itself passes to the knowledge of its Maker, what is this, except to see the door opposite the door? However much it strives, the soul is not able fully to fathom itself; how much less the greatness of Him who was able to make the soul. But when, striving and straining, we desire to see somewhat of the invisible Nature, we are fatigued and beaten back and driven off; and if we are not able to penetrate to what is within, yet already from the outer

door we see the inner one. For the very effort of the looking is the door, because it shows somewhat of that which is inside, although there be not yet the power of entering (*Hom. in Ezech*. II, v.).[3]

Commonly he who is most carried away in contemplation is most harried by temptation; and so, often it is wont to happen to some who make good progress that while contemplation carries their mind above itself, temptation also immediately follows, that it be not puffed up by those things to which it is carried; so that the temptation may weigh it down lest the contemplation should puff it up, and the contemplation raise it up lest the temptation should sink it. For if contemplation so raises the mind that temptation was altogether wanting, it would fall into pride; and if temptation so weighed it down that contemplation did not raise it up, it would surely fall into sin (*Hom. in Ezech*. II. ii. 3). [4]

MORALIA ON JOB
It is necessary that whoever eagerly prosecutes the exercises of contemplation, first question himself with particularity, how much he loves. For the force of love is an engine of the soul, which, while it draws it out of the world, lifts it on high (*Mor*. vi. 58).[5]

Sometimes the soul is admitted to some unwonted sweetness of interior relish, and is suddenly in some way refreshed when breathed on by the glowing spirit; and is the more eager the more it gains a taste of something to love. And it desires that within itself which it feels to taste sweet within, because it has in truth, from the love of its sweetness, become vile in its own sight; and after having been able in whatever way to enjoy it, it discovers what it has hitherto been without it. It endeavours to cling closely to it, but is kept back from its strength by its own remaining weakness; and because it is unable to contemplate its purity, it counts it sweet to weep, and sinking back to itself, to strew the tears of its own weakness. For it cannot fix its mind eye on that which it has with hasty glance seen within itself, because it is compelled by its own old habits to sink downwards. It meanwhile pants and struggles and endeavours to go above itself, but sinks back, overpowered with weariness, into its own familiar darkness. A soul thus affected has to endure itself as the cause of a stubborn contest against itself, and all this controversy about ourselves causes no small amount of pain, when we are engaged in it, whatever pleasure may be blended therewith (*Mor.* xxiii. 43).[6]

The intervening mist of evil is first washed away from the eye of the mind by burning sorrow; and then it is illuminated by the bright coruscations of the unencompassed Light flashing upon above it. When this is in any way seen, the mind is absorbed in a sort of rapturous security; and carried beyond itself, as though the present life had ceased to be, it is in a way remade in a certain newness [it is refreshed in a manner of a kind of new being: Oxf. Lib.]. There the mind is besprinkled with the infusion of heavenly dew from an inexhaustible fountain; there it discerns that it is not sufficient for that to which it has been carried, and from feeling the Truth, it sees that it does not see how great Truth itself is (*Mor.* xxiv. 11).[7]

Whoever is so rapt by contemplation, as, being raised up by divine grace, already to engage his thought on the choir of angels, and fixed on things on high to hold himself aloof from all action below, is not contented with beholding the glory of angelic brightness, unless he is able to behold Him also Who is above angels. For the vision of Him is alone the true refreshment of our mind. Hence, from these choirs of angels he directs the eye of his mind to contemplate the glory of the Majesty on high; and not seeing it, he is still hungry; and at length [in the next life] seeing it he is satisfied. But while weighed down by the interposition of the corruptible flesh, we cannot see God as He is (*Mor.* xxxi. 99-100).[8]

In contemplation it is the divine Wisdom that is contemplated, and even touched: When in contemplation we are brought to the contemplation of Wisdom, the mere immensity thereof, which by itself lifts man to itself, denies the human mind full knowledge, so that it should by touching (tangendo) love this Wisdom, and yet never by passing through penetrate it (*Mor.* xxii. 50).[9]

After the struggles of labour [of contemplation], after the waves of temptations, the mind is often hung aloft in a transport (in excessu suspenditur), in order that it may contemplate a knowledge of the divine Presence (*Mor.* xxiv. 12).[10]

Whatever progress any one may have made when placed in this

life, he does not as yet see God in His real appearance (per speciem), but in enigma and through a glass. Holy men raise themselves up to lofty contemplation, and yet they cannot see God as He is. They resolutely direct the keenness of their intention, but they cannot yet behold Him nigh, the greatness of Whose brightness they are not able to penetrate. For the mist of our corruption darkens us from the incorruptible Light; and when the light can both be seen in a measure, and yet cannot be seen as it is, it shows how distant it is. And if the mind already saw it perfectly it would not see it as it were through fog [or darkness— 'per calignem'] (*Mor.* xxxi. 101).[11]

Every man that apprehends something of the Eternal Being by contemplation, beholds the same through His co-eternal Image. When then His Eternity is perceived as far as the capability of our frail nature admits, His Image is set before the eyes of the mind, in that when we really strain towards the Father, as far as we receive Him we see Him by His Image, i.e., by His Son. And by that Image which was born of Himself without beginning, we strive in some sort to obtain a glimpse of Him who hath neither beginning nor ending (*Mor.* v. 63, 64).[12]

DIALOGUES
In two ways are we led out of ourselves: either by sinful thoughts we fall below ourselves, or by the grace of contemplation we are raised above ourselves. The Prodigal fell below himself; but Peter, whose mind was rapt in ecstasy, was out of himself, indeed, but above himself. Each 'returned to himself'—the former when, conscience smitten, he forsook his evil ways; the latter when from the height of contemplation he returned to the normal state of intellect as before. When the ardour of contemplation bears one aloft, he leaves himself beneath himself (*Dial.* ii. 3).[13]

While [Saint] Benedict was standing at the window of the tower, beseeching Almighty God, suddenly, at dead of night, looking out he saw that a light shed from above had dissipated all the darkness of the night, and was shining with such splendor that the light that had shone forth amid the darkness surpassed the day. And a very wonderful thing followed in that spectacle; for, as afterwards he himself narrated, the whole world, gathered as it were under one ray of the sun, was brought before his eyes. And while he fixed the steady gaze of his eyes in the splendor of the shining light, he saw the soul of Germanus, bishop of Capua, carried to heaven by the angels in a fiery ball.

To the soul that sees the Creator every created thing is narrow. For however little it be of the light of the Creator that it beholds, all that is created becomes to it small: because by the very light of the inmost vision the bosom of the mind is enlarged, and it is so expanded in God that it is above the world. But the seer's soul itself becomes also above itself, and when in the light of God it is rapt above itself, it is broadened out interiorly; and while raised aloft it looks downwards, it understands how small is that which in its lowly estate it could not understand. Therefore the man of God, who, looking on the fiery globe, saw also angels returning to heaven, assuredly could see these things only in God's light. And so, what wonder it is if he saw the world gathered together before him, who, being raised up in the light of his mind, was out of the world? And that the world is said to have gathered before his eyes, it is not that the heaven and earth were contracted, but the seer's mind was enlarged, who, being rapt in God, could see without difficulty all that is beneath God. In that light, therefore, which shone on his outward eyes, there was a light in his inward mind, which, by ravishing the seer's mind to things above, showed him how small were all things below (*Dial.* ii. 35).[14]

John Climacus is part of the hesychastic tradition that taught the unceasing repetition of the Jesus prayer, in conjunction with a certain bodily posture, outer and "mystical" eyes fixed on the heart, controlled breathing, and a strict mental concentration.

JOHN CLIMACUS

We know almost nothing about the life of St. John Scholasticus, except that he spent 40 years in solitude at Tholas in the Sinai desert before becoming abbot of the monastery on Mount Sinai. He wrote the ascetical-mystical classic, the *Klimax* (*Ladder*), from which his name is derived. Its 30 chapters symbolize the 30 years of Christ's hidden life.

As the selected texts illustrate, the book evinces his intimate and passionate experiences of God. Although a hatred of the body and the world *seems* to set the tone for the book, the selected texts clearly indicate that John saw the monk's real war as that against self-love and the demons. So, as Christ's "real servant," the monk has promised to master his mysterious nature and to conquer the demons for a life of unceasing communion with God in Christ.

Moreover, the monk breaks with the world and practices virtues with a view to a life of brotherly love, humility, stillness (*hesychia*), prayer, serenity (*apatheia*), and passionate love of God. This is nothing short of a "resurrection of the soul before the body," as John contends. Thus, John offers an exceptional exposition of the ascetical foundations of mysticism and the mystical foundations of *radical* asceticism that sanctify, transform, and unite the entire person with God.

John was a master at disclosing human motivation. He possessed a deeply analytical mind, acute powers of observation, and deep insights into human nature—especially its uncanny ability to deceive itself. He is one of the most humane of ascetical teachers who spoke little about physical, but much about inner asceticism and the need for the Holy Spirit's help. The selected text on gluttony illustrates John's eloquence in describing the vices, their "sons and daughters," human impotence, and the "sweet" experience of the Holy Spirit's aid.

The selected texts also illustrate a paradox: severe, but graced, self-discipline can be viewed as a kind of personal "tough love" that integrates and transforms a person in what contemporary people understand as a "self-actualized" way. The extravagant penances, eccentricities, and "holy follies" of those in the "Prison," or the isolation monastery used to punish those with faults, must be seen in the context of the deep desire for God that motivated these men. They denied nature "for what is above."

Severity transformed their nature. The selected texts show that the monk's ego-strength, wisdom, humanity, integrated personalities, penetrating discernment, conviction of being a light to the world, and passionate love for God are the fruits of such a life—fruits that can come only from God's Spirit. Moreover, have not contemporary persons, such as Solzhenitszn, Jacobo Timmerman, Viktor Frankl, and Nelson Mandela attested to experiencing some connection between extreme hardship and the discovery of hitherto inner and unsuspected resources?

The monks withdrew to the desert, not to escape the world, but to serve it through their battle against self-love and the demons. They knew that in their passionate love of God and neighbor, they resembled God, because "love, by its nature, is a resemblance of God."[1] Although the monk may seem like a figure best left in the past, it can be argued that all persons discover authentic human and Christian living only if they discover the "monk" in themselves. Who is not called to withdraw deliberately at times from "normal" life, to face one's own desert, and to wage war against self-love, one's demons, and the demons ripping apart the social fabric? Furthermore, are not the monks always with us, even if in bogus form? For example, are not many of the often bizarre, contemporary lifestyles and techniques touted to promote self-actualization and self-realization illustrations of the hunger for a new monasticism?

The selected texts show that John Climacus is part of the hesychastic tradition. The tradition taught the unceasing repetition of the Jesus prayer ("Lord Jesus Christ, Son of God, have mercy on me [a sinner]"), in conjunction with a certain bodily posture, outer and "mystical" eyes fixed on the heart, controlled breathing, a voiding of the mind of all images, and a concentration that allows no idle thought to enter the heart. The true hesychast fights to "fix your mind to your soul [heart] as to the wood of a cross."

As the texts indicate, hesychasm results in a prayer that "holds the world together," as well as direct experience of God, raptures in the Lord, humility, serenity (*apatheia*), and stillness of soul (*hesychia*). The fire of the Holy Spirit awakens in the heart. One is transported and transformed into Christ's light, the divine light that surrounded Jesus on Mt. Tabor. Therefore, John is a proponent of an apophatic, light mysticism, not the apophatic mysticism of darkness we have already seen.

Moreover, for John, the genuine hesychast possesses uncanny discernment. He not only knows which of his thoughts come from God, which from the self, and which from the devils, but he can also discern another's state of soul by observing his body language.

The selections indicate that John emphasized the importance of genuine repentance and tears, as did many of the Desert Fathers. Authentic repentance and "tears of the soul" result in the soul "mingling with God." Tears wash away post-baptismal sins; without them, fewer people would be saved.

Finally, the brief section on dreams has been included to indicate that the Fathers of the Church cannot be called on to support the extravagant contemporary claims made for the spiritual and mystical significance of dreams.

After reading the selections, it will be easy to appreciate why one commentator wrote of the *Ladder*: "With the exception of the Bible and the service books, there is no work in Eastern Christendom that has been studied, copied, and translated more often than *The Ladder of Divine Ascent* by St. John Climacus."[2] Although written mainly for monks, John Climacus' ascetical and mystical classic influenced far wider circles throughout history. Its popularity in the East can be compared with the popularity of *The Imitation of Christ* in the West.[3]

THE TEXTS

THE MONK AS WARRIOR

By what rule of manner can I bind this body of mine? By what precedent can I judge him? Before I bind him he is let loose, before I can condemn him I am reconciled to him, before I can punish him I bow down to him and feel sorry for him. How can I hate him when my nature disposes me to love him? How can I break away from him when I am bound to him forever? How can I escape from him when he is going to rise with me? How can I make him incorrupt when he has received a corruptible nature. How can I argue with him when all the arguments are on his side?

If I try to bind him through fasting, then I am passing judgment on my neighbor who does not fast—with the result that I am handed over to him again. If I defeat him by not passing judgment I turn proud—and I am in thrall to him once more. He is my helper and my enemy, my assistant and my opponent, a protector and a traitor. I am kind to him and he assaults me. If I wear him out he gets weak. If he has a rest he becomes unruly. If I upset him he cannot stand it. If I mortify him I endanger myself. If I strike him down I have nothing left by which to acquire virtues. I embrace him. And I turn away from him.

What is this mystery in me? What is the principle of this mixture of body and soul? How can I be my own friend and my own enemy? Speak to me, my yoke-fellow, my nature! I cannot ask anyone else about you. How can I remain uninjured by you? How can I escape the danger of my own nature? I have made a promise to Christ that I will fight you, yet how can I defeat your tyranny? But this I have resolved, namely, that I am going to master you.

And this is what the flesh might say in reply: "I will never tell you what you do not already know. I will speak the knowledge we both have. Within me is my begetter, the love of self. The fire that comes to me from outside is too much pampering and care. The fire within me is past ease and things long done. . . . "[4]

[Gluttony is speaking]. . . . "My firstborn son is the servant of Fornication, the second is Hardness of Heart, and the third is Sleepiness. From me flow a sea of Dirty Thoughts, waves of Filth, floods of unknown and unspeakable Impurities. My daughters are Laziness, Talkativeness, Breezy Familiarity, Jesting, Facetiousness, Contradiction, Stubbornness, Contempt, Disobedience, Stolidity of Mind, Captivity, Boastfulness, Audacity, Love of Worldly Things, followed by Impure Prayer, Distracted Thoughts, and sudden and often unexpected Catastrophies, with which is linked that most evil of all my daughters, namely, Despair. . . . The thought of death is my enemy always, but nothing human can really wipe me out. He who has received the Paraclete prays to Him against me; and the Paraclete, when entreated, does not allow me to act passionately. But those who have never tasted Him inevitably seek pleasure in my sweetness . . . . "[5]

. . . . we have countless hidden enemies—evil enemies, harsh, deceitful, wicked enemies with fire in their hands, wishing to set the Lord's temple alight with the flame that is in it. These enemies are powerful, unsleeping, incorporeal and unseen. No novice should heed the devilish words of his foes as they murmur: "Do not wear out your body, in case you fall prey to disease and weakness." Hardly anyone can be found in this day and age willing to bring low the body, although they may deny it the pleasure of abundant food. The aim of the demon is to make our entrance into the stadium weak and lethargic, and a fitting end will follow this beginning.

The real servants of Christ, using the help of spiritual fathers and also their own self-understanding, will make every effort to select a place, a way of life, and abode, and the exercises that suit them. Community life is not for everyone, because of gluttonous tendencies, and the solitary life is not for everybody, on account of the tendency to anger. Let each seek the most appropriate way.

All monastic life may be said to take one of three forms. There is the road of withdrawal and solitude for the spiritual athlete; there is the life of stillness [hesychia] shared with one or two others; there is the practice of living patiently in community. . . .[6]

THE PENITENTIAL AND TRANSFORMED MONK

Angels are a light for monks and the monastic life is a light for all men. Hence monks should spare no efforts to becoming a shining example in all things, and they should give no scandal in anything they say or do. For if the light becomes dark, then all the deeper will be the darkness of those living in the world . . . .[7]

The monk is ever embattled with what he is, and he is the unfailing warder of his senses. The monk has a body made holy, a tongue purified, a mind enlightened. Awake or asleep, the monk is a soul pained by the constant remembrance of death. Withdrawal from the world is a willing hatred of all that is materially prized, a denial of nature for the sake of what is above nature . . . .

An unbreakable bond of love joined these men together, and more wonderful was their freedom from all familiarity and idle chatter. Above all, they strove never to injure a brother's conscience. And if ever someone showed hatred of another, the shepherd banished him like a convict to the isolation monastery.

. . . Among these holy fathers I saw things that were really profitable and worthy of admiration. I saw a fraternity assembled and united in the Lord and with a wonderful combination of action and contemplation. They were so taken up with the things of heaven and they practiced so much good that they had little need of the promptings of the superior, and it was out of their own good will that they stirred each other to divine vigilance. They had certain holy and divine exercises that were laid down, studied, and established . . . .

Even in the refectory they did not cease from mental prayer [a concentrated state of recollection in the depths of the heart], and by secret signs and gestures these holy men reminded each other of it . . . .

Many of these holy fathers became experts in active life and in spirituality, in discernment and humility. Among them was the awful and yet angelic sight of men grey-haired, venerable, preeminent in holiness . . . . There is no one among them who is silly and foolish . . . . They are openly gentle, kindly, radiant, genuine, without hypocrisy, affectation, or falsity of either speech or disposition . . . .[8]

[In the isolation monastery] . . . there were men in hardship and bowed down to the end of their lives, going about each day in sadness, their bodies' wounds stinking of rottenness and yet unnoticed by them. They forgot to eat their bread; their drink was mixed with tears. They ate dust and ashes instead of bread; their bones stuck to their flesh and they were dried up like grass . . . . You could see the tongues on some of them dry and hanging from their mouths in the manner of dogs. Some punished themselves in the blazing sun, others tortured themselves in the cold, while others, again, drank only as much water as would keep them from dying of thirst . . . . With knees like wood, as a result of all the prostrations, with eyes dimmed and sunken, with hair gone and cheeks wasted and scalded by many hot tears, with faces pale and worn, they were no different from corpses. Their breasts were livid from all the beatings, which had even made them spit blood. There was no rest for them in beds, no clean and laundered clothing. They were bedraggled, dirty, and verminous . . . .[9]

. . . . I stayed thirty days in that prison [isolation monastery] before returning to the main monastery. . . . It seems to me that those who have fallen and are penitent are more blessed than those who have never fallen and who do not have to mourn over themselves, because through having fallen, they have pulled themselves up by a sure resurrection . . . .[10]

THE HESYCHAST

Stillness of soul is the accurate knowledge of one's thoughts and is an unassailable mind . . . . It is always on the watch at the doors of the heart, killing or driving off invading notions. What I mean by this will be well understood by the man who practices stillness [hesychia] in the deep places of the heart . . . . The start of stillness is the rejection of all noisiness as something that will trouble the depths of the soul. The final point is when one has no longer a fear of noisy disturbance, when one is immune to it. He who when he goes out does not go out in his intellect is gentle and wholly a house of love, rarely moved to speech and never to anger. Strange as it may seem, the hesychast is a man who fights to keep his incorporeal self shut up in the house of the body . . . .[11]

The following are the signs, the stages, and the proofs of practicing stillness in the right way—a calm mind, a purified disposition, rapture in the Lord, the remembrance of everlasting torments, the imminence of death, an insatiable urge for prayer, constant watchfulness, the death of lust, no sense of attachment, death of worldliness, an end to gluttony, a foundation for theology [the direct experience of God], a well of discernment . . . .[12]

Place strict and unsleeping guards at the gateway of your heart. Practice inward stillness [hesychia] amid the twistings and the turbulence of your limbs . . . . Keep your soul undisturbed while tumult rages about you. . . . Fix your mind to your soul as to the wood of a cross, strike it with alternating hammer blows like an anvil . . . . It must be keep calm and unstirred . . . .[13]

Stillness is worshipping God unceasingly and waiting on Him. Let the remembrance of Jesus [the Jesus Prayer context] be present with your every breath. Then indeed you will appreciate the value of stillness . . . .

Prayer is by nature a dialogue and a union of man with God. Its effect is to hold the world together. It achieves a reconciliation with God . . . . Make the effort to raise up, or rather, to enclose your mind within the words of your prayer; and if, like a child, it gets tired and falters, raise it up again . . . . The beginning of prayer is the expulsion of distractions from the very start by monologistos [a repeated short prayer]; the middle state is the concentration on what is being said or thought; its conclusion is rapture in the Lord . . . .[14]

After a long spell of prayer, do not say that nothing has been gained, for you have already achieved something. For, after all, what higher good is there than to cling to the Lord and to persevere in unceasing union with Him? . . . . Do not form sensory images during prayer, for distraction will certainly follow . . . . When fire comes to dwell in the heart it resurrects prayer; and after prayer has been revived and taken up into heaven, a descent of fire takes place into the upper chamber of the soul . . . Prayer is a devout coercion of God ... Now love is greater than prayer ... Love, by its nature, is a resemblance to God, insofar as this is humanly possible ... Love is the greatest of them all.[15]

DISCERNMENT

When prayer is over, wait patiently and you will observe how mobs of demons, as though challenged by us, will try to attack us after prayer by means of wild fantasies. Watch carefully and you will note those that are accustomed to snatch away the first fruits of the soul ... [16]

A perfectly purified man can look into the soul of his neighbor—not of course into its actual substance—and can discern its present state. He who progresses further can even tell the state of the soul from the body ... It is characteristic of the perfect that they always know whether a thought comes from within themselves, or from God, or from the demons ... The eyes of the heart are enlightened by discernment to things seen and unseen ...[17]

LIGHT MYSTICISM

There is the way of bodily tears and there is the way of the tears of the soul. There is the way of the contemplation of what is before us and the way of the contemplation of what remains unseen. There is the way of things heard at second hand and the way of spontaneous joy within the soul. There is the way of stillness and the way of obedience. And in addition to these there is the way of rapture, the way of the mind mysteriously and marvelously carried into the light of Christ .... You will know that you have this holy gift [humility] and not be led astray when you experience an abundance of unspeakable light together with an indescribable love of prayer ...[18]

TEARS

The tears that come after baptism are greater than baptism itself ... Baptism washes off those evils that were previously within us, whereas the sins committed after baptism are washed away by tears. The baptism received by us as children we have all defiled, but we cleanse it anew with our tears. If God in His love for the human race had not given us tears, those being saved would be few indeed and hard to find ...[19]

. . . Prayer is the mother and daughter of tears . . . [20]

Tears come from nature, from God, from suffering good and bad, from vainglory, from licentiousness, from love, from the remembrance of death, and from numerous other causes . . . Tears can wash away sins as water washes away something written. And as some, lacking water, use other means to wipe off what is written, souls lacking tears beat and scour away their sins with grief, groans, and deep sorrow . . . [21]

Real repentance, mourning scrubbed of all impurity, and holy humility among beginners are as different and distinct from one another as yeast and flour from bread. The soul is ground and refined by visible repentance. The waters of true mourning bring it to a certain unity. I would even go so far as to speak of a mingling with God. Then, kindled by the fire of the Lord, blessed humility is made into bread and made firm without the leaven of pride.[22]

DREAMS

A dream is the stirring of the mind during the body's rest . . . But the man who believes in dreams is like someone running to catch up with his own shadows . . . , shows his inexperience, while the man who distrusts every dream is very sensible.[23]

One of the greatest theologians of the Greek Fathers, Maximus Confessor experienced and taught that the Church's liturgy, in conjunction with asceticism and contemplation, bestows mystical loving knowledge of the Trinity.

MAXIMUS CONFESSOR

Maximus Confessor has been called one of the greatest theologians of the Greek Fathers and the last independent theologian of the Byzantine church. In him, the Alexandrian and Cappadocian traditions came to full fruition. So great were his accomplishments and his influence—especially in perfecting the Christology of the Fathers—that he belongs almost equally to both the Eastern and Western Christian churches.

A prominent aristocrat of Constantinople, Maximus's mastery of the Bible, the Fathers, and the pre-Christian philosophers indicates that he received a broad Christian and humanistic education. As first-secretary to the emperor Heraclius, he clearly belonged to the upper levels of his society.

However, after only three years of imperial service, Maximus changed his life radically by entering a monastery at Chrysopolis on the other side of the Bosphorus. A few years later, his love for monastic spirituality brought him to the monastery of St. George at Cyzicus where he remained until the Persian invasion of 626 forced him into exile. From Crete and Cyprus, he eventually made his way to North Africa.

Maximus was a prolific, theological genius whose profoundly Christian sense kept his speculation solidly rooted in the Church's entire life. Subtle, but never abstract, his mystical theology is redo-

ca. 580-662

lent with experience derived from a rich liturgical life and deep personal prayer. He became an opponent of Monothelitism—the view that denied that Christ had a human will. Convinced that Monothelitism's watering down of Christ's full humanity would have a devastating effect on Christian life, Maximus clashed with Pyrrhus, the ex-patriarch of Constantinople, over the latter's Monothelitism. In 649, at the invitation of Pope Martin I, Maximus attended the Lateran synod in Rome that formally condemned this doctrine.

Emperor Constans II had Maximus and Pope Martin I arrested and brought to Constantinople to be tried for treason. Exiled to Bizye in Thrace, Maximus's tongue and right hand were cut off because he refused to comply with the the imperial interdict on Monothelitism. Banished with his disciples to Lazica, he died there within a few years.

The texts from *The Four Hundred Chapters on Love* were selected to illustrate Maximus's great love of the monastic life. Using the same lapidary, pithy writing style of the Desert Fathers, Maximus speaks passionately about Light mysticism, and the pure, distractionless, ceaseless, rapturous prayer that illuminates and transforms the monk into the divine Light. For him, the "active," or ascetical, life often rewards its adherents with distractionless prayer; the contemplative life, with instantaneous rapture as soon as the mind turns to God.

These texts also show that Maximus accepted the Evagrian three-stage ascent to God that consists of asceticism, natural contemplation, and supreme gnosis. However, Maximus shrewdly disengaged it from its questionable cosmogeny. Although he insisted, as Evagrius did, upon spiritual combat against the passions, passionate thoughts and memories, and the demons, Maximus put more emphasis upon self-love as the "mother of all vices" and the necessity of charity to take the lead in rooting out vice and implanting the virtues.

Because God is love, genuine love of neighbor cannot be dissociated from pure prayer borne on the wings of love. For Maximus, trinitarian graces transform even the monk's concupiscence and lower desires into one immense loving desire for God. However, unlike Evagrius—who seems to have confused the soul's knowledge of itself with the knowledge of God—Maximus stresses supreme gnosis as a "supreme ignorance of the supremely Unknowable."

Thus, like Pseudo-Dionysius, Maximus is a proponent of negative theology, of apophaticism. As these texts and the selections from the difficult *Chapters on Knowledge* illustrate, Maximus insists that God is the transcendent, completely incomprehensible God who is totally beyond all images and concepts.

In tension with Maximus's apophaticism is his penetrating incarnationalism, or "trinitarian Christocentrism" (Jaraslov Pelikan). Although God cannot be comprehended, God can still be grasped to some extent by the human mind because the Word became flesh. As the texts reveal, Maximus viewed affirmative (kataphatic) theology as focusing upon the Word *made flesh*; negative (apophatic) theology, upon the Word *as God*. Thus, in one stroke Maximus prevented the best in Dionysian apophaticism from becoming empty speculation or "speculative nihilism" by linking it inextricably to the trinitarian Christ.

Maximus's Word mysticism also brings out his ardent love of Scripture. Every word on the Sacred Page reveals *the* Word. Kataphatic theology makes the Word flesh; apophatic theology makes the Word spirit. Moreover, Maximus considered everything that happened before the incarnation as a preparation for Christ; everything after Christ as our divinization in and through Christ.

Thus, Maximus's incarnationalism has also made him the doctor of *theosis*, or divinization. God became incarnate so that we might "become partakers of the divine nature" (2 Pet. 1:4). *The Chapters on Knowledge* frequently emphasize a descent-ascent plan: "the Word of God . . . became son of man and man himself . . . to make men gods and sons of God."

Maximus was able to articulate a profoundly Christian apophaticism that emphasized the incomprehensible trinitarian God and a kataphaticism that stressed how much can be known about the Trinity because of the incarnation. These he kept in a fruitful tension through his appreciation of worship as an appropriate vehicle for comprehending the incomprehensible and for expressing the ineffable, as the text from *The Church's Mystagogy* illustrates. Maximus viewed mystagogy as an initiation into the Church's liturgy and the liturgy as the springboard into the experience of mystery itself. The goal of the Church's liturgy is to bestow, through asceticism and contemplation, mystical loving knowledge of the Trinity, that is, supreme gnosis.[1]

THE TEXTS

THE FOUR HUNDRED CHAPTERS ON LOVE[2]
First Century

1. Love is a good disposition of the soul by which one prefers no being to the knowledge [mystical experience] of God. It is impossible to reach the habit of this love if one has any attachment to earthly things.

9. If the life of the mind is the illumination of knowledge and this is born of love for God, then it is well said that there is nothing greater than love.

10. When in the full ardor of its love for God the mind goes out of itself, then it has no perception at all either of itself or of any creatures. For once illuminated by the divine and infinite light, it remains insensible to anything that is made by him, just as the physical eye has no sensation of the stars when the sun has risen.

12. When through love the mind is ravished by divine knowledge and in going outside of creatures has a perception of divine transcendence, then according to the divine Isaiah, it comes in consternation to a realization of its own lowliness.

63. We carry along with us the voluptuous images of the things we once experienced. Now the one who overcomes these voluptuous images completely disdains the realities of which they are images. In fact, the battle against memories is more difficult than the battle against deeds, as sinning in thought is easier than sinning in deed.

71. Perfect love does not split up the one nature of men on the basis

of their various dispositions but ever looking steadfastly at it, it loves all men equally, those who are zealous as friends, those who are negligent as enemies. It is good to them and forbearing and puts up with what they do. It does not think evil at all but rather suffers for them, if occasion requires, in order that it may even make them friends if possible. If not, it does not fall away from its own intentions as it ever manifests the fruits of love equally for all men. In this way also our Lord and God Jesus Christ, manifesting his love for us, suffered for all mankind and granted to all equally the hope of resurrection, though each one renders himself worthy either of glory or of punishment.

86. When the mind is completely freed from the passions, it journeys straight ahead to the contemplation of created things and makes its way to the knowledge of the Holy Trinity.

94. Through the working of the commandments the mind puts off the passions. Through the spiritual contemplation of visible realities it puts off impassioned thoughts of things. Through the knowledge of invisible realities it puts off contemplation of visible things. And finally this it puts off through the knowledge of the Holy Trinity.

Second Century

1. The one who truly loves God also prays completely undistracted, and the one who prays completely also truly loves God. But the one who has his mind fixed on any earthly thing does not pray undistracted; therefore the one who has his mind tied to any earthly thing does not love God.

6. There are two supreme states of pure prayer, one corresponding to those of the active life, and the other to the contemplative. The first arises in the soul from the fear of God and an upright hope, the second from divine desire and total purification. The marks of the first type are the drawing of the one's mind away from all the world's considerations, and as God is present to one, as indeed he is, he makes his prayers without distractions or disturbance. The marks of the second type are that at the very onset of prayer the mind is taken hold of by the divine and infinite light and is conscious neither of itself nor of any other being whatever except of

him who through love brings about such brightness in it. Then, when it is concerned with the properties of God, it receives impressions of him which are clear and distinct.

26. The mind that has succeeded in the active life advances in prudence; the one in the contemplative life, in knowledge [mystical experience of God]. For to the former it pertains to bring the one who struggles to a discernment of virtue and vice, while to the latter, to lead the sharer to the principles of incorporeal and corporeal things. Then at length it is deemed worthy of the grace of theology [direct communion with God in pure prayer] when on the wings of love it has passed beyond all the preceding realities, and being in God it will consider the essence of himself through the Spirit, insofar as it is possible to the human mind.

48. For the mind of the one who is continually with God even his concupiscence abounds beyond measure into a divine desire and whose entire irascible element is transformed into divine love. For by an enduring participation in the divine illumination it becomes altogether shining bright, and having bound its passible element to itself, as I said, turned it around to a never-ending divine desire and an unceasing love, completely changed over from earthly things to divine.

54. A monk is a man who separates his mind from material things and who devotes himself to God by self-mastery, love, psalmody, and prayer.

59. Keep yourself away from self-love, the mother of vices, which is the irrational love of the body. From it surely arise the first three passionate and capital thoughts, gluttony, greed, and vainglory, which have their starting point in the seemingly necessary demands of the body and from which the whole catalogue of vices comes about. Therefore, as was said, one must necessarily keep away from and do battle with this self-love with full determination, for when this is overcome then are all its offspring likewise brought into line.

61. It is said that the supreme state of prayer is when the mind passes outside the flesh and the world and while praying is completely without matter and form. The one who preserves this state

without compromise really "prays without ceasing."

Third Century

44. The virtues separate the mind from the passions; spiritual contemplations separate it from simple representations; then pure prayer sets it before God himself.

97. When the mind receives the representations of things, it of course patterns itself after each representation. In contemplating them spiritually it is variously conformed to each object contemplated. But when it comes to be in God, it becomes wholly without form and pattern, for in contemplating the one who is simple it becomes simple and entirely patterned in light.

98. The perfect soul is the one whose affective drive is wholly directed to God.

99. The perfect mind is the one that through genuine faith supremely knows in supreme ignorance the supremely unknowable, and in gazing on the universe of his handiwork has received from God comprehensive knowledge of His Providence and judgment on it, as far as allowable to men.

Fourth Century

36. The unutterable peace of the holy angels is attained by these two dispositions: love for God and love for one another. This holds true as well for all the saints from the beginning. Thus we have been beautifully told by the Savior that "on these two commandments depend the whole law and the prophets."

77. Who enlightened you with the faith of the holy, adorable, and consubstantial Trinity? Or who made known to you the incarnate dispensation of one of the holy Trinity? Or who taught you about the principles of incorporeal beings and those concerning the origin and end of the visible world, or about the resurrection from the dead and eternal life, or about the glory of the kingdom of heaven and the awful judgment? Was it not the grace of God dwelling in you, which is the pledge of the Holy Spirit? What is greater than this grace, or what is better than this knowledge or wisdom?

14. When the Word of God becomes bright and shining in us, and his face is dazzling as the sun, then also will his clothes be radiant, that is, the clear and distinct words of the Holy Scripture of the Gospels now no longer veiled. Then Moses and Elijah will stand beside him, that is, the more spiritual meanings of the Law and the Prophets.

18. The one who prays ought never to halt his movement of sublime ascent toward God. For just as we should understand the ascent "from strength to strength" as the progress in the practice of the virtues, "from glory to glory" as the advance in the spiritual knowledge of contemplation, and the transfer from the letter of Holy Writ to its spirit, so in the same way the one who is settled in the place of prayer should lift his mind from human matters and the attention of the soul to more divine realities. This will enable him to follow the one who has "passed through the heavens, Jesus the Son of God," who is everywhere and who in his incarnation passes through all things on our account. If we follow him, we also pass through all things with him and come beside him if we know him not in the limited condition of his descent in the incarnation but in the majestic splendor of his natural infinitude.

21. In Christ who is God and the Word of the Father there dwells in bodily form the complete fullness of deity by essence; in us the fullness of deity dwells by grace whenever we have formed in ourselves every virtue and wisdom, lacking in no way which is possible to man in the faithful reproduction of the archetype. For it is not unnatural thereby that the fullness of deity dwell also in us by adoption, expressed in the various spiritual ideas.

22. Just as the human word which proceeds naturally from the mind is messenger of the secret movements of the mind, so does the Word of God, who knows the Father by essence as Word knows the Mind which has begotten it (since no created being can approach the Father without him), reveal the Father whom he knows. As the Word of God by nature he is spoken of as the "messenger of the great plan of God."

23. The great plan of God the Father is the secret and unknown mystery of the dispensation which the only-begotten Son revealed by fulfilling in the incarnation, thus becoming a messenger of the great plan of God the eternal Father. The one who knows the meaning of the mystery and who is so incessantly lifted up both in work and in word through all things until he acquires what is sent down to him is likewise a messenger of the great plan of God.

24. If it was for us that the Word of God in his incarnation descended into the lower parts of the earth and ascended above all the heavens; while being himself perfectly unmoved, he underwent in himself through the incarnation as man our future destiny. Let the one who is moved by a love of knowledge mystically rejoice in learning of the great destiny which he has promised to those who love the Lord.

25. If the Word of God and God the Son of the Father became son of man and man himself for this reason, to make men gods and sons of God, then we must believe that we shall be where Christ is now as head of the whole body having become in his human nature a forerunner to the Father on our behalf. For God will be in the "assembly of the gods," that is, of those who are saved, standing in their midst and apportioning there the ranks of blessedness without any spatial distance separating him from the elect.

33. The one who engages in a pursuit of wisdom out of devotion and stands prepared against the invisible forces should pray that both the natural discernment (with its proportionate light) and the illuminating grace of the Spirit remain with him. The former trains the flesh in the acquisition of virtue through asceticism while the latter illuminates the mind to select the companionship of wisdom before all others, according to the Scripture, "He works the destruction of the strongholds of evil and of every pretension which raises itself up against the knowledge of God." Joshua the son of Nun clearly shows this by asking in prayer, "Stand still, O sun, at Gibeon," that is, that the light of the knowledge of God be kept secure for him in the mountain of spiritual contemplation, "and the moon in the valley," that is, that the natural discernment which lies in the frailty of the flesh remain steadfast through virtue.

34. Gibeon is the higher mind, and the valley is the flesh which is weighed down by death. And the sun is the Word who illuminates the mind and inspires it with the power of contemplative experience and delivers it from every ignorance. The moon is the law of nature which persuades the flesh to subject itself lawfully to the spirit by accepting the yoke of the commandments. The moon is symbolic of nature in that it is changeable; but in the saints it remains unchanging through the unchangeable habit of virtue.

37. In the active person the Word grows fat by the practice of virtue and becomes flesh. In the contemplative it grows lean by spiritual understanding and becomes as it was in the beginning, God the Word.

38. The one who is involved in the moral teaching of the Word through rather earthly examples and words out of consideration for his hearers is making the Word flesh. On the other hand, the one who expounds mystical theology using the sublimest contemplative experiences is making the Word spirit.

39. The one who speaks of God in positive affirmations is making the Word flesh. Making use only of what can be seen and felt he knows God as their cause. But the one who speaks of God negatively through negations is making the Word spirit, as in the beginning he was God and with God. Using absolutely nothing which can be known he knows in a better way the utterly Unknowable.

40. The one who through asceticism and contemplation has known how to dig in himself the wells of virtue and knowledge as did the patriarchs will find Christ within as the spring of life. Wisdom bids us to drink from it, saying, "Drink waters from your own vessels and from your own springs." If we do this we shall discover that his treasures are present within us.

73. So long as we see the Word of God take flesh in the letter of Holy Writ in a variety of figures we have not yet spiritually seen the incorporeal and simple and singular and only Father as in the incorporeal and simple and singular and only Son. As the Scripture says, "The one who has seen me has seen the Father," and also, "I am in the Father and the Father is in me." It is, therefore, very necessary for a deep knowledge that we first study the veils of the state-

ments regarding the Word and so behold with the naked mind the pure Word as he exists in himself, who clearly shows the Father in himself, as far as it is possible for men to grasp. Thus it is necessary that the one who seeks after God in a religious way never hold fast to the letter lest he mistakenly understand things said about God for God himself. In this case we unwisely are satisfied with the words of Scripture in place of the Word, and the Word slips out of the mind while we thought by holding on to this garment we could possess the incorporeal Word. In a similar way did the Egyptian woman lay hold not of Joseph but of his clothing, and the men of old who remained permanently in the beauty of visible things and mistakenly worshiped the creature instead of the Creator.

74. The meaning of Holy Writ reveals itself gradually to the more discerning mind in loftier senses when it has put off the complex whole of the words formed in it bodily, as in the sound of a gentle breeze. Through a supreme abandonment of natural activities, such a mind has been able to perceive sense only in a simplicity which reveals the Word, the way that the great Elijah was granted the vision in the cave at Horeb. For Horeb means "newness," which is the virtuous condition in the new spirit of grace. The cave is the hiddenness of spiritual wisdom in which one who enters will mystically experience the knowledge which goes beyond the senses and in which God is found. Therefore, anyone who truly seeks God as did the great Elijah will come upon him not only on Horeb, that is, as an ascetic in the practice of the virtues, but also in the cave of Horeb, that is, as a contemplative in the hidden place of wisdom which can exist only in the habit of the virtues.

76. The divine apostle Paul said that he knew in part the knowledge of the Word. But the great evangelist John said that he saw his glory: "We have seen his glory, the glory as the only begotten of the Father, full of grace and truth." And why did St. Paul say that he knew in part the knowledge of the divine Word? For he is known only to a certain extent through his activities. The knowledge of himself in his essence and personhood remains inaccessible to all angels and men alike and he can in no way be known by anyone. But St. John, initiated as perfectly as humanly possible into the meaning of the Word's incarnation, claims that he has seen the

glory of the Word as flesh, that is, he saw the reason or the plan for which God became man, full of grace and truth. For it was not as God by essence, consubstantial to God the Father, that the only begotten Son gave this grace, but as having in the incarnation become man by nature, and consubstantial to us, that he bestows grace on us who have need of it. This grace we receive from his fullness always in proportion to our progress. Therefore, the one who keeps sacred the whole meaning of the Word of God's becoming incarnate for our sake will acquire the glory full of grace and truth of the one who for our sake glorifies and consecrates himself in us by his coming: "When he appears we shall be like him."

THE CHURCH'S MYSTAGOGY[4]
Chapter Twenty-One

What is signified by the conclusion of the mystical service [the eucharistic liturgy] *when the hymns are sung, that is "One is Holy," and so forth.*

The profession "One is Holy, [one is Lord, Jesus Christ, to the glory of God the Father"] and what follows, which is voiced by all the people at the end of the mystical service, represents the gathering and union beyond reason and understanding which will take place between those who have been mystically and wisely initiated by God and the mysterious oneness of the divine simplicity in the incorruptible age of the spiritual world. There they behold the light of the invisible and ineffable glory and become themselves together with the angels on high open to the blessed purity. After this, as the climax of everything, comes the distribution of the sacrament, which transforms into itself and renders similar to the causal good by grace and participation those who worthily share in it. To them is there lacking nothing of this good that is possible and attainable for men, so that they also can be and be called gods by adoption through grace because all of God entirely fills them and leaves no part of them empty of his presence.

The desert monk, Isaac the Syrian, taught a three-stage ascent to God consisting of asceticism, then of contemplation resulting in psychosomatic integration, and finally of a state of "no prayer" beyond all activity that is simply the ecstatic contemplation of the divine light of the holy Trinity.

ISAAC THE SYRIAN

Relatively little is known about Isaac the Syrian (also known as Isaac of Nineveh) except that he withdrew to desert solitude only five months after his episcopal consecration. There he devoted himself to the study of Scripture, went blind because of his austere life, and then dictated the rest of his five treatises on the monastic life to his disciples.[1] These treatises made a tremendous impact on the monastic movements, especially in the Syrian and in the Eastern churches.

Undoubtedly a mystic and a thinker of unusual clarity and richness, Isaac wrote to guide his monks in reaching ecstatic contemplation of God which foreshadows the glories of heaven. The selected texts illustrate that, for Isaac, "perhaps only a single man in every generation" attains the mystical summit because of the body's appetites, the heart's passionate thoughts, the devil's wiles, and God's complete inaccessibility—except through grace.

The texts were selected to illustrate how Isaac clarified, deepened, and made a unique contribution to the influential Evagrian tradition. Like Evagrius, Isaac taught a three-stage ascent to God. In the first stage, the monk engages in *praktike,* that is, the asceticism required to battle the demons and the body's bondage to the passions. The proper battlefield for *praktike* is the solitude of the desert; the weapons, fasting, vigils, psalmody, and the study of Scripture.

As the monk grows in self-control, reverential fear of the Lord increases. Without this ascetical phase, any attempts by the monk at a contemplative life are as fruitless as a young, wingless bird's attempt to fly.

During the second stage, Isaac maintained with Evagrius that the monk must labor to recapture the soul's (*nous*) original serenity (*apatheia*) lost because of its union with an unruly body. As the texts indicate, natural contemplation bestows the insight into the transitory nature of all things and a "contempt for the world." This realization destroys the devil's sway over the monk, and voids the heart of its passionate thoughts. But the monk also comes to the positive conviction of God's care for him and God's love for all creatures, especially rational ones.

No longer moved by "things corruptible," the monk experiences mystical tears, *apatheia*, and psychosomatic integration. The selected texts show that Isaac expected "only a few" to attain the stage of "pure prayer." At this stage, God's grace makes possible "contemplation," "spiritual prayer," "knowledge" (*gnosis*), and "sometimes revelations of intelligible things." Through a "steadfastness of mind," the monk prays without distraction, and is given astonishing "intellections," or insights into the soul's and creation's mysterious nature.

But in contrast to Evagrius, Isaac spoke of a third stage that is totally beyond even the highest of prayer. His light mysticism focuses upon a state of "no prayer," or the "fruit of pure prayer." In this state, all activity ceases and pure prayer flowers into the ecstatic contemplation of the divine light of the holy Trinity. The mystical experience of the trinitarian divine light ravishes and captivates the soul. It becomes "unconscious," that is, totally forgetful of the world and of itself. The soul rests ecstatically in total passivity in God's glory. Its "sublime" unknowing becomes prayer itself. Without thoughts and free will, "no prayer" gazes "into ecstasy at the unattainable things . . . " in wonder and amazement. Of course, this paradise stage is transitory. Nonetheless, it is an actual foretaste of the resurrected life after death.

This reading also underscores that, for Isaac, all prayer—even the highest state of no prayer—is inextricably connected with psalmody and liturgy, especially the Eucharist.[2]

THE TEXTS

HOMILY FORTY-NINE[3]

The first thought that by God's loving kindness descends into a man, that enters into his heart and guides his soul to life, is the thought of the transitoriness of his nature. This thought is naturally followed by a disdain for the world, and every good movement that leads a man to life enters him from this. And it is this that the divine power which accompanies man lays down as a foundation when it wishes to manifest life in him. If he does not extinguish this thought by involvement in the affairs of life and by vain talk, and if he rears it in his soul by continual concentration within himself and by contemplating it, this thought will lead him to profound divine vision which no man can express. Satan greatly abhors this thought and makes war upon it with all his might to expunge it from man's heart. And if it were possible, he would give a man dominion over the whole world, could he but by this distraction erase this thought from his mind. And if he were able, as it was said, he would gladly do this, for the cunning one knows that if this thought abides in a man, his mind will no longer remain on this earth of delusion, and his machinations against him will not touch him. Now we do not say this concerning that first thought which stirs in us the remembrance of death by reminding us, but concerning the fullness of this activity, which unshakeably establishes in a man the remembrance of death, and which, by his meditation upon it, brings him to a state of continual wonder. The former thought is corporeal, but the latter is a spiritual *theoria* and wondrous grace. This divine vision is arrayed in luminous intuitions. He who possesses it will not gaze searchingly at the world again nor will he cleave to his body.

In very truth, O beloved brethren, if God would send forth this true *theoria* to mankind but for a short while, the world would remain without succeeding generations . . . .

ON THE SECOND ACTIVITY UPON MAN

When a man progresses in good discipline and succeeds in mounting the step of repentance, when he draws nigh the experience of the divine vision that results from divine vision and its practice, and when a gift from on high descends upon him that he may taste the sweetness of spiritual knowledge, a second activity after the first will arise. Firstly he becomes certain of God's providence for every man, he is illumined by His love for creation, and he is filled with wonder at His governance of rational beings and at His great care for them. This is the beginning of the sweetness of God and the fire of His love, which is kindled in the heart and consumes the passions of the soul and body. A man will be conscious of this power when he ponders thoughtfully upon, scrutinizes, and discerns in a spiritual manner all the diverse natures of creation and everything he encounters. Wherefore, through such zealous and divine diligence and through his good conscience a man begins to be stirred to divine love and straightway he is made drunk by it as by wine; his limbs become limp, his mind stands still in awestruck wonder, and his heart is captivated by God. He becomes, as I said, like a man drunk with wine. The more the inner senses grow strong, the more this divine vision gains in strength. And the more a man struggles to live a righteous life, to be watchful, and to labour in reading and prayer, the more its power is established and made fast within him. In very truth, O brethren, a man comes to this at times when he does not remember himself, that he is clad with a body, and he does not know that he is found in this world.

The second activity is the beginning of spiritual *theoria*, and this is the beginning of every revelation in the intellect; by this activity the intellect grows and becomes powerful in hidden things, and by this the intellect advances to other revelations which surpass the nature of man. In a word, guided by the hand of the second activity, all divine *theoria* and all the revelations of the Spirit which the saints receive in this world, and whatever gifts and revelations human nature can come to know in this life pass over to a man. This is the root of our perception of our Creator. Blessed is the man who has kept well this good seed once it has fallen into his soul, and has given it increase, and has not lost it by scattering it in vain concerns and in the distractions of transient and fleeting things! But to our God be glory unto the ages. Amen.

HOMILY TWENTY-THREE[4]

The sweetness of prayer is one thing, and the divine vision of prayer is another; and the second is more honourable than the first, as a mature man is more perfect than an immature child. Sometimes verses become sweet in a man's mouth, and during prayer one verse is chanted numberless times and does not permit him to continue to the next, for he can find no satiety therein. But sometimes a certain divine vision is born of prayer, and the prayer of the man's lips is cut short, and stricken with awe by this vision he becomes as if were a body bereft of breath. This (and the like) we call the divine vision of prayer, and not, as fools affirm it to be, some image and form, or a representation of the imagination. And further, in this divine vision of prayer there exists measures and distinctions of gifts. Till this point there is still prayer, for the mind has not yet passed to where there is no prayer: that state is above prayer. The movements of the tongue and the heart in prayer are keys; what comes after them, however, is the entrance into the secret chambers. Here let every mouth, every tongue become silent, and let the heart (the treasury of the thoughts), and the intellect (the ruler of the senses), and the mind (that swift-winged and most shameless bird), and their every device be still. Here let those who seek tarry, for the Master of the house has come.

On Pure Prayer

Even as the whole force of the laws and commandments given by God to men terminate in the purity of the heart, according to the word of the Fathers, so all the modes and forms of prayer which men pray to God terminate in pure prayer. For sighs, prostrations, heart-felt supplications, sweet cries of lamentation, and all the other forms of prayer have, as I have said, their boundary and their domain in pure prayer. But once the mind crosses this boundary, from the purity of prayer, even to that which is within, it no longer possesses prayer, or movement, or weeping, or dominion, or free will, or supplication, or desire, or fervent longings for things hoped for in this life or in the age to come. Therefore, there exists no prayer beyond pure prayer. Every movement and every form of prayer lead the mind this far by the authority of free will; for this reason there is a struggle in prayer. But beyond this boundary there is awestruck wonder and not prayer. For what pertains to prayer has ceased, while a certain divine vision remains, and the mind does not pray a prayer. Every mode of prayer originates from a motion, but once the intellect enters into spiritual movements, there is no longer prayer. Prayer is one thing, and the divine vision of prayer is another, even though each takes its inception from the other. For prayer is the seed, and the divine vision is the harvesting of the sheaves . . . . [T]hen he remains entirely motionless in his divine vision. Every prayer is a supplication, or a request, or a thanksgiving, or an offering of praise. Diligently seek out whether there exists one of these modes of prayer, or a request of something, when the intellect crosses that boundary and enters into that realm. . . .

Just as among ten thousand men scarcely one will be found who has fulfilled the commandments and what pertains to the Law with but a small deficiency, and who has attained to such limpid purity of soul, so only one man among thousands will be found who after much vigilance has been accounted worthy to attain to pure prayer, and to break through that boundary, and gain experience of that mystery . . . . But as to that mystery which is after pure prayer and lies beyond it, there is scarcely to be found a single man from generation to generation who by God's grace has attained thereto.

Prayer is a supplication, a care, and a desire of something. . . . The motions of prayer are delimited by these movements . . . . But when the mind fervently embraces one of these motions during the time of supplication—corresponding to the compulsion of the occasion—and when on account of its great ardor the course of the motion is drawn by the eye of faith to enter within the veil of the heart, then henceforth the entrances of the soul are closed by this to alien thoughts, the same which are called strangers and which the Law forbids entrance into the Tabernacle of Witness. This is named the acceptable sacrifice of the heart and pure prayer. Its boundaries are, again, until this point. But what lies beyond cannot be called prayer.

. . . any prayer that can be prayed is inferior to what is spiritual; and anything that is spiritual is free of movement. And if a man can scarcely pray with purity, what shall we say concerning spiritual prayer? The Fathers were wont to call every good motion and spiritual activity by the name of prayer . . . Sometimes, spiritual prayer is called by some *theoria* and by others knowledge, and again by some others *noetic vision* . . . 'But when our soul is moved by the operation of the Spirit toward those Divine things, then both sense and their operations are superfluous when the soul has become like unto the Godhead by an incomprehensible union, and is illumined in her movements by the ray of the sublime light.'

. . . The saints of the age to come do not pray with prayer when their intellects have been swallowed up by the Spirit, but rather with awestruck wonder they dwell in that gladdening glory. So it is with us, at the time when the intellect is deemed worthy to perceive the future blessedness, it forgets itself and all things of this world, and no longer has movement with regard to anything. Wherefore with confidence one may dare to say the free will guides and moves every virtue and every order of prayer (whether performed in the body or in the mind), and even the intellect itself, that sovereign over the senses. But as soon as the governance and stewardship of the Spirit rule the intellect, their steward of the senses and the thoughts, then a man's nature is deprived of its free will, and is led by another guidance, and does not direct itself. Where, then, will there be prayer, when a man's nature has not authority over itself, but is led whither it knows not by some other power, and is not able to direct the movements of the mind in that which it chooses, but at that moment is held fast in a captivity by which it is guided whither it does not perceive? . . . Therefore, shall there be prayer in a man who is thus taken captive and does not even have cognizance of himself? . . .

Question: Why, then, is this ineffable grace called by the name of prayer, if it is not prayer?

Answer: This, we say, is because it is granted to the worthy at the time of prayer, and has its inception from prayer. For, according to the testimony of the Fathers, there is no other time of visitation appropriate to this most glorious grace, save the time of prayer. Verily, for this reason it is called by the name of prayer, because the intellect is led by prayer toward that beatitude, and because prayer is its cause, and at no other time does it take place, as the writings of the Fathers explain. Indeed, we see how many of the saints (as it is also recorded in the narration of their lives) are ravished noetically while they stand at prayer . . . because at this time more than all others a man is prepared and collected so as to give his attention to God, and he yearns for and awaits mercy from Him. . . During the time of prayer, however, the vision of the mind gives heed only to God, and stretches forth to Him with all its movements, and it offers Him the heart's supplication with eagerness and constant fervour . . . For, lo, we observe that when we are offering the visible Sacrifice everyone has made ready and has taken their stand in prayer, seeking mercy from the Deity, making supplication and concentrating their intellect upon God, then the Holy Spirit comes upon the bread and the wine which are set upon the altar table . . . From this he begins to understand the incomprehensible things, for the Holy Spirit moves in each man according to his measure, and taking material from that which a man prays, He moves within him, so during prayer his prayer is bereaved of movement, and his intellect is confounded and swallowed up in awestruck wonder, and forgets the very desire of its own entreaty. The intellect's movements are immersed in a profound drunkenness, and it is not in this world; at such a time there will be no distinction between soul and body, nor the remembrance of anything, . . . and it is terminated only by the light of the Holy Trinity through awestruck wonder . . .

. . . Therefore, as I have said, one must not call this gift and grace spiritual prayer, but the offspring of pure prayer which is engulfed by the Holy Spirit. At that moment the intellect is yonder, above prayer, and by discovery of something better, prayer is abandoned. Then the intellect does not pray with prayer, but it gazes into ecstasy at incomprehensible things which surpass this mortal world, and is silenced by its ignorance of all that is found there. This is the unknowing which has been called more sublime than knowledge. This is the unknowing concerning which it has been said, 'Blessed is the man who has attained the unknowing that is inseparable from prayer,' of which may we be deemed worthy by the grace of the only-begotten Son of God, to Whom be all glory, honour, and worship, now, and always, and unto the ages of ages. Amen.

Against the scholasticism and formalism of his day, Symeon the new theologian maintained that theology was a mystical wisdom given by the Holy Spirit only after total purification through rigorous asceticism. This great mystic of the Eastern Christian tradition also claimed to be "theodidact," that is, one taught directly by God.

SYMEON THE NEW THEOLOGIAN

The Eastern Christian tradition emphasizes that the true theologian is one who has been taught by God through mystical experience of the mystery of the Trinity's indwelling in the soul. Thus, the Orthodox Church canonized Symeon and bestowed upon him the title "New Theologian." Just as it had surnamed both St. John the Evangelist and St. Gregory of Nazianzus, "the Theologian," the Orthodox Church honored Symeon because he was so deeply rooted in the tradition of the great mystical theologians of the East.

The "Enthusiastic Zealot" was born in Galatia in Paphogoria (Asia Minor) of a Byzantine provincial noble family. His uncle, who had an important position at the imperial court, brought Symeon to Constantinople at an early age for his secondary education. After meeting Symeon the Studite, a monk of the Stoudion Monastery in Constantinople, the younger Symeon refused to go on for higher studies. The Studite had introduced his young charge to the mystical experience of the indwelling Trinity.

Although Symeon was in charge of a patrician's household and later entered imperial service, he began to give himself to long nightly prayer. Wounded by God's love, drawn to the "terrifying and attractive beauty of God," and receiving visions of the Trinity and Christ as light, he desired to enter a monastery. Through the Spirit-filled assistance of Symeon the Studite, his spiritual director, Symeon was able to end his backsliding, laxity, and immorality. When he was 27 years old, Symeon finally entered the monastery at Stoudion where he experienced a conflict between the common life at the monastery and total obedience to his charismatic spiritual father. Thus, he followed the Studite's advice and transferred to the monastery of St. Mamas, where he gave himself to great penances, long hours of contemplation, and the copying of the Scriptures.

Within three years, he was tonsured monk, ordained a priest, and elected abbot. Symeon insisted that all Christians—especially his monks—must progress in the explicit experience of the triune indwelling in their souls. He also maintained that his own mystical experiences were in some way normative for all. Thus, he encountered great resistance from some in his monastery—almost to the point of incurring physical harm.

It must be emphasized that in the Byzantine Christian world of Symeon's day, the monasteries were too often social vehicles for the maintenance of order and unity throughout the empire. They possessed wealth and indulged in complicated liturgical celebrations that did little to engender genuine piety. The ninth-century monastic reforms initiated by St. Theodore the Studite contributed partially to the imposition even on parish life of the monastic Office and the more formalized practices of prayer and worship. In addition, by divorcing theology from living Christian experience, especially from mystical experience, Byzantine scholastic theology threatened the Church's vital patristic heritage. Thus, Symeon directed his fiery zeal against the somewhat formalized Byzantine spirituality of his day.

His archenemy was Archbishop Stephen of Nicomedia, the chief adviser to and the official theologian of the Constantinople's Patriarch. This formidable scholastic theologian eschewed Symeon's view that theology was a mystical wisdom given by the Holy Spirit only after total purification through rigorous asceticism. Furthermore, Symeon claimed to be a "theodidact," that is, one taught directly by God. He appealed to his own mystical experiences as normative and maintained that his writings were inspired by the Holy Spirit. Stephen branded these claims as ignorant and obscurant enthusiasm that denied, in essence, legitimate ecclesiastical authority and jurisdiction. Symeon added fuel to the fire by contending that a charismatic, non-ordained spiritual father could forgive sins and that a sinful priest could not. However, it would seem that Symeon had in mind a spiritual father's charismatic ability to free sinners from their enslavement to sin.

Both the continued harassment from Stephen and the burdens of office prompted Symeon to resign as abbot in 1005. In 1009, after an ecclesiastical trial, he was banished to the small town of Paloukiton across the Bosporus. Eventually exonerated by both the Emperor and the Patriarch, he was offered an archbishopric. He declined, and continued his life of asceticism, contemplation, and writing for the 13 remaining years of his life at the monastery of St. Marina that he had reconstructed.

Symeon is definitely the most personal of all Byzantine writers. His writings are a mirror of the man. Written and given as conferences when he was abbot, the *Catecheses*, or *Discourses*,[1] is his central work. *The Hymns of Divine Love*[2] is essentially the discourses in poetic form. In his numerous theological and ethical treatises, Symeon shows himself as the guardian of the patristic teaching on mystical theology that emphasized authentic theology as an apophatic wisdom given by the Holy Spirit and transcending human reasoning. His *Practical and Theological Chapters* instructs monks and others in Christian asceticism and contemplation.

In most of his works, Symeon gives a traditional presentation of themes dear to the Eastern Fathers: spiritual combat versus the passions and the demons, constant vigilance, spiritual sobriety, abiding sorrow for sins, the gift of tears, purity of heart, fasting, discernment, *apatheia*, sensitive love of God's will, fasting, charity, and divinization (*theosis*). His works are redolent with the conviction that for the sake of the perfection of *universal* love, one must engage in spiritual combat and mystical prayer. His descriptions of the apophatic experience of the Trinity and of Jesus Christ as a deifying light and fire in a soul surrendering all for God are unsurpassed in the Christian mystical tradition.

Symeon excelled in presenting the Holy Spirit as Sanctifier, as the one who effects Christian asceticism and holiness, as the one through whom Christ speaks directly to the human heart. For Symeon, Christ is conceived spiritually and substantially in the mystic by way of the Holy Spirit. Mystical union with the Trinity experienced as a triple light in unity is also caused by the Holy Spirit. At St. Mamas, Symeon had experienced the descent of the Holy Spirit upon him as fire and light. Symeon maintains that this experience transformed him into light and fire and deified him; that is, it made him a god by grace and by adoption.

However, for Symeon, the chief work of the Holy Spirit is stirring the Christian to genuine repentance and bestowing the gift of mystical tears that soften the heart. For Symeon, "baptism in the Holy Spirit" is the deepened awareness of sins committed after baptism. This baptism also bestows a deeper consciousness of Jesus as Lord and Savior. Through the Spirit, Symeon experienced the habitual presence of Christ in his heart, often ecstatically. This "formless form" of light transformed Symeon into the light and fire of Christ.

The selection illustrates Symeon's trinitarian and Christ centered light mysticism, his emphasis upon deification, and his bold, paradoxical apophatic language. It likewise illustrates a theme found in most of the great Christian mystics: God's attractive beauty is also terrifying. God's light illuminates the mystic not only to God's holiness, but also to the mystic's sinfulness and radical need of constant repentance. Such repentance is also a sign of deep mystical union with God.[3]

THE TEXT

HYMNS OF DIVINE LOVE

HYMN 25[4]

Concerning the contemplation of the divine light received by the author and how the divine light is not understood while in darkness. How struck by awe by the excessiveness of the revelations, he recalls his human weakness and accuses himself.

How shall I describe, Master, the vision of Your countenance?
How shall I speak of the unspeakable contemplation of Your
beauty?
How can the sound of any word contain Him whom
the world cannot hold?
How can anyone express Your love for mankind?
For I was seated in the light of a lamp that was shining on me.
And it was illuminating the darkness and the shadows of night.
It seemed indeed to me that in the light I was occupied in reading,
but as if I were scrutinizing the words and examining the
 propositions.
Then as I was meditating, Master, on these things,
suddenly You appeared from above, much greater than the sun
and You shone brilliantly from the heavens down into my heart.
But all the rest, I was seeing as a deep shadow.
However in the middle there was a column of light,
cutting through the air completely
and it passed from the heavens down to me, miserable one.
At once I forgot the light of the lamp.
I did not remember any longer that I was inside the house.
I was seated in what seemed to me to be a shadowy atmosphere.
Moreover, I forgot completely my body even.
I said to You and now I say it from the bottom of my heart:
"Have mercy on me, Master, have mercy on me, Unique One!"
on me who have never really served You at all, O Savior,
but who from my youth served only to anger You.
I had my share in every kind of vice of the flesh and soul,
and I committed innumerable sins, unheard of sins,
more than all other men, more than brute beasts,
having surpassed all the reptiles and wild animals.
It is therefore toward me You must demonstrate Your mercy,
toward me who have sinned so irrationally, exceeding more
than all others.
It was You Yourself who said that it was not the healthy
who had need of
a physician, Christ, but the sick.
And I have a great sickness and have been so negligent,
so pour out Your great pity upon me, O Word!

But, O what intoxication of light, O what movements of fire!
Oh, what swirlings of the flame in me, miserable one that I am,
coming from You and Your glory!
The glory I know it and I say it is Your Holy Spirit,
who has the same nature with You and the same honor, O Word,
He is of the same race, of the same glory,
of the same essence, He alone with Your Father
and with You, O Christ, O God of the universe!
I fall in adoration before You.
I thank You that You have made me worthy to know as much as it is
the power of Your divinity.
I thank You that You, even when I was sitting in darkness,
revealed Yourself to me, You enlightened me,
You granted me to see the light of Your countenance
that is unbearable to all.
I remained seated in the middle of the darkness, I know,
but while I was there surrounded by darkness
You appeared as light, illuminating me completely from Your total
light.
And I became light in the night, I who was found
in the midst of darkness.
Neither the darkness extinguished Your light completely,
nor did the light dissipate the visible darkness,
but they were together, yet completely separated,
without confusion, far from each other, surely, but not at all mixed,
except in the same spot where they filled everything, so it seems to
me.
Likewise I am in the light, yet I am found in the middle of the darkness.
So I am in the darkness, yet still I am in the middle of the light.
And I say, who will help me in the middle of my darkness
to find a light which the darkness cannot receive?
For how can darkness receive within itself a light
and without being dissipated by the light, it still remains
in the middle of the light?
O awesome wonder which I see doubly,
with my two sets of eyes, of the body and of the soul!
Listen, now. I am telling you the awesome mysteries of a double
God who came to me as a double man.

He took upon Himself my flesh and He gave me His Spirit
and I became also god by divine grace, a son of God by adoption.
O what dignity, what glory!
As a man saddened by sorrow, I see my own misery
and I consider my weakness and I lament.
I am indeed completely unworthy to live, I well know it.
But taking courage in His grace and considering the beauty
which He has given me, this sight fills me with joy.
Then as far as I am human, I know that I see nothing
of the divine realities,
and I am totally cut off from the invisible.
But by divine adoption I see that I have become god
And I have become a participator of intangible things.
Insofar as I am human, I have nothing of the transcendent
and divine realities,
but insofar as I have received mercy through the kindness of God,
I possess Christ, Lord, the Benefactor of all things.
For this reason again, Master, I fall down before You
and ask that I not fail in the hopes I have placed in You,
as being my life, honor and glory and kingdom,
but also as even now You have allowed me to look upon You, Savior, so also after death grant me to see You!
I do not say how much, O Merciful One,
but generously and mercifully, with the look of Your pity,
such as You even now look upon me
and fill me with Your joy and Your divine sweetness.
Yes, my Creator and Fashioner, guard over me with Your hand.
And do not abandon me, no, do not bear any malice toward me!
My great indifference, O Master, do not measure,
but make me worthy by Your light right to the end
to continue without hesitation along the way of Your commandments
and in the very light of Your hands, O all-Merciful One,
let me place my spirit as You rescue me from all my enemies,
from darkness,
fire, eternal punishment, O Word.
Yes, You whose compassion is great, whose mercy is unspeakable,
deign to consign my soul into Your hands,

just as even now I am in Your hand, Savior.
Do not then allow sin to be an obstacle along my path
to cut me off, to snatch me from out of Your hand.
But may the terrible prince of darkness and corrupter of souls
be put to shame in seeing me, O Master, ensconced in Your palm,
just as even now he does not dare to draw near me,
for he sees that I am protected by Your grace!
Do not condemn me, Christ, do not push me into Hell!
Do not cast my soul into the abyss of death,
because I dare to pronounce Your name,
I who am completely sordid, stained and impure.
May the earth not open up and devour me,
O Word, I, the great transgressor, who am completely unworthy,
both to live and to speak!
May fire not descend upon me and at once devour me
for saying without having the right, "Lord have mercy!
May You, rich in mercy, the Lover of mankind by nature, not wish
to enter into judgment against me!"
For when should I really be able to cry out, I who am sin itself?
What then should I express who am the condemned one,
who from my mother's womb have offended You immeasurably
and up to the present am so insensitive to Your magnanimity.
I who have descended a thousand times into the depth of Hell
and who have been pulled out from there by Your divine goodness?
I who have sullied the members and the flesh of my soul and body
as no other living human?
I, crazed by pleasures, a lover, shameless, and perverse and deceit-
ful in the soul's evil?
I who have not kept, O Christ, even one of Your commandments?
What will I offer in my defense, what response will I make to You?

In what spiritual frame of mind should I bear Your accusations,
O my God?
If You lay bare all my disorders and actions,
O King immortal, do not show them to all,
because I shudder at thinking of the deeds of my youth
and to speak of them fills me with fright and covers me with shame.
For if You would wish to reveal these to all,
my confusion would be worse than every sort of punishment.

For who, after seeing my audacities, after seeing my debaucheries,
after seeing my impure embraces, after seeing my shameful actions
which even now sully me when I call them to mind,
would not be stupefied, would not tremble,
would not cry out and at once turn away their looks and say:
"Take away, Master, such a totally sordid person!
Order that the hands be quickly bound along with the feet of
this wretch
and that he be cast quickly into the dark fire,
so that he may no longer be looked at by us,
Your faithful servants!"
Yes, it is proper, Master, this is truly just, that all those men
so express it and You Yourself carry it out,
and that I be cast into fire, prodigal and perverse sinner that I am.
But You descended to save the prodigals and the perverse.
Do not totally shame me, Christ, in the day of judgment,
when You place Your sheep on Your right hand
and place me and the goats on Your left.
But may Your immaculate light, the light of Your countenance,
hide my works and the nudity of my soul,
and clothe me with joyfulness
so that with confidence without shame,
I may be placed at the right hand
with the sheep and with them
I may glorify You forever and ever. Amen.

Known as the "reasonable mystic" and the "learned lover," the Cistercian William of St. Thierry is a witness to and an example of the Golden Age of monasticism and mysticism. He lived and wrote convincingly about the human desire to know God in perfect love.

WILLIAM OF ST. THIERRY

Few have written so profoundly and convincingly about the human desire to *know* God in perfect *love* as William of St. Thierry. Known as the "reasonable mystic," the "learned lover," and one of the most original minds of the 12th century, his writings disclose a cultivated, curious, eclectic mind, united to a heart burning with the love of God. In William, one finds not only a profound thinker with an exacting, startlingly original, yet impeccably orthodox mind, but also a deeply contemplative and passionate religious spirit inclined to solitude for the sake of knowing God. Here is a contemplative who pushes reason to its limits and knows that, eventually, reason must kneel before the Trinity's ineffable mystery to find its fulfillment in love.

Psychologist, moralist, theologian, experienced mystic, spiritual guide, and reformer of the monastic life, William has been called a witness to and a paradigm of the Golden Age of monasticism and mysticism. He was immensely popular with his contemporaries, not only because of his theological and mystical profundity, but also because of his urbanity and attractive personality. Although theologically different from his great friend, Bernard of Clairvaux, numerous writers ascribed Bernard's name to William's works. Only in the 20th century has "Pseudo Bernard," or "Bernard's alter ego," been appreciated on his own.

William was born in Liege of noble parentage, and received an excellent education at the Laon (or Rheims) Cathedral school. However, before completing his studies, William's contemplative spirit led him to enter the Benedictine abbey of St. Nicasius of Rheims. Within three years, he befriended Bernard of Clairvaux, the man who soon became his ideal.

After only six years of monastic life, he was elected abbot of the abbey of St. Thierry. Zealous in both his religious and secular responsibilities, William, nonetheless, felt hemmed in by the burdens of office. On numerous occasions he requested Bernard that he be allowed to enter the monastery of Clairvaux to satisfy his desire for solitude and to be close to his friend. But Bernard resolutely refused.

While in office, William found time to write *The Nature and Dignity of Love, On Contemplating God, Grace and Free Will, On the Sacrament of the Altar*, numerous treatises on the Fathers, a commentary on the *Song of Songs*, and his *Prayers* and *Meditations* that reflect his ardent soul in a way reminiscent of Augustine's *Confessions*.

After 15 years as abbot, William resigned to take the white habit of the Cistercian monks at Signy, an abbey established by his good friend Bernard. In his thirst for ever deeper solitude, William often visited the austere and strictly contemplative eremetical Carthusians of Mount Dieu.

During this period, William wrote *The Mirror of Faith* and *The Enigma of Faith*, works aimed at strengthening the faith of and consoling the monks at Signy and Mount Dieu. William maintained that "speaking about God has certain special words which are rational but not intelligible except in the reasoning of faith, not however in the reasoning of human understanding."[1] For William, in order to "perceive the ineffable in an ineffable way"[2] reason must be shaped by faith in such a way that the "reasoning of faith" may conflict with ordinary human reason. William was a *mystical* theologian, not a speculative one. This may account for his polemics against the theologians, Peter Abelard and William of Conches, who formed part of the intellectual environment of that period.

Like many others in the Christian mystical tradition, William saw no opposition—as some commentators incorrectly maintain—between mysticism and the Bible. The Bible was his primary source, for even when he did not directly quote it, the Bible's influence thoroughly permeates his works. The monastic liturgy and the psalter likewise influence his works, as well as the Latin Fathers, especially Augustine. William also had access to the Greek Fathers through the Latin translations of John Scotus Eriugena.

Like the Greeks, William emphasized that everything comes from God, subsists in God, and must return to God. However, William applied this Greek emanation-return schema only to the individual soul. Essentially a gift of God's grace, the return to God demands the "active life," that is, the asceticism required to eradicate all disorder, vice, and sin in the soul and to establish it in virtue. Asceticism makes the flesh obey reason, submits reason to the spirit, and restores the spirit's original dynamism for the trinitarian life.

However, William does not emphasize asceticism and the acquiring of virtue for their own sake. Like his predecessors in the Christian mystical tradition, William contends that asceticism exists only for the sake of the mystical contemplation that guides and crowns it. Contemplation—which only the Holy Spirit can teach—effects true spiritual union with God, or deification. Nonetheless, this life is open to all genuinely disciplined persons.

The selected text is taken from *The Golden Epistle* (originally called the *Treatise on the Solitary Life*), written toward the end of William's life. A brilliant blending of his creative theology and of his profound contemplative experience, this work, dedicated to the Mount Dieu Carthusians, eulogizes the Cistercian way of life and breathes forth the hunger for God that animated the monastic movements of his century. William discusses the "animal," the "rational," and the "spiritual" man, or the beginner, the progressive, and the perfect in the spiritual life. This work, especially the section on *The Spiritual Man*, offers an excellent summary of his teachings on the contemplative experience of God.

One should note from this selection how skillfully William blends Scriptural texts, words, and allusions to drive home a particular point. For him, the truly spiritual person must progress from "inclining" to, "clinging" to, "enjoying," and "uniting in spirit" with God. The Holy Spirit not only brings about this unity, but is this unity itself. The spiritual person is the perfect person, and perfection consists in becoming by grace what God is by nature, therefore willing only what God wills. The spiritual person becomes so closely united to God that only this mortal life itself prevents perfect union.

By God's "creative grace," the human person is created in God's image through the triune unity of the human spirit's memory, understanding, and will. Although sin has adversely affected this image, God's "illuminating grace" enables the image to be restored through the acquiring of virtue. Moreover, it is illuminating grace that accompanies and brings about mystical experience, and the eventual loving knowledge or knowing love which is union with God.

The truly spiritual person realizes the need for asceticism, self-knowledge, custody of, and purity of heart because "this ineffable reality can be seen only in an ineffable way." Even brief glimpses of God's countenance, "O face, face of my soul," purify the person, often render the person ecstatic, and transform the person into itself. In and through contemplation the spiritual person learns discretion and discernment. Like so many others in the Christian mystical tradition, William taught the purifying, illuminating, and transforming effects of mystical contemplation.

William grappled with the problem of how love could be knowledge. For him, only the "perception of enlightened love" can grasp the ineffable. He says, "When the soul reaches out in love to anything, a certain change takes place in it by which it is transmuted into the object loved."[3] By becoming connatural with God, the person attains a loving knowledge or a knowing love of God, "an understanding that comes from love." However, "that knowledge [of God] is best known in this life by unknowing; the highest knowledge that a man can here and now attain consists in knowing in what way he does not know."[4] Nonetheless, William maintained that through contemplative experience a person does come to know God. "And yet, O Majesty transcending understanding," he prayed, "to the soul that loves you, you do seem understandable. For though no faculty of soul or spirit can ever comprehend you, nevertheless, the man who loves you in his loving understands you totally."[5] The soul may know best how it does not know, but for William genuine love of God is understanding, and vice versa.

The originality of William's mystical theology resides in the way he inserts the human spirit's knowledge and love of God into the inner-trinitarian life. Because the Holy Spirit is not only the reciprocal love of the Father and the Son, but also their mutual knowledge, and because our love and knowledge of God *is* the Holy Spirit itself, William contends that at the higher stages of the contemplative experience, love of God is also knowledge of God. The Holy Spirit is actually not love, but charity, the enlightening knowledge of the hidden God, the knowing love at the Trinity's depths. Because of the Holy Spirit's delicate and subtle role in the spiritual person's contemplative experience, one loves in knowing and knows in loving.

Love is inextricably connected with faith, and vice versa. William prayed aloud: "Why do you not believe, O infidel? Surely because you do not love! You do not believe because you do not love; you do not love because you do not believe."[6] For William, love is a kind of violent will. His mysticism is not bridal, but possesses the simplicity, directness, and trust of love that a young child has for its mother.

One should also note William's Cistercian warm, ardent love of the human Jesus. The contemplation of trinitarian "Beauty" transforms the spiritual person into a person of self-emptying love. In fact, the sections referring to Christ should be read in the context of William's *On Contemplating God*, wherein he compares himself to Moses who hid in the cleft of the rock and saw God's back. However, for William, the rock is the "rock of the Christian faith." Moreover, he says: "And sometimes, when I gaze with longing, I do see the 'back' of him who sees me; I see your Son Christ 'passing by' in the abasement of his incarnation."[7] Thus, the spiritual person does not "cease to arouse his neighbor to the same if he loves him as himself." The unity of spirit espoused by William unites a person not only to God but also to one's neighbor. Unity of spirit, deification, is spiritually fecund and demonstrates its power in self-emptying love. The Cistercian ideal was to be poor with the poor of Christ.[8]

THE TEXTS

THE SPIRITUAL MAN

THE PERFECTION OF MAN IN THIS LIFE
When the object of thought is God and the things which relate to God and the will reaches the stage at which it becomes love, the Holy Spirit, the Spirit of life, at once infuses himself by way of love and gives life to everything, lending his assistance in prayer, in meditation or in study to man's weakness. Immediately the memory becomes wisdom and tastes with relish the good things of the Lord, while the thoughts to which they give rise are brought to the intellect to be transformed into affections. The understanding of the one thinking becomes the contemplation of one loving and it shapes it into certain experiences of spiritual or divine sweetness which it brings before the gaze of the spirit so that the spirit rejoices in them.

250. And then, insofar as it is possible for man, worthy thoughts are entertained of God, if indeed the word "thought" (*cogitatio*) is correct where there is no impelling principle (*cogit*) nor anything impelled (*cogitur*), but only awareness of God's abundant sweetness leading to exultation, jubilation and a true experience of the Lord in goodness on the part of the man who has sought him in this simplicity of heart.

251. But this way of thinking about God does not lie at the disposal of the thinker. It is a gift of grace, bestowed by the Holy Spirit who breathes where he chooses, when he chooses, how he chooses and upon whom he chooses. Man's part is continually to prepare his heart by ridding his will of foreign attachments, his reason or intellect of anxieties, his memory of idle or absorbing, sometimes even of necessary business, so that in the Lord's good time and when he sees fit, at the sound of the Holy Spirit's breathing the elements which constitute thought may be free at once to come together and

do their work, each contributing its share to the outcome of joy for the soul. The will displays pure affection for the joy which the Lord gives, the memory yields faithful material, the intellect affords the sweetness of experience . . . .

256. As to the basic desire, first of all the object of desire should be considered, then the extent to which it is desired and the way in which it is desired. If a man's basic desire is for God he should examine how much and in what way he desires God, whether to the point of despising self and everything which either exists or can exist, and this not only in accordance with reason's judgment but also following the mind's inclination, so that the will is now something more than will: love, dilection, charity, and unity of spirit.

257. For such is the way in which God is to be loved. "Love" is a strong inclination of the will toward God, "dilection" is a clinging to him or a union with him; "charity" is the enjoyment of him. But "unity of spirit" with God for the man who has his heart raised on high is the term of progress toward God. No longer does it merely desire what God desires, not only does it love him, but it is perfect in its love, so that it can will only what God wills.

258. Now to will what God wills is already to be like God, to be able to will only what God wills is already to be what God is; for him to will and to be are the same thing. Therefore it is well said that we shall see him fully as he is when we are like him, that is when we are what he is. For those who have been enabled to become sons of God have been enabled to become not indeed God, but what God is: holy, and in the future, fully happy as God is. And the source of their present holiness and their future happiness is none other than God himself who is at once their holiness and their happiness.

XVI. 259. Resemblance to God is the whole of man's perfection. To refuse to be perfect is to be at fault. Therefore the will must always be fostered with this perfection in view and love made ready. The will must be prevented from dissipating itself on foreign objects, love preserved from defilement. For to this end alone were we created and do we live, to be like God; for we were created in his image.

260. There is however a likeness to God which is lost only with life itself, left to every man by the Creator of all men as evidence of a better and more sublime likeness that has been lost. It is possessed regardless of acceptance or refusal, alike by the man who is capable of conceiving it and by the man who is so stupid that he cannot conceive it. It consists in the fact that, as God is everywhere, and is present with the whole of his being in his creation, so every living soul is in like manner present in its body . . . .

261. But there is another likeness, one closer to God, inasmuch as it is freely willed. It consists in the virtues and inspires the soul as it were to imitate the greatness of Supreme Good by the greatness of its virtue and his unchangeable eternity by its unwearying perseverance in good.

262. In addition to this there is yet another likeness, of which something has been said already. It is so close in its resemblance that it is styled not merely a likeness but unity of spirit. It makes man one with God, one spirit, not only with the unity which comes of willing the same thing but with a greater fullness of virtue, as has been said: the inability to will anything else.

263. It is called unity of spirit not only because the Holy Spirit brings it about or inclines a man's spirit to it, but because it is the Holy Spirit himself, the God who is Charity. He who is the Love of the Father and Son, their Unity, Sweetness, Good, Kiss, Embrace and whatever else they can have in common in that supreme unity of truth and truth of unity, becomes for man in regard to God in the manner appropriate to him what he is for the Son in regard to the Son through unity of substance. The soul in its happiness finds itself standing midway in the Embrace and the Kiss of Father and Son. In a manner which exceeds description and thought, the man of God is found worthy to become not God but what God is, that is to say man becomes through grace what God is by nature . . . .

266. He it is who gives life to man's spirit and holds it together, just as it gives life to its body and holds it together. Men may teach how to seek God and angels how to adore him, but he alone teaches how to find him, possess him and enjoy him. He himself is the anxious quest of the man who truly seeks, he is the devotion of the

man who adores in spirit and truth, he is the wisdom of the man who finds, the love of him who possesses, the gladness of him who enjoys.

267. Yet whatever he bestows here on his faithful of the vision and knowledge of God is but as in a mirror and a riddle, as far removed from the vision and the knowledge that is to be in the future as faith is from truth or time from eternity. This is true even when what we read in the book of Job happens: "He hides the light in his hands and commands it to mount on high, then he tells his beloved that it belongs to him and that he can ascend to it" (Job 36:32f.).

XVIII. 268. For the man who is chosen and loved by God is sometimes shown a certain light of God's countenance, just as light that is enclosed in man's hands appears and is hidden at the will of him who holds it. This is in order that what he is allowed to glimpse for a passing moment may set the soul on fire with longing for the full possession of eternal light, the inheritance of full vision of God.

269. To make him realize to some extent what he lacks, grace sometimes as if in passing touches the affections of the lover and takes him out of himself, drawing him into the light of true reality, out of the tumult of affairs into the joys of silence, and to the slight extent of which he is capable, showing him for a moment, for an instant, ultimate reality as it is in itself. Sometimes it even transforms the man into a resemblance of ultimate reality, granting him to be, to the slight extent of which he is capable, such as it is.

270. Then when he has learned the difference between the clean and the unclean he is restored to himself and sent back to cleanse his heart for vision, to fit his spirit for likeness, so that if at some future date he should again be admitted to it he may be the more pure for seeing and able to remain for a longer time in the enjoyment of it.

271. For the limits of human imperfection are never better realized than in the light of God's countenance, in the mirror which is the vision of God. Then in the light of true reality man sees more and more what he lacks and continually corrects by means of likeness whatever sins he has committed through unlikeness, drawing near by means of likeness to him from whom he has been separated by

unlikeness. And so clearer vision is always accompanied by clearer likeness.

272. It is impossible indeed for the supreme Good to be seen and not loved, or not to be loved to the full extent to which vision of it has been granted. So eventually love arrives at some likeness of that love which made God like to man by accepting the humiliation of our human lot in order that man might be made like to God by receiving the glorification of communion in the divine life. Then indeed it is sweet for man to be abased together with supreme Majesty, to become poor together with the Son of God, to be conformed to divine Wisdom, to make his own the mind which is in Christ Jesus our Lord.

XIX. 273. For here there is wisdom with devotion, love with fear, exultation with trembling, when God is thought of and understood as brought down unto death, the death of the Cross, to the end that man might be exalted to the likeness of the Godhead. For here there flows the rushing stream that gladdens God's city, the remembrance of his abounding sweetness in the understanding and consideration of the benefits he has conferred on us.

274. In this regard man is easily led to love God by thinking about or contemplating what is worthy of love in him, which of itself shines upon the affections of the contemplative: his power and strength and glory and majesty and goodness and beatitude. But what especially carries man away in his spiritual love into the object of his love is that God in himself is whatever there is lovable in him; he is in the whole of himself what he is, if one can speak of a whole where there is no part.

275. In his love of this good the devout man who has been so affected centers himself upon it in such a way as not to be distracted from it until he becomes one or one spirit with him. Once arrived at this point he is separated and kept at a distance only by the veil of this mortality from the Holy of Holies and from that supreme beatitude of highest heaven. Yet since he already enjoys it in his soul through his faith and hope in him whom he loves, he is able to bear what is left of this life also with a more ready patience.

XX. 276. This is the goal for which the solitary strives, this is the end he has in view, this is his reward, the rest that comes after his labors, the consolation for his pains; and this is the perfection and the true wisdom of man.

277. For when that "taking up by the Lord, the Holy One of Israel, our King" (Ps 88:19) befalls the man of God, the wise and devout soul, with grace to enlighten and assist it, in the contemplation of supreme Good gazes also upon the laws of unchangeable Truth to the extent that it is found worthy to attain to them by means of understanding that comes of love. From this it forms for itself a way of life which is heavenly and a model of holiness.

For it gazes upon supreme Truth and everything which derives truth from it, upon supreme Good and everything which derives goodness from it, upon supreme Eternity and everything which derives from it. It models itself upon that Truth, that Charity and that Eternity while directing its life here below. It does not fly above those eternal realities in its judgment but gazes up at them in desire or clings to them by love, while it accepts the realities of this created world to adapt and conform itself to them, not without using its judgment to discriminate, its power to examine and its mind to appreciate.

278. This process gives rise to holy virtues, the image of God is formed anew in man and that divine life is set in order from which the Apostle complains that certain men have become estranged. Virtue also takes on its true rigor, those two elements which constitute the perfection of the contemplative and the active life, concerning which, according to the ancient translators, we read in Job: "Behold piety is wisdom, while to abstain from evil is knowledge" (Job 28:28).

287. Now this is the life of God of which we spoke a little while before, not so much an advance in reason as an attachment of the affections to perfection in wisdom. For the fact that a man relishes these things makes him wise and it is because he has become one spirit with God that he is spiritual. And this is the perfection of man in this life.

292. Just as the spirit has perception of corporeal things through the bodily senses, so it knows things pertaining to reason or the spirit

only through itself. But the things of God it can seek or expect to understand only by God's gift. Indeed it is lawful and possible for man possessed of reason to think and enquire sometimes of some things which concern God, such as the sweetness of his goodness, the power of his strength, and other like matters. But what he is in himself, his essence, can only be grasped by thought at all insofar as the perception of enlightened love reaches out to it.

XXIV. 293. Yet God is to be attained by faith and, to the extent that the Holy Spirit helps our weakness, by thought as Eternal Life living and bestowing life; the Unchangeable and immutably making all changeable things; the Intelligent and creating all understanding and every intellectual being; Wisdom that is the source of all wisdom; fixed Truth that stands fast without any swerving, the Source of all truth and containing from eternity the principles of all things that exist in time.

XXV. 296. Since this ineffable reality can be seen only in an ineffable way, the man who would see it must cleanse his heart, for it cannot be seen or apprehended by means of any bodily likeness in sleep, any bodily form in waking hours, any investigation of the mind, but only by humble love from a clean heart.

297. For this is the face of God which no one can see and live in the world. This is the Beauty for the contemplation of which everyone sighs who would love the Lord his God with his whole heart and his whole soul and his whole mind and his whole strength. Neither does he cease to arouse his neighbor to the same if he loves him as himself.

298. When eventually he is admitted to this vision he sees without any doubt in the light of truth the grace which forestalls him. When he is thrown back on himself he understands in his blindness that his uncleanness is out of keeping with its purity. And if he loves he takes pleasure in weeping, neither is it without much groaning that he is forced to return to himself.

299. We are wholly unequal to the task of conceiving this reality, but he whom we love forgives us, he of whom we confess we can neither speak nor think worthily, and yet we are stimulated and drawn on by his love or the love of his love to speak and to think

of him.

300. It is for one who entertains such thoughts to abase himself in everything and to glorify in himself the Lord his God, to become of no worth in his own eyes as he contemplates God, to subject himself to every human being for the love of his Creator, to offer up his body as a holy victim, living, pleasing to God, the worship due from him as a rational creature. But before everything he should not think highly of himself, beyond his just estimation but have a sober esteem of himself, according to the measure of faith which God has apportioned to him. He should not entrust his treasures to men's mouths but conceal them in his cell and hide them away in his conscience, so as to have this inscription always in the forefront of his conscience and on the front of his cell: "My secret is my own, my secret is my own" (Is 24:16).

THE END OF DOM WILLIAM'S EPISTLE TO THE BRETHREN OF MONT DIEU.

*The "mellifluous teacher," Bernard of Clairvaux,
viewed the relationship between the divine Word
and the individual soul as a spiritual marriage between the heavenly Bridegroom and the human
bride. The sacramental humaneness of his mysticism, with love as its central focus, shaped Christian piety, spirituality, and mysticism from his day
to this.*

BERNARD OF CLAIRVAUX

Bernard of Clairvaux may well be the apotheosis of the monastic
tradition in the medieval period. In his day, he was one of the most
powerful figures in Christendom. He was instrumental in securing
the election of Innocent II to the papacy in preference to the anti-
pope, Analectus II, and influenced the papacy when one of his disciples became Pope Eugene III in 1145.

During his life of prodigious and ceaseless activity, Bernard undertook sensitive missions for popes and kings, had tremendous influence over popes, bishops, and councils, and was the eloquent
preacher of the Second Crusade. He also gave himself wholeheartedly to the theological controversies and ecclesiastical politics of his
times. He was called "the conscience of all Europe." Passionately in
love with God, Christ, and Mary, he maintained a vigorous contemplative life to the end of his life.

Because Bernard believed that everything in Scripture is meaningful if approached in love, he thinks and speaks like the Scriptures.
His is the method of Augustine, Origen, and most of the Fathers,
but the ease, fluency, and clarity with which he makes the hidden
sense flow from the text earned him the title, *Doctor mellifluous*. Due
to his extraordinary, mystical penetration of Scripture, the Fathers,

the liturgy, and psalmody, and his awesome artistic power to describe and communicate this to others, he has been aptly described as "the last of the Fathers, and not inferior to the earliest." The structure of his sentences causes his works to sound like a soul sighing or singing hymns to God. His erudition was such that many in the Christian tradition contend that everything he wrote is a masterpiece. The sacramental humaneness of his mysticism and spirituality, with love as its central focus, shaped Catholic piety, spirituality, and mysticism from his day to this.

Born of an especially holy mother at Fontaines-les-Dijon in Burgandy, Bernard received an education commensurate with his noble lineage and lively intellect. However, when he was 21 years old, he decided to become a monk at Cîteaux, the Cistercian protomonastery, at this time in its first fervor with strict rules. He convinced his brothers, his uncle, and several other noblemen to take the same step.

Within three years he was chosen abbot for a new foundation in the solitary valley of Clara Vallis, or Clairvaux. Clairvaux soon became a model of strict observance, and Bernard averred that—for all practical purposes—there was no salvation outside Cîteaux. Convinced of the superiority of the Cisterician life for the practice of Christian perfection, Bernard railed against the alleged disciplinary decadence of the Cluniacs who observed a modified version of the rule of St. Benedict. He attracted thousands to the cloistered, contemplative life, established 68 foundations, and had almost direct authority over 164 of the 350 houses that existed across the whole of Europe.

Bernard was preeminently a monk whose theology aimed at a clear, intelligent, affective exposition of the faith in order to dispose a person to prayer and contemplation. Thus, he eschewed the incipient scholasticism of his day for its emphasis upon great subtlety in reasoning and its claims to be a "scientific" theology. Bernard placed knowledge squarely in the context of the ascent of the soul to God and was convinced that the profoundest and most significant truths come from and are validated by mystical experience. With others in the Christian mystical tradition, he taught that love is itself a knowing.

His spirituality and mysticism are profoundly Christocentric. As he says, "Write what you will, I shall not relish it unless it tells of Jesus. Talk or argue about what you will, I shall not relish it if you exclude the name of Jesus. Jesus is to me honey in the mouth, music in the ear, a song in the ear."[1] For Bernard, it is essential to "remember" Christ in order to "imitate" him. By praying the mysteries of the life, death, and resurrection, Bernard desires that the "affections for our Lord Jesus should be both tender and intimate, to oppose the sweet enticements of sensual life."[2]

For Bernard, the invisible God assumed flesh because God "wanted to recapture the affections of carnal men who were unable to love in any other way, by first drawing them to the salutary love of his own humanity, and then gradually to raise them to a spiritual love."[3] Thus, he strongly suggested praying with a "sacred-image of the God-man." Bernard writes even more emphatically: "I have said that wisdom is to be found in meditating on these truths [Christ's life, death, and resurrection]. For me they are the source of perfect righteousness, of the fullness of knowledge, of the most efficacious graces, of abundant merits . . . This is my philosophy, one more refined and interior, to know Jesus and him crucified."[4] Still, as profitable as meditations on Christ's humanity may be, Bernard viewed them as "imperfect," because they are tinged with "carnal love." The proficient in the spiritual life love Christ with "rational" and "spiritual love."

This cast of mind, in conjunction with an eagerness to be the champion of orthodoxy, led him to condemn with polemical vehemence Abelard at the Council of Sens (1140) and to attack both Gilbert de la Porrée and Arnold of Brescia as grave dangers to the faith. However, "if at times he appeared somewhat impetuous and obstinate, nothing could conceal the *caritas* which illuminated his character and writings, and caused him to denounce the persecution of the Jews, and to insist that prayer, preaching, and the life of self-denial and worship should be the *militia* of Church and state, monk and layman, alike."[5] Even his enemies were edified by Bernard's great asceticism, holiness, absence of egotism, self-sacrifice, humility, and whole-hearted service.

Central to Bernard's theology is the notion that Love created us out of love to share Love itself, and then redeemed us after we had sinned. God's gift of both the Incarnation and the Mother of God are proof of this. Moreover, the ultimate and culminating end of all theology, the summit of all God's works, is mystical experience.

Bernard's 86 sermons allegorically interpret the *Song of Songs;* they summarize his mystical theology. Like Origen and Augustine, Bernard views the relationship between the Divine Word and the individual soul as a spiritual marriage between the heavenly Bridegroom and the human bride. But unlike them, he fully developed the notion of spiritual marriage.

Commenting on the biblical words, "Let him kiss me with the kiss of his mouth," Bernard draws an analogy between kissing Christ's feet, hand, and mouth and the purgative, illuminative, and unitive way. As he says, "these kisses were given to the feet, the hand and the mouth, in that order. The first is the sign of genuine conversion of life, the second is accorded to those making progress, the third is the experience of only a few of the more perfect."[6]

Thus, the remote preparation for the mystical kiss of the mouth is the asceticism required to obtain solid virtue. The proximate preparation—recollection and introversion—is profoundly affective. For Bernard, the soul's Bridegroom will reveal himself "only to the one who is proved to be a worthy bride by intense devotion, vehement desire and the sweetest affection. And the Word who comes to visit will be clothed in beauty, in every aspect a Bridegroom."[7] What the bride really desires and asks for is "to be filled with the grace of this threefold knowledge [of the Father, Son, and Holy Spirit], filled to the utmost capacity of mortal flesh . . . . Furthermore, this revelation, which is made through the Holy Spirit, not only conveys the light of knowledge but also lights the fire of love . . ."[8]

A portion of Sermon 1 was selected to show Bernard's great esteem for the *Song of Songs* and to illustrate his conviction that personal experience is necessary to plumb the mysteries of this marriage song heard in the heart. In Sermon 41, Bernard gives the earliest account in the Christian tradition of the distinction between apophatic contemplation (in which both reason and the imagination play no part) and *revelatory* contemplation. In the latter, the purely spiritual experiences of God are translated into *communicable* images and language. With an eloquence unusual even for Bernard, he describes the role the angels play to produce in the imagination and mind the images, concepts, and language through which God's pure light can be comprehended and communicated to others.

Sermon 52 illustrates Bernard's conviction that contemplation is a foretaste of heaven and a mystical (bridal) sleep that vivifies the mystical senses. But he also viewed it as a type of ecstatic dying to the world and as an apophatic, imageless—therefore, "angelic"— contemplation of God. For St. John of the Cross, bridal sleep is the most apostolic work a person can do for the Church, because therein a person does what he or she was created for: to love and to be loved.

The selected text from Sermon 74 is one of the most stunning attempts in the entire Christian mystical tradition to describe the mystical experience. When the Word invades the soul, he cannot be perceived by the senses. However, the heart, or the person's deepest center, suddenly becomes alive and its most secret faults are disclosed. When the Word leaves, it is like a boiling pot removed from the stove. The Life of the soul's life seems to have disappeared.

Sermons 83 and 85 describe spiritual marriage and spiritual fecundity. The Word actually takes the soul as his bride, and two become one in spirit, yet remain two. Spousal mysticism emphasizes a differentiated unity. In other words, love actually makes two one, but also enhances personal identity. Love makes the soul equal to God, God by participation, but not simply God. Also, Bernard emphasizes that bridal love loves God for his own sake. Although as bride, the soul desires the Bridegroom's embrace, as mother she loves her children, that is, her neighbor.[9]

THE TEXTS

ON THE SONG OF SONGS[10]

SERMON 1
VI. 11. But there is that other song, which, by its unique dignity and sweetness, excels all those I have mentioned and any others there

might be; hence by every right do I acclaim it as the *Song of Songs*. It stands at a point where all the others culminate. Only the touch of the Spirit can inspire a song like this, and only personal experience can unfold its meaning. Let those who are versed in the mystery revel in it; let all others burn with desire rather to attain to this experience than merely to learn about it. For it is a melody that resounds abroad by the very music of the heart, not a trilling on the lips but an inward pulsing of delight, a harmony not of voices but of wills. It is a tune you will not hear in the streets, these notes do not sound where crowds assemble; only the singer hears it and the one to whom he sings—the lover and the beloved. It is preeminently a marriage song telling of chaste souls in loving embrace, of their wills in sweet accord, of the mutual exchange of the heart's affection.

SERMON 4[11]

III. 3. We should take note of the kind of pendants they offer her [the bride]: they are made of gold and studded with silver. Gold signifies the splendor of the divine nature, the wisdom that comes from above. The heavenly goldsmiths to whom this work is committed, promise that they will fashion resplendent tokens of the truth and insert them in the soul's inward ears. I cannot see what this may mean if not the construction of certain spiritual images in order to bring the purest intuition of divine wisdom before the eyes of the soul that contemplates, to enable it to perceive, as though puzzling reflections in a mirror, what it cannot possibly gaze on as yet face to face. The things we speak of are divine, totally unknown except to those who have experienced them. While still in this mortal body, while still living by faith, while the content of the clear interior light is still not made clear, we can, in part, still contemplate the pure truth. Any one of us who has been given this gift from above may make his own the words of St. Paul: "Now I know in part;" and: "We know in part and in part we prophesy." But when the spirit is ravished out of itself and granted a vision of God that suddenly shines into the mind with the swiftness of a lightning-flash, immediately, but whence I know not, images of earthly things fill the imagination, either as an aid to understanding or to temper the intensity of the divine light. So well-adapted are they to the divinely illuminated senses, that in their shadow the utterly pure and brilliant radiance of the truth is rendered more bearable to the mind and more capable of being communicated to others. My opinion is that they are formed in our imaginations by the inspirations of the holy angels, just as on the other hand there is no doubt that evil suggestions of an opposite nature are forced upon us by the bad angels.

4. Perhaps, too, we have here those puzzling reflections seen by the Apostle in the mirror [1 Cor 13:12] and fashioned, as I have said, by angelic hands from pure and beautiful images, which I feel bring us in contact somehow with the being of God, that in its pure state is perceived without any shadow of corporeal substances. The elegance of the imagery that so worthily clothes and reveals it I attribute to angelic skill. That this is so is more distinctly conveyed by another version: "We, the artificers, will make you images of gold, with silver decorations." "With silver decorations" and "studded with silver" mean the same thing. To me they seem to signify not merely that the angels produce these images within us, but that they also inspire the elegance of diction which so fittingly and gracefully embellishes with greater clarity and keener enjoyment our communication of them to the audience.

SERMON 52[12]
2. That in heaven it is like this, as I read on earth, I do not doubt, nor that the soul will experience for certain what this page suggests, except that here she cannot fully express what she will there be capable of grasping, but cannot yet grasp. What do you think she will receive there, when now she is favored with an intimacy so great as to feel herself embraced by the arms of God, cherished on the breast of God, guarded by the care and zeal of God lest she be roused from her sleep by anyone till she wakes of her own accord.

II. 3. Well then, let me explain if I can what this sleep is which the Bridegroom wishes his beloved to enjoy, from which he will not allow her to be awakened under any circumstances, except at her good pleasure . . . This sleep of the bride, however, is not the tranquil repose of the body that for a time sweetly lulls the fleshly senses, nor that dreaded sleep whose custom is to take life away completely. Farther still is it removed from that deathly sleep by which a man perseveres irrevocably in sin and so dies. It is a slumber which is vital and watchful, which enlightens the heart, drives away death, and communicates eternal life. For it is a genuine sleep that does not stupefy the mind but transports it. And—I say it without hesitation—it is a death, for the apostle Paul in praising people still living in the flesh spoke thus: 'For you have died, and your life is hid with Christ in God.'

4. It is not absurd for me to call the bride's ecstasy a death, then, but one that snatches away not life but life's snares, so that one can say: 'We have escaped as a bird from the snare of the fowlers'. In this life we move about surrounded by traps, but these cause no fear when the soul is drawn out of itself by a thought that is both powerful and holy, provided that it so separates itself and flies away from the mind that it transcends the normal manner and habit of thinking; for a net is spread in vain before the eyes of winged creatures. Why dread wantonness where there is no awareness of life? For since the ecstatic soul is cut off from awareness of life though not from life itself, it must of necessity be cut off from the temptations of life . . . How good the death that does not take away life but makes it better; good in that the body does not perish but the soul is exalted.

5. Men alone experience this. But, if I may say so, let me die the death of angels that, transcending the memory of things present, I may cast off not only the desire for what are corporeal and inferior but even their images, that I may enjoy pure conversation with those who bear the likeness of purity.

III. This kind of ecstasy, in my opinion, is alone or principally called contemplation. Not to be gripped during life by material desires is a mark of human virtue; but to gaze without the use of bodily likenesses is the sign of angelic purity. Each, however, is a divine gift, each is a going out of oneself, each a transcending of self, but in one, one goes much farther than in the other.

6. Consider therefore that the bride has retired to this solitude, there, overcome by the loveliness of the place, she sweetly sleeps within the arms of her bridegroom, in ecstasy of spirit. Hence the maidens are forbidden to waken her until she herself pleases.

SERMON 74[13]

II. 5. Now bear with my foolishness a little. I want to tell you of my own experience, as I promised. Not that it is of any importance . . . . I admit that the Word has also come to me—I speak as a fool—and has come many times. But although he has come to me, I have never been conscious of the moment of his coming. I perceived his presence, I remembered afterwards that he had been with me; sometimes I had a presentiment that he would come, but I was never conscious of his coming or his going. And where he comes from when he visits my soul, and where he goes, and by what means he enters and goes out, I admit that I do not know even now; as John says: 'You do not know where he comes from or where he goes.' There is nothing strange in this, for of him was it said, 'Your footsteps will not be known.' The coming of the Word was not perceptible to my eyes, for he has not color; nor to the ears, for there was no sound; nor yet to my nostrils, for he mingles with the mind, not the air; he has not acted upon the air, but created it. His coming was not tasted by the mouth, for there was not eating or drinking, nor could he be known by the sense of touch, for he is not tangible. How then did he enter? Perhaps he did not enter because he does not come from outside? He is not one of the things which exist outside us. Yet he does not come from within me, for he is good, and I know there is no good in me. I have ascended to the highest in me, and look! the word is towering above that. In my curiosity I have descended to explore my lowest depths, yet I found him even deeper. If I look outside myself, I saw him stretching beyond the furthest I could see; and if I looked within, he was yet further within. Then I knew the truth of what I had read, 'In him we live and move and have our being'. And blessed is the man in whom he has his being, who lives for him and is moved by him.

6. You ask then how I knew he was present, when his ways can in no way be traced? He is life and power, and as soon as he enters in, he awakens my slumbering soul; he stirs and soothes and pierces my heart, for before it was hard as stone, and diseased. So he has begun to pluck out and destroy, to build up and to plant, to water dry places and illuminate dark ones; to open what was closed and to warm what was cold; to make the crooked straight and the rough places smooth, so that my soul may bless the Lord, and all

that is within me may praise his holy name. So when the Bridegroom, the Word, came to me, he never made known his coming by any signs, not by sight, not by sound, not by touch. It was not by any movement of his that I recognized his coming; it was not by any of my senses that I perceived he had penetrated to the depths of my being. Only by the movement of my heart, as I have told you, did I perceive his presence; and I knew the power of his might because my faults were put to flight and my human yearnings brought into subjection. I have marvelled at the depth of his wisdom when my secret faults have been revealed and made visible; at the very slightest amendment of my way of life I have experienced his goodness and mercy; in the renewal and remaking of the spirit of my mind, that is of my inmost being, I have perceived the excellence of his glorious beauty, and when I contemplate all these things I am filled with awe and wonder at his manifold greatness.

7. But when the Word has left me, all these spiritual powers become weak and faint and begin to grow cold, as though you had removed the fire under the boiling pot, and this is a sign of his going. Then my soul must needs be sorrowful until he returns, and my heart again kindles within me—the sign of his returning. When I have had such experience of the Word, is it any wonder that I take to myself the words of the Bride, calling him back when he has withdrawn? For although my fervor is not as strong as hers, yet I am transported by a desire like hers. As long as I live the word 'return', the word of recall for the recall of the word, will be on my lips.

As often as he slips away from me, so often shall I call him back. From the burning desire of my heart I will not cease to call him, begging him to return, as if after someone who is departing, and I will implore him to give back to me the joy of his salvation, and restore himself to me.

SERMON 83[14]

3. Such conformity weds the soul to the Word, for one who is like the Word by nature shows himself like him too in the exercise of his will, loving as she is loved. When she loves perfectly, the soul is wedded to the Word. What is lovelier than this conformity? What is more desirable than charity, by whose operation, O soul, not con-

tent with a human master, you approach the Word with confidence, cling to him with constancy, speak to him as to a familiar friend, and refer to him in every matter with an intellectual grasp proportionate to the boldness of your desire? Truly this is a spiritual contract, a holy marriage. It is more than a contract, it is an embrace: an embrace where identity of will makes of two one spirit. There need be no fear that inequality of persons should impair the conformity of will, because love is no respecter of persons. It is from loving, not revering, that love receives its name. Let someone filled with horror or stupor or fear or wonder be content with reverence; where there is love all these are unimportant. Love is sufficient for itself; when love is present it absorbs and conquers all other affections. Therefore it loves what it loves, and it knows nothing else. He who is justly honored, held in awe, and admired, prefers to be loved. He and the soul are Bridegroom and Bride. What other bond or compulsion do you look for between those who are betrothed, except to love and be loved?

II. This bond is stronger even than nature's firm bond between parents and children. 'For this', it says in the Gospel, 'a man will leave his father and his mother and cleave to his bride.' You see how strong this feeling is between bride and bridegroom—it is stronger not only than other affections, but even than itself.

4. Now the Bridegroom is not only loving; he is love. Is he honor too? Some maintain that he is, but I have not read it. I have read that God is love, but not that he is honor. It is not that God does not desire honor, for he says, 'If I am a father, where is my honor?' Here he speaks as a father, but if he declares himself to be a husband I think he would change the expression and say, 'If I am a bridegroom, where is my love?' For he had previously said, 'If I am the Lord, where is my fear?' God then requires that he should be feared as the Lord, honored as a father, and loved as a bridegroom. Which of these is highest and most lofty? Surely it is love. Without it fear brings pain, and honor has no grace. Fear is the lot of a slave, unless he is freed by love. Honor which is not inspired by love is not honor but flattery. Honor and glory belong to God alone, but God will receive neither if they are not sweetened with the honey of love. Love is sufficient for itself; it gives pleasure to itself, and for its

own sake. It is its own merit and own reward. Love needs no cause beyond itself, nor does it demand fruits; it is its own purpose. I love because I love; I love that I may love. Love is a great reality, and if it returns to its beginnings and goes back to its origin, seeking its source again, it will always draw afresh from it, and thereby flow freely. Love is the only one of the motions of the soul, of its senses and affections, in which the creature can respond to its Creator, even if not as an equal, and repay his favor in some similar way . . . Now you see how different love is, for when God loves, he desires nothing but to be loved, since he loves us for no other reason than to be loved, for he knows that those who love him are blessed in their very love.

5. Love is a great reality, but there are degrees to it. The bride stands at the highest. Children love their father, but they are thinking of their inheritance, and as long as they have any fear of losing it, they honor more than they love the one from whom they expect to inherit. I suspect the love which seems to be founded on some hope of gain. It is weak, for if the hope is removed it may be extinguished, or at least diminished. It is not pure, as it desires some return. Pure love has no self-interest. Pure love does not gain strength through expectation, nor is it weakened by distrust. This is the love of the bride, for this is the bride—with all that means. Love is the being and the hope of a bride. She is full of it, and the bridegroom is contented with it. He asks nothing else, and she has nothing else to give. That is why he is the bridegroom and she the bride; this love is the property only of the couple. No one else can share it, not even a son.

. . . but the love of a bridegroom—or rather of the Bridegroom who is love—asks only the exchange of love and trust. Let the Beloved love in return. How can the bride—and the bride of Love—do other than love? How can Love not be loved?

6. Rightly, then, does she renounce all other affections and devote herself to love alone, for it is in returning love that she has the power to respond to love. Although she may pour out her whole self in love, what is that compared to the inexhaustible fountain of his love? The stream of love does not flow equally from her who loves and from him who is love, the soul and the Word, the Bride

and the Bridegroom, the Creator and the creature—any more than a thirsty man can be compared to a fountain. Will the Bride's vow perish, then, because of this? Will the desire of her heart, her burning love, her affirmation of confidence, fail in their purpose because she has not the strength to keep pace with a giant, or rival honey in sweetness, the lamb in gentleness, or the lily in whiteness? Because she cannot equal the brightness of the sun, and the charity of him who is Charity? No. Although the creature loves less, being a lesser being, yet if it loves with its whole heart nothing is lacking, for it has given all. Such love, as I have said, is marriage, for a soul cannot love like this and not be beloved; complete and perfect marriage consists in the exchange of love. No one can doubt that the soul is first loved, and loved more intensely, by the Word; for it is anticipated and surpassed in its love. Happy the soul who is permitted to be anticipated in blessedness so sweet. Happy the soul who has been allowed to experience the embrace of such bliss! For it is nothing other than love, holy and chaste, full of sweetness and delight, love utterly serene and true, mutual and deep, which joins two beings, not in one flesh, but in one spirit, making them no longer two but one. As Paul says: 'He who is united to God is one spirit with him.'

SERMON 85[5]

13. But notice that in spiritual marriage there are two kinds of birth, and thus two kinds of offspring, though not opposite. For spiritual persons, like holy mothers, may bring souls to birth by preaching, or may give birth to spiritual insights by meditation. In this latter kind of birth the soul leaves even its bodily senses and is separated from them, so that in her awareness of the Word she is not aware of herself. This happens when the mind is enraptured by the unutterable sweetness of the Word, so that it withdraws, or rather is transported, and escapes from itself to enjoy the Word. The soul is affected in one way when it is made fruitful by the Word, in another when it enjoys the Word: in the one it is considering the needs of its neighbor; in the other it is allured by the sweetness of the Word. A mother is happy in her child; a bride is even happier in her bridegroom's embrace. The children are dear, they are the pledge of his love, but his kisses give her greater pleasure. It is good to save many souls, but there is far more pleasure in going aside to be with

the Word. But when does this happen and for how long? It is sweet intercourse, but lasts a short time and is experienced rarely! This is what I spoke of before, when I said that the final reason for the soul to seek the Word was to enjoy him in bliss.

The English Cistercian, Aelred of Rievaulx, has been
called the teacher of mystical friendship. Because God
is friendship, Aelred saw human friendships as a love
by which persons participate in the innertrinitarian
life. Friendship causes and is caused by a loving
knowledge that in its higher stage is a form of mysti-
cal contemplation.

AELRED OF RIEVAULX

One of three sons, Aelred was born around 1110 shortly after his father Eliaf, the last of the hereditary priests of the Northumbria region, moved from Durham to Hexam. As recipient of the tradition
of learning in his noble family, he spent much of his youth in the
court of the half-English King, Daniel I. Because of his intelligence
and winning personality, he became popular and successful in
court. But worldly success was not enough for him. While on an official journey, Aelred became plagued by a sense of self-disgust and
superficiality, and decided to become a Cistercian monk.

This was the Golden Age of Cistercian monasticism. In less than a
century more than 500 Cistercian monasteries had sprung up in Europe. These great monks were "pioneers," clearers of forests, drain-
ers of swamps, reclaimers of land, and excellent farmers. But they
were also great intellectuals whose unprecedented spirituality
shifted the emphasis away from the stern Lord to a warm, personal
love of the person of Jesus Christ.

Because of Aelred's personal charm, shrewd intellect, oratorical eloquence, and literary gifts, this contemporary of the great Bernard of
Clairvaux was soon to be known as the "Bernard of the North."
From a relatively early age, he had also attained a reputation for holiness and wisdom. As abbot of the monastery at Rievaulx, he led a

life of tireless activity, even during his last years when he was chronically ill. In the period of anarchy following the death of Henry I, Aelred was entrusted with important matters of state.

His Cistercian training added the *lectio divina* and a love of Scripture to his love of the secular classics. The Rule of Saint Benedict and the patristic tradition—especially Augustine's *Confessions*—also became his patrimony. As one of the greatest writers of medieval England, he wrote numerous influential sermons, a meditation on Jesus' boyhood, a letter on Christian asceticism, and his two classics, The *Mirror of Charity* and *On Spiritual Friendship*.

Typical Cistercian emphases are found in Aelred's writings:

1) Christians must live the mysteries of Christ's life, death, and resurrection;
2) Affectivity and Christ's humanity must play a more dominant role in Christian spirituality;
3) Christ communicates himself to the person by way of his Church;
4) Mary's mediation in the salvific process is necessary;
5) Asceticism is a preparation for the "Lord's visitations" in the heart;
6) The crown of charity is contemplation during which the soul enjoys "sabbath" rest.

Aelred taught that through contemplation one attained a goal rarely achieved elsewhere: the sabbath rest of God in the soul. God's stillness silences the soul's faculties, puts an end to preoccupation with self and others, and teaches the heart and intellect the mysteries of the inner-trinitarian life.

Aelred focused upon the attraction, intention, and fruition of love. Despite his emphasis upon the affective side of love, he stressed still more love's intention, that is, the act of reason that discerns what is genuine Christian joy for the human heart. But the judgment that something is truly good may or may not produce enjoyable feelings.

Aelred is the "doctor" of spiritual love. His emphasis upon human friendship as a Christian good rooted in God's and Christ's love is unique in the Christian mystical tradition. Unlike the reserve shown in this area by the Fathers and the monastic authors, Aelred viewed friendship as a Christian virtue, a form a charity by which a person participated in the innertrinitarian life. For Aelred, God is friendship, and he who dwells in friendship dwells in God. He considered the friendless person a "beast." As he says, "scarcely any happiness whatever can exist among mankind without friendship, and a man is to be compared to a beast if he has no one to rejoice with him in adversity, no one to whom to unburden his mind if any annoyance crosses his path or with whom to share some unusually sublime or illuminating inspiration . . . He is entirely alone who is without a friend."[1]

Aelred taught that love is still pure even when directed toward another, and not directly to God. Love of God cannot conflict with love of friends because all love is one and grounded in God. Aelred viewed the monastery as a school of spiritual love and friendship, for genuine love builds community. Human, earthly friendship mirrors the great love the saints in heaven have for each other. Because frienship causes and is caused by loving knowledge, Aelred considered it as wisdom that in its higher stages in a form of mystical contemplation.

But Aelred was no teary-eyed romantic. Only good, moral people are capable of friendship; friendship for carnal or material gain is pseudo-friendship. Moreover, friendship had to be firmly anchored in Christ and the Scriptures. As he says, "for now nothing which had not been sweetened by the honey of the most sweet name of Jesus, nothing which had not been seasoned with the salt of Sacred Scripture, drew my affection so entirely to itself."[2]

The texts were selected to illustrate Aelred's great love and perceptive insights into the Christian significance of spiritual friendship. The description of the mystical experience engendered by the comingling of Aelred's loving spirit with the loving spirits of all his brethren is one of the most striking passages in the Christian mystical tradition. The texts also bring out Aelred's insistence upon the "honor," "truth," "good will," and Christ-centered basis of friendship. When the spirits of two friends mingle, they receive Christ's kiss, but through the other. Then the person sighs for the kiss of Christ alone, that is, the Holy Spirit.[3]

THE TEXTS

ON SPIRITUAL FRIENDSHIP

MUTUAL LOVE[4]

Therefore you will not deny that he is most fortunate who rests in the inmost hearts of those among whom he lives, loving all and being loved by all, whom neither suspicion severs nor fear cuts off from this sweetest tranquility . . .

The day before yesterday, as I was walking the round of the cloister of the monastery, the brethren were sitting around forming as it were a most loving crown. In the midst, as it were, of the delights of paradise with the leaves, flowers, and fruits of each single tree, I marveled. In that multitude of brethren I found no one whom I did not love, and no one by whom, I felt sure, I was not loved. I was filled with such joy that it surpassed all the delights of this world. I felt, indeed, my spirit transfused into all and the affection of all to have passed into me, so that I could say with the Prophet: "Behold, how good and how pleasant it is for brethren to dwell together in unity."

THE KISS OF CHRIST[5]

And so in friendship are joined honor and charm, truth and joy, sweetness and good will, affection and action. And all these take their beginning from Christ, advance through Christ, and are perfected in Christ. Therefore, not too steep or unnatural does the ascent appear from Christ, as the inspiration of the love by which we love our friend, to Christ giving himself to us as our Friend for us to love, so that charm may follow upon charm, sweetness upon sweetness and affection upon affection. And thus, friend cleaving to friend in the spirit of Christ is made with Christ but one heart and one soul, and so mounting aloft through degrees of love to friendship with Christ, he is made one spirit with him in one kiss. . .

There is, then, a corporeal kiss, a spiritual kiss, and an intellectual kiss. The corporeal kiss is made by the impression of the lips; the spiritual kiss by the union of spirits; the intellectual kiss through the Spirit of God, by the infusion of grace . . .

. . . the spiritual kiss is characteristically the kiss of friends who are bound by one law of friendship; for it is not made by contact of the mouth but by the affection of the heart; not by a meeting of lips but by a mingling of spirits, by the purification of all things in the Spirit of God, and, through his own participation, it emits a celestial savor. I would call this the kiss of Christ, yet he himself does not offer it from his own mouth, but from the mouth of another, breathing upon his lovers that most sacred affection so that there seems to them to be, as it were, one spirit in many bodies . . .

The soul, therefore, accustomed to this kiss and not doubting that all this sweetness comes from Christ, as if reflecting within itself and saying, "Oh, if only he himself had come!" sighs for the kiss of grace and with the greatest desire exclaims: "Let him kiss me with the kiss of his mouth." So that now, after all earthly affections have been tempered, and all thoughts and desires which savor of the world have been quieted, the soul takes delight in the kiss of Christ alone and rests in his embrace, exulting and exclaiming: "His left hand is under my head and his right hand shall embrace me."

GOD IS FRIENDSHIP[6]

Ivo. What does this all add up to? Shall I say of friendship what John, the friend of Jesus, says of charity: "God is friendship"?

Aelred. That would be unusual, to be sure, nor does it have the sanction of the Scriptures. But still what is true of charity, I surely do not hesitate to grant to friendship, since "he that abides in friendship abides in God, and God in him". . .

And, a thing even more excellent than all these considerations, friendship is a stage bordering upon that perfection which consists in the love and knowledge of God, so that man from being a friend of his fellowman becomes the friend of God, according to the words of the Savior in the Gospel: "I will not now call you servants, but my friends."

FRIENDSHIP IS WISDOM[7]

And yet, if you consider carefully what has been said about friendship, you will find it so close to, or even replete with, wisdom, that I might almost say friendship is nothing else but wisdom.

Richard of St. Victor was the first to create a systematic theology of the mystical life. To him, the Scriptures contain the patterns of the interior life. Symbolically, they embody the journey from ascetical purification to self-knowledge and culminate in the contemplative awareness of God's deepest mysteries.

RICHARD OF ST. VICTOR

This 12th-century spiritual giant was a gifted preacher, spiritual director, theologian, and contemplative whose writings have had immense influence throughout the ages. Dante praised Richard of St. Victor for his "suprahuman" contemplative ability. St. Bonaventure considered him to be not only the "modern" master of contemplation but also the equal of the early Fathers of the Church. To this day, Richard of St. Victor is appreciated for both his theological prowess and his mystical genius while known as the teacher of contemplation and charity.

Little is known of Richard's early life except that he may have been born in Scotland. At a young age, he entered the abbey of St. Victor, located on the Seine's left bank at the outskirts of the busy university city of Paris. The abbey followed the rule of St. Augustine and enjoyed great esteem for its disciplined community life, which was dedicated to contemplation and rigorous study of the Bible and the Fathers of the Church. The monks of the abbey were also known for their exceptionally beautiful liturgies. Because of St. Victor's proximity and openness to the theological schools of Paris, it participated in and contributed to that age's "new" theology, that is, Scholasticism, a form of philosophical and theological inquiry based upon formal and exceptionally rigorous methods of reasoning. Thus, the monks were well-known for their theological sophistication.

Richard was a faithful disciple of Hugh of St. Victor, whom he correctly called "the best theologian of our time." Hugh imparted to Richard an exceptional skill in the theological methods of the day. However, differing from Hugh's more "scientific" approach, Richard emphasized that truth is reached by meditation and contemplation, not by rational induction. Only contemplation can ultimately penetrate God's material and spiritual creation, as well as the mystery of the divine essence and Trinity. With love as its driving force, it is satisfied with nothing less than the vision of God.

Richard's deeply contemplative attitude toward theology contrasts sharply with the rationalistic emphases of both Abelard and Peter the Lombard. But as the disciple of Hugh of St. Victor, he gave rational dialectics a greater role in the theological enterprise than either William of St. Thierry or St. Bernard. Both William and Bernard seemingly confused knowledge and love. Richard's subtle, original mind grasped that love is born of knowledge and that speculation must come before contemplation.

For example, although Richard considered the Trinity to be the supreme object of contemplation and a reality, "above and beyond" reason, he did not hesitate to wrestle with the "necessary reasons" for the Trinity's existence. His penetrating theological treatise on the Trinity cogently argues that God, as perfect love, cannot remain in himself but must go out to another person of equal dignity and worth. To Richard, the second divine person "proceeds" from love. Furthermore, perfect love demands a third person to whom the first two can communicate the delights of their love, or who can be the object of their common love. Since perfect love must be given, received, and shared in community, God, as perfectly one in essence, must give, receive, and share this love in a trinity of persons.

However, Richard specialized and excelled in mystical theology, and as such he was the first to create a systematic theology of the mystical life. His two masterpieces, The *Twelve Patriarchs* (also known as *Benjamin Minor*) and *The Mystical Ark* (also known as *Benjamin Major*), evince a subtle mind, psychological perception, and a skillful analysis of the soul's faculties. Moreover, Richard directs his psychological and theological profundity toward a thoroughly practical goal: the instruction of others in the ascetical-mystical ascent to God.

The Sacred Page nourished Richard's thought. For him, the Scriptures contain the patterns of the interior life. Symbolically, they embody the journey from ascetical purification to self-knowledge and culminate in the contemplative awareness of God's deepest mysteries. The Scriptures reveal their spiritual sense to Richard not only in and through their words but also, and especially, in biblical persons and events. Richard uses biblical persons to express and relate various spiritual states. When a person attains a particular state, he or she becomes a particular biblical person. Richard focuses primarily on the patriarch Jacob and his children but also upon the *Song of Songs* and Jesus' transfiguration. Richard preferred the mystical and tropological (figurative) interpretations of Scripture. Nonetheless, he based these solidly upon the Scriptures' literal meaning and took great care that his allegories were consistent with the analogy of faith, that is, the Church's overall faith.

His Twelve Patriarchs, subtitled "On the Soul's Preparation for Contemplation," begins with the line, "Benjamin a young man in ecstasy of mind" (Psalm 67:28, Vulgate) and tropologically interprets the patriarch, Jacob, and his children as representing successive stages of awareness. Mystical ascent, to Richard, demands an exacting interior asceticism, the acquisition of virtue and moderation, and a redirection of one's affections, mind, and will toward God in order to attain peace and quiet in mind and body. It is also instructive that in his *Mystical Ark*, Richard stresses the importance of psalmody and liturgy as a means of achieving harmony and recollection.

To Richard, discipline of the imagination, or mind, is even more important than bodily discipline. Reason, symbolized by Rachel, must give birth to discretion, symbolized by Joseph. When Benjamin—who symbolizes ecstatic contemplation—is born, Rachel dies, for contemplation transcends reason.

The Mystical Ark is aptly subtitled "On the Grace of Contemplation," and it tropologically interprets the ark of the covenant. This work brilliantly analyzes the different kinds of contemplation, the objects of contemplation, and the human-divine means required for attaining contemplative states. To Richard, contemplation "is the free, more penetrating gaze of the mind, suspended with wonder concerning the manifestations of wisdom" (I,4). It is also "a pene-trating and free gaze of the soul extended everywhere in perceiving things" (I,4). Contemplatives must focus on material creatures, dis-cover the divine reason for their existence, ponder both the spiri-tual soul and the angelic realm, and transcend to the divine nature and the Trinity. To Richard, contemplation enlarges the mind, raises it up, and finally "alienates" it in ecstatic love.

Although Richard is a link between the great mystical awakening in medieval Europe and renewed interest in Pseudo-Dionysius, his mysticism is decidedly affirmative (kataphatic). Mystical ascent pro-ceeds by way of a love that desires to *know* ever-more deeply. Rich-ard says in the *Twelve Patriarchs* that "where there is love, there is seeing" (XIII) and that love drives the person to know. Yet, unlike those in the mystical tradition who assign a priority either to love or to knowledge, Richard deftly shows their reciprocal relationship.

Although Richard teaches that reason dies in mystical ecstasy, one must always return to reason after the experience. Nonetheless, a Dionysian, negative (apophatic) redolence does permeate his works. As he says, "although we may retain in memory something from that [ecstatic] experience and see it through a veil, as it were, and as though in the middle of a cloud, we lack the ability to com-prehend or call to mind either the manner of seeing or the quality of the vision. And marvelously, in a way remembering, we do not remember; and not remembering, we remember; while seeing we do not discern; looking at, we do not examine; and as we direct our attention to something, we do not penetrate it" (IV,23).

The selection has been taken from Richard's most mature work, *Of the Four Degrees of Passionate Charity*. To Richard, the Trinity is the di-vine community of love and contemplation's supreme object. Hence, love must be the contemplative's all and truth. Few pas-sages in mystical literature have analyzed so skillfully the power, beauty, and transforming quality of human yearning, the divine call, and the final outpouring of love in which the mutual embrace of lovers causes the contemplative to die in God and to rise in the humble Christ.

The selected text illustrates that, to Richard, love not only wounds and chains a person but also reduces that person to a singular and insatiable desire for the beloved. Richard then transposes his analysis to a love that thirsts for God, then thirsts to go to God, then thirsts to be in God, and finally thirsts in the way God thirsts. This thirst for God enkindles the affections, attracts the person into himself or herself, purges all disorder, and unifies the person. God's love calls the soul above and beyond itself into ecstatic dissolution through which it melts into God's own life, forgets everything—including itself—for God's sake, and submits to his or her divine remolding into the image of the humble Christ.

One should also note Richard's emphasis upon liberating, divine visitations in which God is felt as a burning fire but is not seen. Eventually, the contemplative sees the inaccessible, divine light but cannot reach it. However, the divine light binds the soul and empties the imagination, memory, and mind of everything except God. The divine light causes the contemplative to swoon in delight and to melt into God's life to become God by participation. Yet, by dying in God, the contemplative is raised in Christ and rendered spiritually fertile in a perfect charity willing to lay down his or her life for others. It must be emphasized that to Richard, contemplation results not only in an ever-deepening penetration of the mysteries of creation and the Trinity, not only in divine revelations and transforming union with God but also in Christ's perfect charity that transforms human community through the humble service of others.[1]

THE TEXTS

OF THE FOUR DEGREES OF PASSIONATE CHARITY[2]
I am wounded by love. Love urges me to speak of love. Gladly do I give myself up to the service of love, and it is sweet and altogether lovely to speak about love. . . . Behold! I see some men wounded, others bound, languishing, fainting, and all for love. Charity wounds, charity binds, makes a man sick, causes him to faint. Which of these is not powerful, not passionate? These are the four steps of passionate love which we are soon to consider. . . .

But let us return to that degree of love which we first mentioned and called 'wounded love.' Do you not feel as if sometimes you were shot through the heart when the fiery dart of this love penetrates the inmost mind of man, pierces his affections so that he can in no way contain or hide the burning of his desire. He burns with desire, his affections are stirred, he is in fever and gasps, sighing deeply and drawing long breaths. These are certain signs of a wounded soul, groans and sighs, a pale and averted face. But this degree offers some respite and allows for the cares and anxieties of necessary business. After the manner of feverish men who are troubled by this illness, sometimes they burn more fiercely, then, by attending to their affairs, they feel some relief. But after a short interval, they burn again, greater heat supervenes, and the broken spirit is once more set on fire and burns more fiercely. Thus, the fever of love, often waning but always returning more acutely, gradually weakens the spirit, wears down and exhausts the strength, until it completely conquers the soul and lays it low. It occupies the soul wholly with thoughts about itself, engrosses and controls it wholly, so that it cannot tear itself away or consider anything else, and so it passes from the first to the second degree.

For we said the first degree was wounding love and the second binding love. For the soul is surely and undoubtedly bound when it cannot forget this one thing or think about anything else. Whatever it does or says, it is always turning this over in its mind and keeping it continually in memory. It dreams of love when sleeping, and waking it thinks of it all the time. It is easy, I think, to understand how this degree, which does not allow man's mind to be quiet even for an hour, surpasses the former. For often wounding is less than binding. . . .

Love rises up to the third degree of passion when it excludes every other love, when it loves nothing but the one, or for the sake of the one. In this third degree of passionate love, nothing can give any satisfaction but the one thing and nothing is known but the one. The soul loves one and is devoted to one, it thirsts for and desires the one, it clings to one, sighs for him, is kindled by him, rests in him. In him alone is it re-created and satisfied. . . .

In the first degree, love pierces the affections; in the second, it binds the thoughts; in the third it destroys action. The whole of man is in these, and what can he have beyond this? If therefore everything that belongs to a man is made captive, what more can be done to him? If this power of love possesses, if the greatness of love absorbs everything how can it increase still more?. . . .

Therefore, the fourth degree of passionate love is that in which nothing at all can satisfy the desire of the passionate soul. This degree, in that it has once passed beyond the bounds of human power, is, unlike others, unlimited in its expansion, for it always finds something that it can still desire. Whatever it may do, or whatever may be done to it, does not satisfy the desire of the ardent soul. . . What is there, I ask, that could penetrate a man's heart more deeply, crucify it more cruelly, agitate it more wildly?. . .

So now we have four degrees of violence in the passion of love, and we have discussed them above. The first degree of violence is when the mind cannot resist its desires; the second when it cannot forget them; and third is when nothing else pleases it; the fourth and last when even this love cannot satisfy it. In the first, love is insuperable; in the second, inseparable; in the third, singular; in the fourth, insatiable. Love is insuperable when it will not yield to any other feeling; inseparable when it never leaves the memory; singular when it will have no companion; insatiable when it cannot be satisfied. And though different things may be noticed about each degree, we should more especially note the excellence of love in the first degree, its passion in the second, its violence in the third, its surpassing greatness in the fourth. For how excellent is the love that exceeds all other affection. How great is the vehemence of love that will not allow the mind to be still. How violent that love which expels every other affection violently. How surpassing the zeal that is not satisfied by anything. . . .

In the first degree, God is loved with the heart, the soul, and the mind but not wholly by any one of these. In the second, he is loved with all the heart; in the third, with all the soul; in the fourth, with all the strength. Love of the heart is a love arising from deliberate consideration; love of the soul is love arising from affection; deliberation belongs to the heart, but desire belongs to the soul. . . . To love with the heart is to love by judgement and deliberation; to love with the soul is to love because of desire and affection. The first is with effort, the second according to desire. To love with one's whole heart, soul, and all one's strength is to concentrate all one's efforts, desires, and powers upon this one thing. . . .

Let us go deeper and speak more openly. In the first degree, the soul thirsts for God; in the second, she thirsts to go to God; in the third, she thirsts to be in God; in the fourth, she thirsts in God's way. She thirsts for God when she desires to experience what that inward sweetness is that inebriates the mind of man, when he begins to taste and see how sweet the Lord is. She thirsts for God when she desires to be raised above herself by the grace of contemplation and to see the Lord in all his beauty, that she may truly say: "For I have seen the Lord face to face, and my life is preserved." She thirsts in God, when in ecstasy she desires to pass over into God altogether, so that having wholly forgotten herself she may truly say: "Whether in the body or out of the body I cannot tell." She thirsts in God's way when, by her own will—I do not mean in temporal matters only but also in spiritual things—the soul reserves nothing for her own will but commits all things to God, never thinking about herself but about the things of Jesus Christ, so that she may say: "I came not to do my own will but the will of the Father who is in heaven." In the first degree, God enters the soul and she turns inward into herself. In the second, she ascends above herself and is lifted up to God. In the third, the soul, lifted up to God, passes over altogether into Him. In the fourth, the soul goes forth on God's behalf and descends below herself. In the first, she enters into herself; in the second, she goes forth from herself. In the first, she reaches her own life; in the third, she reaches God. In the first, she goes forth on her own behalf; in the fourth, she goes forth because of her neighbor. In the first, she enters in by meditation; in the second, she ascends by contemplation; in the third, she is led into jubilation; in the fourth, she goes out by compassion. In the first degree, a spiritual feeling sweeter than honey enters into her and inebriates her with its sweetness, so that she has honey and milk on her tongue and her lips distill the honeycomb. . . This is the first consolation which they who renounce the world receive, and it generally confirms them in their good intention. . . .

In this state, the Lord often visits the hungry and thirsty soul; often he fills her with inward delight and makes her drink with the sweetness of his Spirit. In this state, the Lord often descends from heaven and visits him who sits in darkness and the shadow of death. Often the glory of the Lord abides over the tabernacle of the covenant. Nevertheless, he reveals his presence but without showing his face. He infuses his sweetness but does not show his fair beauty. His loveliness is felt, but his form is not discerned. Even now, the clouds and darkness are round about him and his throne is in the pillar of the cloud. Gentle and soothing is that which is felt, but altogether dark what is seen. For he does not yet appear in the light, and though he be seen in the fire, the fire is a burning rather than an illumination. For he kindles the affection but does not yet illuminate the intellect. He inflames the desire but does not yet enlighten the intelligence. In this state, the soul can feel her beloved, but she cannot see him. And if she does see him, it is as one sees by night. . . . When the mind therefore goes forward to the grace of contemplation with great effort and ardent desire, it moves, as it were, into the second degree of love, where it deserves to look, by divine shewing, upon that which the eye cannot see nor the ear hear nor shall it enter the heart of man, so that it may truly say: "But to us, God hath revealed them by his spirit." Did not he, who saw the angels ascending and descending and God leaning on the ladder, deserve to receive that grace. Whence it is written: "I have seen the Lord face to face and my life is preserved.". . .

And what will the happiness of the vision be if there is such a delight in remembering it? Therefore, the shewing of the divine light in this state and the wonder of the revelation arising from it, together with the perennial memory thereof, bind the soul indissolubly so that she is not able to forget the happiness of her experience. And as in the earlier degree the delight which she has tasted satisfies the soul and transfixes the affections, so in this degree the brightness she has looked upon binds the thoughts that she may neither forget it nor think about anything else. In the second degree, as has been said, in the heaven of heavens, that inaccessible light may be seen but not reached, for if it could be reached, it would not be inaccessible. . . .

Therefore, the third degree of love is when the mind of man is ravished into the abyss of divine light so that the soul, having forgotten all outward things, is altogether unaware of itself and passes out completely into its God and fulfills what is written, "Yea those also who do not believe shall dwell in the Lord God." In this state, it is wholly subdued, the host of carnal desires are deeply asleep, and there is silence in heaven, as it were, for half an hour. In this state, where the soul is abstracted from itself, ravished into that secret place of divine refuge, when it is surrounded on every side by the divine fire of love, pierced to the core, set alight all about, then it sheds its very self altogether and puts on that divine life, and being wholly conformed to the beauty it has seen, passes wholly into that glory. . . .

As soon as she is admitted to that inner secret of the divine mystery, through the greatness of her wonder and the abundance of joy, she is wholly dissolved in herself, or rather into him who speaks, and she begins to hear words that it is not lawful for man to utter and to understand the strange and hidden things of God. In this state, she who cleaves to the Lord is one spirit with Him. In this state, as we have said, the soul is altogether melted into him whom she loves and is herself fainting away. . . When in this way the soul has been reduced in the divine fire, softened to the very core, and wholly melted, nothing is wanting except that she should be shown what is God's goodwill, all-pleasing and perfect, even the form of perfect virtue, to which she must be conformed. For just as metal workers, when the metals are melted and the moulds set out, shape any form according to their will and produce any vessel according to the manner and mould that has been planned, so the soul applies herself in this degree to be readily at the beck and call of the divine will; indeed, she adapts herself with spontaneous desire to every demand of God and adjusts her own will as the divine good pleasure requires. And as liquefied metal runs down easily wherever a passage is opened, so the soul humbles herself spontaneously to be obedient in this way, and freely bows herself in all acts of humility according to the order of divine providence. In this state, the image of the will of Christ is set before the soul so that these words come to her: "Let this mind be in you, which was also in Christ Jesus: who, being in the form of God, thought it not robbery to be equal with God, but emptied himself and became obedient unto death, even to death on the cross." This is the form of the humility of

Christ to which every man must conform himself who desires to attain to the highest degree of perfect charity. For greater love has no man than this, that a man lay down his life for his friends. Those who are able to lay down their lives for their friends have reached the highest peak of charity and are already placed in the fourth degree of charity. . . . Therefore, in the third degree, the soul is glorified; in the fourth, she is humbled for God's sake. In the third, she is conformed to the divine light; in the fourth, she is conformed to the humility of Christ. And though, in the third, she is in a way almost in the likeness of God, nevertheless, in the fourth, she begins to empty herself, taking the form of a servant, and begins to be found in fashion as a man. In the third degree, she is, as it were, put to death in God; in the fourth, she is raised in Christ. . . .

How utterly wondrous and amazing! The more he hopes from God, the more he abases himself for God. The more he rises up in boldness, the more he descends in humility. Just as the goal to which he ascends by confidence is above man, so is the point to which he descends by patience beyond man.

Therefore, as we have said, in the first degree, the soul returns to itself; in the second, it ascends to God; in the third, it passes out into God; in the fourth, it descends below itself. In the first and second, it is raised; in the third and fourth, it is transfigured. In the first, it ascends to itself; in the second, it transcends itself; in the third, it is conformed to the glory of Christ; in the fourth, it is conformed to the humility of Christ. Again, in the first, it is led back; in the second, it is transferred; in the third, it is transformed; in the fourth, it is resurrected.

Hildegard of Bingen is an exceptional example of the
visionary-prophetic mystics who graced the German
Benedictine and Cistercian convents during the 12th
and 13th centuries. Her mystical ecstasies, captivating
visions, and prophecies flowed into and from intense
apostolic service.

HILDEGARD OF BINGEN

Hildegard of Bingen is one of the most fascinating women of the
medieval period. Not only was she the most significant woman author and musical composer of the Middle Ages; she was also an abbess, the founder of a monastery, a religious reformer, a natural
scientist, a seer, and a great mystic. Her prophetic and visionary
mysticism profoundly marked her age and earned her the epithets
Teutonic Prophetess and Sibyl of the Rhine.

Born in 1098 of a noble family in Bermersheim, near Alzey in Rhein-
Hessen, Hildegard began to have visions when she was only five
years old. When she reached the age of eight, her parents entrusted
her to the care of Jutta of Spanheim, the Benedictine abbess at the
Disibodenberg monastery, where Hildegard eventually took the
habit. Upon Jutta's death, Hildegard became the abbess. Ten years
later, because of a revelation, she founded a monastery at
Rupertsberg, near Bingen, as well as other daughter houses.

Hildegard composed 77 songs, *Symphonia armonie celestium*
revelationum, which were gathered for a liturgical cycle. Although
these subtle, unusual songs show a dependence upon Gregorian
chant, they are musically unique. Only someone of powerful voice
and a God-filled heart can do them justice.[1] Hildegard was convinced that heavenly music embraces the human spirit and causes
in it a resounding symphony. To her, therefore, the source, mean-

ing, sense, and task of liturgical music is to restore the heavenly voice with which Adam praised God before he fell into sin.

Hildegard wrote a mystical treatise with a Jeremianic tone, the *Liber vitae meritorum*. It contains apocalyptic denunciations of the evil in the temporal and spiritual realms, as well as chiliastic and prophetic themes. Another mystical treatise, the *Liber divinorum operum simplicis hominis* or *De operatione dei*, is a penetrating cosmology with theodicy that emphasizes the eventual victory of good over evil. She also wrote an *Explication of the Rule of St. Benedict; Lives of St. Rupert and St. Disibode; Exposition on the Gospels;* books on pharmacology, medicine, and natural history; numerous allegorical homilies, a morality play, and two other esoteric works. For diversion, she authored the fascinating *Lingua ignota,* a book about a secret language of 800 words and a 25-letter alphabet.

Her letters to popes, cardinals, bishops, abbots, kings, emperors, nuns, monks, and people from all walks of life illustrate how deeply she was involved in the great political, ecclesiastical, intellectual, and religious currents of her times. This was a period of great spiritual awakening, of heightened sensitivity to the corruption in both Church and State, and of immense longing for a richer spiritual life.

Because of Emperor Frederick I's ("Barbarossa") "obstinacy" in promoting schism by setting up the three "Emperor popes," Hildegard actually threatened him with a (spiritual?) sword. When an episcopal interdict endangered the well-being of her monastery, she held fast because of a divine revelation, and the matter was eventually resolved in her favor. Seriously ill and incapacitated during her last years of life, Hildegard still insisted on being carried from place to place to continue exhorting, preaching to, encouraging, warning, and urging people to heed the divine word imparted to her.

Hildegard is an exceptional example of the "bridal mystics" and "visionary-prophetic mystics" who graced the German Benedictine and Cistercian convents during the 12th and 13th centuries. These women of extraordinary wisdom and practical charity experienced themselves as the spouses of either divine Wisdom and/or Jesus Christ.

Moreover, they all received extraordinary, yet oddly similar, mystical ecstasies, captivating visions, and prophecies. Their spousal union with God occurred not only at the core of their souls but also in and through dramatic visions and inner words (locutions) that commanded them in God's name to encourage and admonish others. For this reason, Hildegard's bridal, visionary, and prophetic mysticism flowered into intense apostolic service that actively fought the moral and religious laxity, the many social injustices, and the numerous heretical movements of her day.

Her masterpiece is the *Scivias* ("Know the ways [of the Lord]"), a book read by Pope Eugene III and several bishops. This work is a collection of 26 visions treating of the relationship between God, the cosmos, the human person, and major theological themes. "It happened that, in the year 1141 of the Incarnation of the Son of God, Jesus Christ," she wrote, "when I was 42 years and seven months old, Heaven was opened and a fiery light of exceeding brilliance came and permeated my whole brain, and inflamed my whole heart and my whole breast, not like a burning but like a warming flame, as the sun warms anything its rays touch. And immediately I knew the meaning of the exposition of the Scriptures, namely the Psalter, the Gospel and the other catholic volumes of both the Old and the New Testaments, though I did not have the interpretation of the words of their texts or the division of the syllables or the knowledge of cases or tenses."[2] In fact, Hildegard experienced a double light: God's light as it shines in the human heart and the "shadow of the living light" that bathes all creation. This light enabled her to grasp the sacramental transparency of all creation. She saw all things in God and God in all things.[3] Through genuine symbols—not fabricated images—she beheld and perceived the architectonic unity-in-difference that exists between God and all creatures.

Hildegard maintained that she saw visions not "in dreams, or sleep, or delirium, or by the eyes of the body, or by the ears of the outer self, or in hidden places; but I received them while awake and seeing with a pure mind and the eyes and ears of the inner self, in open places, as God willed it."[4] The purity of the divine light and the crystal clarity of these God-given visions so vivified her spiritual senses that she was able to express her experiences and visions of God in melody, tone, word, and symbol with biblical soundness, theological profundity, and artistic mastery.

The selected text illustrates her visionary mysticism, as well as her rich trinitarian mysticism, the central role played by Christ therein, and how Christianity's central truths are inextricably linked to the inner trinitarian life. To her, humanity is the heart of the cosmos because of the Son's incarnation. The text illustrates also that the basic element of her visions is the symbol, that is, a reality that actually contains what is symbolized and is different from it. She also used primordial words, or words that defy definition because they express reality itself and contain reality's mysteries within them. The dialogue structure—common to many mystics—should likewise be noted.[5]

THE TEXTS

SCIVIAS[6]

BOOK TWO

VISION TWO
The Trinity

Then I saw a bright light, and in this light the figure of a man the color of a sapphire, which was all blazing with a gentle glowing fire. And that bright light bathed the whole of the glowing fire, and the glowing fire bathed the bright light; and the bright light and the glowing fire poured over the whole human figure, so that the three were one light in one power of potential. And again I heard the living Light, saying to me:

1 On the perception of God's mysteries

This is the perception of God's mysteries, whereby it can be distinctly perceived and understood what is that Fullness, Whose origin was never seen, and in Which that lofty strength never fails that founded all the sources of strength. For if the Lord were empty of His own vitality, what then could have been his deeds? And therefore in the whole work it is perceived Who the Maker is.

2 On the Three Persons

Therefore you see a *bright light*, which without any flaw of illusion, deficiency or deception designates the Father; *and in this light the figure of a man the color of sapphire*, which without any flaw of obstinacy, envy or iniquity designates the Son, Who was begotten of the Father in Divinity before time began, and then within time was incarnate in the world in Humanity; *which is all blazing with a gentle glowing fire*, which fire without any flaw of aridity, mortality or darkness designates the Holy Spirit, by Whom the Only-Begotten of God was conceived in the flesh and born of the Virgin within time and poured the true light into the world. *And that bright light bathes the whole of the glowing fire, and the glowing fire bathes the bright light; and the bright light and the glowing fire pour over the whole human figure, so that the three are one light in one power of potential.* This means that the Father Who is Justice, is not without the Son or the Holy Spirit; and the Holy Spirit, Who kindles the hearts of the faithful, is not without the Father or the Son; and the Son, Who is the plenitude of fruition, is not without the Father or the Holy Spirit. They are inseparable in Divine Majesty, for the Father is not without the Son, nor the Son without the Father, nor the Father and the Son without the Holy Spirit, nor the Holy Spirit without Them. Thus these three Persons are one God in the one and perfect divinity of majesty, and the unity of Their divinity is unbreakable; the Divinity cannot be rent asunder, for it remains inviolable without change. But the Father is declared through the Son, the Son through Creation, and the Holy Spirit through the Son incarnate. How? It is the Father Who begot the Son before the ages; the Son through Whom all things were made by the Father when creatures were created; and the Holy Spirit Who, in the likeness of a dove, appeared at the baptism of the Son of God before the end of time.

3 People must not forget to invoke the One God in Three Persons

Hence let no person ever forget to invoke Me, the sole God, in these Three Persons, because for this reason I have made Them known to Man, that he may burn more ardently in My love; since it was for love of him that I sent My Son into the world, as my beloved John testifies, saying:

4 John on the charity of God

"By this the charity of God has appeared toward us: that God has sent His Only-Begotten Son into the world, that we may live by Him. In this is charity, not that we have loved God, but that He has loved us, and sent His Son to be a propitiation for our sins" [1 John 4:9-10]. What does this mean? That because God loved us, another salvation arose than that we had had in the beginning, when we were heirs of innocence and holiness; for the Supernal Father showed His charity in our dangers, though we deserved punishment, in sending by supernal power His Holy Word alone into the darkness of the world for the people's sake. There the Word perfected all good things, and by His gentleness brought back to life those who had been cast out because of their unclean sins and could not return to their lost holiness. What does this mean?

That through this fountain of life came the embrace of God's maternal love, which has nourished us unto life and is our help in perils, and is the deepest and sweetest charity and prepares us for penitence. How? God has mercifully remembered His great work and His precious pearl, Man, whom He formed from the mud of the earth and into whom He breathed the breath of life. How? By devising the life of penitence, which will never fail in efficacy. For through his proud suasion the cunning serpent deceived Man, but God cast him into penitence, which calls for the humility the Devil did not know and could not practice; for he knew not how to rise up to the right way.

Hence this salvation of charity did not spring from us, and we were ignorant and incapable of loving God for our salvation; but He Himself, the Creator and Lord of all, so loved His people that for their salvation He sent His Son, the Prince and Savior of the faithful, Who washed and dried our wounds. And He exuded the sweetest balm, from which flow all good things for salvation. Therefore, O human, you must understand that no misfortune or change can touch God. For the Father is the Father, the Son is the Son, and the Holy Spirit is the Holy Spirit, and these Three Persons are indivisible in the Unity of the Divinity. How?

5 On the three qualities of a stone

There are three qualities in a stone and three in a flame and three in a word. In the stone a cool dampness and solidity to the touch and sparkling fire. It has cool dampness that it may not be dissolved or broken; solidity to the touch that it may make up habitations and defenses; and sparkling fire that it may be heated and consolidated into hardness. Now this cool dampness signifies the Father, Who never withers and Whose power never ends; and this solidity of touch designates the Son, Who was born of the Virgin and could be touched and known; and the sparkling fire signifies the Holy Spirit, Who enkindles and enlightens the hearts of the faithful. What does this mean?

As a person who in the body often touches the cool dampness of stone falls sick and grows weak, so one who in his unsteady thoughts rashly tries to contemplate the Father loses his faith. And as people build their dwellings and defend themselves against their enemies by handling the solidity of stone, so too the Son of God, Who is the true cornerstone, is the dwelling of the faithful people and their protector from evil spirits. And as sparkling fire gives light to dark places by burning what it touches, so also the Holy Spirit drives out unbelief and consumes the blight of iniquity.

And as these three qualities are in one stone, so the true Trinity is in the true Unity.

6 On the three qualities in a flame

Again, as the flame of a fire has three qualities, so there is one God in three Persons. How? A flame is made up of brilliant light and red power and fiery heat. It has brilliant light that it may shine, and red power that it may endure, and fiery heat that it may burn. Therefore, by the brilliant light understand the Father, Who with paternal love opens His brightness to His faithful; and by the red power, which is in the flame that it may be strong, understand the Son, Who took on a body born from a Virgin, in which His divine wonders were shown; and by the fiery heat understand the Holy Spirit, Who burns ardently in the minds of the faithful. But there is no flame seen where there is neither brilliant light nor red power nor fiery heat; and thus also where neither the Father nor the Son nor the Holy Spirit is known God is not properly worshipped.

Therefore as these three qualities are found in one flame, so Three Persons must be understood in the Unity of the Divinity.

7 On the three causes of human words

And as the three causes for the production of words are seen, so the Trinity in the Unity of the Divinity is to be inferred. How? In a word there is sound, force and breath. It has sound that it may be heard, meaning that it may be understood, and breath that it may be pronounced. In the sound, then, observe the Father, Who manifests all things with ineffable power; in the meaning, the Son, Who was miraculously begotten of the Father; and in the breath, the Holy Spirit, Who sweetly burns in Them. But where no sound is heard, no meaning is used and no breadth is lifted, there no word will be understood; so also the Father, Son and Holy Spirit are not divided from one another, but do Their works together.

So as there are three causes for one word, the celestial Trinity is likewise in the celestial Unity. So as in a stone there exists and there operates no cool dampness without solidity to the touch and sparkling fire, or solidity to the touch without cool dampness and sparkling fire, or sparkling fire without cool dampness and solidity to the touch; and as in a flame there exists and there operates no brilliant light without red power and fiery heat, or red power without brilliant light and fiery heat, or fiery heat without brilliant light and red power; and as in a word there exists and there operates no sound without meaning and breath, or meaning without sound and breath, or breath without sound and meaning, but all keep indivisibly together to operate; so also these Three Persons of the true Trinity live inseparably in the majesty of the Divinity and are not divided from each other.

Thus, O human, understand the One God in Three Persons. In the foolishness of your mind you think that God is so powerless that He cannot truly live in three Persons, but only exists weakly in one. What does this mean? God is, in three Persons, the true God, the First and the Last.

8 On the unity of essence

But the Father is not without the Son, or the Son without the Father, or the Father and the Son without the Holy Spirit, or the Holy Spirit without Them; for these three Persons are inseparable in the Unity of the Divinity. How? A word sounds from a person's mouth, but the mouth does not sound without a word, nor does the word sound without life. Where does the word stay? In the person. And from whence does it go forth? From the person. And how? Because the person is living. Thus the Son is in the Father, Whom the Father sent into the dark world for human salvation, conceived in the Virgin by the Holy Spirit. As the Son is the Only-Begotten in the Divinity, He is the only-begotten in virginity; as he is the Only One of the Father, He is the only-born of the Mother; as the Father begot Him before time began, the Virgin Mother bore the same Only One within time, and after childbirth remained a virgin.

Therefore, O human, in these Three Persons recognize your God, Who created you in the power of His Divinity and redeemed you from damnation. And do not forget your Creator, as Solomon urges you when he writes:

9 Words of Solomon

"Remember your Creator in the days of your youth, before the time of affliction comes, and the years draw nigh of which you shall say: They please me not" [Ecclesiastes 12:1]. What does this mean? With your mental powers remember Him Who created you when, in the days of your false confidence, you think it is possible for you to walk according to your own desires, and raise yourself on high to throw yourself into the abyss, and stand in prosperity to fall into calamity. For the force of life in you always strives to perfect itself, until the time when it is complete. How? From birth a child grows up to full stature and remains an adult, leaving the mental license that is in foolish behavior and thinking carefully about how to manage his affairs, as he did not do in the foolishness of childhood. So let the person of faith do too. Let him leave childish behavior and grow up to fullness of virtue and persevere in its strength, leaving the pride of his desire, which pants after foolish vice; but let him with anxious care meditate what may be useful for him, though before he stooped childishly to childish ways.

Therefore, O human, embrace your God in the daylight of your strength, before the hour comes for the purgation of your works, when all things will be manifest and nothing will be overlooked, when the time comes that will be complete and will never end; about which times your humanity murmurs a little, saying, "These things do not please me, for I do not understand whether they will give me good fortune or calamity." For the human mind always wavers on this subject, since when it does good works it is anxious about whether or not they please God, and when it does bad ones it is afraid to lose forgiveness and salvation.

But let the one who sees with watchful eyes and hears with attentive ears welcome with a kiss My mystical words, which proceed from Me Who am life.

The Carthusian monk, Guigo II, called "the angelic," may be the first in the western mystical tradition to present prayer as a ladder with discrete rungs that one must methodically climb. One must first read Scripture, actively meditate upon the readings, and then stir one's heart in fervent prayer to God with the hope that God will then awaken the mystical senses.

GUIGO II

Guigo II, surnamed "the angelic," was the ninth prior of La Grande-Chartreuse and superior general of the Carthusian Order. His writings faithfully reflect the medieval western monastic mystical tradition, as found in Augustine, Anselm, Bernard, and Bonaventure. Attracted to the biblical imagery found in the books of Exodus and the Song of Songs, Guigo often depicted the soul as a chaste virgin who will know no husband save Christ.

His most famous work, *The Ladder of Monks*, aptly subtitled *A Letter on the Contemplative Life*, may very well be the first sketch of methodical prayer given in the western mystical tradition. In speaking of prayer in terms of a ladder with discrete rungs, this work contrasts somewhat with the earlier monastic tradition that viewed prayer more in terms of the soul's disposition.

Although not as popular as the *Ladder*, his *Twelve Meditations* reflects the same Carthusian spirit: a humane asceticism tinged with anti-intellectualism, deep love of Jesus Christ, and an ardent desire for mystical union with God.

Legend has it that after his death, the new prior went to Guigo's grave and commanded him to stop performing so many miracles. This attests to the reverence and esteem in which he must have

d. 1188

been held.

The texts were selected to illustrate Guigo's four-rung ladder in the ascent to God. His method underscores his love of Scripture and his approach to *lectio divina*. One must first read Scripture, actively apply one's understanding (meditation) to the readings and then lift up one's heart to God in fervent prayer. God may then reward the person by awakening the mystical senses so that the soul can hear, taste, smell, touch, and see something of "God's glory."

For Guigo, contemplative wisdom is strictly God's gift, and a gift that transforms a person from being "carnal" to being "spiritual." Thus, all affectivity is reordered into a loving desire for face to face vision of God. But this gift is given only to the pure of heart who have prepared themselves in solitude, silence, and humility in order to experience God's presence in the heart. Love is the "cross of the spirit" that nails us to Christ. Only if one sacramentally and spiritually eats Christ's body and drinks his blood can one love Christ. And only those who love Christ imitate and follow him.

Guigo employs some of the favorite images of the apophatic tradition; nonetheless, he does not hesitate to aver that, in Christ, the pure of heart are able to "see" God clearly in this life.[1]

THE TEXTS

THE LADDER OF MONKS[2]

One day when I was busy working with my hands I began to think about our spiritual work, and all at once four stages in spiritual exercises came into my mind: reading, meditation, prayer, and contemplation. These make a ladder for monks by which they are lifted up from earth to heaven. It has few rungs, yet its length is immense and wonderful, for its lower end rests upon the earth, but its top pierces the clouds and touches heavenly secrets. . . .

Reading is the careful study of the Scriptures, concentrating all one's powers on it. Meditation is the busy application of the mind to seek with the help of one's own reason for knowledge of hidden truth. Prayer is the heart's devoted turning to God to drive away evil and obtain what is good. Contemplation is when the mind is in some sort lifted up to God and held above itself, so that it tastes the joys of everlasting sweetness. . . .

Reading seeks for the sweetness of a blessed life, meditation perceives it, prayer asks for it, contemplation tastes it. Reading, as it were, puts food whole into the mouth, meditation chews it and breaks it up, prayer extracts its flavor, contemplation is the sweetness itself which gladdens and refreshes. Reading works on the outside, meditation on the pith, prayer asks for what we long for, contemplation gives us delight in the sweetness which we have found. To make this clearer, let us take one of many possible examples.

I hear the words read: "Blessed are the pure in heart, for they shall see God." This is a short text of Scripture, but it is of great sweetness, like a grape that is put into the mouth filled with many senses to feed the soul. When the soul has carefully examined it, it says to itself, There may be something good here. I shall return to my heart and try to understand and find this purity, for this is indeed a precious and desirable thing. . . . So, wishing to have a fuller understanding of this, the soul begins to bite and chew upon this grape, as though putting it in a wine press, while it stirs up its power of reasoning to ask what this precious purity may be and how it may be had.

When meditation busily applies itself to this work, it does not remain on the outside, it is not detained by unimportant things, climbs higher, goes to the heart of the matter, examining each point thoroughly. It takes careful note that the text does not say: "Blessed are the pure in body," but the "pure in heart," for it is not enough to have our hands clean from evil deeds, unless our minds are cleansed from impure thoughts.

. . . . Do you not see how much juice has come from one little grape, how great a fire has been kindled from a spark, how this small piece of metal, "Blessed are the pure in heart, for they shall see God," has acquired a new dimension by being hammered out on the anvil of meditation? And even more might be drawn from it at the hands of someone truly expert. I feel that "the well is deep," but I am still an ignorant beginner, and it is only with difficulty that I have found something in which to draw up these few drops. When the soul is set alight by this kindling, and when it receives a first intimation of the sweetness, not yet by tasting but through its sense of smell, when the alabaster box is broken; and from this it deduces how sweet it would be to know by experience the purity that meditation has shown to be so full of joy.

But what is it to do? It is consumed with longing, yet it can find no means of its own to have what it longs for; and the more it searches the more it thirsts. As long as it is meditating, so long as it is suffering, because it does not feel that sweetness which, as meditation shows, belongs to purity of heart, but which it does not give. A man will not experience this sweetness while reading or meditating "unless it happened to be given from above"... that sweet-tasting knowledge that rejoices and refreshes the soul in which it dwells with a sweetness beyond telling. . . . This wisdom comes only from God. . . .

So the soul, seeing that it cannot attain by itself to that sweetness of knowing and feeling for which it longs, and that the more "the heart abases itself," the more "God is exalted," humbles itself and betakes itself to prayer, saying: Lord you are not seen except by the pure of heart. I seek by reading and meditating what is true purity of heart and how it may be had, so that with its help I may know you, if only a little. Lord, for long have I meditated in my heart, seeking to see you face to face. It is the sight of you, Lord, that I have sought; and all the while in my meditation the fire of longing, the desire to know you more fully, has increased. When you break for me the bread of sacred Scripture, you have shown yourself to me in that breaking of bread, and the more I see you, the more I long to see you, no more from without, in the rind of the letter, but within, in the letter's hidden meaning. . . . So give me, Lord, some pledge of what I hope to inherit, at least one drop of heavenly rain with which to refresh my thirst, for I am on fire with love.

So the soul by such burning words inflame its own desire makes known its state, and by such spells it seeks to call its spouse. But the Lord, whose eyes are upon the just and whose ears can catch not only the words, but the very meaning of their prayers, does not wait until the longing soul has said all its say, but breaks in upon the middle of its prayer, runs to meet it in all haste, sprinkled with sweet heavenly dew, anointed with the most precious perfumes, and he restores the weary soul, he slakes its thirst, he feeds its hunger, he makes the soul forget all earthly things: by making it die to itself he gives it new life in a wonderful way, and by making it drunk he brings it back to its true senses. And just as in the performance of some bodily functions the soul is so conquered by desire that it loses all use of reason, and man becomes as it were wholly carnal, so on the contrary in this exalted contemplation all carnal motives are so conquered and drawn out of the soul that in no way is the flesh opposed to the spirit, and man becomes, as it were, wholly spiritual. . . .

But do not fear, bride of the spouse, do not despair, do not think yourself despised, if for a little while he turns his face away from you. These things all work together for your good, and your profit from his coming and from his withdrawal. He comes for your consolation, he goes away to put you on your guard, for fear that too much consolation should puff you up, and that you, having the spouse always with you, should begin to despise your brethren, and to attribute this consolation not to his grace but to your natural powers. For this grace the spouse bestows when he pleases and to whom He pleases. . . .

For a short time he allows us to taste how sweet he is, and before our taste is satisfied he withdraws; and it is in this way, by flying above us with wings outspread, that he encourages us to fly and says in effect: See now, you have had a little taste of how sweet and delightful I am, but if you wish to have your fill of this sweetness, hasten after me, drawn by my sweet-smelling perfumes, lift up your heart to where I am at the right hand of God the Father. There you will see me not darkly in a mirror but face to face, and "your heart's joy will be complete and no one shall take this joy away from you". . . .

Let us gather together by way of summary what we have already said at length, so that we may have a better view by looking at it altogether. You can see, from what has already been said by way of examples, how these degrees are joined to each other. One precedes the other, not only in the order of time but of causality. Reading comes first, and is, as it were, the foundation; it provides the subject matter we must consider for meditation. Meditation considers more carefully what is to be sought after; it digs, as it were, for the treasure which it finds and reveals, but since it is not in meditation's power to seize upon the treasure, it directs us to prayer. Prayer lifts itself up to God with all its strength, and begs for the treasure it longs for, which is the sweetness of contemplation. Contemplation when it comes rewards the labors of the other three; it inebriates the thirsting soul with the dew of heavenly sweetness. Reading is an exercise of the outward senses; meditation is concerned with the inward understanding; prayer is concerned with desire; contemplation outstrips every faculty. The first degree is proper to beginners, the second to proficients, the third to devotees, the fourth to the blessed.

At the same time these degrees are so linked together, each one working also for the others, that the first degrees are of little or no use without the last, while the last can never, or hardly ever, be won without the first. For what is the use of spending one's time in continuous reading, turning the pages of the lives and sayings of holy men, unless we can extract nourishment from them by chewing and digesting this food so that its strength can pass into our inmost heart?. . . But how is it possible to think properly and to avoid meditating upon false and idle topics, overstepping the bounds laid down by our holy fathers, unless we are first directed in these matters by what we read or what we hear?. . .

Again, what use is it to anyone if he sees in his meditation what is to be done, unless the help of prayer and the grace of God enable him to achieve it?. . . From this we learn that if meditation is to be fruitful, it must be followed by devout prayer, and the sweetness of contemplation may be called the effect of prayer. . . .

TWELVE MEDITATIONS
I[3]
"It is good for me, Lord, that you have humbled me, so that I might learn your true ways". . . And now I see that no one can be at peace until he has become humble. Humility and peace: how good it is for a man to be humbled so that he can attain to peace. Then indeed will he sit alone and be silent. He who is not alone cannot be silent.

And he who is not silent cannot hear when you speak to him. The scripture says: "the words of the wise are as a goad" to those who listen to them in silence. Let all my world be silent in your presence, Lord, so that I may hear what the Lord God may say in my heart. Your words are so softly spoken that no one can hear them except in a deep silence. But to hear them lifts him who sits alone and in silence completely above his natural powers, because he who humbles himself will be lifted up. He who sits alone and listens will be raised above himself. But where? This surely does not mean a lifting up of the body? No: It means of the heart. But how can his heart be above himself? It can because he forgets himself, does not love himself, thinks nothing of himself. Of what then does he think? Of that which is above him, his highest good, his God. And the more he sees and loves God, the more he sees and loves himself. Of what then does he think? Of that which is above him, his highest good, his God. And the more he sees and loves God, the more he sees and loves himself.

IV[4]

"All who belong to Christ, crucify their flesh". . . . The cross of our flesh is our body's mortification. The cross of the soul is the fear of God. The fear of God chastens the soul, so that it does not stray to right or left.

There is a third cross of the spirit, which is love. The Apostle says, "I am nailed with Christ to the cross: who will separate me from the love of Christ?" This was why the blessed Andrew would not be taken down from his cross. This cross is the love that gives us a heart of flesh, a soft and tender heart. So we see that this most gentle victim, Christ, was crucified because of his great love. Therefore, whoever attains to this third cross passes through the cloud between him and God and pours out his prayer in His very presence. And so for six days the cloud veiled Moses on Mount Sinai. But on the seventh day the Lord called to him from the midst of the dark cloud. The Lord's glory appeared like burning fire upon the top of the mountain in the sight of the children of Israel. And Moses went into the midst of the cloud, and climbed to the top of the mountain. What are we to understand by these six days during which Moses was concealed by the cloud, except these six virtues by which he attained to wisdom? Only at the top of the mountain of wisdom does the burning fire of love give us sight of God's glory. And whatever is below this seventh degree of wisdom is to be considered as darkness and cloud. Let the first cross, then, crucify the flesh through fear and reverence and knowledge, so that lechery may be chastised by fear, arrogance by reverence, excess by knowledge. Let the second cross win for the soul fortitude, counsel and understanding, so that it may terrify the devil, and guide by counsel its neighbor, by understanding itself. The third cross transcends all this, and gathered into the unity of love may sleep in true peace and takes its rest.

X[5]

"He who eats my flesh and drinks my blood will have eternal life."

. . . Love, therefore, is placed in the center of the soul, like a heart in the body, and these three of which we have spoken, faith, meditation and understanding, flow and take full shape to serve love's purpose, so that all subsequent qualities proceed from love and are directed by it. First, imitation proceeds from love; for who is there who would not wish to imitate what he loves? Unless you love Christ you will not imitate Him, that is, you will not follow him. . . .

This is what it means to eat the body of Christ spiritually: to have pure faith in Him, and carefully meditating upon that same faith, always to seek, and understanding what we seek, to find, and to imitate as much as we can what we love, and in imitating Christ, to cling to Him steadfastly, and clinging to Him, to be made one with Him for all eternity.

Francis of Assisi has been called "another Christ" who as the Poverello *captured the hearts and imaginations of people the world over in a way unprecedented in Christian history. In September 1224 on Mount Alvernia, he received that "final seal" (Dante), the first documented stigmata in the Christian tradition.*

FRANCIS OF ASSISI

Saint Francis of Assisi has been called the "seraphic" saint, the "angel of the sixth seal," the "second Moses," and even "another Christ." As a faithful mirror of Christ, the *Poverello* has captured the hearts and imaginations of people the world over in a way unprecedented in Christian history.

The founder of the Order of Friars Minor, the Poor Clares, and the Third Order was born in Assisi in central Italy of a wealthy middle-class linen family. He received the normal education of his times, but also learned Latin and French. The ideals of medieval chivalry, as expressed in the songs of troubadours, appealed to him for he wished to find glory in being a knight selflessly devoted to high ideals, loyal to his lord, courteous to all, and compassionate with the poor and the weak. Undoubtedly his fun-loving, gentle, generous, and somewhat playboy nature accounted for his popularity with his peers.

After spending a year as a prisoner of war during the battle between Assisi and Perugia and undergoing a serious illness, he headed for Rome to fight for the Pope. However, he received a revelation at Spoleto, returned to Assisi, and began a life of solitary prayer. Christ-crucified appeared to him, and Francis began working with the poor on whom he lavishly spent his father's money.

Christ again appeared, and said, "Francis, go and repair my Church which, as you see, is falling into ruins."

Undoubtedly upset by Francis's strange ways, his father hauled his son into the bishop's court to retrieve some of the money he had spent on the poor. The 25-year-old Francis stripped himself before all assembled to dramatize his total renunciation of the world for the sake of Christ-crucified. Thus Francis began his 25 year vocation as Christ's knight-fool.He quickly attracted disciples. Twelve Friars Minor journeyed to Rome where Pope Innocent III verbally approved Francis's proto-rule based on Matthew 10:5-14 for a new religious order. Returning to Assisi and living in extreme destitution, the preaching of Francis and his companions resulted in a strong penitential movement that eventually became the Third Order. Wishing to reactivate the Church's missionary spirit, he undertook several unsuccessful journeys to preach to the Muslims in Spain and North Africa. Francis risked his life to preach to the Sultan in Egypt.

Ridden with malaria and suffering from glaucoma, he returned to Italy in 1220, only to undergo great spiritual trials. Interiorly, he experienced a sword-like pain which often stabbed his heart throughout the day. Exteriorly, as his order grew, he experienced the tensions between those attracted to the literal and deliberate imitation of Christ poor and suffering and those attracted to a more conventual life for the sake of a better active, intellectual, and missionary apostolate. His strong personality kept the legally unstable order together during his lifetime, but the Franciscan "Spiritual" and "Conventual" controversy was soon to erupt.

In September 1224 on Mount Alvernia, he received that "final seal" (Dante), the first documented stigmata in Christian history. He bore now the wounds of the crucified Christ not only in spirit, but also on his body. During two more years of increasingly painful illness, Francis composed his classic hymn, *Canticle of Brother Son*, which expressed profound Christian love for God and creation.

Francis's participation in the hierarchical, sacramental Church never wavered. He had embraced fully the crucified and eucharistic Christ whose wounds he wore on his person. Having renounced the world, he wanted only to have, to know, and to be totally like Christ crucified. In this way, he found all things in God and God in all things. The *Poverello* was canonized by Pope Gregory IX on July 16, 1228.

Francis left the Christian tradition no written patrimony. But Leo, Masseo, and Giles—his closest friends and followers—transmitted directly and orally Francis's and their words and deeds which eventually found written form in Brother Ugolino's *Actus Beati Francisci et Sociorum Ejus (The Deeds of St. Francis and His Companions)*. The *Actus* had a tremendous influence in the history of Christian spirituality and mysticism, especially in its Italian condensation, *I Fioretti di San Francesco (The Little Flowers of St. Francis)*.

The texts were selected to illustrate one event in Francis's life that has riveted the Christian imagination: his reception of Christ's wounds on his body through the vision of the seraphic angel on Mt. Alvernia in September 1224. He experienced the stigmata as a "martyrdom of love," and as a substitute for actual martyrdom. Francis was promised that just as Christ had descended into limbo to lead souls to paradise, so would the stigmatized Francis each year on his feast day.

Francis composed the "Canticle of Brother Sun" to praise the Creator of all things. In it, he prays that the "Most High" be praised for "Brother Sun," "Sister Moon and the Stars," "Brother Wind," "Sister Water," "Sister Mother Earth," and even (what is often forgotten by those who overly romanticize this hymn) "Sister Bodily Death."

The last text is one of the most famous prayers ever composed by a saint.[1]

THE TEXTS

THE STIGMATA[2]

The next day came, that is, the Feast of the Cross. And St. Francis, sometime before dawn, began to pray outside the entrance of his cell, turning his face toward the east. And he prayed this way: "My Lord, Jesus Christ, I pray you to grant me two graces before I die:

the first is that during my life I may feel in my soul and in my body, as much as possible, that pain which you, dear Jesus, sustained in the hour of your most bitter Passion. The second is that I may feel in my heart, as much as possible, that excessive love with which you, O Son of God, were inflamed in willingly enduring such suffering for us sinners". . . .

Having received this promise, St. Francis began to contemplate with intense devotion the passion of Christ and his infinite charity. And the fervor of his devotion increased so much within him that he utterly transformed himself into Jesus through love and compassion. And while he was thus inflaming himself in this contemplation, on that same morning he saw coming down from heaven a seraph with six resplendent and flaming wings. As the seraph, flying swiftly came closer to St. Francis, so that he could perceive him clearly, he noticed that he had the likeness of a crucified man and his wings were so disposed that two wings extended above his head, two were spread out to fly, and the other two covered his entire body.

Seeing this, St. Francis was very much afraid, and at the same time he was filled with joy and grief and amazement. He felt intense joy from the friendly look of Christ, who appeared to him in a very familiar way and gazed at him very kindly. But on the other hand, seeing him nailed to the cross, he felt boundless grief and compassion. Next he was greatly amazed at such an astounding and extraordinary vision, for he knew well that the affliction of suffering is not in accord with the immortality of the seraph. And while he was marveling thus, he who was appearing to him revealed to him that this vision was shown to him by divine providence in this particular form in order that he should understand that he was to be utterly transformed into the direct likeness of Christ crucified, not by physical martyrdom, but by enkindling of the mind. . . .

During that seraphic apparition Christ, who appeared to St. Francis, spoke to him certain secret and profound things which the saint was never willing to reveal to anyone while he was alive, but after his death he revealed them, as is recorded. And these were the words: "Do you know what I have done?" said Christ. "I have given you the stigmata, which are the emblems of my passion, so that you may be my standard-bearer. And as I descended into limbo on the day when I died and took from there by virtue of these stigmata of mine all the souls that I found there, so I grant to you that every year on the day of your death you may go to purgatory and by virtue of your stigmata you may take from there and lead to paradise all the souls of your three orders, that is, the friars minor, the sisters, and the continent, and also others who have been very devoted to you, whom you may find there, so that you may be conformed to me in death as you are in life."

Now when, after a long time and a secret conversation, this wonderful vision disappeared, it left a most intense ardor and flame of divine love in the heart of St. Francis, and it left a marvelous image and imprint of the passion of Christ in his flesh. For soon there began to appear in the hands and feet of St. Francis the marks of nails such as he had just seen in the body of Jesus crucified, who had appeared to him in the form of a seraph. For his hands and feet seemed to be pierced through the center with nails, the heads of which were in the palms of his hands and in the upper part of his feet outside the flesh, and their points extended through the back of the hands and the soles of the feet so far that they seemed to be bent and beaten back in such a way that underneath their bent and beaten-back point—all of which stood out from the flesh—it would have been easy to put the finger of one's hand as through a ring. And the heads of the nail were round and black. Likewise in his right side appeared the wound of a blow from a spear, which was open, red, and bloody, and from which blood often issued from the holy breast of St. Francis and stained his habit and breeches.

THE CANTICLE OF BROTHER SUN[3]
Most High Almighty Good Lord,
Yours are the praises, the glory, the honor, and all blessings!
To You alone, Most High, do they belong.
And no man is worthy to mention You.
Be praised, my Lord, with all Your creatures,
Especially Sir Brother Sun,
By whom you give us the light of day!
And he is beautiful and radiant with great splendor.
Of You, Most High, he is a symbol!

Be praised, my Lord, for Sister Moon and the Stars!
In the sky You formed them bright and lovely and fair.
Be praised, my Lord, for Brother Wind
And for the Air and cloudy and clear and all Weather,
By which You give sustenance to Your creatures!
Be praised, my Lord, for Sister Water,
Who is very useful and humble and lovely and chaste!
Be praised, my Lord, for Brother Fire,
By whom You give us light at night,
And he is beautiful and merry and mighty and strong!
Be praised, my Lord, for our Sister Mother Earth,
Who sustains and governs us,
And produces fruits with colorful flowers and leaves!
Be praised, my Lord, for those who forgive for love of You
And endure infirmities and tribulations.
Blessed are those who shall endure them in peace,
For by You, Most High, they will be crowned!
Be praised, my Lord, for our Sister Bodily Death,
From whom no living man can escape!
Woe to those who shall die in mortal sin!
Blessed are those whom she will find in Your most holy will,
For the Second Death will not harm them.
Praise and bless my Lord and thank Him
And serve Him with great humility.

THE PRAYER OF ST. FRANCIS
Lord, make me an instrument of your peace.
Where there is hatred, let me sow love;
Where there is injury, pardon;
Where there is doubt, faith;
Where there is darkness, light;
And where there is sadness, joy.
O Divine Master,
Grant that I may not so much seek to be consoled as to console;
To be understood as to understand; To be loved as to love.
For it is in giving that we receive;
It is in pardoning that we are pardoned;
And it is in dying that we are born to eternal life.

Giles of Assisi was one of St. Francis's early compan-
ions. Famous for frequent and prolonged mystical ec-
stasies, Giles also experienced the transformative
power of mystical friendship.

GILES OF ASSISI

Born in Assisi of a peasant family, Giles, also called Aegidius, was
one of Francis's early companions and accompanied him to Rome
for Pope Innocent III's approval of the new religious order's proto-
rule. After an aborted missionary journey to Tunis, he spent most of
his life at remote hermitages in manual labor and in contemplation.

Famous for frequent and prolonged mystical ecstasies, Giles was
praised by Francis for his contemplative spirit. This man of mystical prayer became well-known for his discerning spiritual advice.
Such was his acclaim that Bonaventure and Pope Gregory visited
him for the benefit of their interior lives. Toward the end of his life,
Giles became an outspoken critic of relaxation and intellectual
pride among the ʳanciscans. His work, the *Golden Sayings*,[1] is a
Christian classic. Beatified by Pope Pius VI in 1777, Giles is the only
companion of Francis to attain this honor.

The first text was chosen to illustrate an experience of mystical ecstasy. Giles feels as if his body is dying and the soul is being taken
from it. This God-given state empowers him to contemplate the
beauty of his own soul, to learn "divine secrets," and inspires him
"to labor still more in the service of God." Mystically married to
God, Giles becomes a parent of transcendental life for others.

The second text was selected to illustrate an experience not uncom-
mon among mystics: mystical friendship. In the "light of divine wisdom" and in the "eternal mirror," Giles and St. Louis have their

hearts revealed to each other. As we have already seen, one of history's most famous mystical experiences occurred during Augustine's conversation with Monica at Ostia. Aelred of Rievaulx attested to his mystical experience of communal love. Teresa of Avila and John of the Cross, as well as Francis de Sales and Jane Francis de Chantal, also experienced the mystical power of friendship rooted in Christ.

The third selection illustrates Giles's four births: physical, sacramental, entrance into his religious order, and seeing God. Giles asserts that his face-to-face mystical vision of God transcends both faith and hope. Instead of saying, "I believe in one God," he now says," I know one God." However, most mystics and mystical theologians would deny that mystical experience transcends faith and hope.[2]

●

THE TEXTS

MYSTICAL ECSTASY[3]
And when God looked upon him [Giles] and his many good works, the hand of the Lord came over him. And there—among other graces conferred on him—one night while he was praying, he was so filled with divine consolation that it seemed to him the Lord wished to draw his soul out of his body that he might clearly see some divine secrets and that he might be inspired to labor still more in the service of God.

He began to feel as if his body was dying, beginning with his feet, until his soul passed out of his body. And it pleased our creator who placed the soul in the body, while his soul was out of the body, it took great pleasure in gazing at itself, because of the remarkable beauty with which the Holy Spirit had adorned it. For it was exceedingly subtle and radiant, beyond all conception, as he himself declared when he was near death. Then that very soul was rapt in an ecstasy in which he contemplated some heavenly secrets which he revealed to no one.

HEART SPEAKS TO HEART[4]
When Saint Louis, the king of France, decided to make a pilgrimage

to the holy places and heard of Brother Aegidius's [Giles] reputation for holiness, he resolved in his heart to visit him. . . . The porter went and told Brother Aegidius that a pilgrim at the gate desired to see him. Immediately Giles knew through the spirit who it was. And stepping out of his cell as if drunken, he came running to the gate, and both men fell into a wondrous embrace and, kneeling, gave each other kisses of great devotion, as if they had been friends from ancient times. When they had given each other the signs of fervent love, neither spoke a word to the other, but they parted, each one keeping silence in his own way. . . .

Then the brothers complained to Brother Aegidius, saying, "O Brother Aegidius, why did you not want to say anything to so great a king, who came from France in order to see you and to hear a good word from you?"

Answered Aegidius, "Dearest brothers, do not be surprised that he could say nothing to me, nor I to him; for the moment we embraced, the light of divine wisdom revealed his heart to me and mine to him. And standing in the eternal mirror we learned with complete comfort what he had intended to say to me and I to him, without noises of the lips and the tongue, and better than if we had spoken with lips.

SEEING GOD; LOSING FAITH AND HOPE[5]
Once [Giles] said, "I know a man who saw God so clearly that he lost all faith." Another time Brother Andreas said to him, "You say that in a vision God took away your faith; tell me, if it pleases you, whether you have hope." He answered, "He who has no faith, how should he have hope?" Brother Andreas said to him, "Do you not believe that God, it it please him, can give a pledge of eternal life?"

Brother Aegidius said that he had been born four times. "The first time," he said, "I was born of my physical mother, the second time in the sacrament of baptism, the third time when I entered this holy order, the fourth time when God granted me the grace of his appearance."

Then Brother Andreas said to him, "If I should go into distant lands and someone asked me whether I knew you and how you fared, I could answer thus: 'It is thirty-two years since Brother Aegidius was born, and before he was born he had faith, but after his birth he lost his faith.'"

Brother Aegidius answered, "As you have said, so it is. True, before then I did not have faith as perfectly as I should have had it; nevertheless God took it from me. But even from him who has it in a perfect manner, the way one should have it, God will take it away. After that I did such things that I deserve to have a rope tied around my neck and be dragged in shame through all the streets of the city."

Again Brother Andreas said, "If you have not faith, what would you do if you were a priest and had to celebrate high mass? How would you say, 'I believe in one God'? It seems that you would have to say, 'I know one God.'" Then Brother Aegidius answered with a very joyous countenance and sang in a loud voice, "I know one God, the Almighty Father."

The Flemish Beguine, Hadewijch, is perhaps the most sublime exponent of love mysticism in the Western tradition. This deeply emotional, ecstatic, visionary, and bridal form of mysticism contends that God allows himself to be experienced as love by a person who ardently desires to be united with God in this life.

HADEWIJCH OF ANTWERP

This Flemish Beguine is perhaps the most sublime exponent of love mysticism in the Western mystical tradition. Love mysticism contends that God allows himself to be experienced as Love by a person who ardently desires to love and to be united with God in this life. In addition, this love is usually deeply emotional, ecstatic, visionary, and bridal. So traumatic is this holy madness at times that the visionary's physical well-being and even life are endangered.

Hadewijch was a Beguine, that is, a woman who lived a semi-religious community life, but without vows. The Beguines were pious women who seem to have rejected both a woman's constricted life at court and the stricter obligations of the cloistered life. Much like the primitive monastic tradition in which a spiritual father gathered disciples around him without ecclesiastical sanction, the early stages of the Beguine movement saw laywomen uniting in much the same way. Embracing a loose form of community life, apostolic poverty, contemplation, and recitation of the hours, they also studied, taught, gave spiritual direction, and cared for the sick and the needy.

The name "Beguine" may be derived either from the name of Lambert le Bègue (d.1177), a revivalist preacher at Liége, or from the gray cloth of their distinctive garb. Perhaps because of their threatening independence, holiness of life, good works—and, occasionally, eccentricities and unorthodox beliefs—the Beguines were frequently the object of clerical and lay criticism. Nonetheless, Pope Honorius III gave them full ecclesiastical authorization in 1216.

The Beguines' spirituality was influenced by the Crusades. Sharply focused on the mysteries of the humanity of Christ's life, especially his childhood and passion, this spirituality was also strongly eucharistic and Marian.

The main theme throughout Hadewijch's writings is the tumultuous longing for the infinite joy of possessing a God who is love. She had experienced this love so deeply that she learned in a vision: "The seraph who had lifted me up placed me upon it [a seat] and said to me: 'Behold, this is love, whom you see in the midst of the countenance of God's nature; she has never yet been shown here to a created being. . . .'"[1] Hadewijch never sought or clung to her ecstatic experiences, but saw them as part of her need to "grow up" in the Lord. She experienced that she became the brave knight of divine Love who knows "what love teaches with love and how love honors the loyal lover with love."[2]

The joys and sufferings encountered by the soul in its longing for God fill Hadewijch's works. Love is an abyss not only of joy, bliss, peace, and "unheard of songs," but also of violent storms and terrifying, horrible, and awesome places. For her, "to carry love means a propensity, a longing, a desire, a service, an incessant exercise of burning will. But to feel love means the awareness of being in the liberty of love. But to be love surpasses all."[3]

The Hadewijch corpus shows astonishing literary versatility, tremendous emotional and intellectual range, and profound spirituality and mysticism. In some love mysticisms, affective and religious emotions become an end in themselves and never take advantage of theological and doctrinal support. This is definitely not the case with Hadewijch who had assimilated scripture, the church's liturgy, Augustine, William of St. Thierry, and other church fathers.

Moreover, her theological exemplarism provides a solid foundation for her love mysticism. According to this view, the human person is created in the image of God, but the image was sullied by Adam's sin. Because the soul is "Christ's mother," it must give birth to the divine infant. In this way, it recovers its trinitarian image and ascends to the triune God.

One also finds elements of an "ontological" mysticism (*Wesensmystik*) in Hadewijch. This speculative mysticism emphasizes the unity-in-difference between God as Being and the person as a being. It ponders the extreme "nakedness" (devoid of all concepts and images) of the divine-human intercourse in the soul's "ground." It stresses that the whole spiritual life consists in a return to God by poverty, detachment, and nakedness. Extreme forms of *Wesensmystik* emphasized that persons attained their goal by keeping themselves free from all works, save "pure love alone," a love that eventually annihilates them in the abyss of the divine essence. Through pure love, they become God.

However, Hadewijch never tires, for christological reasons, of emphasizing the need to live a fully human ascetical-mystical life. While maintaining that one is never absorbed into the divine, Hadewijch insists that one must "become God with God." For her, when plunged in love, one returns to the world with "impressionable senses" that are even more open to all worldly reality and a readiness to serve others.

Her 31 *Letters* illustrate her educated intelligence, the striking artistry of her prose writing, the importance of self-knowledge, and how the mystical life is the full flowering of the truths of faith. *Poems in Stanzas* show, in 45 poems, her lyric and poetic genius that made full use of the themes, imagery, and techniques of the troubadours who sang the praises of courtly love. In fact, Hadewijch fused the poetry of courtly love, the latin sequence of the church's liturgy, and a christianized *Minne* (love) mysticism that created a new genre of medieval mystical poetry.

She also had numerous visions "in the spirit" and "out of the spirit." Her 14 recorded visions emphasize the necessity of becoming "one with God in fruition." *Poems in Couplets* illustrate her aphoristic and improvising mastery in underscoring God's love for us and our love for God. Some of these poems are deeply eucharistic. They teach that when we eat Christ, he eats us, for the "heart of each devours the other's heart."

Hadewijch's love, or "seraphic," mysticism is deeply trinitarian and christogical. Like the great Eastern church fathers before her, Hadewijch sees the Father as the source without source of the divine life and fecundity. The human person "lives the Trinity" by emulating the trinitarian inhalation into unity and exhalation into Trinity by turning inward in contemplation and outward in virtue and apostolic service, an idea that Ruusbroec was to develop. If one is to "grow up in order to be God with God," one must "live God and man." Said christologically, "We all indeed wish to be God with God, but God knows there are few of us who want to live as men with his humanity, or want to carry his cross with him, or want to hang on the cross with him and pay humanity's debt to the full."[4] Hadewijch's Christology points out the human paradox: to be divine, one must be fully human, as Christ was. Her "to live God and Man" became a sharp sword against the Brethren of the Free Spirit who wanted to be God without remaining human.

The first selected text is perhaps the most beautiful description in the Christian mystical tradition of the soul's greatness. Only the soul can reach God's abyss; only God can reach and satisfy the soul's abyss.

The second selection illustrates Hadewijch's poetic and literary genius. One senses her passionate love of Love and her willingness to allow Love to conquer her so that she may conquer Love. In the agony and ecstasy of love, "love, by Love, sees to the depths of the Beloved," and attains true freedom. Love also enlightens the soul's darker half to make the soul one in divine light.

The third text was selected to illustrate Hadewijch's ecstatic visionary love mysticism. She is so full of desire to satisfy and be satisfied by her Beloved that she is mad with love. This madness affects her heart, veins, and even threatens to break her bodily. Hadewijch ardently longs to be conformed fully to "his Humanity" and "to grow up to be God with God."

In ecstatic vision, she sees an eagle (common in her writings), a Child at the altar, and the "Man." This vision brings out her eucharistic mysticism: the Christ Child comes from the altar to give her the sacrament. However, it is the "Man" who actually gives her the

"Sacrament," the chalice, and then takes her into his arms. As she melts into her Beloved, they are "one without a difference."

This medieval woman possesses an astonishing subtlety of feeling in her ability to teach us how to grow in trinitarian love by living Christ both in his divinity and humanity.[5]

THE TEXTS

LETTER 18[6]

GREATNESS OF THE SOUL
... 63. Now understand the deepest essence of your soul, what "soul" is. Soul is a being that can be beheld by God and by which, again, God can be beheld. Soul is also a being that wishes to content God; it maintains a worthy state of being as long as it has not fallen beneath anything that is alien to it and less than the soul's own dignity. If it maintains this worthy state, the soul is a bottomless abyss in which God suffices to himself; and his own self-sufficiency ever finds fruition to the full in this soul, as the soul, for its part, ever does in him. Soul is a new way for the passage of God from his depths into his liberty; and God is a way for the passage of the soul into its liberty, that is, into his inmost depths, which cannot be touched except by the soul's abyss. And as long as God does not belong to the soul in his totality, he does not truly satisfy it. ...

LETTER 19[7]

TO HAVE NOTHING BUT GOD
God be with you and give you
True knowledge of the methods of Love;
May he enable you to understand
What the Bride says in the Song of Songs:
I to my Beloved, and my Beloved to me!
If anyone allowed Love to conquer him,
He would then conquer Love completely.
I hope this will be your experience;

And although we are waiting long for the event,
Let us thank Love for everything.
He who wishes to taste veritable Love,
Whether by random quest or sure attainment,
Must keep to neither path nor way.
He must wander in search of victory over Love,
Both on the mountains and in the valleys,
Devoid of consolation, in pain, in trouble;
Beyond all the ways men can think of,
That strong steed of Love bears him.
For reason cannot understand
How love, by Love, sees to the depths of the Beloved,
Perceiving how Love lives freely in all things.
Yes, when the soul has come to this liberty,
The liberty that Love can give,
It fears neither death nor life.
The soul wants the whole of Love and wants nothing else.
—I leave rhyme: What mind can say eludes me.

27. For with nothing the mind says can one put into words the theme of Love, which I desire and want for you. I say no more; here we are obliged to speak with our soul. Our theme is boundless; for this theme—Love—which we take, is God himself by nature (cf. 1 Jn 4:16). Veritable Love never had the restrictions of matter but is free in the rich liberty of God, always giving in richness, and working with pride, and growing in nobleness.

37. Oh, may you full grow up according to your dignity, to which you were called by God from all eternity! How can you endure it that God has fruition of you in his Essence, and you do not have fruition of him? How I feel about that is something I must be silent about; read what you have here; as you will, I shall keep silence. God must work according to his pleasure. I can say as Jeremiah said: *You have deceived me, O Lord,* and I am glad to have been deceived by you (Jer. 20:7).

46. The soul who is most untouched is the most like to God. Keep yourself untouched by all men in heaven and on earth, until the day when God is lifted up above the earth and draws you and all things to himself (John 12:32). Some say that he meant by this, upon

the cross on which he was lifted up. But when God and the blessed soul are united he, together with the blessed soul, will be exalted from the earth in all beauty. For when the soul has nothing else but God, and when it retains no will but lives exclusively according to his will alone; and when the soul is brought to nought and with God's will wills all that he wills, and is engulfed in him, and is brought to nought—then he is exalted above the earth, and then he draws all things to him; and so the soul becomes with him all that he himself is.

62. The souls engulfed in God who are thus lost in him are illuminated on the side by the light of Love, as the moon receives its light from the sun. The simple knowledge then received by them in this new light, from which they come and in which they dwell—this simple light then catches their darker half, so that the two halves of the soul become one; and then there is full light.

69. If you had demanded this light to choose your Beloved, you would be free. For these souls are united and clothed with the same light with which God clothes himself (Ps. 103:2).

73. How these two halves of the soul become one—there is much to say on this point. I do not dare to say anything more about it, for my sad lot with regard to Love is too hard; and besides, I fear that the aliens may plant nettles where roses should stand.

77. Here we now drop the subject. God is with you.

VISION 7[8]

On a certain Pentecost Sunday a vision at dawn. Matins were being sung in the church, and I was present. My heart and my veins and all my limbs trembled and quivered with eager desire and, as often occurred with me, such madness and fear beset my mind that it seemed to me I did not content my Beloved, and that my Beloved did not fulfill my desire, so that dying I must go mad, and going mad I must die. On that day my mind was beset so fearfully and so painfully by desirous love that all my separate limbs threatened to break, and all my separate veins were in travail.

14. The longing in which I then was cannot be expressed by any language or any person I know; and everything I can say about it

would be unheard-of to all those who never apprehended Love as something to work for with desire, and whom love had never acknowledged as hers. I can say this about it: I desire to have full fruition of my beloved, and to understand and taste him to the full. I desire that his humanity should to the fullest extent be one in fruition with my humanity, and that mine then should hold its stand and be strong enough to enter into perfection until I content him, who is perfection itself, by purity and unity, and in all things to content him fully in every virtue. To that end I wished he might content me interiorly with his God-head, in one spirit, and that for me he should be all that he is, without withholding anything from me. For above all the gifts that I ever longed for, I chose this gift: that I should give satisfaction in all great sufferings. For that is the most perfect satisfaction: to grow up in order to be God with God. For this demands suffering, pain, and misery, and living in great new grief of soul: but to let everything come and go without grief, and in this way to experience nothing else but sweet love, embraces, and kisses. In this sense I desired that God give himself to me, so that I might content him.

42. As my mind was beset with fear, I saw a great eagle flying toward me from the altar, and he said to me: "If you wish to attain oneness, make yourself ready!"

45. I fell on my knees and my heart beat fearfully, to worship the beloved with oneness, according to his true dignity; that indeed was impossible to me, as I know well, and as God knows, always to my woe and to my grief.

50. But the eagle turned back and spoke: "Just and mighty Lord, now show your great power to unite your oneness in the manner of union with full possession!"

53. Then the eagle turned around again and said to me: "He who has come, comes again; and to whatever place he never came, he comes not."

57. Then he came to the altar, showing himself as a child; and that child was in the same form as he was in his first three years. He turned toward me, in his right hand took from the ciborium his body, and in his left hand took a chalice, which seemed to come

from the altar, but I do not know where it came from.

64. With that he came in the form and clothing of a man, as he was on the day when he gave us his body for the first time; looking like a human being and a man, wonderful, and beautiful, and with glorious face, he came to me as humbly as anyone who actually belongs to another. Then he gave himself to me in the shape of the sacrament, in its outward form, as the custom is; and then he gave me to drink from the chalice, in form and taste, as the custom is. After that he came himself, took me entirely in his arms, and pressed me to him; and all my members felt his in full felicity, in accordance with the desire of my heart and my humanity. So I was outwardly satisfied and fully transported. Also then, for a short while, I had the strength to bear this; but soon, after a short time, I lost that manly beauty outwardly in the sight of his form. I saw him completely come to nought and so fade and all at once dissolve that I could no longer recognize or perceive him outside me, and I could no longer distinguish him within me. Then it was to me as if we were one without difference. It was thus: outwardly, to see, taste, and feel, as one can outwardly taste, see, and feel in the reception of the outward sacrament. So can the beloved, with the loved one, each wholly receive the other in full satisfaction of the sight, the hearing, and the passing away of the one in the other.

94. After that I remained in a passing away in my beloved, so that I wholly melted away in him and nothing any longer remained to me of myself; and I was changed and taken up in the spirit, and there it was shown me concerning such hours.

Bonaventure has been called "the prince of mystics."
It was his genius to integrate the Franciscan love of
Christ's humanity with the Dionysian joy of finding
God ultimately beyond all things in a mystical ec-
stasy of "superluminous darkness."

BONAVENTURE

Because of the theological acumen and the religious fervor of his spirituality, the Christian world bestowed upon Bonaventure soon after his death in 1274 the title "Devout Teacher." Six years after his canonization by Pope Sixtus IV in 1482, Pope Sixtus V designated him "Doctor Seraphicus" of the Church. Late in the 19th century, Pope Leo XIII called Bonaventure "the Prince of Mystics." In our own century, noted medievalist and philosopher Etienne Gilson said that Bonaventure wrote "the most complete synthesis that Christian mysticism has ever seen." In fact, many commentators aver that what Bonaventure achieved in his century for spirituality and mysticism may be compared to what Thomas Aquinas achieved for theology: the apotheosis of the Christian tradition.

In his person, Bonaventure combined the simplicity of Francis of Assisi and Franciscan intellectualism. All Bonaventure's writings focus upon the person's union with God. By effecting a profound melding of philosophical speculation and mystical affectivity, Bonaventure eschewed both pure intellectualism and naive emotionalism. Theoretical reflection enriched his spirituality and mysticism; but mystical experience remained at the heart of his speculative reflections.

Like Francis, Bonaventure found God in all things and all things in God. Like Augustine, he focused upon God in the soul's depths; finally, like the great Dionysius, Bonaventure saw all creatures flowing out of God and finding their way back to the "superessential, superdivine, supereminent, super-unknown" Trinity. It was Bonaventure's genius to integrate the Franciscan love of Christ's humanity with the Dionysian joy of finding God ultimately beyond all things in a mystical ecstasy of "superluminous darkness." Thus, Bonaventure interlaced the sensible, the psychological, and the metaphysical with the mystical.

Bonaventure was born John di Fidanza into a well-to-do family in the small town of Bagnoregio, near Viterbo, some 60 miles north of Rome. He left for studies at the University of Paris when he was 17 years old. Nine years later he entered the Franciscan Order, received the name Bonaventure, and continued his studies under Alexander of Hales, the illustrious Franciscan theologian at the University of Paris.

Within a few years, Bonaventure began to lecture at the University of Paris and wrote numerous scholastic treatises, eventually becoming the head of the Franciscan theological school there. During this period, he joined with Thomas Aquinas to defend the new mendicant orders—especially in their emphasis upon poverty—against the attacks of the secular masters at the university.

In 1257, he was elected General of the Franciscan Order, a position he held for 17 years. As general, Bonaventure wrote a number of spiritual works, sermons, and two biographies of St. Francis. Because he prudently maintained a moderate course in the conflict between the Franciscan Spirituals (who desired a strict imitation of St. Francis) and the Conventuals (who saw the need for more adaptation), he managed to shape those ideals into institutional forms that have existed to the present day. He is rightly called the second founder of the Franciscans and the chief architect of their enduring spirituality.

Pope Clement IV wanted to make Bonaventure archbishop of York, an honor he promptly declined. However, Pope Gregory X gave him the red hat in 1273 by making him cardinal archbishop of Albano. Bonaventure spent the next year aiding the Pope to prepare for the Second Council of Lyons at which Bonaventure died on July 15, 1274. Nonetheless, Bonaventure was the major instrument for church reform, for reconciling the mendicant orders and the secular clergy, and for the tentative reconciliation between the Roman and Greek Churches.

The selection is taken from Bonaventure's *The Soul's Journey Into God*. It may well be the most concise, comprehensive, architectonic mystical treatise ever written. The text illustrates that St. Francis of Assisi's deep love for the crucified Christ prompted both Bonaventure's journey into God and the writing of this classic. Bonaventure, long attracted to St. Francis, described him as "the outstanding follower of Jesus Christ." In the prologue to the longer of the two biographies of St. Francis, he wrote: "I recognized that God saved my life through him, and I realize that I have experienced his power in my very person."[1]

The selected texts also illustrate the major role Christ plays in Bonaventure's *mystical* journey *into* God. Bonaventure places Christ at the beginning, in the middle, and at the end of the *Journey* to underscore, like Francis before him, that only through the crucified Christ is the journey possible. However, in this treatise, Bonaventure focuses upon the mystical Christ, the soul's Bridegroom, the God-man who is the gateway and door to ecstatic mystical contemplation, the greatest coincidence of opposites, that is, "the first and the last, the highest and the lowest, the circumference and the center, *the Alpha and the Omega* [Apoc. 1:8], the caused and the cause, the Creator and the creature. . . ."[2]

The mystical Christ, the very life of the soul's life, the Christ who heals and transforms the soul's mystical senses, and then plunges it into its deepest depths, dominates the *Journey*. Bonaventure's description of the mystical senses is also noteworthy.

However, Bonaventure's emphasis upon the mystical Christ must be comprehended in the context of his *Tree of Life*, his meditations on Christ's life, death, and resurrection that evoke a simple and direct devotion to Christ's humanity. Only someone who can say with Bonaventure while pondering Christ crucified, "O human heart, you are harder than any hardness of rocks, if at the recollection of such great expiation you are not struck with terror, nor moved with compassion, nor shattered with compunction nor softened with devoted love,"[3] is prepared to follow the mystical Christ into the divine darkness of mystical ecstasy.

Bonaventure contemplates God, as he is reflected in creation, in sensation, in the soul's memory, understanding, and will, and in the soul's graced faculties. He also contemplates God as being and as the good. Moreover, this selection should be read in the context of Bonaventure's profound trinitarian theology. With Pseudo-Dionysius, Bonaventure focuses upon the Trinity as the self-diffusive good. Like the Greek Fathers, Bonaventure views the Father as the womb, or the "fontal fullness" (*fontalis plenitudo*) of divine fecundity, the Son as the Father's perfect image, and the Holy Spirit as the mutual love of Father and Son, or Gift, in and through whom all gifts are given.

The world is the overflow and expression of divine fecundity. In generating the Son, the Father likewise effects the eternal reasons for everything that exists. Thus, the Son as eternal exemplar is the link between the Father and all creation. Bonaventure can contemplate all creatures as reflecting God's power, wisdom, and goodness because of his exemplarism: all creatures have their archetypes in the divine mind and flow out of the divine fecundity.

Hence, all creatures are shadows, echoes, pictures, vestiges, representations, or footprints of the Trinity. One should note the eloquence with which Bonaventure rejoices in creation's intelligible structure as a reflection of the Son's wisdom. Of course, contemplation on the soul's faculties and their elevation by grace discloses an even more intimate reflection of the Trinity, because memory, understanding, and will are created and graced in the Trinity's image and likeness.

Bonaventure was a strong proponent of the triple way of the soul's journey into God. However, purgation, illumination, and union should not be considered as three successive ways, because Bonaventure contends that the activity proper to each way is always concomitant with the other ways. The purgative way focuses upon the outer man, disciplines the senses and the passions, and leads to inner peace. Only frequent confession, the examination of one's conscience, and meditation can assuage "the sting of conscience" that animates this way. "The beam of intelligence" disciplines reason, enlightens the spirit, and teaches the person to know Christ and to follow him ever more closely. "The living flame of wisdom" initiates the unitive way by engendering loving knowledge of God. It concentrates the spirit by turning it away from all creatures, feeds it by turning the heart towards its spouse, and raises it above all things to the incomprehensible God who is "all delight." In summary, the purgative way expels sins; the illuminative leads to the imitation of Christ; and the unitive way brings about union with the spouse. The threefold way causes the repose of peace, the splendor of truth, and the sweetness of love.

The selection offers a look at Bonaventure's Christian architectonic, cosmic vision centered on the Trinity, Christ, and creation. It is a masterpiece of the Franciscan journey from St. Francis, to the crucified Christ, to the mystical Christ, to a sacramental grasp of all creation, to God as being, to the triune God—all ultimately grasped in the darkness of ecstatic love.[4]

THE TEXTS

THE SOUL'S JOURNEY INTO GOD

PROLOGUE[5]

2. Following the example of our most blessed father Francis, I was seeking this peace with panting spirit—I a sinner and utterly unworthy who after our blessed father's death had become the seventh Minister General of the Friars. It happened that about the time of the 33rd anniversary of the saint's death, under the divine impulse, I withdrew to Mount La Verna, seeking a place of quiet and desiring to find there peace of spirit. While I was there reflecting on various ways by which the soul ascends into God, there came to mind, among other things, the miracle which had occurred to blessed Francis in this very place; the vision of a winged seraph in the form of the crucified. While reflecting on this, I saw at once that this vision represented our father's rapture in contemplation and the road by which this rapture is reached.

3. The six wings of the seraph can rightly be taken to symbolize the six levels of illumination by which, as if by steps or stages, the soul

can pass over to peace through ecstatic elevations of Christian wisdom. There is no other path but through the burning love of the crucified. . . . For no one is in any way disposed for divine contemplation that leads to mystical ecstasy unless like Daniel he is a man of desires (Dan. 9:23).

CHAPTER ONE[6]

ON THE STAGES OF THE ASCENT INTO GOD AND ON CONTEMPLATING HIM THROUGH HIS VESTIGES IN THE UNIVERSE

2. . . . In relation to our position in creation, the universe itself is a ladder by which we can ascend into God. Some created things are vestiges, others images; some are material, others spiritual; some are temporal, others everlasting; some are outside us, others within us. In order to contemplate the first principle, who is most spiritual, eternal and above us, we must pass through his vestiges, which are material, temporal and outside us. This means *to be led in the path to God.* We must also enter into our souls, which is God's image, everlasting, spiritual and within us. This means *to enter in the truth of God.* We must go beyond to what is eternal, most spiritual and above us, by gazing upon the First Principle. . . .

3. This threefold division . . . reflects also the threefold substance in Christ, who is our ladder: bodily, spiritual, and divine.

4. Corresponding to this threefold movement, our mind has three principle perceptual orientations. The first is toward exterior material objects and is the basis for its being designated as animal or sensual. The second orientation is within itself and into itself and is the basis for its being designated as spirit. The third is above itself and is the basis for its being designated as mind. By all of these we should dispose ourselves to ascend into God so as to love him *with our whole mind, with our whole heart and with our whole soul* (Mark 12:30; Matt. 22:37; Luke 10:27). In this consists both perfect observance of the Law and Christian wisdom.

6. Just as there are six stages in the ascent into God, there are six stages in the powers of the soul, through which we ascend from the lowest to the highest, from the exterior to the interior, from the tem-

poral to the eternal. These are the senses, the imagination, reason, understanding, intelligence, and the summit of the mind or the spark of conscience. We have these stages implanted in us by nature, deformed by sin and reformed by grace. They must be cleansed by justice, exercised by knowledge and perfected by wisdom.

7. . . . All this is done through Jesus Christ . . . . He has taught the knowledge of truth according to the threefold mode of theology: symbolic, literal and mystical, so that through the symbolic we may rightly use sensible things, through the literal we may rightly use sensible things and through the mystical we may be lifted above to ecstasy.

8. Whoever wishes to ascend to God must first avoid sin, which deforms our nature, then exercise his natural powers mentioned above: by praying, to receive restoring grace; by a good life, to receive purifying justice; by meditating, to receive illuminating knowledge; and by contemplating, to receive perfecting wisdom. Just as no one comes to wisdom except through grace, justice and knowledge, so no one comes to contemplation except by penetrating meditation, a holy life and devout prayer. . . .

15. Whoever, therefore, is not enlightened by such splendor of created things is blind; whoever is not awakened by such outcries is deaf; whoever does not praise God because of all these effects is dumb; whoever does not discover the First Principle from such clear signs is a fool. Therefore, open your eyes, alert the ears of your spirit, open your lips and *apply your heart* [Prov. 22:17] so that in all creatures you may see, hear, praise, love and worship, glorify and honor your God lest the whole world rise against you. . . .

CHAPTER TWO[7]

ON CONTEMPLATING GOD IN HIS VESTIGES IN THE SENSE WORLD

1. Concerning the mirror of things perceived through sensation, we can see God not only through them as through his vestiges, but also in them as he is in them by his essence, power and presence. This type of consideration is higher than the previous one; therefore it

holds second place as the second level of contemplation by which we are led to contemplate God in all creatures which enter our minds through our bodily senses.

11. From the first two stages in which we are led to behold God in vestiges, like the two wings covering the seraph's feet, we can gather that all the creatures of the sense world lead the mind of the contemplative and wise man to the eternal God. For these creatures are shadows, echoes and pictures of that first, most powerful, most wise and most perfect Principle, of that eternal source, light and fulness, of that efficient, exemplary and ordering art. They are vestiges, representations, spectacles proposed to us and signs divinely given so that we can see God. . . .

12. The creatures of the sense world signify *the invisible attributes of God*. . . . For every creature is by its nature a kind of effigy and likeness of the eternal Wisdom, but especially one that in the book of scripture has been elevated through the spirit of prophecy to prefigure spiritual things; and most especially, those creatures in whose likeness God wished to appear through the ministry of angels; and most especially, a creature which God willed to institute as a symbol and which has the character not only of a sign in the general sense but also of a sacrament.

CHAPTER THREE[8]

ON CONTEMPLATING GOD THROUGH HIS IMAGE
STAMPED UPON OUR NATURAL POWERS

1. The two previous stages, by leading us into God through his vestiges, through which he shines forth in all creatures, have led us to the point of reentering into ourselves, that is, into our mind, where the divine image shines forth. Here it is that, now in the third stage, we enter into our very selves; and, as it were, leaving the outer court, we should strive to see God through a mirror in the sanctuary, that is, in the forward area of the tabernacle. Here the light of truth, as from a candelabrum, glows upon the face of our mind, in which the image of the most blessed Trinity shines in splendor. Enter into yourself, then, and see that your soul loves itself most fervently; that it could not love itself unless it knew itself, nor know itself unless it remembered itself, because our intellects grasp only

what is present in our memory. From this you can observe, not with the bodily eye, but with the eye of reason, that your soul has a threefold power. Consider, therefore, the operations and relationships of these three powers, and you will be able to see God through yourself as through an image, which is to see *through a mirror in an obscure manner* (1 Cor. 13:12).

CHAPTER FOUR[9]

ON CONTEMPLATING GOD IN HIS IMAGE REFORMED BY THE GIFTS OF GRACE

2. When one has fallen down, he must lie there unless someone lends a helping hand for him to rise. So our soul could not rise completely from the things of sense to see itself and the Eternal Truth in itself unless Truth, assuming human nature in Christ, had become a ladder, restoring the first ladder that had been broken in Adam. Therefore, no matter how enlightened one may be by the light of natural and acquired knowledge, he cannot enter into himself *to delight* within himself *in the Lord* unless Christ be his mediator. . . .

3. . . . . When by faith the soul believes in Christ as the uncreated word and splendor of the Father, it recovers spiritual hearing and sight: its hearing to receive the words of Christ and its sight to view the splendors of that light. When it longs in hope to receive the inspired word, it recovers through desire and affection the spiritual sense of smell. When it embraces in love the word incarnate, receiving delight from him and passing over into him through ecstatic love, it recovers its sense of taste and smell. Having recovered these senses, when it sees its spouse and hears, smells, tastes and embraces him, the soul can sing like the bride in the *Canticle of Canticles*, which was composed for the exercise of contemplation in this fourth stage. *No one* grasps this *except him who receives* (Apoc. 2:17), since it is more a matter of affective experience than rational consideration. For in this stage, when the inner senses are restored to see the highest beauty, to hear the highest harmony, to smell the highest fragrance, to taste the highest sweetness, to apprehend the highest delight, the soul is prepared for spiritual ecstasy through devotion, admiration and exultation according to the three exclamations in the *Canticle of Canticles*. . . .

CHAPTER FIVE[10]

ON CONTEMPLATING THE DIVINE UNITY THROUGH ITS PRIMARY NAME WHICH IS BEING

1. We can contemplate God not only outside us and within us but also above us: outside through his vestiges, within through his image and above through the light which shines upon our minds, which is the light of eternal truth, since "our mind itself is formed immediately by Truth itself." Those who have become practiced in the first way have already entered the court before the tabernacle; those practiced in the second way have entered the sanctuary; and those practiced in the third way enter with the high priest into the holy of holies where the cherubim of glory stand over the ark overshadowing the mercy seat. By these cherubim we understand two modes or stages of contemplating the invisible and eternal things of God: one is concerned with the essential attributes of God and the other with those proper to the persons.

2. The first method fixes the gaze primarily and principally on being itself, saying that God's primary name is *He who is* [Exod. 3:14]. The second method fixes the gaze on the good itself, saying that this is God's primary name. The first looks chiefly to the Old Testament which proclaims most of all the unity of the divine essence. Hence Moses was told: *I am who am* [Exod. 3:14]. The second method looks to the New Testament which determines the plurality of persons by baptizing *in the name of the Father and of the Son and of the Holy Spirit* [Matt. 28:19]. . . .

3. Let him who wishes to contemplate the invisible things of God in the unity of his essence fix his attention first on being itself, and let him see that being itself is so certain in itself that it cannot be thought not to be. . . .

4. Strange, then, is the blindness of the intellect, which does not consider that which it sees first and without which it can know nothing. The eye, concentrating on various differences of color, does not see the very light by which it sees other things; and if it does see this light, it does not advert to it. In the same way, the mind's eye, concentrating on particular and universal being, does not advert to being itself, which is beyond every genus, even though it comes to

our minds first and through it we know other things. Hence it is most truly apparent that "as the eye of the bat is in regard to light so is the eye of our mind in regard to the most evident things of nature." Thus our mind, accustomed to the darkness of beings and the images of the things of sense, when it glimpses the light of the supreme being, seems to itself to see nothing. It does not realize that this very darkness is the supreme illumination of our mind (cf. Ps.138:11), just as when the eye sees pure light, it seems to itself to see nothing.

5. . . .Therefore that being which is pure being and simple being and absolute being is primary being, eternal, utterly simple, most actual, most perfect and supremely one. . . .

CHAPTER SIX[11]

ON CONTEMPLATING THE MOST BLESSED TRINITY IN ITS NAME WHICH IS GOOD

1. After considering the essential attributes of God, the eye of our intelligence should be raised to look upon the most blessed Trinity, so that the second cherub may be placed alongside the first. Now just as being itself is the root principle of viewing the essential attributes, and the name through which the others become known, so the good itself is the principal foundation for contemplating the emanations.

2. See, then, and observe that the highest good is without qualification that than which no greater can be thought. And it is such that it cannot be rightly thought not to be, since to be is in all ways better than not to be; it is such that it cannot rightly be thought of unless it be thought of as three and one. For good is said to be self-diffusive; therefore the highest good must be most self-diffusive. But the greatest self-diffusion cannot exist unless it is actual and intrinsic, substantial and hypostatic, natural and voluntary, free and necessary, lacking nothing and perfect. Therefore, unless there were eternally in the highest good a production which is actual and consubstantial, and a hypostasis as noble as the producer, as in the case in a producing by way of generation and spiration, so that it is from an eternal principle eternally coproducing so that there would

be a beloved and a cobeloved, the one generated and the other spirated, and this is the Father and the Son and the Holy Spirit. . . .

6. But if you are the other cherub contemplating the properties of the persons, and you are amazed that communicability exists with individuality, consubstantiality with plurality, configurability with personality, coequality with order, coeternity with production, mutual intimacy with sending forth, because the Son is sent by the Father and the Holy Spirit by both, who is nevertheless with them and never departs from them. . . .

CHAPTER SEVEN[12]

ON SPIRITUAL AND MYSTICAL ECSTASY IN WHICH REST IS GIVEN TO OUR INTELLECT WHEN THROUGH ECSTASY OUR AFFECTION PASSES OVER ENTIRELY INTO GOD

1. . . . After our mind has beheld God outside itself through his vestiges and in his vestiges, within itself through his image and in his image, and above itself through the similitude of the divine Light shining above us and in the Light itself, insofar as this is possible in our state as wayfarers and through the exercise of our mind, when finally in the sixth stage our mind reaches that point where it contemplates in the First and Supreme principle and in *the mediator of God and men* [1 Tim. 2:5], Jesus Christ, those things whose likenesses can in no way be found in creatures and which surpass all penetration by the human intellect, it now remains for our mind by contemplating these things, to transcend and pass over not only this sense world but even itself. In passing over, Christ is the way and the door. . . .

3. This was shown also to blessed Francis, when in ecstatic contemplation on the height of the mountain—where I thought out these things I have written—there appeared to him a six-winged seraph fastened to a cross. . . There he passed over into God in ecstatic contemplation and became an example of perfect contemplation as he had previously been a man of action, like another Jacob and Israel, so that through him, more by example than by word God might invite all truly spiritual men to this kind of passing over and spiritual ecstasy.

4. In this passing over, if it is to be perfect, all intellectual activities

must be left behind and the height of our affection must be totally transferred and transformed into God. This, however, is mystical and most secret, which *no one knows except him who receives it* [Apoc. 2:17], no one receives it except him who desires it, and no one desires except him who is inflamed in his very marrow by the fire of the Holy Spirit whom Christ sent into the world. And therefore the Apostle says that this mystical wisdom is revealed by the Holy Spirit.

6. But if you wish to know how these things come about, ask grace not instruction, desire not understanding, the groaning of prayer not diligent reading, the spouse not the teacher, God not man, darkness not clarity, not light but the fire that totally inflames and carries us into God by ecstatic unctions and burning affections. This fire is God and *his furnace is in Jerusalem* [Is. 31:9]; and Christ enkindles it in the heat of his burning passion, which only he truly perceives who says: *My soul chooses hanging and my bones death* [Job 7:15]. Whoever loves this death can see God because it is true beyond doubt that *man will not see me and live* [Exod. 33:20]. Let us, then, die and enter into the darkness; let us impose silence upon our cares, our desires and our imaginings. With Christ crucified let us *pass out of this world to the Father* [John 13:1] so that when the Father is shown to us, we may say with Philip: *It is enough for us* [John 14:8]. Let us hear with Paul: *My grace is sufficient for you* [2 Cor. 12:9]. Let us rejoice with David saying: *My flesh and my heart have grown faint; You are the God of my heart, and the God that is my portion forever. Blessed be the Lord forever and all the people will say: Let it be; let it be. Amen* [Ps. 72:26; 105:48].

HERE ENDS THE SOUL'S JOURNEY INTO GOD

One of the great mystics of the Helfta (Germany) con-
vent, the God-intoxicated nun, Mechtild of Magde-
burg, is known as the "Lord's nightingale." Her love
mysticism stressed the mutual craving between God
and the soul that results in the "noble dance of praise"
with Christ who had revealed to her the mysteries of
his sacred heart.

MECHTILD OF MAGDEBURG

Mechtild of Magdeburg, "the Lord's nightingale," was born of a
noble family in Saxony. When she was only 12 years old, she received such a powerful experience of the Holy Spirit that from that
moment on she saw God in everything and everything in God.
Moreover, this experience protected her from serious sin throughout her life. When she was about 23, Mechtild became a Beguine in
Magdeburg. Years later, she became a Dominican tertiary, thereby
intensifying her life of asceticism, contemplation, and practical charity.

After a serious illness in 1281, Mechtild felt moved by God to write
about her experiences. She says, "I cannot write nor do I wish to
write—but I see this book with the eyes of my soul and hear it with
the ears of my eternal spirit and feel in every part of my body the
power of the Holy Spirit. . . . The writing in this book flowed out of
the living Godhead into the heart of Sister Mechtild."[1] Thus, her
mystical classic is called, *The Flowing Light of the Godhead.*

However, the book is actually a series of disconnected composi-
tions of varying length, written on loose sheets of paper. Mechtild
wrote spiritual poems, prose, songs of divine love, allegories, moral
reflections, admonitions, and practical advice on daily conduct.
These sheets also describe visions, revelations, and mystical experi-

ences of the highest order. Heinrich of Halle, her Dominican spiritual director, collected these papers and gave them the order the book now has.

Mechtild of Magdeburg is another example of the love, bridal, visionary, and prophetic mysticism of that period. Her writings show the skill with which she used the literary and artistic devices of her day, especially those of the Minnesingers, to describe her God-intoxication. "Love alone" was the foundation of her life and of her writings. As she says, "I was created in Love, therefore nothing can console or liberate my nobleness save Love alone."

Mechtild's love mysticism underscores the mutual craving between God and the soul, and the supreme value of interiorly experiencing it. As she wrote, "God has enough of all good things save of intercourse with the soul; of that He can never have enough."[2] Neither could the soul have enough of this love, for the love by which the soul loves is Love. In this context, hell can only be "eternal hatred." But this all-powerful Love also embraces and suffuses all creation. Therefore, her cosmic and sacramental vision is not limited to the relationship between God and the soul.

The joy and playfulness of the mystical dance between God, the soul, and all creation permeate Mechtild's writings. But she also speaks forcefully of the trials, tribulations, and total self-emptying required to live by "love alone." Only by loving the "nought and fleeing the I" does one succeed in living by "love alone." If one wishes to follow God into the "wine cellar" to "drink the unmingled wine," which guarantees genuine intoxication with Love, one must calculate the cost of such wine: "Thou must spend more than thou hast" and "squander" your "all," and become "poor and naked."[3] Paradoxically, only when Mechtild experienced the "Blessed Forsakenness of God" did she realize that "the more deeply I sink, the more sweetly I drink of Thee."[4] Only one who passes through the spiritual dark night in perfect imitation of Christ's passion and death can drink the unmingled wine.

Mechtild's writings also demonstrate a profound grasp of the mystery of Christ's sufferings, mercy, and love. Christ called her to dedicate herself "to the light of my divinity flowing into all hearts that live without guile." With the eyes of her soul, she had seen "the beautiful manhood of Jesus Christ." Christ had also revealed to her the mysteries of his sacred heart.

Her writings often focus upon Christ as a beautiful youth who personifies Love and invites her to participate in the mystical dance that circles inward and upward to the Father in the Holy Spirit. Because of the Christ-centeredness of her mysticism, she bitterly denounced the Brethren of the Free Spirit for committing "a sin that is worse than all other sins." She writes that these people "would be so holy as to draw themselves up into the eternal Godhead and pass by the eternal holy humanity of our Lord Jesus Christ."[5] In company with many in the Christian mystical tradition, Mechtild contended that no spirituality and mysticism worthy of the name Christian can bypass Christ's humanity for an allegedly higher and purer spirituality.

Her writings disclose a person of largesse, spontaneity, nobility, freedom, intelligence, clarity, and poetic imagination in describing delicate inner experiences. Like Hildegarde of Bingen and Hadewijch, the subjective pole of her mystical experiences is not the spirit's primordial unity, but the mystical senses. Herein lies the extraordinary clarity of her visions and the power of her imagery and symbols.

Because of Mechtild's extraordinary experiences and her outspoken denunciations of corruption in the clergy and religious life, she was severely criticized, denounced as a heretic, and forced to flee to the convent of Helfta. Her condemnations were severe because she, a true daughter of the Church, wrote, "I hold holy Church much more worthily than anything of my own."[6]

Helfta was a center widely known for its mystical and literary talent. There she was warmly received by Mechtild of Hackeborn and Gertrude the Great, two other outstanding mystics of Mechtild's ilk. Her mystical and literary skills fully matured at Helfta, where she remained for the rest of her life. Although her contemporaries regarded her as a saint, she was never canonized.

The text was selected to illustrate Mechtild's skillful use of images and poetry, as well as her fondness for dialogue as a literary device to express the rhythm of divine-human intercourse. This text is perhaps the most beautiful in the Christian mystical tradition on the mystical dance and deification, that is, "the soul being fashioned in the very nature of God." Within a trinitarian framework, Mechtild speaks of the necessity of being clothed with the virtues before the soul can meet her lover. The Old Testament, the longing of the prophets, our Lady, the saints—the entire Church—prepare and lead the soul to the "noble Dance of Praise" with Christ, the beautiful youth. But Mechtild emphasizes the necessity of grace, for the soul cannot dance "unless thou [Christ] lead me." When the senses complain that no one can endure the presence of God's burning and blinding glory, the soul cries out that just as fish live in water and birds in the air, it must live in God. Scorning as "childish" everything less than being Love's Bride, the soul is willing to endure anything—"thy self must go"—to experience the divine intercourse and to realize that "where two lovers come secretly together, they must often part, without parting."[7]

THE TEXTS

THE FLOWING LIGHT OF THE GODHEAD[8]
44. *Of the way of love in seven things, of three bridal robes and of the dance*

God speaks

Ah! loving soul! Wouldst thou know where thy way lies?

Soul

Yes! Holy Spirit! Show it to me!

HOLY SPIRIT
Thou must overcome the need of remorse, the pain of penitence, the labor of confession, the love of the world, temptation of the devil, pride of the body, and annihilation of self-will which drags so many souls back that they never come to real love. Then, when thou hast conquered most of thine enemies, thou art so wearied, that thou criest out—Ah! beautiful youth! Where shall I find thee?

THE YOUTH
I hear a voice
Which speaks somewhat of love.
Many days have I wooed her
But never heard her voice.
Now I am moved
I must go to meet her,
She it is who bears grief and love together,
In the morning, in the dew in the intimate rapture
Which first penetrates the soul.

HER WAITING-MAIDS, THE FIVES SENSES SPEAK
Lady! Thou must adorn thyself!

SOUL
Ah! Love! Whither shall I go?

THE SENSES
We have heard a whisper,
The Prince comes to greet thee,
In the dew and the song of the birds!
Tarry not, Lady!
And so the soul puts on a shift of humility, so humble that
nothing could be more humble. And over it a white robe of
chastity, so pure that she cannot endure words or desires which
might stain it. Next she wraps herself in a mantle of holy desire
that she has woven out of all the virtues.

Thus she goes into the woods, that is the company of holy people.
The sweetest nightingales sing there day and night and she hears
also many pure notes of the birds of holy wisdom. But still the
youth does not come. She sends her messengers, for she would
dance. He sends her the faith of Abraham, the longings of the
prophets, the chaste modesty of our Lady St. Mary, the sacred perfection of our Lord Jesus Christ and the whole company of his elect.
Thus there is prepared a noble dance of praise. Then the youth
comes and speaks to her—

Maiden! thou shalt dance merrily
Even as mine elect!

ca. 1210-1297   *TEXTS*, MECHTILD OF MAGDEBURG   251

THE SOUL
I cannot dance O Lord, unless Thou lead me.
If Thou wilt that I leap joyfully
Then must Thou Thyself first dance and sing!
Then will I leap for love
From love to knowledge,
From knowledge to fruition,
From fruition to beyond all human sense
There will I remain
And circle evermore.

THE YOUTH
Thy Dance of Praise is well done.
Now shalt thou have thy will
Of the Virgin's Son.
For thou art weary! Come at midday
To the shade by the brook
To the resting place of love.
There thou mayst cool thyself.

THE SOUL
Ah! Lord! that is too much
That Thou shouldst companion my love;
Where the heart has no love of itself,
It will be ever aroused thereto by Thee!
Then wearied by the dance, the soul says to the senses,
"Leave me! I must cool myself!" The senses answer, "Lady! Wilt
thou be refreshed by the tears of Mary Magdalene? Can they
suffice thee?"

SOUL
Hush! ye know not what I mean!
Hinder me not! I would drink of the unmingled wine!

SENSES
Lady! In virgin Mary
The love of God is ready for thee!

SOUL
That may be so. For me

It is not the highest.

SENSES
Thou mayest cool thyself
In the blood of the martyrs.

SOUL
I have been martyred so many a day
I can no longer go that way.

SENSES
Many pure souls abide
By the counsel of confessors.

SOUL
Their counsel will I obey
And yet—I cannot go that way!

SENSES
In the wisdom of the Apostles
Thou wilt find sure refuge?

SOUL
Their wisdom have I in my heart,
It bids me choose the better part.

SENSES
Lady! The angels are clear and bright
And full of Love;
If thou wouldst cool thyself,
Ascend to them above.

SOUL
The angels joy is woe to me
Unless my Lord, my Love, I see.

SENSES
In holy austerity cool thyself and save
That which God to John Baptist gave.

SOUL
Pain and suffering do not appal,
Yet Love rules ever over all.

SENSES

Ah! Lady! wouldst thou be refreshed,
Bend thee down to the Virgin's knee
To the tiny Babe and taste and see
How the angels drink of Eternity,
In the milk of the joy of the Maid!

SOUL
That is a childish joy
To suckle and rock a Babe!
But I am a full-grown Bride
I must to my lover's side!

SENSES
Ah! Lady! Comest thou there
Then are we blinded
So fiery is the glory of the Godhead
As thou well knowest—
That all the flame and all the glow
In Heaven above and earth below
Which burneth and shineth—
All doth flow from God Himself;
From His Divine breath,
Through His Divine lips
From the counsel of the Holy Spirit—
Who may abide it, even one hour?

SOUL
Fish cannot drown in the water,
Birds cannot sink in the air,
Gold cannot perish
In the refiner's fire.
This has God given to all creatures
To foster and seek their own nature,
How then can I withstand mine?

I must to God—
My Father through nature,
My Brother through humanity,
My Bridegroom through Love,
His am I for ever!
Think ye that fire must utterly slay my soul?
Nay! Love can both fiercely scorch
And tenderly love and console.
Therefore be not troubled!
Ye shall still teach me.
When I return
I will need your teaching
For the earth is full of snares.
Then the beloved goes in to the Lover, into the secret
hiding place of the sinless Godhead.... And there, the soul being
fashioned in the very nature of God, no hindrance can come
between it and God.
Then our Lord said—
Stand, O Soul!

SOUL
What wilt thou Lord?

THE LORD
Thy SELF must go!

SOUL
But Lord, what shall happen to me then?

THE LORD
Thou art by nature already mine!
Nothing can come between Me and thee!
There is no angel so sublime
As to be granted for one hour
That is given thee for ever.
Therefore must thou put from thee
Fear and shame and all outward things.
Only of that of which thou art sensible by nature
Shalt thou wish to be sensible in Eternity.
That shall be thy noble longing,

Thine endless desire,
And that in My infinite mercy
I will evermore fulfil.

SOUL

Lord, now I am naked soul
And thou a God most Glorious!
Our two-fold intercourse is Love Eternal
Which can never die.
Now comes a blessed stillness
Welcome to both. He gives Himself to her
And she to Him.
What shall now befall her, the soul knows:
Therefore am I comforted.
Where two lovers come secretly together
They must often part, without parting.
Dear friend of God! I have written down this, my way of love,
for thee. May God give it to thee in thy heart. AMEN.

*Because she reflected deeply upon the theological sig-
nificance of mystical union with God in the soul's
depths, another Helfta mystic, Gertrude the Great,
stands out as a proponent of ontological mysticism. Ecstatic visions instructed her about Christ's wounds
and heart as the supreme symbol of God's self- giving
love and about the efficacy of a holy life lived for others.*

GERTRUDE THE GREAT

We know nothing about the birthplace, the family, or the circumstances under which this illustrious mystic was entrusted to the
care of the Helfta nuns in Thuringia (Germany) when she was only
five years old. But we do know that she received a good education,
showed intellectual promise, became a skilled Latinist, worked as a
copyist in the monastery scriptorium, and was called "Great" because of her theological sophistication and mystical acumen. Well
known are her *Exercitia Spiritualia,* seven contemplations on the
awareness of grace that permeates Christian life, and her
Revelationes or *Legatus divinae pietatis (Herald of God's Loving Kindness),* consisting of five books, the second of which certainly comes
from Gertrude's hand; the others, from her notes.

In her revelations, Gertrude accuses herself of having been more interested in intellectual pursuits than in her spiritual well-being.
However, when she was about 25 years old, she had numerous illuminations and a special vision of the young and beautiful Christ.
Made ecstatically aware of the loving bond existing between Christ
and her, Gertrude perceived that this union would eradicate her
sins and reorder her passions. Moreover, she soon experienced nup-
tial union with Christ and participation in the trinitarian life of
peace and splendor.

It must be emphasized that Gertrude's mystical life began and came to fruition in a monastic context, as did that of all the great Helfta mystics. Her profound experiences occurred, deepened, and reached full maturity through the study of Scripture, spiritual reading, communal prayer, the chanting of the Divine Office, and eucharistic celebrations. For example, often during the chanting of the Office, Gertrude saw mystically the divine face and experienced the embraces and kisses of the Trinity. As one would expect, many of her ecstasies, illuminations, revelations, and wounds of love took place during Mass.

Through ecstatic visions, Gertrude perceived and understood Christ's heart and wounds as the supreme symbol of God's self-giving love. She gloried in the heart and wounds that Christ gave her not only as a pledge of his love but also as a place of refuge and rest. Like her Helfta sisters, Gertrude expressed this somewhat emotional and romantic mysticism in the literary language of her day: the language of courtly love and of the minnesingers.

One finds scattered references to Christ's sacred heart in the writings of Bernard, William of St. Thierry, and Richard of St. Victor. However, with the mystical experiences of the saving and transforming power of Christ's sacred heart and wounds, the Helfta nuns laid the foundation for a devotion that has played a significant role in the spiritual life of numerous Christians right up to the present day.

But the Helfta mystics were also intellectually and theologically sophisticated, and Gertrude was no exception. For example, she perceived her heart not only as God's abode but also as the bridge uniting Christ's humanity and divinity. Her heart mysticism also focused much more on the purging, illuminating, and transforming significance of Christ's heart and wounds, and much less upon an aspect that was to dominate later devotion: sadness because of the bleeding heart that suffers from ingratitude. Moreover, one finds in Gertrude's writings an attempt to reflect upon the philosophical and theological significance of mystical union with God in the soul's depths. Thus, Gertrude both knew and contributed to the abstract and speculative Low Countries' ("Low Land") and Rhineland "ontological" mysticism (*Wesensmystik*) of that period.

Through her revelations, Gertrude learned that God was like a mighty emperor who had not only ladies-in-waiting (contemplatives) but also men-at-arms (those in the active apostolate). Therefore, both contemplation and any activity that afforded the opportunity to exercise patience, humility, and practical charity pleased the Lord.

However, Gertrude also experienced in mystical contemplation that her life of union with Christ had an apostolic effect upon the entire mystical body, the Church. Her mysticism instructed her about the efficacy of a holy life lived *for others*. Because of her marital union with Christ, his merits became her merits and could be passed on to repentant sinners. It must be emphasized that the visionary, bridal Helfta mystics were also service mystics. Thus, Gertrude lived a busy monastic life that extended practical charity and apostolic service far beyond the monastic walls to people from all walks of life.

The texts were selected to illustrate Gertrude's visionary, bridal, and service mysticism centered on Christ, his heart, and his wounds. When she received Christ's wounds in her heart, she experienced their purgative effect and her growth in virtue. In ecstatic love, the Christ Child is born in her heart, deifies her, and transforms her into an icon of his presence. When Gertrude's soul is imprinted by the *trinitarian* Christ like wax by a hot seal, her soul melts into Christ with the realization that his love "could not be hindered from communicating itself." In the concluding selection, Gertrude sees into Christ's pierced side and "there came forth from his blessed and inmost Heart a pure and solid stream, like crystal." She is instructed that her illness will sanctify her but for the sake of a more effective love of others. The frequency with which her visions contain inner words, or mystical locutions, should also be noted.[1]

THE TEXTS

THE LIFE AND REVELATIONS OF SAINT GERTRUDE
Chapter IV[2]

Of the stigmata imprinted in the heart of Gertrude, and her exercises in honor of the Five Wounds. I believe it was during the winter of the first or second year when I began to receive these favors, that I met the following prayer in a book of devotions:

"O Lord Jesus Christ, Son of the living God, grant I may aspire toward Thee with my whole heart, with full desire and with thirsty soul, seeking only Thy sweetness and Thy delights, so that my whole mind and all that is within it may most ardently sigh to Thee, who art our true Beatitude. O most merciful Lord, engrave Thy Wounds upon my heart with Thy most precious Blood, that I may read in them both Thy grief and Thy love; and that the memory of Thy wounds may ever remain in my inmost heart to excite my compassion for Thy sufferings and to increase in me Thy love. Grant me also to despise all creatures, and that my heart may delight in Thee alone. Amen."

. . . Being seated in the refectory, as I said before, I thought attentively on these things, when I perceived that the grace that I had so long asked by the aforesaid prayer was granted to me, unworthy though I am; for I perceived in spirit that Thou hadst imprinted in the depths of my heart the adorable marks of Thy sacred Wounds, even as they are on Thy Body; that Thou hadst cured my soul in imprinting these Wounds on it; and that, to satisfy its thirst, Thou hadst given it the precious beverage of Thy love.

But my unworthiness had not yet exhausted the abyss of Thy mercy; for I received from Thine overflowing liberality this remarkable gift—that each time during the day in which I endeavored to apply myself in spirit to those adorable Wounds, saying five verses of Psalm 103, "Bless the Lord, O my soul," I have never failed to receive some new favor. At the first verse, "Bless the Lord, O my soul," I deposited all the rust of my sins and my voluptuousness at the Wounds of Thy blessed Feet; at the second verse, "Bless the Lord, and never forget all He hath done for thee," I washed away all the stains of carnal and perishable pleasures in the sweet bath of Blood and Water which Thou didst pour forth for me; at the third verse, "Who forgiveth all thine iniquities," I reposed my spirit in the Wound of Thy Left Hand, even as the dove makes its nest in the crevice of the rock; at the fourth verse, "Who redeemeth thy life from destruction," I approached Thy Right Hand and took from thence all that I needed for my perfection in virtue; and being thus magnificently adorned, I passed to the fifth verse, "Who satisfieth thy desire with good things," that I might be purified from all the defilement of sin and have the indigence of my wants supplied, so that I might become worthy of Thy presence—though of myself I am utterly unworthy—and might merit the joy of Thy chaste embraces. . . .

Chapter VI[3]

Of the intimate union of the infant jesus with her heart.

. . . It was on that most sacred night in which the sweet dew of Divine grace fell on all the world, and the heavens dropped sweetness, that my soul, exposed like a mystic fleece in the court of the monastery, having received in meditation this celestial rain, was prepared to assist at this Divine Birth, in which a Virgin brought forth a Son, true God and Man, even as a star produces its ray. In this night, I say, my soul beheld before it suddenly a delicate Child, but just born, in whom were concealed the greatest gifts of perfection. I imagined that I received this precious gift in my bosom with the tenderest affection. As I possessed it within me, it seemed to me that all at once I was changed into the color of this Divine Infant, if we may be permitted to call that color which cannot be compared to anything visible.

Then I understood the meaning contained in those sweet and ineffable words: "God will be all in all" (I Corinthians 15:28); and my soul, which was enriched by the presence of my Beloved, soon knew, by its transports of joy, that it possessed the presence of its Spouse. Then it received these words with exceeding avidity, which were presented as a delicious beverage to satisfy the ardor of its thirst: "As I am the figure of the substance of God, my Father, in His Divinity, so also you shall be the figure of My substance in My Humanity, receiving in your deified soul the infusions of My Divinity, as the air receives the brightness of the solar rays, that these rays may penetrate you so intimately as to prepare you for the closest union with Me.". . .

Chapter VII[4]

The Divinity is imprinted upon the soul of Gertrude as a seal upon wax.

. . . and having received the Food that gives life immediately after the Procession, I thought only of God and myself; and I beheld my soul, under the similitude of wax softened by the fire, impressed like a seal upon the bosom of the Lord; and immediately I beheld it surrounding and partly drawn into this treasure-house, where the ever-peaceful Trinity abides corporally in the plenitude of the Divinity and resplendent with its glorious impression. . . .

Chapter VIII[5]

Of the admirable union of her soul with God.

. . . But since we may understand the invisible things of God, in some measure, by those that are visible—as I have before remarked—I saw (to express as far as I can that which is inexpressible) that the part of His blessed Heart where the Lord received my soul on the Feast of the Purification, under the form of wax softened by the fire, was, as it were, dropping a sweat, which came forth with violence, even as if the substance of the wax was melted by the excessive heat hidden in the depth of this Heart. This sacred reservoir attracted these drops to itself with surprising force, powerfully and inexpressibly, and even so inconceivably that one saw evidently that love, that could not be hindered from communicating itself, had an absolute power in this place, where it discovered secrets that were so great, so hidden, and so impenetrable. . . .

Chapter IX[6]

Of another admirable manner in which St. Gertrude was closely united to God.

Soon after, during the fast when I was confined to bed for the second time by a severe sickness and the other sisters were occupied elsewhere so that I was left alone one morning, the Lord, who never abandons those who are deprived of human consolation, came to verify these words of the prophet: "I am with him in tribulation" (Psalm 91). He turned His right Side toward me, and there came forth from His blessed and inmost Heart a pure and solid stream, like crystal; and on His Breast there was a precious ornament, like a necklace, which seemed to alternate between gold and rose-color. Then our Lord said to me: "This sickness that you suffer will sanctify your soul; so that each time you go forth from Me, like the stream which I have shown you, for the good of your neighbor, either in thought, word, or act, even then, as the purity of the crystal renders the color of the gold and the rose more brilliant, so the cooperation of the precious gold of My Divinity, and the rose of the perfect patience of My Humanity, will render your works always agreeable to Me by the purity of your intention.". . .

The writings of the God-intoxicated Italian Francis-can, Jacopone da Todi, contain some of the fiercest love poetry, one of the most beautiful hymns of praise to St. Francis and his stigmata, and one of the most sublime eulogies to Dame Poverty in the Christian mystical tradition.

JACOPONE DA TODI

The scion of an aristocratic Umbrian family in Todi, Jacopone married and worked as a *notatio*, a profession that mixed accounting and law. When he was 47 years old, his wife died. For unknown reasons, Jacopone became a *bizzocone*, a ragged public penitent. Ten years later he entered the order of the Franciscans and took part in the raging conflict within the order between the latitudinarian group of Conventuals and the stricter one of Spirituals. Jacopone had spent much time meditating on the life of Francis of Assisi. Like Francis, he had a passionate love for Dame Poverty and an ardent desire to emulate Christ crucified. Thus, Jacopone may have become a Spiritual intentionally in order to suffer the severe persecutions they were then enduring.

Shocked by the mediocrity and corruption he saw in society, in the Franciscan order, and in the Church, he found hope in the election to the papacy of Pier da Morrone, a 70-year-old abbot of an order of hermits and a friend of many Spirituals. But Jacopone's hopes were quickly dashed. Within a few months, the "angel-pope" Celestine V made what Dante bitterly called "the great refusal": He resigned. The venal, greedy, politically ambitious, and ruthless Cardinal Benedetto Gaetani became the new pope, Boniface VIII. Filled with fury, Jacopone, other Spirituals, and rebellious cardinals signed the Longhezza Manifesto, which denounced the conclave that elected

Boniface VIII and demanded a new election.

The rebellion failed. Jacopone was excommunicated, stripped of his Franciscan habit, and imprisoned in an underground cell at the monastery of San Fortunato in Todi, where he spent nearly 10 years before his release by Pope Benedict XI. That he returned to the Franciscans and spent his last years at the Monastery of San Lorenzo in Collazzone in great peace demonstrates the friar's spiritual depths.

It is against this background that one must read *The Lauds*,[1] undoubtedly the most powerful Italian religious poetry before Dante. It is also unparalleled as prison literature. Jacopone's God-intoxication permeates these writings, which contain some of the fiercest love poetry in the Christian mystical tradition. Like his counterparts in the Muslim tradition, the Sufis, Jacopone uses invocation and incantation to stir up the heart, then to maintain its swelling and ascent, and finally to send the ecstatic heart diving into Love itself.

Through Christ's incarnation and crucifixion, Jacopone experienced mystically the madness of the divine love. As he says, "for love of man You seem to have gone mad! . . . Jesus cannot cure Himself of love; He seems to be out of His senses."[2] Thus, Jacopone responds accordingly when he says, "Love, you are driving me to madness; I can do no more."[3] As the selected texts illustrate, Jacopone considers madness for the love of Christ to be the highest wisdom because of God's mad love for him. "Love, Love-Jesus" becomes his frequent refrain.

Jacopone sings of a soul drowning in ecstatic love. The soul, like a "drop of wine" that is poured into the sea, loses "all sense of self and self-consciousness" and "becomes one with God."[4] Thus fused with God, the soul becomes divine; united with Christ, it becomes "almost Christ." As the soul drinks in this love, it is imbibed by Love. And so, in "lofty self-annihilation," "two are made one" in a "true union that admits no division."[5] Inebriated by Love emptying itself to the point of death on a cross, Jacopone became the fool of Love who heard all creation shout this Love.

Thus, Love was the reason for his strident paeans to self-hatred, self-annihilation, and uncompromising poverty. Through his experiences of the madness of divine love, this crotchety Old Testament-like prophet of Love simultaneously grasped the awesomeness of his sins, his radical creaturehood, and his inability to love as greatly as he was loved. Jacopone could be churlish, coarse, boorish, shrill, wrathful, and excessive toward whomever tried to diminish the vision Love reveals through the incarnate and crucified Christ. This is the proper context for understanding the self-hatred that he vents in the last selected text.

To Jacopone, the wisdom of St. Francis as manifest in his stigmata only pointed up the hypocrisy, sham, and mediocrity of his own heart. So, teaching that a heart was only as big as the love it contained, he waged a relentless war against his weak, vacillating, unredeemed self. Paradoxically, his vehement denunciations of world and self are redolent with the sense of having been redeemed and loved by God. The man, willing to give away all creation for the sake of Love, discovers that as a "new creature born in Christ," all things are his.

Against the man he so fiercely hated, Pope Boniface VIII, Jacopone wishes to use two swords: self-hatred and such ardent love of neighbor that "do what you will, this love will overcome you."[6] In the final analysis, Jacopone tasted that "I am the only enemy that stands between me and salvation."

The first of the following texts was selected to illustrate Jacopone's vehement love mysticism. Laud 90 reveals him as a man wounded, haunted, possessed, and mad with love, as a man willingly giving himself and all creation for love. So inebriating are the agonies and ecstasies of drowning in divine Love and being clothed with Christ that he wishes to die of love.

The second selection reveals how profoundly St. Francis and the stigmata captured the Christian imagination. This text is perhaps the most beautiful hymn of praise to Francis and the stigmata in the Christian tradition.

The third and fourth selections focus upon Jacopone's Franciscan love of Dame Poverty. It, too, may be the most sublime hymn of praise to poverty in the Christian mystical tradition.

The final selection is the most captivating expression of Christian self-hatred ever recorded. Again, it must be understood in the context of how deeply Jacopone had experienced the "Love, Love" that all creation shouts. It is one side of his mysticism of joy in the world and of his final confession that sums up Franciscan mysticism: "Thou art the Love wherein the heart loves Thee."[7]

THE TEXTS

THE LAUDS

90 THE LAMENT OF THE SOUL FOR THE INTENSITY OF IN-
FUSED CHARITY[8]
Why do you wound me,
cruel charity,
Bind me and tie me tight?
My heart all trembling,
in fragments, Encircled by flames,
Like wax melts into death.
I ask for respite. None is granted.
My heart, cast into a blazing furnace,
Lives and dies in that fire.

Before my heart knew this, all unsuspecting
I asked for the grace to love you, O Christ
Confident that love would be a gentle peace,
A soaring to a height and leaving pain behind.
Now I feel torment I could never have imagined
For that searing heat rends my heart.
This love is beyond image or similitude—
My heart beats no longer, and in joy I die. . . .

For this Love I have renounced all,
Traded the world and myself;
Were I the lord of creation
I would give it all away for Love.
And yet Love still plays with me,
Makes me act as if out of my senses,

Destroys me and draws me I know not where—
But since I sold myself I have no power to resist. . . .

. . . Stones will liquify before Love lets me go.
Intense desire flames high, fusing my will—
Oh, who could separate me from this Love?

Neither iron nor fire can pry us apart;
The soul now dwells in a sphere
Beyond the reach of death and suffering.
It looks down on all creation and basks in its peace.
My soul, how did you come to possess this good?
It was Christ's dear embrace that gave it to you. . . .

At the sight of such beauty I am swept up
Out of myself to who knows where;
My heart melts, like wax near fire.
Christ puts His mark on me, and stripped of myself
(O wondrous exchange!) I put on Christ.
Robed in this precious garment,
Crying out its love,
The soul drowns in ecstasy! . . . .

United with Christ she is almost Christ;
Fused with God she becomes divine. . . .

A new creature is born in Christ:
I hasten to put on the new man,
And Love continues to rise in the veins,
A knife blade cutting into the heart,
A heat that sears all power of thought.
Christ in His beauty draws me to Him,
Locks me in His embrace, and I cry out:
"Love for whom I hunger, let me die of love!". . . .

"Once I spoke, now I am mute;
I could see once, now I am blind.
Oh, the depths of the abyss in which,
Though silent, I speak; fleeing, I am bound;
Descending, I rise; holding, I am held;
Outside, I am within; I pursue and am pursued.

Love without limits, why do You drive me mad
And destroy me in this blazing furnace?. . . .

Christ, You have pierced my heart,
And now You speak of orderly love.
How can I experience love of that sort
Once united with You?
Just as a red-hot iron
Or forms touched by burning colors of dawn
Lose their original contours,
So does the soul immersed in You, O Love . . . .

"Love, Love you have wounded me,
Your name only can I invoke;
Love, Love, I am one with You,
Let me embrace You alone.
Love, Love, You have swept me up violently,
My heart is beside itself with love;
I want to faint, Love; may I always be close to You:
Love, I beseech You, let me die of love.

"Love, Love-Jesus, I have come to port;
Love, Love-Jesus, You have led me there.
Love, Love-Jesus, comfort me;
Love, Love-Jesus, You have set me afire.
Love, Love-Jesus, consider my needs:
Keep me always in Your embrace,
United with You in true charity,
The supreme realization of unifying love.

"Love, Love," the world cries out,
"Love, Love," shouts all of creation.
Love, Love, so inexhaustible are You
That he who clasps You close desires You all the more!
Love, Love, perfect circle, he who enters into You
With his whole heart loves You forever. For You are warp and
woof
Of the robe of him who loves You, filling him with such
delight
That he calls out again and again, "Love"! . . .

"Love, Love-Jesus, full of desire,
Love, I want to die in Your embrace.
Love, Love-Jesus, my sweet Spouse, I ask You for death.

Love, Love-Jesus, my delight,
You surrender Yourself to me, make me one with You:
Consider that I am faint with love of You.
Love, and know not where I am.
Jesus, my hope, drown me in Love.

61 ST. FRANCIS AND THE SEVEN VISIONS OF THE CROSS[9]

O truly poor Francis, patriarch of our times,
Yours is a new banner, emblazoned with seven crosses. . . .

That Christ you saw said to you,
"Come and lovingly embrace this noble cross;
If you would follow Me, become as nothing,
Hate yourself and love your neighbor." . . .

The seventh apparition came as you prayed with great devotion
On the craggy heights of La Verna—
An awesome vision of a six-winged seraphim, crucified.
It sealed you with the stigmata—side, hands, and feet.

The man who hears a brief account finds this hard to believe,
Yet many there were who saw these marks
While you were still alive and well,
And on your death many came to touch them.

Among others, Saint Claire came,
Bringing with her her sisters;
Greedy for such treasure she tried in vain
To pull out those nails with her teeth:

The nails were made of flesh, hardened like iron,
The flesh was as fair as a child's.
It had lost the traces of the many winters;
Love had made it radiant, beautiful to gaze on.

That wound in your side was like a scarlet rose.
All that saw wept at the marvel:
Its likeness to that of Christ

Made the heart sink into an abyss of love. . . .

[These wounds] flowed freely as the friars gazed upon this
vision
Of fiery love. The precious balsam of holiness
That lies hidden in the heart
Had burst forth from the wounds of Francis. . . .

The burning love of Christ, whose depths are lost to sight,
Enfolded Francis, softened his heart like wax,
And there pressed its seal, leaving the mark
Of the One to whom he was united. . . .

Who knows the intensity of that fire?
We can only know that the body could not contain it
And it burst out through the five wounds,
That all might see that it dwelt therein.

No saint ever bore such signs upon his body—
Sacred mystery, revealed by God!
It is best to pass over this in silence;
Let only those who have experienced it speak. . . .

O my arid soul, dry of tears, run—take the bait;
Drink of these waters and never turn away
Until you are drunk with love.
Oh, that we might die at this sacred spring!

59 ON HOLY POVERTY, QUEEN OF CREATION[10]
Lady Poverty, burning with charity,
Vast is your dominion!

France and England are mine, from sea to sea;
So firm is my grip, No one takes up arms against me.
Mine is Saxony, mine is Gascony,
Mine are Burgundy and all of Normandy. . . .

Since my will is centered in God, who possessed all,
I wing with ease from earth to heaven.
Since I gave my will to God
All things are mine and I am one with them
In love, in ardent charity.

... Poverty, deepest wisdom, you are slave to nothing,
And in your detachment you possess all things.
To have contempt for things is to possess them without risk;
They cannot block the path to perfection. ...

God does not dwell in a heart that's confined,
And a heart is only as big as the love it holds:
In the great heart of Poverty God has room to dwell. ...

This heaven is founded on *nichil* [no-thing],
Where purified love lives in Truth.
You see that things are not as they seemed to you,
So high a state has been reached. ...

Where Christ enters in, the old world is swept away,
Lover and beloved are fused in wondrous union.
Love no longer needs the heart,
Nor knowledge the intelligence—our will is His.

To live as myself and yet not I,
My being no longer my being,
This is a paradox
We cannot pretend to understand!

Poverty is having nothing, wanting nothing,
And possessing all things in the spirit of freedom.

48 THE ILLS AND EVILS FRATE JACOPONE CALLED
DOWN ON HIMSELF IN AN EXCESS OF CHARITY[12]
Send me illness, O Lord,
I beg of You, out of courtesy!

Hurl down quartian ague, tertian fever,
Chills every day and swollen dropsy!
Give me toothache, headache, and stomach cramps,
Pains in my guts and spasms of choking.
Give me pleuritis and burning eyes,
Let my left side swell with a tumor;
Visit me with a violent case of tuberculosis,
Let me suffer perpetual delirium. ...

Let my mouth be full of ulcerous sores,
Have me suffer from epilepsy, falling into fire and water,
My whole body utterly broken by illness.
Come blindness, loss of speech and hearing,
Wretchedness, poverty and palsy.
May my stench keep everyone at a distance,
With no one to help me in my misery:
Let them abandon me in the horrible gulch of Rigoverci. . .

Let me be buried in the stomach of a ravenous wolf,
Who will shit the relics in a bramble patch.

Let those who come there, expecting miracles after my death,
Be accompanied by evil spirits,
Feel howling terror, have doomsday visions.
Let anyone who hears the mention of my name shudder
And cross himself to ward off the danger of an ugly encounter.
All this I call down on myself, O Lord, is not adequate vengeance,
For You created me as Your beloved,
And I, ungrateful wretch, put You to death.

Angela of Foligno, "the nightingale of the Ineffable,"
may be the most remarkable woman Franciscan in the
Christian mystical tradition. Few mystics have as-
serted with such boldness as Angela that they saw
God "as clearly as possible in this life."

ANGELA OF FOLIGNO

Born in Foligno in Umbria of a wealthy family, Angela of Foligno is one of a group of more than 100 holy women who lived in Italy during the period from 1200 to 1500. She may well be the most remarkable and significant woman Franciscan in the Christian mystical tradition. If one considers the profundity of her mystical life, the extraordinary phenomena she experienced, her highly gifted mind, the skill with which she described these experiences, the interaction of her visionary and apostolic mysticisms, and the far-reaching influence she exerted both during her lifetime and during the 16th and 17th centuries, it is astonishing that she remains relatively unknown today.

For many years, Angela lived such a dissolute life of sin that she feared sacramental confession. When she was approximately 40 years old, she experienced a mysterious conversion in which a dream of St. Francis of Assisi played a role. After the conversion, Angela's desire (and perhaps a genuine divine revelation) prompted her to pray for the death not only of her mother— whom Angela considered a "hindrance" to her spiritual progress—but also of her husband and child. Her prayers were answered.

Angela became a member of the "Third Order" of St. Francis, an expansion of the Franciscan rule. The first and second orders consisted of Franciscan friars and nuns bound by ecclesiatical vows to an austere life of poverty, chastity, and obedience. The Third Order comprised people from all walks of life who possessed the Franciscan spirit and wished to associate with kindred souls in formal or informal groups. Members of the Third Order lived under mitigated Franciscan rules and were spiritually directed by the friars. Although they did not take religious vows, they did promise solemnly to strive for perfection. It is only in this communal context that Angela's spirituality and mysticism can be understood.

Angela offers a penetrating description of her "twenty steps of penance" that more or less begin with sacramental confession and end with mystical visions, revelations, illuminations, understandings, and consolations. Many of these steps consist of focusing upon the suffering and crucified Christ and upon Mary and John the Evangelist at the foot of the cross. These contemplations bestowed on Angela an exceptional sensitivity to God's omnipotence and love, as well as a deep insight into the seriousness of her sins. God also taught her that the beginning and end of true wisdom is "to know God and ourselves."

Commentators have called Angela a "bit-by-bit" mystic because of her many years of intense purification. As she gradually embraced full material poverty, she experienced *everything* as a barrier to full union with the "divine Goodness" and to transformation into Christ, the "true book of Life." Angela's desire for total poverty, radical asceticism, and profound contemplation also expressed itself in heroic service to the poor and sick of Foligno, especially to the lepers in the local hospital.

Shortly after her conversion, Angela says that she experienced God writing the Lord's Prayer into her heart so that she penetrated its deepest meaning. Now she truly knew the prayer "by heart." "Divine sweetnesses" constantly penetrated her spirit, and on one occasion, she was swept with an intellectual illumination that left her in ecstasy for eight days. She had numerous visions through her *soul's* eyes of God's goodness, beauty, power, humility, wisdom, justice, and love. She also had a dark, but profoundly loving, vision of the Trinity and one "wherein she beheld God as clearly as is possible in this life." Many of her visions focus on Christ's passion, her mystical entrance into Christ's pierced side, the eucharist, Mary, and on her own "spiritual" children. But unlike many mystics who suffered their visions as burdens, Angela called hers "consolations."

One of the most striking of her mystical experiences was that of the Holy Spirit who embraced Angela and chided her for not loving as much as she was loved. The Holy Spirit also instructed her that she would not be satisfied until she loved with the same love with which she was loved. Then the Spirit spoke these words to her soul: "Oh my daughter, who art sweeter unto Me than I am unto thee; temple of My delight, thou dost possess the ring of My love and art promised unto Me, so that henceforth thou shalt never leave Me. The blessing of the Father, the Son, and the Holy Spirit be upon thee and thine understanding."[1] After this experience, she could speak only of God, and she perceived all earthly reality in its relationship with God.

Even Angela's death was strikingly mystical. Christ himself washed her soul in his "precious blood" and presented her to his Father, who then showed Angela to her bridegroom, the eternal word.

Before her full transformation into God, however, Angela had suffered several years of mystical purgation. Severe temptations, bodily torments from demons, and excruciating fear that her beloved visions had been only demonic delusions plagued her. During a moment of extreme distress, she cried out: "Oh Love, heretofore have I never known Thee. Why leavest Thou me in this manner?"[2] She feared she would die from the intense pain of Love's absence. Then she grieved even more profoundly because death did not come.

As is common among the great mystics, the sense that God had just reason to abandon her dominated the final stage of her dark night of the spirit. Her every vice awakened, and she was plunged into the deepest spiritual darkness possible. Dying mystically, Angela proved her love to be genuine through humble, steadfast acceptance of contempt and hardships. God taught her that all good comes not from oneself but from uncreated Love. Thus was she born to the inner freedom to love Love as much as Love loved her.

In one especially perceptive chapter, Angela describes how one may know "that God has entered the soul."[3] The soul experiences unexpected fire, love, and sweetness. It knows—but not with full assurance—that God is present. On occasion, the soul mystically sees God, hears his words, and experiences great illuminations. Then God "embraces" the soul and produces such "unction" that the soul cannot doubt his presence. Even the body and psyche perfectly obey the spirit and outwardly radiate the light and love within.

The Franciscan tone of her work is unmistakable. Like Francis, she modeled her life on the poor, suffering, humiliated, and crucified Christ—not the Christ of glory or the almighty Lord (*Pantokrator*). So powerfully did God's love as manifested on the cross penetrate her spirit that she received some of Christ's wounds on her body. And like Francis, she perceived that the "world is full of God."

During the last 12 years of Angela's life, she enjoyed a wide reputation as a spiritual director and teacher. As the guiding light for a large group of people in Italy and elsewhere, she wrote many letters of spiritual counsel, spoke out against the heresies of her day, and was designated "Mistress of Theology" by the many theologians and priests who sought her advice. Her wisdom and ardent virtue converted the young, brilliant Umberto da Casale from a self-indulgent friar into a person who eventually became a luminary of the "Spirituals"—the more conservative wing of the Franciscan movement.

The text was selected because few mystics have asserted with such boldness that they saw God "as clearly as possible in this life." Prior to vision eight, Angela had a "visionless" vision of the Trinity in total but exquisite darkness. But the eighth vision takes her beyond the darkness into the trinitarian light and transforms her. Angela now perceives with "clarity, sweetness, and assurance" how God is in all things, how Christ is present in the eucharist, and how deliciously beautiful is her own soul. This vision "enlarged" her mind so that she understands and knows God better, learns divine secrets, and plumbs the mysteries of the Scriptures.

However, the experience of her indestructible union with God as a foretaste of heavenly glory and the joy that transcends all previous joys is the most significant aspect of Angela's vision. There is no text in the Christian mystical tradition that speaks so eloquently of the joy "in the unspeakable manifestation of God."

This vision engendered in the inner "chamber" of Angela's soul an unassailable sense of God's presence, although of varying intensity. It withdrew her from all concepts and images, even those of Christ's humanity. However, because she had been made experientially one with Christ, she "constantly rejoiced in the humanity of Christ,"[4] undoubtedly in a way beyond form or figure.

The selected text also indicates a paradox: The mystics comprehend what they claim is beyond comprehension; they speak about what they maintain is beyond words. Angela frequently protests that what she sees and experiences is beyond words, images, and the mind. To speak about it, she calls "blasphemy." It makes her tongue "dumb." She avers that she cannot even "stammer" about what she sees and experiences. Nonetheless, Angela writes with eloquence, conciseness, and clarity about what she declares to be inexpressible. She is the nightingale of the ineffable.[5]

THE TEXT

THE BOOK OF DIVINE CONSOLATION[6]

EIGHTH VISION AND CONSOLATION, WHEREIN SHE BE-
HELD GOD AS CLEARLY AS IS POSSIBLE IN THIS LIFE, IN
WHICH VISION SHE ACQUIRED STRENGTH IN GOOD IN-
TENTIONS AND IN THE PERFECT DELIGHT IN GOD
Being thus exalted in spirit during the time of Lent, therefore, I was joined with God in a manner other than was customary for me. Methought I was in the midst of the Trinity, in a manner higher and greater than was usual, for greater than usual were the blessings I received, and continually were there given unto me gifts full of delight and rejoicing most great and unspeakable. All this was so far beyond anything which had heretofore happened unto me that verily a divine change took place in my soul, which neither saint nor angel could describe or explain. This divine change, or operation, was so profound that no angel or other creature, howsoever wise, would comprehend it, wherefore do I say again that it seemeth

unto me to be evil-speaking and blasphemy if I do try to tell of it.

Here I am drawn forth out of all things wherein I did formerly take delight, such as the life and humanity of Christ and the consideration of those most deep companions whom God had greatly loved from all eternity and had given unto His Son. Likewise did He draw me forth from the aforesaid delight, that is to say, the poverty, suffering, and contempt borne by His Son (wherein I was accustomed to find my repose and my bed); also was I withdrawn from that darkness, in the vision of which I had so greatly rejoiced. And finally I was drawn out of all former states with so much unction and in sleep, that I could in no wise comprehend it, and do only know that now I have not those things.

In these divine benefits and operations which were accomplished in my soul, God did first present Himself unto it thus ineffably in His works; then did He manifest and reveal Himself fully unto the soul, bestowing upon it great gifts, with indescribable clearness and certainty.

There are two ways wherein God showeth Himself unto the soul. One way is when He showeth Himself intimately, and it doth then know Him to be present, as He is present in every creature and in everything that hath being; as much in demons as in good angels, in hell as in Paradise, in adultery and murder, in all good works, and in all things which exist, both beauteous and ill-favored. When I have this unity, therefore, I do rejoice in God no less when I see a bad angel and an evil deed than when I see a good angel or deed; and in this manner doth He most often present Himself unto my soul. And this presentation doth bring enlightenment, with great truth and divine grace, so that when the soul beholdeth this it cannot offend in any way.

Moreover, this enlightenment bringeth many divine benefits unto the soul; for example, when it becometh aware that God is already present, it doth deeply humble itself and is confused by reason of its sins. Also it receiveth much wisdom and divine consolation with great joy.

God showeth Himself in another and more special manner, very different from the foregoing, which likewise giveth joy, but different from the former joy. For here He draweth all the soul unto Himself and worketh many divine things in it, with much greater grace and an unspeakable depth of joy and enlightenment; so that, without any other gifts, this presentation of God is the blessing possessed by saints in the eternal life.

Of the gifts received by the saints in the life eternal, however, some have more and some less. But of these it is impossible to speak, as I have already said, because my words are so feeble that they do deface and blaspheme rather than justly describe. I will only say that amongst these gifts is the enlargement of the mind, whereby it becometh more capable of understanding and knowing God; for when He presenteth Himself unto the soul, He doth reveal and make Himself manifest and doth thus enlarge it to receive gifts and sweetness never known before and greater and deeper than hath been described.

Unto the soul (now drawn out of all darkness) is then vouchsafed the utmost knowledge of God which I do think could be granted. And it is given with so much clearness, sweetness, and certainty, and hath such depth, that the human heart cannot attain it, nor can my heart ever return again to the understanding and knowledge thereof, or to the imagining of aught regarding it, saving only when the supreme God doth vouchsafe unto the soul to be exalted even unto that which the heart cannot reach [on its own]. Therefore is it not possible to say anything whatsoever concerning it, or to find words wherewith to express it; neither can the imagination or the understanding in any way reach unto it, so immeasurably doth it exceed all things.

Thus do we perceive that by nothing that we can think or say can God be exalted. The Holy Scriptures are so far above us that no man—be he the wisest in all the world and possessing all the knowledge it is possible to have in this life—can fully and perfectly know and understand them; there is none whose intelligence would not be always overcome by them.

Of these most excellent and divine workings in the soul whereby God doth manifest Himself, can man in no wise speak or even stammer. But inasmuch as my soul is ofttimes uplifted to know the di-

vine secrets, I do understand wherefore the Holy Scriptures were
written, what they do appear to affirm and deny, that which is easy
and that which is difficult, and why some derive no profit from
them, and why those who do observe them are saved by them.
Thus have I an advantage in knowing these things, and after learning the secrets of God, I can speak some few words with certainty;
yet are my words outside of those divine and ineffable workings,
and in no way do they approach nigh unto them, but rather do they
spoil and blaspheme, as I have always said.

Therefore do I say that if all divine consolations, all spiritual joys,
all heavenly delights which ever were in this world, if all the saints
who have lived from the beginning of the world until now were to
expound and show forth God, if all the worldly delights, both good
and evil, which ever existed were all to be converted into one good
and spiritual joy which should endure until I were made perfect, I
would not, even that I might obtain all this, give or exchange, even
for the space of the twinkling of an eye, that joy which I have in the
unspeakable manifestation of God.

These things I have spoken that I might in some way instill into the
hearts of men the conviction that this unspeakable blessing is infinitely above all those aforesaid things. And I possess it not only for
the space of the opening and shutting of an eye, but ofttimes for a
good while. In that way do I have it with much effect, but in another way—that is to say, with less effect—do I have it almost continually. And albeit I do feel a little of both grief and joy from
without, yet within my soul there is a chamber into which there entereth no sort of grief or joy of any virtue whatsoever, nor anything
else that can be named or expressed. But unto it there entereth that
greatest Good, and in that manifestation of God (which I do blaspheme in thus naming it, seeing that I have no word wherewith to
speak of it perfectly) lieth the whole truth.

In Him, therefore, do I understand and possess all truth that is in
heaven and earth and hell and in all creatures; and so great is the
truth and the certainty that were the whole world to declare the
contrary, I would not believe it, yea, I should mock at it. For I behold Him who is everything; I perceive how surely in Him are all
created things; I likewise perceive how He hath made me capable

of perfectly understanding the aforesaid matters in a way better than there had been until I saw in that great darkness wherein I did so rejoice. For I do behold myself thus alone with God, wholly clean, wholly pure, wholly sanctified, wholly upright, wholly assured, and wholly celestial in Him, and when I am in this state, I do remember naught else.

Once when I was in that state, the most high God spake thus unto me: "Daughter of divine wisdom, perfect temple of delight, joy of joys; daughter of true peace, in thee reposeth the Holy Trinity and the whole truth, and thus thou holdest Me and I hold thee."

One of the operations of the soul vouchsafed unto it by our Lord God is that with great rejoicing I do most fully understand how God entereth into the most holy Sacrament of the Altar, together with that most high and noble company. But when I remain outside of that state I do perceive myself to be full of sin, obedient unto sinfulness, unjust, unclean, wholly false, and earthly. Nevertheless, I do stay quiet, having in me a divine and constant unction, above all which I have ever felt in all my days.

I came not unto that aforesaid state of mine own self, but I was led and drawn thereunto by God; so that, albeit of mine own self I should not have known how to desire or ask for it, I am now in that state continually. Ofttimes is my soul uplifted to God without my will or consent, and when I am not hoping or thinking to receive aught from Him, my soul is suddenly exalted and dominated by Him. And when thus exalted I understand the whole world and do believe myself in heaven with God instead of upon the earth. This state is far more excellent than any other I have experienced; it is so full of satisfaction, so clear, ennobling, and enlarging that I never felt any other state approaching unto it.

This manifestation of God have I experienced more than a thousand times, and each one was different from the others. Thus once at the Feast of Saint Mary at Candlemas I did have that unspeakable manifestation of God, and while it was being revealed unto the soul, the soul did behold a representation of itself; and it beheld itself more noble and high than it could possibly imagine or understand, and I could not otherwise have believed that either mine own soul or the souls of those in Paradise could be of such nobility. For my soul did then behold itself in such wise that it could not understand itself. If, therefore, the soul which is finite and circumscribed could not comprehend its own self, how much less could it comprehend its Creator who is immense, infinite, and boundless?

Then did my soul present itself before God with the utmost assurance; it had no fear whatsoever, but it went into God's presence with the greatest joy it had ever felt, with a new and most excellent pleasure, in a manner so miraculous, so new and clear that my own soul could never have understood such a thing. At this meeting of my soul with God (when I saw and understood the aforesaid unspeakable manifestation of God), the most high God spake unto me certain words which I do not desire should be written down; and when the soul returned unto itself, it found and retained within itself the consciousness that it could endure all suffering and torment for God's sake and that by nothing whatsoever that could be done or said could it henceforth be separated from God.

Then did my soul exclaim and say, "Oh, most sweet Lord, who can separate me from Thee?" And I heard a voice make answer that nothing could separate me from Him because of His grace.

All these things did I hear spoken by God in a manner more wondrous than I can describe. It was likewise told me that the aforesaid unspeakable manifestation of God is that Good enjoyed by the saints in the life eternal, and that this Good is naught else save this, but otherwise experienced and so different from the other that the lowest of the saints who hath the least in the life eternal hath yet more than can be given unto any soul before the death of the body.

That is what my soul hath understood in that marvelous manifestation of God.

The Spanish "Fool of Love," Ramon Lull, espouses in lovely poems and often cryptic fables a "seraphic" mysticism of love and a "cherubic" mysticism of understanding which stresses that will, understanding, and memory must ascend in contemplation of the Beloved.

RAMON LULL

Born in Palma, Majorca, shortly after the end of Muslim domination, Ramon Lull grew up in an atmosphere permeated by a variety of religious traditions and ethnic groups. During his years of service as a page at the Majorcan royal court, he composed troubadour-style love songs for his mistresses, a hobby he continued even after his marriage.

While composing one of these songs at 30 years of age, Christ crucified appeared to Lull. This vision occurred five times and transformed the worldly troubadour into Christ's troubadour. Now, Lull desired only to sing of God's love and to be a "Fool of Love." Attracted to the Franciscan ideals of poverty and self-emptying love, he eventually became one of the most distinguished members of the Franciscan Third Order.

The desire both to convert the Arabic-speaking world and to achieve a Christian-Muslim synthesis haunted him. Thus, this Majorcan missionary lived in, wrote to, preached to, and held discussions with almost half of the medieval world. Highly unusual for Lull's day was his conviction that Islam was not a false but only an incomplete religion. His tolerant spirit both valued and emphasized the importance of God's grace in conversion. In his later years, he became less tolerant, and was imprisoned, banished, and deported by Muslims on numerous occasions, and he was finally stoned to death by North African Moors when well into his eighties. Although never canonized, Lull was beatified by Pope Pius IX in 1858, and is revered as *Doctor Illuminatus* by the Franciscans.

In 1272, on Mount Ramada, Lull had a mystical illumination in which he saw the entire world in relationship to God's attributes. This "cherubic" experience convinced him that all human wisdom pales before mystical knowledge. For this reason, he stressed that memory and reason must also join will in the ascent to God.

Ironically, however, *Doctor Illuminatus* is perhaps best known as the "Fool of Love." His "seraphic" mysticism of love proceeds by way of Franciscan folly for the sake of Love. Lull's most famous work, *The Book of the Lover and Beloved* (part of a much larger work, the *Blanquerna*[1]), was composed as a guide to contemplation and contains one short passage for each day of the year. Replete with Franciscan tenderness, love of God, and devotion to the incarnation and Christ's passion, it is redolent with Islamic modes of mystical expression.

At first glance, the work appears to be a collection of love aphorisms. However, the three main characters—the Lover, the Beloved, and Love—give the book its unity. The Lover denotes the seeking Christian and, at times, Christ himself. The Beloved is God, whom the Lover seeks on a long and dangerous journey. Love is a mysterious transcendent person that represents both the love of the Lover and the Beloved. Lull's book attained such popularity that it has been called the second-greatest devotional book in the Western World, second only to *The Imitation of Christ*.

The texts were selected to illustrate Lull's poetic skills and his use of often cryptic fables (in imitation of the Muslim Sufis) to underscore the book's ideal: perfect union of the Beloved and the Lover. Although the "Lover and the Beloved are distinct beings," "they are one reality in essence." "As water mingles with wine" and "as heat is with light," so do Lover and the Beloved become one. In fact, the relationship among Lover, Beloved, and Love offers a "demonstration of the Trinity."

The selections also bring to light Lull's Christ-centered mysticism. Because of Christ's divine and human natures, the Beloved descends to empower the Lover to ascend. Although the Lover's heart may soar, the Beloved must still be loved "in the abyss of this world" and contemplated "in tribulations and trials."

Lull's "seraphic" mysticism of love and "cherubic" mysticism of understanding underscores that will, understanding, and memory must ascend in contemplation of the Beloved. The light from the Beloved banishes all darkness and sin. Through light, the Beloved "reveals himself to his lovers." Nonetheless, the madness of love sometimes takes away will and reason, leaving only the "remembrance of his remembrance of his Beloved."

Selected text no. 97 is one of the loveliest paeans to Love in the Christian mystical tradition; nos. 277, 348, 350, 351, some of the most cryptic and intriguing. For Lull, love is both a "bondage" and "liberty." He lived what he wrote: "In whatever you do, you must love, for this is Love's command."[2]

THE TEXTS

THE BOOK OF THE LOVER AND BELOVED[3]

1. The Lover asked his Beloved if there was anything remaining in him which was still to be loved. And the Beloved answered that he still had to love that by which his own love could be increased.

26. The birds sang dawn hymns, and the Lover who is the dawn, woke. The birds ended their song, and the Lover died in the dawn for his Beloved."

27. The bird sang in the garden of the Beloved. The Lover came and said to the bird, "If we do not understand one another in speech, we can make ourselves understood by love, for in your song I see my Beloved before my eyes."

47. The Lover was all alone in the shade of a fair tree. Men passed by that place, and they asked him why he was alone. And the Lover answered, "I am alone now that I have seen you and heard you. Until now, I was in the company of my Beloved."

50. Whether Lover and Beloved are near or far is all the same, for

their love mingles as water mingles with wine. They are joined as closely as heat is with light. They agree and are as closely united as Essence and Being.

54. The Lover went through the city like one who was a fool, singing of his Beloved, and men asked him if he had gone mad. He answered, "My Beloved has taken my will, and I have yielded up to him my understanding. So there is nothing left in me except memory by which I remember my Beloved."

56. The heart of the Lover soared to the heights of the Beloved, so that he might not be prevented from loving him in the abyss of this world. And when he reached his Beloved, he contemplated him with sweetness and delight. But the Beloved led him down again to this world so that he might contemplate him in tribulation and griefs.

67. The Lover was gazing on a place where he had seen his Beloved. And he said, "Ah, place, which recalls the blessed haunts of my Beloved. You will tell my Beloved that I suffer trials and adversities for his sake." And that place answered, "When your Beloved hung on me, he bore greater trials and adversities for love of you than all other trials and adversities that Love could give to its servants."

72. Many people were with the Lover, who complained that his Beloved did not increase his love and that Love gave him trials and sorrows. The Beloved replied that the trials and sorrows for which he blamed Love were the increase of love itself.

78. The Lover cried aloud to all men and said, "Love bids you love always—in walking and sitting, waking and sleeping, in speech and in silence, in buying and selling, weeping and laughing, joy and sorrow, gain and loss. In whatever you do, you must love, for this is Love's commandment."

97. They asked the Lover, "Where do you come from?" He answered, "From love." "To whom do you belong?" "I belong to love." "Who gave birth to you?" "Love." "Where were you born?" "In love." "Who brought you up?" "Love." "How do you live?" "By Love." "What is your name?" "Love." "Where do you come from?" "From Love." "Where are you going?" "To love." "Where

do you live?" "In love." "Have you anything except love?" "Yes," he answered, "I have faults, and I have sins against my Beloved." "Is there pardon in your Beloved?" "Yes," answered the Lover, "in my Beloved there is mercy and justice, and therefore I am lodged between fear and hope."

100. The light of the Beloved's dwelling place came to enlighten the dwelling of the Lover, to cast out its darkness, and to fill it with joys, griefs, and thoughts. And the Lover cast everything out of his dwelling so that there would be room in it for his Beloved.

114. While the Lover was walking in this way, he found a hermit sleeping near a pleasant spring. The Lover woke the hermit, and asked him if he had seen the Beloved in his dreams. The hermit answered that, whether he was awake or asleep, his own thoughts, too, were held captive in the prison of Love. The Lover greatly rejoiced because he had found a fellow prisoner, and they both wept, for the Beloved has only a few lovers like this.

124. They asked the Lover, "What is the greatest darkness?" He answered, "The absence of my Beloved." "And what is the greatest light?" "The presence of my Beloved."

139. The Lover forgot everything that existed beneath the high heavens, so that his understanding might soar higher toward a knowledge of the Beloved, whom his will desired to contemplate and preach.

152. The Beloved silenced his Lover, and the Lover received comfort by gazing upon his Beloved.

163. Love and Indifference met in a garden where the Lover and the Beloved were talking in secret. And Love asked Indifference what was his intention in coming to that place. He replied, "So that the Lover may cease to love, and the Beloved may cease to be honored." The words of Indifference greatly displeased the Beloved and the Lover, and their love was increased so that it might vanquish and destroy Indifference.

201. "Tell us, Lover! Do you possess riches?" "Yes," he replied, "I have love." "Do you possess poverty?" "Yes," he replied, "because my love is no greater, and because it fills so few others with love

that they may exalt the honor of my Beloved."

206. There was an eclipse in the heavens and darkness over all the earth. And it recalled to the Lover that for a long time sin had banished his Beloved from his will, and so the darkness had banished the light from his understanding. This is that light by which the Beloved reveals himself to his lovers.

211. Love and loving, Lover and Beloved, are so closely united in the Beloved that they are one reality in Essence. And Lover and Beloved are distinct beings, which agree, without any contrary element or diversity in Essence. Therefore the Beloved is to be loved above all other objects of affection.

226. The will of the Lover desired to soar on high so that he might greatly love his Beloved. So he commanded the understanding to soar as high as it might, and in the same way the understanding commanded the memory. So all three mounted to the contemplation of the Beloved in his honors.

227. The will of the Lover left him and gave itself up to the Beloved. And the Beloved gave it into the captivity of the Lover so that he might love and serve him.

249. Love destroyed all that was in the heart of his faithful Lover so that he might live and have free course there. And the Lover would have died if he had not had remembrance of his remembrance of his Beloved.

258. The Beloved is far above Love. The Lover is far beneath it. And Love, which lies between these two, makes the Beloved descend on the Lover, and makes the Lover rise toward the Beloved. This ascending and descending are the beginning and the life of that love by which the Lover suffers and the Beloved is served.

259. On the right side of Love stands the Beloved, and on the left side is the Lover. And so he cannot reach the Beloved unless he passes through Love.

261. The Beloved made for his Love Two like himself, to be equally loved in honor and worth. And the Lover bore equal love for all Three, although love is one only in significance of the essential Unity of One in Three.

295. "Tell us, Fool! What is love?" He answered, "Love is that which throws the free into bondage, and gives liberty to those who are in bonds." And who can say whether love is nearer to liberty or bondage?

297. "O Beloved," said the Lover, "I come to you, and I walk in you, for you call me. I go to contemplate contemplation in contemplation, with contemplation of your virtue. I am in your virtue, and with your virtue I come to your virtue, from which I take virtue. And I greet you with your greeting, which is my greeting in your greeting, by which I hope for eternal greeting in blessing of your blessing, in which I am blessed in my blessing."

300. "O Beloved, in the prison house of love you hold me enthralled by your love, which has enamored me of itself, through itself and in itself. For you are nothing else to me but love, in which you make me to be alone, with your love and your honors for my only company. For you alone are in me alone, who am alone with my thoughts, because your aloneness in virtues makes me praise and honor its worth without fear of those who do not know you and do not have you alone in their love."

328. The Lover lifted up the powers of his soul and mounted the ladder of humanity to glory in the Divine Nature. And by the Divine Nature he caused the powers of his soul to descend and glory in the human nature of his Beloved.

348. As the Lover contemplated his Beloved, his understanding conceived subtleties, and his will was enkindled with love. In which of the two do you think his memory grew more fruitful in thinking on his Beloved?

350. The Lover gazed upon himself so that he might be a mirror in which to behold his Beloved, and he gazed upon his Beloved as in a mirror in which he might have knowledge of himself. Which of these two mirrors do you think was nearer to his understanding?

351. Theology and Philosophy, Medicine and Law met the Lover who inquired of them if they had seen his Beloved. The first wept, the second was doubtful, but the other two were glad. What do you think is the significance of each of these happenings to the Lover

who is seeking his Beloved?

362. Two lovers met. One revealed his Beloved, and the other comprehended him. And there was a dispute about which of those two was nearer to his Beloved. For the solution, the Lover took knowledge from the demonstration of the Trinity.

[Appendix] The Lover one day went into a cloister, and the monks asked him if he, too, were a Religious. "Yes," he answered, "of the Order of my Beloved." "What rule do you follow?" "The rule of my Beloved." "To whom are you vowed?" He answered, "To my Beloved." "Do you possess your will?" He answered, "No, it is given to my Beloved." "Have you added anything to the rule of your Beloved?" "Nothing can be added to that which is already perfect." "And why," continued the Lover, "do you who are Religious not take the Name of my Beloved? May it not be that, as you bear the name of another, your love may grow less, and that, hearing the voice of another, you may not catch the voice of my Beloved?"

[Appendix] The Lover gazed at the rainbow, and it seemed to him as if it were of three colors. And he cried, "O marvellous distinction of three, for the three together are one! And how can this be in the image unless it be so of itself, in truth?"

The founder of Rhineland mysticism, Meister Eckhart, was first and foremost a high-powered philosopher and mystical theologian who speculated about the divine-human intercourse in the "spark of the soul" and the implications of that union for authentic Christian living.

MEISTER ECKHART

Born in a Thuringian village called Hochheim, the founder of Rhineland mysticism entered the Dominican Order at Erfurt when he was approximately 15 years old. Because of his prodigious intellectual promise, Eckhart was sent to study at Europe's most prestigious university, Paris, and later, at Cologne. He received his Master's degree from Paris—hence his moniker, "Meister"—and taught there on three different occasions. Later, Eckhart spent ten years teaching theology at Strasbourg where he also attained fame as a preacher and spiritual director.

Eckhart earned more than the academic respect of his Dominican confreres. Several positions of high authority in his Order interlaced with his academic career. However, in 1326, the Franciscan Archbishop summoned Eckhart to Cologne and charged him with heresy. His famous *Defense* (*Rechtfertigungsschrift*)[1] vigorously denies that the two lists of propositions drawn up from his writings are heretical, and contains the now-famous statement: "For I am able to err, but I cannot be a heretic, since one has to do with the intellect and the other with the will."

Appealing to the Holy See, Eckhart left for Avignon to defend himself but died before the case was concluded. On March 27, 1329, Pope John XXII condemned the two lists of propositions according to their "obvious meaning," a relatively benign condemnation prompted by Eckhart's undoubtedly orthodox intent and sincere submission to Church authority.

Many factors led to Eckhart's condemnation. He participated in the Dominican-Franciscan controversy of the age. The Franciscans advocated a return to Augustinian theology; the Dominicans championed Scholasticism. Many designated Scholasticism a new enlightenment because of its readiness to enrich theology with Greek (especially Aristotle), Arabic, and Hebrew sources; others branded it as paganism in disguise.

Because the Dominicans were loyal to the pope, Eckhart was also the target for the antipapal partisans of Louis of Bavaria. Moreover, Eckhart had close associations with the Beguines, that is, women's groups devoted to evangelical simplicity, deep prayer, and practical charity, but whose extreme members led to the movement's condemnation at the Council of Vienne in 1312.

It must be admitted that Eckhart's modes of expression, despite their profundity, are at times infelicitous. He seems to have given insufficient attention to the intellectual ability of his audience and to how easily some of his expressions could be misunderstood. Eckhart occasionally succumbed to intellectual abstraction founded on little more than wordplay. Even his greatest supporters admit that not all his statements can be defended.

It must be emphasized that Eckhart was not a mystic in the strict sense, that is, someone who experienced radical purification or illumination by God, let alone union with or transformation into God. This pious and holy priest was first and foremost a high-powered *philosopher* and mystical *theologian* who speculated about the divine-human intercourse in the "spark of the soul" and the implications of that union for authentic Christian living. It is in this sense that Eckhart is a proponent of "ontological" mysticism (*Wesensmystik*).

Moreover, an inextricable connection exists between Eckhart the mystical theologian and Eckhart the Dominican for whom preaching was a primary vocation. In the service of God's word, he dared to speak poetically, to push language to its limits, and to make use of audacious paradoxes to captivate his audiences. His profound message, his unusual ways of expressing it, and his key insights make him difficult to read, understand, and, at times, appreciate. Some commentators contend that Eckhart did for the German language what Dante did for Italian.

Despite his posthumous condemnation, he had a tremendous influence on the German speculative ontological mysticism of John Tauler, Henry Suso, John Ruusbroec, and others in Germany, Switzerland, and the Low Countries. Eckhart also fathered various popular spiritual movements in these areas in the 14th and 15th centuries.

Eckhart enjoyed a resurgence in the 19th century, but he remains a controversial and enigmatic figure. For example, he has been called a monist, a pantheist, a quietist, a mystic of pure inwardness, a this-worldly mystic, a reformer before the Reformation, the father of German idealism, a medieval Zen master, a source for Nazi thinking, the first Marxist, and the darling of those who dogmatize that a mystic must necessarily be an iconoclast.

However, for all his originality, Eckhart has deep roots in medieval scholastic philosophy and theology, Christian neo- Platonism, and the Fathers of the Church. And he must also be understood as a brilliant, profound, pious Dominican preacher and friar with unquestionable loyalty to the Christian faith and to the Church. In fact, attacks on the blatant ecclesiastical abuses of his day are noticeably absent from his writings. But the fact remains that this key figure in Western mysticism remains difficult to categorize.

The first three of the following selections focus on one of Eckhart's favorite themes: the mode of existence of a creature in the divine "womb" prior to its actual creation. In its "primal existence," the creature was a "pure being" and so deeply united with God that God was not "god" (the false god created by the human mind), and the creature could not be conceived of apart from its divine existence.

The texts also stress another significant theme: "the spark of the soul," the Eckhardian icon for the divine-human relationship at its deepest level. To Eckhart, the divine-human union existing from all eternity in the divine mind perdures in the created soul's spark and is of such intensity because (to use another Eckhart image) "the eye in which I see God is the same eye in which God sees me. My eye and God's eye are one eye and one seeing, one knowing, and one loving."[2] Furthermore, the soul's spark is both "virgin"—because empty of all created things—and "wife"—because therein does the Father give birth to the Son and the Holy Spirit springs forth.

This is the proper context for understanding Eckhart's emphasis upon spiritual poverty. If one is to experience the ineffable divine-human union, the birth of the Son, and the spiration of the Holy Spirit in the spark of the soul, one must be emptied of everything—even "god." One must get rid of "god" for God and be "too poor to have a god." Thus, the person must annihilate self in all created things and become "as untrammeled by humanness as he was when he came from God," for God must pour himself into a perfectly empty soul.

Eckhart's radical negative way (apophaticism) is another reason for his emphasis upon perfect spiritual poverty. "Because God's unconditioned being is above god and all distinctions," only the totally naked soul perceives the uncreated light that sees God directly. Only in perfect self-annihilation does one grasp that God and the soul are one.

As the selected texts illustrate, the fully naked soul bursts forth to meet the naked Godhead in the divine desert "untrammeled by humanness." When the person is "as he was when he came from God," Father, Son, Holy Spirit, and the divine essence disappear into the desert Godhead from whence they came. Then the person experiences that he or she is perfectly one with God.

Some commentators benignly interpret Eckhart's bold assertions. They contend that Eckhart is merely emphasizing the creature's impotence to comprehend God and to conceptualize the nature of the divine indwelling. They assert that Eckhart's teaching on the soul's spark is his way of underscoring that God should not be conceived "as being outside the self." The spark-of-the-soul theology allows for a mysticism that finds God in all things, even in the most ordinary.

However, other commentators argue correctly that Eckhart's "spark of the soul" is nonincarnational and worlddenying and reduces the divine-human relationship to one of pure interiority. Nothing matters except this inner core. Thus, Eckhart paved the way for quietism, the view that God "wants to work in us without us." Self-annihilation, according to this view, acts only to suppress all inner activity. It calls for complete passivity and eschews striving for virtue, active prayer, and the sacramental life.

These same commentators maintain rightly that Eckhart seemingly identifies the soul's spark and God, obliterating the unity-in-difference between God and creatures. His emphasis on God's radical oneness "beyond all distinctions," in which Father, Son, Holy Spirit, and divine essence disappear creates a new god: a totally unknown Godhead that has nothing to do with the known triune God of revelation. For other commentators, Eckhart's god is a "quarternity," that is, a four-some god comprised of a Trinity and a distinct Godhead.

The last text was selected to illustrate a more moderate Eckhart who teaches three paths to God. One walks the first path by seeking and finding God in all things; the second "pathless" path, "beyond self and all things, beyond will and images," requires the voiding of the mind of all created things. The third path is both a path and a "being-at-home," because one follows Christ who is the way. God leads a person on the third path of the "one beloved Christ" "by the light of his Word" and "embraced by the love of the Spirit."[3]

THE TEXTS

BLESSED ARE THE POOR[4]
Now, there are two kinds of poverty. One is external poverty, and it is good and much to be praised in people who take it upon themselves willingly, for the love of our Lord Jesus Christ, for he himself practiced it in the earthly realm. Of this poverty I shall say nothing more, for there is another kind of poverty, an inward poverty. . . . He is a poor man who wants nothing, knows nothing, and has nothing. . . . For if one wants to be truly poor, he must be as free from his creature will as when he had not yet been born. For, by the ever-

lasting truth, as long as you will do God's will and yearn for eternity and God, you are not really poor, for he is poor who wills nothing, knows nothing, and wants nothing.

Back in the Womb from which I came, I had no god and merely was, myself. I did not will or desire anything, for I was pure being, a knower of myself by divine truth. Then I wanted myself and nothing else. And what I wanted, I was, and what I was, I wanted, and thus, I existed untrammeled by god or anything else. But when I parted from my free will and received my created being, then I had a god. For before there were creatures, God was not god, but, rather, he was what he was. When creatures came to be and took on creaturely being, then God was no longer God as he is in himself, but god as he is with creatures.

Now we say that God, insofar as he is only god, is not the highest goal of creation, nor is his fullness of being as great as that of the least of creatures, themselves in God. . . . Therefore, we pray that we may be rid of god, and taking the truth, break into eternity, where the highest angels and souls, too, are like what I was in my primal existence, when I wanted what I was and was what I wanted. Accordingly, a person ought to be poor in will, willing as little and wanting as little as when he did not exist. This is how a person is poor, who wills nothing. . . . More: he shall be quit and empty of his own knowledge, as he was when he did not exist, and let God achieve what he will and be as untrammeled by humanness as he was when he came from God.

Now the question is raised: In what does happiness consist most of all? Certain authorities have said that it consists in loving. Others say that it consists in knowing and loving, and this is a better statement. But we say that it consists neither in knowledge nor in love, but in that there is something in the soul, from which both knowledge and love flow and which, like the agents of the soul, neither knows nor loves. To know this is to know what blessedness depends on. This something has no "before" or "after," and it waits for nothing that is yet to come, for it has nothing to gain or lose. Thus, when God acts in it, it is deprived of knowing that he has done so. What is more, it is the same kind of thing that, like God, can enjoy itself. . . .

ca. 1260-ca. 1328 *TEXTS*, MEISTER ECKHART 297

If it is the case that a man is emptied of things, creatures, himself, and god, and if still god could find a place in him to act, then we say: as long as that [place] exists, this man is not poor with the most intimate poverty. For God does not intend that man shall have a place reserved for him to work in, since true poverty of spirit requires that man shall be emptied of god and all his works, so that if God wants to act in the soul, he himself must be the place in which he acts—and that he would like to do. . . .

Thus we say that a man should be so poor that he is not and has not a place for God to act in. To reserve a place would be to maintain distinctions. *Therefore I pray God that he may quit me of god,* for [his] unconditioned being is above god and all distinctions. It was here [in unconditioned being] that I was myself, wanted myself, and knew myself to be this person [here before you], and therefore, I am my own first cause, both of my eternal being and of my temporal being. To this end I was born, and by virtue of my birth being eternal, I shall never die. It is of the nature of this eternal birth that I *have been* eternally, that I *am* now, and *shall be* forever. What I am as a temporal creature is to die and come to nothingness, for it came with time, and so with time it will pass away. In my eternal birth, however, everything was begotten. I was my own first cause as well as the first cause of everything else. If I had willed it, neither I nor the world would have come to be! If I had not been, there would have been no god. There is, however, no need to understand this.

A great authority says: "His bursting forth is nobler than his efflux." When I flowed forth from God, creatures said: "He is a god!" This, however, did not make me blessed, for it indicates that I, too, am a creature. In bursting forth, however, when I shall be free within God's will and free, therefore, of the will of god and all his works, and even of god himself, then I shall rise above all creature kind, and I shall be neither god nor creature, but I shall be what I was once, now, and forevermore. I shall thus receive an impulse which shall raise me above the angels. With this impulse, I receive wealth so great that I could never again be satisfied with a god, or anything that is a god's, nor with any divine activities, for in bursting forth I discover that God and I are One. Now I am what I was and I neither add to nor subtract from anything, for I am the un-moved Mover, that moves all things. Here, then, a god may find no "place" in man, for by his poverty the man achieves the being that was always his and shall remain his eternally. Here, too, God is identical with the spirit and that is the most intimate poverty dis-coverable. . . .

THE BIRTH OF THE SON IN THE SOUL[5]

. . . .Those in hell are in everlasting torment, but they would not want to lose their lives, not the devils or the souls of men, for their life is so precious that it flows without any medium from God into the soul. And because it flows from God without medium they want to live. What is life? God's being is my life. If my life is God's being, then God's existence must be my existence and God's is-ness is my is-ness, neither less nor more. . . .

The Father gives birth to his Son in eternity, equal to himself. "The Word was with God, and God was the Word" (John 1:1); it was the same in the same nature. Yet I say more: He has given birth to him in my soul. Not only is the soul with him and he equal with it, but he is in it, and the Father gives his Son birth in the soul in the same way as he gives him birth in eternity and not otherwise. He must do it whether he likes it or not. The Father gives birth to his Son without ceasing; and I say more: He gives birth not only to me, his Son, but he gives birth to me as himself and himself as me and to me as his being and nature. . . .

In the innermost source, there I spring out in the Holy Spirit, where there is one life and one being and one work. Everything God per-forms is one; therefore he gives me, his Son, birth without any dis-tinction. My fleshly father is not actually my father except in one little portion of his nature, and I am separated from him; he may be dead and I alive. Therefore, the heavenly Father is truly my Father, for I am his Son and have everything that I have from him, and I am the same Son and not a different one. Because the Father per-forms one work, therefore his work is me, his Only-Begotten Son without any difference.

"We shall all be completely transformed and changed into God" (2 Corinthians 3:18). See a comparison. In the same way, when in the sacrament bread is changed into the Body of the Lord, however many pieces of bread there were, they still become one Body. Just so, if all the pieces of bread were changed into my finger, there would still not be more than one finger. But if my finger were changed into the bread, there would be as many of one as the other. What is changed into something else becomes one with it. I am so changed into him that he produces his being in me as one, not just similar. By the living God, this is true! There is no distinction.

The Father gives his Son birth without ceasing. Once the Son has been born he receives nothing from the Father because he has it all, but what he receives from the Father is his being born. In this we ought not to ask for something from God as if he were a stranger. . . . One should not accept or esteem God as being outside oneself, but as one's own and as what is within one; one should not serve or labor for any recompense, not for God or for his honor or for anything that is outside oneself, but only for that which one's own being and one's own life is within one. . . . God and I, we are one. I accept God into me in knowing; I go into God in loving. There are some who say that blessedness consists not in knowing but in willing. They are wrong; for if it consisted only in the will, it would not be one. . . .

THE DIVINE DESERT[6]

. . . I say the same about the man who has annihilated himself in himself and in God and in all created things; this man has taken possession of the lowest place, and God must pour the whole of himself into this man, or else he is not God. I say in the truth, which is good and eternal and enduring, that God must pour out the whole of himself with all his might so totally into every man who has utterly abandoned himself that God withholds nothing of his being or his nature or his entire divinity, but he must pour all of it fruitfully into the man who has abandoned himself for God and has occupied the lowest place. . . .

Sometimes I have spoken of a light that is uncreated and not capable of creation and that is in the soul. I always mention this light in my sermons; and this same light comprehends God without a medium, uncovered, naked, as he is in himself; and this comprehension is to be understood as happening when the birth takes place.

Here I may truly say that this light may have more unity with God than it has with any power of the soul, with which, however, it is one in being. . . .

That is why I say that if a man will turn away from himself and from all created things, by so much will you be made one and blessed in the spark in the soul, which has never touched either time or place. This spark rejects all created things, and wants nothing but its naked God, as he is in himself. It is not content with the Father or the Son or the Holy Spirit, or with the three Persons so far as each of them persists in his properties. I say truly that this light is not content with the divine nature's generative or fruitful qualities. I will say more, surprisingly though this is. I speak in all truth, truth that is eternal and enduring, that this same light is not content with the simple divine essence in its repose, as it neither gives nor receives; but it simply wants to know the source of this essence, it wants to go into the simple ground, into the quiet desert, into which distinction has never gazed, not the Father, nor the Son, nor the Holy Spirit. In that innermost part, where no one dwells, there is contentment for that light, and there it is more inward than it can be to itself, for the ground is a simple silence, in itself immovable, and by this immovability all things are moved, all life is received by those who in themselves have rational being. . . .

THE RIM OF ETERNITY[7]
. . . Now take note what the rim of eternity is. The soul has three paths to God. One is to seek God in all creatures through all kinds of activity and with flaming love. . . . The second path is a pathless path, free yet bound, raised aloft and wafted off almost beyond self and all things, beyond will and images. However, it does not stand firmly on its own. This is what Christ meant when he said: "Happy are you, Peter. Flesh and blood have not enlightened you," rather, "your being raised up into the intellect [did]. In this you called me God" ("My heavenly Father revealed it to you") (Matthew 16:17). St. Peter did not see God bare [directly], but he had certainly been drawn up by the power of the heavenly Father above all created powers of comprehension to the rim of eternity. . . . Thus you should understand that St. Peter stood on the rim of eternity and was not seeing God in unity [as he is] in his "ownness."

The third path is called a path and yet a being-at-home. It is to see God immediately in his ownness. Dear Christ says, "I am the way, the truth, and the life" (John 14:6). One Christ, one Person; one Christ, one Father; one Christ, one Spirit; three, one; three: way, truth, and life; one beloved Christ in whom all this is. Outside this path, bordering it, are all creatures acting as means. To be led into God on this path by the light of his Word and to be embraced by the love of the Spirit of them both—this is beyond anything one can express in words. Now listen to something astounding. How wondrous to be within and without, to grasp and to be embraced, to see and to be what is seen, to hold and to be held: This is the final end where the spirit remains at rest in the unity of blissful eternity. . . .

"The father of English literature," Richard Rolle,
lived and wrote with the conviction that those who
love God will experience God's fire, warmth, music,
and sweetness not merely in their souls' depths but
with their entire person.

RICHARD ROLLE

Born in the village of Thornton, near Pickering, in the diocese of
York, Hilton studied at Oxford but left before obtaining his degree.
Oxford emphasized philosophy and secular subjects, but Rolle was
captivated by theology and biblical studies. Moreover, those
"puffed up with their complicated arguments" were compromising
his spiritual values. Fashioning a rough hermit's habit out of his
father's raincoat and two of his sister's tunics, Rolle ran away from
home to embrace the eremetical life.

A prolific author of Latin and English devotional treatises and poetry, Rolle was the most widely read spiritual writer up to the time
of the Reformation. Widely acknowledged as a genuine pioneer of
vernacular writing and even as "the father of English literature," he
may have had the gift of "automatic writing," that is, inspired writing produced with little or no conscious effort by the author in an
ecstatic or semi-ecstatic state. Moreover, for centuries, many in England revered him as saint because of his practical tenderness and
compassion toward the sick, the poor, and the neglected, as well as
the miracles performed on their behalf, both during and after his
lifetime.

His most significant work, *The Fire of Love*, is a passionate, sometimes impetuous, defense of the eremetical life that Rolle considered superior to communal, religious life and to the busy life of the
clergy. But unlike the lazy tramps of his time (the *girovagi*), true her-

mits, according to Rolle, "have one controlling motive: They live loving God and their neighbor; they despise worldly approval; they flee, so far as they may, from the face of man; they hold all men more worthy than themselves; they give their minds constantly to devotion; they hate idleness; they withstand manfully the pleasures of the flesh; they taste and seek ardently heavenly things; they leave earthly things on one side without coveting them; and they find their delight in the sweetness of prayer."[1]

Rolle emphasizes throughout his writings that the human soul is made for God *alone*; hence, *only* God can fill it. This love-haunted, love-possessed, love-raptured man insists that only love of God makes us blessed and that love not centered on God is not love at all. Moreover, love of God and of the world cannot coexist in the same soul.

Rolle uses a language redolent of ecstatic transports. After years of solitary prayer, Rolle received intoxicating, melting, ravishing, and annihilating experiences of the Beloved's embraces. His "seraphic" mysticism of love focuses upon God as inner fire, sweetness, and heavenly melody and song. Because of his experiences of the heavenly music, Rolle also possessed a heightened sense of the angelic world. For him, the contemplatives sit among the seraphim, those angels burning with the love of God for all eternity. As he says: "Completely absorbed in supreme love," an "indescribable love blazes in their souls" and make them "love God with such sweetness and devotion. Fundamentally they know nothing within themselves but spiritual heat, heavenly song, divine sweetness."[2]

Due to Rolle's *seeming* emphasis upon the psychosomatic effects of contemplation and his minimal statements on mystical purgation, two later influential English mystics, Walter Hilton and the author of the *Cloud of Unknowing*, distrusted Rolle as a spiritual guide. To this day, Rolle has often been dismissed as overly emotional and superficial.

But Rolle wrote the *Fire of Love* with warmth, gusto, confidence, and an overwhelming conviction that those who love God will experience his warmth, music, and sweetness not merely in the depths of their soul but with their *entire* person. The most trustworthy mystics in the Christian tradition likewise experienced this. It must also be emphasized that Rolle preferred the rapture of love which lifts up the mind to God during contemplation to the more extreme psychophysical trances. One finds in his ardent, affectionate spirituality and mysticism a balance and common sense typical of the English (and other) mystics.

The texts that follow were selected to illustrate Rolle's seraphic mysticism of love and his fierce imagery of burning and passion. He depicted union with God as convivial and sensual participation in a medieval banquet replete with things pleasing to sight, hearing, tasting, smelling, and touching. The selections show Rolle's appreciation for the gift of conversion, God's grace which had transformed his carnal into spiritual desires. One detects his uncompromising aversion to materialism, the values of his age, and his extreme rejection of the "lovers of this world."

The selections also indicate that Rolle "moved from place to place." Thus, he was not a conventional hermit who had received episcopal approval for his way of life. This required proof that he could support himself, either by undertaking some public work (ferryboat operation, small farm, etc.) or by endowment. Neither did Rolle become a total recluse, that is, one totally confined to one house and "enclosed" by a formal episcopal ceremony.

The texts explain Rolle's progressive, purgative, illuminative, and unitive ascent to God. After he had turned his back on the world, the "door of Heaven swung back." God revealed his "face," and the "door remained opened" (heavenly illumination) for almost three years. Then, Rolle entered the banquet hall to enjoy the fire, light, warmth, heavenly song, and sweetness of the unitive life, as much as it is possible here for "mortal man."

The living flame of love penetrated his heart so powerfully that it felt as if "real fire" heated the heart area. He had to keep feeling his breast to make "sure there was no physical reason for it." Because this love intensified his love of Christ and his service of God, he discerned it as God's gracious gift. Although some commentators minimize the somatic dimension of this experience, it must be emphasized that certain contemplative states do produce intense bodily heat, as the practioners of kundalini yoga know.

The texts illustrate, too, the fierce imagery of burning and passion, as well as the enthralling image of Divine Music using Rolle as its human instrument. In him, mysticism had truly taken on musical form. The indented text is a sample of Rolle's poetic outpouring to Christ that fill his writings. The rough, incantatory nature of his poetry evinces a dynamic, vibrant spirit.

The last selection is one of the most beautiful on devotion to Jesus' name in the Christian mystical tradition. Shortly after his conversion, Rolle had experienced the power of using the name to dispel severe demonic temptations, "terrors," and spiritual tepidity. Moreover, use of the name "Jesus" can cause mystical purgation, illumination, and union.

This text also brings out Rolle's anti-intellectualism. For him, if one loves in heart and *deed*, nothing more is needed. He was truly Love's hobo.[3]

THE TEXTS

THE FIRE OF LOVE [4]

CHAPTER 15
As adolescence dawned in my unhappy youth, present, too, was the grace of my Maker. It was He who curbed my youthful lust and transformed it into a longing for spiritual embrace. He lifted and transferred my soul from the depths up to the heights, so that I ardently longed for the pleasures of heaven more than I had ever delighted in physical embraces or worldly corruption. The way all this worked out, if I were minded to publish it, obliges me to preach the solitary life. For the inbreathing Spirit meant me to follow his life and love its purpose. And this, from that moment, with all my limitations, I have sought to do. Yet I was still living amongst those who flourished in the world, and it was their food I used to eat. And I used to listen to that kind of flattery which all too often can drag the most doughty warriors from their heights down to hell itself. But when I rejected everything of this sort to set myself to one purpose, my soul was absorbed with love for my Maker.

I longed for the sweet delights of eternity, and I gave my soul over to love Christ with every ounce of my power. And this she has received from the Beloved, so that now it is solitude that seems most sweet, and those comforts which in their madness men treasure are counted nothing.

From then on, I continually sought quiet, and that although I went from one place to another. . . . From the time my conversion of life and mind began until the day the door of Heaven swung back and his Face was revealed, so that my inner eye could contemplate the things that are above and see by what way it might find the Beloved and cling to him, three years passed—all but three or four months. But the door remained open for nearly a year longer before I could really feel in my heart the warmth of eternal love.

I was sitting in a certain chapel, delighting in the sweetness of prayer or meditation, when suddenly I felt within myself an unusually pleasant heat. At first I wondered where it came from, but it was not long before I realized that it was from none of his creatures but from the Creator himself. It was, I found, more fervent and pleasant than I had ever known. But it was just over nine months before a conscious and incredibly sweet warmth kindled me, and I knew the infusion and understanding of heavenly, spiritual sounds— sounds which pertain to the song of eternal praise and to the sweetness of unheard melody; sounds which cannot be known or heard save by him who had received them, and who himself must be clean and separate from the things of earth.

While I was sitting in that same chapel, and repeating as best I could the night-psalms before I went in to supper, I heard, above my head it seemed, the joyful ring of psalmody, or perhaps I should say, singing. In my prayer, I was reaching out to heaven with heartfelt longing when I was aware, in a way I cannot explain, of a symphony of song, and in myself I sensed a corresponding harmony at once wholly delectable and heavenly, which persisted in my mind. Then and there my thinking itself turned into melodious song, and my meditation became a poem, and my very prayers and psalms took up the same sound. The effect of this inner sweetness was that I began to sing what previously I had spoken; only I sang inwardly, and that for my Creator . . . . Meanwhile, wonder seized me that I should be caught up into such joys while I was still an exile, and that God should give me gifts, the like of which I did not know I could ask for, and such that I thought that not even the most holy could have received in this life. From this I deduced that they are not given for merit, but freely to whomever Christ wills. All the same, I fancy that no one will receive them unless he has a special love for the name of Jesus, and so honors it that he never lets it out of his mind, except in sleep. Anyone to whom this is given will, I think, achieve this very thing.

From the time my conversion began until, by the help of God, I was able to reach the heights of loving Christ, there passed four years and three months. When I had attained this high degree, I could praise God with joyful song indeed! And there that blessed state has remained since that initial impetus: and so it will continue to the end. In fact, it will be more perfect after death, for though it is here that joyful love and burning charity begin, it is there, in the kingdom of heaven, that it will receive its most glorious fulfillment. But a man who has passed through these states in his life profits to no small degree, yet he does not ascend to a higher stage, for he is one who has been confirmed in grace, as it were, and so far as mortal man can be, is at rest . . . .

So, Jesus, I want to be praising you always,
such is my joy.
When I was down and out, you stooped to me and associated me with those
sweet ministers who through the Spirit give
out those lovely and heavenly melodies. I will
express my joy and gratitude because you have
made me like one of those whose superb song
springs from a clear conscience. Their soul
burns with their unending love. And your
servant, too, when he sits in prayer, glows
and loves in his fervor. His mind is
transformed; he burns with fire; indeed, he
expands in the vehemence of his longing. And
virtue, beautiful, true, lovely, and
faultless, flourishes before the face of his

Creator. His song suffuses his whole being,
and with its glad melody lightens his burden,
and brightens his labor . . . .

And now, my brothers, I have told you how I came to the fire of
love: not in order that you should praise me but rather that you
might glorify God. From him I have received whatever I have had
of good. It is so that you who are aware that *everything under the
sun is vanity* might be moved to imitate, not denigrate.

THE FORM OF LIVING[5]

CHAPTER 9

If you wish to be on good terms with God and have his grace direct
your life and come to the joy of love, then fix this name "Jesus" so
firmly in your heart that it never leaves your thought. And when
you speak to him using your customary name "Jesu," in your ear it
will be joy, in your mouth honey, and in your heart melody, because
it will seem joy to you to hear that name being pronounced, sweetness to speak it, cheer and singing to think it. If you think of the
name "Jesu" continually and cling to it devotedly, then it will
cleanse you from sin and set your heart aflame; it will enlighten
your soul, remove turbulence, and eliminate lethargy; it will give
the wound of love and fill the soul to overflowing with love; it will
chase off the the devil and eliminate terror, open heaven, and create
a mystic. Have "Jesu" in your mind, because it expels all wickedness and delusion from his lover; and greet Mary frequently, both
day and night. Great will be the love and joy you feel if you are willing to act in accordance with this instruction. There is no need for
you to be very eager for a lot of books: Hold on to love in heart and
deed, and you've got everything which we can talk or write about.
For the fulfillment of the law is love: On that, everything depends.

Steeped in the magnificent Orthodox liturgy of the fa-
mous Mount Athos monastery, Gregory Palamas is
one of the leading spokesmen of the Greek patristic
tradition and an ardent defender of the hesychast way
of life. No one has written so cogently as Gregory on
Christian apophatic prayer and the body's role in con-
templation.

GREGORY PALAMAS

Gregory Palamas has been called one of the leading spokesmen of
the Greek patristic tradition and the last great mystical theologian
of medieval Mount Athos. This fascinating Byzantine figure was
born in Constantinople of a noble family with connections at the
court of Emperor Andronicus II. While receiving a liberal education
at the imperial university, he befriended the mystical-minded met-
ropolitan of Philadelphia. When he was 22 years old, he entered the
famous Mount Athos monastery, the center par excellence of Byzantine spirituality.

Turkish raids in 1325 prompted him and some of his companions to
go to Thessalonica where they formed a semimonastic community.
After ordination to the priesthood, Palamas and 10 others retired to
a hermitage near Beroea where he lived the hesychastic (*hesychia*=
rest) life of one who rests in God. The hesychast monk spent five
days a week in solitude and in the constant repetition of the Jesus
Prayer, with weekends in community for eucharist and spiritual
conversation.

Returning to Mount Athos in 1331, Palamas continued his hesychast way of life. However, he was soon to be embroiled in a bitter
theological, ecclesiastical, and theological strife that continued for
most of his life. In 1347, he became archbishop of Thessalonica. He

was kidnapped and held for ransom by the Turks from 1354 to 1355 and died in 1359. He was canonized in 1368.

One key source of Orthodox spirituality and mysticism was ecclesiastical and hierarchical: the magnificent Orthodox liturgy. The other significant source was hesychasm. With deep roots in the Desert Fathers, the hesychasts emphasized the unceasing repetition of the Jesus Prayer, "Lord Jesus Christ, Son of God, have mercy on me," or simply the invocation of the name "Jesus."

Controlled breathing and bodily posture consisting of a bowed head and eyes fixed on the heart or body's center were recommended to facilitate this constant prayer. Thereby the hesychasts strove to make the mind (*nous*) descend into the heart in order to attain divinization (*theosis*).

Unlike the intellectualistic orientation of Origen, Evagrius, and Pseudo-Dionysius, the hesychasts' immediate aim was to secure the union of the mind with the *heart* so that their prayer became the prayer of a heart totally dedicated to Jesus. Therefore, they directed their spiritual combat more against inordinate desires and less against distracting thoughts. By reorienting their prayer to the biblical heart, they eliminated the *tendency*, as found in Origen, Evagrius, and Pseudo-Dionysius, to pray with a mind detached from matter in order to reach the abstract One of the Greeks. The hesychasts' prayer of the heart focused on the living, triune One and the incarnate word.

For those chosen by God, the prayer of the heart leads to the vision of the Holy Spirit as uncreated grace. This vision brings about the divinization process. Moreover, the Holy Spirit reveals himself as a transforming divine light that can be seen in this life by those with graced mystical eyes. This "Taboric light" is identical with the light that filled Christ during his transfiguration on Mount Tabor, namely, the uncreated "energy" of the Godhead.

The Taboric light dispels the hesychast's darkness like a lamp in the night. Then it becomes like a full moon in the sky of the heart. Finally, it becomes like the rising sun and prompts the monk to dialogue and union with Christ, now master of the heart.

The hesychast method of prayer, and especially its psychosomatic aspects, were fiercely attacked by Barlaam, a Calabrian monk philosopher. For this antimystical, Platonic humanist the human body could play no role in pure prayer nor be transformed by divine light. He ridiculed the hesychasts as omphalopsychites—those who have their soul in their navels. He denounced them as heretical Messalians, that is, the "praying people" who contended that they could see the Trinity with their physical eyes. Barlaam's philosophical negative way (apophaticism) forced him to deny that one could have a direct experience of God.

From 1338 to 1341, Gregory Palamas wrote nine treaties *For the Defense of Those Who Practice Sacred Quietude,* three groups of three books also called *Triads,* against Barlaam. These treatises offer a magnificent exposition of the Orthodox position on the deification of the human person in Christ and an invincible defense of the hesychasts' position.

Palamas won the day over Barlaam. The *Hagioritic Tome* was accepted by four councils of Constantinople, at which the Byzantine Church affirmed the orthodoxy of hesychast spirituality and mysticism. The *Tome* sanctioned the view that mystical experience is the normal counterpart of a properly oriented ascetical life. Furthermore, it teaches that mystical experience is a foretaste of heaven and a direct experience of God.

The texts that follow were selected to illustrate Palamas's uncompromising rejection of disembodied Platonic prayer. For Barlaam and other Platonists, the body was evil. Thus, during contemplation, the mind must be disciplined to "go out" of the body. One must empty the mind of everything to engender a dizzying emptiness that resulted in intellectual fainting. This corpse-like contemplation required an ascetical life that produced "insensibility" (*analgesia*) that Palamas—in the tradition of the Fathers—branded as "petrification."

In contrast, Palamas's richly *incarnational* spirituality and mysticism centers on the Word made *flesh.* Christian asceticism is orientated toward reordering the passions, not uprooting them. Asceticism, especially those practices "painful to the [sense of] touch," are especially helpful in liberating the whole body-person from disordered passions and engendering "impassibility" (*apatheia*) or genuine Christian psychosomatic wholeness.

Palamas teaches that controlled breathing, concentrating the eye on a point in the body, and unifying oneself "at the center of the belly" (the *hara* of yoga) causes "unified recollection." With the Spirit's grace, the hesychast method of prayer leads to loving knowledge of God that divinizes the entire body-person, resulting in love of neighbor.

The texts also demonstrate Palamas's positive apophaticism. Because Palamas worshipped the ineffable, incomprehensible God, he had experienced "something" beyond both knowing and unknowing. To him, contemplation is more than transsensual and transintellectual negation. Through purity of heart and the Spirit, one attains the "ineffable vision" of God, "participation in divine things," union, and "perfect love [for one's] neighbor." The visionless vision of God may transcend the entire body-person; nonetheless, it is one in which the entire body-person participates. I know of no other author in the Christian mystical tradition who has written so profoundly on genuine Christian apophatic prayer and the body's role in contemplation.

The selected texts contain one of the most beautiful descriptions of Tabor-light mysticism. Because "the divinity of the Word on the mountain [Tabor] glorified with divine light the body conjoined to it," contemplatives are able to behold the "garment of their deification" through Spirit-given illuminations.[1]

THE TEXTS

B. APOPHATIC THEOLOGY AS POSITIVE EXPERIENCE[2]
I. iii. 4.

The human mind also, and not only the angelic, transcends itself, and by victory over the passions acquires an angelic form. It, too, will attain to that light and will become worthy of a supernatural vision of God, not seeing the divine essence, but seeing God by a revelation appropriate and analogous to Him. One sees, not in a negative way—for one does see something—but in a manner superior to negation. For God is not only beyond knowledge but also beyond unknowing . . . .

5. So, when the saints contemplate this divine light within themselves, seeing it by the divinizing communion of the Spirit, through the mysterious visitation of perfecting illuminations—then they behold the garment of their deification, their mind being glorified and filled by the grace of the Word, beautiful beyond measure in His splendor; just as the divinity of the Word on the mountain glorified with divine light the body conjoined to it. For "the glory which the Father gave Him," He Himself has given to those obedient to Him, as the Gospel says, and "He willed that they should be with Him and contemplate His glory."

17. . . . Contemplation, then, is not simply abstraction and negation; it is a union and a divinization which occurs mystically and ineffably, by the grace of God, after the stripping away of everything from here below which imprints itself on the mind, or rather after the cessation of all intellectual activity; it is something which goes beyond abstraction (which is only the outward mark of the cessation). This is why every believer has to separate God from all His creatures, for the cessation of all intellectual activity and the resulting union with the light from on high is an experience and a divinizing end, granted solely to those who have purified their hearts and received grace . . . .

18. Do you now understand that in place of the intellect, eyes, and ears they acquire the incomprehensible Spirit and by Him hear, see, and comprehend? For if all their intellectual activity has stopped, how could the angels and angelic men see God except by the power of the Spirit? This is why their vision is not a sensation, since they do not receive it through the senses; nor is it intellection, since they do not find it through thought or the knowledge that comes thereby but after the cessation of all mental activity . . . .

On the other hand, the mind does not acquire it simply by elevating itself through negation . . . . Thus, beyond prayer, there is the ineffable vision and ecstasy in the vision and the hidden mysteries. Similarly, beyond the stripping away of beings, or rather after the cessation [of our perceiving or thinking of them] accomplished not only in words but in reality, there remains an unknowing which is beyond knowledge; though indeed a darkness, it is yet beyond radiance, and, as the great Denys says, it is in this dazzling darkness that the divine things are given to the saints.

Thus the perfect contemplation of God and divine things is not simply an abstraction; but beyond this abstraction, there is a participation in divine things, a gift and a possession rather than just a process of negation. But these possessions and gifts are ineffable . . .

C. THE HESYCHAST METHOD OF PRAYER AND THE TRANSFORMATION OF THE BODY[3]
I. ii.

1. My brothers, do you not hear the words of the Apostle, "Our bodies are the temple of the Holy Spirit which is in us," and again, "We are the house of God"? For God Himself says, "I will dwell in them and will walk in them, and I shall be their God." So why should anyone who possesses mind grow indignant at the thought that our mind dwells in that whose nature it is to become the dwelling place of God? How can it be that God at the beginning caused the mind to inhabit the body? Did even He do ill? Rather, brother, such views befit the heretics, who claim that the body is an evil thing, a fabrication of the Evil One . . . .

2. This is why we set ourselves against this "law of sin," and drive it out of the body, installing in its place the oversight of the mind and in this way establishing a law appropriate for each power of the soul and for every member of the body . . . . He who has purified his body by temperance, who by divine love has made an occasion of virtue from his wishes and desires, who has presented a mind purified by prayer, acquires and sees in himself the grace promised to those whose hearts have been purified. He can then say with Paul: "God, who has ordered light to shine from darkness, has made His light to shine in our hearts, in order that we may be enlightened by the knowledge of the glory of God in the face of Jesus Christ"; but he adds, "We carry this treasure in earthen vessels." So we carry the Father's light in the face of Jesus Christ in earthen vessels, that is, in our bodies, in order to know the glory of

the Holy Spirit . . . .

3. . . . Thus our heart is the place of the rational faculty, the first rational organ of the body. Consequently, when we seek to keep watch over and correct our reason by a rigorous sobriety, with what are we to keep watch, if we do not gather together our mind, which has been dissipated abroad by the senses, and lead it back again into the interior, to the selfsame heart which is the seat of the thoughts?... Can you not see, then, how essential it is that those who have determined to pay attention to themselves in inner quiet should gather together the mind and enclose it in the body, and especially in that "body" most interior to the body, which we call the heart?

4. . . . to make the mind "go out," not only from fleshly thoughts but out of the body itself, with the aim of contemplating intelligible visions—that is the greatest of Hellenic errors, the root and source of all heresies, an invention of demons, a doctrine which engenders folly and is itself the product of madness. That is why those who speak by demonic inspiration become beside themselves, not knowing what they are saying. As for us, we recollect the mind not only within the body and heart but also within itself.

6. The Father of lies . . . has found accomplices who have even composed treatises toward this end, and who seek to persuade men (even those who have embraced the higher life of hesychasm) that it would be better for them to keep the mind *outside* of the body during prayer. They do not even respect the clear and authoritative words of John, who writes in his *Ladder of Divine Ascent*, "The hesychast is one who seeks to circumscribe the incorporeal in his body."

That is exactly the tradition, and our spiritual Fathers have also handed it down to us, and rightly so. For if the hesychast does not circumscribe the mind in his body, how can he make to enter himself the One who has clothed himself in the body, and Who thus penetrates all organized matter, insofar as He is its natural form?. . .

7. You see, brother, how John teaches us that. . . it is absolutely necessary to recall or keep the mind within the body, when one determines to be truly in possession of oneself and to be a monk worthy

of the name, according to the inner man.

On the other hand, it is not out of place to teach people, especially beginners, that they should look at themselves and introduce their own mind within themselves through control of breathing. A prudent man will not forbid someone who does not as yet contemplate himself to use certain methods to recall his mind within himself, for those newly approaching the struggle find that their mind, when recollected, continually becomes dispersed again. It is thus necessary for such people constantly to bring it back once more; but in their inexperience, they fail to grasp that nothing is more difficult to contemplate and more mobile and shifting than the mind.

This is why certain masters recommend them to control the movement inward and outward of the breath and to hold it back a little; in this way, they will also be able to control the mind together with the breath—this, at any rate, until such time as they have made progress, with the aid of God, have restrained the intellect from becoming distracted by what surrounds it, have purified it and truly become capable of leading it to a "unified recollection." One can state that this recollection is a spontaneous effect of the attention of the mind, for the to-and-fro movement of the breath becomes quieted during intensive reflection, especially with those who maintain inner quiet in body and soul . . . .

8. . . . How should such a one not gain great profit if, instead of letting his eye roam hither and thither, he should fix it on his breast or on his navel, as a point of concentration? For in this way, he will not only gather himself together externally, conforming as far as possible to the inner movement he seeks for his mind; he will also, by disposing his body in such a position, recall into the interior of the heart a power which is ever flowing outward through the faculty of sight. And if the power of the intelligible animal is situated at the center of the belly, since there the law of sin exercises its rule and gives it sustenance, why should we not place there "the law of the mind which combats" this power, duly armed with prayer, so that the evil spirit who has been driven away, thanks to the "bath of regeneration," may not return to install himself there with seven other spirits even more evil, so that "the latter state becomes worse than the first"?

II. ii.

5. When we return to interior reflection, it is necessary to calm the sensations aroused by external activities . . . . It is the body in particular which suffers as regards sensation, especially when we fast and do not provide it with nourishment from without . . . . For as all who have experienced ascetical combat, sensation painful to the touch is of the greatest benefit to those who practice inner prayer . . . .

6. In every case, those who practice true mental prayer must liberate themselves from the passions and reject any contact with objects which obstruct it, for in this way they are able to acquire undisrupted and pure prayer . . . . For it is the case that if we cannot taste mental prayer, not even, as it were, with the slightest touch of our lips, and if we are dominated by passionate emotions, then we certainly stand in need of the physical suffering that comes from fasting, vigils, and similar things, if we are to apply ourselves to prayer. This suffering alone mortifies the body's inclination to sin, and moderates and weakens the thoughts that provoke violent passions. Moreover, it is this which brings about within us the start of holy compunction, through which both the stain of past faults is done away and the divine favor especially attracted, and which disposes one toward prayer . . . .

7. To become "insensible" is in effect to do away with prayer; the Fathers call this "petrification." Was not this man Barlaam the first to . . . criticize those who have real knowledge because they feel physical pain? Indeed, certain of the Fathers have declared that fasting is of the essence of prayer: "Hunger is the stuff of prayer," they say. Others say it is its "quality," for they know that prayer without compunction has no quality . . . . And again: "Prayer is the mother of tears and also their daughter." Do you not see that physical distress not only causes no obstacle to prayer but contributes largely to it . . . .

9. . . . This spiritual grace in the heart, alas, you call "fantasy of the imagination, presenting to us a deceptive likeness of the heart." However, those judged worthy of this grace know that it is not a fantasy produced by the imagination and that it does not originate with us nor appear only to disappear; but rather, it is a permanent

energy produced by grace, united to the soul and rooted in it, a fountain of holy joy that attracts the soul to itself, liberating it from multiform and material images and making it joyfully despise every fleshly thing. . . .

As to that which takes place in the body, yet derives from a soul full of spiritual joy, it is a spiritual reality, even though it does work itself out in the body. . . . Conversely, the spiritual joy which comes from the mind into the body is in no way corrupted by the communion with the body but transforms the body and makes it spiritual, because it then rejects all the evil appetites of the body; it no longer drags the soul downward but is elevated together with it. Thus it is that the whole man becomes spirit, as it is written: "He who is born of Spirit, is spirit." All these things, indeed, become clear by experience.

12. Our philosopher brings the further objection: That to love those activities which are common to the passionate part of the soul and to the body serves to nail the soul to the body and to fill the soul with darkness. But what pain or pleasure or movement is not a common activity of both body and soul?. . .

For just as the divinity of the Word of God incarnate is common to body and soul, since He has deified the flesh through the mediation of the soul to make it also accomplish the works of God; so similarly, in spiritual man, the grace of the Spirit, transmitted to the body through the soul, grants to the body also the experience of things divine, and allows it the same blessed experience as the soul undergoes. The soul, since it experiences divine things, doubtless possesses a passionate part, praiseworthy and divine: or rather, there is within us a single passionate aspect which is capable of thus becoming praiseworthy and divine.

When the soul pursues this blessed activity, it deifies the body also; which, being no longer driven by corporeal and material passions . . . returns to itself and rejects all contact with evil things. Indeed, it inspires its own sanctification and inalienable divinization, as the miracle-working relics of the saints clearly demonstrate. . . .

19. . . . Impassibility [apatheia] does not consist in mortifying the passionate part of the soul but in removing it from evil to good and

directing its energies toward divine things . . . and the impassible man is one who no longer possesses any evil dispositions but is rich in good ones, who is marked by the virtues, as men of passion are marked by evil pleasures; who has tamed the irascible and concupiscent appetites (which constitute the passionate part of the soul) to the faculties of knowledge, judgment, and reason in the soul, just as men of passion subject their reason to the passions. For it is the misuse of the powers of the soul which engenders the terrible passions, just as the misuse of the knowledge of created things engenders the "wisdom which has become folly."

But if one uses these things properly, then through the knowledge of created things, spiritually understood, one will arrive at knowledge of God; and through the passionate part of the soul which has been orientated toward the end for which God created it, one will practice the corresponding virtues: With the concupiscent appetite, one will embrace charity, and with the irascible, one will practice patience. It is thus not the man who has killed the passionate part of the soul who has the preeminence, for such a one would have no momentum or activity to acquire a divine state and right dispositions and relationship with God; but rather, the prize goes to him who has put that part of his soul under subjection, so that by its obedience to the mind, which is by nature appointed to rule, it may ever tend toward God, as is right, by the uninterrupted remembrance of Him. Thanks to this remembrance, he will come to possess a divine disposition and cause the soul to progress toward the highest state of all, the love of God. Through this love, he will accomplish the commandments of Him whom he loves, in accord with Scripture, and will put into practice and acquire a pure and perfect love for his neighbor, something that cannot exist without impassibility.

20. Such is the way which leads through impassibility to perfect love, an excellent way which takes us to the heights. . . .

A cautious disciple of Meister Eckhart and a severe critic of the excessive passivity in the spirituality of the Brethren of the Free Spirit, Tauler preached often in praise of the active life. This Rhineland mystic also emphasized that the Trinity is an "imageless image" who dwells in and is united inextricably with the soul's inmost depths.

JOHANNES TAULER

Many commentators consider Meister Eckhart to be the greatest mystical theologian of the 14th century. His disciple, Johannes Tauler, became the Rhineland's most influential preacher and spiritual director. Though born into a well-off family of the newly ascendant merchant class in Strasbourg, Tauler entered the Dominican Order when he was approximately 15 years old. He received a good education, and during his general studies in Cologne, he indirectly became a disciple of Eckhart. He also met John Ruusbroec, the famous Flemish mystic, and befriended the other renowned Rhineland Dominican mystic, Henry Suso.

It must be emphasized that Tauler lived in a time of trial and upheaval. The conflict between Church and Empire resulted in the pope's exile to Avignon, and great plagues and famines were ravaging Europe. Tauler lived and worked in Strasbourg and Basel, vital centers of learning and commerce. As a mendicant preacher and spiritual director, he came into close contact with the emerging burgher class, many Dominican nunneries, the Beguines, the Brethren of the Free Spirit, and the Friends of God.

The Friends of God was an informal association of people from many walks of life. Nourished by Eckhart's intellectualism and the older German visionary mysticism, they sought a richer and deeper interior life. Tauler not only added clarity, balance, and nuance to Eckhart's system but also propagated, expanded, and transposed its intellectualism into a more affective and practical mystical theology. In this way, Tauler kept the powerful movement within mainstream Christianity.

The Brethren of the Free Spirit was also a loose association of Christians intent upon living a more intense spiritual life. The more extreme Brethren claimed the continuous inspiration of the Holy Spirit, sinlessness, and even identity with God. Nothing mattered except passive surrender to the Spirit. Thus, they eschewed asceticism, virtue, active prayer, and Christian life. Passivity (quietism) and licentiousness often reigned supreme.

Perhaps because of the Brethren's excessive passivity, Tauler preached often in praise of the active life. His sermons illustrate his practical appreciation of farmers, artisans, and craftsmen—without denigrating the aristocracy and its values. Although Tauler never recovered from Eckhart's tragic end, his sermons are gentle, easy of tone, and free of bitterness. But if they were practical and crafted with less linguistic boldness than Eckhart, they likewise encouraged a profound interior life. True to Eckhart's apophatic mysticism, Tauler was more sensitive to the needs of a practical, active spirituality. Because the Friends of God freely adopted his sermons, Tauler had a remarkably wide social impact. In fact, for many centuries, he had a far greater impact than Eckhart on European (not only Rhineland) spirituality and mysticism. Thus, Tauler is a spiritual master in his own right and deserves his title, *Doctor Illuminatus*.

Medieval monastic mysticism focused upon the Latin tradition, Dionysian elements, practical spirituality, the will, and an explicit imitation of Christ. In contrast, medieval Dominican mysticism was more intellectual, neo-Platonic, and emphasized merging with the divine abyss. The sometimes shrill tone of Dominican mysticism's apophaticism was, in part, a reaction to the older German visionary mysticism.

Tauler shared Eckhart's view that the human person preexists in God's mind in essential unity in and with God before his or her creation. Therefore, the mystic's goal is the return of the created spirit into God.

However, Tauler transposes the neo-Platonist mysticism of ascent in a Christian way. Before ascending into God, one must descend into the deepest humility by imitating Christ's self-emptying. In contrast to Eckhart's emphasis upon the birth of the mystical Christ in the soul, Tauler focuses more upon the Trinity's birth. Detachment, self-emptying, self-denial, abandonment—the "labor of the night"—are required for immersion into the "hidden abyss" of the Trinity whose "imageless Image" is in the soul. The entire process is inextricably linked to Christ's passion and death, for to have a "soul full of God," one must have a "body full of suffering."

For example, Christ's five wounds enable the person to escape the five prisons of love of creatures, self-love, inordinate attachment to reason, dependence upon religious feelings and visionary experiences, and self-will. Christ's passion points the way to the innermost part of the soul wherein the hidden darkness of the "supreme, superabundant Unity unfolds into Trinity." Yet, one does not discover in Tauler's writings the ardent love of the man Jesus found in many other Christian mystics.

In contrast to Eckhart's focus upon reason (*Vernunft*), Tauler emphasizes root-will (*Gemüte*). Grounded in and emerging from the soul, this active power is essentially the unity of intellect and will. Root-will empowers a person to be passive actively. When one is drawn into the soul's created and uncreated ground, one voluntarily surrenders to the attraction of the "unfathomable abyss."

Contemporary commentators maintain that Eckhart and Tauler underscore detachment and self-emptying as the means to "turn into the depth of your ground and remain there." In so doing, one gives birth to the Son in the spark of the soul, just as the Father gives birth to the Son from all eternity. This "breakthrough" can occur at any time and in any way. Thus, these commentators contend that "breakthrough-mysticism" is not the same as the classical three-fold path of purgation, illumination, and union.

But this assertion assumes that the three-fold path is a step-by-step process and not simultaneous. These commentators overlook that the detachment and self-emptying necessary for sinking back into the divine abyss require a process of purgation, illumination, and union.

The following text was selected to illustrate how Tauler elevated the German vernacular language to a level beyond that of scholarly Latin. It also exemplifies Tauler's preaching style: he spends no time with the literal meaning of the feast day, gives a brief theological discourse, and then explains in detail the feast's mystical meaning.

The selection also highlights Tauler's trinitarian mysticism. To him, all the Church's feast days find their "consummation" here, because the Trinity is *the* Christian mystery. Tauler emphasizes that the Trinity is an "imageless Image" that dwells in and is united inextricably with the soul's inmost depths. God's grace allows the person free access to this ground where the "soul possesses everything by grace which God possesses by nature."

Thus, Tauler exhorts his listeners to cease being so concerned with external affairs, to appreciate the limits of external devotions, and to melt into the soul's ground. Here the Trinity is born in a darkness transcending all sense and intellectual activity. One must listen to one's own ground, for it is the anchor point of one's life, the beacon of critical discernment. To remain there even briefly has enormous practical effect both for oneself and for others. Discipline, recollection, humility, and true love of God are required if one is to gaze "upon God with one's entire spirit" by love's attraction.[1]

THE TEXT

Sermon 29[2]

[FEAST OF THE BLESSED TRINITY II]
Quod scimus loquimur, et quod vidimus testamur
We speak of what we know, and we bear witness
to what we have seen (John 3:11)
The second interpretation of the Holy Trinity tells us how its image-

less Image dwells in reality in the inmost ground of the soul. Here man can find by grace what God possesses by nature, if only he will let himself sink into that ground, and if he frees himself from all sensual images.

Our dear Lord said: "We speak of what we know, and we bear witness to what we have seen; and our witness you do not receive. If I have spoken of earthly things to you and you do not believe, how will you believe if I shall speak to you of heavenly things?" These words are taken from the Gospel of the exalted feast of the sublime, lofty, and most glorious Trinity. And all the feasts we have observed throughout this year, whatever they commemorated, have led up to this one feast and found their consummation in it, just as the course which creatures run, especially rational creatures, has its goal and end in the Holy Trinity, for in a sense it is both beginning and end. When we come to speak of the Most Blessed Trinity, we are at a loss for words, and yet words must be used to say something for this sublime and ineffable Trinity. To express it adequately is as impossible as touching the sky with one's head. For everything we can say or think can no more approach the reality than the smallest point of a needle can contain Heaven and earth; indeed, a hundred, a thousand times, and immeasurably less than that.

It is utterly impossible for our intellect to understand how the lofty, essential Unity can be single in essence and yet threefold in Persons; how the Persons are distinct from each other; how the Father begets the Son; how the Son proceeds from the Father and yet remains within Him (by comprehending Himself, the Father utters His Eternal Word); how from this comprehension that proceeds from Him, there streams forth an ineffable love, which is the Holy Spirit; and how these wondrous Processions stream back again in essential unity, in ineffable self-delight and self-enjoyment; how the Son and the Holy Spirit are also one. And yet there is an inexpressibly vast distinction between the Persons, although they proceed in an ineffable way in unity of nature. On this subject, a staggering amount of things could be said, and yet nothing would have been said to convey how the supreme, superabundant Unity unfolds into Trinity.

To experience the working of the Trinity is better than to talk about it. In fact, one shies away from a busy scrutiny of this mystery, especially as the words are borrowed from the world as we know it, and also because of the disproportion between the subject and our intelligence, to which all this is unutterably high and hidden. For this subject even surpasses the understanding of the Angels. So let us leave the learned discourses to the scholars: They have to engage in them in order to safeguard the Faith. And they have written weighty volumes on the subject. It is for us to believe in simplicity.

Saint Thomas says: "No one should go beyond what those doctors affirmed, who have experienced and pursued these truths at the source, where they have received them from the Holy Spirit." And though there is no subject more joyous and sweet to the taste, there is also nothing more grievous than falling into error concerning it. Therefore, stop your disputations on that mystery, and believe it in simplicity, entrusting yourselves wholly to God. Even for the great scholars, there is no better way than this, and yet they have never been more subtle in their reasoning than now. You, however, should allow the Holy Trinity to be born in the center of your soul, not by the use of human reason, but in essence and in truth; not in words, but in reality. It is the divine mystery we seek, and how we are truly its Image; for this divine Image certainly dwells in our souls by nature, actually, truly, and distinctly, though of course not in as lofty a manner as it is in Itself.

Above all, cherish this very sweet Image which dwells in you in such a blessed and unique manner. Nobody can express adequately its nobility, for God is in this Image, indeed he is the Image, in a way which surpasses all our powers of comprehension.

Scholars discuss this Image a great deal, trying to express in various natural ways its nature and essence. They all assert that it belongs to the highest faculties of our soul, which are memory, intellect, and will; that these faculties enable us to receive and enjoy the Blessed Trinity. This is indeed true, but it is the lowest degree of perception, leaving the mystery in the natural order. Saint Thomas says that the perfection of the Image lies in its activity, in the exercise of the faculties; that is, in the active memory, in the active intellect, and in the active will. Further than that, Saint Thomas will not go.

Other theologians, however, state—and here we have something of far greater significance—that the Image of the Blessed Trinity rests in the most intimate, hidden, and inmost ground of the soul, where God is present essentially, actively, and substantially. Here God acts and exists and rejoices in Himself, and to separate God from this inmost ground would be as impossible as separating Him from Himself. This is God's eternal decree; He has ordained that He cannot and will not separate Himself. And thus, in the depth of this ground, the soul possesses everything by grace which God possesses by nature. In the measure in which man surrenders himself and turns to that inmost ground, grace is born in the highest way.

A pagan master, Proclus, has this to say on the subject: "As long as man is occupied with images inferior to himself and as long as he does not go beyond them, it is unlikely that he will ever reach this depth. It will appear as an illusion to really believe that this ground exists within us; we doubt that it can actually exist in us. Therefore," he continues, "if you wish to experience its existence, you must abandon all multiplicity and concentrate your attention on this one thing with the eyes of your intellect; and if you wish to rise higher, you must put aside all rational methods, for reason is now beneath you, and then you may become united with the One." And he calls this state a divine darkness: still, silent, at rest, and above all sense perception.

Beloved, it is a disgraceful thing that a pagan philosopher understood and attained this truth, while we are so far from both. Our Lord expressed the same truth when he said: "The kingdom of God is within us." It is to be found in the inmost depth, beyond the activity of our faculties. And so we read in today's Gospel: "We speak of what we know, and we bear witness to what we have seen; and our witness you do not receive." Indeed, how could a person who lives merely by his senses receive this witness? To those who subscribe to such a way of life, that which is beyond the senses appears as an illusion. As our Lord says: "As the heavens are exalted above the earth, so are my ways exalted above your ways, and my thoughts above your thoughts." And Our Lord says the same thing today: "If I have spoken to you of earthly things and you believe not, how will you believe if I shall speak to you of heavenly things?" Recently, I spoke to you about wounded love, and you said that you could not understand me, and yet we were dealing only with earthly things. How can you expect to understand things spiritual and divine?

You are concerned with so many external affairs, always busy with one thing or another; this is not the witness of which Our Lord said: "We bear witness to what we have seen." This witness is to be found in your inmost ground, beyond sensual images; within this ground, the Heavenly Father begat His only-begotten Son, swifter a million times than the twinkling of an eye. And this happens in the swiftness of eternity that is forever new, in the inexplicable splendor of His own Being. Whoever wishes to experience this must turn inward, far beyond these exterior and interior faculties, beyond all that the imagination has ever acquired from outside, so that he may sink and melt into that ground. Then the power of the Father will come and call the soul into Himself through His only-begotten Son, and as the Son is born of the Father and returns into Him, so man is born of the Father in the Son, and flows back into the Father through the Son, becoming one with Him. Thus Our Lord says: "You will call me Father and will not cease to walk after me. This day have I begotten you, through and in my Son." And now the Holy Spirit pours Himself out in inexpressible and overflowing love and joy, flooding and saturating the ground of the soul with His wondrous gifts.

. . . To remain in that state of interior union for just one second is worth more than all exterior works and rules; and it is in the depth of this ground that we should pray for our friends, living or dead. That would be far more efficacious than reciting a hundred thousand Psalters.

This, then, is the true witness: "The Holy Spirit, testifying to our spirit that we are the children of God." And thus we receive this testimony in our hearts, as it says in today's Gospel. In Heaven, that means in the heaven within our souls, there are three who bear witness: the Father, the Word, and the Spirit. They are your witnesses who give the true testimony that you are a child of God. They illuminate the depth of your ground, and thus your own ground becomes your witness. And this witness also testifies against you and against all the disorders within you; and this testimony enlightens your reason, whether you like it or not, and reveals your whole life to you, if you will only listen. Listen carefully to this testimony, and live accordingly if you wish to be saved at the Day of Judgment. If you reject it by your words and deeds and by your whole life, the same witness will condemn you at the last day, and that will be your fault and not God's. Beloved, always listen to this witness within, and you will never regret it.

You have sailed down the Rhine in order to take up a life of poverty. But if you fail to reach this ground within you, no amount of traveling will get you there. Do not waste your energy! Shed all outward attachments, turn inward, and seek the deepest ground of your soul; exterior precepts and techniques will be of no avail. In the lives of the Fathers, we read of a good husband who fled into the forests to avoid these obstacles; he had as many as two thousand brethren under his care, all seeking this same interior ground. And his wife had a community of many under her care. This ground, however, is a single, hidden solitude, utterly sublime, a darkness forever accessible to your free will. No path of the senses will ever lead you there. And then you will say: "I love spiritual people and would like nothing better than helping those who have felt God's touch and have received interior illumination." Whoever draws such people away from the higher graces, enforcing exterior practices upon them, prepares a terrible judgment for himself. Trying to force such souls into pious exercises puts more obstacles in their way than did the pagans and the Jews. And so I warn you, who are so ready to judge with cutting remarks and disdainful gestures, to be indeed careful in dealing with such spiritual people.

And now, if you wish to contemplate the Holy Trinity within you, keep these three points in mind. First, keep God alone before your eyes, His honor, and not your own. Secondly, in all your works and exterior activities, keep a close watch over yourself; be constantly mindful of your utter nothingness, and observe carefully what occupies you most. Thirdly, ignore what goes on around you: If it is not your business, do not pay attention to it; it will take care of itself. If things are good, let them be so; if they are bad, do not criticize and ask questions. Turn into the depth of your ground and remain there, so that you may hear the voice of the Father Who calls you. He calls you to Himself and endows you with such riches that, if it

ca. 1300-1361

were necessary, you could answer all questions of the entire clergy in the Church; of such clarity and brilliance are the gifts God bestows upon His lovers.

And should you forget everything that has been said here, keep in mind these two little points: First, be truly humble, throughout your entire being, not only in mind and in outward conduct; think lowly of yourself, and see yourself honestly for what you are. And secondly, let the love you bear God be a true one; not just what is usually understood by the term, which refers only to emotions, but a love that embraces God most ardently. Such love is a far cry from what is usually meant by religious feeling, which is situated in the senses. What I mean here transcends all sensible experience; it is a gazing upon God with one's entire spirit, a being drawn by love, just as a runner is drawn, or an archer, who has a single goal before his eyes.

May the Blessed Trinity grant us to arrive at this inmost ground where its true image dwells.

AMEN.

Also a disciple of Meister Eckhart, Suso is the greatest poet and lyricist of all the German mystics. He speaks of the soul's return to God as a "breakthrough" and of God as "the Nothing" and the "deep abyss." He experienced and taught the devotional foundation of mysticism and the mystical dimension of authentic devotion.

HENRY SUSO

Henry Suso had the misfortune to live during the waning of the Middle Ages—a time of pestilence and hunger, the "Babylonian captivity" of the papacy at Avignon, the decline of philosophy and theology, and the need for reform both in the mendicant Orders and in the wider Church. He also suffered the shock of seeing Eckhart, the master he so loved and revered, condemned by the Church. Moreover, history would tend to treat Suso simply as one of Eckhart's disciples, thus obscuring his uniqueness as a spiritual and mystical writer.

The introduction to Suso's partially autobiographical work, *The Life of the Servant*, begins: "There was a preacher in Germany, a Swabian by birth, whose name is written in the book of the living. He longed to be, in name and in deed, the Servitor of Eternal Wisdom."[1] This humble, modest preacher came from a region of Germany renowned for military prowess, knights, able administrators, poetry, music, and minnesingers. Just as his ancestors had served their liege lords, Suso desired to serve the heavenly Lord and to sing the praises of eternal wisdom. Undoubtedly, his Swabian background enabled him to become the greatest poet and lyricist of all the German mystics—their minnesinger in prose.

Because of the variety of his works, we know more about Suso than any other German mystic. His *Little Book of Truth*[2] gives proof of his philosophical and theological skills; his masterpiece, *The Little Book of Eternal Wisdom*, demonstrates his emotionally powerful, vividly imaginative, and concrete writing and his prudent and practical mysticism; his *Sermons* and *Letters*[3] show his discerning spiritual direction; and his Life furnishes significant autobiographical information.

Henry Suso (German, *Seuse*) was born of an aristocratic, worldly father and a saintly mother. At 13 years of age, he joined the Dominicans and went through their standard course of studies at Constance, Strasbourg, and Cologne, where Eckhart was his teacher.

Suso confessed to living a lukewarm religious life for some 15 years before experiencing a profound conversion that espoused him to "Eternal Wisdom" and reoriented his life to heroic austerity and deep prayer. Around 1327, he wrote the *Little Book of Truth*, a work that some commentators claim is one of the most obscure in German mysticism. But the obscurity is cleared if one reads it as a fierce attack on two views of the Brethren of the Free Spirit: that a truly spiritual person cannot sin and can become God without qualifications.

Its main theme focuses on genuine self-abandonment that leads to mystical union. Suso conceded that during moments of ecstatic rapture, the person knows and loves without knowing it. Nonetheless, against the Brethren of the Free Spirit, he maintained that during this unselfconscious experience, the distinction between God and the creature remains.

Although not an apology for Eckhart, this work explains several of his main themes in an orthodox way while reverently admitting that he often lacked clarity. Suso shows how Eckhart's themes had been perverted, misunderstood, and even quoted in support of the Brethren's false doctrine, and he illustrates this by way of the "Wild Man" (Chapter 6).

Reminiscent of Eckhart, Suso speaks of the return to God as a "breakthrough" and of God as "the Nothing" and the "deep abyss." The soul's blessedness consists in contemplating the "naked Godhead." But in contrast to Eckhart, Suso does not sever the incomprehensible Godhead from the God of revelation. Less speculative and intellectual than Eckhart, Suso underscores the affective, psychological, and personal aspects of sinking into the divine abyss. More cautious and more attentive to peoples' pastoral needs than Eckhart, Suso often corrects his master via Bernard's and Bonaventure's affective mysticism and Aquinas's theology.

Suso's *Little Book of Eternal Wisdom*—later translated by him into Latin and titled *The Clock of Wisdom*—has been called one of German mysticism's finest fruits. In some circles, only the *Imitation of Christ* displaced it in popularity. "The ideas here expressed are simple," writes Suso, "and the words are even simpler, for they proceed from a simple soul and are meant for simple persons who still have failings to overcome." The book offers a hundred meditations on Christ's passion in the form of a dialogue between the "servant" (not always Suso) and "Eternal Wisdom."

Suso experienced and taught the devotional foundation of mysticism and the mystical dimension of authentic devotion. Thus, his spirituality and mysticism highlight devotion to Jesus' sacred heart, his holy name, eternal wisdom, the eucharist, and the immaculate heart of Mary.

Suso also stressed a tender, personal love of Jesus Christ. To him, the way to the highest mystical union is the contemplation and imitation of Christ's sufferings. He castigated both those who view Christ only "from within and not from without" (the Brethren of the Free Spirit) and those who view Christ "only from without and not from within." The former he disparaged as "only" contemplatives—not "active"; the latter, as overzealous ascetics who have overlooked the "inner Christ." According to him, neither group was in touch with their true human nature.

In Suso's view, a person lives a genuine spiritual life by way of corporeal austerities, acceptance of exterior and interior trials, total detachment from creatures, self-renunciation, and complete abandonment to God's will. In keeping with the German apophatic mystical tradition, Suso focused on a form of imageless ecstasy. In this state, the contemplative experiences undifferentiated union with God and the preexistent oneness of all creatures in God ("creatures have existed eternally in God as their eternal exemplar"). On the other hand, he also underscores the ontological distinction between God and creatures. But unlike the earlier tradition, which taught that the purgative, illuminative, and unitive ways occurred simultaneously, Suso popularized the notion of a consecutive, three-fold way.

The *Life of the Servant* originated in conversations and correspondence between Suso and Elsbeth Stägel, his spiritual daughter. Although it has been called a "charming Christian biography," the *Life* is more the story of a soul. It shows the hand of a later genial hagiographer, making it difficult to distinguish fact from fiction. Historians suggest that toward the end of his life, Suso collected his High German works into a single volume that he called *The Exemplar.*

When approximately 40 years old, Suso stopped teaching to become a wandering preacher and a spiritual director. For the most part, his active ministry was directed to Dominican nuns and the Friends of God in Switzerland and the Upper Rhine. Exiled at one time for his loyalty to the Pope during the papal disputes with Louis of Bavaria, Suso also suffered physical hardship, hostility, calumny, and persecution as a defender of Eckhart and for his association with women, many of whom he encouraged to enter monasteries. Falsely accused of paternity by a woman he had helped, he was forced into exile and died in Ulm.

The following texts were selected to illustrate his apophatic, ecstatic conversion, his espousal to eternal wisdom, and the dalliance and playfulness in the divine life. The texts also underscore his skillful use of the language and imagery of both courtly love and the minnesingers. His lovely hymn to suffering is one of most beautiful in the Christian mystical tradition.[4]

THE TEXTS

A SUPERNATURAL EXPERIENCE[5]
One day when he was feeling more wretched than usual, he made his way to the choir after the midday meal and settled himself in one of the lower stalls on the right-hand side. It was January 21, the

feast of St. Agnes. As he stood there alone, a perfect specimen of melancholia, his soul was mysteriously transported, either in the body or out of the body. Human words fail when it comes to describing what he saw and heard in this ecstasy; it was a vision without form or mode but containing in itself the form and mode of every pleasurable sensation. His heart was simultaneously hungry and appeased; his wishes were stilled, and every desire found its fulfillment. He did nothing but stare into the brilliant reflection, oblivious of himself and all creatures, forgetful of the passage of time. It was a sweet foretaste of heaven's unending bliss.

After about an hour he returned to his senses and said to himself: "If that was not a foretaste of heaven, then I do not know what heaven is. Now I am fully convinced that every suffering that can possibly come my way is a cheap price to pay for such a gain. Alas, dear God, where was I and where am I now? Oh, that the memory of this hour may always stay fresh in my mind."

Leaving the choir, he made his way into the cloister, looking the same as before in outward appearance, but inwardly like a man returned from another world. The memory of the vision he had seen caused him anguish of body and desolation of spirit; he now longed for not the companionship of creatures but the heavenly joys he had tasted so briefly. He went about his duties silent and unnoticed, his soul reliving the bliss of God's touch, experiencing time and again the brightness of heavenly visions, and it seemed to him as if he were floating on air.

Like a dish that retains the taste of porridge which has been poured out, so his spiritual faculties preserved the delicious heavenly flavor of this vision for a long time and hungered for another supernatural experience.

HIS SPIRITUAL ESPOUSALS WITH ETERNAL WISDOM[6]
The vision in the choir on Saint Agnes' day was followed by a period of renewed fervor for the Servitor, a spiritual springtime in which he courted Divine Wisdom as a knight offers love tokens to his fair bride. This interval is more fully described in the Little Book of Eternal Wisdom, published in German and Latin, which he composed under God's inspiration.

He had always been quite affectionate by nature. Now his heart was captivated by Lady Wisdom who, under the guise of a gracious maiden and clothed in velvet and adorned with diamonds, gladdened all hearts by her fair words. In the refectory, while listening to the reader ministering to the spiritual nourishment of the brethren, he first saw the beauty of the countenance of Eternal Wisdom. The passage being read, which contrasted with the fickleness of earthly love with the constancy of divine love, captivated his soul as the panther charms his prey with a magic scent. This happened frequently, especially when the Books of Wisdom were read . . . .

He said to himself: "Help me! That's the plain truth. There is only one thing for me to do; she [Eternal Wisdom] shall be my bride, and I will be her Servitor. Oh God, if I could catch one glimpse of her, speak to her for a few moments. What is this love which can color everything with its brightness? Is this loved one God or human, man or woman, knowledge or wisdom? Or what else can it be?"

While he was turning these questions over in his mind, picturing this beloved in the various symbolic expressions of Scripture, she showed herself to him floating high above him on a cloud-covered throne, shining like the morning star, as dazzling as the sun. Her crown was eternity; her raiment, bliss; her conversation, sweetness; her embrace, the fullness of delight. She was far, yet near; present, yet absent; high as the hills and low as the grass. She permitted him to approach her and at the same time kept him at a distance. She reached to the highest heaven and touched the lowest depths. She swept from end to end mightily and ordered all things graciously. At one moment he thought he saw in her a beautiful maiden, and presently he saw her as a noble youth. Sometimes she showed herself to him as a wise mistress, at other times as a queenly fiancée. His heart missed a few beats when she drew near and tenderly addressed him: "Praebe, fili, cor tuum mihi"—"My son, give me your heart" (Proverbs 23:26). Like a lovesick swain struck dumb by emotion, he fell on his knees in gratitude and consent.

Afterward, he would often turn his mind and heart inward to gaze on his loveliest love and whisper to himself: "Oh, tell me, what is the source of love and bliss? From what fountain do the rivers of tenderness, beauty, deep contentment, and delight flow? Is it not from the spring of the naked Godhead, ageless as the heavens and fresh as the morning dew? Get ready for the plunge, my soul. We will dive into the bottomless depth of all goodness. No one can hinder us. Oh, restless source of all rest, I embrace you to my heart's content."

Having said this, he clasped to himself the first cause of all good, wherein his spiritual craving for beauty, love, and happiness was completely satisfied.

He adopted another practice at this time. Whenever he listened to melodious vocal or instrumental music or heard someone tell of the delights of human friendship, he immediately took refuge in the heart of him whose intimacy is sweeter than all earthly joys. The number of times he mystically wooed his heart's beloved in this way cannot be counted. When he enjoyed the familiar presence of Eternal Wisdom he felt like a smiling babe held securely on its mother's lap, hungrily nuzzling its head against her breast. This comparison made him exclaim: "Alas, dear Lord, how honored I should be if I had a princess for a bride. What a far greater distinction comes to me in being wedded to the Queen of all hearts and Mediatrix of all graces. In her, I have all riches and absolute power. Nothing earthly holds any more attraction for me!"

These and similar reflections absorbed all his spiritual and sensitive faculties; his whole life, intellectual and artistic, was caught up in one triumphant hymn, *Super salutem* (Wisdom 7:10- 11). "You are my heart's delight and beauty above all earthly joy and comeliness. Happiness came to me in your wake and all my longings finds fulfillment in you."

HOW LOVABLE GOD IS[7]
The Servitor: Lord, I meditate on the call of love which you spoke in the Book of Wisdom: "Come to me, all you that yearn for me, and be filled with my fruits; you will remember me as sweeter than honey, better to have than the honeycomb" (Sirach 24:19-20).

Gentle Lord, so great is the loving tenderness with which you offer yourself that all hearts ought to yearn ardently to receive you. The life-giving words of endearment which flow from your precious mouth have so deeply wounded many youthful hearts that all earthly love was completely extinguished in them. Ah, gentle Lord, my heart pines, my spirit yearns, my whole soul longs to hear you tell me of your love. Speak then, my only chosen Consoler, one little word to the soul of your lovely handmaid whose heart is wakeful while she sleeps in your shadow.

Answer of Eternal Wisdom: Hearken, my daughter, and see; incline your ears toward me; convert yourself so thoroughly as to forget yourself and all creatures.

I am in myself the incomprehensible Good, unbeginning and unending, which has never been expressed nor ever will be. I can make hearts feel my inward presence, but no tongue can adequately describe me. However, since I give myself, the supernatural, immutable Good, to every creature according to its receptivity, I shall wrap the sun's radiance in a cloth and tell you in earthly words the spiritual meaning concerning myself and my sweet love. . . .

Listen further. I am of princely birth, of noble lineage. I am the beloved Word of the Father's heart, of him whose eyes find happiness gazing into the delightful depths of his own pure Fatherland, my natural Sonship, and the agreeable, flame-winged love of the Holy Spirit.

I am the throne of blessedness,
The crown of happiness.

If a man were to remain in a blazing furnace until the last day just in order to get a glimpse of me, he would not have deserved to look at my clear eyes, my gentle mouth, my roseytinted cheeks, and my person so comely and perfect in every respect. . . .

In the Godhead I play a game of delight
Which thrills the angels by its very sight.
A thousand years to them do seem
As transient as a passing dream.
All the blessed gaze wonderingly upon me. Their eyes are riveted on mine, their hearts are inclined to me, and their souls are bowed in unceasing worship.

Unalloyed happiness is his who, holding my fair hand, dances with

me the dance of heavenly bliss. His steps are secure for all eternity.
One living word from my mouth is more
than angels' songs harmonious,
than rarest harp melodious,
than silver strings far sweeter.

You see, therefore, that it is delightful for the enamored soul to love
me, and bliss for her to embrace and kiss me. Indeed, every heart
should break with desire for me. I am small and assiduous and
present at all times to the pure soul. I am secretly with her,
Eating or sleeping,
Walking or driving,
Here and there, everywhere. . . .

The Servitor: Ah, tender, lovely flower of the field, you are my
heart's only treasure. These truths are familiar to the enamored soul
of anyone who has ever experienced your love in a spiritual embrace, but strange-sounding to the man whose heart and soul are
yet earthbound.

Ah, beloved, incomprehensible Good, in this joyous hour, this
sweet moment, I must disclose to you a hidden wound which your
love has inflicted on my heart. Love, divided love is like water in
fire; you know that true, fervent love cannot endure any duality.
Ah, gentle Lord, my soul's only Master, that is why my heart craves
so intensely, to be particularly loved by you and pleasing to your divine eyes. But it seems to me that many hearts are intensely loved
by you and highly agreeable to you. Dear Lord, what possibility of
special love remains in me?

Answer of Eternal Wisdom: I am a lover of such a nature that I am
not diminished by oneness nor multiplied by plurality. I am at all
times as completely occupied with your interests and intent on
your love as if I had no other ties. . . .

ON THE INFINITE NOBILITY OF TEMPORAL SUFFERING[8]
Gentle Lord, tell me now, what is this suffering which you consider
so intrinsically useful and desirable? I earnestly desire that you tell
me more about it, so that, in case you send it to me, I will accept it
lovingly and cheerfully from your fatherly hand.

Answer of Eternal Wisdom: I mean every suffering, whether it be voluntarily embraced or involuntarily encountered, in which latter case a man makes a virtue out of necessity. In both cases, one does not wish to be free of it [suffering] against my will but orders it in loving, humble patience to my eternal praise. The more voluntary the suffering, the nobler it is and the more agreeable to me. . . .

I reside in a pure soul as in a paradise of all delights; therefore, I cannot permit that it seek pleasure or delight in any creature. Because by nature the soul is inclined to dangerous pleasure, I pay no attention to its likes and dislikes, and to prevent its escape from me, I surround the streets with thorns and stop up all the breaches with calamities. I strew its course with suffering so that it will be unable to put down the foot of its heart's content anywhere except in the sublimity of my divine nature.

. . . Now hear the strains vibrating from the lute of a God-suffering man. The music swells full and melodious. To the world, suffering is an infamy, but to me it is an immense dignity. Suffering is the extinguisher of my wrath and the purchaser of my favor. Suffering endears men to me, because a suffering man resembles me. Suffering is a hidden blessing, precious beyond purchase, and if a man knelt before me and begged a hundred years for the privilege of suffering, he would not deserve it. It converts a worldly man into a heavenly man. Suffering makes a man a stranger to the world and gives him instead my continual intimacy. It decreases friends and increases grace.

He whom I lovingly embrace must be completely denied and forsaken by the whole world. Suffering is the safest, shortest, and quickest way. . . .

Patience in suffering is a living sacrifice, a sweet odor of precious balsam before my divine countenance and a marvel ascending to heaven in the sight of the entire celestial host. No valiant knight was ever watched as intently during the tournament as the entire celestial host gazes at a man suffering bravely. All the saints are the cupbearers of a suffering man, because they have previously experienced it time and again, and they cry out in unison that it is free from poison and a wholesome drink. Patience in suffering is a greater work than raising the dead or performing miracles; it is a narrow way that leads infallibly to heaven's gate. Suffering associates a man with the martyrs, reflects honor upon him, and helps him to conquer all his enemies. . . . With a clear voice, it will lead the eternal chorus, which sings wholeheartedly a new song which the angels cannot sing because they have never experienced suffering. To epitomize: worldlings call sufferers "the poor," but I call them "the blessed," because they are indeed predestined.

*John Ruusbroec has been called the greatest contem-
plative and mystical writer in the Christian tradition. He has also been praised as the most articulate
trinitarian mystic of the West, unmatched in his
power to describe the soul's union with God.*

JOHN RUUSBROEC

John Ruusbroec, "the Admirable," has been called the greatest contemplative and mystical writer in the Christian tradition. He has
also been praised as the most articulate trinitarian mystic of the
West, unmatched in his power to describe the unitive life. Yet, if
those who know something about the Christian tradition are asked
to list the great mystics, rarely is Ruusbroec named first—if he is
named at all.

John was born in Ruusbroec, South Brabant, about five miles from
Brussels. When he was 11 years old, he went to live with an uncle
of his who was a canon of a Brussels cathedral, the collegiate
church of St. Gudula. Ordained at the age of 24, Ruusbroec spent 26
years at St. Gudula's. There he maintained close contact with the
local Beguines.

At 50 years of age, Ruusbroec, along with two companions, retired
for a more contemplative life to the forest of Soignes, Groenendaal
(green valley), just outside Brussels, where they eventually became
Augustinians. Here Ruusbroec lived the "God-seeing" life for 38
years before dying at the age of 88.

This mystical genius not only reached the most exalted heights of
mystical contemplation but also possessed the theological profundity and the limpid prose to express it. In contrast to the many mystics who complain of their inability to capture and express what

they have experienced, Ruusbroec finds his own language adequate. His numerous works attest to his eloquence as well as his productivity.

Ruusbroec directed his treatises against the extreme claims and aspirations of the Brethren of the Free Spirit. Some of the Brethren were militant in their dualism, pantheism, and quietism. For example, Bloemardinne, the female apostle of "seraphic love"—and perhaps Ruusbroec's first opponent—proclaimed that her love as one of the Brethren was as pure as that of the seraphim—even of God himself. Thus, to avoid distracting the deified spirit, she counseled permitting the flesh to do whatever it wanted. She and other Brethren assumed that they had reached such an intimate union with God that they were above Church, sacraments, virtue, and law. In fact, they averred a form of autotheism, that one can become God in this life, in the full and strict sense.

The texts printed here were selected to illustrate both Ruusbroec's vigorous repudiation of the Brethren's claims and the profundity of his mystical theology. Ruusbroec rejected the Brethren's pseudomysticism because they confused their unfruitful state of "bare emptiness" with the genuine experience of God and even asserted that they were God. Moreover, their psychological quietism would lead them not only to eternal death but also to such "restlessness," "anxiety," and "despair" that they would "die like rabid dogs."

The selections underscore Ruusbroec's contention that even the highest stages of the mystical life demand a threefold unity with God. The first aspect—union with God "through an intermediary"— calls for asceticism, virtue, good works, and a full participation in the Church's sacramental life. Genuine union with God is impossible without God's grace, the active striving for virtue, and a fully Christian life.

The second aspect—union with God "without intermediary"—impels the contemplative to follow a "homeward-turning love" to the "topmost part of [his] spirit" and, with a mind "bare and devoid of images," to adhere to God in "fathomless love." In what may be the most beautiful passage in the Christian mystical tradition, Ruusbroec depicts the "strife of love" between God's Spirit and the contemplative's spirit when they unite. During this encounter, the person experiences "the highest distinction" possible, that is, the "essential distinction between the soul's being and God's being."

During the third aspect—union with God "without difference"—the contemplative no longer rests at the soul's summit. Rather, he or she is plunged into the "modeless abyss" of unspeakable bliss wherein the Trinity gives way to its "essential Unity." Resting in the Trinity's heart, the contemplative also experiences the preexisting oneness of all things in God.

It must be emphasized that, to Ruusbroec, no one way of uniting with God is perfect without the other two. The genuine contemplative life consists of a *simultaneous*—not consecutive—unified life of virtue, interiority, virtue, interiority, differentiated and undifferentiated union with God. The selections show how Ruusbroec links these three unions with the "fulfillment of Christ's prayer."

The texts furthermore illustrate Ruusbroec's profound trinitarian exemplarism. Like the heart's systole and diastole, the Trinity lives in eternal contraction from the trinity of persons to the triune unity and expansion from the unity to the plurality of persons. In contrast to Eckhart's Godhead above both the persons and the divine essence, Ruusbroec retrieves the view of the Greek Fathers that there is one God because there is one Father. Light and love are eternally begotten and spirated from the divine darkness. The "wild desert" of the Godhead is fertile with love. The divine silence speaks an eternal word of love. In other words, the ever Three are ever One, ever at work and ever at rest.

Finally, the selected texts show Ruusbroec's trinitarian exemplarism with respect to the human spirit. To him, the human spirit is a living mirror upon which the Trinity has imprinted its image. Memory, intellect, and will proceed from the oneness of the human spirit. This threefold oneness by nature should also be possessed supernaturally, that is, by the Trinity's communication of its own life. Thus, the human spirit's relationship to the Trinity, and even to itself, partakes in the divine movements within the triune unity.

In imitation of the Trinity and its "inflow" and "outflow" of love, the authentic contemplative is equally ready for contemplation and action and is perfect in both. Lost in the Trinity's unity, the contemplative is nonetheless always anchored to the person of Jesus Christ. United with God in a union beyond all distinctions, the contemplative is nevertheless able to feel the distinction between the human spirit and God. Experiencing all creatures in their preexistent oneness with God—finding all things in God—the contemplative also experiences them in their otherness and distinctness and finds God in all things. As Ruusbroec, the "ecstatic Doctor," says: "That we might blissfully possess the essential Unity and clearly contemplate the Unity in the Trinity—may the divine love grant us this, for it turns no beggar away. Amen. Amen."[1]

THE TEXTS

THE LITTLE BOOK OF CLARIFICATION[2]
PART ONE: UNION THROUGH AN INTERMEDIARY

A. THE NATURE OF THIS UNION
In the first place, I say that all good persons are united with God through an intermediary. This intermediary is God's grace, together with the sacraments of the holy Church, the divine virtues of faith, hope, and love, and of a virtuous life in accordance with God's commandments. To these there is joined a dying to sin, to the world, and to all the inordinate desires of our nature. In this way, we remain united to the holy Church, that is, to all good persons, and are obedient to God and of one will with him, just as a good religious community is united with its superior. Apart from this union, no one can be pleasing to God or be saved.

You can thus understand that we are united with God through an intermediary, both here in grace and later in glory. There is much difference and diversity in this intermediary as regards both the way persons live and the reward they receive, just as I have told you. St. Paul understood this well when he said that he wished to be freed from the body and to be with Christ (Philippians 1:23). But he did not say that he himself would be Christ or God, as some unbelieving and perverse persons now claim, saying that they have no God but are so dead to themselves and so united with God that they have become God.

B. THE AUTOTHEISTIC-QUIETISTIC DEVIATION FROM THE TRUTH

These persons have turned inward to the bareness of their being by means of an undifferentiated simplicity and a natural inclination, with the result that they think eternal life will be nothing other than a purely existing, blessed state of being which has no distinctions of order, holiness, or merit. Some of these persons are so insane that they say that the Persons in the Godhead will disappear, that nothing will remain there for all eternity except the essential substance of the Godhead, and that all blessed spirits will be so simply absorbed with God in a state of essential blessedness that nothing will remain apart from this—neither will nor action nor the distinct knowledge of anything created.

These persons have gone astray into the empty and blind simplicity of their own being and are trying to become blessed in their bare nature, for they are united in so simple and empty a way to the bare essence of their soul and to God dwelling within them that they have no ardor or devotion to God, whether exteriorly or interiorly. At the highest point of their introversion, they feel nothing but the simplicity of their own being, dependent upon God's being. They take this undifferentiated simplicity which they possess to be God himself, because they find natural rest in it. They accordingly think that they themselves are God in the ground of their simple oneness, for they lack true faith, hope, and love. Because of this bare emptiness which they experience and possess, they claim to be without knowledge and love and to be exempt from the virtues. They therefore strive to live apart from conscience, however much evil they do. They ignore all the sacraments, all the virtues, and all the practices of the Holy Church, for they think they have no need of these, believing that they have passed beyond them all—according to them, only those who are imperfect need such things. . . .

. . . They claim that the highest holiness consists in a person's following his own nature in every respect, without restraint, so that he might live in a state of emptiness according to the inclination of his spirit and turn outward to satisfy the flesh in accordance with every movement of corporeal desire, so as all the more quickly to be freed of such an image and be able to return without hindrance to the bare emptiness of his spirit.

This is the hellish fruit which grows out of their unbelief and nourishes that unbelief right up to the death which is eternal, for when the time has come and their nature is weighed down with bitter woe and fear of death, then they are interiorly filled with images, restlessness, and anxiety. They lose their state of empty, restful introversion, fall into such despair that no one can console them, and die like rabid dogs. Their emptiness brings them no reward, and those who have performed evil deeds and die in them go to the eternal fire, as our faith teaches. . . .

PART THREE: UNION WITHOUT DIFFERENCE

A. THE GROUND OF THIS UNION WITHIN THE GODHEAD
That last-named feeling [of transrational changeless beatitude] is our superessential beatitude, which consists in the enjoyment of God and of all his beloved. This beatitude is the dark stillness which always stands empty. To God, it is essential, but to all creatures, it is superessential. Here the Persons give way and lose themselves in the maelstrom of essential love, that is, in the blissful Unity, and nevertheless remain active as Persons in the work of the Trinity. . . .

. . . By means of the relations of the Persons in the Godhead, there is an ever-new sense of contentment accompanied by a new outflow of love in a new embrace in the Unity. This is beyond time, that is, without any before or after, in an eternal now. In this embrace in the Unity, all things are brought to their perfection; in the outflow of love, all things are accomplished; and in the living, fruitful nature, all things have their possibility of occurring. In this living, fruitful nature, the Son is in the Father, and the Father is in the Son, while the Holy Spirit is in them both, for this is a living, fruitful Unity which is the source and beginning of all life and all becoming. Here all creatures are therefore one being and one life with God—apart from themselves, in their eternal origin. But as the Persons proceed outward in distinct ways, then the Son has created and ordered all creatures to their own essential being. He has also recreated human beings to the greatest extent possible through his grace and his death and has adorned with love and virtues those who belong to him, bringing them back with him to their source. There the Father, the Son, and all the beloved are enveloped and embraced in the bond of love, that is, in the Unity of the Holy Spirit. This is the same Unity which is fruitful in the processions of the Persons and which in their return is an eternal bond of love which will never be broken.

B. OUR THREEFOLD PARTICIPATION IN GOD'S BEATITUDE
All who know themselves to be enveloped in this bond will remain eternally blessed. Such persons are rich in virtue, clear in contemplation, and simple in their enjoyable rest, for as they turn inward, God's love reveals itself as flowing out with all that is good, as attracting inward into unity, and as being superessential and devoid of mode in eternal rest. They are therefore united with God through an intermediary and without intermediary and also without difference.

UNION THROUGH AN INTERMEDIARY
In their inward vision, God's love is seen as a good common to all as it flows forth in heaven and on earth. They feel the holy Trinity inclined toward them and being within them in the fullness of grace. They are therefore adorned with every virtue, with holy exercises, and with good works, both from without and from within, and are thus united with God through the intermediary of his grace and of their own holy way of life. . . .

UNION WITHOUT INTERMEDIARY
Secondly, in their inward vision, these same interior and enlightened persons have God's love before them whenever they wish, drawing or calling them to union, for they see and feel that the Father and the Son, through the Holy Spirit, have embraced themselves and all the elect and are being brought back with eternal love to the Unity of their nature. This Unity is constantly drawing and calling to itself all that has been born of it, whether in a natural way or through grace. Enlightened persons are therefore raised up with a free mind above reason to a vision which is bare and devoid of images. Here lives the eternal call of God's Unity. With a bare and im-

ageless understanding, these persons pass beyond all activity, all exercises, and all things and enter the topmost part of their spirit. There their bare understanding is pervaded with eternal resplendence, just as the air is pervaded with the light of the sun. So, too, is their bare and uplifted will transformed and pervaded with fathomless love, just as a piece of iron is penetrated by fire, while their bare and uplifted memory feels itself caught up and set firm in a fathomless state devoid of images. In this way the created image is united above reason in a threefold way with its eternal image, which is the source of its being and life. This source is held fast and possessed essentially and in unity through a simple act of contemplating in imageless emptiness. A person is thus raised above reason, threefold in unity and one in trinity.

. . . In this storm of love, two spirits struggle—the Spirit of God and our spirit. God, by means of the Holy Spirit, inclines himself toward us, and we are thereby touched in love; our spirit, by means of God's activity and the amorous power, impels and inclines itself toward God, and thereby God is touched. From these two movements there arises the struggle of love, for in this most profound meeting, in this most intimate and ardent encounter, each spirit is wounded by love. These two spirits—that is, our spirit and the Spirit of God—cast a radiant light upon one another and each reveals to the other its countenance. This makes the two spirits incessantly strive after one another in love. Each demands of the other what it is, and each offers to the other and invites it to accept what it is. This makes these loving spirits lose themselves in one another. God's touch and his giving of himself, together with our striving in love and our giving of ourselves in return—this is what sets love on a firm foundation.

Nevertheless, the creature does not become God, for this union occurs through grace and through a love which has been turned back to God. For this reason, the creature experiences in his inward vision a difference and distinction between himself and God. Even though the union is without intermediary, the manifold works which God performs in heaven and on earth are hidden from the spirit. Although God gives himself as he is with clear distinction, he does so in the essential being of the soul, where the soul's powers are unified above reason and undergo a transformation wrought by

God in an undifferentiated way. There everything is full and overflowing, for the spirit feels itself to be but one truth, one richness,
and one unity with God, but there is nevertheless an essential inclination to go onward, and that is an essential distinction between
the soul's being and God's being. This is the highest distinction
which a person can experience.

UNION WITHOUT DIFFERENCE

After this follows the unity without difference, for God's love is to
be considered not only as flowing forth with all that is good and as
drawing back to unity, but also as being above and beyond all distinction in a state of essential enjoyment in accordance with the
bare essential being of the Godhead. For this reason, enlightened
persons find within themselves an essential act of gazing inward
which is above reason and apart from reason; they also find an inclination toward blissful enjoyment which transcends all particular
forms and beings and which immerses them in a modeless abyss of
fathomless beatitude, in which the Trinity of the divine Persons possess their nature in the essential Unity. There the state of beatitude
is so simple and so modeless that in it, every essential act of gazing,
every inclination, and every distinction of creatures pass away, for
all exalted spirits melt away and come to nought by reason of the
blissful enjoyment they experience in God's essential being, which
is the superessential being of all beings. There they fall away from
themselves and become lost in a state of unknowing which has no
ground. There all light is turned into darkness and the three Persons give way before the essential Unity, where without distinction
they enjoy essential bliss.

This bliss is essential to God alone; to all spirits, it is superessential,
for no created being can be one with God's being and have its own
being perish. If that happened, the creature would become God,
and this is impossible, for God's essential being can neither de-
crease nor increase and can have nothing taken away from it or
added to it. Nevertheless, all loving spirits are one enjoyment and
one beatitude with God, without difference, for that blessed state of
being which is the enjoyment of God and of all his beloved is so
simple and undifferentiated that there is within it neither Father
nor Son nor Holy Spirit as regards the distinction of Persons, nor is

there any creature either. Rather, all enlightened spirits are there raised above themselves into a modeless state of blissful enjoyment which overflows whatever fullness any creature has ever received or ever could receive. There all exalted spirits are, in their super-essential being, one enjoyment and one beatitude with God, without difference. This beatitude is so simple and undifferentiated that no distinction could ever enter within it. This is what Christ desired when he prayed to his heavenly Father that all his beloved might be made perfectly one, even as he is one with the Father in the blissful enjoyment through the Holy Spirit (cf. John 17:21-23). He thus prayed and desired that he might be one in us and we one in him and in his heavenly Father in blissful enjoyment through the Holy Spirit. I consider this the most loving prayer which Christ ever prayed for our salvation.

THESE THREE UNIONS AS THE FULFILLMENT OF
CHRIST'S PRAYER

You should also note that his prayer was threefold, as St. John has described it for us in this same Gospel. He first prayed that we should be with him, so that we might see the glory, which his Father had given him (John 17:24). It is for this reason that I said in the beginning that all good persons are united with God through the intermediary of God's grace and their own virtuous life. God's love is always flowing into us with new gifts. All who take heed of this are filled with new virtues, with holy exercises, and with all good things, just as I have told you previously. This union through the fullness of grace and glory, in both body and soul, begins here and lasts for all eternity.

Secondly, Christ prayed that he might be in us and we in him. We find this in many places in the Gospel. This is the union without intermediary, for God's love not only flows outward but also draws inward toward unity. All who experience and perceive this become interior and enlightened persons and have their higher powers raised above all their exercises into their bare essential being. There these powers are simplified in their essential being, above reason, and thereby become full and overflowing. In this simplicity, the spirit finds itself united with God without intermediary. This union, together with the exercises which are proper to it, will last for all eternity, just as I have said previously.

Thirdly, Christ prayed the highest prayer, namely, that all his beloved might be made perfectly one, even as he is one with the Father (John 17:23)—not in the way that he is one single divine substance with the Father, for that is impossible for us, but in the sense of being one in the same unity in which he, without distinction, is one enjoyment and one beatitude with the Father in essential love.

Christ's prayer is fulfilled in those who are united with God in this threefold way. They will ebb and flow with God and constantly stand empty in possession and enjoyment; they will work and endure and fearlessly rest in their superessential being; they will go out and enter in and find their nourishment both without and within; they are drunk with love and sleep in God in a dark resplendence.

A Dominican tertiary, Catherine taught that God is "First Truth" and charity itself who is madly in love with us. God is the "peaceful sea" in which we must drown. Catherine's is a mystical contemplation in action, a mysticism that expresses and fulfills itself sacramentally in social and political activity.

CATHERINE OF SIENA

Caterina di Giacomo di Benincasa was born in the Fontebranda district of Siena, the 24th of 25 children of a prosperous Sienese wool dyer. When seven years old, she vowed her virginity to Christ; when 15, Catherine cut off her hair to defy her parents' efforts to have her marry. At 18, she received the Dominican habit, becoming a *Mantellata*, a member of the Dominican Third Order, a loose federation of women—usually widowed—who lived at home, took the habit, received spiritual direction from Dominican friars, and cared for the poor and the sick.

Leaving her home only for Mass, Catherine lived in solitude in her room; at 19, she experienced mystical marriage with Christ. During this time, the learned Bartolomeo de'Dominici became her confessor and lifelong friend. When Catherine was 21, she felt the need to rejoin her family and to help the *Mantellate* in their practical works of mercy. Great austerity, solitude, and silent contemplation, as well as vigorous social work for the poor, sick, and dying, became her way of life. At the age of 23, Catherine experienced her "mystical death," a four-hour God-given ecstasy in which her body seemed dead. She also maintained she received the stigmata, though only she could see them.

The distinguished Dominican reformer Raymond of Capua, whom she considered both a "father and son" given to her by "gentle

Mary," became her confessor and spiritual director. During the last five years of her life, Catherine was involved in the religiopolitical problems of the Italian city-states and barely escaped assassination. Highly influential in mitigating the antipapal forces in her region, she also preached in favor of a crusade, the reform of the clergy, and the return of the Avignon papacy to Rome; her prophetic gifts actually played a role in Pope Gregory XI's decision to move back to Rome. His successor, Urban VI, seeking her support for his legitimacy, called Catherine to Rome in 1379 in a vain attempt to win back the schismatics. The Great Schism was the saddest disappointment in Catherine's life.

In the beginning of 1380, Catherine became so sick that she could not eat, and she refused water as well. Incessant prayer, mystical ecstasies, and self-oblation became her apostolate for the Church. Dying at the age of 33, she was canonized in 1461 by the Sienese Pope Pius II and five centuries later (1970), she was declared Doctor of the Church by Pope Paul VI. Through her impact upon Raymond of Capua, she indirectly influenced the Dominican reforms after her death. It is an indication of Catherine's reputation among her contemporaries that her book, *The Dialogue,* along with her biography by Raymond of Capua, were among the first books to see print in England, Germany, Italy, and Spain.

Although Catherine had no formal schooling and learned to read only when she was 30, she addressed almost every class of society of her day. She was a tireless teacher who dictated—often in ecstasy—almost 400 letters as well as her famous book, *The Dialogue.* Members of her community recorded for posterity 24 of her ecstatic prayers. These writings reveal an extraordinary integration of the best of the Western mystical tradition and the Bible. In fact, her own message is that of the Scriptures and of the Fathers. However, Catherine's originality can be found in her inner life that lived this message; it consists, too, in the way she used the Sienese dialect to express what she had absorbed.

Catherine taught that God is "First Truth" and charity itself, who is madly in love with us. God is the "peaceful sea" in which we must drown. Because Christ's open heart is the revelation of God's heart, it reveals that we were created out of boundless love, for love, and to share in this love for all eternity. She also emphasized the "engrafting" of God into human nature through the incarnation. On the day of his circumcision, Christ espoused the entire human race with the ring of his flesh. Catherine also depicts Christ as a nursing mother. As she perceives it, the way to God is a lived dynamic of knowledge and love for the crucified Christ. The summit is not only union with God but also an insatiable hunger for the salvation of others.

The Dialogue is Catherine's crowning work, "my book," as she fondly referred to it. Entrusting *The Dialogue* to Raymond, she bequeathed it to her followers as a compendium of her teachings. In it, Catherine addresses four petitions to God: for herself, that she be allowed to suffer in atonement for sins; for the reform of the Church; for the whole world; for divine providence in all things, but specifically in regard to a "certain case that had arisen." God responds to each of these petitions while she is in ecstasy, to which she reacts with thanksgiving.

Her book is difficult reading but a rewarding one because Catherine uses a layered logic that seems repetitious, yet adds new meanings and shadings as she progresses. By using Christ as a "bridge" and as a "door," one meets God—the "peaceful sea"—in the heart, in ecstasy, and in helping one's neighbor. Catherine's bridge image is famous:

This bridge, my only begotten Son, has three stairs.
Two of them he built on the wood of the most holy
cross, and the third even as he tasted the great
bitterness of the gall and vinegar they gave him to
drink. You will recognize in these three stairs three
spiritual stages. . . . At the first stair, lifting the
feet of her [the soul's] affections from the earth,
she stripped herself of sin. At the second, she
dressed herself in love for virtue. And at the third,
she tasted peace.[1]

This bridge must be used to cross the threatening waters of evil and sin to reach not dry land but God, the peaceful sea in which one drowns.

Perhaps more important than her dramatic mystical experiences and her powerful sacramental expressions is the way Catherine's life filled her mysticism and mysticism her life. Hers is a mystical contemplation in action, a mysticism that expressed and fulfilled itself sacramentally in social and political activity. In line with many others in the Christian tradition, Catherine's mysticism and activity are two sides of the same coin, the systole and diastole of her mystical heart.

The texts that follow were selected to illustrate Catherine's exquisitely sacramental mysticism and the powerful symbols and images through which she expresses it. The first reading centers on Catherine's experience of ecstatic rapture in which God totally fills her memory, understanding, and will. Love causes the soul to be more united to God than to its body, so the body actually levitates. Catherine teaches that only bodily fragility prevents her continuous ecstatic union with God, although "grace. . . [and] its feeling" remained permanently with her.

The first reading also offers a good summary of her mystical ascent to God: virtue, the "bridge of the teaching of Christ crucified," one's spirit "inebriated" with Christ's blood and "aflame" with the fire of his love, and finally "drowning" in the Godhead, the "peaceful sea."

The second reading, on the five kinds of tears, can also be read as Catherine's compendium of the steps to mystical union. Perfect weeping is given only to those first washed by Christ's blood who then taste the sweetness of God's love. Perfect weeping requires the disinterested love of both God and neighbor. Spirit-inspired longings of love cause "tears of fire," that is, the desire to belong totally to God. At the stage of "unitive tears," one longs only to have Christ crucified as the pattern for one's life. Catherine depicts the crucified Christ as the "nipple" of the divine breast that one suckles to be filled with the milk from the "high eternal Godhead." In the stage of unitive tears, Catherine hears God say about her: "She is another me, made so by the union of love."

The last selection is perhaps the most riveting letter in the Christian mystical tradition. Catherine wrote this letter shortly after comforting Niccolò di Toldo during his last hours before being beheaded for pro-papal activities.

This letter illustrates Catherine's precious blood mysticism. She begins every letter with "my greetings in the precious blood of God's Son" and exhorts her reader to drown in Christ's blood. Catherine's blood mysticism is a form of sacred heart mysticism. This blood flows from the wound in Christ's side wherein the "bride rests in the bed of fire and blood." This blood is also the divine wine that warms and inebriates. The theme of Jesus as "blood and fire" runs throughout her writings.

The letter illustrates her own desire for martyrdom. When Niccolò's head falls into her hands, Catherine has a vision of Christ receiving the beheaded's blood into his side, then Niccolò's soul being washed in Christ's blood, and finally the Holy Spirit's "hands" locking him into Christ's side where he rests in peace. The fragrance of the beheaded's blood mingles with her own and Christ's, and awakens Catherine's desire for the "wedding" of her own martyrdom in which one drowns "in the blood and fire pouring from the side of God's Son."[2]

THE TEXTS

THE DIALOGUE

79. I [God] said that these [perfect] souls are given the feeling (of my presence) never to lose it. But I do leave them in another fashion. The soul that is chained within the body is incapable of constantly experiencing union with me, and because of her incapacity I withdraw—not my grace or its feeling, but the union. For once souls have risen up in eager longing, they run in virtue along the bridge of the teaching of Christ crucified and arrive at the gate with their spirits lifted up to me. When they have crossed over and are inebriated with the blood and aflame with the fire of love, they taste in me the eternal Godhead, and I am to them a peaceful sea with which the soul becomes so united that her spirit knows no movement but in me. Though she is mortal she tastes the reward of the

immortals, and weighted down still with the body, she receives the lightness of the spirit. Often, therefore, the body is lifted up from the ground because of the perfect union of the soul with me, as if the heavy body had become light.

[This does not happen] because its heaviness has been taken away but because the union of the soul with me is more perfect than the union between the soul and the body. And for this reason the strength of the spirit united with me lifts the body's weight off the ground, and the body is, as it were, immobile, so completely bedraggled by the soul's emotion that (as you recall having heard about several persons) it would have been impossible to go on living had not my goodness encircled it with strength. . . . This is why I withdraw that union for a while and make the soul return to the vessel that is her body, so that the body's feeling, which has been completely lost because of the soul's emotion, returns. For the soul does not really leave the body (this happens only in death), but her powers and emotions are united with me in love. Therefore the memory finds itself filled with nothing but me. The understanding is lifted up as it gazes into my Truth. The will, which always follows the understanding, loves and unites itself with what the eye of the understanding sees.

When these powers are gathered and united all together and immersed and set afire in me, the body loses its feeling. For the eye sees without seeing; the ear hears without hearing; the tongue speaks without speaking . . . ; the hand touches without touching; the feet walk without walking. All the members are bound and busied with the bond and feeling of love. By this bond they are subjected to reason and joined with the soul's emotion so that, as if against their own nature, they all cry out to me, the eternal Father, with one voice, asking to be separated from the soul, and the soul from the body.[3]

88. *Then God, gentle First Truth, spoke:*

First of all, there are the tears of damnation, the tears of this world's evil ones. Second are the tears of fear, of those who weep for fear because they have risen up from their sins out of fear of punishment.

Third are those who have risen up from sin and are beginning to taste me. These weep tenderly and begin to serve me. But because their love is imperfect, so is their weeping. The fourth stage is that of souls who have attained perfection in loving their neighbors and love me without any self-interest. These weep, and their weeping is perfect. The fifth stage (which is joined to the fourth) is that of sweet tears shed with great tenderness. I will tell you, too, about tears of fire, shed without physical weeping, which often satisfy those who want to weep but cannot. And I want you to know that a soul can experience all of these different stages as she rises from fear and imperfect love to attain perfect love and the state of union.[4]

89. . . . I want you to know that all tears come from the heart. Nor is there any other bodily member that can satisfy the heart as the eyes can. . . .[5]

91. . . . I [God] still have to tell you, if I would fully answer your desire, about some souls who want the perfection of tears though it seems they cannot have it. Is there another way [to that perfection than by] physical tears? Yes. There is the weeping of fire, of true holy longing, and it consumes in love. [A soul so consumed] would like to dissolve her very life in weeping in self-contempt and for the salvation of souls, but she seems unable to do it.

I tell you, these souls have tears of fire. In this fire, the Holy Spirit weeps in my presence for them and for their neighbors. I mean that my divine charity sets ablaze with its flame the soul who offers me her restless longings without any physical tears. These, I tell you, are tears of fire, and this is how the Holy Spirit weeps. Since the soul cannot do it with tears, she offers her desire to weep for love of me. And if you open your mind's eye, you will see that the Holy Spirit weeps in the person of every one of my servants who offers me the fragrance of holy desire and constant humble prayer.[6]

96. I [God] have told you about the fruit of the third kind of tears. Next comes the fourth and last, the stage of unitive tears. This is not separated from the third, as I have told you. The two are joined together just as charity for me and for your

neighbors: They season each other. But the soul has grown so much by the time she reaches the fourth stage that she not only suffers patiently but gladly longs for suffering—so much so that she spurns every amusement, no matter what the source, simply to be able to pattern herself after my Truth, Christ crucified. Such a soul receives the fruit of spiritual calm, an emotional union with my gentle nature in which she tastes milk, just as an infant when quieted rests on its mother's breast, takes her nipple, and drinks her milk through her flesh. This is how the soul who has reached this final stage rests on the breast of my divine charity and takes into the mouth of her holy desire the flesh of Christ crucified. . . .

See then, gentle daughter, how delightfully glorious is this state in which the soul enjoys such union at charity's breast that her mouth is never away from the breast nor the breast without milk. Thus the soul is never without Christ crucified nor without me, the eternal Father, whom she finds when she tastes the high eternal Godhead. O who could imagine how that soul's powers are filled! Her memory is filled with constant remembrance of me as she lovingly drinks in my blessings. [What she drinks in] is not so much my blessings in themselves, but my loving charity in giving them to her. Especially, [what she drinks in] is the blessing of creation, for she sees that she is created in my image and likeness. At the first stage she had recognized the punishment that follows ingratitude for this blessing, and so she rose up from her wretchedness through the blessing of the blood of Christ, in which I created her anew in grace. I cleansed her soul's face of the leprosy of sin, and so she discovered the second state. There she tasted the sweetness of loving me and disgust for the sin in which she saw she had been so displeasing to me that I had taken out her punishment on the body of my only-begotten Son.

After this, she discovered the coming of the Holy Spirit who convinced and will continue to convince the soul of truth. When does the soul receive this light? After she has recognized my benefits to her in the first and second stages, she receives the perfect light. Then she knows the truth about me, the eternal Father: that in love I have created her to give her eternal life. This is the truth, and I have revealed it to her in the blood of Christ crucified. Once the soul has come to know this, she loves it, and she shows her love by genuinely loving what I love and hating what I hate. Thus she finds herself in the third stage of charity for her neighbors.

So the memory, all imperfect past, is filled at this breast because it has remembered and held without itself my blessings. Understanding receives the light. Gazing into the memory, it comes to know the truth, and shedding the blindness of selfish love, it remains in the sunlight of Christ crucified in whom it knows both God and humanity. Beyond this knowledge, because of the union [with me] that she has realized, the soul rises to a light acquired not by nature nor by her own practice of virtue but by the grace of my gentle Truth who does not scorn any eager longing or labors offered to me.

Then the will, which follows understanding, unites itself [with me] in a most perfect and burning love. And if anyone should ask me what this soul is, I would say: She is another me, made so by the union of love. . . . Not even the soul's own will stands between us, because she has become one with me.[7]

LETTER 31 (TO FRATE RAIMONDO DA CAPUA, IN OR NEAR PISA)[8]

In the name of Jesus Christ crucified and of gentle Mary. Very loved and dearest father and my dear son in Christ Jesus, I, Caterina, servant and slave of God, send you my greetings in the precious blood of God's Son, which is permeated with the fire of his blazing charity. This is what my soul desires: to see you in this blood—you, Nanni, and Iacomo. Son, I see no other way of our attaining the most basic virtues we need. No, dearest father, your soul could not attain them—this soul of yours that has become my food. Not a moment passes that I am not eating this food at the table of the gentle Lamb who was slain in such blazing love. I am saying that unless you are drowned in the blood, you will not attain the little virtue of true humility, which is born from hatred as hatred is from love, and so come forth in the most perfect purity as iron comes out purified from the furnace.

So I want you to shut yourself up in the open side of God's Son, that open hostelry so full of fragrance that sin itself is made fragrant. There the dear bride rests in the bed of fire and blood. There she sees revealed the secret of the heart of God's Son. *Oh overflowing cask, you give drink and fill to drunkenness every loving desire. You give joy and illumine all our understanding. You so fill all our remembrance that we are overcome and can neither hold nor understand nor love anything other than this good gentle Jesus, blood and fire, ineffable love!* Once my soul has been blessed with seeing you so drowned, I want you to act like a person who draws water with a pail. I mean, with a boundless desire pour the water over the heads of your brothers and sisters who are our members bound together in the body of the sweet bride. . . .

Up, up, my dearest father, and let's sleep no longer, for I'm hearing news that makes me no longer want either bed or rest. I've already begun by receiving a head into my hands. It was sweeter to me than the heart can imagine or the tongue speak or the eye see or the ear hear. . . . I went to visit the one you know and he was so comforted and consoled that he confessed his sins and prepared himself very well. He made me promise for the love of God that when the time came for the execution, I would be with him. This I promised and did.

In the morning, before the bell, I went to him, and he was greatly consoled. I took him to hear Mass, and he received holy communion, which he hadn't received in a long time. His will was in accord with and submissive to God's will. His only fear now was of not being strong at the final moment. But God's measureless and burning goodness tricked him, creating in him such affection and love through his love for me in God that he could not do without God! He said, "Stay with me; don't leave me alone. That way I can't help but be all right, and I'll die happy!" His head was resting on my breast. I sensed an intense joy, a fragrance of his blood—and it wasn't separate from the fragrance of my own, which I am waiting to shed for my gentle Spouse Jesus.

With my soul's desire growing, and sensing his fear, I said, "Courage, my dear brother, for soon we shall reach the wedding feast. You will go forth to it bathed in the sweet blood of God's Son, with the sweet name of Jesus, which I don't want ever to leave your memory. I shall wait for you at the place of execution.". . .

I waited for him at the place of execution. I waited there in continual prayer and in the presence of Mary and of Catherine, virgin and martyr. Before he arrived, I knelt down and stretched my neck out on the block, but I did not succeed in getting what I longed for up there. . . .

Then he arrived like a meek lamb, and when he saw me, he began to laugh and wanted me to make the sign of the cross on him. When he had received the sign, I said, "Down for the wedding, my dear brother, for soon you will be in everlasting life!" He knelt down very meekly; I placed his neck [on the block] and bent down and reminded him of the blood of the Lamb. His mouth said nothing but "Gesù!" and "Caterina!" and as he said this, I received his head into my hands, saying, "I will!" with my eyes fixed on divine Goodness.

Then was seen the God-Man as one sees the brilliance of the sun. [His side] was open and received blood into his own blood— received a flame of holy desire (which grace had given and hidden in his soul) into the flame of his own divine charity. After he had received his blood and desire, [Jesus] received his soul as well and placed it all-mercifully into the open hostelry of his side. Thus, First Truth showed he was receiving him only through grace and mercy and not for anything he had done. Oh how boundlessly sweet it was to see God's goodness! With what tenderness and love he awaited that soul when it had left its body—the eye of his mercy turned toward it—when it came to enter into his side bathed in its own blood, which found its worth in the blood of God's Son. Once he had been so received by God (who by his power was powerful enough to do it), the Son, Wisdom and Word incarnate, gave him the gift of sharing in the tormented love with which he himself had accepted his painful death in obedience to the Father for the welfare of the human race. And the hands of the Holy Spirit locked him in. . . . Now that he was hidden away where he belonged, my soul rested in peace and quiet in such a fragrance of blood that I couldn't bear to wash away his blood that had splashed on me. Ah, poor wretch that I am, I don't want to say any more. With the greatest envy I remained on earth!

It seems to me that the first stone is already laid. So don't be surprised if I impose on you only my desire to see you drowned in the blood and fire pouring out from the side of God's Son. No more apathy now, my sweetest children, because the blood has begun to flow and to receive life!

The anonymous author of The Cloud of Unknowing *is considered to be the mystical genius of 14th-century England. As an outstanding example of the Christian apophatic tradition, he stressed that only love, not knowledge, can fully comprehend God and that one must be specifically called to apophatic mysticism through discernible signs.*

THE ANONYMOUS AUTHOR OF THE CLOUD OF UNKNOWING

Although some commentators consider him to be the mystical genius of 14th-century England, the astonishing fact is that the identity of this mystic, theologian, and spiritual director who wrote the highly celebrated *Cloud of Unknowing* has never been established. Yet this anonymous author's mystical depth, theological acumen, psychological shrewdness, and soundness of spiritual direction was such that he has even been called the English equivalent of St. John of the Cross, whom many consider the Church's greatest mystic and mystical writer.

Nor was *The Cloud of Unknowing* the only work of this esteemed author. He also penned *The Epistle of Prayer, Assessment of Inward Stirrings*, and *The Book of Privy Counselling,* perhaps his most mature piece of writing. These may be the first works in Middle English about the mystical quest for God. The same author also translated and adapted into Middle English Pseudo-Dionysius' *Mystica Theologica*, Richard of St. Victor's *Benjamin Minor,* and two of Bernard of Clairvaux's sermons.

Possessing both considerable literary beauty and practicality, this writer's books and treatises focus upon the essentials of the mystical life. They evince his personal experience as well as his masterful assimilation of the Western mystical tradition. However, our author does not merely repeat the tradition, offer a compilation of it, or simply recount his own mystical experiences. With a sure touch and serene authority, he transposes the Western tradition and his own mystical wisdom into a competent guide for the seeker of the contemplative way to God.

The anonymous author teaches a highly introspective form of mysticism that turns a person's inner eye not to finding God in all things but to finding God in the depths of the "mirror" of darkness, that is, the soul emptied of *everything* except naked love. He is an outstanding example of the Christian apophatic mystical tradition which stresses that only love, not knowledge, can fully comprehend God. He therefore prefers to speak about what God is not. Through mystical love, "there is a negative knowledge which understands God." Thus, his teaching is neither a medieval form of Transcendental Meditation nor yogic nescience that does not require love as a driving force. To him, love is mysticism's business.

Through the pen of this author, the purgation, illumination, and union caused by the "tiny dart of love" in the depths of one's spirit are presented in a compact, unsystematic way. What nourishes this inner flame is the forgetting of all created things. When "naked love," that is, love shorn of all concepts and images, takes hold at the root of the contemplative's being, it tortuously causes all the sins of the person's life to arise. Eventually, one suffers not from the painful remembrance of past sins but from the acute realization that one is a sinner, a "lump of sin." As the tiny flame of love heals the scars of past sins and removes the "lump," the contemplative suffers from not being able to forget his or her self. Thus, one experiences the self as a "cross" between oneself and God. In time, one agonizes over not being able to love as much as one is loved. This entire process cleanses people of all sinfulness and increases their capacity to love.

However, God also illuminates contemplatives through ecstatic revelations of God's superabundant goodness and beauty. Paradoxically, the splendor of spiritual light blinds, yet opens the inner eye to an experience of God "as he really is." Moreover, contemplatives experience that "God is their being, but they are not God's being." Naked love effects such a radical union between God and contemplatives that they are as close to God "by grace" as God is to himself "by nature." They have become one in grace.

The first of the following readings was selected to illustrate the anonymous author's simple, yet powerful, apophatic contemplative technique. It must be emphasized that he presupposes the reader to be a person experienced in asceticism, self-knowledge, moderation in all things, vocal and liturgical prayer, meditation, study, Scripture, sacramental confession, and in obedience to a spiritual father. In addition to the foundation of a full Christian life, he presupposes that one has been *specifically called* to the contemplative life by discernible signs that will be explained below.

The author recommends lifting up one's heart in love and rejecting all thoughts of and desire for creatures. One must place everything—even thoughts about God, Christ, Mary, and the like—into a "cloud of forgetting" that arises between the contemplative and all created things. This process causes a "darkness," a "cloud of unknowing" to arise between God and the contemplative. One then prays in "naked love." Only love shorn of all knowledge can "feel and see God in this life." The author also suggests selecting a short, meaningful word—not to concentrate on its meaning but simply to use as a mantra to beat back distractions.

The second text was chosen to show that apophatic prayer is not for everyone. God may give this grace to anyone from any walk of life; nonetheless, God does not call everyone to this "singular" way of life. If the tiny dart of love *constantly* intrudes in one's life and becomes a "barrier to ordinary prayer," and if one is *constantly* aroused to contemplation whenever one hears or reads about it, then—and only then—can one undertake apophatic contemplation.

The third selection focuses on mystical discernment. To our anonymous author, once naked love sufficiently cleanses and illuminates a person, it becomes the heart of everything that person does. It may first gently prod a contemplative's heart to do this or that. If resisted, the "tiny dart of love" becomes like a needle in the heart that points to and insists upon a certain course of action.

The fourth selection also illustrates that God does not give everyone a contemplative vocation and that "the devil has his contemplatives." Because apophatic contemplation is fraught with dangers, the author emphasizes the importance of adequate preparation, the gentle attraction of grace, and the presence of certain signs that indicate a contemplative vocation. The genuine contemplative heeds the advice of a cleansed conscience, common sense, a spiritual director, reason, and the scriptures.

On the other hand, "pseudocontemplatives" often embrace the way of brute force, straining, morbid introspection, facile iconoclasm, or degenerate passivity. By forcing the forgetting of all created things, they end up with an unhealthy otherworldly fixation leading to physical, emotional, and spiritual deterioration. Frenzy, eccentric mannerisms, pride, intellectual conceit, and sensuality are their hallmarks.

The author also teaches that naked love may show itself as ecstatic or as the gentle, peaceful, silent love permeating all the contemplative's daily activities. Mystical love heals, integrates, and transforms the human personality as it graciously but firmly directs the person toward God and neighbor. To our author, contemplative love is in itself apostolic: it is the best thing we can do both for ourselves and for our neighbor.[1]

THE TEXTS

"How the Work of Contemplation Shall Be Done"

This is what you are to do: lift your heart up to the Lord, with a gentle stirring of love desiring him for his own sake and not for his gifts. Center all your attention and desire on him and let this be the sole concern of your mind and heart. Do all in your power to forget everything else, keeping your thoughts and desires free from involvement with any of God's creatures or their affairs whether in general or in particular. Perhaps this will seem like an irresponsible attitude, but I tell you, let them all be; pay no attention to them. . . .

And so diligently persevere in it until you feel joy in it. For in the beginning it is usual to feel nothing but a kind of darkness about your mind, as it were, a *cloud of unknowing*. You will seem to know nothing and to feel nothing except a naked intent toward God in the depths of your being. Try as you might, this darkness and cloud will remain between you and your God. You will feel frustrated, for your mind will be unable to grasp him, and your heart will not relish the delight of his love. But learn to be at home in this darkness. Return to it as often as you can, letting your spirit cry out to him whom you love. For if, in this life, you hope to feel and see God as he is in himself it must be within this darkness and this cloud. But if you strive to fix your love on him forgetting all else, which is the work of contemplation I have urged you to begin, I am confident that God in his goodness will bring you to a deep experience of himself. . . .[2]

When I speak of darkness, I mean the absence of knowledge. If you are unable to understand something or if you have forgotten it, are you not in the dark as regards this thing? You cannot see it with your mind's eye. Well, in the same way, I have not said "cloud" but *cloud of unknowing*. For it is a darkness of unknowing that lies between you and your God.

If you wish to enter into this cloud, to be at home in it, and to take up the contemplative work of love as I urge you to, there is something else you must do. Just as the cloud of unknowing lies above you, between you and your God, so you must fashion a *cloud of forgetting* beneath you, between you and every created thing. The cloud of unknowing will perhaps leave you with the feeling that you are far from God. But no, if it is authentic, only the absence of a *cloud of forgetting* keeps you from him now. Every time I say "all creatures," I refer not only to every created thing but also to all their circumstances and activities. I make no exception. You are to concern yourself with no creature, whether material or spiritual, nor with their situation and doings, whether good or ill. To put it briefly, during this work, you must abandon them all beneath the *cloud of forgetting*. . . .

Yes, and with all due reverence, I go so far as to say that it is equally useless to think you can nourish your contemplative work by considering God's attributes, his kindness, or his dignity; or by thinking about our Lady, the angels, or the saints; or about the joys of heaven, wonderful as these will be. I believe that this kind of activity is no longer of any use to you. Of course, it is laudable to reflect upon God's kindness and to love and praise him for it; yet it is far better to let your mind rest in the awareness of him in his naked existence and to love and praise him for what he is in himself. . . .[3] A naked intent toward God, the desire for him alone is enough.

If you want to gather all your desire into one simple word that the mind can easily retain, choose a short word rather than a long one. A one-syllable word such as "God" or "love" is best. But choose one that is meaningful to you. Then fix it in your mind so that it will remain there come what may. This word will be your defense in conflict and in peace. Use it to beat upon the cloud of darkness above you and to subdue all distractions, consigning them to the cloud of forgetting beneath you. Should some thought go on annoying you demanding to know what you are doing, answer with the one word alone. If your mind begins to intellectualize over the meaning and connotations of this little word, remind yourself that its value lies in its simplicity. Do this, and I assure you these thoughts will vanish. Why, because you have refused to develop them with arguing. . . .[4]

As I have already explained to you, this simple work is not a rival to your daily activities. For with your attention centered on the blind awareness of your naked being united to God's, you will go about your daily rounds, eating and drinking, sleeping and waking, going and coming, speaking and listening, lying down and rising up, standing and kneeling, running and riding, working and resting. In the midst of it all, you will be offering to God continually each day the most precious gift you can make. This work will be at the heart of everything you do, whether active or contemplative.[5]

"Signs of a Contemplative Vocation"[6]

You will notice, first of all, that I have given you two kinds of evidence for discerning whether or not God is calling you spiritually to contemplation. One was interior and the other exterior. Now it is my conviction that for discerning a call to contemplation, neither one, by itself, is sufficient proof. They must occur together, both indicating the same thing, before you may rely on them without fear of error.

The interior sign is that growing desire for contemplation constantly intruding in your daily devotions. And there is much I can tell you about that desire. It is a blind longing of the spirit and yet there comes with it, and lingers after it, a spiritual sight that both renews the desire and increases it. . . .

So carefully observe your daily devotions, and see what is happening. If they are filled with the memory of your own sinfulness, considerations of Christ's Passion, or anything else pertaining to the ordinary Christian way of prayer I have described before, know that the spiritual insight accompanying and following this blind desire originates in your ordinary grace. And this is a sure sign that God is not stirring you or calling you to a more intense life of grace as yet. Rather, he is giving you this desire as food and strength to go on waiting quietly and working in your ordinary grace.

The second sign is exterior and it manifests itself as a certain joyful enthusiasm welling up within you, whenever you hear or read about contemplation. I call it exterior because it originates outside you and enters your mind through the windows of your bodily senses (your eyes and ears) when you read. As for the discernment of this sign, see if that joyful enthusiasm persists, remaining with you when you have left your reading. If it disappears immediately or soon after and does not pursue you in all else you do, know that it is not a special touch of grace. If it is not with you when you go to sleep and wake up, and if it does not go before you, constantly intruding in all you do, enkindling and capturing your desire, it is not God's call to a more intense life of grace, beyond what I call the common door and entry for all Christians. In my opinion, its very transience shows that it is simply the natural joy any Christian feels when he reads or hears about the truth and more especially a truth like this, which so profoundly and accurately speaks of God and the perfection of the human spirit.

But when the joyful enthusiasm which seizes you as you read or hear about contemplation is really the touch of God calling you to a higher life of grace, you will notice very different effects. So abounding will it be that it will follow you to bed at night and rise with you in the morning. It will pursue you through the day in everything you do, intruding into your usual daily devotions like a barrier between you and them.

Moreover, it will seem to occur simultaneously with that blind desire which, in the meantime, quietly grows in intensity. The enthusiasm and the desire will seem to be part of each other; so much so, that you will think it is only one desire you feel, though you will be at a loss to say just precisely what it is that you long for.

Your whole personality will be transformed, your countenance will radiate an inner beauty, and for as long as you feel it, nothing will sadden you. A thousand miles would you run to speak with another who you knew really felt it, and yet when you got there, find yourself speechless. Let others say what they will, your only joy would be to speak of it. Your words will be few, but so fruitful and full of fire that the little you say will hold a world of wisdom (though it may seem nonsense to those still unable to transcend the limits of reason). Your silence will be peaceful, your speech helpful, and your prayer secret in the depths of your being. Your self-esteem will be natural and unspoiled by conceit, your way with others gentle, and your laughter merry as you take delight in everything with the joy of a child. How dearly you will love to sit apart by yourself, knowing that others, not sharing your desire and attraction, would only hinder you. Gone will be all desire to read or hear books, for your only desire will be to hear of it.

Thus, the mounting desire for contemplation and the joyful enthusiasm that seizes you when you read or hear of it meet and become one. These two signs (one interior and one exterior) agree, and you may rely on them as proof that God is calling you to enter within and begin a more intense life of grace.

Mystical Discernment[7]

And then your heart's experience will know well how to tell you when to speak and when to be silent. It will guide you with discernment in all your living without error and teach you in mystical manner how you are to begin and leave off in all your natural doings with a great and perfect discernment. And if, by grace, you can make a habit of this loving awareness and exercise yourself in it constantly, then, if you need to speak, follow a normal diet, or dwell in company, or do anything else that belongs to the good and common custom of human nature and Christian men, it will first gently move you to speak or to do the natural ordinary thing, whatever it is. And if you fail to do it, this awareness will wound you as sorely and painfully as if your heart were pierced and let you have no peace until you do it. And in the same way, if you happen to be speaking or doing anything else that belongs to normal human activity, and it is necessary and profitable to you to be still and set yourself to the contrary, such as fasting in place of eating, living alone instead of in company, and all other such works of singular holiness, this loving awareness will move you to do these things.

Thus, by experience of this blind stirring of love for God, the contemplative will arrive at the grace of discernment. . . .

And so you may confidently rely on this gentle stirring of love in your heart and follow wherever it leads you, for it is your sure guide in this life and will bring you to the glory of the next. This little love is the essence of a good life and without it no good work is possible. Basically, love means a radical personal commitment to God. This implies that your will is harmoniously attuned to his in an abiding contentedness and enthusiasm for all he does.

"The Devil's Contemplatives"[8]

Neglecting the inspiration of grace and excited by vanity and conceit, he [the devil's contemplative] strains his endurance so morbidly that in no time he is weary and enervated in body and spirit. Then he feels the necessity to alleviate the pressure he has created by seeking some empty material or physical compensation as a relaxation for mind and body.

Should he escape this, his spiritual blindness and the abuse he inflicts on his body in this pseudocontemplation (for it can hardly be called spiritual) may lead him to arouse his passions unnaturally or work himself into a frenzy. And all this is the result of pseudospirituality and maltreating the body. It is instigated by his enemy, the fiend, who takes advantage of his pride, sensuality, and intellectual conceit to deceive him.

Yet, unfortunately, many people believe that the excitement they feel is the fire of the love kindled in their breasts by the Holy Spirit. From this deception and the like spring evils of every kind, much hypocrisy, heresy, and error. For this sort of pseudoexperience brings with it the false knowledge of the fiend's school just as an authentic experience brings with it the understanding of the truth taught by God. Believe me when I say that the devil has his contemplatives as surely as God has his. . . .

The spiritual and physical comportment of those involved in any sort of pseudocontemplation is apt to appear very eccentric, whereas God's friends always bear themselves with simple grace. Anyone noticing these deluded folk at prayer might see strange things indeed! If their eyes are open, they are apt to be staring blankly like a madman or peering like one who saw the devil, and well they might, for he is not far off. Sometimes their eyes look like the eyes of wounded sheep near death. Some will let their heads droop to one side, as if a worm were in their ears. Others, like ghosts, utter shrill piping sounds that are supposed to pass for speech. They are usually hypocrites. Some whine and whimper in their desire and eagerness to be heard. . . .

Anyone observing them would undoubtedly notice many other grotesque mannerisms, although a few are so clever that they are able to maintain a respectable front in public. Should they be observed off guard, however, I believe that their sham would be evident, and anyone with the audacity to contradict them will certainly feel their wrath. Yet they believe that all they do is for God and in the service of truth. But I am convinced that unless God intervenes with a miracle to make them renounce this specious nonsense, their way of "loving God" will drive them straight into the devil's clutches stark raving mad. I am not saying that everyone under the devil's influence is afflicted with all these affectations, though this is not impossible. But all his disciples are corrupted with some of them or with others like them, as I will explain now, God willing.

There are those so laden with all sorts of eccentric and effeminate mannerisms that when they listen, they have a coy way of twisting their heads up and to one side, gaping with open mouths. One would think they were trying to hear with their mouths instead of their ears! Some, when they speak, will rudely point their fingers on their own hands or breast or at those to whom they are lecturing. Others can neither sit, stand, nor lie down without moving their feet or gesturing with their hands. Some row their arms as though they were trying to swim over a great water. Others, again, are forever grinning and giggling with every word like giddy schoolgirls or silly clowns with no breeding. . . .

I am not implying that these mannerisms are greatly sinful in themselves or that all who employ them are necessarily great sinners. My point is that if these affectations dominate a person to where he is enslaved by them, they are evidence of pride, sophistry, exhibitionism, or curiosity. At the very least, they betray a fickle heart and restless imagination of one sadly lacking in a true contemplative spirit.

Walter Hilton's writings are almost a complete guide to the spiritual life of the 14th-century English mystics. Hilton's message is simple: Single-minded devotion to Jesus is the way to Jerusalem, "the vision of peace."

WALTER HILTON

Very little is known about the person considered by some commentators to be one of the 14th-century mystical giants. Hilton led the eremitical life for several years before becoming a canon of the Augustinian Priory of Thurgarton near Southwell, Nottinghamshire, about 1375. Although he lived in a period of tremendous religious and political upheaval—the Great Western Schism, the middle of the Hundred Years' War, the Peasants' Revolt of 1381, the Lollard movement, and the Augustinian battles versus the disciples of Wycliffe—his writings exhibit an almost ethereal serenity.

This master of the Western mystical tradition wrote a *Letter on the Mixed Life, Commentaries on Psalms 90 and 91, The Goad of Love,* and the famous *Scale of Perfection.* The *Scale* has been called the most lucid, balanced, and complete treatise on the interior life of the late Middle Ages and an almost complete guide to the spiritual life of the 14th-century English mystics. Because of its practical advice for even nonmystics, the *Scale* became an immediate favorite of the laity when it was first published in 1494.

In the *Scale*, Hilton broke away somewhat from the medieval tradition that tended to restrict perfection to the cloister. Instead, he focused on perfection as the fullness of Christian charity. In the *Goad of Love*, he taught that one need not withdraw from the world to seek Christ, who can be found especially among the sick. However, those who desire the perfection of contemplation, that is, the vision of Jesus, must lose their taste for the world and seek physical solitude whenever possible to attain solitude of heart.

In order to understand the selected texts, one must keep in mind Hilton's teachings on the three degrees of contemplative life. The first degree consists of the "tasteless and cold," but good, knowledge attained through study, especially of Scripture. The second degree consists of love on fire with devotion but without understanding. The third degree occurs only after grace has weaned a person from the world and raptured that person in enlightening and "soft, sweet, burning love." "Love on fire with contemplation" requires a special grace given only to a few. Moreover, to Hilton, only those vowed to a solitary life have its "full use."

The first text, "The Parable of the Pilgrim," was selected because it is considered to be a masterpiece of spiritual writing. It illustrates the devotional and affective basis of Hilton's mysticism as well as his homey style. Hilton's message is simple: Single-minded devotion to Jesus is the way to Jerusalem, "the vision of peace." In order to attain contemplation, which Hilton identifies as "the vision of Jesus," the pilgrim must reform his or her life through sacramental penance, respect for the Church's teachings, and humility. The pilgrim must also leave everything, conquer the enemies of bodily passion and demonic trickery, use whatever devotional practices deepen love for Christ, and realize that "you have nothing until you feel the love of Jesus within you."

The second text illustrates both Hilton's warm, Christ-centered mysticism and his intriguing apophaticism. To him, Jesus is both our deepest desire and its object. Because love of Jesus is both a "true day" and a "blessed night," the ardent desire to know and love Jesus casts the person into a "glowing darkness" that extinguishes the world's false lights. The more one "thinks of nothing" except the desire for Jesus, the more one experiences the light of his love. Diverting one's attention from worldly things produces an inner darkness that opens the spiritual eye. Christ's true light intensifies until the person is clothed in light and "wholly ablaze."

This pragmatic, ardent, shrewd mystical teacher offers sound advice on the beginnings of prayer as an awareness of God to the heights of mystical marriage. Despite his simplicity, profundity, and former renown, Hilton seems undeservedly neglected in our age.[1]

THE TEXTS

THE SCALE OF PERFECTION

THE PARABLE OF THE PILGRIM[2]

A man once wished to go to Jerusalem, and since he did not know the way, he called on another man, who, he hoped, knew the way, and asked him for information. The other man told him that he would not reach it without great hardship and effort. "The way is long," he said, "and there is great danger from thieves and bandits, as well as many other difficulties which beset a man on this journey. Furthermore, there are many different roads which seem to lead toward it, but every day men are killed and robbed, and never reach their goal. But I guarantee one road which will lead you to the city of Jerusalem if you will keep to it. On this road your life will be safe, but you will have to undergo robbery, violence, and great distress."

The pilgrim replied: "I do not mind how much hardship I have to undergo on the road, so long as my life is spared and I reach my destination. So tell me all you know, and I faithfully promise to follow your instructions." The other answered, "I will set you on the right road. See that you carry out my instructions. Do not allow anything that you may see, hear, or feel on the road to delay you. Do not stop for it, look at it, take pleasure in it, or fear it. Keep on your way without halting, and remember that your goal is Jerusalem; that is what you want, and nothing else. If you are robbed, beaten, insulted, and treated with contempt, do not retaliate if you value your life. Resign yourself to such injuries and disregard them, lest you suffer worse things. And if people delay you with foolish tales and lies in order to distract you and make you abandon your pilgrimage, turn a deaf ear to them and make no reply save that you wish to reach Jerusalem. And if people offer you gifts or provide opportunities for you to enrich yourself, disregard them: keep your mind constantly on Jerusalem. If you will keep to this road and do as I have said, I guarantee that you will not be killed, and that you will arrive at the place for which you long."

Spiritually interpreted, Jerusalem is the vision of peace, and symbolizes contemplation in the perfect love of God. For contemplation is nothing other than the vision of Jesus, who is our true peace. Therefore, if you really desire to attain this blessed vision of true peace and to be a true pilgrim to Jerusalem, I will set you on the right road as far as I can, although I have never been there myself. The beginning of this high road that you must travel is reformation in faith, which . . . is grounded in humility, faith, and the laws of the Church. And if you have been reformed by the sacrament of penance according to the laws of the Church, you can rest assured that, despite your earlier sins, you are on the right road. If you wish to make swift and substantial progress along this road, you must constantly bear in mind two things, humility and love. That is, I am nothing, and I want only one thing. Fix the true meaning of these words permanently in your subconscious mind and purpose, so that they will guide you even when you are not thinking of them. Humility says, "I am nothing, I have nothing." Love says, "I desire one thing only, which is Jesus." When deftly touched by the finger of reason, these two strings, secured by the thought of Jesus, make sweet harmony in the harp of the soul, for the lower you strike on one, the higher the sound on the other. Under the influence of humility, the less you feel that you are or possess, the greater will be your love and longing for Jesus. I am not speaking merely of the kind of humility that a soul feels at the sight of its own sin or weakness or of the sorrows of this life or when it sees the better lives of other Christians; for although this kind of humility is sound and wholesome, it is still of an elementary and worldly type, not pure, gentle, and perfect. I am speaking rather of the humility that a soul feels by grace as it contemplates the infinite being and wondrous goodness of Jesus. And if you cannot yet see this with the eyes of the soul, do believe in its reality. For having once caught a glimpse of his being, whether by true faith or by spiritual experience, you will see yourself not only as the most wretched of men but as worthless, even though you had never sinned. This is perfect humility, for in comparison to Jesus, who is all, you are nothing. You should also realize that you possess nothing, like a vessel that stands empty, incapable of filling itself; for however many good works you perform, spiritual or bodily, you have nothing until you feel the love of Jesus within you. It is this precious liquor alone that can fill your soul and no other. And since this alone is so precious and noble, you must realize that whatever you may have or achieve is of no value or satisfaction without the love of Jesus. Put everything else behind you and forget it; only then can you have what is best of all.

A real pilgrim going to Jerusalem leaves his house and land, wife and children; he divests himself of all that he possesses in order to travel light and without encumbrances. Similarly, if you wish to be a spiritual pilgrim, you must divest yourself of all that you possess; that is, both of good deeds and bad, and leave them all behind you. Recognize your own poverty, so that you will not place any confidence in your own work; instead, be always desiring the grace of deeper love, and seeking the spiritual presence of Jesus. If you do this, you will be setting your heart wholly on obtaining the love of Jesus and whatever spiritual vision of himself that he is willing to grant, for it is to this end alone that you have been created and redeemed; this is your beginning and your end, your joy and your bliss. . . .

Now that you are on the road and know your proper destination, you must begin your journey. The departure consists entirely of spiritual—and when necessary, bodily—activity, and you must direct this activity wisely in the following way. I regard any activity that you undertake as excellent provided that it suits your particular calling and conditions of life and that it fosters this high desire for the love of Jesus and makes it more sincere, more comforting, and more productive of all virtues. It may be prayer, meditation, reading, or working, but so long as the activity is one which deepens the love of Jesus in your heart and will and withdraws your thoughts and affections from worldly trivialities, it is good. . . . For although the desire and longing of your heart for Jesus should be constant and unchanging, you are at liberty to vary your spiritual exercises in order to stimulate this desire, and they may well be changed when you feel that grace moves you to do so.

The relation of spiritual activities to desire is similar to that of sticks to fire. For the more sticks are laid on the fire, the greater is the fire: similarly, the more varying spiritual exercises that a man performs to stimulate his desire for God, the stronger and more ardent it will be. Therefore, if you are free and not bound by any particular obligation, consider carefully which activity is best suited to you, and which most fosters your desire for Jesus, and undertake it. Do not deliberately bind yourself to an unchangeable routine which would prevent your heart loving Jesus freely should you receive a special visitation of grace. . . .

You are now on the road, and you know how to proceed. . . . Your chief enemies are the bodily desires and foolish fears which the corruption of human nature stirs up in your heart and which would stifle your desire for the love of God and take full possession of your heart. These are your deadliest enemies. There are also others, for evils spirits employ all their tricks to deceive you. . . .

However, so long as you are on the road, they will not cease to harass you; at one time, they will intimidate and threaten you, at another, they will try to flatter you and seduce you, to make you abandon your purpose and turn back. . . .

. . . Fix your thoughts on Jesus, and do not allow any trouble to disturb you or occupy your attention. Remember what you have learned: you are nothing, you have nothing, and loss of worldly goods is nothing, for you desire nothing but the love of Jesus. So continue both your journey to Jerusalem and your present exercise. . . .

THE SECURE AND GLOWING DARKNESS
If you wish to learn the nature of this desire, it is in fact Jesus himself. He implants this desire within you and is himself both the desire and the object of your desire. If you could only understand this, you would see that Jesus is everything and Jesus does everything. You yourself do nothing; you simply allow him to work within your soul, accepting sincerely and gladly whatever he deigns to do in you. . . .

Therefore, when your mind is touched by his grace and you feel yourself moved by a strong desire to please and love Jesus, you can be sure that Jesus is within you, for it is he whom you desire. Fix your eyes on him, for he does not come in bodily form but invisibly, with the hidden presence of his power. See him spiritually if you can; trust him and follow him wherever he goes, for he will guide you on the right road to Jerusalem, which is the vision of peace in contemplation. . . .

But the everlasting love of Jesus is true day and blessed night, for God is both love and light, and he is everlasting. . . . But anyone who realizes that the love of this world is false and transitory, and therefore wishes to abandon it and seek the love of God, cannot at once experience his love but must remain awhile in the night. He cannot pass suddenly from one light to the other, that is, from the love of this world to the perfect love of God. This night is nothing other than a complete withdrawal of the soul from earthly things by an intense desire to love, see, and know Jesus and the things of the spirit. This is a real night, for just as night is dark, hiding all created things and bringing all bodily activity to a halt, similarly, one who sets himself to think of Jesus and to desire his love alone must try to withdraw his thoughts and affections from created things. In so doing, his mind and his affections will be set free from enslavement to anything of a nature inferior to his own. If he can do this, then it is night for him, for he is in darkness.

But this is a night pregnant with good, a glowing darkness, for it shuts out the false love of his world and ushers in the dawn of the true day. Indeed, the darker this night, the nearer the true day of the love of Jesus, for the further the soul in its longing for Jesus retires from the clamor of worldly desires and impure thoughts, the nearer it approaches to experiencing the light of his love. . . .

By "thinking of nothing" I mean that the soul attains recollection, stability, and integrity, so that it cannot be compelled against its will to think of, or be drawn toward, any sinful, vain, or worldly thing. The soul may then be said to think of nothing, because its thoughts are not attracted to earthly things. This nothing brings a rich reward, and this night is full of great consolation to the soul that desires the love of Jesus. For it is undisturbed by any earthly thought, and is free to think of Jesus alone. For although the soul has banished all thoughts of the world, it is actively engaged in the contemplation of Jesus.

What, then, is the nature of this darkness? It arises solely from a grace-inspired desire to have the love of Jesus. This desire and longing for the love of God, to see him and to possess him, drives out of the heart all worldly considerations and affections. It moves the soul to recollection and to ponder how it may come to this love; in this way it brings it into this precious nothing. But the soul is not in complete darkness and nothingness during this time, for although it conceals it from the false light, it does not entirely conceal it from the true light. For Jesus, who is both love and light, is in this darkness, whether it brings pain or peace. He is at work in the soul, moving it to anguish with desire and longing for the light, but not as yet allowing it to rest in love, nor showing it his light. This state is called night and darkness, because the soul is hidden from the false light of the world and has not yet fully enjoyed the true light but is awaiting the blessed love of God which it desires. . . .

This darkness and night, then, springs solely from the soul's desire and longing for the love of Jesus, combined with a blind groping of the mind toward him. . . . So respond wholeheartedly to the stirrings of grace, and learn to live in this darkness. When you grow accustomed to it, you will soon find peace, and the true light of spiritual knowledge will grow within you; not all at once but imperceptibly and little by little. . . .

For remember that although your soul dwells in this peaceful darkness untroubled by thoughts of the world, it is not yet at the end of its journey, for it is not yet clothed in light or wholly ablaze with the fire of love. It is fully conscious of something beyond itself which as yet it neither knows nor possesses, but it has an ardent longing for it. The object of its longing is nothing other than the vision of Jerusalem. . . .

Julian's visionary mysticism makes her unique among the English mystics. She is well-known for calling both God and Jesus "Mother," and for her statement: "I wille make all thynge wele, I shalle make all thynge wele, I maye make alle thynge wele and I can make alle thynge wele."

JULIAN OF NORWICH

We know almost nothing about Julian's life, not even her given name. Since she lived the solitary, enclosed life of an anchoress in a "cell" adjoining the parish church of St. Julian in Conisford at Norwich (opposite the house of the Augustinian friars), the name "Julian" was probably adopted in honor of the saint of the church to which the hermitage was attached.

We do know from her writings that in her youth, Julian prayed for three graces from God. First, she desired to participate deeply in Christ's passion. Craving to suffer with Christ, as did those who loved him, Julian envied Mary Magdalene who had witnessed Christ's sufferings at the foot of the cross. Second, she prayed for a sickness unto death wherein she would experience no earthly comfort but all kinds of pain, both physical and spiritual. In short, deep devotion to Christ's passion—a devotion that pervaded the Western church in Julian's era—stamped her spirituality. Third, she also pleaded for three "wounds": the wound of contrition, the wound of compassion, and the wound of "willful" longing for God.

In the year 1373, during an illness thought to be fatal, Julian was privileged to have a vision of Christ crucified. As she gazed upon the figure on the cross, she "suddenly saw the red blood trickling down from under the crown, all hot, flowing freely and copiously, a living stream, just as it seemed to me that it was at the time when the crown of thorns was thrust down upon his blessed head."[1]

Revelations about the indwelling of the Trinity in the soul, God's love for humanity, and other spiritual illuminations accompanied this vision. Julian recorded this experience and her initial reflections upon it in what is now called the *Short text* of her *Sixteen Revelations of Divine Love, or Showings*. Julian is an example of a visionary mystic, that is, of someone mystically purged by, illuminated by, and united to God through visions. Her God-given life was bestowed in and through visions and remained inseparable from them. The visionary character of her revelations makes Julian unique among the English mystics, except for Margery Kempe, who was a generation younger.

Realizing that her showings were meant not for her alone but for all Christians, Julian prayed and reflected upon the meaning of her extraordinary experiences for almost 20 years. The *Long text* exemplifies that, in the case of some mystics, mystical experience matures only through profound theological reflection and vice versa. The text not only describes her mystical experiences, but it also attempts to explain their doctrinal significance. This 20-year mystical process gave creative expression to all the main areas of Christian doctrine to form a work of comprehensive unity.

Based upon the evidence of her text, most commentators conclude that Julian was a learned woman, far exceeding what could be expected of women in her day. She read English and Latin, was well-versed in the rules of classical Latin rhetoric, and kept abreast of contemporary spiritual literature. In addition, her writings exhibit a knowledge of many patristic writers known in her time only in learned circles. Thus, Julian rightly deserves the title, "the first woman of letters in the English language."

Because of their philosophical training, some mystics express their mystical experiences in abstract, technical language. In contrast, Julian's genius resides in her ability to articulate inchoate contemplative insights through powerful symbols and images that capture the emotional and spiritual intensity of the original experience. In other words, Julian not only describes what happened to her but also puts the reader in touch with the actual experience. Because of her unusual mystical and theological skill, some commentators have suggested making Julian, in addition to Teresa of Avila and Catherine of Siena, the third woman Doctor of the Church.

The absence from Julian's text of allusions to the disasters of the late 14th century in England and the world is somewhat remarkable. These included the epidemic and long-ranging effects of the Black Death, the Hundred Years' War, the Peasants' Revolt of 1381, the Lollard controversy, the troubled reign of Richard II, the prosecution of heresy throughout Europe, and the Great Schism. Yet she is tremendously concerned about the effects of sin and suffering on human faith in God. But as the selected texts here reproduced indicate, God instilled in her an unshakable trust in his invincible love and mercy through numerous revelations.

The first text is the vision of the little hazelnut. Julian experienced all her visions as signs of God's "familiar," or "homely," courteous, and intensely personal love. The vision illustrates a paradox experienced by most Christian mystics: God made, loves, and preserves even the tiniest speck of his creation. However, only God satisfies the human heart's immense longing, because "God is everything that is good." Thus, one can despise as "nothing" everything created.

The second text is perhaps the most famous statement of Christian optimism in the entire mystical tradition. Because of Julian's God-given tasting of the inner-trinitarian life, she attested that God said, "I wille make all thynge wele, I shalle make all thynge wele, I maye make alle thynge wele and I can make alle thynge wele. . . ."

The third text was chosen because the parable of the Lord and the servant is the key to understanding her entire mystical theology. What Julian knows about the mystery of sin and evil clashes harshly with the revelation of depth, intensity, and familiarity of God's love. As she understands it, God's love overlooks sin, turns it into honor, and instructs her that all will be well. In order to resolve Julian's perplexity over why all things will be well—despite sin and the possibility of damnation—God revealed this parable and instructed her to pay attention to *every* detail.

The Lord (God) loves the servant (Adam/Christ). The servant's "good will" prompts him to rush out in loving service of his Lord, but he falls and is injured. The worst part of the fall is his inability now to "turn his face to see the Lord's gaze of love." To Julian, God is revealed as unconditional love because Jesus, Adam, and the entire human race are one by a "true union made in heaven." Thus, God does not punish sin; sin punishes itself. One finds in Julian a graphic example of benign apocatastasis, the theory that one may hope that all will be saved.

The fourth text was selected because it is one of the greatest hymns to God's love in the Christian mystical tradition. Why did God create? Out of love. How does Julian know? Love instructed her. Why did Love instruct her. Because of Love. "Love is his meaning" in everything.

The final text illustrates Julian's acute experience of the feminine side of God, of the Motherhood of the Trinity and of Christ. It must be emphasized that both her trinitarian and incarnational mysticisms ground her experience of and insight into the reality that "as truly as God is our Father, so truly is God our Mother." And Christ is our true Mother because all things were created in and for Christ, because he took on human nature and died for us, now feeds us, and allows us to rest upon his breast to gaze into his open wound to "show us there a part of the Godhead and of the joys of heaven. . . ."[2]

THE TEXTS

SHOWINGS
"No bigger than a hazelnut"[3]

At the same time as I saw this sight of the head bleeding, our good Lord showed a spiritual sight of his familiar love. I saw that he is to us everything which is good and comforting for our help. He is our clothing, who wraps and enfolds us for love, embraces us and shelters us, surrounds us for his love, which is so tender that he may never desert us. And so in this sight I saw that he is everything which is good, as I understood.

And in this he showed me something small, no bigger than a hazelnut, lying in the palm of my hand, as it seemed to me, and it was round as a ball. I looked at it with the eye of my understanding and thought: What can this be? I was amazed that it could last, for I thought that because of its littleness it would suddenly have fallen into nothing. And I was answered in my understanding: It lasts and always will, because God loves it; and thus everything has being through the love of God.

In this little thing I saw three properties. The first is that God made it, the second is that God loves it, the third is that God preserves it. But what did I see in it? It is that God is the Creator and the protector and the lover. For until I am substantially united to him, I can never have perfect rest or true happiness,—until, that is, I am so attached to him that there can be no created thing between my God and me.

This little thing which is created seemed to me as if it could have fallen into nothing because of its littleness. We need to have knowledge of this, so that we may delight in despising as nothing everything created, so as to love and have uncreated God. For this is the reason why our hearts and souls are not in perfect ease, because here we seek rest in this thing which is so little, in which there is no rest, and we do not know God who is almighty, all wise and all good, for he is true rest. God wishes to be known, and it pleases him that we should rest in him; for everything which is beneath him is not sufficient for us. And this is the reason why no soul is at rest until it has despised as nothing all things which are created. When it by its will has become nothing for love, to have him who is everything, then is it able to receive spiritual rest.

And also our good Lord revealed that it is very greatly pleasing to him that a simple soul should come naked, openly, and familiarly. For this is the loving yearning of the soul through the touch of the Holy Spirit, from the understanding which I have in this revelation: God, of your goodness give me yourself, for you are enough for me, and I can ask for nothing which is less which can pay you full worship. And if I ask anything which is less, always I am in want; but only in you do I have everything.

"I shall make all things well"[4]

And so our good Lord answered to all the questions and doubts which I could raise, saying most comfortably: I may make all things well, and I can make all things well, and I shall make all things well, and I will make all things well; and you will see yourself that every kind of thing will be well. When he says "I may," I understand this to apply to the Father; and when he says "I can," I understand it for the Son; and when he says "I will," I understand it for the Holy Spirit; and when he says "I shall," I understand it for the unity of the blessed Trinity, three persons and one truth, and when he says "You will see yourself," I understand it for the union of all men who will be saved in the blessed Trinity.

The Parable of the Lord and the Servant[5]

And then our courteous Lord answered very mysteriously by revealing a wonderful example of a lord who has a servant and gave me sight for the understanding of them both. . . The lord sits in state, in rest and in peace. The servant stands before his lord, respectfully, ready to do his lord's will. The lord looks on the servant very lovingly and sweetly and mildly. He sends him to a certain place to do his will. Not only does the servant go, but he dashes off and runs at great speed, loving to do his lord's will. And soon he falls into a dell and is greatly injured; and then he groans and moans and tosses about and writhes, but he cannot rise or help himself in any way. And in all this, the greatest hurt which I saw him in was lack of consolation, for he could not turn his face to look on his loving lord, who was very close to him, in whom is all consolation; but like a man who was for the time extremely feeble and foolish, he paid heed to his feelings and his continued distress, in which distress he suffered seven great pains. . . .

I was amazed that this servant could so meekly suffer all this woe; and I looked carefully to know if I could detect any fault in him or if the lord would impute to him any kind of blame; and truly, none was seen, for the only cause of his falling was his good will and his great desire. And in spirit, he was as prompt and as good as he was when he stood before his lord, ready to do his will. . . .

For 20 years after the time of the revelation except for three months, I received an inward instruction, and it was this: You ought to take heed to all the attributes, divine and human, which were revealed in the example, though this may seem to you mysterious and ambiguous. . . . I understood that the lord who sat in state, in rest and peace, is God. I understood that the servant who stood before him was shown for Adam, that is to say, one man was shown at that time and his fall, so as to make it understood how God regards all men and their falling. For in the sight of God, all men are one man, and one man is all men. This man was injured in his powers and made most feeble, and in his understanding he was amazed, because he was diverted from looking on his lord, but his will was preserved in God's sight. I saw the lord commend and approve him for his will, but he himself was blinded and hindered from knowing this will. And this is a great sorrow and a cruel suffering to him, for he neither sees clearly his loving lord, who is so meek and mild to him, nor does he truly see what he himself is in the sight of his loving lord. And I know well that when these two things are wisely and truly seen, we shall gain rest and peace, here in part and the fullness in the bliss of heaven, by God's plentiful grace.

And this was a beginning of the teaching which I saw at the same time, whereby I might come to know in what manner he looks on us in our sin. And then I saw that only pain blames and punishes, and our courteous Lord comforts and succors, and always he is kindly disposed to the soul, loving and longing to bring us to his bliss. . . . And the loving regard which he kept constantly on his servant, and especially when he fell, it seemed to me that it could melt our hearts for love and break them in two for joy. . . .

In the servant is comprehended the second person of the Trinity, and in the servant is comprehended Adam, that is to say all men. And therefore when I say "the Son," that means the divinity which is equal to the Father, and when I say "the servant," that means Christ's humanity, which is the true Adam. The lord is God the Father, the servant is the Son, Jesus Christ, the Holy Spirit is the equal love which is in them both. When Adam fell, God's Son fell; because of the true union which was made in heaven, God's Son could not be separated from Adam, for by Adam I understand all mankind. Adam fell from life to death into the valley of this wretched world and after that into hell. God's Son fell with Adam into the valley of the womb of the maiden who was the fairest daughter of Adam, and that was to excuse Adam from blame to heaven and on earth; and powerfully he brought him out of hell. By the wisdom and the goodness which were in the servant is understood God's Son; by the poor laborer's clothing and the standing close by on the left is understood Adam's humanity with all the harm and weakness which follow. For in all this our good Lord showed his own Son and Adam as only one man. The strength and the goodness that we have is from Jesus Christ; the weakness and blindness that we have is from Adam, which two were shown in the servant.

And so has our good Lord Jesus taken upon him all our blame; and therefore our Father may not, does not wish to, assign more blame to us than to his own beloved Son Jesus Christ. So he was the servant before he came to earth, standing ready in purpose before the Father until the time when he would send him to do the glorious deed by which mankind was brought back to heaven. That is to say, even though he is God, equal with the Father as regards his divinity, but with his prescient purpose that he would become man to save mankind in fulfillment of the will of his Father, so he stood before his Father as a servant, willingly taking upon him all our charge. And then he rushed off very readily at the Father's bidding, and soon he fell very low into the maiden's womb, having no regard for himself or for his cruel pains.

The white tunic is his flesh, the scantiness signifies that there was nothing at all separating the divinity from the humanity. The tight fit is poverty, the age is Adam's wearing, the wornness is the sweat of Adam's labor, the shortness shows the servant-laborer.

And so I saw the Son stand, saying in intention: See, my dear Father, I stand before you in Adam's tunic, all ready to hasten and run. I wish to be on earth to your glory, when it is your will to send me. How long shall I desire it? Very truly, the Son knew when was the Father's will, and how long he would desire it, that is to say as regards his divinity, for he is the wisdom of the Father. Therefore, this meaning was shown for understanding of Christ's humanity. For all mankind, which will be saved by the sweet Incarnation and the Passion of Christ, all is Christ's humanity, for he is the head, and we are his member, to which members the day and the time are unknown when every passing woe and sorrow will have an end, and everlasting joy and bliss will be fulfilled, which day and time all the company of heaven longs and desires to see. And all who are under heaven will come there; their way is by longing and desire, which desiring and longing was shown in the servant standing before the lord, or, otherwise, in the Son standing before the Father in Adam's tunic. For the longing and desire of all mankind which will be saved appeared in Jesus, for Jesus is in all who will be saved, and all who will be saved are in Jesus; all is of the love of God, with obedience, meekness and patience, and the virtues which befit us.

Also in this marvelous example I have teaching within me, as it were, the beginning of an ABC, whereby I may have some understanding of our Lord's meaning, for the mysteries of the revelation are hidden in it, even though all the showings are full of mysteries.

The Motherhood of God and of Christ[6]

. . . So our Lady is our mother, in whom we are all enclosed and born of her in Christ, for she who is mother of our savior is mother of all who are saved in our savior; and our savior is our true Mother, in whom we are endlessly born and out of whom we shall never come.

Plenteously, fully and sweetly was this shown; and it is spoken of in the first revelation, where it says that we are all enclosed in him, and he is enclosed in us. And it is spoken of in the 16th revelation, where he says that he sits in our soul, for it is his delight to reign blessedly in our understanding, and sit restfully in our soul, and to dwell endlessly in our soul, working us all into him. . . .

And so in our making, God almighty is our loving Father, and God all wisdom is our loving Mother, with the love and the goodness of the Holy Spirit, which is all one God, one Lord. And in the joining and the union he is our very true spouse and we his beloved wife and his fair maiden, with which wife he was never displeased; for he says: I love you and you love me, and our love will never divide in two.

I contemplated the work of all the blessed Trinity, in which contemplation I saw and understood these three properties: the property of the fatherhood, and the property of the motherhood, and the property of the lordship in one God. In our almighty Father we have our protection and our bliss, as regards our natural substance, which is ours by our creation from without beginning; and in the second person, in knowledge and wisdom we have our perfection, as regards our sensuality, our restoration, and our salvation, for he is our Mother, brother, and savior; and in our good Lord the Holy Spirit we have our reward and our gift for our living and our labor, endlessly surpassing all that we desire in this marvelous courtesy, out of his great plentiful grace. For all our life consists of three: In the first we have our being, and in the second we have our increasing, and in the third we have our fulfillment. The first is nature, the second is mercy, the third is grace.

As to the first, I saw and understood that the high might of the Trinity is our Father, and the deep wisdom of the Trinity is our Mother, and the great love of the Trinity is our Lord; and all these we have in nature and in our substantial creation. And furthermore, I saw that the second person, who is our Mother, substantially the same beloved person, has now become our mother sensually, because we are double by God's creating, that is to say substantial and sensual. . . .

. . . And our substance is in our Father, God almighty, and our substance is in our Mother, God all wisdom, and our substance is in our Lord God, the Holy Spirit, all goodness, for our substance is whole in each person of the Trinity, who is one God. And our sensuality is only in the second person, Christ Jesus, in whom is the Father and the Holy Spirit; and in him and by him we are powerfully taken out of hell and out of the wretchedness on earth, and gloriously brought up into heaven, and blessedly united to our substance, increased in riches and nobility by all the power of Christ and by the grace and operation of the Holy Spirit.

. . . So Jesus Christ, who opposes good to evil, is our true Mother. We have our being from him, where the foundation of motherhood begins, with all the sweet protection of love which endlessly follows.

As truly as God is our Father, so truly is God our Mother, and he revealed that in everything, and especially in these sweet words where he says: I am he; that is to say: I am he, the power and goodness of fatherhood; I am he, the wisdom and the lovingness of motherhood; I am he, the light and the grace which is all blessed love; I am he, the Trinity; I am he, the unity. . . .

. . . Our great Father, almighty God, who is being, knows us and loved us before time began. Out of this knowledge, in his most wonderful deep love, by the prescient eternal counsel of all the blessed Trinity, he wanted the second person to become our Mother, our brother, and our savior. From this it follows that as truly as God is our Father, so truly is God our Mother. Our Father wills, our Mother works, our good Lord the Holy Spirit confirms. . . .

And so Jesus is our true Mother by nature by our first creation, and he is our true Mother in grace by his taking our created nature. All the lovely works and all the sweet loving offices of beloved motherhood are appropriated to the second person, for in him we have this godly will, whole and safe forever, both in nature and in grace, from his own goodness proper to him.

I understand three ways of contemplating motherhood in God. The first is the foundation of our nature's creation; the second is his taking of our nature, where the motherhood of grace begins; and the third is the motherhood at work. And in that, by the same grace, everything is penetrated, in length and in breadth, in height and in depth without end; and it is all one love.

. . . Our Mother in nature, our Mother in grace, because he wanted altogether to become our Mother in all things, made the foundation of his work most humbly and most mildly in the maiden's womb . . . arrayed and prepared himself in this humble place, all ready in our poor flesh, himself to do the service and the office of motherhood in everything. The mother's service is nearest, readiest and surest: nearest because it is most natural, readiest because it is most loving, and surest because it is truest. No one ever might or could perform this office fully, except only him. We know that all our mothers bear us for pain and for death. . . .

The mother can give her child to suck of her milk, but our precious Mother Jesus can feed us with himself, and does, most courteously and most tenderly, with the blessed sacrament, which is the precious food of true life; and with all the sweet sacraments he sustains us most mercifully and graciously . . . .

The mother can lay her child tenderly to her breast, but our tender Mother Jesus can lead us easily into his blessed breast through his open side, and show us there a part of the Godhead and of the joys of heaven, with inner certainty of endless bliss. . .

"Love was his meaning"[7]

And from the time that it [her showing] was revealed, I desired many times to know in what was our Lord's meaning. And 15 years after and more, I was answered in spiritual understanding, and it was said: What, do you wish to know your Lord's meaning in this thing? Know it well, love was his meaning. Who reveals it to you? Love. What did he reveal to you? Love. Why does he reveal it to you? For love. Remain in this, and you will know more of the same. But you will never know different, without end.

So I was taught that love is our Lord's meaning. And I saw very certainly in this and in everything that before God made us, he loved us, which love has never abated and never will. And in this love he has done all his works, and in this love he has made all things profitable to us, and in this love our life is everlasting. In our creation we had beginning, but the love in which he created us was in him from without beginning. In this love we had our beginning, and all this shall we see in God without end.

Thomas à Kempis wrote one of the greatest classics of Catholic spirituality, The Imitation of Christ, *a book second only to the Bible in popularity in the Western Church. As an outstanding summary of the best in the New Devotion movement, Thomas'* Imitation *illustrates the relationship between deep piety and mysticism found in some mystical texts.*

THOMAS À KEMPIS

Thomas Hemerken was born in Kempen near Düsseldorf in the Rhineland diocese of Cologne, Germany. From 1393 to 1398, he was educated in Deventer under the direction of Florentius Radewijns, the successor of the famous Geert de Groote, founder of the Brothers of the Common Life and father of the *Devotio Moderna* (new devotion). Instead of joining the Brothers as planned, Thomas entered the newly founded monastery of the Canons Regular of St. Augustine at Mount St. Agnes, where his older brother was prior. Except for three years, he spent the rest of his life transcribing manuscripts—even an entire Bible—and writing numerous works.

Thomas has been called the most outstanding representative of the "new devotion," that is, new in contrast to the old 13th and 14th century highly scholastic and speculative mysticism rooted in Eckhart and Tauler. The new devotion emphasized a radical imitation of Christ to combat the cooling of Christian ardor among the Catholics of the Low Countries. Permeated with Cistercian and Franciscan emotion, but not "charismatic" or "enthusiastic" in the contemporary sense, this spiritual movement stressed the devotional reading of Scripture and a deep love for Christ's humanity, his passion, and the eucharist. It also taught that the avoidance of vice, the practice of virtue, ascetical self-abnegation, solitude, separation from the world, and methodical meditation open to mystical contemplation produced a devout, interior person of compunction. But the new devotion showed little concern for the active apostolate, opposed the humanism of its day, and despised culture and purely human values.

Out of this movement came the greatest classic of Catholic spirituality, *The Imitation of Christ*, a book second only to the Bible in popularity in the Western Church. More than 700 extant manuscripts of this work and translations into more than 50 languages attest to its status as one of the most famous Christian devotional book in history. Numerous statesmen, philosophers, poets, founders of religious orders, saints, and mystics have regarded it as their favorite book.

Since the 16th century, however, the authorship of the *Imitation* has been the subject of great controversy, and no less than 25 individuals have been named as its author. But most contemporary scholarship agrees that Thomas à Kempis wrote four distinct treatises at different times for the young religious at Mount St. Agnes. The treatises were eventually bound together and called *The Imitation of Christ*.

Drawing heavily upon the scriptures, the Fathers, and the spiritual notebooks of quotations used by members of the new devotion, the *Imitation* offers a series of meditative reflections for the attainment of virtue, for progressing in the interior life, and for uniting with Christ. Therefore, like the Bible, it should be read meditatively, pondered, and savored. Offering no new knowledge or intellectual speculation, it presents the truths of the new devotion in simple language. It exhorts its readers to seek ardently what is interior, true, and eternal.

The first treatise focuses on renouncing all that is vain, illusory, and pleasing to the senses. One must seek humility, desire to be unknown, and desire only the eternal. The second treatise teaches that since the Kingdom of God is within, it cannot be attained by the senses or by mere human knowledge. One must follow the crucified Christ to reach union with God.

The third treatise is the longest. Although it repeats the same themes as the first two, there is more about grace and love. It is written as a dialogue between Jesus, the soul's beloved, and the disciple who wishes only to clothe himself with Christ crucified. It teaches what all mystics know: "Son, as much as thou canst go out of thyself, so much wilt thou be able to enter into me."

The fourth treatise focuses on the blessed sacrament as the acme of the doctrine presented in the first three. The desired union with God can be obtained sacramentally by participating in Jesus' eucharistic supper and sacrifice.

The readings presented here were selected to illustrate the relationship between deep piety and mysticism found in some mystical texts. They clearly indicate the *Imitation*'s eucharistic and Christ-centered mysticism, as well as its rejection of vain learning and the world. Christ and God alone satisfy the human heart, so the self and all else must be despised and forgotten. However, only grace can awaken the mystical senses to enjoy God's and Christ's "visitations" in the heart's innermost center. And only grace enables a person to empty the self so that God's light and love may illuminate and unite the person with the Lord himself. The *Imitation*'s central message is simple: "Let me love Thee more than myself and myself only for Thee, and all others in Thee. . . ."[1]

THE TEXTS

THE IMITATION OF CHRIST
To be united with Christ in the Blessed Sacrament[2]

Who will give me, O Lord, that I may find Thee alone, that I may open my whole heart to Thee and enjoy Thee as my soul desireth; and that now no man may despise me nor any created thing move me or regard me, but that Thou alone speak to me, and I to Thee, as the beloved is wont to speak to his beloved, and a friend to entertain himself with his friend. This I pray for, this I desire, that I may be wholly united to Thee, and may withdraw my heart from all created things, and by the Holy Communion, and often celebrating, may more and more learn to relish heavenly and eternal things.

Ah! Lord God, when shall I be wholly united to thee and absorbed in Thee and altogether forgetful of myself? Thou in me and I in Thee and altogether forgetful of myself? Thou in me and I in Thee; and so grant us both to continue in one. . . . Verily Thou art my peacemaker, in whom is sovereign peace and true rest; out of whom is labor and sorrow and endless misery. . . .

There is nothing that I can give Him that will please Him better than if I give up my heart entirely to God and unite it closely to Him. Then all that is within me shall rejoice exceedingly when my soul shall be perfectly united to my God; then will He say to me: If thou wilt be with Me, I will be with thee: and I will answer Him: Vouchsafe, O Lord, to remain with me, and I will willingly be with Thee. This is my whole desire, that my heart may be united to Thee. . . .

When I think of the many devout persons who, so piously and with such love in their hearts, approach your sacrament, Lord, my face reddens with shame realizing that I go to your altar and the table of holy communion with a tepid and indifferent heart.

Why am I so dry and have so lukewarm a heart? Why am I not fully on fire when in your presence, my God? Why am I not so powerfully attracted and enkindled as many of the devout are? They have such a fervent desire to receive holy communion and their hearts so brim with love that they cannot hold back their tears. Their souls and bodies long for you, long from their very depths, O God, the fountain of life, and it is only by receiving your body with all delight and spiritual yearning that they can allay or satisfy their hunger.

How genuine their burning faith! A sure and convincing proof of your sacred presence! Indeed, the devout truly recognize their Lord in the breaking of the bread; their hearts burning so strongly within because Jesus walks with them.

Christ Speaks Interiorly to the Faithful soul

Blessed is that soul which heareth the Lord speaking within her and from His mouth receiveth the word of comfort. Blessed ears which receive the accents of the divine whisper and take no notice of the whispers of the world. Blessed ears indeed, which hearken to truth itself teaching within and not to the voice which soundeth without. Blessed eyes which are shut to outward things and attentive to the interior. Blessed they who penetrate into internal things and endeavor to prepare themselves more and more by daily exercises to the attainment of heavenly secrets.[3]

I would willingly speak My words to thee and reveal My secrets to thee, if thou wouldst diligently observe My coming and open to Me the door of thy heart. . . .

Frequently doth He visit the internal man sweet in His communication with him, delightful His consolation, much peace, and a familiarity exceedingly to be admired. . . .[4] If thou hadst once perfectly entered into the interior of Jesus and experienced a little of His burning love, then wouldst thou not care at all for thy own convenience or inconvenience, but wouldst rather rejoice at reproach, because the love of Jesus makes a man despise himself. A lover of Jesus and of truth and a true internal man that is free from inordinate affections, can freely turn himself to God and in spirit elevate himself above himself, and rest in enjoyment. . . .[5]

O my most beloved spouse, Jesus Christ, most pure lover, Lord of the whole creation, who will give me the wings of true liberty to fly and repose in Thee?. . . When shall I fully recollect myself in Thee, that through the love of Thee I may not feel myself but Thee alone, above all feeling and measure in a manner not known at all?. . .[6] O Jesus! the brightness of eternal glory, the comfort of a soul in its pilgrimage, my tongue cannot express the sentiments of my heart, but my silence itself speaks to Thee. . . .[7] In silence and quiet the devout soul goes forward and learns the secrets of the Scriptures.[8]

Nothing But God[9]

What can be more at rest than a simple eye that aims at nothing but God? And what can be more free than he who desires nothing upon earth? A man ought, therefore, to pass and ascend above everything created and perfectly forsake himself and in ecstasy of mind stand and see that Thou, the Creator of all, infinitely transcendest all creatures. And unless a man be at liberty from all things created, he cannot freely attend to things divine. And this is the reason why there are found so few contemplative persons, because there are few that wholly wean themselves from transitory and created things. For this, a great grace is required, which may elevate the soul and carry her up above herself. And unless a man be elevated in spirit and set at liberty from all creatures and wholly united to God, whatever he knows and whatever he has is of no great weight. . . . Unspeakable indeed is the sweetness of Thy contemplation, which Thou bestowest on those that love Thee.

My God and My All[10]

My God and my all! Enough is said to him that understands; and it is delightful to him that loves to repeat it often. For when Thou art present, all things yield delight; but when Thou art absent, all things are loathsome. Thou givest tranquillity to the heart and great peace and pleasant joy. . . .

But they that follow Thee by despising the things of this world and mortifying the flesh, are found to be wise indeed, for they are transported from vanity to truth, from the flesh to the spirit. Such as these have a relish of God, and what good soever is found in creatures, they refer to the praise of their Maker. But great, yea very great, is the difference between the relish of the Creator and the creature, of eternity and of time, of light uncreated and of light enlightened.

O light eternal! transcending all created lights, dart forth Thy light from above, which may penetrate the most inward parts of my heart. Cleanse, gladden, enlighten, and quicken my spirit with its powers that I may be absorbed in Thee with ecstasies of joy. Oh, when will this blessed and desirable hour come when Thou shalt fill me with Thy presence and become to me all in all?

Vain Learning[11]

I [Christ] am He who teaches men knowledge, and I give a more clear understanding to little ones than can be taught by man.... I am He that in an instant elevates a humble mind to comprehend more reasons of the eternal truth than could be acquired by ten years' study in the schools. I teach without noise of words, without confusion of opinions, without ambition of honor, without contention of arguments. I teach to despise earthly things, to loathe things present, to see and relish things eternal, to flee honors, to endure scandals, to repose all hope in Me, to desire nothing out of Me, and above all things, ardently to love Me. For a certain person, by loving Me entirely, learned divine things and spoke wonders. . . . But to some I speak things common, to others things more particular; to some I sweetly appear in signs and figures, to others in great light I reveal mysteries.

The Desire for Eternal Life[12]

Son, when thou perceivest a longing after eternal bliss to be infused into thee from above, and thou desirest to go out of the dwelling of this body, that thou mayst contemplate My brightness, without any shadow of change, enlarge thy heart, and with all thy affections embrace this holy inspiration. Return very great thanks to the divine bounty, which deals so favorably with thee, which mercifully visits thee, ardently incites thee, and powerfully raises thee up, lest by thy own weight thou fallest down to the things of the earth. For it is not by thy own thought or endeavor that thou attainest this; but only by the favor of heavenly grace and the divine visit. . . .

The Doctrine of Truth[13]

He to whom all things are one and who draws all things to one and who sees all things in one, may be steady in heart and peaceably repose in God. . . .

The more a man is united within himself, and interiorly simple, the more and higher things doth he understand without labor; because he receiveth the light of understanding from above.

To Subdue Nature[14]

This grace [to subdue nature] is a supernatural light and a certain special gift of God and the proper mark of the elect and pledge of eternal salvation, which elevates a man from the things of the earth to the love of heavenly things, and from carnal makes him spiritual. Wherefore, the more nature is kept down and subdued, the greater abundance of grace is infused; and the inward man, by new visitations, is daily more reformed according to the image of God.

Hymn to Love[15]

Love is an excellent thing, a great good indeed, which alone maketh light all that is burdensome and equally bears all that is unequal. For it carries a burden without being burdened and makes all that which is bitter sweet and savory.... Nothing is sweeter than love; nothing stronger, nothing higher, nothing more generous, nothing more pleasant, nothing fuller or better in heaven or on earth; for love proceeds from God and cannot rest but in God above all created things.

The lover flies, runs, and rejoices; he is free and not held. He gives all for all and has all in all, because he rests in one sovereign good above all, from whom all good flows and proceeds. He looks not at the gifts but turns himself to the giver above all goods. Love often knows no measure but is inflamed above all measure.... Love watches, and sleeping slumbers not. When weary is not tired; when straitened is not constrained; when frightened is not disturbed, but like a living flame and a torch all on fire it mounts upward and securely passes through all opposition....

Give increase to my love that I may learn to taste with the interior mouth of the heart how sweet it is to love and to swim and to be dissolved in love. Let me be possessed by love, mounting above myself with great fervor and wonderment. Let me sing the canticle of love, let me follow my Beloved on high, let my soul lose herself in Thy praises, rejoicing exceedingly in Thy love. Let me love Thee more than myself and myself only for Thee, and all others in Thee, who truly love Thee as the law of love commands, which shines forth from Thee.

Mystic, married laywoman, and humanitarian, Catherine has been called the only mystical genius of her age. To her, purgatory is nothing more than God's fiery love, cleansing, healing, and transforming the person into himself so that "our being is then God."

CATHERINE OF GENOA

The youngest of five children in the noble Fieschi family, Catherine desired to enter an Augustinian convent at the age of 13. Her older sister was already a contemplative nun, and Catherine undoubtedly had the gift of prayer when quite young. But despite her noble family's ties to Pope Innocent IV, she was refused entry because of her age. For financial and political advantages, when she was 16 years old, her family married her off to the dissolute and irresponsible Giuliano Adorno.

Bitter loneliness eventually caused her to seek succor in a frivolous and seemingly immoral life. But on March 22, 1473, during a Lenten confession, she had a sudden, overwhelming experience of God as pure love and a penetrating contrition for her sins. In the aftermath of this conversion, the cross-bearing Christ appeared to Catherine and further deepened her conversion. In contrast to many mystics, who are gradually and experientially purified by, illuminated by, and united to pure love, Catherine's transformation into God seems to have occurred almost instantaneously.

From that moment, Catherine's inner life was possessed by pure love, and often ecstatically so, while the poor of Genoa's slums and busy hospital administration work consumed her public life. Thus, her ecstatic, mystical love expressed and sacramentalized itself in her identification with the poor, sick, and suffering of Genoa. Her penitential "holy follies," such as eating lice and kissing the sores of syphilitics, must be understood in the context of the reckless joy in God's love that may be found in many saints. To them, love of God expresses itself partially in extreme penances.

God taught Catherine mystically that he, as pure love, was her total fulfillment, while life was a conflict between pure love and self-love. Only by the grace of pure love could the person emerge victorious in spiritual combat.

During Advent and Lent, for approximately 23 years, Catherine subsisted solely on water and daily eucharist. However, her energy did not diminish, and she continued to give herself fully both to an intense spiritual life and to the needs of the poor and sick. It must be emphasized that daily communion was most unusual in Catherine's day. Her acceptance of her husband's bankruptcy and of Thobis, the child he fathered with his mistress, also ran counter to the social customs of her age.

Although Catherine wrote no works, her confessor and confidant, Cattaneo Marabotto, and her spiritual son, Ettore Vernazza, faithfully recorded her adages and instructions, while adding their own comments and interpretations. Catherine's *Purgation and Purgatory* is a collection of her sayings and teachings about spiritual purgation both here and in the next life. Her *Spiritual Dialogue* is an account of her inner journey. It is written like a mystery play in which various figures—Soul, Body, Self-Love, Human Frailty, and Spirit—represent different aspects of the same person.

A woman of vibrant spirituality, Catherine was loyal to the hierarchical Church despite the laxity, venality, and decadence that permeated it. The failure of Church leaders to support the many reform movements was soon to result in the disintegration of Western Europe's religious unity engendered by the Protestant Reformation. Looking at the times and works of this mystic, married laywoman and humanitarian, one can easily understand why commentators have called Catherine the only genius of her age. She was canonized on May 18, 1737.

Catherine serves as a bridge between the mystics of the late Middle Ages and those of the 16th and 17th centuries. She had considerable influence on later French mysticism, German Romanticism, 19th-century American Protestants, and prominent Anglican converts to Catholicism. Giving spiritual birth to Ettore Vernazza, the father of the Oratory of Divine Love, is perhaps Catherine's greatest single historical contribution. Composed of laity and clergy, this highly influential movement focused on individual reform, Church reform, and the care of the poor.

The first of the following texts was selected to illustrate Catherine's dramatic conversion through a series of visions and wounds of love. It brings into sharp focus her eucharistic devotion and her Passion mysticism. The ecstatic experiences of God's love and Christ's redemptive shedding of blood acutely awakened her to three things: 1) God's pure love, 2) an inseparable union with pure love and Christ, and 3) her own sinfulness. These experiences also bestowed upon her the grace to discern her hidden resistances to pure love.

The second selection is the most captivating passage on purgation and purgatory in the Christian mystical tradition. Catherine taught that God does not place a soul in purgatory or hell. The soul seeks its own place. To her, purgatory is nothing more than God's "fiery love," cleansing, healing, and transforming the person into himself so that "our being is then God." It must be emphasized that Catherine experienced—as all the great mystics—this God-given purgation, illumination, and deification process here on earth. As she says, "The things that I speak about work within me in secret and with great power."[1]

THE TEXTS

THE SPIRITUAL DIALOGUE[2]
This soul [Catherine] witnessed many other signs of God's love that are beyond telling. A ray of God's love wounded her heart, making her soul experience a flaming love arising from the divine fount. At that instant, she was outside of herself, beyond intellect, tongue, or feeling. Fixed in that pure and divine love, henceforth she never ceased to dwell in it.

She was also made to understand the extent of her ingratitude and mirror herself in her sins; and she was overcome with such despair and self-loathing that she was tempted to publicly confess her sins. And Catherine's soul cried out, "O Lord, no more world, no more sins!"

She did not view sins principally as sins but as offenses against the goodness of God, His strong love. It was the consciousness of that that made her turn against herself and do her utmost to translate that love into deeds.

In this resolve, the ray of God so united her to Him that from this time on, no force or passion could separate them from one another. In witness of this union, some three days later, when she had not yet confessed, she felt the pull of Holy Communion, which from that day on never left her. No priest or friar objected to this need, the daily reception of the Blessed Sacrament, for such was the will of God. . . .

One day there appeared to her inner vision Jesus Christ incarnate crucified, all bloody from head to foot. It seemed that the body rained blood. From within, she heard a voice say: "Do you see this blood? It has been shed for your love, to atone for your sins." With that she received a wound of love that drew her to Jesus with such trust that it washed away all that previous fright, and she took joy in the Lord.

She was also granted another vision, more striking yet, beyond telling or imagination. God showed her the love with which He had suffered out of love for her. That vision made her turn away from every other love and joy that did not come directly from God. In that vision, Catherine saw the evil in her soul and the purity of God's love. The two never left her. Had she dwelt on that vision any longer than she did, she would have fainted, become undone.

The vision made her dwell constantly on the evil of man, which could not have been greater, considering the great love of God, a love that never ceased doing the soul as much good as it could; and in turning her gaze upon herself, Catherine saw how much evil there was in her. That experience made her think of man in terms of the very opposite of the goodness of God, and this thought made her almost despair. Had God not tempered this vision, body and soul would both have perished. But now, Catherine became such an enemy of herself that when she had to use her name for one reason or another, she preferred to say "we." She waged resolute war on the self-love that survived in her. Were an angel to have spoken well of her, she would not have believed him, so certain was she of the evil in her.

Because of that evil, which she felt to be irremediable, she almost despaired; still, trusting God, she said: "Lord, I make you a present of myself. I do not know what to do with myself. Let me, then, Lord, make this exchange: I will place this evil being into your hands. You are the only one who can hide it in your goodness and so rule over me that nothing will be seen of my own proper self. On your part, you will grant your pure love, which will extinguish all other loves in me and will annihilate me and busy me so much with you that I will have no time or place for anything or anyone else."

The Lord accepted. As a consequence, those preoccupations never troubled Catherine again. And with that, God sent her a ray of His love so burning and deep that it was an agony to sustain. Issuing from the fountain of Christ, that love, wounding the soul, stripped it of all other loves, appetites, delights, and selfishness. The soul cried out, sighed deeply, and in its transformation was taken out of itself.

God deeply impressed upon her the fountains of Christ with their fiery, bloody drops of love for man. He also impressed on her the vision of man, but limited the attendant suffering, so that at one and the same time she could endure both visions. Armed with this love, she was sure of overcoming any obstacles or devils, for she was in her fortress, God. Trusting in His goodness, she could endure the sight of her lower self.

Thus, all that was not Pure Love meant nothing to her. She felt no attraction to any food that was not strictly necessary, nor to frequenting friends, even close ones. She was very drawn to solitude, to God Himself alone; and God gave her the gift of prayer so that she would be on her knees for six or seven hours. . . . God, who now ruled over her, took away the instinct for the things of the world and the self. He gave her other and better preferences. . . . Now she looked constantly at the ground, never laughed or smiled or glanced at passersby. So absorbed was she that the outside world seemed almost not to exist. Outwardly, she seemed very unhappy, but within her there was a great joy. . . .

[Catherine's] spirit by now was able to discern the smallest imperfection in it and act on that knowledge. It dealt with Human Frailty with dispatch and brooked no opposition. . . . Pure Love does not attach itself to pleasure or feeling, bodily or spiritual. . . . Love must be naked.

PURGATION AND PURGATORY[3]
At the moment of death, therefore, the soul goes to its appointed place with no other guide for it but the nature of its sins; and in the case of mortal sin, hell is its proper place. Were the sinful soul not there, where the justice of God wills it, the soul would be in a still greater hell. . . . So it is with purgatory. Once separated from the body, the soul, no longer in that original state of purity, aware that the impediments it faces cannot be removed in any other way, hurls itself into purgatory. Should the soul find that the assigned place is not sufficient to remove its impediment, then it would experience a hell far worse than purgatory. In that insufficiency, the soul would see itself cut off from God; and compared with God's love, the suffering of purgatory is a small matter. . . .

The greatest suffering of the souls in purgatory. . . is their awareness that something in them displeases God, that they have deliberately gone against His great goodness. . . . All that I have said is as nothing compared to what I feel within, the witnessed correspondence of love between God and the Soul; for when God sees the Soul pure as it was in its origins, He tugs at it with a glance, draws it, and binds it to Himself with a fiery love that by itself could annihilate the immortal soul. In so acting, God so transforms the soul in Him that it knows nothing other than God; and He continues to draw it up into His fiery love until He restores it to that pure state from which it first issued. As it is being drawn upward, the soul feels itself melting in the fire of that love of its sweet God. . . .

That is why the soul seeks to cast off any and all impediments, so that it can be lifted up to God; and such impediments are the cause of the sufferings of the souls in purgatory. Not that those souls dwell on their suffering; they dwell rather on the resistance they feel in themselves against. . .His intense and pure love bent on nothing but drawing them up to Him. . . .

Once stripped of all its imperfections, the soul rests in God, with no characteristics of its own, since its purification is the stripping away of the lower self in us. Our being is then God. Even if the soul were to remain in the fire, still it would not consider it a suffering; for those would be the flames of divine love, of eternal life. . . . Though this fire can be experienced in this life, I do not believe that God allows such souls to remain long on earth, except to show His mighty works. . . . If man were to be aware of the many hidden flaws in him, he would despair.

These flaws are burned away in the last stage of love. God then shows that weakness to man, so that the soul may see the workings of God, of that flaming love. Things man considers perfect leave much to be desired in the eyes of God, for all the things of man that are perfect in appearance—what he seeks, feels, knows—contaminate him.

If we are to become perfect, the change must be brought about in us and without us; that is, the change is to be the work not of man but of God. This last stage of love is the pure and intense love of God alone. In this transformation, the action of God in penetrating the soul is so fierce that it seems to set the body on fire and to keep it burning until death. The overwhelming love of God gives it a joy beyond words. . . .

. . .These things that I speak about work within me in secret and with great power. . . .

Francisco de Osuna wrote what may well be the Span-
ish masterpiece of Franciscan mysticism, The Third
Spiritual Alphabet. His premise is that friendship and
communion with God are possible in this life through
cleansing one's conscience, entering one's heart, rest-
ing in loving stillness, and then rising above the heart
to God alone.

FRANCISCO DE OSUNA

When Francisco de Osuna was born in Seville, Ferdinand of
Aragon (1451-1516) and Isabella of Castile (1451-1504) ruled Spain,
a budding European superpower. In 1492, Granada, the last Moor-
ish fortress, fell. The ideas of the "Reconquista" influenced Spain's
social and political life. In 1492, in the service of Isabella the Catholic, Columbus discovered the New World. The oceans were being
explored, and exotic lands beckoned. New inventions transformed
customs and morals. Furthermore, Spain's spiritual ruler, Cardinal
Francisco Jiménez de Cisneros, was a man intent on transforming
its spiritual life. Spain's political and mystical golden ages were to
coincide.

Although little is known about Francisco de Osuna's life, he was
clearly acknowledged as a master of the spiritual life during the
16th century. At the dawn of Spain's golden age of mysticism,
Osuna assimilated and put his unique stamp on the spiritual and intellectual crosscurrents of his day: the vernacular Bible, Islamic mysticism, Spanish Erasmianism, and the rediscovery of the Fathers,
the Greek philosophers, and Pseudo-Dionysius. A prolific author of
more than 500 works, Osuna wrote what may well be the Spanish
masterpiece of Franciscan mysticism, *The Third Spiritual Alphabet.*

Teresa of Avila's uncle, Don Pedro, gave her a copy of the *Alphabet* in 1537. Osuna's book became her guide, set her on her inner journey, and led her to mystical prayer within nine months. She later used this book to teach her own nuns the value and sweetness of recollection, of the consciousness of God's presence in the depths of the heart.

In the midst of the controversy over the nature of genuine mystical prayer that raged during the 1520s between the proponents of recollection (*recogimiento*) and those who advocated abandonment to God's will (*dejamiento*), Osuna accomplished two things: 1) he explained with unusual subtlety and spiritual perspicacity the nature of authentic recollection, and 2) he exposed the quietist tendency in *dejamiento*.

Osuna begins with the premise that "friendship and communion with God are possible in this life of exile."[1] The best way to accomplish this is through recollection, that is, by cleansing one's conscience, entering one's heart, resting in a loving stillness, and then rising above the heart to God alone.

Much more than a technique, recollection is an organic process of prayer that requires mental concentration, the active directing of the mind, and God's grace. Essentially prayer, it includes vocal prayer, active ("acquired") contemplation, and passive ("infused") contemplation. Recollection aims at quieting the exterior person, then drawing the inner person into the heart so that the soul's powers are united to its "highest" part where God's image dwells. At times, God can be seen in the soul as if he were an image in a calm pool of water. Recollection unites the soul to God so that it experientially shares God's life.

Osuna belongs to the apophatic tradition, which emphasizes that God is best known by a loving unknowing. Not to think of anything (*no pensar nada*) requires emptying the mind and heart in order to be filled lovingly with God. Therefore, in some sense, thoughts are the contemplative's greatest enemy.

Yet Osuna contends that "neither the Sacred Humanity nor any created thing in itself can impede contemplation, however lofty."[2] His mitigated apophatic mysticism does not insist that all thoughts— good and holy thoughts included—be cast into a cloud of forgetting for the sake of praying with a naked mystical love. To him, vocal prayer, prayer with holy thoughts, and an ecstatic prayer of love that silences the soul's "lower" functions can and should dwell in one and the same person. In short, the prayer of naked love may punctuate a person's life, but no one can remain constantly in this state.

Franciscan graciousness and emotion permeate his teaching on recollection. Not force, but a graced love honed by benign austerity molds the heart and makes it alert, poised, guarded, receptive, and, at times, lovingly ecstatic. Then the heart draws love from everything and refers it to God. Thus, recollection includes an effort to still the mind, touches of stillness, and ecstatic union with God—an experiential ebb and flow into and out of God.

Osuna's second accomplishment—his rejection of the pseudomystical, passive tendency in *dejamiento*—must be understood in the context of his teaching on recollection. For some of its practioners, *dejamiento* degenerated into pseudomystical quiet that overemphasized passivity, rejected all effort during prayer, ridiculed and rejected the sacramental life, averred that abandonment bestowed impeccability, and resulted in sexual aberrations and excesses.

Some commentators evaluate Osuna in terms of his influence on Teresa of Avila and John of the Cross, two titans of mysticism who quickly overshadowed him. Others call attention to the bridge he forged between the earlier Spanish giant, Ramon Lull, and the later masters, Teresa and John. But Osuna was more than a bridge and a precursor. One finds in his writings—especially on the relationship between the apophatic *no pensar nada* and kataphatic contemplation—insights, emphases, subtleties, and modes of expression that go beyond the great Teresa and John. Even the tone of his work and the atmosphere it creates must be savored for its own sake and the gentle, welcoming way it attracts one to the life of prayer.

The first text here included was selected because it is one of the loveliest paeans to humility in the Christian mystical tradition. Osuna views humility as the foundation of the spiritual life, for it nurtures charity and renders a person "capable of receiving God."

The second selection illustrates Osuna's indirect criticism of those who advocated quietist, angelic contemplation. According to him, one must follow and imitate Christ both in his divinity and in his humanity.

The remaining texts were selected to clarify Osuna's views on recollection. A general attitude of recollection throughout the day is requisite for special recollection—for seeking God in the heart. By stilling all created things and the soul itself, one not only "rests within oneself" in the "sepulcher of the heart," but also the soul contemplates itself contemplating. It then "retires above itself" in the "lively awareness of God alone." Osuna speaks powerfully about transcending the activity of the senses, the memory, and the imagination by damming up the soul with love to force it up to God. "Sweet fire" will seize it, illuminate it, and expand it "like a glove we blow into." The person experiences the ecstatic giving of self and the receiving of God. Even when the soul falls back to itself, it contemplates "the image of God in its own clear waters. . . ."[3]

THE TEXTS

HUMILITY IS THE FOUNDATION FOR ALL[4]

Humility is the basis for every devotion and the root of every tree that is to bear fruit. If the word root applies to charity, then let humility be the fertilizer that nourishes the trees and makes them bountiful. . . . Humility is the first entry into religion, as it was Christ's first step into the world. . . . Humility has always been the cornerstone of sanctity. . . .

The purpose of humility corresponds to that of recollection, for in both we are to become emptied of ourselves so that our hearts may be filled more with God. . . . Quiet is the property of recollection and gentleness of humility, and both virtues are proper to the person of heart, who is the inner, spiritual person who hides within in order to find God who dwells within us. . . .

Some define humility as pusillanimity and the low, vile disposition of people inclined to pettiness. . . the appearance of ill health and common gestures, clothing, and manners. . . the cowardice and fear that dominate some people and prevent their striving for greater things. . . . These things are not humility, nor do they have anything to do with it. . . . [H]umility and magnanimity are such beloved sisters and companions that one is not found without the other. . . . [H]umility does not remain at the level of scorning honors but flies to the sublimity of spiritual graces. . . .

O humility, sublime virtue, mother and source of virtues, who could find the means to praise you and a heart generous enough to love you sincerely? You are lovable before God and all men; you subject devils with your quiet subjection. Even your adversary, pride, esteems your habit and seeks to wear it so as to appear more valuable. You widen and deepen the heart in order to discover the increasingly abundant spring of graces and to make it capable of receiving God. . . . You magnified the greatest of men, Christ, and the greatest angel perished by not loving you. . . . You alone know how greatly creatures need God and how our services to him are truly new gifts that he secretly bestows on us.

Another Manner of Following Christ[5]

As Christ has two natures, so there are two ways of following him. As Saint Jerome explains, if it is one thing to imitate Christ as man and another to imitate him as God, then it is also one thing to follow him as man and another to follow him as God. . . .

Our exterior person, or animal body, is born to labor and run after Christ in the ways described: following him in hardship and penitence and poverty in all things. But our soul with its superior part is a very swift bird, born to fly to divinity. . . .

. . . hence, those who follow Christ in his Divinity also wish to know God and to see him in a loftier understanding and spiritual vision that will satisfy the soul. . . .

It seems very wrong to want your soul to follow Christ's Divinity if your body refuses to follow his Humanity. The one is the foundation for the other.

Three Stages of Prayer[6]

The first form or manner of prayer is vocal. . . . Even though this prayer of the Lord [Our Father] is. . . the most excellent of vocal prayers, we should not forsake other vocal prayer, or we might run the risk of becoming tired of the one. . . . The second kind of prayer is that within our hearts, wherein we do not pronounce the words vocally with the mouth. . . . [T]his prayer consists of holy thoughts. . . . The third kind of prayer is called mental or spiritual prayer, in which the highest part of the soul is lifted more purely and affectionately to God on the wings of desire and pious affection strengthened by love. . . . [G]enuine love. . . withdraws from creatures and becomes recollected with God, [knowing that] it will be entirely received by him. . . .

It should be observed that man's giving himself to God and God himself to man is such a perfect exchange of gifts that when one gives himself, it seems as if God is in the person totally and entirely. I mean that if faith did not enlighten the man who possessed God, he would almost say that God was contained in himself and outside of him he was not. . . . The exchange in which recollected people give themselves to God is sometimes so generous that they reserve nothing for themselves and so lose their wills and power to choose; they remember God and give themselves so completely to him that they forget themselves as totally as if they did not exist.

These three forms of prayer not only pertain to states [beginners, proficients, the perfect] and the people in them but are often found in each person individually according to his particular temperament. Sometimes a person is more ready for one kind of prayer than another, and at times he is helped more quickly than he expected, but then he may fall so low as to have to start again from the beginning.

Two Kinds of Recollection[7]

One is general, the other is special. The first consists of an understanding we must hold as securely in our hearts as we grip the reins to restrain a runaway horse. This general recollection is our way of going continuously alert with our hearts pacified and sealed, caring not for human things . . . a spiritual emptying whereby we realize that the heart has no other task than to approach God. . . . Special recollection is when you retire secretly to pray silently to the Lord, leaving aside absolutely every other occupation and business so as to devote yourself exclusively to total recollection without your concern being fragmented.

God Is to Be Sought in the Heart[8]

Inasmuch as our lives are to be directed to no other end than seeking God, from whom we departed and to whom we are to return . . . the eternal Father in the law of nature also imprints it on our souls so that the highest part and reason always desire what is best, even though our evil freedom may contradict it. . . .

Given the wide variety of people who undertake to seek God as they are obliged, there must necessarily be diverse kinds of seeking, though the finding itself and the object of the quest will be the same. . . .

God . . . is so kind and courteous that he frees them of their burden by going out to them in welcome, irrespective of the road they travel in their quest. . . . Although these and other similar ways of seeking God may be good, I think it best to search for him in our hearts. . . . If the Kingdom of God is within us, then we only delay and make detours if we go forth in search by withdrawing to external considerations and become distracted by them. In the example of the Magdalen, let us often return to the sepulcher of the heart, even though the disciples and other women may have departed. *Magdalen* means magnificent, and she is the will that magnifies and exalts God. It should often return to the sepulcher where Christ rests after the labor of the passion, that sepulcher being the heart of one for whom he died. The disciples are the five senses, which withdraw from this exercise because they cannot reach it, and the women are the unnecessary imagination, fancy, and sensitive memory. That which chiefly remains is the will that like Magdalen sighs and longs to find what is lost, returning again and again to the same place, which is the heart, for our letter advises: "Retire into yourself often in silence and hope," [and] "Drink the water from your own cisterns and the streams of your own well.". . .

In almost the same way, the soul that is not hardened and despairing, though it may look like a dry, spent cistern, can receive the inflowing, clean water sent by the Lord if it turns inward so that with natural desire awakened and brought to life, the heart will become a well capable of receiving a plenitude of grace. Then the heart can produce devotion and love for God that will swell into streams of living water of inner devotion, leaping and surging to eternal life. Having turned inward so that we may ascend beyond ourselves to God, we return to the source of consolation of eternal grace. No one can rise to God, however, if he does not first enter within himself. The more forcefully and deeply he plunges inward, the higher his ascent, for he who is thus humbled will be exalted.

How This Letter Applies to Beginners and Proficients[9]

.... beginners ... we should advise them to retire into themselves and take courage.... First, we must frequently examine our past life and shed bitter tears of sorrow.... [W]e must have the silence that ... comes with patience and then this essential patience must be joined with the hope of succeeding. This labor is more than human, for human energy does not suffice: The Lord must extend his hand to ordain silence so we can hear his majesty....

Only the proficient ... truly do draw inward often, tasting great sweetness in God, who lulls them to sleep and quiets them and creates peace in them.... The proficients' manner of working spiritually is to withdraw and rest within themselves.... Such people act more in God than in themselves.

How the Perfect Practice Prayer[10]

The perfect draw the most deeply into themselves.... Although it is difficult to clarify the difference between the perfect and the proficient, it may be said that the second withdraw from all negligence and distraction into their hearts to enjoy spiritual silence and hope for the Lord's grace, whereas the perfect retire above themselves, for it is one thing to turn into yourself and quite another to turn above yourself.... [This] adds to recollection another operation in the soul, whereby it contemplates itself as being recollected. The soul is like someone who, standing guard, pauses to reflect on what he is doing without being diverted from his duty, for the second operation of reflection does not violate the silence but provides for the soul insight into itself....

What shall we say of the grace that is usually experienced in this twofold devotion when the will is so inflamed in the breast that we feel an unbearable sweet fire, a fire as intense as those of the world but, unlike them, painless and so delectable that we wish it to burn forever in the heart and inner being?. . . . [T]he understanding is so illumined and instructed that it seems to have been given a key into wisdom itself. . . . Memory is so calm as to be occupied in absolutely nothing whatsoever. . . . In the breast and at times throughout the entire being we feel our vital spirits and physical forces retract inward, and, even more significant, we are aware of a marvelous dilation whereby the soul is expanded like a glove we blow into. . . . The soul with its senses closed off in silence mounts higher and, standing, is raised up to God. . . .

So dam up with reeds the fountain of your soul whose love, Richard [of St. Victor] says, always springs forth, so that it will be forced to rise. Should it not rise, if it remains quiet and at rest within itself, it will see the image of God reflected in its own clear waters, more resplendent there than in any other thing, provided the disturbing turmoil of thoughts dies down. . . .[11]

The recollected watch the flocks of their senses so as to drive away evil thoughts that come to disquiet them. But they must turn their attention to themselves and notice what they do. . . . That we both watch and guard means that the first recollection gives rise to a second one that is born from a new grace infused into the soul that it may turn to itself and that the soul should carefully protect. . . . The second form of recollection is a lively awareness of the first, and the third is the simple remembrance of God alone whose presence we keep in the memory with no further assistance.

Three Kinds of Silence[12]

There are three kinds of quiet or silence in recollection. . . . The first is when all phantasies, imaginations, and kinds of visible things cease in the soul; it thus calms all created things. . . . The second kind of quiet in recollection is when the perfectly still soul feels a kind of spiritual idleness. . . [and] is appropriately compared to hearing because the listener not only calms everything else but also wishes everything to be quiet to him so he can more perfectly turn to the one who addresses him. . . . The first silence is with respect to other things as they concern us; the second is a deep rest wherein we become quiet to ourselves and turn to God with expectant, open submissiveness.

The third quiet of the understanding is accomplished in God when the soul is entirely transformed in him and tastes his sweetness abundantly, resting in his sweetness as if in a wine cellar. Silent, quiet, desiring nothing more, it is content; it falls asleep in its very self, forgetful of its human weakness, for it sees itself made like God, united in his image and garbed with his clarity as was Moses after he entered the cloud encircling the mountain. . . . In this third state of quiet, the understanding is so stilled and sealed, or it might be more accurate to say so occupied, that it understands nothing of the many things said to it, nor does it consider anything happening around it, for though it hears them, it understands them not. . . .

This letter does not say to quiet the intelligence but the understanding. . . . [T]he comprehension of invisible things belongs to pure intelligence; the intelligence is said to be pure when the understanding is fixed on a supreme truth without the intervention of the imagination. . . . [P]ure intelligence considers the invisible invisibly and sees the spiritual actually and essentially, knowing it is neither bound nor attached to external appearance.

"To be with the trinitarian Christ to serve" may well sum up Ignatian mysticism. His profound trinitarian, Christ-centered, eucharistic, priestly, and "hyperpapal" mysticism enabled Ignatius to find God in all things and all things in God. A master of the discernment of spirits, he has been called "the mystic of moods and thoughts."

IGNATIUS OF LOYOLA

Although Ignatius of Loyola is undoubtedly one of the most profound and original mystics in Christian history, he is better known for his role as an ascetic, a spiritual director, a champion of the poor and the sick, a reformer of the Church, a counter-reformer, an advisor to popes, cardinals, bishops, kings, princes, and other heads of state, the founder of the Society of Jesus, the leader of men, the initiator of worldwide missionary activity, and an educational innovator. His well-known *Spiritual Exercises* changed the history of spirituality from the 16th century to the present day. In short, his apostolic successes and those of the Jesuits from his time to the present seem to have overshadowed the importance of his mysticism. However, Ignatius' pastoral activities must be understood as the full flowering of his mysticism into every human dimension.

Born in the austere castle of the Loyolas in the Basque region of northern Spain, Iñigo López de Oñaz y Loyola, together with five sisters and 12 brothers, grew up in a noble Catholic family that prided itself on its military past and its fidelity to the king. His family may have first designated him for the clerical state, but Iñigo felt a strong attraction to an adventuresome military career.

When he was 14 years old, Iñigo was sent to a relative, the chief treasurer of the royal court. Under his tutelage and care, Iñigo received the basic formation of a Spanish gentleman and courtier. Women, gambling, dueling, and a tremendous desire for glory dominated his life until he received a disabling leg wound at the battle of Pamplona in 1521. During his long, boring convalescence at Loyola, Iñigo spent many hours daydreaming about the stories of courtly love he had read in the trashy literature of the age. But upon reading and pondering books on the life of Christ and the lives of the saints, God awakened him to his sinful past and instilled in him a tremendous desire to atone for these sins by going to Jerusalem and imitating the austerities of the great saints.

Before he undertook his penitential pilgrimage to Jerusalem, Iñigo spent three days at Montserrat to prepare for a general confession. There he divested himself of his remaining earthly goods, clothed himself in sackcloth, and spent a night in vigil before the altar of the Black Madonna. Then he moved on to Manresa where, for almost a year, he indulged his thirst for long hours of prayer and great penances. The intensity of his mystical purgation nearly drove him to suicide. But it was also at Manresa that God enlightened him so profoundly that he became "another man" and received numerous mystical gifts.

He spent the following year walking in Christ's footsteps in the Holy Land, thus fulfilling his dream to be near Christ in his historical existence. When external circumstances made it clear that it was not God's will that he remain in the Holy Land, Iñigo decided to study for the sake of a more effective apostolate. From Alcalá, and then Salamanca, he went to the famed University of Paris where he not only obtained advanced degrees in theology but also gathered companions around him in mystical friendship. Here he called himself Ignatius, perhaps out of devotion to Ignatius of Antioch who had great reverence for the name of Jesus.

In 1537, Ignatius and several of his companions were ordained and went to Rome to place themselves at the Pope's disposal. In a small chapel at La Storta, some six miles north of Rome, Ignatius saw the Eternal Father with his cross-bearing Son. The Father spoke interiorly to Ignatius' heart: "I shall be favorable to you [plural] at Rome," and "I want you, my Son, to take this man as your servant." Then Christ said to Ignatius: "I want you [singular] to serve us [Father and Son]." The graces at La Storta confirmed Ignatius' trinitarian, Christ-centered, service and ecclesial mysticism.

In Rome, Ignatius and his cohorts identified themselves as the companions of Jesus (thus, Society of Jesus, *Compañía de Jesús*), and continued to do what had been a part of Ignatius' life ever since his conversion: caring for the poor, the sick, the dying, and those in need of religious instruction. He and his companions decided to form a new religious order that was soon approved by Pope Paul III.

In conjunction with the founding of the Society of Jesus, Ignatius authored one of the basic documents in the history of religious life in the modern era, the Jesuit *Constitutions*, that was to be immensely influential in the formation of new religious congregations. Moreover, the Pope also formally approved Ignatius' *Spiritual Exercises*, for which Pope Pius IX later declared Ignatius the patron saint of spiritual exercises and retreats.

It was from a tiny Roman room that Ignatius, the "immobile missionary," played a key role as a reformer of the Church, one of the principal figures in the Counterreformation, director of vast, worldwide missionary activities, and occasional sensitive diplomat for the Church. Moreover, as the founder of colleges and universities, Ignatius was to be the spark that kindled the often astonishing success of Jesuit secondary education and its fostering of humanism from the 16th century to the present. Because of his pastoral work in Rome, as well as the founding of charitable institutions there, Ignatius has also been called the "apostle of Rome." Pope Gregory XV canonized him in 1622.

The first two of the following selections are taken from Ignatius' autobiography, *A Pilgrim's Journey*, which he dictated to one of his companions a few years before his death. They illustrate how God, during Ignatius' recuperation at Loyola, taught him discernment of spirits, that is, how to perceive and understand to some degree the different stirrings that are produced in the soul—the good, that they may be accepted; the bad, that they may be rejected. Ignatius learned not only that God, angels, and the devil moved him for various reasons but also discovered the connection between certain thoughts and emotional states.

ca. 1491-1556

These selections (together with the one taken from his letter to Sister Teresa Rejadell) can be read as a summary of Ignatius' teaching on the discernment of spirits. They underscore that it is characteristic of the devil to discourage and harass those zealous to serve God, while it is characteristic of God to console them, to make everything easy, to enlighten, reveal his will, and point out the right path. These texts were chosen to illustrate why Ignatius has been called a master of the discernment of spirits and the "mystic of moods and thoughts." *Discreet* love is perhaps the hallmark of Ignatian mysticism and spirituality.

It was also during the period of recovery that God awakened in Ignatius the desire to do penance, go to Jerusalem, and serve. "To be with the trinitarian Christ to serve" may well sum up Ignatian mysticism. Ignatius expected those he directed to find God in all things, not only in contemplation. To one truly "mortified," that is, someone who prefers God's will to his own, contemplation in action—or union with God, even in the midst of supposedly distracting activity—is not only possible; it is expected of him. Ignatius' "contemplation to attain the love of God" requires a person to ask "for an intimate knowledge of the many blessings received, that filled with gratitude for all, [that person] may *in all things love and serve* the Divine Majesty." This, too, is a good summary of Ignatian mysticism and spirituality.

The selections also show the importance of visions in Ignatius' mystical life. Only if they brought about lasting transformations did Ignatius consider them God-given.

The texts also focus on what Ignatius considered the most important period in his life: Manresa. His foundational experience of enlightenment on the banks of the Cardoner river transformed him into a new man with profound insight into all matters of faith and many matters of learning.

The next excerpts come from Ignatius' *Spiritual Diary*—two small notebooks from a much larger, lost packet—which covers the period from February 2, 1544, to February 27, 1545. It should be remembered that Ignatius was at the time writing the *Constitutions* and deliberating on a minor point of Jesuit poverty. The Diary is perhaps the most remarkable document on trinitarian mysticism ever written in any language. It offers an astonishing record of Ignatius' mystical intimacy with each person of the Trinity, the Divine Essence, the God-man, and Mary. It also highlights his mysticism of mediation. Mystical tears, trinitarian visions and illuminations, various kinds of locutions, profound mystical consolations, mystical touches, and experiences of reverential love, mystical repose, and melodic inner voices permeate this short document.

However, it must be emphasized that Ignatius sought mystical experiences not for themselves but in order to learn God's will and have it confirmed. In fact, Ignatius usually closed his letters, numbering nearly 7,000, with the words, "May Christ our Lord help us all with His bountiful grace, so that we may know His holy will and perfectly fulfill it."[1]

THE TEXTS

A PILGRIM'S JOURNEY[2]

8. . . .When he thought of worldly matters, he found much delight, but after growing weary and dismissing them, he found that he was dry and unhappy. But when he thought of going barefoot to Jerusalem and of eating nothing but vegetables and of imitating the saints in all the austerities they performed, he not only found consolation in these thoughts, but even after they had left him, he remained happy and joyful. He did not consider, nor did he stop to examine, this difference until one day his eyes were partially opened and he began to wonder at this difference and to reflect upon it. From experience, he knew that some thoughts left him sad while others made him happy, and little by little he came to perceive the different spirits that were moving him; one coming from the devil, the other coming from God.

9. He gained not a little light from this lesson, and he began to think more seriously about his past life and how greatly he needed to do penance for it. It was at this time that the desire to imitate the saints came to him, and without giving any consideration to his present circumstances, he promised to do, with God's grace, what they had

done. His greatest desire, after regaining his health, was to go to Jerusalem, as previously stated, and to observe the fasts and to practice the discipline as any generous soul on fire with God is accustomed to do.

10. With these holy desires of his, the thoughts of his former life were soon forgotten, and this was confirmed by a vision in this manner: One night, as he lay sleepless, he clearly saw the likeness of our Lady with the holy Child Jesus, and because of this vision he enjoyed an excess of consolation for a remarkably long time. He felt so great a revulsion for his past life, especially for his sins of the flesh, that it seemed to him that all the images that had been previously imprinted on his mind were now erased. Thus, from that hour until August 1553, when this is being written, he never again consented, not even in the least matter, to the motions of the flesh. Because of this effect in him, he concluded that this had been God's doing, though he did not dare to specify it any further, nor say anything more than to affirm what he had said above. His brother interpreted his external change, as did other members of the household, to mean that an interior change had taken place in his soul.

27. . . . During this period [at Manresa], God was dealing with him in the same way a schoolteacher deals with a child while instructing him. This was because either he was thick and dull of brain or because of the firm will that God Himself had implanted in him to serve Him—but he clearly recognized and has always recognized that it was in this way that God dealt with him. Furthermore, if he were to doubt this, he would think he was offending the Divine Majesty. One can see how God dealt with him in the following five examples.

28. First. He was greatly devoted to the Most Holy Trinity, and every day he prayed to each of the three Persons. But while doing the same to the Most Holy Trinity, the thought came to him, why four prayers to the Trinity? But this thought caused him little or no trouble since it was of so little importance. One day, as he was saying the Hours of Our Lady on the monastery steps, his understanding was raised on high, so as to see the most Holy Trinity under the aspect of three keys on a musical instrument, and as a result he shed many tears and sobbed so strongly that he could not control

himself. Joining in a procession that came out of the monastery, that morning he could not hold back his tears until dinnertime, and after he had eaten he could not refrain from talking, with much joy and consolation, about the Most Holy Trinity, making use of different comparisons. This experience remained with him for the rest of his life so that whenever he prayed to the Most Holy Trinity he felt great devotion.

29. Second. One day it was granted him to understand, with great spiritual joy, the way in which God had created the world. He seemed to see a white object with rays stemming from it, from which God made light. He neither knew how to explain these things nor did he fully remember the spiritual lights that God had then imprinted on his soul.

Third. It was likewise in Manresa—where he stayed for almost a year, and after experiencing divine consolations and seeing the fruit that he was bringing forth in the souls he was helping—that he abandoned those extremes he had previously practiced and began to cut his nails and hair. One day, while in town and attending Mass in the church attached to the above-mentioned monastery, he saw with inward eyes, at the time of the elevation of the body of the Lord, some white rays coming from above. But after so long a time, he is now unable to adequately explain this; nevertheless, he clearly saw with his understanding how our Lord Jesus Christ was present in that most holy Sacrament.

Fourth. During prayer, he often, and for an extended period of time, saw with inward eyes the humanity of Christ, whose form appeared to him as a white body, neither very large nor very small; nor did he see any differentiation of members. He often saw this in Manresa; and if he were to say 20 times or 40 times, he would not presume to say that he was lying. He saw it again while he was in Jerusalem, and once more when he was on his way to Padua. He has also seen our Lady in similar form, without differentiation of members. These things that he saw at that time fortified him and gave such great support to his faith that many times he thought to himself: If there were no Scriptures to teach us these matters of faith, he would still resolve to die for them on the basis of what he had seen.

Fifth. One time he went, following his devotion, to a church a little more than a mile from Manresa, which I believe was called St. Paul's. The road ran next to the [Cardoner] river. As he went along, occupied with his devotions, he sat down for a while with his face toward the river, which there ran deep. As he sat, the eyes of his understanding began to open; not that he saw a vision, but (he came) to understand and know many things, matters spiritual and those pertaining to faith and learning. This took place with such great clarity that everything appeared to him to be something new. And it happened to enlighten his understanding in such a manner that he thought of himself as if he were another man and that he had an intellect different from the one he had before. He cannot expound in detail what he then understood, for they were many things, but he can state that he received such a lucidity in understanding that during the course of his entire life—now having passed his 62nd year—if he were to gather all the help he received from God and everything he knew and add them together, he does not think they would add up to all that he received on that one occasion.

THE SPIRITUAL DIARY[3]
14. Friday Feb. 15. During my first prayer, when I named the Eternal Father etc., there came a feeling of interior sweetness that continued. . . [A] mighty impulse to weep and sob gripped me, and I seemed to see or feel that the Heavenly Father showed Himself propitious and kind—to the point of making clear to me that he would be pleased if Our Lady, whom I could not see, would intercede. While preparing the altar after I had vested, and during mass, I experienced great impulses and wept very copiously and intensely, sobbing violently. Often, I could not speak. The same continued after mass. During much of this time, before, during, and after mass, I felt and saw clearly that Our Lady was very propitious, pleading before the Father. Indeed, during the prayers to the Father and the Son, and at His consecration, I could not but feel or see her, as though she were part, or rather portal, of the great grace that I could feel in my spirit. At the consecration, she showed that her own flesh was in that of her Son with so many intuitions that they could not be written. . . .

23. Sunday, Feb. 24. During the customary prayer, from the beginning to the end, inclusive, I was helped by grace very far inside and

gentle, full of devotion, warm, and very sweet. While preparing the altar and vesting, the name of Jesus was shown me; I felt great love, confirmation, and an increased resolve to follow him; I wept and sobbed. Throughout mass, very great devotion and many tears so that quite often I lost the power of speech; all the devotion and feelings had Jesus as their object. I could not turn myself to the other Persons, except insofar as the First Person was the Father of such a Son: then I began to exclaim spiritually, "How He is Father, and how He is Son."

26. Wednesday, Feb. 27. . . . I entered the chapel and while praying felt, or to put it more exactly, I saw, not by natural power, the Blessed Trinity and also Jesus, who was representing me, or placing me before the Trinity or acting as mediator close to the Blessed Trinity, that I might communicate in that intellectual vision. On feeling and seeing in this way, I was covered in tears and love, but with Jesus as the object, and toward the Blessed Trinity, [I felt] a respect of submission more like a reverential love than anything else. Later I felt in a similar way that Jesus was performing the same task when I thought of praying to the Father, for it seemed, and I could feel within me, that He was doing everything before the Father and the Blessed Trinity. . . . When I write this, my understanding feels drawn to see the Blessed Trinity and appears to see, although not distinctly as before, three Persons. During mass, when I said the prayer that begins, "Domine Jesu Christe, Fili Dei vivi," etc., it seemed to me in spirit that whereas before I had seen Jesus, as I said, (then what I saw was) white, that is His humanity, on this occasion my feeling in my soul was different, i.e., I was aware not of the humanity alone, but of Jesus as being completely my God etc. with a fresh rush of tears and great devotion etc.

28. Friday, Feb. 29. . . . When out of the house, in the church before mass, I caught sight of the homeland of Heaven or the Lord of it, insofar as I understood the three Persons and how within the Father were the second and the third. . . .

31. Monday, Mar. 3. . . .Throughout mass, great love and devotion, and very many tears; this devotion and love had for their object the Blessed Trinity. I had not special knowledge or separate visions of the three Persons but a simple awareness or a representation of the

Blessed Trinity. Also, I occasionally had the same sensations with Jesus for their object: I seemed to be under His shadow as though He were my guide—but without diminution in the grace I was receiving from the Blessed Trinity; on the contrary I seemed to be more united with the Divine Majesty. During the prayers to the Father, I was unable, and had no desire, to find devotion, except the few times that the Persons made themselves seen in Him. In this way, everything, either mediately or immediately, transformed itself into the Blessed Trinity. . . .

34. Thursday, Mar. 6. . . . On pronouncing the words "Te igitur," I felt and saw, not obscurely but brightly, the very Being or Essence of God, appearing as a sphere, a little larger than the sun appears; from this Essence, the Father seemed to be going or deriving, so that when I said, "Te," that is, "Father," the image of the Divine Essence came to me before that of the Father. During this representation and vision of the Being of the Blessed Trinity, I could not distinguish or have sight of the other Persons. . . .

. . . After I had unvested and was praying at the altar, once more the same Being and spherical vision allowed itself to be seen: In some way I saw all three Persons as I had seen the first, viz., the Father in one part, the Son in another, and the Holy Spirit in another, all three coming forth or having their derivation from the Divine Essence, without leaving the spherical vision. . . .

28. Monday, Mar. 10. During the customary prayer, considerable devotion, especially from the middle onwards. Before the preparatory prayer, I experienced a new devotion: I thought or decided that I should live, or be, like an angel to perform the duty of celebrating mass: Very gently, some water came to my eyes. . . .

29. Tuesday, Mar. 11. . . . During these periods, I partly saw many times the Divine Being and sometimes with the Father as object, i.e., first the essence and then the Father. . . .

14. Sunday, Mar. 30. Many tears before mass. . . . At this period of time, it occurred to me that my humility, reverence, and submission should be not of a man who fears but of a man who loves. So strongly did this impress itself on my soul that with great faith I said: "Give me a lover's humility," and so also concerning my rever-

ence and submission. As I said the words, I experienced new visitations. So also I tried to check the tears in order to attend solely to this loving humility, etc. Later in the day, I felt great joy when I remembered this. I resolved not to stop there but afterward to entertain the same sentiment, viz., that of loving humility, etc., toward creatures, unless, on occasions, it were for the honor of God Our Lord to conduct myself differently; as it says in today's Gospel, "I should be a liar like you." During these periods, several times, I had the vision of the Divine Being in the form of a circle as before.

46. Sunday, May 11. Tears during mass; very many and continuous tears during mass; the internal *loquela* [inner voices] of the mass seemed even more divinely granted, as I had prayed for it this very day, because during the week, I had sometimes experienced the external *loquela*, and sometimes not, but the internal more rarely, although on Saturday, I found it a little more clear. So also during all the masses of the week, although I was not so visited with tears, yet I experienced greater quiet or contentment throughout mass from the pleasure of the *loquela*, with the devotion I could feel, than at other times when, during part of the mass, I had tears. Those tears that came today seemed completely different from all others in the past; they came so slowly, seemed so from within, and were so gentle, without clamor or great impulses. I thought they came from deep inside, though I cannot explain it. During the internal and external *loquela*, I felt wholly moved to the divine love and to this gift of *loquela*, divinely granted; I felt within me a great harmony accompanying the internal *loquela*, but I cannot express it.

57. Thursday, May 22. Many tears before mass, both in my room and in the chapel; no tears during the greater part of the mass; there was much *loquela*. However, I began to have doubts about the pleasure and delight caused by the *loquela* lest it were due to an evil spirit, seeing that the spiritual visitation of tears had ceased. A little while I thought I was taking excessive pleasure in the tone of the *loquela*, that is, in the mere sound, without paying sufficient attention to the meaning of the words and the *loquela*. At once the tears came, very many and very often, so that I realized that I was being instructed in the method I should follow. And I hoped for greater learning in the future.

May the grace and love of Christ our Lord be our never-failing protection and help.

Your letter, which I received a few days ago, brought with it much joy in the Lord, whom you are serving and whom you desire to serve even more earnestly and to whom we must attribute all of the good that we see in creatures. . . .

. . . The enemy is leading you into error in two things, but not in any way to make you fall into a sin that would separate you from God our Lord. He tries rather to upset you and to interfere with your service of God and your peace of mind. In the first place, he proposes and leads you on to false humility. And in the second, he gives you an exaggerated fear of God, with which you are altogether too much occupied.

In the first place, then, the enemy as a rule follows this course. He places obstacles and impediments in the way of those who love and begin to serve God our Lord, and this is the first weapon he uses in his efforts to wound them. He asks, for instance: "How can you continue a life of such great penance, deprived of all satisfaction from friends, relatives, possessions? How can you lead so lonely a life, with no rest, when you can save your soul in other ways and without such dangers?" He tries to bring us to understand that we must lead a life that is longer than it will actually be, by reason of the trials before us, and which no man ever underwent. He fails to remind us of the great comfort and consolations which our Lord is wont to give to such souls, who, as new recruits in our Lord's service, surmount all these obstacles and choose to suffer with their Creator and Lord. The enemy will then try his second weapon, which is pride and vainglory. He will endeavor to make the individual see that there is a great deal of goodness and holiness in him and puts him in a high position above his merits. If the servant of God is proof against these darts, humbling and abasing himself and refusing consent to the suggestions of the enemy, the enemy draws his third weapon, which is false humility. . . . In this way, he tries to prevent him from speaking of any of the blessings he has received. . . . His purpose is to prevent him from producing fruit in others as well as in himself. For he knows that when such a person recalls to mind what he has received, he is always helped in regard to greater things. . . .

. . . if the enemy uplifts us, we must abase ourselves by recounting our sins and miseries. If he keeps us down and depresses us, we must raise ourselves up in true faith and hope in our Lord by recalling the blessings we have received and with how much love and affection He is waiting to save us. The enemy does not care whether he speaks the truth or whether he lies. His sole purpose is to overcome us. . . .

. . .the second point. The enemy, having instilled a fear in us that has some appearance of humility—a false humility—aims to prevent us from speaking of good, holy, and profitable things. He will then confront us with a much worse fear, the fear that we are separated and estranged from our Lord. . . .

For a clearer understanding of this fear and its origin, I will call your attention briefly to two lessons which our Lord usually gives, or permits. The first is an interior consolation which casts out all uneasiness and draws one to a complete love of our Lord. In this consolation, He enlightens some, and to others He reveals many secrets as a preparation for later visits. In a word, when this divine consolation is present, all trials are pleasant and all weariness rest. He who goes forward with this fervor, warmth, and interior consolation finds every burden light and sweetness in every penance or trial, however great. This consolation points out and opens up the way we are to follow and points out the way we are to avoid. It does not remain with us always, but it will always accompany us on the way at the times that God designates. All this is for our progress.

But when this consolation is absent, the other lesson comes to light. Our ancient enemy sets up all possible obstacles to turn us from the way on which we have entered. He makes use of everything to vex us, and everything in the first lesson is reversed. We find ourselves sad without knowing why. We cannot pray with devotion, nor contemplate, nor even speak or hear of the things of God with any interior taste or relish. Not only this, but if he sees that we are weak and much humbled by these harmful thoughts, he goes on to suggest that we are entirely forgotten by God our Lord and leads us to think that we are quite separated from Him and that all that we have done and all that we desire to do is entirely worthless. He thus endeavors to bring us to a state of general discouragement. We can thus see what causes our fear and weakness: It is a too-prolonged gaze at such times on our miseries. We allow ourselves to be laid low by his misleading suggestions. For this reason, it is necessary to be aware of our opponent. If we are in consolation, we should abase and humble ourselves and reflect that soon the trial of temptation will come. And when temptation, darkness, or sadness comes upon us, we must go contrary to it without permitting ourselves to pay any attention to the unpleasant impressions caused in us and hope patiently for the consolation of our Lord, which will cast out all our uneasiness and scatter all the clouds.

It remains for me to speak of how we ought to understand what we think is from our Lord and, understanding, how we ought to use it to our advantage. For it frequently happens that our Lord moves and urges the soul to this or that activity. He begins by enlightening the soul; that is to say, by speaking interiorly to it without the din of words, lifting it up wholly to His divine love and ourselves to His meaning without any possibility of resistance on our part, even should we wish to resist. This thought of His, which we take, is of necessity in conformity with the commandments, the precepts of the Church, and obedience to our superiors. It will be full of humility because the same divine Spirit is present in all. But we can frequently be deceived, however, because after such consolation or inspiration, when the soul is still abiding in its joy, the enemy tries, under the impetus of this joy, to make us innocently add to what we have received from God our Lord. His only purpose is to disturb and confuse us in everything.

At other times, he makes us lessen the import of the message we have received and confronts us with obstacles and difficulties, so as to prevent us from carrying out completely what had been made known to us. Right here there is more need of attention than anywhere else. We may often have to control the desire we feel and speak less of the things of God our Lord; at other times, we may speak more than the satisfaction or movement we feel prompts in us. We act thus because in this matter we should give more heed to the good of others than to our own desires. When the enemy thus tries to magnify or diminish the communication received, we must proceed for the purpose of helping others. . .

In closing I beg the most holy Trinity to bestow upon us all plentiful grace to know God's most holy will and perfectly to fulfill it.

Teresa of Avila, the Spanish Carmelite reformer, may well be the most important woman mystic in the Christian tradition due to her penetrating descriptions of the various levels of mystical prayer, mystical marriage, mystical fecundity, of the relationship between mystical prayer and Christ's humanity, and of various secondary mystical phenomena.

TERESA OF AVILA

To attain the title Doctor of the Church, a person must possess great sanctity, distinguished learning, and be proclaimed Doctor by either a Pope or an ecumenical council. Because this title is associated with the Church's own teaching office and had been bestowed only upon men, some theologians assumed that a woman could not hold the title. However, on September 27, 1970, Pope Paul VI solemnly declared St. Teresa of Avila a Doctor of the Church and a teacher of "marvelous profundity," the first woman to be so honored.

The granddaughter of a Christianized Jew (*converso*), Teresa de Ahumada was one of 10 children born in Avila to religiously sensitive parents. When Teresa was 14, her mother died. Unable to cope with her bereavement and influenced by the bad example of favorite cousins, Teresa became so frivolous that her father sent her to Our Lady of Grace boarding school in Avila. There, inspired by a holy nun and by her pious uncle Don Pedro, who supplied her with spiritual books, Teresa, against her father's wishes, entered the Carmelite Monastery of the Incarnation when she was 20 years old.

Contrary to common belief, life at the monastery was austere. Furthermore, the inner battle between self-love and love of God undermined Teresa's health. She became a paralytic for almost three years. Near death, she claimed to have been cured through St. Joseph's intercession. For the next 18 years, she struggled with prayer because she did not seem to realize that genuine prayer can coexist with turmoil in superficial levels of the psyche. Her final conversion and total surrender to God took place "after nearly 20 years of a stormy sea," that is, when she was about 40 years old.

A few years later, Teresa set out to correct irregularities in Carmelite life and in 1562 founded the first convent of the new Carmelite reform. She speaks of the next five years at the Monastery of St. Joseph as "the most restful years of my life."

In 1567, she met John of the Cross, "the father of my soul," and persuaded him to initiate a similar reform for Carmelite men. After 12 years of tensions, hostilities, opposition, and successes, the Carmelites of the Primitive Rule were given independent jurisdiction from the other Carmelites. Teresa continued the work of the Reform, traveled widely to establish new foundations, and eventually succumbed to the ill health that had plagued most of her life.

Teresa of Avila excelled as a spiritual and mystical writer. In what may be her most personal and captivating book, *The Book of Her Life (Book of God's Mercies)*, Teresa discusses the first 20 years of her life and focuses upon her family life, her sins, the graces she received, and her vocation to serve God perfectly. In the second section, Teresa offers a magnificent treatise on prayer. Likening the soul to a garden, she speaks of four ways in which a gardener can water it. She compares hauling water with buckets to the labor involved in meditative prayer; watering by way of a windlass to the restful prayer of recollection and quiet; watering by way of an irrigation ditch to the prayer in which the soul's faculties "sleep," while the soul's deepest part enjoys God's undisturbed presence; and finally, the watering by a downpour of torrential rains to the prayer of union in which the soul actually dies and finds the self alive in God.

In the book's third part, she describes some events of her extraordinary mystical life: ecstasies, raptures, wounds of love, a vision of her place in hell, visions of Christ's humanity, and the like. In the fourth section, Teresa speaks of mystical marriage and spiritual fecundity. Her mystical experiences and her fruitfulness life of service are two sides of the same coin.

In *The Way of Perfection*, Teresa offers practical advice on prayer to her Carmelite nuns. This book contains her profoundly beautiful commentary on the Lord's prayer. *The Book of Her Foundations* narrates events connected with the founding of her many Carmelite monasteries, as well as writings on the perfect contemplation and the many mystical favors given to her nuns.

Among the minor works, her *Meditations on the Song of Songs* (actually, only on a few verses of it) must be mentioned. In fact, Teresa sees the Song of Songs as a paradigm of what transpires between God and the soul. Despite her lack of formal training and only limited access to the Bible, this small work illustrates her penetrating knowledge and deft use of Scripture.

In her masterpiece, *The Interior Castle*, Teresa describes the human soul as an extremely beautiful castle of clear crystal or diamond that contains many rooms, paralleling the many heavenly mansions. God himself dwells in the center of this castle and continually invites the person to come inside to remain in his truth and love.

The Teresian mystical journey consists in entering the castle and proceeding through seven "mansions" that contain innumerable rooms in order to encounter the King at the central mansion. No one person will pass through all the castle's rooms, nor does Teresa attempt to describe them all. As she says, "it is impossible that anyone understand them all since there are many."[1]

This castle is entered by way of prayer and meditation. To Teresa, "mental prayer . . . is nothing else than an intimate sharing between friends; it means taking time frequently to be alone with Him who we know loves us."[2] In her view, humility is the foundation of prayer. However, induced by a sense of false humility, she gave up prayer for more than a year. God eventually taught her that to neglect prayer out of feelings of unworthiness, or for any other reason, was the most serious temptation of her life. The worst time she ever had, Teresa confessed, came after she abandoned prayer.

Teresa's profound love of Jesus Christ and his role in her mysticism cannot be overemphasized. It is striking that she returns to the topic of *meditating* upon Christ's sacred humanity in the sixth mansion, or the penultimate dwelling, of the interior castle after discussing raptures, mystical wounds of love, visions, locutions, and the prayer of union. Teresa flatly contradicts those who advocate apophatic prayer and insist that thoughts, images, and even Christ's humanity prevent one from reaching the higher stages of prayer.

When she first began to delight in the prayer of quiet, she admitted that no one could have persuaded her to meditate upon Christ's humanity. But with a little more experience, Teresa called this period of prayer without Christ an "act of high treason," even though she acted that way unknowingly. Eventually, she found a new love for Christ's humanity, and stated in a way highly characteristic of her prayer: "But to withdraw completely from Christ or that this divine Body be counted in a balance with our own miseries or with all creation, that I cannot endure."[3] Moreover, she taught explicitly that one cannot enter the innermost mansion without Jesus as one's guide. The selected texts that follow illustrate the role that Christ's humanity played for her even in the ultimate mansion.

It must be stressed that Teresa lacked a formal education and that her eminent learning was first and foremost "infused," that is, God-given. Her mystical erudition flowed from her mystical love, for often during prayer she received the grace both to understand and to express various aspects of her inner and outer life. For example, she experienced that "the soul sees that in an instant it is wise; the mystery of the Blessed Trinity and other sublime things are so explained that there is no theologian with whom it would not dispute in favor of the truth of these grandeurs."[4] Thus, Teresa lived what she wrote and insisted that she spoke of "nothing [that] I have not experienced myself or seen in others [or received understanding of from our Lord in prayer.]"[5]

The selections come from the fifth and seventh dwellings of Teresa's mystical gem, *The Interior Castle*. In the fifth dwelling, God suspends and completely lulls the faculties. Even in these advanced stages of the mystical life, Teresa stresses the need for asceticism, devotion, the sacraments, and meditation. But God himself rewards the person with his own life. In what may be one of the loveliest analogies in Christian mystical literature, Teresa leaves aside the images of castle and water to compare the soul to a silkworm. In the prayer of union, God becomes the actual cocoon in which the soul dies to itself only to emerge transformed as a small, white butterfly.

Paradoxically, the prayer of union bestows both profound peace and great restlessness. Despite the extraordinary calm in her soul's core, Teresa likewise experienced great pain from her inability to love enough and her realization that she could not do more.

The selected texts also illustrate the number of extraordinary phenomena that accompanied God's purifying, illuminating, and transforming awakening of the triune life in Teresa's depths. If past commentators tended to overemphasize these occurrences at the expense of the key experience—God's self-communicating life to the person—contemporary commentators tend to distinguish too sharply between them. God communicated himself to Teresa in and through these unusual experiences, and they are an inextricable part of her mysticism.

Teresa brings up short those who misunderstand this prayer by introducing the theme of spiritual greed. She chides those avaricious in prayer, who cling more to its comforts than to God himself. Moreover, to Teresa, genuine union with God consists as well in compassion for others and love of neighbor.

In the seventh dwelling, Teresa explains that although God had really united the person to Himself in the fifth mansion by the prayer of union and in the sixth mansion by raptures, the soul was left blinded and deaf like St. Paul encountering Christ on the road to Damascus. God removed Teresa's inner blindfold and unplugged her mystical ear through an intellectual vision of the Trinity. Permanently aware of the triune indwelling and more alert in God's service, Teresa now experienced her "spirit" as permanently contemplative and her "soul" as prepared to undertake anything for God. In short, as a contemplative in action, she felt as both Mary and Martha.

A profound vision of Christ's humanity initiated Teresa into the most interior mansion. She saw Christ with the "eyes of her soul." Because of the overwhelming power of the vision and of Christ's words, she realized that Christ had never before appeared to her at this depth. This vision was succeeded by extremely delicate intellectual visions of Christ's humanity, in which she found that her spirit had become inseparably one with God in a foretaste of heavenly life. Moreover, unlike mystical betrothal—which she compared to two joined candles producing one flame but which can be separated—spiritual marriage is like the indissoluble unity of rain falling into the ocean.[6]

THE TEXTS

THE INTERIOR CASTLE

THE FIFTH DWELLING PLACES[7]
CHAPTER 2
. . . Explains the prayer of union through an exquisite comparison. . . .

2. You must have already heard about His marvels manifested in the way silk originates, for only He could have invented something like that. The silkworms come from seeds about the size of little grains of pepper. (I have never seen this but heard of it, and so if something in the explanation gets distorted, it won't be my fault.) When the warm weather comes and the leaves begin to appear on the mulberry tree, the seeds start to live, for they are dead until then. The worms nourish themselves on mulberry leaves until, having grown to full size, they settle on some twigs. There, with their little mouths, they themselves go about spinning silk and making some very thick little cocoons in which they enclose themselves. The silkworm, which is fat and ugly, then dies, and a little white butterfly, which is very pretty, comes forth from the cocoon. Now, if this were not seen but recounted to us as having happened in other times, who would believe it? Or what reasonings could make us conclude that a thing as nonrational as a worm or a bee could be so diligent in working for our benefit and with so much industriousness. And the poor worm loses its life in the challenge. . . .

3. Let's return to what I was saying. The silkworm is like the soul that starts to live when, by the heat of the Holy Spirit, it begins to benefit through the general help given to us all by God and

through the remedies left by Him to His Church, by going to confession, reading good books, and hearing sermons, which are the remedies that a soul, dead in its carelessness and sins and placed in the midst of occasions, can make use of. It then begins to live and sustain itself by these things, and by good meditations, until it is grown. Its being grown is what is relevant to what I'm saying, for these other things have little importance here.

4. Well once this silkworm is grown. . . it begins to spin the silk and build the house wherein it will die. I would like to point out here that this house is Christ. Somewhere, it seems to me, I have read or heard that our life is hidden in Christ or in God (both are the same), or that our life is Christ. . . .

5. Well see here, daughters, what we can do through the help of God: His Majesty Himself, as He does in this prayer of union, becomes the dwelling place we build for ourselves. It seems I'm saying that we can build up God and take Him away, since I say that He is the dwelling place and we ourselves can build it so as to place ourselves in it. And, indeed, we can! Not that we can take God away or build Him up, but we can take away from ourselves and build up, as do these little silkworms. For we will not have finished doing all that we can in this work when, to the little we do—which is nothing—God will unite Himself in His greatness and give it such high value that the Lord Himself will become the reward of this work. Thus, since it was He who paid the highest price, His Majesty wants to join our little labors with the great ones He suffered so that all the work may become one.

6. Therefore, courage, my daughters. Let's be quick to do this work and weave this little cocoon by getting rid of our self-love and self-will, our attachment to any earthly thing, and by performing deeds of penance, prayer, mortification, obedience, and of all the other things you know. Would to heaven that we would do what we know we must; and we are instructed about what we must do. Let us die; let this silkworm die, as it does in completing what it was created to do! And you will see how we see God, as well as ourselves placed inside His greatness, as is this little silkworm within its cocoon. . . .

7. Now, then, let's see what this silkworm does, for that's the reason

I've said everything else. When the soul is, in this prayer, truly dead to the world, a little white butterfly comes forth. Oh, greatness of God! How transformed the soul is when it comes out of this prayer after having been placed within the greatness of God and so closely joined with Him for a little while—in my opinion, the union never lasts for as much as a half hour. Truly, I tell you that the soul doesn't recognize itself. Look at the difference there is between an ugly worm and a little white butterfly; that's what the difference is here. The soul doesn't know how it could have merited so much good—from where this good may have come, I mean, for it well knows that it doesn't merit this blessing. It sees within itself a desire to praise the Lord; it would want to dissolve and die a thousand deaths for Him. It soon begins to experience a desire to suffer great trials without its being able to do otherwise. There are the strongest desires for penance, for solitude, and that all might know God; and great pain comes to it when it sees that He is offended. . . . As I have said, if after God brings a soul here it makes the effort to advance, it will see great things.

8. Oh, to see the restlessness of this little butterfly, even though it has never been quieter and calmer in its life, is something to praise God for! And the difficulty is that it doesn't know where to alight and rest. Since it has experienced such wonderful rest, all that it sees on earth displeases it, especially if God gives it this wine often. Almost each time, it gains new treasures. It no longer has any esteem for the works it did while a worm, which was to weave the cocoon little by little; it now has wings. How can it be happy walking step by step when it can fly? On account of its desires, everything it can do for God becomes little in its own eyes. It doesn't wonder as much at what the saints suffered now that it understands through experience how the Lord helps and transforms a soul, for it doesn't recognize itself or its image. The weakness it previously seemed to have with regard to doing penance it now finds is its strength. . . .

9. . . . So, there is no reason to be surprised that this little butterfly seeks rest again since it feels estranged from earthly things. Well then, where will the poor little thing go?. . . . O Lord, what new trials begin for this soul?. . .

10. I don't mean to say that those who arrive here do not have

peace; they do have it, and it is very deep. For the trials themselves are so valuable and have such good roots that although very severe, they give rise to peace and happiness. From the very unhappiness caused by worldly things arises the ever so painful desire to leave this world. Any relief the soul has comes from the thought that God wants it to be living in this exile; yet even this is not enough, because in spite of all these benefits, it is not entirely surrendered to God's will. . .although it doesn't fail to conform itself. But it conforms with a great feeling that it can do no more because no more has been given it, and with many tears. Every time it is in prayer, this regret is its pain. . . .

11. . . . Even were we to meditate for many years, we wouldn't be able to feel them as painfully as does this soul now. . . . The grief that is felt here is not like that of this world. We can, with God's favor, feel the grief that comes from thinking about these things a great deal, but such grief doesn't reach the intimate depths of our being as does the pain suffered in this state, for it seems that the pain breaks and grinds the soul into pieces, without the soul's striving for it or even wanting it. Well, what is this pain? Where does it come from? I shall tell you.

12. Haven't you heard it said of the bride. . .that God brought her into the inner wine cellar and put charity in order within her? Well, that is what I mean. Since the soul now surrenders itself into His hands and its great love makes it so surrendered that it neither knows nor wants anything more than what He wants with her (for God will never, in my judgment, grant this favor save to a soul that He takes for His own), He desires that, without its understanding how, it may go forth from this union impressed with His seal. For indeed the soul does no more in this union than does the wax when another impresses a seal on it. The wax doesn't impress the seal upon itself; it is only disposed—I mean by being soft. And even in order to be disposed, it doesn't soften itself but remains still and gives its consent. Oh, goodness of God; everything must be at a cost to You! All you want is our will and that there be no impediment in the wax.

13. Well now you see here, Sisters, what our God does in this union so that this soul may recognize itself as His own. He gives from

what He has, which is what His Son had in this life. He cannot grant us a higher favor. . . .

CHAPTER 3
Continues on the same subject. . . .

11. When I see souls very earnest in trying to understand the prayer they have and very sullen when they are in it—for it seems they don't dare let their minds move or stir lest a bit of their spiritual delight and devotion be lost—it makes me realize how little they understand of the way by which union is attained; they think the whole matter lies in these things. No, Sisters, absolutely not; works are what the Lord wants. He desires that if you see a Sister who is sick, to whom you can bring some relief, you have compassion on her and not worry about losing this devotion; and that if she is suffering pain, you also feel it; and that, if necessary, you fast so that she might eat—not so much for her sake as because you know it is your Lord's desire. This is true union with His will. . . .

THE SEVENTH DWELLING PLACES[8]
CHAPTER 1
Treats of the great favors God grants souls that have entered the seventh dwelling places.

5. . . . Now then, when His Majesty is pleased to grant the soul this divine marriage. . ., He first brings it into His own dwelling place. He desires that the favor be different from what it was at other times when He gave the soul raptures. I really believe that in rapture He unites it with Himself, as well as in the prayer of union . . . . But it doesn't seem to the soul that it is called to enter into its center, as it is here in this dwelling place, but called to the superior part. These things matter little; whether the experience comes in one way or another, the Lord joins the soul to Himself. But He does so by making it blind and deaf. . . . Yet when He joins it to Himself, it doesn't understand anything; for all the faculties are lost.

6. In this seventh dwelling place, the union comes about in a different way: Our good God now desires to remove the scales from the soul's eyes and let it see and understand—although in a strange way—something of the favor He grants it. When the soul is brought into that dwelling place, the Most Blessed Trinity, all three

Persons, through an intellectual vision, is revealed to it through a certain representation of the truth. First, there comes an enkindling in the spirit in the manner of a cloud of magnificent splendor; and these Persons are distinct, and through an admirable knowledge the soul understands as a most profound truth that all three Persons are one substance and one power and one knowledge and one God alone. It knows in such a way that what we hold by faith, it understands, we can say, by sight—although the sight is not with the bodily eyes nor with the eyes of the soul, because we are not dealing with an imaginative vision. Here, all three Persons communicate themselves to it, speak to it, and explain those words of the Lord in the Gospel: that He and the Father and the Holy Spirit will come to dwell with the soul that loves Him and keeps His commandments.

7. Oh, God help me! How different is hearing and believing these words from understanding their truth in this way! Each day, this soul becomes more amazed, for these Persons never seem to leave it any more, but it clearly beholds, in the way that was mentioned, that they are within it. In the extreme interior, in some place very deep within itself, the nature of which it doesn't know how to explain, because of a lack of learning, it perceives this divine company.

8. You may think that as a result the soul will be outside itself and so absorbed that it will be unable to be occupied with anything else. On the contrary, the soul is much more occupied than before with everything pertaining to the service of God; and once its duties are over, it remains with that enjoyable company. If the soul does not fail God, He will never fail, in my opinion, to make His presence clearly known to it. It has strong confidence that since God has granted this favor, He will not allow it to lose the favor. Though the soul thinks this, it goes about with greater care than ever not to displease Him in anything.

9. It should be understood that this presence is not felt so fully—I mean so clearly—as when revealed the first time or at other times when God grants the soul this gift. For if the presence were felt so clearly, the soul would find it impossible to be engaged in anything else or even to live among people. But even though the presence is not perceived with this very clear light, the soul finds itself in this

company every time it takes notice. . . .

10. It seems that the divine Majesty desires, through this wonderful company, to prepare the soul for more. Clearly, the soul will be truly helped in every case to advance in perfection and to lose the fear it sometimes had of the other favors He granted it. . . . Such was the experience of this person, for in everything, she found herself improved, and it seemed to her, despite the trials she underwent and the business affairs she had to attend to, that the essential part of her soul never moved from that room. As a result, it seemed to her that there was, in a certain way, a division in her soul. And while suffering some great trials a little after God granted her this favor, she complained of that part of the soul, as Martha complained of Mary, and sometimes pointed out that it was there always, enjoying that quietude at its own pleasure, while leaving her in the midst of so many trials and occupations that she could not keep it company.

11. This will seem to you, daughters, to be foolishness, but it truly happens in this way. Although we know that the soul is all one . . . one understands with certitude that there is some kind of difference, a difference clearly recognized, between the soul and the spirit, even though they are both one. So delicate a division is perceived that sometimes it seems the one functions differently from the other, and so does the savor the Lord desires to give them seem different. It also seems to me that the soul and the faculties are not one but different. There are so many and such delicate things in the interior that it would be boldness on my part to set out to explain them.

CHAPTER 2
Continues on the same subject. . . .

. . . The first time the favor is granted [spiritual marriage], His Majesty desires to show Himself to the soul through an imaginative vision of His most sacred humanity so that the soul will understand and not be ignorant of receiving this sovereign gift. With other persons, the favor will be received in another form. With regard to the one of whom we are speaking, the Lord represented Himself to her, just after she had received Communion, in the form of shining splendor, beauty, and majesty, as He was after His resurrection, and told her that now it was time she consider as her own what belonged to Him and that He would take care of what was hers. . . .

2. It may seem that this experience was nothing new, since at other times the Lord had represented Himself to the soul in such a way. The experience was so different that it left her indeed stupefied and frightened: first, because this vision came with great force; second, because of the words the Lord spoke to her; and also because in the interior of her soul, where He represented Himself to her, she had not seen other visions except the former one. You must understand that there is the greatest difference between all the previous visions and those of this dwelling place. Between the spiritual betrothal and the spiritual marriage the difference is as great as that which exists between two who are betrothed and two who can no longer be separated.

3. . . . it should be understood that in this state, there is no more thought of the body than if the soul were not in it, but one's thought is only of the spirit. In the spiritual marriage, there is much less remembrance of the body because this secret union takes place in the very interior center of the soul, which must be where God Himself is, and in my opinion, there is no need of any door because everything that has been said up until now seems to take place by means of the senses and faculties, and this appearance of the humanity of the Lord must also. But that which comes to pass in the union of the spiritual marriage is very different. The Lord appears in this center of the soul not in an imaginative vision but in an intellectual one—although more delicate than those mentioned—as He appeared to the apostles without entering through the door when He said to them *pax vobis* [peace be with you]. What God communicates here to the soul in an instant is a secret so great and a favor so sublime—and the delight the soul experiences so extreme—that I don't know what to compare it to. I can only say that the Lord wishes to reveal for that moment, in a more sublime manner than through any spiritual vision or taste, the glory of heaven. One can say no more—insofar as can be understood—than that the soul, I mean the spirit, is made one with God. . . . He doesn't want to be separated from the soul.

4. The spiritual betrothal is different, for the two often separate. And the union is also different because, even though it is the joining of two things into one, in the end, the two can be separated and each remains by itself. We observe this ordinarily, for the favor of union with the Lord passes quickly, and afterward the soul remains without that company; I mean, without awareness of it. In this other favor from the Lord, no. The soul always remains with its God in that center. Let us say that this union is like the joining of two wax candles to such an extent that the flame coming from them is but one, or that the wick, the flame, and the wax are all one. But afterward, one candle can be easily separated from the other, and there are two candles; the same holds for the wick. In the spiritual marriage the union is like what we have when rain falls from the sky into a river or fount; all is water, for the rain that fell from heaven cannot be divided or separated from the waters of the river. Or it is like what we have when a little stream enters the sea; there is no means of separating the two. Or, like the bright light entering a room through two different windows; although the streams of light are separate when entering the room, they become one.

6. And that [the soul's] life is Christ is better understood, with the passing of time, by the effects this life has. Through some secret aspirations, the soul understands clearly that it is God who gives life to the soul. These aspirations come very, very often in such a way that they can in no way be doubted. The soul feels them very clearly, even though they are indescribable. But the feeling is so powerful that sometimes the soul cannot avoid the loving expressions that they cause, such as O Life of my life! . . . .

Along with Teresa of Avila, John of the Cross is considered to be the cofounder of the Discalced Carmelites. Called the greatest mystic in the Christian tradition, his writings have become almost the norm for interpreting the mystical ascent to God. His analysis of the dark night of the soul is unrivaled.

JOHN OF THE CROSS

John of the Cross has been called the greatest mystic in the Christian tradition. The saint's extraordinary mystical experiences, sublime poetry, and mystical theology offer a singular guide to the life of perfection. John had a decisive influence on the Christian mystical tradition. In fact, his writings have become almost the norm for interpreting the mystical ascent to God. Thus, in 1926, Pope Pius XI proclaimed him a Doctor of the Church.

Juan de Yepes y Alvárez was born about 25 miles north of Avila in Fontiveros, Spain. John's father, Gonzalo de Yepes, was disowned by his wealthy Toledo silk-merchant family when he married a poor woman not of his social class. Moreover, Gonzalo died when John was only two years old. Thus, John experienced both poverty and sorrow from an early age.

When John was 20, he entered the Carmelite Order at the monastery of Santa Ana in Medina del Campo. He attended the University of Salamanca, and was ordained a priest in 1567. The following year, John helped Teresa of Avila to restore austerity to her Carmelite convent, and then founded a Discalced (shoeless) Carmelite monastery in 1569. Because of his success in restoring the Primitive Rule to the friars of the Mitigation, he is considered—along with Teresa of Avila—to be a cofounder of the Discalced Carmelites.

Because the reform movement created resistance as well as political and ecclesiastical intrigues, great turmoil filled much of John's life thereafter. Kidnapped by disgruntled members of his own order in 1578, John was held in captivity for approximately nine months in Toledo, where he wrote some of his great lyric poetry. But after his escape, he rose to positions of responsibility in his order, did much administrative work, and wrote his most significant works.

Forced out of office because of a renewed clash within the reform movement, he retired to the solitude of La Peñuela monastery in Andalusia. Efforts were then made to have him expelled from the movement. He became ill and went to Ubeda because no one knew him there. Mistreated by the prior, he soon succumbed to his illness.

John wrote his major works during the last 14 years of his life, that is, after he had attained intellectual, spiritual, and mystical maturity. One work, *The Ascent of Mount Carmel—The Dark Night*, is written as an allegory in which the lover sings of her good fortune in having departed "one dark night" to be united with her beloved. It then speaks of the wonderful results of this union of love. In this work, John delineates how one reaches "the high state of perfection" attained only in the dark night of naked faith.

Composed in love overflowing into mystical knowledge, *The Spiritual Canticle* describes in lyric verse the exchange of love that transpires between the soul and Christ, its bridegroom. *The Living Flame of Love* deals "with a love within this very state of transformation that has a deeper quality and is more perfect."[1] In fact, this state is the "highest degree of perfection one can reach in this life."[2]

St. John of the Cross may be compared to an experienced, yet uncompromising, mountain climber. Impressed with the breathtakingly beautiful view from the top, John refuses to allow the one he is guiding to look around or to rest until they reach the summit. John's radical apophaticism emphasizes a mystical journey during the night of faith and rejects all secondary mystical phenomena systematically and unhesitatingly. The following quotation sets the tone of his mystical enterprise: "To reach satisfaction in all, desire its possession in nothing. To come to the knowledge of all, desire the knowledge of nothing. To come to possess all, desire the possession of nothing. To arrive at being all, desire to be nothing."[3]

The real subject of John's works is God. An incredible certitude of God's presence permeates these writings. His beautiful, passionate, mysterious poetry—followed by lengthy commentary—is systematically and theologically structured. It is also didactic and evocative. His works instruct the reader in how to attain life's goal: perfect loving union with God in which one actually becomes God by participation. John's uniqueness makes him more than simply one mystic in the Christian tradition. To study his works in depth is to discover most of what is to be found in the other Christian mystics, although with different emphasis and another psychological disposition.

John wrote "to explain the dark night through which a soul journeys toward that divine light of perfect union with God . . . through love."[4] By blending mystical poetry, which he calls "expressions of love arising from mystical understanding,"[5] with discursive commentary, John systematically explains the classical purgative, illuminative, and unitive states that culminate in transformation into God. First, one enters in a "twilight" of the senses in which the world of appearances is transcended. Second, one moves into a total night of the spirit in which the self dies. Third, one journeys toward the noonday sun involving spiritual betrothal and marriage once a mystical dawn occurs.

John's comparison of the contemplative to a "turtledove" in stanza 34 of *The Spiritual Canticle* is a perfect symbol of his entire spirituality and mysticism. According to John, the turtledove never lands, perches, rests, eats, or drinks until it has found its mate. Only then will it enjoy anything. John emphasizes the single-minded pursuit of a beloved who seeks the contemplative even more.

To understand John's somewhat austere single-mindedness, it is imperative to read all his works in the context of the awesomely beautiful descriptions of the deepening of loving union with God, as found in *The Living Flame of Love*. That work, John's masterpiece on mystical marriage, should be read before his more intimidating *Ascent of Mount Carmel—The Dark Night*. Too many people read the imposing and seemingly impossible *Ascent—Night* and never read *The Living Flame*. But the hollowing-out process described in the *Ascent—Night* can be understood only in terms of the being-filled-with-God process described in *The Living Flame*.

The selections presented here focus on the most profound depiction of the purgative way in the Christian mystical tradition. According to John, "to love is to labor to divest and deprive oneself for God of all that is not God." But he stresses that human effort alone cannot remove all hindrances to becoming God by participation. Only God can effect the required purgation. Moreover, contemplation is God's secret flowing into the soul.

The texts were selected to illustrate the signs John gives to indicate that God is purifying the senses. These signs indicate the transition from "acquired" contemplation to "infused" contemplation, or mystical contemplation in the strict sense. Despite the profound dryness that God instills in the senses, the person begins to experience a profound peace and joy at the depths of his or her spirit.

The excerpts highlight two important themes: 1) God's self-communication to the soul *is* the dark night of the spirit; and 2) there is nothing in this self-communication that gives the spirit pain. But due to the spirit's resistance and to its small capacity to love, it must undergo a transformative mystical death.

The dark night of the spirit accomplishes three things: 1) it completes the purgation of the senses; 2) it purifies the person's entire conscious, preconscious, and unconscious life, enabling the total person to obey love alone; and 3) it enlarges the person's capacity to receive love and to love equally in return.

The final text was selected to indicate the poetic song of love sung by the soul at the contemplative summit.[6]

THE TEXTS

THE DARK NIGHT[7]

BOOK I
CHAPTER 7
5. It is enough to have referred to the many imperfections of those who live in this beginner's state to see the need there is that God put them in the state of proficients. He does this by introducing

them into the dark night, of which we shall now speak. There, through pure dryness and interior darkness, He weans them away from the breast of these gratifications and delights, takes away all these trivialities and childish ways, and makes them acquire the virtues by very different means. No matter how earnestly the beginner in all his actions and passions practices the mortification of self, he will never be able to do so entirely—far from it—until God accomplishes it in him passively by means of the purgation of this night . . . . The verse, then, is: One dark night.

CHAPTER 8
The beginning of the exposition of this dark night. An explanation of verse 1 of the first stanza.

1. This night, which as we say is contemplation, causes two kinds of darkness, or purgation, in spiritual persons according to the two parts of the soul, the sensory and the spiritual.

Hence, the one night, or purgation, will be sensory, by which the senses are purged and accommodated to the spirit; and the other night, or purgation, will be spiritual, by which the spirit is purged and denuded, as well as accommodated and prepared for union with God through love.

The sensory night is common and happens to many; these are the beginners of whom we shall treat first. The spiritual night is the lot of very few, of those who have been tried and are proficient and of whom we shall speak afterward.

2. The first purgation, or night, is bitter and terrible to the senses. But nothing can be compared to the second, for it is horrible and frightful to the spirit. . . .

CHAPTER 9
Signs for discerning whether a spiritual person is treading the path of this sensory night and purgation.

1. Because the origin of these aridities may not be the sensory night and purgation, but sin and imperfection or weakness and lukewarmness or some bad humor or bodily indisposition, I will give some signs here for discerning whether the dryness is the result of

this purgation or of one of these other defects. I find there are three principal signs for knowing this.

2. The first is that as these souls do not get satisfaction or consolation from the things of God, they do not get any out of creatures either. Since God puts a soul in this dark night in order to dry up and purge the sensory appetites, He does not allow it to find sweetness or delight in anything.

Through this sign, it can in all likelihood be inferred that this dryness and distaste is not the outcome of newly committed sins and imperfections. If this were so, some inclination or propensity to look for satisfaction in something other than the things of God would be felt in the sensory part. . . .

Yet, because the want of satisfaction in earthly or heavenly things could be the product of some indisposition or melancholic humor, which frequently prevents one from being satisfied with anything, the second sign, or condition, is necessary.

3. The second sign for the discernment of this purgation is that the memory ordinarily turns to God solicitously and with painful care, and the soul thinks it is not serving God but turning back, because it is aware of this distaste for the things of God. Hence, it is obvious that this aversion and dryness is not the fruit of laxity and tepidity, for a lukewarm person does not care much for the things of God nor is he inwardly solicitous about them. . . .

4. The reason for this dryness is that God transfers His goods and strength from sense to spirit. Since the sensory part of the soul is incapable of the goods of spirit, it remains deprived, dry, and empty, and thus, while the spirit is tasting, the flesh tastes nothing at all and becomes weak in its work. . . . And since, also, its spiritual palate is neither purged nor accommodated for so subtle a taste, it is unable to experience the spiritual savor and good until gradually prepared by means of this dark and obscure night; the soul rather experiences dryness and distaste because of a lack of the gratitude it formerly enjoyed so readily.

6. . . .This [interior] food is the beginning of contemplation that is dark and dry to the senses. Ordinarily this contemplation, which is secret and hidden from the very one who receives it, imparts to the

soul, together with the dryness and emptiness it produces in the senses, an inclination to remain alone and in quietude. And the soul will be unable to dwell upon any particular thought, nor will it have the desire to do so.

If those in whom this occurs know how to remain quiet, without care or solicitude about any interior or exterior work, they will soon in that unconcern and idleness delicately experience the interior nourishment. This reflection is so delicate that usually, if the soul desires or tries to experience it, it cannot . . . .

7. . . . The reason is that now, in this state of contemplation, when the soul has left discursive meditation and entered the state of proficients, it is God who works in it. He therefore binds the interior faculties and leaves no support in the intellect or satisfaction in the will or remembrance in the memory. At this time, a person's own efforts are of no avail but an obstacle to the interior peace and work God is producing in the spirit through that dryness of sense. Since this peace is something spiritual and delicate, its fruit is quiet, delicate, solitary, satisfying, and peaceful and far removed from all these other gratifications of beginners, which are very palpable and sensory. . . .

8. The third sign for the discernment of this purgation of the senses is the powerlessness, in spite of one's efforts, to meditate and make use of the imagination, the interior sense, as was one's previous custom. At this time, God does not communicate Himself through the senses as He did before, by means of the discursive analysis and synthesis of ideas, but begins to communicate Himself though pure spirit by an act of simple contemplation, in which there is no discursive succession of thought. The exterior and interior senses of the lower part of the soul cannot attain to this contemplation. As a result, the imaginative power and fantasy can no longer rest in any consideration nor find support in it. . . .

CHAPTER 10
The conduct required of souls in this dark night.

4. The attitude necessary in the night of sense is to pay no attention to discursive meditation, since this is not the time for it. [People] should allow their soul to remain in rest and quietude, even though

it may seem very obvious to them that they are doing nothing and wasting time, and even though they think this disinclination to think about anything is due to their laxity. Through patience and perseverance in prayer, they will be doing a great deal without activity on their part. All that is required of them here is freedom of soul, that they liberate themselves from the impediment and fatigue of ideas and thoughts and care not about thinking and meditating. They must be content simply with a loving and peaceful attentiveness to God, and live without the concern, without the effort, and without the desire to taste or feel Him. All these desires disquiet the soul and distract it from the peaceful quiet and sweet idleness of the contemplation which is being communicated to it.

6. Accordingly, a person should not mind if the operations of his faculties are being lost to him; he ought to desire rather that this be done quickly so that he may be no obstacle to the operation of the infused contemplation which God is bestowing, that he may receive it with more plenitude and make room in his spirit for the enkindling and burning of the love that this dark and secret contemplation bears and communicates to his soul. For contemplation is nothing else than a secret and peaceful and loving inflow of God, which, if not hampered, fires the soul in the spirit of love.

BOOK II

CHAPTER 5
Begins to explain how this dark contemplation is not only night for the soul but also affliction and torment.

1. This dark night is an inflow of God into the soul, which purges it of its habitual ignorance and imperfections, natural and spiritual, and which the contemplatives call infused contemplation, or mystical theology. Through this contemplation, God teaches the soul secretly and instructs it in the perfection of love without its doing anything or understanding how this happens.

Insofar as infused contemplation is loving wisdom of God, it produces two principal effects in the soul: It prepares the soul for the union with God through love by both purging and illuminating it. Hence, the same loving wisdom that purges and illumines the blessed spirit, purges and illumines the soul here on earth.

2. Yet a doubt arises: Why, if it is a divine light (for it illumines and purges a person of his ignorances), does the soul call it a dark night? In answer to this, there are two reasons why this divine wisdom is not only night and darkness for the soul but also affliction and torment. First, because of the height of divine wisdom, which exceeds the capacity of the soul. Second, because of the soul's baseness and impurity; and on this account, it is painful, afflictive, and also dark for the soul.

3. To prove the first reason, we must presuppose a certain principle of the Philosopher: that the clearer and more obvious divine things are in themselves, the darker and more hidden they are to the soul naturally. . . . The brighter the light, the more the owl is blinded; and the more one looks at the brilliant sun, the more the sun darkens the faculty of sight, deprives it, and overwhelms it in its darkness.

Hence, when the divine light of contemplation strikes a soul not yet entirely illuminated, it causes spiritual darkness, for it not only surpasses the act of natural understanding, but it also deprives the soul of this act and darkens it. That is why St. Dionysius and other mystical theologians call this infused contemplation a "ray of darkness"—that is, for the soul not yet illuminated and purged. . . . For this great supernatural light overwhelms the intellect and deprives it of its natural vigor. . . . As a result, when God communicates this bright ray of His secret wisdom to the soul not yet transformed, He causes thick darkness in its intellect. . . .

5. In regard to the first cause of one's affliction: because the light and wisdom of this contemplation is very bright and pure, and the soul in which it shines is dark and impure, a person will be deeply afflicted in receiving it within himself. When eyes are sickly, impure, and weak, they suffer pain if a bright light shines on them.

The soul, because of its impurity, suffers immensely at the time this divine light truly assails it. When this pure light strikes in order to expel all impurity, a person feels so unclean and wretched that it seems God is against him and that he is against God.

. . . Clearly beholding its impurity by means of this pure light, although in darkness, the soul understands distinctly that it is worthy neither of God nor of any creature. And what most grieves it is that it thinks it will never be worthy and that there are no more blessings for it. The divine and dark light causes deep immersion of the mind in the knowledge and feeling of one's own misery and evils; it brings all these miseries into relief so that the soul sees clearly that of itself it will never possess anything else. . . .

6. A person suffers affliction in the second manner because of his natural, mortal, and spiritual weakness. Since this divine contemplation assails him somewhat forcibly in order to subdue and strengthen his soul, he suffers so much in his weakness that he almost dies, particularly at times when the light is more powerful. Both the sense and the spirit, as though under an immense and dark load, undergo such agony and pain that the soul would consider death a relief. . . .

CHAPTER 6
Other kinds of affliction suffered in this night.

1. The two extremes, divine and human, which are joined here, produce the third kind of pain and affliction the soul suffers here. The divine extreme is the purgative contemplation, and the human extreme is the soul, the receiver of this contemplation. Since the divine extreme strikes in order to renew the soul and divinize it (by stripping it of the habitual affections and properties of the old man to which it is strongly united, attached, and conformed), it so disentangles and dissolves the spiritual substance—absorbing it in a profound darkness—that the soul at the sight of its miseries feels that it is melting away and being undone by a cruel spiritual death; it feels as if it were swallowed by a beast and being digested in the dark belly, and it suffers an anguish comparable to Jonas's when in the belly of the whale [Jonah 2:1-3]. It is fitting that the soul be in this sepulcher of dark death in order that it attain the spiritual resurrection for which it hopes.

2. . . .But what the sorrowing soul feels most is the conviction that God has rejected it and with an abhorrence of it, cast it into darkness. The thought that He has abandoned it is a piteous and heavy affliction for the soul. . . .

When this purgative contemplation oppresses a man, he feels very vividly indeed the shadow of death, the sighs of death, and the sorrows of hell—all of which reflect the feeling of God's absence, of being chastised and rejected by Him, and of being unworthy of Him as well as the object of His anger. The soul experiences all this and even more, for now it seems that this affliction will last forever.

3. A person also feels forsaken and despised by creatures, particularly his friends. . . .

4. Another excellence of dark contemplation, its majesty and grandeur, causes a fourth kind of affliction to the soul. This property makes the soul feel within itself the other extreme—its own intimate poverty and misery. Such awareness is one of the chief afflictions it suffers in the purgation. . . .

Since God purges both the sensory and spiritual substance of the soul and its interior and exterior faculties, it is fitting that it be brought into emptiness and poverty and abandonment in these parts and left in dryness and darkness. For the sensory part is purified by aridity, the faculties by the void of their apprehensions, and the spirit by thick darkness.

5. God does all this by means of dark contemplation. And the soul not only suffers the void and suspension of these natural supports and apprehensions, which is a terrible anguish (like hanging in midair, unable to breathe), but it is also purged by this contemplation. As fire consumes the tarnish and rust of metal, this contemplation annihilates, empties, and consumes all the affections and imperfect habits the soul contracted throughout its life. Since these imperfections are deeply rooted in the substance of the soul, it usually suffers besides this poverty and this natural and spiritual emptiness an oppressive undoing and an inner torment . . . in order to burn away the rust of the affections the soul must, as it were, be annihilated and undone in the measure that these passions and imperfections are connatural to it.

6. . . . God humbles the soul greatly in order to exalt it greatly afterward. And if He did not ordain that these feelings, when quickened in the soul, be soon put to sleep again, a person would die in a few days. Only at intervals is one aware of these feelings in all their intensity. Sometimes the experience is so vivid that it seems to the

soul that it sees hell and perdition open before it. These are the ones who go down into hell alive [Psalm 55:15], since their purgation on earth is similar to that of purgatory. For this purgation is that which would have to be undergone there. The soul that endures it here on earth either does not enter purgatory or is detained there for only a short while. It gains more in one hour here on earth by this purgation than it would in many there.

CHAPTER 7
A continuation of the same subject; other afflictions and straits of the will.

1. The afflictions and straits of the will are also immense. Sometimes these afflictions pierce the soul when it suddenly remembers the evils in which it sees itself immersed, and it becomes uncertain of any remedy. To this pain is added the remembrance of past prosperity, because usually, persons who enter this night have previously had many consolations in God and rendered Him many services. They are now sorrowful in knowing that they are far from such good and can no longer enjoy it. . . .

3. . . . Added to this, because of the solitude and desolation this night causes, is the fact that a person in this state finds neither consolation nor support in any doctrine or spiritual director. Although his spiritual director may point out many reasons for being comforted on account of the blessings contained in these afflictions, he cannot believe this. Because he is so engulfed and immersed in that sentiment of evil by which he so clearly sees his own miseries, he believes his directors say these things because they do not understand him and do not see what he sees and feels. Instead of consolation, he experiences greater sorrow thinking that the director's doctrine is no remedy for his evil. . . .

7. . . . Thus, although a person suffering this purgation knows that he loves God and that he would give a thousand lives for Him (he would, indeed, for souls undergoing these trials love God very earnestly), he finds no relief. This knowledge rather causes him deeper affliction. For in loving God so intensely that nothing else gives him concern, and aware of his own misery, he is unable to believe that God loves him. He believes that he neither has nor ever will have within himself anything deserving of God's love but rather

every reason for being abhorred not only by God but by every creature forever. He grieves to see within himself reasons for meriting rejection by Him whom he so loves and longs for. . . .

CHAPTER 9
Although this night darkens the spirit, it does so to give light.

1. It remains to be said, then, that even though this happy night darkens the spirit, it does so only to impart light concerning all things; and even though it humbles a person and reveals his miseries, it does so only to exalt him; and even though it impoverishes and empties him of all possessions and natural affection, it does so only that he may reach out divinely to the enjoyment of all earthly and heavenly things, with a general freedom of spirit in them all. . . .

10. Let us examine now why this light of contemplation, which is so gentle and agreeable and which is the same light to which the soul must be united and in which it will find all its blessings in the desired state of perfection, produces such painful and disagreeable effects when in these initial stages it shines upon the soul.

11. We can answer this question easily by repeating what we already explained in part; that is, there is nothing in contemplation of the divine inflow which of itself can give pain; contemplation rather bestows sweetness and delight. The cause for not experiencing these agreeable effects is the soul's weakness and imperfection at the time, its inadequate preparation, and the qualities it possesses contrary to this light. Because of these, the soul has to suffer when the divine light shines upon it.

THE LIVING FLAME OF LOVE[8]
Stanzas Which The Soul Recites

In the intimate union with God, its beloved Bridegroom

1. O living flame of love
That tenderly wounds my soul
In its deepest center! Since
Now You are not oppressive,
Now consummate if it be Your will!
Tear through the veil of this sweet encounter!

2. O sweet cautery,
O delightful wound!
O gentle hand! O delicate touch
That tastes of eternal life
And pays every debt!
In killing You changed death to life.

3. O lamps of fire!
In whose splendors
The deep caverns of feeling,
Once obscure and blind,
Now give forth, so rarely, so exquisitely,
Both warmth and light to their Beloved.

4. How gently and lovingly
You awake in my heart,
Where in secret You dwell alone;
And in your sweet breathing,
Filled with good and glory,
How tenderly You swell my heart with love.

The works of Francis de Sales, "the heavenly patron of all writers," illustrate why he has been called the teacher of a lived theology of the heart that implants an attitude of suavity in the depths of the human spirit. Affective and effective love, "the ecstasy of work and life," ground his mysticism.

FRANCIS DE SALES

The 16th-century Counter-Reformation brought about massive reforms throughout the Catholic Church. In Spain, Ignatius of Loyola, Teresa of Avila, and John of the Cross were only three examples of the profound renaissance of spirituality and mysticism that accompanied these reforms. In the 17th century, however, France took center stage.

Francis de Sales was one of the many prominent French men and women who experienced, taught, and creatively wrote about the interior life during the Counter-Reformation. As Bishop of Geneva for 20 years, he cofounded the Order of the Visitation. As a devoted pastor, eloquent preacher, and perceptive spiritual director, he also inspired a variety of religious congregations founded under his patronage. The success of this "devout humanist"—a mystic, a saint, and a Doctor of the Church—was rooted in his passionate love of God and a compassion for humanity.

Born the eldest of 13 children at the castle of Sales in Savoy, Francis received at Annecy, Paris, and Padua the education befitting a Renaissance gentleman destined for a brilliant secular career. His life, however, took another turn.

At only four years of age, Francis had uttered prophetically: "God's and my mother's love I hold most dearly." And despite the Calvinistic ambience of his day, which nurtured in him an early conviction that he was predestined to eternal damnation, he was still determined to live in "disinterested love" for God. While kneeling before the statue of the Black Madonna in the Parisian church of St. Étienne, his heart heard the words that undid the eternal decree: "I do not call myself the Damning One, my name is Jesus." Like "leprous scabs," the dark weights in his soul fell away, and his victorious optimism of joyful love of God was born in the depths of his spirit.

In 1593, Francis was ordained. Burning with a counter-reformer's missionary ardor, he undertook the task of reclaiming for Catholicism the Chablis, an area on Lake Geneva's southern shore that had been forcibly converted to Calvinism. Often exposed to great danger and enduring many hardships, Francis reconverted the Chablis with his holiness, personal charm, eloquent preaching, skilled debating, and a series of short, popular writings, known as the *Controversies*. His lesser known work, *The Standard of the Cross*, also dates from this period.

In 1602, Francis became bishop of Geneva, where he remained despite better offers—until he died. A zealous pastor, he drew people to God by love and gentleness. Everything Francis did flowed from his deep tasting of God as love, shaped and matured by his cares, sufferings, and labors for the Church. To him, there is a "correspondence" between God, the source and foundation of love, and the human person, created out of love, worthy of love, capable of love, and made for love. He labored to win the hearts of his people, for he knew that to win the heart was to win the entire person.

His highly influential book, *Introduction to the Devout Life*, speaks of a spirituality that looks beyond the cloister to the diocesan clergy and to the laity. It presupposes that all people are called to holiness, to total dedication to Christ. The *Introduction* is Francis's summa of spiritual direction for people in the world.

Because of the Jesuit influence on his education and his interior life, the book contains the active, pragmatic emphases of the Ignatian spirituality of his time. Its lucidity, warmth, charm, and optimism about the goodness of human nature led many to devotion in a manner that contrasts with the more militant spiritualities of the

Counter-Reformation. It has been said of him that he sweetened everything but attenuated nothing. Moreover, Francis, "the heavenly patron of all writers," contributed to the development of the modern French language.

Influenced by the writings of Teresa of Avila, Francis desired to found a religious order for women less austere than the Carmelites but, nonetheless, dedicated to the contemplative life and to the care of the poor and the sick. Given the traditional practice of enclosure for religious women, his vision was somewhat radical for his time.

In 1610, he and Jeanne de Chantal, a young widow and spiritual friend, cofounded the Order of the Visitation of Mary. The order flourished in his lifetime. But in 1618, the archbishop of Lyons altered its original shape by insisting upon full enclosure.

Connected with Jeanne de Chantal and the Visitation is his masterpiece, *Treatise on the Love of God*. Presupposing someone "advanced in devotion," Francis desired "solely" to present "in a simple, natural way, without art and still more without dissimulation, an account of the birth, progress, decay, operations, properties, benefits, and excellences of divine love."[1] He addresses his instructions to "Theotimus," that is, "the human spirit as it desires to make progress in holy love."[2] Emphasizing affective and effective love, the work is permeated with warmth and charm. As a history of Francis's own love of God, it illustrates why he has been called the teacher of a lived theology of the heart that implants an attitude of "suavity" in the depths of the human spirit.

Francis remains solidly rooted in the kataphatic mystical tradition, stressing that knowledge is required for love. Although he emphasizes human passivity in relationship to God's action in the depths of the human person, Francis nonetheless urges his reader to be a "mystical bee," that is, to ponder God's holy mysteries "in order to extract from them the honey of divine love."[3] In fact, meditation to Francis is not a beginner's preoccupation but "mystical rumination" needed "to arouse the will to holy and salutary affections and resolutions . . . [and] to discover motives for love or some heavenly affection."[4]

To Francis, meditation gives birth to contemplation. When meditation "produces the honey of devotion,"[5] it is transformed into contemplation. He views contemplation as "the mind's loving, unmixed permanent attention to the things of God."[6] Moreover, to Francis, "meditation is the mother of love, but contemplation is its daughter."[7]

Francis is also known as the teacher of "holy indifference," that is, a total and loving abandonment of self-will and an embracing of God's will as it is manifested in one's life. To live the good news of Jesus Christ, one must have radical trust in God's loving providence and surrender totally to God's guidance and dispensation. Central to Francis's vision is that "God's will is God's love," and that one must love God for God's sake, not for one's own. As he says, "the climax of loving ecstasy is when our will rests not in its own contentment but in God's, or when it has contentment not in its own will but in God's."[8]

The following selections contain some of the loveliest and most striking images used in the Christian mystical tradition to depict the soul's union with God: ivy penetrating a tree, a nursing infant and its mother's breast, honeybees attracted to sound and smell, and the like. When asked who is more united to God, a sleeping saint or a person in the prayer of union, Francis replied that the saint is already united to God. The other is being united.

The texts were also selected to illustrate Francis's aversion to quietism. He underscores both the person's complete dependence upon God and the different ways in which the person must cooperate with and consent to God's grace.

For Francis, the highest types of union with God are suspension and rapture. Lifted up and out of oneself, one consents to being thrown into God and to desiring God for God's sake, not for one's own contentment. Again, Francis uses striking images to illustrate union with God. No Christian mystic has stressed as he has the importance of affections and love in ecstasy. Cold ecstasies, that is, ecstasies that affect the intellect more than the will, are immediately suspect, for they are usually induced by the demons. Exceptionally cogent is his emphasis upon the most sacred ecstasy of all, the "ecstasy of work and life." One lives truly out of and above oneself through renunciation and self-denial by true imitation of Christ.[9]

THE TEXTS

ON THE LOVE OF GOD
BOOK 7[10]

CONCERNING THE SOUL'S UNION WITH GOD, WHICH IS
PERFECTED IN PRAYER
CHAPTER 1
How Love Brings about the Soul's Union with God in Prayer

In this chapter, we will not discuss the general union of the heart
with God but rather certain particular acts and movements that a
soul recollected in God makes by way of prayer so as to be more
and more closely united and joined to his divine goodness. There
is, of course, a difference between joining and uniting one thing to
another and clasping or pressing a thing against or upon another....
Hence, to clasp together is to join in a firm, intimate way, as we see
ivy joined to trees. It is not merely united to them, but it presses on
them and clasps them so strongly that it even penetrates and gets
into their bark.

Comparison of the love little children have for their mothers should
not be rejected because of its pure, innocent character. Consider,
then, a beautiful little child to whom the seated mother offers her
breast. It throws itself forcibly into her arms and gathers up and en-
twines all its little body on that beloved bosom and breast. See how
its mother in turn takes it in, clasps it, fastens it so to speak to her
bosom, joins her mouth to its mouth, and kisses it. Watch again
how that little babe is allured by its mother's caresses, and how on
its part it co-operates in this union of its mother and itself. As much
as it possibly can, it fastens and presses itself to its mother's breast
and face. It seems as if it wants to bury and hide itself completely in
the beloved bosom from which it came. Theotimus, at such a moment there is a perfect union; it is but a single union, yet it proceeds
from both mother and child, although in such wise that it depends
entirely on the mother. She drew the child to herself. She first
clasped it in her arms and pressed it to her bosom. The child's

strength was never sufficient to clasp and hold itself so close to its mother. Yet on its own part the poor little one does as much as it can and joins itself with all its strength to its mother's bosom. It not only consents to the sweet union its mother makes but with all its heart contributes its own feeble efforts. I call them feeble efforts because they are so weak that they resemble attempts at union rather than actual union.

Thus, too, Theotimus, our Lord shows the most loving breast of his divine love to a devout soul, draws it wholly to himself, gathers it in, and as it were, enfolds all its powers within the bosom of his more than motherly comfort. Then, burning with love, he clasps the soul, joins, presses, and fastens it to his sweet lips and to his delightsome breasts, kisses it with the sacred "kiss of his mouth," and makes it relish his breasts, "more sweet than wine." Then the soul is allured by the delights brought by such favors and not only consents and yields to the union God makes but co-operates with all its powers. It forces itself to join and fasten itself more and more closely to God's goodness but in such wise that it fully acknowledges that its union and association with this supreme sweetness completely depend on God's action. Without that action, it could not make the least effort of any kind to be united to him. . . .

In prayer, this union is often made by means of little but frequent flights and advances of the soul toward God. If you watch a little infant joined and united to its mother's breast, you will see that from time to time it presses on and clasps her closer with little movements aroused by the pleasure it takes in drinking her milk. So, too, the heart united to God in prayer often makes certain renewals of its union by movements in which it presses and joins itself more closely to the divine sweetness. . . .

At other times, this union is made not by repeated movements but by the way the heart insensibly continues to press forward and advance in God's goodness. We see how a large, heavy mass of lead, brass, or stone, even though not forced downward, will so work in and sink down and press into the earth where it lies that it finally is buried by the pull of its own weight which makes it unceasingly tend to the center. So, too, if our heart is once joined to God and remains in this union and nothing draws it away, it continues to sink deeper by an insensible progress of that union until it is wholly in God. This is by reason of the sacred inclination given it by holy love to unite itself. . . . Hence, even after it has attained to a simple union it does not cease to act, although imperceptibly, in order to increase and perfect that union more and more. . . .

. . . Happy is the soul that in peace of heart lovingly preserves the sacred sentiment of God's presence! Its union with divine goodness will have continual, although imperceptible, increase, and with infinite mildness, it will suffuse his entire spirit.

When I speak here of the sacred perception of God's presence, I do not mean a sensible perception but that which resides in the summit and supreme point of the spirit, where God's love reigns and carries out its principal exercises.

CHAPTER 2
Concerning the Various Degrees of the Holy Union Made in Prayer

Sometimes this union is made without co-operation on our part except for a simple continuation in which we let ourselves be united to God's goodness without any resistance. We are like a little child lovingly desirous of its mother's breast but so feeble that of itself it cannot make any movement either to get to it or to cling to it once it is there. The child is only happy at being taken up and drawn within its mother's arms and at being pressed by her to her breast. . . .

. . . You see the child hold and press the breast with its mouth, making soft sounds all the while. It draws in the milk so avidly as even to cause its mother pain. But after the fresh milk has to some extent cooled the hungry heat within that little breast and the pleasing vapors it sends to the brain have begun to lull it to sleep, then, Theotimus, you see the child very softly close its little eyes and little by little give way to sleep. Still it does not release the breast, on which it exerts no action but a slow and almost insensible movement of the lips whereby it draws in milk that it swallows imperceptibly. It does this without thinking, but surely not without pleasure. . . . It is the same with the soul that is in repose and quiet before God. In an almost insensible way it draws in the delight of his presence, without thinking, without working, without doing anything by means of any faculty except the highest part of the will, which it moves softly and almost imperceptibly. It uses the will as a mouth whereby the insensible delight and satiety it takes in enjoying God's presence finds entrance. . . .[11]

Sometimes we cooperate, as when we run willingly to assist the sweet force of God's goodness which draws and clasps us to him by his love.

Sometimes it seems that we begin to join and attach to God even before he joins himself to us. This is because we perceive the unitive action on our part without perceiving what God is doing on his part. . . .

Sometimes this union is made so insensibly that our heart neither feels God's operation within nor our cooperation with it, but discovers the union alone insensibly complete. It is like Jacob who without any thought of it found that he was married to Leah. . . .

Sometimes this union is made by the will alone and in the will alone. At other times the intellect has part in it, since the will draws the intellect along. . . .

Sometimes this union is made by all the faculties of the soul. All of them gather around the will, not to unite themselves to God, for they are entirely incapable of doing so, but to add efficacy to the will for making its union. . . . Such are the various kinds of union. . . .

Thus it happens at times that our Lord imperceptibly infuses into the depths of our hearts a certain sweet, suave feeling that bears witness to his presence. Then the powers of the soul—in fact, even the exterior senses, by a certain secret consent—turn toward this most inward part where their most lovable and most cherished spouse is. A new swarm or flight of honeybees that is about to take flight and change its place is called back by a sound made softly on metal basins, the smell of wine mixed with honey, or even the scent of certain aromatic herbs. The swarm is stopped by the attraction of such agreeable things, and enters the hive prepared for it. So too our Savior utters some secret word of love, pours forth the wine of his dilection, which is more delicious than honey, or diffuses into our hearts "the fragrance of his garments," that is, certain perceptions of his heavenly consolations. By such means he causes them to perceive his most loving presence and thus draws to himself all the faculties of the soul, which gather about him and rest in him as in their most desired object. . . .

. . . Honied wine is used not only to draw bees out of the hive and to call them back, but also to pacify them. When bees stir up sedition and mutiny and slay and destroy one another, the beekeeper has no better remedy than to cast honied wine among that enraged little populace. When the individual bees that make up the swarm perceive this sweet and agreeable odor, they become peaceful, give themselves up to the enjoyment of such pleasures, and remain quiet and tranquil. O eternal God, when by your sweet presence you cast "the sweet smell of your ointments" into our hearts—a perfume that gives greater joy than delicious wine and more joy than honey—all the powers of our soul enter into delightful repose with such perfect rest that there is no further feeling except that of the will, which, like a spiritual sense of smell, remains sweetly engaged in sensing without adverting to it the incomparable good of having its God present to it.[12]

CHAPTER 3[13]
Concerning the Supreme Degree of Union by Suspension and Rapture

Whether the union of our soul with God is made imperceptibly or perceptibly, God is always its author. . . .

The perfection of this union consists in two points: It is pure, and it is strong. . . . I can approach a person to speak with him, to see him better, to get something from him, to smell the perfume that he uses, or to gain his assistance. . . . But if I approach and join him solely for the purpose of being near him and enjoying this proximity and union, then it is an approach to a pure and simple union. . . .

When the soul's union with God is in the very highest degree a strict, close union, theologians call it inhesion or adhesion. The reason is that the soul remains so caught up, fastened, attached, and affixed to God's majesty that it cannot easily detach or draw itself away. Consider, I ask you, a man whose attention is caught and held fast by the beauty of some harmonious piece of music, or even by some unseemly thing such as a foolish game of cards. You would like to draw him away from it but you cannot. No matter what his duties are, he cannot be torn away. He even gives up food and drink for this game. . . .

Consider, I ask you, Theotimus, a little child holding fast to the breast and neck of its mother. If you want to take it away and put it in the cradle, since it is time for that, it argues and disputes as best it can against leaving that beloved bosom. If it is made to let go with one hand, it makes a grab with the other. If it is lifted up bodily, it bursts out crying, keeping its heart and eyes where it can no longer keep its body, and it goes on crying for its dear mother until it is rocked asleep. So too the soul that by acts of union has gotten as far as to be taken up and fastened to God's goodness can hardly be drawn away from it except by force and with great pain. We cannot make the soul let go. If we distract its imagination, it does not cease to keep hold by means of intellect. If we pry its intellect loose, it clings by means of the will. If by some violent distraction we make the will abandon its hold, the soul still turns back from moment to moment to its beloved object. It can never be entirely detached from it. As far as it can, it remakes those sweet bonds of union with God by returning frequently to him as if by stealth. . . .

. . .I ask you, my dear Theotimus, who is more united, clasped, and fastened to God? Is it those great saints who are asleep or the soul who is actually at prayer? Without a doubt, it is those admirable lovers. They have more charity, and their affections, although in some manner sleeping, are so engaged and placed in their Master that they cannot be separated from him. "But," you will ask me, "how can it be that a soul in the prayer of union, even in ecstasy, should be less united to God than such as are asleep, be they ever so saintly?" Note what I tell you, Theotimus: the soul at prayer is more advanced in a unitive exercise; the others in union itself. Those saints are united; they are not being united, since they are asleep. The other soul is being united; that is, it is engaged in the actual practice and exercise of union. . . .

CHAPTER 4[14]
Concerning rapture, and the first species of it

An ecstasy is called rapture inasmuch as in it God draws and lifts us up to himself, and rapture is called ecstasy because in it we go out of and above ourselves, and remain there so as to be united to

God. Although the allurements by which we are drawn to God's side are wondrously gentle, sweet, and delightful, still because of the power God's beauty and goodness have to draw the mind's attention and concentration to himself, it seems that it not only lifts us up but ravishes and bears us away. On the contrary, because of the completely voluntary consent and ardent movement by which the enraptured soul flows out after those divine allurements, it seems not only to mount and rise upward but to eject and throw itself out of its very being into the divinity itself. . . .

With regard to sacred ecstasies, my dear Theotimus, they are of three kinds: The first is of the intellect, the second of the affections, and the third of action. The first is in splendor, the second in fervor, and the third in deeds. The first is made by admiration, the second by devotion, and the third by operation. Admiration is aroused in us when we encounter a new truth which we neither knew nor expected to know. If the new truth we meet is joined to beauty and goodness, the admiration that derives from it is full of delight. . . .

Admiration of pleasing things firmly attaches and fastens the mind to the admired object, both by reason of the excellence of the beauty it finds there and also by reason of the novelty of such excellence. The intellect can never be sufficiently satisfied in looking at something it never saw before but which is very agreeable to see. In addition to this, God sometimes grants the soul a light not only clear but increasing, like the break of day. Then, like men who have found a gold mine and continually dig deeper so as to find always more and more of the metal they desire so much, the intellect continues to bury itself deeper and deeper in consideration and admiration of its divine object. Just as wonder has produced philosophy and the careful study of natural things, so also it has caused contemplation and mystical theology. When such wonder is strong, it takes us out of ourselves and above ourselves by the lively attention and application our intellect gives to heavenly things. As a result, it carries us on to ecstasy.

CHAPTER 5[15]
Concerning the Second Species of Rapture

God attracts our minds to himself by his supreme beauty and incomprehensible goodness. . . . So God, Father of all light, supremely good and beautiful, by his beauty draws our intellect to contemplate him, and by his goodness he draws our will to love him. Beautiful, he crowns our intellect with delights and pours his love into our will. As good, he fills our will with his love and arouses our intellect to contemplate it. Love thus arouses us to contemplate and contemplation to love. Hence, it follows that ecstasy and rapture depend wholly on love, for it is love that carries the intellect to contemplation and the will to union. . . .

This rapture of love is brought about in the will in the following manner. God touches it with those sweet allurements, and then, just as a needle touched by a magnet turns and moves toward the north, forgetful of its sensible condition, so the will, touched with heavenly love, is moved forward and born by God. It leaves behind all its earthly inclinations and by this means enters into a rapture, not of knowledge but of fruition, not of admiration but of affection, not of science but of experience, not of sight but of taste and savor. . . . The sight of beauty causes us to love it, and the love for it causes us to gaze at it. A man is seldom warmed by the sun's rays without being given light by them, or receives light without being warmed as well. Love easily makes us admire, and admiration easily makes us love.

Nevertheless, the two ecstasies, that of the intellect and that of the will, do not belong to one another to such an extent that often one may not be without the other. Just as philosophers have had more knowledge than love of their Creator, so good Christians often have more love than knowledge. Consequently, excess of knowledge is not always followed by excess of love. . . . Ecstasy of admiration alone does not make us better, according to what was said of it by him who was lifted up in ecstasy to the third heaven. "If I should know all mysteries and all knowledge, yet do not have charity, I am nothing," he says. Hence the evil spirit can cause ecstasy, if we may say so, and ravish the intellect by proposing it to marvelous conceptions that hold it raised up and suspended above its natural powers. . . .

CHAPTER 6[16]

Concerning the Marks of a Good Rapture, and concerning its Third Species

...Therefore, that we may distinguish divine from human and diabolical ecstasies, God's servants have provided us with many tests. For my own part, it will suffice to put before you two marks of a good and holy ecstasy. The first is that sacred ecstasy never seizes and influences the intellect as much as it does the will, which it moves, warms, and fills with strong affection for God. Hence, if an ecstasy is more beautiful than good, more bright than warm, more speculative than affective, it is gravely doubtful and worthy of suspicion. I do not deny that a man may have raptures and visions, even prophetic visions, without having charity. I well know that just as a man may have charity without having raptures in which he makes prophecies, so too a man may have raptures and make prophecies without having charity. But I affirm that when a man in rapture has more light in his intellect for wondering about God than warmth in his will to love him, he ought to be on guard. There is danger that this ecstasy is false and may render his spirit puffed up rather than edified. . . .

The second mark of true ecstasy consists in the third species of ecstasy noted above, that is, the ecstasy that is all-holy and all-worthy of love and that crowns the other two. It is the ecstasy of work and life. Complete fulfillment of God's commandments is not within the bounds of human strength, yet it is well within the confines of man's spiritual instincts as being the most conformable to reason and natural light, so that if we live according to God's commandments we do not on that account depart from our natural inclinations. In addition to God's commandments there are certain heavenly inspirations for the fulfillment of which it is necessary not only that God raise us above our powers but also draw us above the instincts and inclinations of our nature. Although these inspirations are not opposed to human reason, yet they exceed it, surpass it, and are above it. Hence by them we live not only a civilized, virtuous, Christian life, but a superhuman, spiritual, devout, ecstatic life, that is, a life that is in every way beyond and above our natural condition.

Not to steal, not to lie, not to commit acts of impurity, to pray to God, not to swear in vain, to love and honor one's father, not to kill—all this is to live according to man's natural reason. To forsake all goods, to love poverty, to name and hold it as one's most delightful mistress, to hold opprobrium, contempt, insults, abjection, persecution, and martyrdom to be joys and blessings, to keep oneself within the limits of most absolute chastity, and finally to live in the world and in this mortal life contrary to all the opinions and maxims of the world, and against the current of the river of this life, by ordinary resignation, renunciation, and self-denial—that is not to live a merely human but rather a superhuman life. This is not to live in ourselves, but out of ourselves and above ourselves. Since no man can in this way go above himself unless the eternal Father draws him, it follows that such a life is a continual rapture and a perpetual ecstasy of action and operation. . . .

CHAPTER 7[17]
How Love is the Life of the Soul; Continuation of the Discussion of the Ecstatic Life

. . . Sometimes we see a person who goes into rapture in prayer. In such raptures he departs from himself and rises above himself up unto God but still has no ecstasy in his life, that is, he does not live a life elevated and united to God by denial of worldly lusts and mortification of his natural will and inclinations through interior gentleness, simplicity, and humility, and above all through constant charity. Theotimus, you must conclude that all such raptures are extremely doubtful and dangerous. They are raptures suited to make men marvel but not to sanctify them. What good can a soul have from being ravished up to God in prayer if in his life and conduct he is ravished by earthly, base, natural affections. To be above oneself in prayer and below oneself in life and works, to be an angel in meditation and a beast in conduct, is . . . to swear by God and to swear by Melchom. In short, it is a sure sign that such raptures and such ecstasies are merely tricks and trumperies of the evil spirit. Blessed are they who live a superhuman ecstatic life and are raised above themselves even though they may never be ravished above themselves in prayer. Many are the saints in heaven who were never in ecstasy or rapturous contemplation. How many martyrs and great saints, both men and women, appear in history who had no other privilege in prayer but that of devotion and fervor! There was never a saint who did not have ecstasy and rapture of life and operation gained by overcoming himself and his natural inclinations.

Theotimus, I ask you, who fails to see that it is concerning ecstasy of life and operation that the great Apostle chiefly speaks when he says, "It is no longer I who live, but Christ lives in me"? He himself explains this in other terms when he says to the Romans that "our old self has been crucified with" Jesus Christ, that with him we are "dead to sin," and that we are risen with him to "walk in newness of life, so that we may no longer be slaves to sin.". . . .

CHAPTER 8[18]
St. Paul's Wonderful Exhortation to an Ecstatic and Superhuman Life

. . .Thus, then, the holy ecstasy of true love is accomplished when we live no more according to human reason and inclinations but above them according to the inspirations and promptings of the divine Savior of our souls.

*In 1654, the French mathematician, scientist,
literateur, poet, philosopher, theologian, and mystic,
Blaise Pascal, experienced the "living God" as "Fire."
His mysticism also focused on the human and divine
sufferings of Jesus Christ. To Pascal, the human heart
knows God with certainty, for God is felt there.*

BLAISE PASCAL

Despite his brief life and his unfinished work, Blaise Pascal was a
genius who continues to fascinate a great variety of people. Mathematician, scientist, literateur, poet, rhetorician, philosopher, theologian, and mystic, the views of this "sublime misanthrope"
permeated much of France's religious atmosphere in the second
half of the 17th century and still influence contemporary French
thought. Self-tormented and intellectually restless, Pascal deline-
ated in a perennially contemporary way the heart's immense longings, its tangles, the will's powerlessness, human fragility, and the
darkness of the "thinking reed" who knows his own misery.

Perhaps because Pascal's mother died when he was three years old,
his father became quite devoted to him and his two sisters, seeing
to it that he received a thorough Catholic education. At 23, Pascal
was converted by several French Jansenists.

In its benign form, Jansenism emphasized the need for evangelical
seriousness, conversion, and moral severity. One must reject the
world totally and submit wholeheartedly to God. Jansenism also refused to compromise with the humanism and "enlightened" skepticism of its day. In its extreme form, Jansenism was Augustinianism
gone sour. Almost fanatically severe, it taught that sin is possible
even without interior free choice, that Christ died only for an elect,
that the virtues of pagans are only vices, that sinful concupiscence

almost completely rules the person, and that most people are doomed to damnation.

Pascal's conversion to a mitigated Jansenism awakened him to what he considered an unChristian desire for scientific renown, so he renounced his scientific work. However, Pascal became ill shortly thereafter and was forced to return to a more "worldly" life .

In 1654, as the first selection indicates, Pascal received his now-famous mystical experience of God that lasted for about two hours. One finds a firsthand account in his *Mémorial*, a scrap of paper, later copied onto parchment and always carried thereafter.

The God-given 1654 occurrence deepened Pascal's already profound appreciation of God's mercy, as well as his acute sense of human nothingness before God's majesty and otherness. His sense of God's awesome holiness may have been initially rooted in his many illnesses and his Jansenistic conversion. Pascal sought even more fervently after this experience to disclose the wretchedness of the human condition without God and the happiness that could be had with God in Christ, the redeemer.

Retiring to the Jansenist monastery at Port-Royal, Pascal wrote his masterpiece of French irony, the *Provincial Letters*, and his *Pensées*, notes for an apology of the Christian religion. He admired Montaigne for his skeptical exposé of rationalism's pretensions and its attack on Christianity. Against Descartes and his ilk, Pascal stressed the primacy of experience over reason but maintained that religious authority did not substitute for scientific evidence. Although a scientist to the end, he valued the "science of the human" above the science of things. For him, science could not reach the essential human truths because it could not probe the mystery of what it ultimately means to be human.

As the selected texts illustrate, Pascal combined a moderate philosophical skepticism with firm religious belief. In religious knowledge, he averred that knowledge was inseparable from love. Although he used reason against anti-Christian freethinkers, Pascal emphasized the necessity for moral preparation for the proper use of reason. However, reason was of limited use concerning God. The heart connaturally, intuitively, directly, and prephilosophically knows God with certainty. For Pascal, the heart's reasons are not sentiments, but certainties.

The first text is Pascal's description of his famous 1654 mystical experience of the "living God" as "Fire." The selection illustrates both his thirst for the "God of Jesus Christ" and his disdain for the philosophy of his day. For him, only the God revealed by Jesus Christ makes the human soul great.

The second selection has been called a "tiny masterpiece" of Christ-centered mysticism. The text can be read as a summary of Pascal's relationship to Christ and as his rewriting of the Gospels' passion narratives. His Passion-mysticism underscores both the human and the *divine* sufferings of Christ, especially his loneliness. It astonishes him that Jesus actually sought "companionship and solace from men" during his agony, illustrating Pascal's jaundiced view of human nature. Nonetheless, because Christ redeemed humanity, Pascal views the human person as a redeemed sinner.

The third selection contains Pascal's best-known statement, "the heart has its reasons." The human heart knows God, for God is felt there. In this passage, Pascal rejects rationalism, for its reduction of God to what reason can comprehend, and fideism, for its naive rejection of "the right use of reason." Whereas rationalism takes the necessary mystery out of Christianity, fideism reduces it to a superstition.

The final text was selected to illustrate the impenetrable darkness of the human condition, human misery without God, and human dignity when united to God. Pascal's analysis of *ennui*, the experience of our nothingness, is worth noting.

In the last years of his life, though very sick, Pascal made great spiritual progress, apparently renounced Jansenism, and died in such terrible agony that some considered him a Christian martyr. His witness to the Christian calling is perhaps as significant as his works.[1]

THE TEXTS

AN EXPERIENCE OF GOD[2]

In the year of Grace 1654, on Monday, 23rd November, Feast of
Saint Clement, Pope and Martyr, and of others in the Martyrology,
and the Eve of Saint Chrysogonus and other Martyrs. From about
half past ten at night until about half-past twelve.

FIRE

"God of Abrahman, God of Isaac, God of Jacob," not of the philosophers and scientists. Certitude. Certitude. Feeling. Joy. Peace. God
of Jesus Christ. "My God and your God." Thy God shall be my
God. Forgetting the world and all things, except only God. He is to
be found only by the ways taught in the Gospel. Greatness of the
human soul. "Righteous Father, the world has not known Thee, but
I have known Thee." Joy, joy, joy, tears of joy. I have fallen away
from Him. "They have forsaken me, the fountain of living water."
"My God, wilt thou forsake me?" May I not be separated from Him
for all eternity. This is life eternal, that they may know Thee, the
only true God, and Jesus Christ, whom Thou has sent. Jesus Christ.
Jesus Christ. I have fallen away from Him; I have fled from Him, denied Him, crucified Him. May I not be separated from Him for eternity. We hold Him only by the ways taught in the Gospel.
Renunciation total and sweet. Total submission to Jesus Christ and
to my director. Eternally in joy for one day of trial upon earth. "I
will not forget thy Word." Amen.

THE MYSTERY OF JESUS[3]

Jesus suffers in his passion the torments inflicted upon him by men,
but in his agony he suffers the torments that he inflicts on himself.
He was troubled. This punishment is inflicted by no human, but by
an almighty hand, and only he that is almighty can bear it.

Jesus seeks some comfort at least from his three dearest friends, and
they sleep. He asks them to bear with him a while, and they abandon him with complete indifference, and with so little pity that it

did not keep them awake even for a single moment. And so Jesus was abandoned to face the wrath of God alone.

Jesus is alone on earth, not merely with no one to feel and share his agony, but with no one even to know of it. Heaven and he are the only ones to know.

Jesus is in a garden, not of delight, like the first Adam, who there fell and took with him all mankind, but of agony, where he has saved himself and all mankind.

He suffers this anguish and abandonment in the horror of the night.

I believe that this is the only occasion on which Jesus ever complained. But then he complained as though he could no longer contain his overflowing grief: "My soul is exceedingly sorrowful, even unto death."

Jesus seeks companionship and solace from men.

It seems to me that this is unique, but he finds none, for his disciples are asleep.

Jesus will be in agony until the end of the world. There must be no sleeping during that time.

Jesus, totally abandoned, even by the friends he had chosen to watch with him, is vexed when he finds them asleep because of the dangers to which they are exposing not him but themselves, and he warns them for their own safety and their good, with warm affection in the face of their ingratitude. And warns them: "The spirit is willing but the flesh is weak."

Jesus finds them asleep again, undeterred by consideration either for him or for themselves, is kind enough not to wake them up and lets them take their rest.

Jesus prays, uncertain of the will of the Father, and is afraid of death. But once he knows what it is, he goes to meet it and offer himself up. Let us be going. He went forth. Jesus asked of men and was not heard.

Jesus brought about the salvation of his disciples while they slept. He has done this for each of the righteous while they slept, in nothingness before their birth and in their sins after their birth.

He prays only once that the cup might pass from him, even then submitting himself to God's will, and twice that it should come if it must be so.

Jesus is weary at heart.

Jesus, seeing all his friends asleep and all his enemies watchful, commends himself utterly to his Father.

Jesus disregards the enmity of Judas, and sees only in him God's will, which he loves; so much so that he calls him friend.

Jesus tears himself away from his disciples to enter upon his agony: We must tear ourselves away from those who are nearest and dearest to us in order to imitate him.

While Jesus remains in agony and cruelest distress, let us pray longer.

We implore God's mercy, not so that he shall leave us in peace with our vices, but so that he may deliver us from them.

If God gave us masters with his own hand, how gladly we ought to obey them! Necessity and events are infallibly such.

"Take comfort; you would not seek me if you had not found me."

"I thought of you in my agony: I shed these drops of blood for you."

"It is tempting me rather than testing yourself to wonder if you would do right in the absence of this or that. I will do it in you if it happens."

"Let yourselves be guided by my rules. See how well I guided the Virgin and the saints who let me work in them."

"The Father loves all I do."

"Do you want it always to cost me the blood of my humanity while you do not even shed a tear?"

"My concern is for your conversion; do not be afraid, and pray with confidence as though for me."

"I am present with you through my word in Scripture, my spirit in the Church, through inspiration, my power in my priests, my prayer among the faithful."

"Physicians will not heal you, for you will die in the end, but it is I who will heal you and make your body immortal."

"Endure the chains and bondage of the body. For the present I am delivering you only from spiritual bondage."

"I am a better friend to you than this man or that, for I have done more for you than they, and they would never endure what I have endured from you, and they would never die for you, while you were being faithless and cruel, as I did, and as I am ready to do, and still do in my elect, and in the Blessed Sacrament."

"If you knew your sins, you would lose heart." "In that case I shall lose heart, Lord, for I believe in their wickedness on the strength of your assurance." "No, for I tell you this can heal you, and the fact that I tell you is a sign that I want to heal you. As you expiate them you will come to know them, and you will be told: 'Behold thy sins are forgiven thee.'"

"Repent then of your secret sins and the hidden evil of those you know."

"Lord, I give you all."

"I love you more ardently than you have loved your foulness. As an unclean beast for the mire."

"May mine be the glory, not thine, worm and clay."

"Acknowledge to your director that in my very words you find an occasion for sin, and for vanity or curiosity."

Pilate's false justice only causes Jesus Christ to suffer. For he has him scourged by his false justice and then put to death. It would have been better to put him to death at once. The falsely righteous are like that. They do both good works and bad to please the world and show that they are not wholly Christ's, for they are ashamed to be. Finally, when it comes to great temptations and opportunities they put him to death.

I see the depths of my pride, curiosity, concupiscence. There is no link between me and God or Jesus Christ the righteous. But he was made sin for me. All your scourges fell upon him. He is more abominable than I, and, far from loathing me, feels honored that I go to him and help him. But he healed himself and will heal me all the more surely. I must add my wounds to his, and join myself to him and he will save me in saving himself.

But none must be added for the future.

Ye shall be as gods, knowing good and evil. We all act like God in passing judgments: "This is good or evil too delighted by events.

Do small things as if they were great, because of the majesty of Christ, who does them in us and lives our life, and great things as if they were small and easy, because of his almighty power.

THE HEART HAS ITS REASONS[4]
The heart has its reasons, which the reason knows not, as we see in a thousand instances. I say that the heart naturally loves the Universal Being, and that it loves itself naturally, according to the measure in which it gives itself to one or the other—to reason, or to God; and it hardens itself against the one or the other, as it pleases. You have cast away the one and kept the other. Do you love by reason?

It is the heart that is conscious of God, and not the reason. This, then, is faith: God sensible to the heart, not to the reason.

Two errors—to exclude reason, and to admit no argument but reason.

Submission, and the right use of reason—this is the essence of Christianity.

If we submit everything to the test of reason, our religion will have nothing of mystery or of the supernatural about it. If our religion violates the rules of reason, it will be absurd—and it will rightly be ridiculed.

THE HUMAN CONDITION[5]
There is nothing upon earth which does not demonstrate either the misery of man or the mercy of God; either the powerlessness of

man without God—or his power in union with God. . . .

Man does not know where he belongs. He has obviously gone astray and has fallen from his proper place. He cannot find his way back to it, though he seeks it everywhere in great anxiety but without success, moving about in impenetrable darkness. . . .

Ennui: Nothing is more unbearable to a man as a condition of complete rest, without passions, without business, without amusements, and without the need for application. It is then that he feels his own nothingness, his abandoned state, his insufficiency, his dependent condition, his powerlessness, the vacuum within. Forthwith there wells up, from the depths of his soul, ennui, blackness, sadness, melancholy, disgust, despair.

Wife, mother, then Ursuline nun, and first woman missionary to Canada, Marie of the Incarnation was mystically espoused to the divine Word. Through sublime trinitarian visitations, she experienced herself as a sacrificial victim of divine love for a more effective apostolate.

MARIE OF THE INCARNATION

Marie of the Incarnation has been called Canada's St. Teresa of Avila. When Marie was only 28 years old, she had attained the fullness of spousal union with the incarnate Word and the summit of trinitarian mysticism. Shortly thereafter, Christ communicated his missionary Spirit, and Marie became the first woman missionary of the new world. In her 40s and 50s, she established a monastery and founded a school for the education of Indian girls. Having mastered the language of the Algonquins, Montagnais, Hurons, and Iroquois, Marie also wrote catechisms and dictionaries in and for these languages. Combined with her spousal and trinitarian mysticism, she experienced an exceptional victim-soul mysticism through which she was immolated for the sake of divine Love and for a more effective apostolate. Although relatively unknown, she is one of the most appealing and profound mystics in the mystical tradition.

Marie of the Incarnation was born Marie Guyart of a silk-merchant family in Tours, France, on October 28, 1599. Christ appeared to her in a dream when she was seven, and asked: "Will you be Mine?" After saying "yes," she awakened to find herself tremendously attracted to goodness.

Marie was drawn to religious life, but she submitted to her parents' wishes and married Joseph Claude Martin. Her husband died, leaving her at age 21, with a son and a failing business. Marie supported herself and her son by helping her sister and brother-in-law in their household and business matters, while sustaining a life of great penance and mystical prayer.

Contrary to her maternal instincts, Marie entrusted her 11- year-old son to her sister and entered the Ursuline monastery at Tours on January 25, 1632. Writing to her son even some 40 years later, Marie admitted that leaving him was like a "living death," which wrests soul from body. However, her spiritual director had acceded to Marie's unusual request to enter religious life because of her extraordinary interior life. In fact, within two months of entering the Ursulines, she attained the mystical summit.

In 1635, Marie had a mysterious dream: She and a companion were led to an "awesome" and "pitiable" land upon which the Blessed Virgin and Christ Child looked. Three years later she met the lady of her dreams, Madeleine de la Peltrie, with whom she and two other Ursuline nuns would set sail for Canada in 1639. After a harrowing sea journey, they landed in Quebec. Despite sickness, poverty, great physical hardships—as well as the intimidation and murder of missionaries and their Indian charges by hostile tribes— Marie and her companions established a monastery and founded a school to educate Indian girls.

Her son, Dom Claude Martin, eventually became a famous Benedictine and collected and published her letters. The letters offer a fascinating insight into her service mysticism and are a source for the study of 17th-century Canadian history.

At Dom Claude's request, Marie also sent her two spiritual autobiographies, known as *The Relation of 1633* (an account of her inner life from childhood up to 1633) and *The Relation of 1654* (the same, but up to 1654). The latter is considered to be her masterpiece and, of all her writings, reveals the most about her extraordinary mystical life. Spontaneity, humor, sincerity, directness, passionate love of God and neighbor, the desire to be a total oblation in God's service, a great variety of mystical experiences, and a surety and psychological finesse in analyzing complex states of soul characterize the work.

Several things stand out in the 1654 account of her inner life. First, only someone who has passed through all the mystical stages and attained spiritual maturity could have written this document. Second, her thirteen states of prayer do not fit the "classical" pattern of mystical ascent. Third, even in the highest states of prayer in which God bound her inner faculties, Marie's prayer contains a kataphatic basis. For her, "the least thought of these divine mysteries pertaining to the adorable Word Incarnate inflames the soul."[1] Finally, her imposing spousal and trinitarian mysticism culminated in the state of "victimhood," that is, perfect spiritual poverty that "has only God in mind."

The first text was selected to illustrate Marie's spousal union with the divine Word. She says that God always gave her premonitions before great graces so that she could prepare herself. In ecstatic union, Marie experienced the Word taking her as his bride and the Holy Spirit enabling her to respond. Illuminated and enkindled in love, her soul sings "a constant bridal hymn."

The next selection describes the climax of Marie's extraordinary trinitarian mysticism. When she was only 26, she had received trinitarian illuminations with respect to the divine attributes that moved her to deeper love of the Trinity. A short time later, the Eternal Word took her as his bride. Finally, through the "greatest gift of all," she experienced the mystery of the triune indwelling: the Father was her Father, the Word her Spouse, and the Holy Spirit the operative principle in all her activity.

The selection also illustrates something unusual: Marie experienced a dark night of the soul tempting her to suicide and blasphemy after her mystical marriage. She even had the experience of an evil spirit entering her and another spirit conquering it.

The next selected text shows that when Marie was approximately 35, Jesus' Spirit missioned her to Canada "to win souls for Christ" by instilling in her soul a Precious Blood mysticism. God the Father both instructed Marie to plead her cause by way of Christ's Sacred Heart and confirmed her service mysticism.

This selection also illustrates Marie's mystical appreciation of Scripture. Whenever she spoke on matters concerning faith and morals, she maintained that the pertinent scriptural passages entered and illuminated her mind. God transformed her not only by his own inner activity but also through these scriptural illuminations. Sacred Scripture was so inextricably tied to her life that Marie "got the reputation of never speaking except in sentences which were passages of Holy Scripture."

The selections indicate, too, that long after her transforming union with the Trinity, Marie experienced mystically the difference between her "spirit" and her "soul" in a purgative and even hellish way. Despite the continual experience of the trinitarian indwelling at the spirit's depths, the sense of God's purity and holiness instilled in her an acute sense of her imperfections and faults. The divine sword separating spirit from soul scours "the corners and turns and labyrinths of corrupt nature." So great was this "purgatory" that Marie spoke of "despairs" in which one is tempted to throw oneself into hell.

Not long before her departure to Canada, Marie received a vision of a "building of extraordinary grandeur. All that I could see was that the building, instead of being constructed of stones, was fashioned of crucified bodies. Some had only their legs pierced; others were attached a little higher up. Some were crucified at the waist while others again had their whole body crucified. But it was only those who were entirely attached who bore it willingly."[2] The last selection indicates that Marie loved her cross. Through penance and her dark nights of the senses and of the spirit, God bestowed on her the state of "victimhood" in and through which she attained "true and substantial poverty of spirit." With the last traces of self-will removed, her spirit sang a perpetual love song of perfect docility to God's will, a song of perfect adherence and adoration.[3]

THE TEXTS

THE RELATION OF 1654

SEVENTH STATE OF PRAYER
XXII.[4]

It has always been my experience that when the Divine Majesty wished to bestow some unusual grace of me, in addition to the remote preparations, I would feel, as the time drew near, that he was disposing me in a special way by a foretaste which was like the peace of paradise. The dignity of this makes it impossible for me to express myself otherwise. With these premonitions I would say to him: "What do you want of me, my Love?" And I would feel his action and, generally, he would effect a change in my state.

. . .This time, although my understanding was enlightened even more than before, it was the will which was important because this grace was concerned entirely with love, and through love my soul found itself wholly in the intimacy and enjoyment of a God of love.

Then, engulfed in the presence of this adorable Majesty, Father, Son, and Holy Spirit, adoring him in the awareness and acknowledgment of my lowliness, the Sacred Person of the Divine Word revealed to me that he was in truth the spouse of the faithful soul. I understood this truth with absolute certainty, and this very understanding became the imminent preparation for this grace to be effected in me. At that moment, this adorable Person seized my soul, and embracing it with indescribable love, united it to himself and taking it as his spouse.

. . .This time my soul recognized the distinct actions of the three divine Persons. When the Sacred Word acted in me, the Father and the Holy Spirit contemplated this action, but this did not hinder their unity because in the Trinity unity and diversity coexist without difficulty and in an indescribable manner so that each Person is free to act of itself.

I would have to have the ability of the seraphim and the other blessed spirits to express what occurred during this ecstasy and rapturous love which so absorbed the understanding that it was powerless to see anything except the treasures it possessed in the Sacred Person of the Eternal Word. Or to express it better: The powers of the soul were completely engulfed and absorbed in the Word who, as its spouse, bestowed on the soul the intimacy and right to be his bride. The soul realizes that in all this, it is the Holy Spirit who is the moving power, enabling it to act thus with the Word. . . .

The soul constantly experiences the action of this gracious initiator who by this spiritual marriage has taken possession of it with so gentle and sweet a fire that it cannot be described. He makes it sing a constant bridal hymn just as he wishes. Neither books nor study can teach this language which is completely divine and heavenly. It comes from that sweet melody of the mutual embrace of the soul and the adorable Word, which, through the kisses of his divine mouth, fills her with his spirit and his life. Thus this bridal hymn is the return and requital of the soul to its beloved Spouse.

EIGHTH STATE OF PRAYER
XXXIII.[5]

. . . One day at evening prayer, just as the signal had been given to begin, I was kneeling in my place in choir when a sudden inner transport ravished my soul. Then the three Persons of the Most Holy Trinity manifested themselves again through the words of the adorable Word Incarnate: "If anyone loves me, my Father will love him; we will come to him and make our dwelling with him" (John 14:23). I then felt the effects of these divine words and the action of the three divine Persons more strongly than ever before. These words, by penetrating me with their meaning, brought me both to understand and to experience. Then the most Holy Trinity, in its unity, took my soul to itself like a thing which already belonged to it, and which it had itself made capable of this divine imprint and the effects of this divine action.

In this great abyss it was shown to me that I was receiving the highest grace of all those communications of the three divine Persons that I had received in the past. This meaning was clearer and more intelligible than any words and occurred in this way: "The first time I revealed myself to you it was to instruct your soul in this great mystery; the second time was for the Word to take your soul for his Spouse; this time, Father, Son, and Holy Spirit are giving themselves in order to possess your soul completely." The effect of this was immediate and as the three divine Persons possessed me, so I possessed them in the full participation of the treasures of the divine magnificence. The Eternal Father was my father; the adorable Word, my Spouse; and the Holy Spirit was he who by his action worked in my soul, fashioning it to support the divine impressions. . . .

XXXV.[6]
Sometime after I had been clothed with the religious habit, temptations began to attack me on all sides, although I was not tempted to leave religious life. I have never been tempted on that score. These were temptations to blasphemy, to immodesty, even to pride, despite the fact that I was experiencing both my weakness and my poverty. I felt insensible and dull in the face of spiritual things and suffered from a spirit of contradiction toward my neighbor and an inclination to destroy myself. It seemed to me that I had been fooled by the devil and that I had deluded myself; I now believed that what had happened to me and what had been considered as coming from God was mere imagination. Everything I had experienced, all that I have described above, rose up before me and caused me to suffer grievously. . . .

. . . On another night while I still heard some sisters walking through the dormitory, suddenly I felt this evil spirit slipping into my bones, into my very marrow and nerves to destroy and annihilate me. I was terrified and I could neither move nor call out to anyone. This went on for a long time. Then, having suffered grievously, I felt in myself a strength and vigor so powerful that it seemed like another spirit come to do battle against the first one, so that in no time it had been conquered and brought to naught. Then I was free. . . . Since that time this has never happened to me again. . . .

NINTH STATE OF PRAYER
XXXIX.[7]
. . . Then at the age of 34 or 35, I entered into that state which, as it were, had been shown me and of which I had remained in expectation. This was an outpouring of apostolic spirit (which is nothing else than the Spirit of Jesus Christ), which took possession of my

soul so that it could no longer live except in him and by him. I was thus wholly dedicated to zeal for his glory so that he would be known, loved, and adored by all peoples whom he has redeemed by his Precious Blood.

My body was in our monastery but my spirit, united to that of Jesus, could not remain shut up there. This apostolic spirit carried me in thought to the Indies, to Japan, to America, to the East and to the West, to parts of Canada, to the country of the Hurons—in short to every part of the inhabited world where there were human souls who belonged by right to Jesus Christ. With inner certainty I saw the demons gaining victory over these poor souls, whom they snatched from the domain of Jesus Christ, our divine Master and Sovereign Lord, who had redeemed them by his Precious Blood.

As I watched this happen so surely, I became jealous, unable to endure the sight. I yearned for these poor souls; I gathered them to my heart; I presented them to the Eternal Father, telling him that it was time he exercised his justice in favor of my Spouse, to whom he had promised all nations for his inheritance. I reminded him that this Divine Son, through the shedding of his blood, had satisfied for all the sins of men who had previously been condemned to eternal death; yet there were still souls who did not live or belong to him. It was these souls whom I carried in my heart and whom I presented to the Eternal Father, begging that they all be given to Jesus Christ, to whom they rightfully belonged.

In spirit I roamed through the vast stretches of the Indies, of Japan and China, and kept company with those laboring to spread the Gospel there. I felt closely united to these workers because I felt that I was one with them in spirit. While it is true that in body I was bound by my rule of enclosure, nevertheless, my spirit did not cease its travels, nor did my heart cease its loving solicitations to the Eternal Father for the salvation of the many millions of souls whom I constantly offered him. The spirit of grace which acted in me moved me to such boldness and familiarity with the Eternal Father that it was impossible for me to do otherwise. "O Father, why do you delay? It is a long time since my Beloved shed his blood. I beg you in the interests of my Spouse," I would say to him, "be faithful to your word, O Father, for you have promised him all nations."

By a light infused into my soul, I saw more clearly than by any human light the meaning of this passage of Holy Scripture that speaks of the sovereign power which the Eternal Father has given the adorable Word Incarnate over all men, and this bright light which revealed so many wonders now kindled in my soul a love which consumed me and increased my longing that this Sacred Word would reign as absolute master—to the exclusion of all the demons—in the souls of all rational creatures. I felt that justice was on my side. The Spirit which possessed me made this clear and compelled me to say to the Eternal Father: "It is only just that my divine Spouse be master. I am wise enough to teach all nations about him. Give me a voice strong enough to be heard to the ends of the earth to proclaim that my divine Spouse is worthy to reign and to be loved by all hearts."

In my eagerness and yearning toward the Eternal Father, I gave tongue, without any effort on my part, to passages from the Apocalypse, which speak of this divine King of nations. I never sought out these passages, but they were urged on me and produced by the Spirit which possessed me. Turning to myself, I found myself in spirit among whole groups of souls who did not know my Spouse and who, therefore, did not pay him homage. I paid homage for all of them. I embraced them and longed to gather them all in the most Precious Blood of this adorable Lord and Master. . . .

XL.[8]

. . . I felt that the Eternal Father was pleased by my entreaties in so just a cause, but that there was something lacking which he wanted of me in order to grant my request. I cast myself at his feet, abasing myself to the very center of my lowliness so that his divine goodness would bestow on me whatever he wanted in order to hear me in the cause of my Spouse.

Then I felt in my soul an effusion and a ray of divine light followed by these words: "Ask of me by the heart of Jesus, my beloved Son; it is through him I will hear you and grant your requests." At this moment the Spirit which moved me united me to this divine heart of Jesus so that I could neither speak nor breathe except in him. I experienced a fresh outpouring of grace through this divine heart and through the spirit of my Jesus which worked marvels in me for the spread of the kingdom of Jesus Christ. All this happened about 1635. . . .

XLI.[9]

One day as I was praying in these dispositions before the Blessed Sacrament, leaning against my prie-dieu, my spirit was suddenly absorbed in God and there was again shown to me this vast country as I have described it before in all its details. Then this adorable Majesty said to me: "It is Canada that I have shown you; you must go there to build a house for Jesus and Mary." These words vivified my soul while at the same time reducing me to indescribable abasement at the command of this infinite and adorable Majesty. He gave me sufficient strength to reply, however: "O my great God, you can do all and I, I can do nothing. If you help me, I am ready. I promise to obey you. May your adorable will be done in me and through me." In this reply there was neither reasoning nor reflection. My response followed upon the heels of the command, my will being at that very moment united to the will of God. Then there followed an ecstasy of love in which this infinite Goodness caressed me in a way no human language can express and from which sprang a profound source of inner strength.

I no longer saw any country except Canada, and my greatest journeyings were in the land of the Hurons, accompanying those who were spreading the Gospel, united in spirit to the Eternal Father under the patronage of the Sacred Heart of Jesus, in order to win souls for him there. I stopped in many places throughout the world, but the country of Canada was my home and my country. My spirit, withdrawn from my body, seemed to have gone beyond me, which caused my body to suffer a great deal. Even while I ate, I was journeying through the country of the savages, working for their conversion and helping missionaries. My days and nights were spent in this way. . . .

Sometimes I was able to see the various reasons for this change of state in which I found myself. Then I was able to speak about it to the adorable Word Incarnate. While I spoke to him insistently, there appeared before me all the faults, imperfections, the impurities which I had committed since being called by the Divine Majesty. What had formerly seemed like nothing to me now seemed horrible in light of the infinite purity of God who demanded exact reparation for all I had experienced. How could one ever express the ways of this divine purity and the demands on souls called to live purely a spiritual life? There is no way to express this or to describe how terrible this divine love can be, penetrating and unrelenting in regard to purity, that irreconcilable enemy of purely human nature.

Even when one feels that one's lower nature has been put to death and believes that one has risen above it so that all is the work of grace, still there remain those corners and turns and labyrinths of corrupt nature whose ways are incomprehensible, known only by the spirit of God. It is he who understands these paths and who can destroy them by his intense and penetrating fire and sovereign power. When he wishes, and is pleased to do so, this is a purgatory more penetrating than lightning—a sword that divides and cuts with subtle sharpness. In this purgatory, one never loses sight of the Sacred Word Incarnate. He who had seemed to be only love and who formerly had consumed the soul by his divine embraces is now he who crucifies it and divides its spirit, except for the very center of the soul which is the dwelling place and throne of God which now appears like an abyss and like a place apart. . . .

Thus, the soul and spirit are honed by this cross and its penetrating thrusts; yet, as I have said, no matter how subtle these thrusts, they never reach the center of the soul which seems not to be in their power. (Although, of course, the soul is a single unity.) It sometimes happens that God, who is the master of this center, seems to hide and leave it for a while; and then it exists in a void—an intolerable state. From thence are born those despairs which would like to throw body and soul into hell.

One time as I was standing near the Blessed Sacrament, I saw a great flame near the window which I thought was the abyss of hell. In a sudden movement my whole being wanted to cast itself down, out of contempt for God. Suddenly his Divine Majesty with secret strength held me back and in a moment this terrifying vision ended. I think that if there had not been some paneling there which I could lean against I would have fallen, so violent was this experience. . . .

THIRTEENTH STATE OF PRAYER
LXV.[11]
Since beginning my second term as superior, the inner state in which Our Lord has led me has been that of victim in a more subtle and intense manner than usual, consuming me in various ways through his Holy Spirit. . . .

I have experienced that there are various degrees in true poverty of spirit. When Our Lord bestowed on me a religious vocation, his mercy taught me the value of this poverty. . . . My whole soul was inclined toward this sublime virtue which I saw held first place in the life of the Son of God. In it I saw all the other virtues affirmed, and I understood that its goal was nothing but pure and unadorned love which, in its simplicity, has only God in mind.

I had not yet realized, however, what the Spirit of God wanted to accomplish in my soul in order that it experience the validity of this spiritual poverty. Since then he has done this again and again in the changes of states in which it has pleased his Divine Majesty to lead me. In order to unify everything, he brought me to a true state of victim and of constant immolation which is so appalling to nature because of its subtlety. One would have to experience this to believe how the creature is reduced even in its noblest faculties. . . .

A Polish immigrant to Germany, convert, and then Franciscan priest, Angelus Silesius wrote the mystical classic, The Cherubinic Wanderer. *His epigrammatic couplets exude a mystical joy, serenity, and an enthusiasm for the divine-human encounter. The "prophet of the Ineffable" expresses the oneness of all things in God prior to creation.*

ANGELUS SILESIUS

Johannes Scheffler was born in the Silesian capital of Breslau of a well-to-do Lutheran, land-owning family who, for religious reasons, emigrated from Poland. Scheffler's parents died when he was young. Financially secure, he was able to study medicine and philosophy at Strasbourg, Padua, and Leiden. While in Holland, he studied the works of Jacob Boehme, the "teutonic philosopher of Görlitz" and Silesian mystic.

Boehme's noted biographer, Abraham von Franckenberg, urged Scheffler to write down his insights, a practice encouraged further by his exposure to Ignatius of Loyola's *Spiritual Exercises.* However, the German speculative mystics, the earlier German visionary mystics, and the Franciscan mystics of the order Scheffler eventually joined, influenced him the most.

Appointed a court physician by Duke Sylvius Nimrod of Württemburg, Scheffler converted to Catholicism and left his position, apparently because of the Court chaplain's intolerance. Returning to Breslau, he entered the Franciscans, was ordained a priest in 1661, and took the name "Angelus Silesius."

Scheffler became a shrill, strident, vitriolic, angry counter-reformation pamphleteer. But he lived a frugal, ascetic life and spent himself in service to the poor, the sick, and the orphaned. His works, *The Holy Joy of the Soul,* and especially his classic, *The Cherubinic Wanderer,* have universal appeal because they exude a mystical joy, peace, serenity, and an enthusiasm for the divine-human encounter. When one considers the horrors, turmoil, sufferings, and animosities that existed in his region both during and in the aftermath of the Thirty Years' War, his profound serenity is all the more remarkable.

Scheffler's mystical genius is revealed in extraordinary rhetorical skills. In the *Wanderer,* one finds a new variety of Christian mystical expressions. For example, he underscores the intimacy of the divine-human intercourse by speaking of it as the "art of kissing God." Scheffler has also been called the prophet (one who "speaks forth") of the Ineffable.

By using old French Alexandrine verse, liturgical expressions, and the Silesian Pietists' *paradoxa* (concatenations of seemingly contradictory scriptural verses), Scheffler wrote epigrammatic couplets. By blending images, themes, paradoxes, aphorisms, antithetical statements, and dissonance, these couplets dazzle, delight, and unite both the mind and heart with the object of their longing: the ineffable God.

If the "symbol leads to thought" (Paul Ricoeur), these epigrams flow from and return to a profoundly mystical life. His epigrams are sparks from a mystical soul, a mysticism expressed, incarnated, and sacramentalized in language, rhythm, and music. They illustrate the unity that often exists between mystical life at a person's core and its psychosomatic expression through all levels of the person's being. These epigrams, much like Japanese *haiku* or a Zen *koan,* baffle the mind, reveal the Ineffable, and exemplify the inextricable unity between life and its expression.

Two selections—"How God Dwells in the Holy Soul" and "The Secret Hart and Its Source"—have been called his most beautiful poems. Some selections illustrate his roots in the German speculative mystical tradition that emphasized God as the "naught," underscoring God's incomprehensibility, abnegation, emptiness, and the paradoxical divine-human union. Other selections manifest his roots in German bridal love mysticism and his ardent Franciscan incarnational mysticism. The selections also illustrate the illuminative ("cherubinic") and the love ("seraphic") elements that enlighten and inflame the spirit with love of the Trinity, Christ, the Cross, and Mary.

Some of his epigrams sound pantheistic, that is, as if Silesius destroys the distinction between the human and the divine. For example, he says: "Tell me, which holy soul will not be God in God?" But the epigrams clearly indicate Silesius' exemplarism and incarnationalism through which he expresses the oneness of all things in God *prior* to creation ("The rose which here on earth is now perceived by me/Has blossomed thus in God from all eternity"), their creation in the Son's image, and the necessity of becoming a son in the Son for the return to God. For Angelus, one is reborn by seeing reality as Adam saw it before the Fall and by participating in the language with which Adam conversed with God prior to the fall.[1]

THE TEXTS[2]

God Has All Names and None

Indeed one can name God by all His highest names
And then again one can each one withdraw again. (5:196, 115)

Who Goes Past God, Sees God

O Bride, if you should seek the bridegroom's face to view,
Go past God and all things, He'll be revealed to you. (5:269, 120)

The Godhead Is Unfathomable

How deep the Godhead is, no one may ever fathom;
Even the soul of Christ in its abyss must vanish. (5:339, 124)

One Abyss Calls the Other

The abyss that is my soul invokes it unceasingly.
The abyss that is my God. Which may the deeper be? (1:68, 42)

The Godhead Is a Naught

The tender Godhead is a naught and more than naught;

Who nothing sees in all, believe me, he sees God. (1:111, 44)

In the Sea a Little Drop Is Also the Sea

All in the sea is sea, even the tiniest drop;
Tell me, which holy soul will not be God in God? (6:173, 134)

The Spiritual Virgin

The Virgin I must be and bring God forth from me,
Should I ever be granted divine felicity. (1:23, 40)

How To Be Child and Father

I am God's child and son, and yet my child is He.
How can it ever happen that both these things should be? (1:256, 50)

The Spark in the Fire

Who is it who can tell the spark within the fire?
And who, once within God, can perceive what I am? (4:137, 95)

The Noblest Prayer

The noblest prayer will a man so much transform
That he becomes himself that which he does adore. (4:140, 95)

God is within and around Me

I am the vase of God, He fills me to the brim,
He is the ocean deep, contained I am in Him. (4:157, 96)

All Men Must Become As One

Multiplicity God shuns; therefore He draws us in,
That all He has created in Christ be one to Him. (5:149, 112)

Not To See God Is To See Nothing

You travel wide and far to scout and see and search;
If God you fail to see, you have nothing observed. (6:248, 136)

God Has No Other Model but Himself

Why God created us the image of His own?
I say because He has simply no other one. (5:239, 117)

God Becomes Me, Because I Was He Before

What I am, God becomes, takes my humanity;
Why has He acted thus? Because I once was He. (5:259, 119)

I, Like God, God, Like Me

God is that which He is; I am that which I am;
And if you know one well, you know both me and Him. (1:212, 48)

The Voice of God

Creatures are but the voice of the Eternal Word:
It sings and sounds its self, in sweetness and in dread. (1:270, 52)

God's Other Self

I am God's other Self, He can in me behold
What from eternity was cast in His own mould. (1:278, 53)

God Loves Himself Alone

Indeed it is quite true, God loves Himself alone
And whom His other Self can in His Son become.

The Power of Return

If you, my soul, return to what has been your source,
You'll be what you have been, that which you honor and love.
(4:134, 94)

God's Portraiture

I know God's Portraiture; he left it in disguise
In all His creatures fair, for you to recognize. (4:164, 97)

The Rose

The rose which here on earth is now perceived by me,
Has blossomed thus in God from all eternity. (1:108, 44)

Nothing Lives Without Dying

If He should live in you, God first Himself must die,
How would you, without death, inherit His own life? (1:33, 41)

How God's Voice Is Heard

The voice of God is heard: Listen within and seek;
Were you but always silent, he'd never cease to speak. (5:330, 124)

The Creature Is Grounded in God

The creature is to God closer than to itself;
Were it destroyed it would with Him and in Him dwell. (1:193, 47)

The Silent Prayer

God far exceeds all words that we can here express
In silence He is heard, in silence worshipped best. (1:240, 49)

Abandonment

Go out and God comes in; die, and you live in God;
Be not, it will be He; be still, God's plan is wrought. (2:136, 63)

When God Likes to Dwell with Us

God, whose sweet bliss it is to dwell within our breast,
Comes then most readily when we our house have left. (5:33, 104).

The Conceiving Soul

The soul that's virginal and naught but God conceives,
Can pregnant be with God as often as it pleases. (4:216, 99)

The Cross Is Love's Most Cherished Place

Tell me where love is found in her most cherished place?
Where to the Cross she's bound, for her Beloved's sake.(5:82, 108)

The Best Book

Too many books cause stress; who reads one thoroughly
(I mean the book of Christ) gets well eternally. (5:87, 109)

Three Kinds of Birth

The Virgin bears the Son of God externally,
I inwardly in spirit, the Father eternally. (5:249, 118)

The Evangelical Shepherd

The Shepherd is God's Son, the Godhead desert is,
Myself I am the sheep, whom He first sought and kissed. (5:316, 123)

He in Me, I in Him

Know, God becomes a child, lies in the Virgin's womb,
That I would grow like Him, His Godhead may assume. (3:16, 72)

The Closest Playmates

Not all is near to God: the Virgin and the Babe,
These two, and they alone, shall be God's playing-mates. (1:296, 54)

The Ineffable Reversal

All things are now reversed: The castle is the cave,
The crib becomes the throne, the night brings forth the day,
The Virgin bears a Child; Reflect, O Man, and say
That heart and mind must be reversed in every way. (3:245, 83)

Love Has Invented It

That God is crucified and can be wounded, hit,
That He the shame endures He is afflicted by,
That He such anguish bears and He can come to die,
Do not astonished be: Love has invented it. (4:52, 90)

One Drinks and Eats God

If you are divinized, you drink and eat your God;
This is forever true, with every piece of bread. (2:120, 63)

What the Saint Does, God does in Him

Himself God acts in saints, performs their actions here:
He walks, stands, lies, sleeps, wakes, eats, drinks, is of good cheer.
(5:174, 113)

The Highest Bliss Save God

The highest bliss in Heaven (save God) shall surely be
Hearts open to each other in pure transparency. (5:187, 114)

The Most Beautiful Thing

Nothing in either world as fair as I can be,
For God, Beauty Itself, has fallen in love with me. (5:232, 117)

God's Nature

Love is God's very nature, He can't act otherwise;
Hence if you would be God, love also without why. (5:243, 118)

Love Forces God

If it was not God's wish to raise me above God
I should compel him thus, by force of sheerest love. (1:16, 39)

The Spiritual Sowing

God is the husbandman, His seed His only Word,
The ploughshare is His Spirit, my heart the sowing ground. (1:64,
42)

How To Measure God

One cannot measure God; yet one can measure Him
By measuring my heart; He is possessed therein. (5:348, 125)

How God Dwells in the Holy Soul

If you should ask how God the Word in you does dwell,
Know that it is like suns flooding the world with light
And like the bridegroom coming in the night
And like the king enthroned in his realm,
A father with his son, a master in his school,
And like a treasure hidden from our sight
And like an honored guest in robes of white
And like a jewel in a crown of gold,
A lily in a flowery field,
And like sweet music at an evening meal.
And like the oil of cinnamon ignited
And like a host in a pure shrine,
A fountain in a garden of cool wine:
Tell me, where else clad in such beauty he is sighted? (6:1, 129)

The Secret Hart and Its Source

The hart runs off to seek a cooling hidden spring,
So that it then may be refreshed and calmed therein.
The soul, in love with God, is rushing toward the source,
From which the purest stream of life comes flowing forth.

The source is Jesus Christ, Who with His bracing draught
Imbues us with true faith, restores us from sin's wrath.
If you drink freely from this Fount and are revived,
Then, holy soul, you have at blessedness arrived. (6:12, 129)

Conclusion

Friend, let this be enough; if you wish more to read
Go and become yourself the writ and that which is. (6:263, 33)

The French Carmelite nun, Thérèse of Lisieux, lived her famous "Little Way" for 10 years before she died at the age of 24. Her vocation was to fill each moment with total and radical self-emptying love and thereby to embrace every vocation. To her, hidden love is an apostolate that affects the entire world.

THÉRÈSE OF LISIEUX

Marie Françoise Thérèse Martin was born in Alenon, France, on January 2, 1873, the youngest of nine children, four of whom had died before her birth. Louis, her father, was refused entrance to a monastery because he knew no Latin. When he was 35 and a successful watchmaker, he married the 27-year-old Zélie Guérin, a successful craftswoman who, for unknown reasons, had also been turned away by a religious order. They lived together as brother and sister for almost a year.

The Martins led an active Catholic sacramental life—unusual for that period of severe Jansenism—and engaged the entire family in the service of the poor and the sick. Family life was of extreme importance to the Martins, and Thérèse was later to recall how God had surrounded her life with love from her first memories.

When Thérèse was four years old, her mother died. Shortly thereafter, the family moved to Lisieux where she experienced eight years of weariness, over-sensitivity, and even religious scrupulosity. For three months in 1883 during this "winter of trial," Thérèse suffered from an illness that produced convulsions, hallucinations, and comas. She claimed that she was instantaneously and miraculously cured while praying before a statue of Our Lady of Victories.

Thérèse later wrote that she had undergone a "complete conversion" after Christmas Eve Mass in 1886, when she experienced charity entering her soul and the need to forget herself for the sake of others. A few days later, while looking at a picture of the crucified Christ, she resolved to remain in spirit at the foot of the Cross to gather up Christ's redemptive blood and to pour it out on needy "souls" because of her burning "thirst" to save them.

Thérèse soon experienced the success of her apostolic mysticism. The unrepentant murderer, Henri Pranzini, kissed the crucifix three times immediately before his execution. Thérèse was convinced that her prayers had converted him. Even in her last years, she referred to him as her "first child."

With an ardent desire to suffer for God and to pray for sinners, Thérèse wanted to enter the Carmelite monastery in Lisieux when she was 14. She was told to wait until she was 21. She and her father petitioned Bishop Hugonin to assist in admitting her. Moreover, when Thérèse, her father, and her sister Céline pilgrimaged to Rome, she personally asked Pope Leo XIII to intervene. He said, "If it is God's will, you will enter," and enter she did on April 9, 1888, at the age of 15.

For the next 10 years, until her slow, excruciating tubercular death before she was 24, Thérèse lived her famous Little Way, an attitude of soul that stamped her entire relationship with God. As she says, "the Almighty had done great things in the soul of His divine Mother's child, and the greatest thing is to have shown her her littleness."[1] Knowing the weakness of human strength, Thérèse never relied on her own. She taught that one should not become discouraged if one falls. Although little children often fall, they are rarely injured. With perfect confidence in and total abandonment to God, she lived expecting everything from God alone. In fact, Thérèse's life is a commentary on St. Paul's, "when I am weak, then I am strong" (1 Corinthians 12:10).

Although Thérèse was a respected member of her Carmelite community, few nuns noticed anything remarkable about her. However, when her autobiography was published about a year after her death, the worldwide reaction to "the very little Sister Thérèse of the Child Jesus and the Holy Face" produced a "hurricane of glory." Thousands of letters poured into Lisieux to sing her praises. Moreover, so evident was she a "miracle of virtues and a prodigy of miracles" that the Holy See waived the normal 50-year waiting period; Pope Pius XI solemnly canonized her on May 17, 1925, with a half-million pilgrims in attendance in St. Peter's square.

Thérèse never traveled much beyond her hometown of Alençon (except for the brief trip to Italy). Nevertheless, she lived her vocation to "suffer for souls" so radically that a few years later Pius XI declared her the "principal patroness, equal to St. Francis Xavier, of all missionaries, men and women, and of the missions in the whole world." On May 3, 1944, Pope Pius XII proclaimed her to be France's second patroness and "the equal of St. Joan of Arc." Thus, the nun who often called herself a "grain of sand" has come to be known as "the greatest saint of modern times."

Some commentators deny that Thérèse was a mystic because her Little Way seems incompatible with mysticism's heights. However, it would be difficult to find a person in the Christian mystical tradition whom God had so radically purified at such an early age. From the age of three, she claimed that she never refused God anything. The least trace of imperfection or infidelity horrified her. In time, her only joy was to suffer for Christ, and she rejoiced that "this unfelt joy is above every other joy."[2]

Moreover, an all-consuming trial of faith accompanied her tubercular sufferings the last year and a half of her life. So crucifying was this "thick darkness" that it even destroyed her natural satisfaction in desiring heaven. Her dark night of the soul revealed heaven's real attraction for her: "Oh! It's Love! To love, to be loved, and to return to the earth to make love loved."[3]

Thérèse maintained, too, that God flooded her soul with a transforming light,[4] which informed her that she would become a great, but hidden, saint until her posthumous glory became evident.[5]

However, the main effect of God's transformative illumination impressed upon Thérèse that her vocation was to love, that she could live only for love. From the age of 14, she experienced "assaults of love" that consumed her like a "veritable flame."[6] These transports reached their zenith in her "Oblation to Merciful Love" on June 9,

1895 when she offered herself totally as a "victim of holocaust" for the salvation of others. "At the age of 14," she says, "I also experienced transports of love. Ah! How I loved God! But it wasn't at all as it was after my Oblation to Love; it wasn't a real flame that was burning me."[7] Inspired with the realization that charity is essentially Jesus' *new commandment* to love others as He loves them, she desired to be a martyr for love in the sense that through her Christ would love all those she was commanded to love.

Thérèse's remarkable recollection puts her mysticism into sharp focus: She never passed more than a few minutes without thinking of God. It is also instructive how often the words "God alone" and "Jesus alone" appear in her writings. She was nothing less than a God-possessed woman. In its profoundest dimension Thérèsian mysticism is one of the "Holy Face," love's victim-face of Isaiah's suffering servant. "These words of Isaiah: 'Who has believed our report? There is no beauty in him, no comeliness, etc.,'" she wrote, "have [been] the whole foundation of my devotion to the Holy Face, or, to express it better, the foundation of all my piety. I, too, have desired to be without beauty, alone in treading the winepress, unknown to everyone."[8]

In short, Thérèse of the Holy Face lived an intense suffering-servant, or victim-soul, mysticism. Victim souls are not those who experience the Cross as the setbacks encountered in great apostolic undertakings, but the ones who manifest God's hand even in life's apparent absurdities: natural failings, physical defects, sickness, old age, and death. More importantly, they have also grasped the redemptive value of suffering, that is, how even hidden, sacrificial love is apostolic. The victim soul mystic is the prime example of the person who allows God alone to determine who and what one is.

Thérèse's desire to be hidden, forgotten, and unrecognized like the holy face of the suffering servant is only the negative side of her victim-soul mysticism. She passionately desired to suffer like Jesus for the world's redemption and succeeded in her vocation to fill each moment with total and radical self-emptying love. Only a few months before her death, she said: "Never would I have believed it was possible to suffer so much! [She didn't receive a single injection of morphine.] Never! Never! I cannot explain this except by the ardent desires I have had to save souls."[9]

Thérèse's greatness comes from her living out of her favorite quotation from St. John of the Cross, "Love is repaid by love alone." She measured sanctity not by great deeds, but through the quality of love with which anything is done. She wanted to cast at Jesus the "flowers of little sacrifices" filled with love. To desire and to succeed in filling each moment with perfect love is not a "little way," but the full flowering of Christian life.

Readers often find Thérèse's flowery and childish language a major obstacle in appreciating her mystical profundity. However, it must be remembered that she wrote to and for the members of her family, not for the general public. Moreover, she used the "precious" religious language of her times.

The text that follows was selected to illustrate the profundity of Thérèse's Little Way, the martyrdom of doing the ordinary extraordinarily well in love. This is one of the most beautiful passages on victim-soul mysticism in the Christian mystical tradition. It indicates Thérèse's conviction that hidden love is the little spark that gives birth to the Church's great lights. It underscores the Church's social nature and the value of praying for others as an apostolate.

The selection also brings out Thérèse's steely determination to be nourished on Truth alone and to fill each moment with self-emptying love. Her crucifying desire to love God and Christ alone, her joy in the dark night, her thirst for souls, and her radical suffering servant mysticism are vividly expressed here. Never in the Christian tradition has such a compelling commentary been lived and written on St. Paul's famous paean to love. In her desire to embrace every vocation, Thérèse learned that love does comprise them all and that her vocation is to love. The selections also amply illustrate that Thérèse had attained to mystical maturity through the fullness of her Christian faith, hope, and love.[10]

THE TEXTS

O my Beloved! this grace [devotion to Venerable Anne of Jesus, foundress of Carmel in France and to the saints] was only a prelude to the greatest graces you wished to bestow upon me. Allow me, my only Love, to recall them to You today, *today* which is the sixth anniversary of *our union.* Ah! my Jesus, pardon me if I am unreasonable in wishing to express my desires and longings which reach even unto infinity. Pardon me and heal my soul by giving her what she longs for so much!

To be your *Spouse,* to be a *Carmelite,* and by my union with You to be the *Mother* of souls, should not this suffice me? And yet it is not so. No doubt, these three privileges sum up my true *vocation: Carmelite, Spouse, Mother,* and yet I feel within me other *vocations.* I feel the *vocation* of the WARRIOR, THE PRIEST, THE APOSTLE, THE DOCTOR, THE MARTYR. Finally, I feel the need and the desire of carrying out the most heroic deeds for You, *O Jesus.* I feel within my soul the courage of the *Crusader,* the *Papal Guard,* and I would want to die on the field of battle in defense of the Church.

I feel in me the *vocation* of the PRIEST. With what love, O Jesus, I would carry You in my hands, when, at my voice, You would come down from heaven. And with what love would I give You to souls. But alas! While desiring to be a *Priest,* I admire and envy the humility of St. Francis of Assisi and I feel the *vocation* of imitating him in refusing the sublime dignity of the *Priesthood.*

O Jesus, my Love, my Life, how can I combine these contrasts? How can I realize the desires of my poor little soul?

Ah! in spite of my littleness, I would like to enlighten souls as did the *Prophets* and the *Doctors.* I have the *vocation of the Apostle.* I would like to travel over the whole earth to preach Your Name and to plant Your glorious Cross on infidel soil. But *O my Beloved,* one mission alone would not be sufficient for me, I would want to preach the Gospel on all the five continents simultaneously and even to the most remote isles. I would be a missionary, not for a few years only but from the beginning of creation until the consummation of the ages. But above all, O my Beloved Savior, I would shed my blood for You even to the very last drop.

Martyrdom was the dream of my youth and this dream has grown with me within Carmel's cloisters. But here again, I feel that my dream is a folly, for I cannot confine myself to desiring *one kind* of martyrdom. To satisfy me I need all. Like You, my Adorable Spouse, I would be scourged and crucified. I would die flayed like St. Bartholomew. I would be plunged into boiling oil like St. John; I would undergo all the tortures inflicted upon the martyrs. With St. Agnes and St. Cecilia, I would present my neck to the sword, and like Joan of Arc, my dear sister, I would whisper at the stake Your Name, O JESUS. When thinking of the torments which will be the lot of Christians at the time of Anti-Christ, I feel my heart leap with joy and I would that these torments be reserved for me. Jesus, Jesus, if I wanted to write all my desires, I would have to borrow Your *Book of Life* [Rv 20:12], for in it are reported all the actions of the saints, and I would accomplish all of them for you.

O my Jesus! What is your answer to all my follies? Is there a soul more *little*, more powerless than mine? Nevertheless even because of my weakness, it has pleased You, O Lord, to grant my *little childish desires* and you desire, today, to grant other desires that are *greater* than the universe.

During my meditation, my desires caused me a veritable martyrdom, and I opened the Epistles of St. Paul to find some kind of answer. Chapters 12 and 13 of the First Epistle to the Corinthians fell under my eyes. I read there, in the first of these chapters, that *all* cannot be apostles, prophets, doctors, etc., that the Church is composed of different members, and that the eye cannot be the hand *at one and the same time* [1 Cor 12:29]. The answer was clear, but it did not fulfill my desires and gave me no peace. But just as Mary Magdalene found what she was seeking by always stooping down and looking into the empty tomb, so I, abasing myself to the very depths of my nothingness, raised myself so high that I was able to attain my end. Without becoming discouraged, I continued my reading, and this sentence consoled me: "*Yet strive after THE BET-*

TER GIFTS, *and I point out to you* a yet more excellent way" [1 Cor 12:31]. And the Apostle explains how all *the most PERFECT gifts* are nothing without LOVE. That *Charity is the EXCELLENT WAY* that leads most surely to God.

I finally had rest. Considering the mystical body of the Church, I had not recognized myself in any of the members described by St. Paul, or rather I desired to see myself in them *all. Charity* gave me the key to my *vocation.* I understood that if the Church had a body composed of different members, the most necessary and most noble of all could not be lacking to it, and so I understood that the Church had *a Heart and that this Heart was BURNING WITH LOVE. I understood it was Love alone* that made the Church members act, and that if *Love* ever became extinct, apostles would not preach the Gospel and martyrs would not shed their blood. I understood that LOVE COMPRISED ALL VOCATIONS, THAT LOVE WAS EVERYTHING, THAT IT EMBRACED ALL TIMES AND PLACES. . . . IN A WORD, THAT IT WAS ETERNAL!

Then, in the excess of my delirious joy, I cried out: O Jesus, my Love. . . . My *vocation,* at last I have found it. . . . MY VOCATION IS LOVE!

Yes, I have found my place in the Church and it is You, O my God, who have given me this place; in the heart of the Church, my Mother, I shall be Love. Thus I shall be everything, and thus my dream will be realized. . .

I am only a child, powerless and weak, and yet it is my weakness that gives me the boldness of offering myself as *VICTIM of Your Love, O Jesus!* In past times, victims, pure, and spotless, were the only ones accepted by the Strong and Powerful God. To satisfy Divine *Justice,* perfect victims were necessary, but the *law of Love* has succeeded to the law of fear, and *Love* has chosen me a holocaust, me, a weak and imperfect creature. Is not this choice worthy of *Love?* Yes, in order that Love be fully satisfied, it is necessary that It lower Itself, and that It lower Itself to nothingness and transform this nothingness into fire.

O Jesus, I know it, love is repaid by love alone, and so I searched and I found the way to solace my heart by giving You Love for

Love. . . . A child of light, I understood that *my desires of being every-thing*, of embracing all vocations, were the riches that would be able to render me unjust, so I made use of them to *make friends*. Remember the prayer of Eliseus to his Father Elias when he dared to ask him for HIS DOUBLE SPIRIT [2 Kgs 2:9], I presented myself before the angels and saints and I said to them: "I am the smallest of creatures; I know my misery and my feebleness, but I know also how much noble and generous hearts love to do good. I beg you, the, O Blessed Inhabitants of heaven, I beg you to ADOPT ME AS YOUR CHILD. *To you alone will be the glory* which you will make me merit, but deign to answer my prayer. It is bold, I know; however, I dare to ask you to obtain for me YOUR TWOFOLD SPIRIT."

Jesus, I cannot fathom the depths of my request; I would be afraid to find myself overwhelmed under the weight of my bold desires. My excuse is that I am *a child*, and children do not reflect on the meaning of their words; however, their parents, once they are placed upon a throne and possess immense treasures, do not hesitate to satisfy the desires of the *little ones* whom they love as much as they love themselves. To please them they do foolish things, even going to the extent of *becoming weak* for them. Well, since I am *the Child of the Church* and the Church is a Queen since she is Your Spouse, O King of kings. The heart of a child does not seek riches and glory (even the glory of heaven). She understands that this glory belongs by right to her brothers, the angels and saints. Her own glory will be the reflected glory which shines on her Mother's forehead. What this child asks for is Love. She knows only one thing: to love you, O Jesus. Astounding works are forbidden to her; she cannot preach the Gospel, shed her blood; but what does it matter since her brothers work in her stead and she, a *little child*, stays very close to the *throne* of the King and Queen. She loves in her brothers' place while they do the fighting. But how will she prove her *love* since *love* is proved by works? Well, the little child *will strew flowers*, she will perfume the royal throne with their *sweet scents* and she will sing in her silvery tones the canticle of *Love*.

Yes, my Beloved, this is how my life will be consumed. I have no other means of proving my love for you other than that of strewing flowers, that is, not allowing one little sacrifice to escape, not one look, one word, profiting by all the smallest things and doing them through love. I desire to suffer for love and even to rejoice through love; and in this way I shall *strewn* flowers before Your throne. I shall not come upon one without *unpetalling* it for You. While I am strewing my flowers, I shall sing, for could one cry while doing such a joyous action? I shall sing even when I must gather my flowers in the midst of thorns, and my song will be all the more melodious in proportion to the length and sharpness of the thorns. . . .

O my Jesus! I love You! I love the Church, my Mother! I recall that *"the smallest act of PURE LOVE is of more value to her than all other works together."* But is PURE LOVE in my heart? Are my measureless desires only but a dream, a folly? Ah! If this be so, Jesus, then enlighten me, for You know I am seeking only the truth. If my desires are rash, then make them disappear, for these desires are the greatest martyrdom to me. However, I feel, O Jesus, that after having aspired to the most lofty heights of Love, if one day I am not to attain them, I feel that I shall have tasted *more sweetness in my martyrdom and my folly* than I shall taste in the bosom of the *joy of the Fatherland,* unless You take away the memory of these earthly hopes through a miracle. Allow me, then, during my exile, the delights of love. Allow me to taste the sweet bitterness of my martyrdom.

Jesus, O Jesus, if the desire of loving You is so delightful, what will it be to possess and enjoy this Love?

How can a soul as imperfect as mine aspire to the possession of the plenitude of *Love*? O Jesus, *my first and only Friend*, You whom I *love* UNIQUELY, explain this mystery to me! Why do You not reserve these great aspirations for great souls, for the *Eagles* that soar in the heights?

I look upon myself as a *weak little bird*, with only a light down as covering. I am not an eagle, but I have only an eagle's EYES AND HEART. In spite of my extreme littleness I still dare to gaze upon the Divine Sun, the Sun of Love, and my heart feels within it all the aspirations of an *Eagle*.

The little bird wills to fly toward the bright Sun which attracts its eye, imitating its brothers, the eagles, whom it sees climbing up towards the Divine Furnace of the Holy Trinity. But alas! The only thing it can do is raise its little wings; to fly is not within its little power.

What will then become of it? Will it die of sorrow at seeing itself so weak? Oh no! The little bird will not even be troubled. With bold surrender, it wishes to remain gazing upon its Divine Sun. Nothing will frighten it, neither wind nor rain, and if dark clouds come and hide the Star of Love, the little bird will not change its place because it knows that beyond the clouds its bright Sun still shines on and that its brightness is not eclipsed for a single instant. . . .

O Jesus, Your *little bird* is happy to be *weak and little*. What would become of it if it were big? Never would it have the boldness to appear in Your presence, to *fall asleep* in front of You. Yes, this is still one of the weaknesses of the little bird: when it wants to fix its gaze upon the Divine Sun, and when the clouds prevent it from seeing a single ray of that Sun, in spite of itself, its little eyes close, its little head is hidden beneath its wings, and the poor thing falls asleep, believing all the time that it is fixing its gaze upon its Dear Star. When it awakens, it doesn't feel desolate; its little heart is at peace and it begins once again its work of *love*. It calls upon the angels and saints who rise like eagles before the consuming Fire, and since this is the object of the little bird's desire the eagles take pity on it, protecting and defending it, and putting to flight at the same time the vultures who want to devour it. These vultures are the demons whom the little bird doesn't fear, for it is not destined to be their *prey* but the prey of the *Eagle* whom it contemplates in the center of the Sun of Love.

O Divine Word! You are the Adored Eagle whom I love and who alone *attracts me!* Coming into this land of exile, You willed to suffer and to die in order *to draw* souls to the bosom of the Eternal Fire of the Blessed Trinity. Ascending once again to the Inaccessible Light, henceforth Your abode, You remain still in this "valley of tears," hidden beneath the appearances of a white host. Eternal Eagle, You desire to nourish me with Your divine substance and yet I am but a poor little thing who would return to nothingness if Your divine glance did not give me life from one moment to the next.

O Jesus, allow me in my boundless gratitude to say to You that Your *love reaches unto folly*. In the presence of this folly, how can You not desire that my heart leap towards You? How can my confidence, then, have any limits? Ah, the saints have committed their *follies* for You, and they have done great things because they are eagles.

Jesus, I am too little to perform great actions, and my own *folly* is this: to trust that Your Love will accept me as a victim. My *folly* consists in begging the eagles, my brothers, to obtain for me the favor of flying towards the Sun of Love with the *Divine Eagles's own wings* [Dt 32:11]!

As long as You desire it, O my Beloved, Your little bird will remain without strength and without wings and will always stay with its gaze fixed upon You. It wants to be *fascinated* by Your divine glance. It wants to become the *prey* of Your Love. One day I hope that You, the Adorable Eagle, will come to fetch me, Your little bird; and ascending with it to the Furnace of Love, You will plunge it for all eternity into the burning Abyss of this Love to which it has offered itself as a victim.

O Jesus, why can't I tell all *little souls* how unspeakable is Your condescension? I feel that if You found a soul weaker and littler than mine, which is impossible, You would be pleased to grant it still greater favors, provided it abandoned itself with total confidence to Your Infinite Mercy. But why do I desire to communicate Your secrets of Love, O Jesus for was it not You alone who taught them to me, and can You not reveal them to others? Yes, I know it, and I beg You to do it. I beg You to cast Your Divine Glance upon a great number of *little* souls. I beg You to choose a legion of *little* Victims worthy of Your LOVE!

The very little Sister Thérèse of the Child Jesus and the Holy Face, unworthy religious of Carmel.

An Italian laywoman who eventually took the vows of the Passionist nuns, Gemma Galgani has been called the "Daughter of the Passion" because of her profound imitation of the Victim of Calvary. She travelled the entire mystical journey and experienced more secondary mystical phenomena than any other mystic in the Christian tradition.

GEMMA GALGANI

Gemma Galgani's spiritual life bears a striking resemblance to that of Thérèse of Lisieux. They were contemporaries, came from large families, suffered much from ill health, died in their early 20's, quickly attained a reputation for sanctity, and were soon canonized for their heroic virtue and for the miracles attributed to their intercession.

Moreover, both Gemma and Thérèse's are paradigms of victim-soul mysticism. Experiencing a profound call to imitate the Victim of Calvary, they both lived for love alone. These two mystics lived as oblations to Divine Love to offer expiation and reparation for the sins of the world.

But here the comparison ends. As we have seen, Thérèse's life was in some ways so ordinary that some commentators deny she was a mystic. But Gemma experienced, in an extraordinary way, God's purifying, illuminating, and transforming power. She also experienced more secondary mystical phenomena than any other mystic in the Christian tradition. Gemma experienced numerous trinitarian, Christ-centered, Marian, and eucharistic illuminations. Raptures, ecstasies, seraphic wounds of love, visions, locutions, the *complete* stigmata, bloody sweat, tears of blood, mystical effluvia (perfumed bodily secretions), satanic attacks, and penetrating discernment of spirits filled her life. Christ had told Gemma in a vision that he wanted her to travel the entire mystical journey; he was faithful to his word.

On March 12, 1878, Gemma Galgani was born the fourth of eight children of fairly well-to-do parents at Camigliano, near Lucca, in Tuscany. When her mother died in 1886, Gemma attended the school run by the sisters of St. Zita but terminated her education because of ill health. Because of her father's eventual bankruptcy, Gemma was exposed to extreme poverty when he died in 1896. A few years later, Cecilia Giannini asked Gemma's brother, as a favor, to allow her to live with the Giannini family in Lucca, where she spent her remaining four years of life. She and Cecilia Giannini, the family matriarch, became close friends and confidants.

In 1902, her illnesses returned. However, extreme physical pain, mental sufferings, and even satanic assaults did not disturb Gemma's extraordinary peace. Six months before her death, she took the vows of the Passionist nuns. Like their calling, her vocation was one of reparation and propitiation. A few months before her death on April 11, 1903, she worked toward establishing a convent for Passionist nuns in Lucca. On May 3, 1940, the "Daughter of the Passion" was canonized. Her fame spread quickly, mainly because of the 1941 publication of her correspondence with her spiritual director, Germano di San Stanislao Ruoppolo, C.P.

Gemma possessed extraordinary spiritual gifts even as a child. Before she was five years old, she spent time meditating upon Christ's passion. Sacramentally confirmed at seven years of age, Gemma received mystical locutions. When she made her First Communion at nine years of age, she experienced mystical union with Christ.

From 1891-1895, she received Communion several times weekly, experienced mystical locutions, and felt called to religious life "to suffer and to assist Jesus in his sufferings." Although serious illness prevented her from becoming a Passionist nun, in 1896 she took a private vow of chastity. Gravely ill from 1898-1899, Gemma attributed her incredible recovery to the intercession of St. Gabriel of l'Addolorata who appeared to her on several occasions.

During a vision of the crucified Christ in Holy Week of 1899, he implanted in her heart the living flame of love and suffering. A few months later, she not only received the stigmata but also all the wounds of the Victim of Calvary: the nail wounds in the hands and feet, the crowning with thorns, the scourging, the lance wound in the side, the left shoulder wound from carrying the cross, the bruised knees from falling under the weight of the cross, the thirst on the cross, and the overall agony of Gethsemani and Calvary.

Gemma also experienced the radical purgation of the dark night of the soul. Concomitant with God's purgative action at the soul's center, Gemma had to endure satanic attacks, as well as great mental and physical suffering. But God's transformative illuminations were many and varied: illuminations concerning the Trinity, God's presence in all things, Christ's divine-human nature, the eucharist, discernment of spirits, and converse with her guardian angel. On the Feast of the Assumption of Mary in 1900, the Blessed Virgin Mary appeared to Gemma, ravished her heart, confirmed her in grace, and married her mystically to her Son.

Gemma had such patience in illness and tribulation and such deep humility that only a few (Cecilia and Father Germano) realized her greatness. In fact, Gemma's sole desire was to be "only a victim" by contemplating and imitating Christ, the victim of the sins of the world. As he had promised her, she would not die until she had drunk the very last drop from his cup of sufferings. But Christ himself would lead her into paradise.

The selections that follow are taken from the long excerpts from Gemma's letters contained in her spiritual director's biography that proved instrumental in her canonization. The selected texts center on her victim-soul mysticism, a mysticism derived in part from her devotion to the Sacred Heart which was in vogue during her day. Gemma possessed a seraphic desire to be consumed with love, to offer herself as a victim of oblation and expiation for the sins of the world. The selections illustrate her passionate desire not to abandon even one seemingly hopeless sinner because Christ's blood had been shed for all. The way Gemma experienced both the agonies and the wounds of Christ at Gethsemani and Calvary is also inextricably tied to her victim-soul mysticism.

It is difficult to find a more ardent and penetrating account of eucharistic mysticism in the Christian mystical tradition. The selections on her ecstatic prayer indicate the incredible facility with which she was united to God and how easily she found God in all things and all things in God. Her visions of and conversations with her guardian angel are unique in the Christian mystical tradition. The role of Mary in her mystical life should also be noted.

Jesus defined part of his mission in terms of defeating Satan. St. Paul maintained that the Christian life involves warfare not only against "flesh and blood," but also against principalities and powers. Many mystics in the Christian tradition experienced Satan's attempt to thwart their union with God firsthand. The selections indicate that Gemma was no exception.

The selections also raise the question of the role secondary mystical experiences have in the mystical life. The Christian mystical tradition attests that unusual mystical experiences often occur with the primary phenomenon of the mystic's experience of God's purifying, illuminating, and transforming self-communication. If past studies tended to overemphasize these extraordinary experiences at the expense of the primary mystical process, contemporary studies distinguish them too sharply.

For example, in Gemma's case, God's purifying, illuminating, and transforming self-communication cannot be distinguished clearly from the extraordinary mystical phenomena she received. In fact, these phenomena are the way she both received and expressed God's loving self-communication. The ordinariness of the extraordinary permeates Gemma's fascinating mystical life.

Thus, those commentators who dismiss these phenomena as "otherworldly," as detracting from genuine Christian living, or as insignificant are in error. Just because many people consider dreams irrelevant to their lives does not mean that in fact they are so, as contemporary psychology attests. The same holds for extraordinary mystical phenomena.

But those commentators who emphasize the "miraculous" nature of extraordinary phenomena likewise seem to be in error. Secondary mystical experiences may be regarded as the echoes, reverberations, radiations, shocks, and percolation of God's purging, illuminating, and unifying self-communication. Gemma's psychosomatic structure assimilated and adjusted to God's self-communication to her deepest core by means of these phenomena. God purified, illuminated, transformed, and integrated Gemma's entire body-person by means of these psychosomatic phenomena. God's loving self-communication demands its enfleshment in the entire body-person which often results in grace's psychosomatic manifestations, or secondary mystical experiences.

Secondary mystical phenomena may be assessed as God's self-communication insofar as it refracts itself into the mystic's full body-person. These phenomena also express symbolically the way the Christian's deepest mystical life reaches the surface mind, various levels of the psyche, and the body. They should be compared, therefore, to the poetry, literature, music, paintings, and sculptures of the world's great artists.

However, God-given secondary mystical experiences never occur alone. The mystic experiences genuine, pathological, and diabolical phenomena during the course of her mystical life. These phenomena reveal not only Gemma's God-induced psychosomatic integration, but also her brokenness and the presence of the demonic. Taken together, therefore, these phenomena manifest God's presence, the devil's presence, and Gemma's own healthy and pathological accommodations and resistances to both the divine and the demonic presence.

Furthermore, it is not surprising that some of these phenomena may reflect Gemma's infantile dreams, inordinate desires, immature projections, and pathological hallucinations. However, others directly countered Gemma's physically, psychologically, and morally pernicious tendencies. Conversion, renewed energy, strength, courage, authority, and peace accompanied them. They bestowed insight, knowledge, and wisdom upon her and deepened her faith, hope, and love.

The Christian mystics unanimously teach that genuine God-induced extraordinary phenomena leave behind in their wake faith, hope, love, humility, heroic virtue, and peace. The enhancement of life at all levels of the person's being attests to their authenticity. They both produce and flow from holiness.

In conclusion, Gemma's extraordinary mystical phenomena need not be overemphasized as miraculous nor dismissed as irrelevant and otherworldly. Her mystical life, her sanctity, her heroic virtue, her passionate desire to participate in Christ's redemptive work cannot be understood without them.[1]

THE TEXTS

A VICTIM OF LOVE

"Would it sadden thee were I to give thee to drink of My chalice even to the last drop?" Jesus, may Thy most Holy will be done. . . .

At that sight [a vision of Christ crucified] I felt such great grief, that thinking of the infinite love of Jesus for us, and of the sufferings He had endured for our salvation, I fainted and fell. After the lapse of an hour or so I came to myself; and then there arose in my heart an immense desire to suffer something for Him Who had suffered so much for me. . . .[2]

"My child, I [Christ] have need of victims, and strong victims. In order to oppose the just wrath of My Divine Father, I need souls who, by their sufferings, tribulations and difficulties, make amends for sinners and for their ingratitude. Oh! that I could make all understand how incensed My Heavenly Father is by the impious world! There is nothing to stay His Hand, and He is now preparing a great chastisement for all the world. . . ."

I [Gemma] am the victim, and Jesus the sacrificing Priest. . . . To suffer, but without any consolation, without any comfort; to suffer, for love alone. . . .[3]

"What correspondence do I [Christ] ever find in My creatures whom I have loved so much? No one any longer cares for My Heart and for My Love. I am forgotten as though I had never loved them and as though I had never suffered for them. My Heart is always in sadness; I am left almost alone in My churches; if many assemble there it is for other motives than worship and I have to suffer the pain of seeing My House become a theatre of amusement. Many through hypocrisy betray Me by sacrilegious Communions. I can bear no more."

Thou knowest O Lord how ready I [Gemma] am to sacrifice myself in everything. I will bear every sort of pain for Thee. I will give every drop of my blood to please Thy Heart and to hinder the outrages of sinners against Thee . . . . O Jesus, do not abandon poor sinners, think of sinners and of me; I want them all saved. . . . That one [a hardened sinner] I want You, Jesus, to remember particularly, because I want him saved together with me.

But what do I hear thee say, Mother [of God]? Abandon that soul? Is it not a question of one belonging to Jesus? Has He not shed all his Blood for this soul?. . . . Oh! rather than abandon a soul! O Mother, it is impossible that Jesus would forsake a soul! Why, He even had mercy on the thief!" . . . .[4]

I would wish to bathe with my blood all those places where Jesus is outraged. I would wish all sinners to be saved, because they have been redeemed by the Precious Blood of Jesus. . . .

I have such a great longing to fly away to my God! O, if I could but hear from you, father [Germano]. For days Jesus has been making me a victim of Love; He is making me die, ah! only of Love. . . . What a precious death! I am not quieted if Jesus does not inflame me a little with His Love that I may be consumed in Him. I would have my heart become ashes, that all should say: Gemma has been burned to ashes for Jesus. . . .

For the last eight days I have felt something mysterious in the region of my heart that I cannot understand. The first days I disregarded it, because it gave me little or no trouble. But today is the third day that this fire has increased. O so much, as to be almost unbearable. I should need ice to put it out, and it hinders my sleeping and eating. It is a mysterious fire that comes from within to the outside. It is however a fire that does not torment me; rather it delights me; but it exhausts and consumes me. Jesus, father, will have made you understand all about it. Great God! How I love Thee, O how I love Thee!. . . .

In order to form an idea of it, imagine that into the very center of this poor heart a red-hot iron, kept continually heated in a furnace, has been introduced; thus I feel myself burning. . . . Thou art on fire, Lord, and I burn. O pain, O infinitely happy Love! O sweet fire! O sweet flames! And wouldst Thou have my heart become a flame? Ah! I have found the flame that destroys and reduces to ashes! Ah! cease, cease, I cannot withdraw my heart from so much fire. What do I say! No, rather come Jesus; I will open my heart to Thee; put Thy Divine fire into it. Thou art Flame, and let my heart be turned into flame. . . .[5]

My heart, father, is the victim of Love, and I shall soon die of love. These flames of love consume my body as well as my heart, and I shall be reduced to ashes. Yesterday as I drew near to Jesus exposed in the Blessed Sacrament I felt myself burning so violently that I was obliged to move away. I was burning all over; it rose even to my face. Viva Gesù! How happens it that so many who are standing close to Jesus do not burn to ashes?[6]

EUCHARISTIC MYSTICISM[7]
And when my [Gemma's] flesh is united with Thine in the Holy Eucharist, make me feel Thy Passion. . . . [She called the Eucharist] the Academy of Paradise where one learns how to love; the school is the supperroom, Jesus is the Master, the doctrines are His Flesh and Blood. . . . Oh! What immense happiness and joy my heart feels before Jesus in the Blessed Sacrament! And if Jesus would allow me to enter the sacred Tabernacle, where He, Soul, Body, Blood and Divinity is present, should I not be in Paradise?. . . . Jesus, Soul of my soul, my Paradise, Holy Victim, behold me all thine. . . .

Listen, Jesus, to what the Confessor asks me: "What do you do Gemma when you are before Jesus?" What do I do? If I am with Jesus Crucified I suffer, and if with Jesus in His Sacrament, I love. . . I stopped for a few minutes to think of this [receiving Communion] and there and then, I felt forced toward Jesus [ecstasy]. This same thing happens to me whenever I think of Jesus, particularly when He invites me to receive Him, and when He tells me that He is coming to repose in my heart. . . .

[Eucharist] is a question of uniting two extremes; God Who is everything and the creature who is nothing; God Who is light and the creature who is darkness; God Who is holiness and the creature who is sin. It is a question of taking part at the Table of the Lord.

There cannot be then enough preparation for it.

THE STIGMATA[8]

We were on the Vigil of the Feast of the Sacred Heart, Thursday evening. All of a sudden, more quickly than usual, I felt a piercing sorrow for my sins; but I felt it so intensely that I have never since experienced anything like it. That sorrow, I might say, almost brought me to death's door. Next I felt all the powers of my soul in recollection. My intellect knew nothing but my sins and offenses against God; my memory recalled them all, and set before me all the torments that Jesus had endured to save me; my will moved me to detest them all and willingly suffer everything to expiate them. A world of thoughts turned in my mind and they were thoughts of grief, love, fear, hope, encouragement.

This recollection was quickly followed by a rapture out of my senses, and I found myself in the presence of my dear heavenly Mother who had my Angel Guardian on her right. He spoke first, telling me to repeat the act of contrition, and when I had done so my Holy Mother said: "My child, in the name of Jesus may all thy sins be forgiven thee." Then she added: "My Son Jesus loves thee beyond measure, and wishes to give thee a grace; wilt thou know how to render thyself worthy of it?" My misery did not know what to answer. Then she added: "I will be a mother to thee; wilt thou be a true child?" She opened her mantle and covered me with it. At that moment Jesus appeared with all His Wounds open; but from those Wounds there no longer came forth blood, but flames of fire. In an instant those flames came to touch my hands, my feet and my heart. I rose to go to bed, and became aware that blood was flowing from those parts where I felt pain. I covered them as well as I could, and then helped by my Angel I was able to get into bed. In the morning I found it difficult to go to Holy Communion, and I put on a pair of gloves to hide my hands. I could not remain standing and felt every moment that I should die. Those pains did not leave me until three o'clock on Friday—the Feast of the Sacred Heart.

THE WOUNDING FROM THE LANCE[9]

This morning about ten o'clock my heart was seeking, seeking. . . . I felt my senses leave me. . . . To the agony of my heart was added an excessive pain through all my members. . . . But before and above all was my sorrow for sin. Oh! excruciating this pain! Were it any greater I could not have outlived it: and I may say the same of the stroke [of the lance that opened her side] I received. . . . My little heart could no longer bear the restraint and has begun to send forth blood in quantities. . . . Jesus has made His strength felt in my soul and my heart not being able to resist it, the wound in that part has opened and poured out blood.

THE CROWING WITH THORNS[10]

At last, this evening [July 19, 1900], after six days of suffering from the absence of Jesus, I have been a little recollected. I went to my prayer as I usually do every Thursday, and began to think of the Crucifixion of Jesus. At first I did not feel anything but after some moments I became rapt in thought, Jesus was near. My state of recollection was followed as usual by the loss of my senses, and I found myself with Jesus Who was suffering terrible pain. How could I bear to see Jesus suffering and not help Him? Then I felt myself consumed by an unquenchable desire to suffer; and begged and entreated of Jesus to grant me this grace. He gratified me at once, and drawing near to me He took the Crown of Thorns from His own Head, placed it on mine, and with His Holy Hands fixed it on my temples. These are painful moments, but happy ones. Thus I passed an hour with Jesus.

THE SCOURGING[11]

Friday [March, 1901] about two o'clock Jesus let me feel some slight blows. Father, I am all scars that cause me a little suffering. Jesus be praised for ever! . . . But are they Thy Stripes, O Jesus? . . . First they were switchings, now they are scourgings.

THE BLOODY SWEAT[12]

Monsignor, one of my aunts, yesterday when I went to my room, followed me in a great rage, and said:—"This evening thou has not thy sister Julia to defend thee, let me see at once whence all that blood has come or I will beat thee into obedience." I remained silent, while she with one hand held my throat and with the other tried to undress me. She did not succeed; just then the bell rang and she left me. . . . But that was not all:—When I was going to bed she returned saying that is was time to put an end to these fooleries and that I had done enough to deceive others. "If thou dost not tell me," she said, "whence that blood has come, I will not allow thee to leave the house alone, or send thee anywhere." You can imagine that at those words I began to cry, and knew not what to do. At last I determined to tell her, and answered thus: "Blasphemies are the cause; I see how much they make Jesus suffer, and I suffer with Him, and my heart suffers, and that blood comes from it!" She then cooled a little and left me alone. . . .

Yesterday Jesus made me suffer greatly. I sweated blood all day; but not at home; it was with Signora Cecilia Giannini. Jesus continually warns me not to let my personal happenings get known; otherwise he punishes me. He always tells me that I ought to be ashamed to let myself be seen by anyone being so full of defects. . . .

THE SHOULDER WOUND FROM CARRYING THE CROSS[13]
"Gemma, wilt thou have it, My Cross? See, this is the present I have prepared for thee." My Jesus, yes, give it me, but give me also strength, because my shoulders are weak; at least that I may not fall under it.". . .

ECSTATIC PRAYER[14]
When I place myself to meditate, I use no effort. My soul immediately feels itself absorbed, in the immense greatness of God, now lost at one point, now at another. But first I begin by making my soul reflect, that being made to the image and likeness of God, He alone has to be her end. Then in a moment, it seems that my soul flies away to God, loses the weight of the body, and finding myself in the presence of Jesus, I lose myself totally in Him. I feel that I love the heavenly Lover of His creatures; the more I think of Him the more I come to know how sweet and lovable He is. Sometimes I think I see in Jesus a divine light and a sun of eternal brightness, a God so great that there is nothing on earth or in heaven that is not subject to Him, a God in Whose Will is all power. . . . I lose myself also in His Goodness and here almost always my mind flies to paradise. . . .

On entering into prayer I behold Jesus not with the eyes of my body but I recognize Him distinctly; because He makes me lapse into a blissful abandonment and in this total surrender I know

Him. His voice is heard by me with such force that, as I have often said, it cuts more than a double-edged sword, so deeply does it enter into my soul. His words are of eternal life. When I thus see Jesus and hear Him I don't seem to perceive beauty of body, nor figure, nor sweet sound, nor charming song; but when I see and hear Him, I see an infinite Light, and immense Good. His voice is not an articulate voice, but it is stronger, and makes itself more felt in my soul than if I heard pronounced words. . . .

FINDING GOD IN ALL THINGS[15]

Imagine that you see a light of immense splendor, that penetrates everything, and at the same time gives life and animation to all, so that whatever exists has its being from this light and in it lives. Thus I see my God and creatures in Him. Imagine a fiery furnace, great as the universe, nay, infinitely greater, that burns everything without consuming anything, and burning illuminates and strengthens, and those who are most penetrated by its flames are happiest, and desire more ardently to be consumed. Thus I see our souls in God.

TRINITARIAN MYSTICISM[16]

I seem to behold three Persons within a boundless light, all three united in one essence; trinity in unity and unity in trinity, and as the essence of the Trinity is but one, so one only is its goodness, one only its beatitude.

GUARDIAN ANGEL EXPERIENCES[17]

[And her guardian angel appeared and said to her]: "Yes I shall be thy guide and inseparable companion. Dost thou not know who it is that gave me charge of thee? It is the merciful Jesus. . . ."

My Angel is a little severe, but I am glad of it. During the past days he brought me to order as often as three or four times a day. . . . Yesterday while at table I raised my eyes and saw the Angel looking at me with a severity that would frighten one. Later when I went to rest a little, O my God, how angry he was! I looked at him but lowered my eyes immediately. "Art thou not ashamed," he said, "to commit faults in my presence?". . . . Every now and then he repeated: "I am ashamed of thee." I prayed also that others might not see him so angry; for if they did no one could come near me. . . . I should have so liked to ask his pardon, but when he is angry there is no chance of his granting it. . . .

The Angel Guardian, while I was making my evening prayer, came near and touched me on the shoulder saying: "Gemma, why such great distaste for prayer?" No, I answered, it is not distaste; I have not been well for two days; and he added: "Do thy part assiduously and Jesus, thou wilt see, wilt love thee still more." I begged of him to ask Jesus for leave to pass the night by me. He disappeared at once, and when he got leave from Jesus to stay he returned. Oh! He was so kind, and when we was about to go I besought him not to leave me yet; but he said: "I must go." Go then, I replied, and salute Jesus for me. He gave a last look at me and said: "It is my wish that thy conversation be no longer with creatures; when thou dost wish to speak, speak with Jesus, and with thy Angel. . . .

SATANIC EXPERIENCES[18]
Be prepared My child; the devil at My bidding shall be the one who by the war he will wage against thee, will give the last touch to the work that I [Christ] will accomplish in thee. . . .

Oh! what torment this gives me, not to be able to pray! What fatigue it costs me! How many efforts does not that wretch [the devil] make to render it impossible for me to pray! Yesterday evening he tried to kill me, and would have succeeded if Jesus had not come quickly to my aid. I was terrified and kept the image of Jesus in my mind, but I could not pronounce His name. . . .

[Gemma reports that she heard these demonic words]: "What art thou doing? Stupid that thou art to think of praying to a malefactor. Look at the harm He [Christ] does thee, keeping thee nailed to the Cross with Himself. How then canst thou care for Him, for Him Whom thou dost not even know—Who makes all who love Him suffer?"

For some days Chiappino [a name she called the devil] has pursued me in every guise and way, and has done all in his power against me. This monster keeps on redoubling all his efforts to ruin me and tries to deprive me of whoever directs and advises me. But even should this happen, I am not afraid. . . .

Once more I have passed a bad night. The demon came before me as a giant of great height. He beat me fiercely all night, and kept saying to me: "For thee there is no more hope of salvation; thou art in my hands." I replied that God is merciful, and that therefore I feared nothing. Then giving me a hard blow on the head he said in a rage, "Accursed be thou!" and disappeared. I went to my room to rest a little and there I found him. He began again to strike me with a knotted rope, and kept on because he wanted me to listen to him while he suggested wickedness. I said no, and he struck me harder, and knocked my head violently against the ground. At a certain moment it came to my mind to invoke Jesus' Holy Abba. I called aloud: "Eternal Father through the most Precious Blood free me!" I don't quite know what happened; that contemptible beast dragged me violently from my bed and threw me, dashing my head against the floor with such force that it pains me still. I became senseless and remained lying there until I came to myself a long time afterward. Jesus be thanked!

Come quickly father [Germano], or at least repeat the exorcisms at a distance; the devil is doing all he can against me. Help me to save my soul, for I fear I am already in the power of Satan. Ah! if you only knew how much I am suffering! Last night how contented he was! He took me by the hair and tore it away saying: "Disobedience, disobedience! now there is no more time to amend; come, come with me"; and he wanted to take me to hell. He remained more than four hours tormenting me, and thus I passed the night. I fear so much that listening to him I may displease Jesus.

Oh! God, I have been in hell, without Jesus, without Mary, without my Angel. If I have come out of it without sin, I owe it, Oh Jesus, to Thee alone. And yet I am contented, because suffering thus and suffering ceaselessly I know that I am doing Thy most Holy Will. . . .

The phrase, "in the heaven of my soul," summarizes the doctrine and inner life of the French Carmelite, Elizabeth of the Trinity. To her, "to remain at the Source" in union and love summed up all holiness and the entire apostolate. Elizabeth averred that her spiritual motherhood, her mission would continue even after death.

ELIZABETH OF THE TRINITY

Elizabeth Catez was born on July 18, 1880 at the military camp of Avor in the district of Farges-en-Septaine (Cher), France, where her father was stationed as a military officer. Both her grandfather and father died when she was seven years old. This vivacious, outgoing, friendly, socially successful, iron-willed girl loved sports, nature, and won first prize for piano at the Conservatory in Dijon. Her musical talent shows itself in the rhythmical cadence of her writings. Pious and gifted for recollection, she enjoyed herself everywhere while praying everywhere.

At 14, Elizabeth took a vow of perpetual virginity and began to think seriously of a vocation to the local Carmelite monastery. When she was 17, she asked permission to enter Carmel, but her mother told her to wait. Nonetheless, as a laywoman, Elizabeth lived the Carmelite life as much as possible before she entered the order at 21. As a member of the zealous Dijon Carmelite community under the able leadership of Mother Germaine of Jesus, Elizabeth deepened her already considerable gifts for silence, recollection, and prayer in the "little cell of her heart."

Elizabeth's spiritual life was also influenced by Père Vallé, the well-known Dijon Dominican preacher, and by her readings of St. Thérèse of Lisieux, St. Teresa of Avila, and St. John of the Cross. She lacked a formal education but possessed an exceptional ability to get to the heart of John's Gospel and the Pauline writings.

Elizabeth deeply appreciated the God "who is all Love" and the mystery of the indwelling Trinity whose spouse she would soon become. For her, the saints had mystically penetrated and assimilated the mystery of how much we are loved by the God who is "all love," the Trinity who creates heaven in us. The key phrase throughout her writings, "in the heaven of my soul," summarizes her doctrine and inner life.

For Elizabeth, the life of the Virgin Mary from the annunciation to the nativity is the perfect exemplar of the interior life. In fact, the goal of Carmelite life is to be an Advent to prepare for God's incarnation—not only in oneself but also in others. "Even in the midst of the world," she wrote, "one can listen to Him in the silence of a heart that beats only for Him." Inner silence, to the extent that even the soul is quiet, is the condition for listening to the instructions of the divine Word dwelling within.

But Elizabeth sought more than constant recollection, unceasing prayer, and the enjoyment of the trinitarian life. She also desired her life to be one of perpetual adoration. In fact, she considered her existence as the "praise of Glory." Moreover, Elizabeth maintained that the person devoted to the trinitarian indwelling could become an apostle of the praise of the Trinity's glory.

Elizabeth viewed her entire Carmelite life as apostolic, as fruitful for others. To be an apostle means to "remain at the Source." For her, two words summed up all holiness and the entire apostolate: Union and Love. "I wish," she wrote, "to be wholly silent, wholly adoring, so that I may enter into Him ever more deeply and be so filled with Him that I can give Him through prayer to these poor souls who are unaware of the Gift of God."[1] Holiness was simple: to live by love.

Elizabeth considered her vocation to be apostolic in another sense. Because Jesus was a victim for the sake of our salvation, she desired to be "another humanity in which He can renew His whole Mystery," especially that of the Passion. She wanted nothing less than mystical death, to have her whole substance consumed, to feel her being distilled drop by drop—but as an oblation for the salvation of others. Her victim soul mysticism reached its peak during the year on her sickbed. She died saying, "I am going to Light, to Love, to Life."

Elizabeth averred that her spiritual motherhood, her mission would continue even after death. "Even in heaven," she wrote, "my mission will be to draw souls by helping them to go out of themselves in order to cling to God by a wholly simple and loving movement, and to keep them in this great silence, which will allow God to communicate Himself to them and to transform them into Himself."[2] She was beatified in 1984.

The selections were chosen to illustrate Elizabeth's emphasis upon a God who is all love, her sense of the mystery of the divine indwelling, our predestination to be Christ's likeness, her desire to suffer for the sake of others, and her affection for others. The texts also illustrate a profound grasp of Christianity's social dimension, of how even hidden prayer and sacrifice influence others, and of how the saints in heaven relate to those on earth. The passage, "To be the Bride of Christ," and Elizabeth's famous prayer to the Trinity can be read as a summary of her mystical life and teaching.[3]

THE TEXTS

"Always believe in Love"[4]

Dear little sister, do you really know what riches you have? Have you ever sounded the bottomless depths of Love? I am going to make known to you the unutterable tenderness that hovers over your soul both night and day. O my Marguerite, with just a perfectly simple gaze, contemplate the "hidden Mystery" that is taking place in your heart: Look, the Holy Spirit chooses you for his temple, You no longer belong to yourself. . .and that is your greatness! Beneath his divine touch, oh, persevere in silence so that he may imprint upon you the likeness of the Lord. You were predestined to bear this resemblance By a mysterious design of the Creator. Truly, you are no longer yourself, but you are becoming Himself, the transformation is taking place at every moment. Give thanks to the

Savior for this sublime decree of his, May your soul be plunged into adoration. . . "Always believe in Love" in spite of everything that happens.

"I feel so much love on my soul"[5]

I feel so much love on my soul; it's like an ocean into which I plunge and lose myself. That is my vision here on earth, while I await the vision face to face in light. He is in me, and I am in him. I have only to love him, to let myself be loved, and to do that always and in everything. To wake up in Love, move about in Love, fall asleep in Love, my soul in his soul, my heart in his heart, my eyes within his eyes, so that by my contact with him, he will purify me and free me from my wretchedness.

"To be the prey of Love"

During the night that preceded the great day [of her Profession], while I was in choir awaiting the Spouse, I understood that my Heaven was beginning on earth—Heaven in faith, with suffering and self-sacrifice for Him whom I love. . . . I so wish to love Him, to love Him as my seraphic Holy Mother Teresa did, even to dying of it, and that is my whole ambition: to be the prey of love. . . .

I do not know if I will have the happiness of giving to my Spouse the witness of my blood of martyrdom, but at least, if I fully live my Carmelite life, I have the consolation of spending myself for Him, for Him alone.

What difference does the work which He wills for me make. Since He is always with me, prayer, the heart-to-heart exchange should never end! I feel Him so alive in my soul. I have only to recollect myself to find Him within me, and that is all my happiness.

He has placed within my heart a thirst for the infinite, and such a great need to love, that He alone can satisfy it. I go to Him, like a little child to its mother, so He may fill, may possess everything, and may take me and carry me away in His arms. I think that we must be so simple with God. . .![6]

It is God who is pleased to immolate His little sacrifice, but this Mass which He is saying with me, and of which His love is the priest, may last a long time yet. Time in the Hand of Him who is sacrificing her does not seem long to the little victim, and she can say that, if she takes the path of suffering, she still stays much more on the road of happiness, of the true happiness, darling Mama, which no one can take from her. . . .[7]

More and more I am drawn to suffering; this desire almost surpasses the one for Heaven, though that was very strong. Never has God made me understand so well that suffering is the greatest pledge of love He can give His creature. Oh, you see, with each new suffering, I kiss the Cross of my Master, and I say to Him: "Thank you, I am not worthy of it," for I think how suffering was the companion of His life, and I do not deserve to be treated as His Father treated Him. In speaking of Jesus Christ, one saint wrote: "Where, then, did He dwell but in suffering?" (and David sang that this suffering was as immense as the sea). Every soul crushed by suffering in whatever form it may occur, can tell itself: I dwell with Jesus Christ, we are living in intimacy, the same dwelling shelters us! The saint of whom I just spoke says that the sign by which we recognize that God is in us and that His love possesses us is that we receive not only patiently but gratefully whatever wounds us and makes us suffer. To reach that state, we must contemplate the God crucified by love, and that contemplation, if it is true, never fails to end in the love of suffering. Darling Mama, receive every trial, every annoyance, every lack of courtesy in the light that springs from the Cross; that is how we please God, how we advance in the ways of love. . . .[8]

"A Carmelite. . . is a soul who has gazed on the Crucified"[9]
A Carmelite, my darling, is a soul who has gazed on the Crucified, who has seen Him offering Himself to His Father as a victim for souls and, recollecting herself in this great vision of the charity of Christ, has understood the passionate love of His soul, and has wanted to give herself as He did! . . . And on the mountain of Carmel in silence, in solitude, in a prayer that never ends, for it continues through everything, the Carmelite already lives as it were in Heaven: "by God alone." The same One who will one day be her beatitude and will fully satisfy her in glory is already giving Himself to her, He never leaves her, He dwells within her soul; more than that, the two of them are but one. So she hungers for silence

that she may always listen, penetrate ever further into His Infinite
Being. She is identified with Him whom she loves, she finds Him
everywhere; she sees Him shining through all things! Is this not
Heaven on earth? You carry this Heaven within your soul, my little
Germaine, you can be a Carmelite already, for Jesus recognizes the
Carmelite from within, by her soul. Don't ever leave Him, do every-
thing beneath His divine gaze, and remain wholly joyful in His
peace and love, making those around you happy!

"Staying at the source"[10]

... Don't you find that in action, when we are carrying out
Martha's role, the soul can remain wholly adoring, buried like Magdalene in her contemplation, staying by this source like someone
who is starving; and this is how I understand the Carmelite's apostolate as well as the priest's. Then both can radiate God, give Him
to souls, if they constantly stay close to this divine source. It seems
to me that we should draw so close to the Master, to be in such communion with His soul, to identify ourselves with all its movements,
and then to go out as He did, according to the will of His Father.
Then it does not matter what happens to the soul, since it has faith
in the One it loves and who dwells within it. During this Lent I
would like, as Saint Paul says, "to be buried in God with Christ" to
be lost in this Trinity who will one day be our vision, and in this divine light penetrate into the depth of the Mystery. Would you pray
that I may be wholly surrendered and that my Beloved Bridegroom
may carry me away wherever He wishes. A Dieu, Monsieur
l'Abbé!, let us remain in His love. Is He not that infinity for which
our souls thirst?

"Molded into the pattern of his death"[11]

How I love the thought from St. Paul that you sent me. It seems to
me as though it were being realized in me on this little bed, which
is the altar on which I am offering myself to Love.

Oh, ask that my likeness to the beloved Image may be each day
more perfect: "Configuratus morti ejus." There again you see what
haunts me, what gives strength to my soul in suffering. If you only
knew what a work of destruction I feel in my whole being. The
road to Calvary opens out before me and I am full of joy to walk

along it like a bride at the side of the divine crucified one. On the 18th, I shall be 26. I don't know whether this year will end for me in time or in eternity, and I ask you as a child asks its father to be kind enough to consecrate me at holy Mass as a victim of praise of God's glory. Oh, consecrate me so completely that I shall no longer be me, but He, and that the Father may recognize him when he looks at me. May I be "molded into the pattern of his death" that I may suffer in myself what is lacking to his passsion for his body which is the Church. Then bathe me in the blood of Christ that I may be strong with his strength.

"The fulfillment of Christ's prayer"[12]

Don't you find that with souls there is no distance at all, no separation? It is surely the fulfillment of Christ's prayer, "Father, that they may be completely one." It seems to me that the souls on earth and those glorified in the light of the beatific vision are so close to one another because they all commune with the same God, with the same Father, who gives himself to those on earth in faith and mystery, and feasts others on his divine glory. But he is the same God and we bear him within us. He is bending over us with all his love, day and night longing to communicate with us, to infuse his divine life into us so as to make us into deified beings who radiate him everywhere. Oh, what power over souls has the apostle who always stays close to the source of living water! Then he can overflow to those around him without his soul ever becoming empty because he is in communion with the Infinite! . . .

"To be the bride of Christ"[13]

To be the bride of Christ! "Bride," I must live all that this name implies of love given and received, of intimacy, of fidelity, of absolute devotion! To be a bride means to be given as He gave Himself; it means to be sacrificed as He was, by Him, for Him. It is Christ making Himself all ours and we becoming "all His!"

To be a bride means to have all rights over His Heart. It is a heart-to-heart exchange for a whole lifetime. It is to live with, always with Christ. It means to rest from everything in Him, and to allow Him to rest from everything in our soul! It means to know nothing else than to love, to love while adoring, to love while making reparation, to love while praying, while asking, while forgetting oneself; to love always in every way!

To be a bride means to have eyes only for Him, our thoughts, haunted by Him, our heart wholly taken over, wholly possessed, as if it had passed out of itself and into Him; our souls filled with His soul, filled with His prayer, our whole being captivated and given. It means, by keeping our gaze always fixed on His, to discover His least sign, His least desire; it means to enter into all His joys, to share all His sadness. It means to be fruitful, a co-redeemer, to bring souls to birth in grace, to multiply the adopted children of the Father, the redeemed of Christ, the co-heirs of His glory.

To be a bride, a bride of Carmel, means to have the flaming heart of Elijah, the transpierced heart of Teresa, his "true bride," because she was zealous for His honor.

Finally, to be taken as bride, a mystical bride, means to have ravished His Heart to the extent that, forgetting all distance, the Word pours Himself out in the soul as in the bosom of the Father with the same ecstasy of infinite love! It is the Father, the Word, and the Spirit possessing the soul, deifying it, consuming it in the One by love.

"Trinity, whom I adore"[14]

O my God, Trinity, whom I adore, help me to forget myself entirely that I may be established in You as still and as peaceful as if my soul were already in eternity. May nothing trouble my peace or make me leave You, O my Unchanging One, but may each minute carry me further into the depths of Your Mystery. Give peace to my soul; make it Your heaven, Your beloved dwelling, and Your resting place. May I never leave You there alone but be wholly present, my faith wholly vigilant, wholly adoring, and wholly surrendered to Your creative Action.

O my beloved Christ, crucified by love, I wish to be a bride for Your heart; I wish to cover You with glory; I wish to love you. . .even unto death! But I feel my weakness, and I ask You to "clothe me with Yourself," to identify my soul with all the movements of Your Soul, to overwhelm me, to possess me, to substitute Yourself for me that my life may be but a radiance of Your Life. Come into me as Adorer, as Restorer, as Savior. O Eternal Word, Word of my God, I want to spend my life in listening to You, to become wholly teachable that I may learn all from You. Then, through all nights, all voids, all helplessness, I want to gaze on You always and remain in Your great light. O my beloved Star, so fascinate me that I may not withdraw from Your radiance.

O consuming Fire, Spirit of Love, "come upon me," and create in my soul a kind of incarnation of the Word: that I may be another humanity for Him in which He can renew His whole Mystery. And You, O Father, bend lovingly over Your poor little creature; "cover her with Your shadow," seeing in her only the "Beloved in whom You are well pleased."

O my Three, my All, my Beatitude, infinite Solitude, Immensity in which I lose myself, I surrender to You as Your prey. Bury Yourself in me that I may bury myself in You until I depart to contemplate in Your light the abyss of Your greatness.

Faustina Kowalska has been called the "Apostle of Divine Mercy." An example of prophetic mysticism, she received divine revelations (concerning a devotion to divine mercy) and a mission to the universal Church that it and its members should heed. No one has written so simply and movingly about the need to pray for others, especially the dying.

M. FAUSTINA KOWALSKA

Helena Kowalska was born on August 25, 1905, in the village of Glogowiec, near Lodz, Poland. After a pious childhood, and without completing her elementary school education, Helena began doing household work in Aleksandrow, and then in Lodz, when she was 14 years old. She entered the Congregation of the Sisters of Our Lady of Mercy in 1925, and took the religious name Mary Faustina, and worked mainly at domestic tasks in various houses of her Congregation. From the time she entered religious life, she was afflicted with ill health, and she died from tuberculosis on October 5, 1938 in Cracow.

Outwardly, Faustina lived the "ordinary" life of an untalented and deeply pious nun. She kept a diary because her confessors, the Rev. M. Sopocko and Father J. Andrasz, S.J., commanded her to do so. Furthermore, Christ himself had ordered her to write so that after her death many others might derive strength and consolation from what she had recorded about divine mercy.

Her diary, *Divine Mercy in My Soul: The Diary of the Servant of God Sister M. Faustina Kowalska, Perpetually Professed Member of the Congregation of Sisters of Our Lady of Mercy,*[1] reveals a person who has traveled the entire mystical path. Moreover, Faustina asserts that God himself assured her that she would become a saint. She also attests that God gave her the mission to make known the divine mercy while praising it both on earth and in heaven.

Her *Diary* indicates that Faustina experienced mystical locutions from Christ, Our Lady, her guardian angel, and some of the saints. Ecstatic visions, mystical transports, an ability to read what was in another's heart (hierognosis), and prophetic insights punctuated her outwardly prosaic life. She often sensed when others were praying for her and when others needed her prayers.

As a "disciple of a crucified Master," Faustina's passion mysticism allowed her to participate fully in Christ's redemptive sufferings and death. Although she was never given the stigmata, she experienced these wounds profoundly on Fridays and during Holy Week.

The selected texts here printed indicate that Faustina was convinced of the authenticity of private revelations concerning the devotion to divine mercy. Thus, she is an example of those mystics in the Christian tradition whose mysticism contains a "prophetic" dimension, that is, those who receive divine revelations and assurance of a mission to the universal Church that it and its members must heed. The lives of these mystics indicate that the line between the mystic and the prophet must not be too sharply drawn.

Faustina maintains that Christ ordered her to have a picture painted of the merciful Christ, to establish the first Sunday after Easter as the Feast of Divine Mercy, to pray the rosary in a particular way to obtain the grace of a merciful death, and to found a religious congregation devoted to the divine mercy (founded after her death by the Rev. Sopocko). Thus, she devoted herself—particularly through her confessor, Sopocko—to the propagation of this devotion to divine mercy, which developed rapidly in Poland and in Polish centers in foreign lands.

The prophetic dimension of Faustina's mysticism manifests itself in yet another way. Her *Diary* states that Christ told her that both her and Sopocko's efforts in regard to this devotion would be severely tested, but would eventually triumph. Twenty years after her death, that is, in 1958, the Holy See, because of inaccurate information it had received, forbade the devotion to divine mercy as it had been popularized and severely censured Sopocko. The censures were revoked in 1978 after consultation with Polish bishops and after the Holy See had gained access to many pertinent original documents.

The devotion to divine mercy enjoyed an immediate renaissance and attained a more solid theological foundation. It is no coincidence that Pope John Paul II's 1980 encyclical, *On the Mercy of God (Dives in misericordia)*, was influenced by Faustina's writings. In fact, as Archbishop of Cracow, Karol Cardinal Wojtyla (Pope John Paul II) in 1967 was deeply involved in the initial informative process for Faustina's beatification. In 1969, this process was formally inaugurated.

The selections also indicate the profundity of Faustina's experience of both God's holiness and her own nothingness. A God-given sensitivity to the least imperfection motivated her to rid herself of everything that hindered the divine communication. Faustina's initial intimacy with God gave way to a dark night of spirit in which she saw only her faults and her sinfulness. She concomitantly experienced demonic assaults, an aversion for the interior life, and a strong sense that she had been justifiably rejected by God. In conjunction with her ill health, community backbiting and envy concerning her divine mission, and the deterioration of her body, this dark night brought her to the brink of despair.

As the texts indicate, she came through this dark night because of her obedience to superiors' command to continue to receive Holy Communion, despite her feelings of unworthiness. One aspect of Faustina's mysticism is eucharistic. Undergoing transforming union, she then experienced almost continual communion with God and the gift to see God almost face to face. Exceptional trinitarian insights and communications punctuated the rest of her life.

The selections underscore Faustina's God-given mission to "win souls" through prayer and sacrifice. Convinced that God asked her to be a victim soul to make reparation for the world's sins and to be the vehicle of God's mercy to hardened sinners—especially at the hour of their death—Faustina consented to becoming such a victim with her entire being. She then received the name "sacrifice," and experienced her "transconsecration."

The texts were in part selected to illustrate her wrath-of-God-the-Father theology that has a long history in the Christian tradition. According to this theology, Christ's sacrificial death appeases the Father's anger engendered by sin. The sacrifice "shields" the sinner from the Father's blazing wrath. Thus, Faustina sought to unite herself to Christ's redemptive passion and death through prayer and sacrifice in order to make reparation for the world's sins. However, it must be emphasized that one need not accept this theology to appreciate the undeservedly neglected insight that prayer and sacrifice do heal and transform the evils caused by sin.

The texts illustrate that, like Thérèse of Lisieux, Faustina experienced mystically that prayer and sacrifice were her mission to the world. In her view, even the most humble task, done through pure love, had more direct apostolic consequences than the sermons of missionaries. Her insights into how one's personal holiness influences the entire Church are especially significant.

As the texts indicate, Faustina stressed the importance of confessors and spiritual directors in one's spiritual life. A good director was one of God's greatest gifts. To her, confessors and directors were identical with Christ.

Unique in the Christian mystical tradition is Faustina's evocative and provocative description of the conversion of a hardened sinner at the hour of his death through her intercession. Perhaps no one has written so simply and movingly about need to pray for others, especially the dying. The texts illustrate why she has been called the "Apostle of Divine Mercy."[2]

THE TEXTS

DIVINE MERCY IN MY SOUL[3]
February 22, 1931

47. In the evening, when I was in my cell, I saw the Lord Jesus clothed in a white garment. One hand [was] raised in the gesture of blessing, the other was touching the garment at the breast. From beneath the garment, slightly drawn aside at the breast, there were

emanating two large rays, one red, the other pale. In silence, I kept my gaze fixed on the Lord; my soul was struck with awe but also with great joy. After a while, Jesus said to me, *Paint an image according to the pattern you see, with the signature: Jesus, I trust in You. I desire that this image be venerated, first in your chapel, and [then] throughout the world.*

48. *I promise that the soul that will venerate this image will not perish. I also promise victory over [its] enemies already here on earth, especially at the hour of death. I Myself will defend it as My own glory.*

49. When I told this to my confessor, I received this for a reply: "That refers to your soul." He told me, "Certainly, paint God's image in your soul." When I came out of the confessional, I again heard words such as these: *My image is already in your soul. I desire that there be a Feast of Mercy, which you will paint with a brush, to be solemnly blessed on the first Sunday after Easter; that Sunday is to be the Feast of Mercy.*

50. *I desire that priests proclaim this great mercy of Mine toward souls of sinners. Let the sinner not be afraid to approach Me. The flames of mercy are burning Me—clamoring to be spent; I want to pour them out upon these souls.*

Jesus complained to me in these words: *Distrust on the part of souls is tearing at My insides. The distrust of chosen souls causes Me even greater pain; despite My inexhaustible love for them, they do not trust Me. Even My death is not enough for them. Woe to the soul that abuses these [gifts].*

51. When I spoke about this to Mother Superior [Rose, telling her] that God had asked this of me, she answered that Jesus should give some sign so that we could recognize Him more clearly.

When I asked the Lord Jesus for a sign as a proof "that You are truly my God and Lord and that this request comes from You," I heard this interior voice: *I will make this all clear to the Superior by means of the graces which I will grant through this image.*

95. A Deeper Knowledge of God and the Terror of the Soul

In the beginning God, lets himself be known as Holiness, Justice, and Goodness—that is to say, Mercy. The soul does not come to know this all at once, but piecemeal, in flashes; that is to say, when God draws near. And this does not last for long, because the soul could not bear such light. . . .

But this same flash, at the same time, allows the soul to know itself as it is; the soul sees its whole interior in a superior light and rises up alarmed and terrified. Still, it does not remain under the effects of terror, but it begins to purify itself, to humble and abase itself before the Lord. These lights become stronger and more frequent; the more the soul is crystallized, the more these lights penetrate it.... At certain moments, the soul, as it were, enters into intimacy with God and greatly rejoices in this; it believes that it has already reached the degree of perfection destined for it because its defects and faults are asleep within it, and this makes it think that they no longer exist. Nothing seems difficult for it; it is ready for everything. It begins to plunge itself into God and taste the divine delights. It is carried along by grace and does not take account of the fact that the time of trial and testing may come. . . .

96. Trials sent by God to a soul which is particularly loved by Him. Temptations and darkness; Satan.

The soul's love [for God] is still not such as God would have it. The soul suddenly loses the tangible perception of God's presence. Various defects and imperfections rise up within it, and it must fight them furiously. All its faults lift up their heads, but the soul's vigilance is great. The former awareness of the presence of God gives place to coldness and spiritual dryness; the soul has no taste for spiritual exercises; it cannot pray, either in the old manner or in the manner in which it had just begun to pray. . . . God has hidden himself from it, and it can find no consolation in creatures. . . . The soul craves passionately for God, but sees its own misery; it begins to sense God's justice. . . . Its mind is dimmed, darkness fills it; unspeakable torment begins. . . . Satan begins his work.

97. Faith staggers under the impact; the struggle is fierce. . . . With God's permission, Satan goes even further: Hope and love are put to the test. These temptations are terrible. God supports the soul in secret, so to speak. . . .

The Trial of Trials, Complete Abandonment—Despair

98. . . . At this point, however, the soul is engulfed in a horrible night. It sees within itself only sin. It feels terrible. It sees itself completely abandoned by God. It feels itself to be the object of His hatred. It is but one step away from despair. . . . [P]rayer is an even greater torment for it, as this prayer seems to arouse God to an even greater anger. . . .

If God wishes to keep the soul in such darkness, no one will be able to give it light. It experiences rejection by God in a vivid and terrifying manner. . . . In the midst of this, the evil spirit adds to the soul's suffering, mocking it: ". . .You have been rejected by God!" This word, *rejected*, becomes a fire which penetrates every nerve to the marrow of the bone. It pierces right through [it]. The soul no longer looks for help anywhere. It shrinks into itself and loses sight of everything; it is as though it has accepted the torture of being abandoned. . . . This is the agony of the soul.

101. . . . When the soul has been saturated through and through by this infernal fire, it is, as it were, cast headlong into great despair. . .

103. Suddenly, I saw the Lord interiorly, and He said to me: *Fear not, My daughter, I am with you.* In that single moment, all the darkness and torments vanished, my senses were inundated with unspeakable joy, [and] the faculties of my soul filled with light.

105. However, in all these sufferings and struggles, I was not omitting Holy Communion. When it seemed to me that I should not communicate, I went, before Holy Communion, to the Directress and told her that I could not approach the Sacrament, because it seemed to me that I should not do so. But she would not permit me to omit Holy Communion, so I went, and I understand now that it was only obedience that saved me. . . .

135. During the third probation, the Lord gave me to understand that I should offer myself to Him so that He could do with me as He pleased. I was to remain standing before Him as a victim offering. . . . When I came to the adoration, I felt within my soul that I had entered the temple of the living God, whose majesty is great and incomprehensible. And He made known to me that even the purest spirits are in His sight. Although I saw nothing externally, God's presence pervaded me. At that very moment, my intellect

was strangely illuminated. A vision passed before the eyes of my soul; it was like the vision Jesus had in the Garden of Olives. First, the physical sufferings and all the circumstances that would increase them; [then] the full scope of the spiritual sufferings and those that no one would know about. Everything entered into the vision: false suspicions, loss of good name. . . . My name is to be: "sacrifice.". . .

136. And the Lord gave me to know that the whole mystery depended on me, on my free consent to the sacrifice given with full use of my faculties. . . . At that moment, I realized I was entering into communion with the incomprehensible Majesty. I felt that God was waiting for my word, for my consent. Then my spirit immersed itself in the Lord, and I said: "Do with me as You please. I subject myself to Your will. As of today, Your holy will shall be my nourishment, and I will be faithful to Your commands, with the help of Your grace. Do with me as You please. . . ."

137. Suddenly, when I had consented to the sacrifice with all my heart and will, God's presence pervaded me. My soul became immersed in God and was inundated with such happiness that I cannot put into writing even the smallest part of it. . . . Aware of this union with God, I felt I was especially loved and, in turn, I loved with all my soul. A great mystery took place during the adoration, a mystery between the Lord and myself. . . . And the Lord said to me, *You are the delight of My Heart; from now on, every one of your acts, even the very smallest, will be a delight to my eyes, whatever you do.* At that moment I felt transconsecrated. My earthly body was the same, but my soul was different; God was now living in it with the totality of His delight. This is not a feeling, but a conscious reality that nothing can obscure.

154. Once, there was adoration at the convent of the Sisters of the Holy Family, I went there in the evening with one of our sisters. As soon as I entered the chapel, the presence of God filled my soul. I prayed as I do at certain times without saying a word. Suddenly, I saw the Lord who said to me, *Know that if you neglect the matter of the painting of the image and the whole work of mercy, you will have to answer for a multitude of souls on the day of judgment. . . .*

299. When, on one occasion, my confessor told me to ask the Lord

the meaning of the two rays in the image, I answered, "Very well, I will ask the Lord."

During prayer I heard these words within me: *The two rays denote Blood and Water. The pale ray stands for the Water which makes souls righteous. The red ray stands for the Blood which is the life of souls.* . . .

These two rays issued forth from the very depths of My tender mercy when My agonized Heart was opened by a lance on the Cross. These rays shield souls from the wrath of My Father. Happy is the one who will dwell in their shelter, for the just hand of God shall not lay hold of him. I desire that the first Sunday after Easter be the Feast of Mercy.

300. *Ask of my faithful servant [Father Sopoko] that, on this day, he tell the whole world of My great mercy; that whoever approaches the Fount of Life on this day will be granted complete remission of sins and punishment. Mankind will not have peace until it turns with trust to My mercy. . . . My Heart rejoices in this title of Mercy.*

301. *Proclaim that mercy is the greatest attribute of God. All the works of My hands are crowned with mercy.*

417. [April] 26 . . .Then I heard the words, *You are a witness of My mercy. You shall stand before My throne forever as a living witness to My mercy.*

438. June 30, 1935. At the very beginning of Holy Mass on the following day, I saw Jesus in all His unspeakable beauty. He said to me that He desired that *such a Congregation be founded as soon as possible, and you shall live in it together with your companions. My Spirit shall be the rule of your life. Your life is to be modeled on Mine, from the crib to My death on the Cross. Penetrate My mysteries, for you will know the abyss of My mercy towards creatures and My unfathomable goodness—and this you shall make known to the world. Through your prayers, you shall mediate between heaven and earth.*

441. Once, the image was being exhibited over the altar during the Corpus Christi procession [June 20, 1935]. When the priest exposed the Blessed Sacrament, and the choir began to sing, the rays from the image pierced the Sacred Host and spread out all over the world. Then I heard these words: *These rays of mercy will pass through you, just as they have passed through this Host, and they will go*

out through all the world. At these words, profound joy invaded my soul.

475. The words with which I entreated God are these: *Eternal Father, I offer You the Body and Blood, Soul and Divinity of Your dearly beloved Son, Our Lord Jesus Christ for our sins and those of the whole world; for the sake of His sorrowful Passion, have mercy on us.*

476. The next morning, when I entered chapel, I heard these words interiorly: *Every time you enter the chapel, immediately recite the prayer which I taught you yesterday.* When I had said the prayer, in my soul I heard these words: *This prayer will serve to appease My wrath. You will recite it for nine days, on the beads of the rosary, in the following manner: First of all, you will say one OUR FATHER and HAIL MARY and the I BELIEVE IN GOD. Then on the OUR FATHER beads, you will say the following words: "Eternal Father, I offer you the Body and Blood, Soul and Divinity of Your dearly beloved Son, Our Lord Jesus Christ, in atonement for our sins and those of the whole word." On the HAIL MARY beads you will say the following words: "For the sake of His sorrowful Passion have mercy on us and on the whole world." In conclusion, three times you will recite these words: "Holy God, Holy Mighty One, Holy Immortal One, have mercy on us and on the whole world.*

767. My communion with the Lord is now purely spiritual. My soul is touched by God and wholly absorbs itself in Him, even to the complete forgetfulness of self. Permeated by God in its very depths, it drowns in His beauty; it completely dissolves in Him—I am at a loss to describe this, because in writing I am making use of the senses; but there, in that union, the senses are not active; there is a merging of God and the soul; and the life of God to which the soul is admitted is so great that the human tongue cannot express it. . . .

769. I have noticed that the Lord grants this grace to souls for two purposes. The first is when the soul is to do some great work which is, humanly speaking, absolutely beyond its power. In the second case, I have noticed that the Lord grants it in order that kindred souls might be guided and set at peace, although the Lord can grant this grace as He pleases and to whomever He pleases. . . .

770. . . . However, just as the Lord plunged me into these torments, so too He brought me out of them. Only this lasted for a few years,

after which I again received this extraordinary grace of union which has continued to this day. Still, during this second period of union, there also have been short interruptions. But for some time now, I have not experienced any interruption at all; on the contrary, I am more and more deeply steeped in God. The great light which illumines the mind gives me a knowledge of the greatness of God; but it is not as if I were getting to know the individual attributes, as before—no, it is different now: in one moment, I come to know the entire essence of God.

771. In that same moment, the soul drowns entirely in Him and experiences a happiness as great as that of the chosen ones in heaven. . . . However, the soul receiving this unprecedented grace of union with God cannot say that it sees God face to face, because even here there is a very thin veil of faith, but so very thin that the soul can say that it sees God and talks with Him. It is "divinized." God allows the soul to know how much He loves it, and the soul sees that better and holier souls than itself have not received this grace. Therefore, it is filled with holy amazement, which maintains it in deep humility, and it steeps itself in its own nothingness and holy astonishment; and the more it humbles itself, the more closely God unites himself with it and descends to it.

The soul, at this moment is, as it were, hidden; its senses are inactive; in one moment, it knows God and drowns in Him. It knows the whole depth of the Unfathomable One, and the deeper this knowledge, the more ardently the soul desires Him.

908. O Jesus, how sorry I feel for poor sinners. Jesus, grant them contrition and repentance. Remember Your own sorrowful Passion. I know Your infinite mercy and cannot bear it that a soul that has cost You so much should perish. Jesus, give me the souls of sinners; let Your mercy rest upon them. Take everything away from me, but give me souls. I want to become a sacrificial host for sinners. Let the shell of my body conceal my offering, for Your Most Sacred Heart is also hidden in a Host, and certainly You are a living sacrifice.

Transform me into Yourself, O Jesus, that I may be a living sacrifice and pleasing to You. I desire to atone at each moment for poor sinners. The sacrifice of my spirit is hidden under the veil of the body;

the human eye does not perceive it, and for that reason it is pure and pleasing to You. O my Creator and Father of great mercy, I trust in You, for You are Goodness Itself. Souls, do not be afraid of God, but trust in Him, for He is good, and His mercy is everlasting.

1129. During Holy Mass, I found myself suddenly united with the Most Holy Trinity. I recognized His majesty and greatness. I was united to the Three Persons. And once I was united to One of these Most Venerable Persons, I was at the same time united to the other Two Persons. . . .

1308. Jesus, I have noticed that You seem to be less concerned with me. *Yes, My child, I am replacing Myself with your spiritual director* [Father Andrasz]. *He is taking care of you according to My will. Respect his every word as My own. He is the veil behind which I am hiding. Your director and I are one; his words are my words.*

1698. I often attend upon the dying and through entreaties obtain for them trust in God's mercy, and I implore God for an abundance of divine grace, which is always victorious. God's mercy sometimes touches the sinner at the last moment in a wondrous and mysterious way. Outwardly, it seems as if everything were lost, but it is not so. The soul, illuminated by a ray of God's powerful final grace, turns to God in the last moment with such a power of love that, in an instant, it receives from God forgiveness of sin and punishment, while outwardly it shows no sign either of repentance or of contrition, because souls [at that stage] no longer react to external things. Oh, how beyond the comprehension is God's mercy! But—horror!—there are also souls who voluntarily and consciously reject and scorn this grace! Although a person is at the point of death, the merciful God gives the soul that interior vivid moment, so that if the soul is willing, it has the possibility of returning to God. But sometimes, the obduracy in souls is so great that consciously they choose hell; they [thus] make useless all the prayers that other souls offer to God for them and even the efforts of God Himself. . . .

1767. *My daughter, I want to instruct you on how you are to rescue souls through sacrifice and prayer. You will save more souls through prayer and suffering than will a missionary through his teachings and sermons alone. I want to see you as a sacrifice of living love, which only then carries weight before Me. You must be annihilated, destroyed, living as if you were dead in the most secret depths of your being. You must be destroyed in that secret depth where the human eye has never penetrated; then will I find in you a pleasing sacrifice, a holocaust full of sweetness and fragrance. And great will be your power for whomever you intercede. Outwardly, your sacrifice must look like this: silent, hidden, permeated with love, imbued with prayer. I demand, My daughter, that your sacrifice be pure and full of humility, that I may find pleasure in it. I will not spare My grace, that you may be able to fulfill what I demand of you.*

I will now instruct you on what your holocaust shall consist of, in everyday life, so as to preserve you from illusions. You shall accept all sufferings with love. Do not be afflicted if your heart often experiences repugnance and dislike for sacrifice. All its power rests in the will, and so these contrary feelings, far from lowering the value of the sacrifice in My eyes, will enhance it. Know that your body and soul will often be in the midst of fire. Although you will not feel My presence on some occasions, I will always be with you. Do not fear; My grace is with you. . . .

1768. *My daughter, in this meditation, consider the love of neighbor. Is your love for your neighbor guided by My love? Do you pray for your enemies? Do you wish well to those who have, in one way or another, caused you sorrow or offended you? Know that whatever good you do to any soul, I accept it as if you had done it to Me.*

1777. *My daughter, know that My Heart is mercy itself. From this sea of mercy, graces flow out upon the whole world. No soul that has approached Me has ever gone away unconsoled. All misery gets buried in the depths of My mercy, and every saving and sanctifying grace flows from this fountain. My daughter, I desire that your heart be an abiding place of My mercy. I desire that this mercy flow out upon the whole world through your heart. Let no one who approaches you go away without that trust in My mercy which I so ardently desire for souls. Pray as much as you can for the dying. By your entreaties, obtain for them trust in My mercy, because they have most need of trust, and have it the least. Be assured that the grace of eternal salvation for certain souls in their final moment depends upon your prayer. You know the whole abyss of My mercy, so draw upon it for yourself and especially for poor sinners. Sooner would heaven and earth turn into nothingness than would My mercy not embrace a trusting soul.*

Paleontologist, world traveler, poet, visionary, and mystic, the French Jesuit priest, Pierre Teilhard de Chardin, sought God in and through science and evolution. He wished to disclose to scientists the ultimate meaning and coherence of the universe that is both personal and loving because of "the science of Christ through all things."

PIERRE TEILHARD DE CHARDIN

Pierre Teilhard de Chardin was a Jesuit priest, distinguished scientist, paleontologist, world traveler, poet, visionary, and mystic. It is difficult to find someone who has lived such an intense spiritual and mystical life as Teilhard and yet was so passionately in love with his era. Intense love for science, the world, and their projects filled his soul. As scientist, Teilhard considered himself a priest performing a holy task. To him, science itself was mysticism, because "the scientist's quest, however positivistic he may claim it to be, is colored or haloed—or rather is invincibly animated, fundamentally by a mystical hope."[1]

Teilhard's genius consisted of uniting and reconciling in himself the two worlds of Christianity and science, the religions of heaven and earth. Within himself, he effected the "transformation...of the 'God of the Gospel' into the 'God of evolution'—a transformation without deformation."[2] Teilhard conceived his life's work as "christifying" evolution and disclosing "Christ the Evolver" at the heart of the evolutionary process. The synthesis of these scientific and mystical views was the hallmark of his abiding genius.

Born of a "gentleman farmer" and a devout mother in Sarcenat,

France, Teilhard entered the Jesuit novitiate at Aix-en-Province in 1899. He was ordained priest in 1911. Throughout his long years of Jesuit training in the classics, philosophy, and theology, he was attracted to the natural sciences, especially to geology and paleontology.

After serving as a stretcher-bearer in World War I, Teilhard completed his doctorate in paleontology at the Sorbonne in 1922. For almost 25 years, he worked in China, took part in numerous scientific expeditions to Central Asia, India, and Burma, and gained a notable reputation as a paleontologist. Returning to Paris to continue his research and writings in 1946, he subsequently undertook an archaeological expedition to South Africa (1951). After that, he settled at the Wenner Gren Foundation in New York City as a research scholar and he died there on Easter Sunday, April 10, 1955.

During his lifetime, Teilhard had been unable to obtain permission from his religious superiors to publish his philosophical, spiritual, and theological writings. Thus, his only published works had been scientific papers. But from 1955 on, his controversial writings were published, and the response received by his daring, brilliant, and creative synthesis of science and religion was exceptional. The essence of his scientific-mystical ideas may be found in *The Phenomenon of Man* and *The Divine Milieu*.

To Teilhard, the key to authenticity is seeing and participating in an evolution that permeates everything and literally converges on the person of Jesus Christ. He attempted to show to the scientist, whose research led to the chaos and meaninglessness of an infinity of galaxies and subatomic particles, that not only was the cosmos held together from above but was actually becoming the cosmic Christ. He wanted to convince believing Christians how important it is to take seriously the evolution of the cosmos, because in the incarnation God had descended into the very depths of matter so that "Christ is all, and in all" (Colossians 3:11). Human progress, evolution, a more humane world, and genuine Christianity were possible only by uniting with God the Evolver who was still creating the world. These ideas are reflected in his *Writings in Time of War*, *The Future of Man*, *Hymn of the Universe*, *The Heart of Matter*, *The Making of a Mind*, *Science and Christ*, and numerous other works.

It was especially Teilhard's scientific work that impelled him to explore the "mystical treasures hidden in the effort to know."[3] Believing that science and religion were the "two conjugated faces or phases of one and the same act of knowledge,"[4] he aroused the suspicion and hostility of scientists and Christians alike for calling their conventional wisdom into question.

This solitary explorer sought God in and through science and evolution. He wanted to show Christians how to discover the mystical vibration inherent in genuine scientific discovery. He also wished to disclose to scientists the ultimate meaning and coherence of the universe that is both personal and loving because of "the science of Christ through all things."[5] In Teilhard's view, Ignatius' finding God in all things applied especially to emphasizing the personal God of love as the source, the motor, and the goal of all scientific work.

According to Teilhard, all human striving, scientific or religious, must eventually lead to worship, adoration, and ecstasy. Science, evolution, religion, and mysticism therefore pertain to the one central longing of the human heart: to find a personal totality that it can ultimately love.

"I believe that the universe is an evolution," Teilhard wrote. "I believe that evolution proceeds toward spirit. I believe that in man, spirit is fully realized in person. I believe that the supremely personal is the Universal Christ."[6] As he saw it, nature's dynamism and direction are toward spirit, the human person, and Christ. Matter must become living and conscious, self-conscious, reflective, and free and finally see God through the eyes of Christ.

The text from "The Mystical Milieu" that follows was selected as a summary of Teilhard's mystical vision. To him, the mystical milieu in which a person lives is of a conjunction of five circles: presence, consistence, energy, spirit, and person. No circle can be understood and appreciated in isolation from the other circles. The selection also illustrates that the Teilhardian mystical journey consists of two phases: a descent into matter that eventually forces the mystic to reverse course; then an ascent to the circles of spirit (self-consciousness and freedom) and of person.

In the circle of presence, Teilhard's love of matter and the created world stands out. To him, the essential aspiration of *all* mysticism is to be united, to become the other, while remaining oneself. Thus, as the selected text indicates, Teilhard abhorred all mysticisms that diminished individuality, personhood, freedom, and self-consciousness. He had experienced profoundly creation's allure, how it enters into us and takes us out of ourselves. However, the mystic becomes aware of an "indefinite fringe of reality surrounding the totality of all created things."

The selected texts highlight that in the circle of consistence, the mystic suffers from the transitory nature of all created things but discovers the "ultimate Element" and the "Sovereign Consistence" that penetrates all things. In experiencing that only God is the Great Stability, the mystic is made free.

In the circle of energy, the mystic bathes in God's light and desires God as "Creative Action." There is a need to become an "instrument" and an actual extension of God's ongoing creative action. In this section, Teilhard emphasizes the need to live and to develop oneself. If one is to adore and to allow oneself to be possessed, one must first have a self to give away. Moreover, only unavoidable suffering is to be accepted.

In the circle of spirit, the mystic sees clearly that evolution's goal is to become self-conscious and free, and man, in Teilhard's understanding, is the "spearhead of evolution." In this circle, the mystic experiences a passion for progress and the realization that one actually co-creates the mystical milieu with God both through one's actions and one's sufferings. To develop science, to increase human freedom, to make the world a more humane place "thickens" the divine milieu. Nonetheless, Teilhard insists that genuine action also requires renunciation. In order to progress, one must become sensitive to the least creative impulse and not cling to pet projects and former accomplishments.

Despite his emphasis on the unifying and transforming power of secular activity, the texts indicate Teilhard's positive assessment of prayer and contemplation. To him, these activities generate nothing less than creative, evolutionary, and cosmic energies.

The selection also illustrates Teilhard's view that one becomes one-self by using one's talents to co-create the world with God. However, one must eventually surrender to setbacks, illnesses, and death. His sense is that one is hollowed out, filled with God, and transformed into a constitutive element in the divine milieu.

In the circle of person, the divine milieu takes on the human-divine face of Jesus. Just as Christ said "this is my body and blood" over the eucharistic bread and wine, Teilhard sees the entire evolutionary process as a cosmic communion. One can find Christ in all things because all things are in fact becoming the cosmic Christ.

The text indicates clearly why Teilhard has been called the mystic of matter, the mystic of evolution, the mystic of a universe actually becoming a person, a mystic of the cosmic Christ, and a mystic of the divine milieu.[7]

THE TEXTS

"THE MYSTICAL MILIEU"[8]
"In him we live and move and have our being"

A: THE CIRCLE OF PRESENCE
A limpid sound rises amidst the silence; a trail of pure color drifts through the glass; a light glows for a moment in the depths of the eyes I love. Three things, tiny, fugitive: a song, a sunbeam, a glance. So, at first, I thought they had entered into me in order to be lost in me. On the contrary: They took possession of me and bore me away.

For if this plaint of the air, this tinting of the light, this communication of a soul were so tenuous and fleeting it was only that they might penetrate the more deeply into my being, might pierce through to that final depth where all the faculties of man are so closely bound together as to become a single point. Through the sharp tips of the three arrows that had pierced me, the world itself had invaded my being and had drawn me back into itself. . . .

I felt my body, my soul, and even my spirit pass into the ethereal tint, unreal in its freshness, that caressed my eyes. Serene and iridescent, its color bathed more than my senses; it in some way impregnated my affections and thoughts. I melted away in it, lost in a strange yearning to attain some individuality vaster and simpler than mine—as though I had become pure light. . . .

The man who is wholly taken up with the demands of everyday living or whose *sole* interest is in the outward appearance of things seldom gains more than a glimpse, at best, of this second phase in our perceptions, that in which the world, having entered into us, then withdraws from us and bears us away with it: he can have only a very dim awareness of that aureole, thrilling and inundating our being, through which is disclosed to us at every point of contact the unique essence of the universe.

The mystic is the *man who is born to* give first place in his experience to that aureole. The mystic only gradually becomes aware of the faculty he has been given of perceiving the indefinite fringe of reality surrounding the totality of all created things, with more intensity than the precise, individual core of their being. . . .

But happy above all he to whom, rising beyond the aesthetic dilettantism and the materialism of the lower layers of life, it is given to hear the reply of all beings, singly and all together: "What you saw gliding past, like a world, behind the song and behind the color and behind the eyes' glance, does not exist just here or there but is a presence existing equally everywhere. . . . In this presence all diversities and all impurities yearn to be melted away."

When he has pursued to the end the vocation contained in all sense-perception—when his eyes have once become accustomed to the Light invisible in which both the periphery of beings and their center are bathed—then the seer perceives that he is immersed in a *universal Milieu*, higher than that which contains the restlessness of ordinary, sensible, apprehended life: a Milieu that *knows no change*, immune to the surge of superficial vicissitudes—a *homogeneous* Milieu in which contrasts and differences are toned down. . . .

Lord, it is you who, through the imperceptible goadings of sense-beauty, penetrated my heart in order to make its life flow out into yourself. . . . [Y]ou unfurled your immensity before my eyes and displayed yourself to me as Universal Being. . . .

Like every natural force [a single fundamental feeling underlying all mystical systems], that passion, as it develops, is liable to checks and perversions, to deviations. It can evaporate in futile poetry, it can be lost in naturalist mysticism, or take the degraded form of godless pantheism. Nevertheless, it remains true that this is the primordial, irrepressibly ebullient passion in the human heart.

If, then, a man is to build up in himself, for God, the structure of a sublime love, he must first of all sharpen his sensibility. By a familiar contact, prudent but untiring, with the most deeply emotive realities, he must carefully foster in himself his feeling for, his perception of, his zest for the Omnipresent which haloes everything in nature. . . .

B: THE CIRCLE OF CONSISTENCE
The basic mystical intuition has just led up to the discovery of a suprareal unity diffused throughout the immensity of the world. . . .

In that milieu, at once divine and cosmic, in which he had first observed only a simplification and, as it were, a spiritualization of space, the seer, faithful to the light given him, now perceives the gradual delineation of the form and attributes of an ultimate *Element* in which all things find their definitive consistence.

. . . The mystic suffers more than other men from the tendency of created things to *crumble into dust:* Instinctively and obstinately, he searches for the stable, the unfailing, the absolute; but so long as he remains in the domain of outward appearances, he meets with nothing but disappointment. . . . And yet everywhere there are traces of, and a yearning for, a unique support, a unique and absolute soul, a unique reality in which other realities are brought together in a synthesis as stable and universal as matter, as simple as spirit.

One must have felt deeply the pain of being plunged into that multiplicity which swirls about one and slips through one's fingers, if one is to be worthy of experiencing that rapture that transports the soul, when, through the unifying influence of that universal Presence, it perceives that reality has become not merely transparent but *solidly* enduring. For this means that the incorruptible principle of the universe is now and forever found and that it extends everywhere: *The world is filled,* and filled with the Absolute. To see this is to be made free. . . .

Beneath what is temporal and plural, the mystic can see only the unique Reality which is the support common to all substances and which clothes and dyes itself in all the universe's countless shades without sharing their impermanence. He knows the joy of feeling that Reality penetrates all things—wherever the mysterious light of the Omnipresent has shone—even into the very stuff of which his mental awareness, in the different forms it assumes, is made up. He soon comes to see the world as no more than the backwash of one essential Thing whose pleasure is to react upon itself, within the conscious mind it supports. . . .

Hitherto, Lord, my attitude toward your gifts has been that of a man who, feeling that he is not alone, tries to distinguish what influence is acting upon him in the darkness. Now that I have found the transparent consistence in which we are all held, I realize that *the mystical effort to see* must give way to *the effort to feel and to surrender myself.* This is the phase of communion. . . .

The power to appreciate and to open the heart is indispensable to the awakening and the maintenance of the mystical appetite. *But all the raptures they bring put together are not so effective as the icy chill of a disappointment* in knowing that you alone, my God, are stable. It is through sorrow, and not through joy, that your Godhead gradually assumes, *in our sentient faculty,* the higher Reality it possesses in the nature of things.

That is why, if some day—if not before, it will at least be on the day I die—everything should begin to fall away from me, if some total catastrophe should tear down the structure, based on all the things I have sought and loved, which makes up my life's work—then, when I see the naked form of your consistence rising up alone from the ruins, I believe that, with the help of your grace, Lord, the words that come to my lips will be the old paean of the ancient world, "Ahh, God!"

C: THE CIRCLE OF ENERGY
1. *Passivity.* But I look for more, Lord, much more! When your Presence bathed me in its light, I sought to find in it the supreme tangi-

ble Reality. Now that I hold you, Sovereign Consistence, and feel that I am carried along by you, I realize that hidden away beneath my yearnings was an unspoken longing not to embrace but to be possessed.

It is not in the form of a ray of light or of a tenuous matter but as fire that I desire you; and it was as fire that I felt your presence in the intuition of my first contact. I shall never, I know well, find rest, unless some active force pours down from you to cover and transform me.

I pray you, divine milieu, already decked with the spoils of quantity and space, show yourself to me as the focus of all energies; and that you may do so, make yourself known to me in your true essence, which is *Creative Action*. . . .

Once again, it is for the mystic to carry out the task of taking possession of the world at that point at which it escapes from other men and to effect the synthesis which, if attempted experientially or on normal philosophical lines, can only bring failure or disaster. The mystic was looking for the devouring fire which he could identify with the Divine that summons him from all sides: Science points it out to him. *See, the universe is ablaze!*. . .

From all these discoveries, each one of which carries him deeper into an ocean of energy, the mystic draws an undiluted joy. And he is always eager for more; he will never feel that he is as fully dominated by the forces of Earth and Air as his yearning to be subject to God's mastery demands. In very truth it is God and God alone whose Spirit stirs up the whole mass of the universe in ferment. . . .

The fact is, creation has never stopped. The creative act is one huge continual gesture, drawn out over the totality of time. It is still going on; and incessantly, even if imperceptibly, the world is constantly emerging a little farther above nothingness. . . .

Thus the mystic recollects himself in hallowed communion with the omnipresent Will. Delectably, he loses himself in the indefinitely renewed consciousness of his universal passivity. . . .

What is there in suffering that commits me so deeply to you?. . . It is because the only element I hanker after in your gifts is the fragrance of your power over me and the touch of your hand upon me. For what exhilarates us human creatures more than freedom, more than the glory of achievement, is the joy of finding and surrendering to a beauty greater than man, the rapture of being possessed. . . .

Blessed, above all, be death and the horror of falling back into the cosmic forces. . . Death causes us to lose our footing completely in ourselves so as to deliver us over to the powers of heaven and earth. This is the final terror—but it is also, for the mystic, the climax of his bliss: It is our final entry, there to remain forever, into the milieu that dominates, that carries us off, that consumes. "Ahh, God!"

2. *Action.* Just as the mystic, in following his innate appetite for the Universal, did not fall into pantheism, so, in surrendering to his preference for passivity, he does not sink into inertia. . . Above all, he is immune from the perversion of loving suffering for its own sake or seeking to suffer simply in order to suffer. In his eyes, the *only* charm of sorrow derives exclusively from its quality of being without any possible doubt, something *involuntary*, of representing eminently what is *in us without us.* . . .

. . .The man who is passionately enamored of the divine milieu will never surrender any essential part of himself, never let himself become less a man, never throw in the sponge when things go wrong: Only in the last extreme will he accept suffering, and then only insofar as it is unavoidable. . . .

God's creative power does not, in fact, fashion us as though out of soft clay. It is fire that kindles life in whatever it touches, a quickening spirit. Therefore, it is *by living* that we must decisively adapt ourselves to it, model ourselves upon it, identify ourselves with it. . . .

Anyone who has the mystic's insight, and who loves, will feel within himself a fever of active dependence and arduous purity seizing upon him and driving him on to the absolute integrity and the utilization of all his powers. . . . He can never rest so long as there remains the least discord between the vibration of his own being and that of the divine milieu. . . . In order to become perfectly resonant to the basic rhythm of reality, the mystic makes himself docile to the least hint of human obligation, the most unobtrusive demands of grace.

To win for himself a little more of the creative energy, he tirelessly develops his thought, dilates his heart, intensifies his external activity. For created beings must work if they would be yet further created.

There are no limits to this communion of an activity that strives to approach the perfection of its first principle. . . . The mystic finds a joy no words can describe in feeling that through his active obedience (which is a very different thing from the passive acceptance that first satisfied him), he *endlessly* adheres *more closely* to the encompassing Godhead. Endlessly, the more perfect an instrument he becomes, the more does he *become one* with the creative Act. . . .

D: THE CIRCLE OF SPIRIT
The force that had been drawing the mystic toward the zone in which all things are fused together now reverses its direction and brings him back to an exact examination of the experiential Multiple, *from the moment he realizes* that the higher element in which he longs to lose himself is not only the beatifying term of human activity but also, to some extent, its product. . . .

As soon as the light grows a little more brilliant, the seat of all action and communion will be revealed to the seer as being situated neither in the divine sphere nor in the created stratum, both properly so called, but in a special reality born of their mutual interaction. The mystical milieu *is not a completed zone* in which beings, once they have succeeded in entering it, remain immobilized. It is a *complex* element, made up of *divinized created being*, in which, as times goes on, the immortal distillation of the universe is gradually assembled. We cannot give it precisely the name of God: It is the kingdom. Nor can we say that it is: It is in the process of *becoming*.

As a result of this new insight, the mystic is reinvigorated by the infusion into him of a life that had hitherto been somewhat alien to his soul. Now that man's labor interests him not simply as *an operation* that brings union with the divine act, but *as a work* (*opus*) which is a condition for the presence of God among us, it becomes possible for him not only to feel the divine milieu but to *form* it and to allow it to encompass him like a continually stronger light. Now that, in order to adhere to God, it is not enough for him to lend himself to purely *operative action*, but to *action* aimed at *achievement*, he has no difficulty, in his mystical drive, in making his own that insatiable ardor which gives the children of the earth their passion for progress. . . .

1. *The Light that Inspires the Battle.* The first necessity is the liberation of Spirit. Spirit is the goal toward which nature's age-long labors are directed. Everything that lives (and that may well mean everything that moves) is driven, from its very beginning, by an urge toward a little more freedom, a little more power, more truth. . . .

The mystic, however, can see the profound and hallowed reason for his insatiable activity, for man's unswerving impulse toward the elusive Something that shines ahead of him. Throughout time, a task greater than individual lives is being achieved. . . . Spirit is coming to birth, the created foundation of the mystical milieu, the cosmic substance into which the Godhead is finally and forever being condensed. God, as he spiritualizes the world, is in the process of penetrating it. . . .

Then, it is really true, Lord? By helping the spread of science and freedom, I can increase the density of the divine atmosphere in which it is always my one desire to be immersed. By laying hold of the Earth I enable myself to cling closely to you. . . .

. . .the perception of God present in all things presupposed in the mystic an intense zest for *the Real*. A little later, adherence to God active in all things, forced him to develop as wide a consciousness as possible, *again of the Real*. And now that he is making his way farther into the immanent God, he is tied, as a person, to an unremitting *fulfillment*, once again of the Real. And this can only mean one thing, that man finds himself inexorably forced, by his passion for union with God, *to give things their highest possible degree of reality*, whether it be in his knowledge of them and his love for them or in their proper being. Lost though he is in his dreams, the mystic is still a supreme realist. . . .

In his love for the Divine, which he sees welling up on all sides with each new advance effected by nature, the mystic flings himself with enthusiasm into *the battle for Light*. . . . Alone among men, the mystic is *certain* that the least of his labors is an *enduring possession*, effective and enduring. For the mystic works within God.

2. *The Fire that Comes Down upon Earth*.

At this stage, however, the initiate is not solely concerned, as he was in the circle of energy, with hastening to the blaze and losing himself in it *while still remaining himself;* the time has come when the created being's own substance, under the mastering influence of God, must become a constitutive element of the regenerated universe. What seeks to be effected is more than a simple union; it is a *transformation*. . . .

Seeing the mystic immobile, crucified, or rapt in prayer, some may perhaps think that his activity is in abeyance or has left this earth: They are mistaken. Nothing in this world is more intensely alive and active than purity and prayer, which hang like an unmoving light between the universe and God. Through their serene transparency flow the waves of creative power charged with natural virtue and with grace. What else is this but the Virgin Mary?

There was a time when, in his eagerness to accept the domination of God, the mystic found himself forced into action. Now, the process is reversed and the very excess of his desire for action weds him to a passivity of a higher order. Through seeking to possess and thoroughly cultivate the world (that so he may feel the presence of God), he has become an ascetic and a contemplative. Through seeking the development of his own nature, he has found the rapture of feeling that suffering is dissolving his being, drop by drop, and replacing it with God. Through loving life, he has come to wish for death, since death alone can destroy his egoism so radically as to enable him to be absorbed in Christ. So, for the third time, we cry again, "Ahh, God!"

E: THE CIRCLE OF PERSON
We have seen the mystical milieu gradually develop and assume a form at once divine and human. At first, we might have mistaken it for a mere projection of our emotions, their excess flowing out over the world and appearing to animate it.

Soon, however, its autonomy became as apparent as a strange and supremely desirable Omnipresence. This universal presence began by drawing into itself all consistence and all energy. Later, embodied in a great wind of purification and conquest that excites man at every stage in his history, it drew us into itself—so fully as to assimilate us to its own nature.

Sometimes, when I scrutinize the world very closely,. . . . I [see] a shadow floating, as though it were the wraith of a universal soul seeking to be born. What name can we give to this mysterious Entity, who is in some small way our own handiwork, with whom, eminently, we can enter into communion, and who is some part of ourselves, yet who masters us, has need of us in order to exist, and at the same time, dominates us with the full force of his absolute Being?

I can feel it: He has a name and a face, but he alone can reveal his face and pronounce his name: Jesus!

. . .Together with all the beings around me, I felt that I was caught up in a higher movement that was stirring together all the elements of the universe and grouping them in a new order. When it was given to me to see where the dazzling trail of particular beauties and partial harmonies was leading, I recognized that it was all coming to center *on a single point*, on a Person: your Person: Jesus!

In that superabundant unity, that Person possessed the virtue of each one of the lower mystical circles. His presence impregnated and sustained all things. His power animated all energy. His mastering ate into every other life, to assimilate it to himself. Thus, Lord, I understood that it was impossible to live without ever emerging from you, without ever ceasing to be buried in You, the Ocean of Life, that life that penetrates and quickens us. Since first, Lord, you said, "This is my body," not only the bread of the altar but (to some degree) everything in the universe that nourishes the soul for the life of Spirit and Grace has become *yours* and has become *divine*—it is divinized, divinizing, and divinizable. Every presence makes me feel that you are near me; every touch is the touch of your hand; every necessity transmits to me a pulsation of your will. And so true is this, that everything around me that is essential and enduring has become for me the dominance and, in some way, the substance of your heart: Jesus!

That is why it is impossible. . . for any man who has acquired even the smallest understanding of you to look on your face without seeing in it the *radiance* of every reality and every goodness. In the mystery of your mystical body—your cosmic body—you sought to feel the echo of every joy and every fear that moves each single one of all the countless cells that make up mankind. And correspondingly, we cannot contemplate you and adhere to you without your Being, for all its supreme multiplicity, transmuting itself as we grasp it into the restructured Multitude of all that you love upon earth: Jesus!

. . . When I think of you, Lord, I cannot say whether it is in this place that I find you more or in that place—whether you are to me Friend or Strength or Matter—whether I am contemplating you or whether I am suffering—whether I rue my faults or find union— whether it is you I love or the whole sum of others. Every affection, every desire, every possession, every light, every depth, every harmony, and every ardor glitters with equal brilliance at one and the same time in the inexpressible *Relationship* that is being set up between me and you: Jesus!

CONCLUSION

The experiences described in this essay are only an *introduction to mysticism*. Beyond the point at which I have stopped, the being in whom the higher cosmic milieu is completely *personified*, reveals, as and when he wills, the beauties of his countenance and heart. There are infinite degrees in the loving initiation of one person into another unfathomable Person.

. . . Of course, all who are admitted to the vision of Christ will not go through the different phases in the order I have described; but if they analyze their passion for the divine, they will see that they have proceeded through the circles, and that their love lies at the center. In particular, they will recognize the role of the created thing in the sharpening of sensibility, which gives the warmth that Charity calls for, and the vast cosmic realities that give God his tangible and palpable being here below. *Amictus (mundo) sicut vestmento—*

clothed (in the world) as in a garment. No one, I think, will understand the great mystics—St. Francis and Blessed Angela and the
others—unless he understands the full depth of the truth that Jesus
must be loved as a world. . . .

When Thomas Merton died in 1968, he was perhaps the world's most famous monk. He became the leading contemplative and a highly prophetic voice of 20th-century America by uniting within himself his monastic vocation to solitude and his need to speak out on contemporary social issues.

THOMAS MERTON

Born of a New Zealand father and an American mother in the Midi region (Prades) of France on January 31, 1915, Merton had a difficult and unhappy childhood. When he was only six years old, his artist mother died. Although loving and caring, his father, also an artist, moved from place to place, and often left the boy alone. Merton was 16 when his father died.

Although Merton received a good education in France, England, and then at Columbia University, his teens and early 20s were years filled with sensuality, confusion, a critical attitude toward religion, and intense searching.

After converting to Roman Catholicism in 1938, while studying at Columbia, Merton entered the Trappist abbey of Our Lady of Gethsemani in Kentucky three years later. His autobiography, *The Seven Storey Mountain* (1948), became an international success not only because of its significant statement about monastic spirituality but also because of its telling account of the spiritual condition of the times.

The diverse genres of his writings are indicative of Merton's range and depth. He wrote personal journals (e.g., *The Sign of Jonas*), devotional meditations (e.g., *New Seeds of Contemplation*), theological essays (e.g., *The Ascent to Truth*), reflections on Far Eastern religions (e.g., *Zen and the Birds of Appetite*), biblical reflections (*Bread in the Wilderness*), poetry (e.g., *Emblems in a Season of Fury*), and collections of essays and reviews (e.g., *Raids on the Unspeakable*). Through these writings, one sees Merton move from the enthusiastic, but somewhat narrow, Catholicism typical of a new convert to the creative openness of the mature man, who tapped the resources of other spiritual traditions and of worlds beyond his own monastery.

Merton reemphasized the primary value of the contemplative life and articulated a monastic spirituality for people in the world. Attuned to the genuine aspirations of American counterculture that were partially consonant with monastic goals, and well-versed in Marxist ideology (especially its criticisms of Western capitalism), Merton also had a good grasp of the Christian tradition: the Scriptures, the Fathers of the Church, the Desert Fathers, and the great mystics. He was more than conversant with contemporary Protestant and Catholic theologies, as well as Far-Eastern religions. In addition, he was well-read in literature, poetry, art, and contemporary psychology. From this base, he addressed the pressing social issues of his day: civil rights, social justice, poverty, urban and international violence, nuclear disarmament, ecumenism, and the East-West religious dialogue.

Merton did not attain experiential purgation by, illumination from, and transforming union with God. Thus, he was not a mystic in the strict sense. Nonetheless, he remained a seeker throughout his life. As a mystical theologian, he reflected upon his primary concern, namely, mystical union with God. His significant literary gifts enabled him to interpret monasticism for outsiders and insiders by retrieving the Christian mystical tradition and explaining it with the above issues and movements in mind. In this way, he made an enormous contribution to contemporary American spirituality.

Merton became the leading contemplative and a highly prophetic voice of the 20th-century American church by uniting and reconciling within himself his monastic vocation to solitude and silence and his strong, prophetic sense of need to speak out on contemporary social issues. Through his writings and example, he trained a generation of Christian contemplatives. At the time of his apparently accidental death by electrocution, while attending an international congress on the future of monasticism in Bangkok, Thailand, he was perhaps the world's most famous monk.

One scholar has written that Merton's "greatest contribution was the particularity of his person and the synthesizing and contemporizing of ancient and universal truths."[1] One sees clearly in Merton's life the lived paradoxes, the partial syntheses, the tensions, the joys, and the agonies of one whose primary concern was union with God in Christ in an age of Auschwitz, Hiroshima, Vietnam, the Watts riots, civil rights, and Aquarius.

As Merton sees it, because everyone shares in Adam's flight from unity with God, all remain in exile not only from God, but also from their own deepest self. Merton distinguishes sharply between a "true self," a "deep self," a "new self," and a "false self," a "shadow self," an "outer self." For the most part, the external, daily self that we seem to know is a fabrication and a distortion of the self made in God's image and likeness. This "worldly self" proclaims itself to be autonomous and to be a god unto itself.

Life's task and goal focus upon attaining one's true identity by returning "to the infinite ground of pure reality." According to Merton, the true self anchors itself only in God. In fact, this "transcendental self" is identified perfectly with God in love and freedom but is metaphysically distinct from God. Because the true self made in God's image seems the very enemy of the daily, familiar self, the quest for authenticity requires a great battle. Moreover, the struggle for God is at the same time a struggle simply to be one's genuine self.

Contemplation, to Merton, forces a person below the surface comforts of basic narcissism to face the hell that exists because of the self's lived lie. God reveals himself to the contemplative only when he has embraced the "wilderness of the human spirit," the inner desert in which he comes face to face with his own nothingness, sinfulness, ignorance, infidelity, helplessness, and need for God.

The contemplative imitates Christ's self-emptying love to the point of death on the cross and experiences an emptiness and a seeming loss of faith that actually deepens faith. Merton sees contemplation as an imitation of Christ's solitary night in the garden. Contemplation must share in the life, death, and resurrection of Jesus Christ and participate spiritually in the union of God and man which is the hypostatic union. The true goal of all Christian prayer, meditation, and contemplation is to effect a loving union with Christ, the incarnate Word, because only in Christ does the true self emerge. One must contain all the divided worlds in oneself but transcend them in Christ.

Merton refused to reduce contemplation to another phase of the active life, to activity accompanied by prayer. Contemplation is both a form of resting in God and a cleaving to the God who creates, redeems, heals, and divinizes the world. Thus, in God, the monk touches the very center where all persons and all created things are actually one. In this way, the contemplative truly enters into the world's very heart to bring about its transformation.

According to Merton, the monk must get to the root of the world's good and evil—not by action and analysis but by simplicity, silence, and solitude. Still, the monk must avoid being a "guilty bystander." He must participate to some extent in the Church's mission, not only by prayer and holiness but also by understanding and concern.

Only a few hours before his death in Bangkok, on December 10, 1968, Merton uttered what may well be his central insight:

Christianity and Buddhism agree that the root
of man's problems is that his consciousness is
fouled up and does not apprehend reality as it
fully is. . . . Christianity and Buddhism alike,
then, seek to bring about a transformation of
man's consciousness. . . [and] to transform and
liberate the truth in each person, with the
idea that it will communicate itself to others.
Of course, the man par excellence to whom this task is deputed is
the monk. And the Christian monk and the Buddhist monk—in
their sort of ideal setting and ideal way of looking
at them—fulfill this role in society. . . . The
whole purpose of the monastic life is to teach
men to live by love.[2]

The first of the following texts was selected to illustrate how skill-fully Merton retrieved the apophatic mystical tradition for his American audience. He also emphasized that contemplation is a *vocation*, not an activity one simply undertakes on one's own. The genuine contemplative knows that the condition of being filled with God is self-emptiness. Waiting in silence for God to speak his Word transforms the contemplative's entire life. Nothing less than a genuine spiritual death suffices for knowing God through love.

To Merton, contemplation is no narcissistic quietism. Nor has it anything in common with the artificial darkness that pseudocontemplation creates, which ends up making an idol of the self. He considered the desire for exotic experiences to result in a "spiritual consumerism" and the chief danger to a genuine, contemporary contemplative life.

The second text was selected to illustrate Merton's view that the contemplative discovers and explores new dimensions of freedom and love that transform both his or her self and that of others. Without deepening, healing, and transforming itself in Christ, activism degenerates into a projection onto others of one's own sinfulness, selfishness, and brokenness. Only contemplation can heal the contemporary person's self-alienation that has dangerous social consequences in our nuclear age.

The third selection focuses on Merton's understanding of "masked contemplation." Like many in the Christian mystical tradition, Merton insisted that contemplation is pure in proportion to its hiddenness. Thus, active and selfless service of others gives rise to an apophatic experience of the hidden God. Selflessness, purity of heart, simplicity, and inner freedom engender an awareness of God that far transcends the superficial experiences that are often, mistakenly, taken for genuine mystical experiences.

The final text was selected to illustrate how Merton emphasizes contemplation as knowing God through love. One must love God for God's sake alone, and not for his gifts, experiences, or even the transformative value of contemplation. Moreover, authentic contemplation—which only God can teach—must overflow to others. How it does affect others concretely will only be known in heaven.[3]

THE TEXTS

CONTEMPLATIVE PRAYER[4]
Contemplative prayer is, in a way, simply the preference for the desert, for emptiness, for poverty. One has begun to know the meaning of contemplation when he intuitively and spontaneously seeks the dark and unknown path of aridity in preference to every other way. The contemplative is one who would rather not know than know. Rather not enjoy than enjoy. He accepts the love of God on faith, in defiance of all apparent evidence. This is the necessary condition, and a very paradoxical condition, for the mystical experience of God's presence and of his love for us. Only when we are able to "let go" of everything within us, all desire to see, to know, to taste and to experience the presence of God, do we truly become able to experience that presence with the overwhelming conviction and reality that revolutionize our entire inner life. . . .

Contemplation is essentially listening in silence, an expectancy. And yet, in a certain sense, we must truly begin to hear God when we have ceased to listen. What is the explanation of this paradox? Perhaps only that there is a higher kind of listening, which is not an attentiveness to some special wavelength, a receptivity to a certain kind of message, but a general emptiness that waits to realize the fullness of the message of God within its own apparent void. In other words, the true contemplative is not the one who prepares his mind for a particular message that he wants or expects to hear, but who remains empty because he knows that he can never expect or anticipate the word that will transform his darkness into light. He does not even anticipate a special kind of transformation. He does not demand light instead of darkness. He waits on the Word of God in silence, and when he is "answered," it is not so much by a word that bursts into his silence. It is by his silence itself suddenly, inexplicably revealing itself to him as a word of great power, full of the voice of God.

But we must not take a purely quietistic view of contemplative prayer. It is not mere negation. Nor can a person become a contemplative merely by "blackening out" sensible realities and remaining alone with himself in darkness. First of all, one who does this of set purpose, as a conclusion to practical reasoning on the subject and without an interior vocation, simply enters into an artificial darkness of his own making. He is not alone with God but alone with himself. He is not in the presence of the Transcendent One but of an idol: his own complacent identity. He becomes immersed and lost in himself, in a state of inert, primitive, and infantile narcissism. His life is "nothing," not in the dynamic, mysterious sense in which the "nothing," *nada*, of the mystic is paradoxically also the all, *todo*, of God. It is purely the nothingness of a finite being left to himself and absorbed in his own triviality. . . .

. . .to become a Yogi and to be able to commit moral and intellectual suicide whenever you please, without the necessity of actually dying, to be able to black out your mind by the incantation of half-articulate charms and to enter into a state of annihilation, in which all the faculties are inactive and the soul is inert, as if it were dead— all this may well appeal to certain minds as a refined and rather pleasant way to getting even with the world and with society, and with God Himself for that matter. . . .

CONTEMPLATION IN A WORLD OF ACTION[5]
What does the contemplative life or the life of prayer, solitude, silence, meditation mean to the man in the atomic age? What can it mean? Has it lost its meaning altogether?

The real purpose of prayer (in the fully personal sense as well as in the Christian assembly) is the deepening of personal realization in love, the awareness of God (even if sometimes this awareness may amount to a negative factor, a seeming "absence"). The real purpose of meditation—or at least that which recommends itself as most relevant for modern man—is the exploration and discovery of new dimensions in freedom, illumination and love, in deepening our awareness of our life in Christ.

What is this in relation to action? Simply this. He who attempts to act and do things for others or for the world without deepening his own self-understanding, freedom, integrity, and capacity to love, will not have anything to give others. He will communicate to them nothing but the contagion of his own obsessions, his aggressiveness, his egocentered ambitions, his delusions about ends and means, his doctrinaire prejudices and ideas. There is nothing more tragic in the modern world than the misuse of power and action to which men are driven by their own Faustian misunderstandings and misapprehensions. We have more power at our disposal today than we have ever had, and yet we are more alienated and estranged from the inner ground of meaning and of love than we have ever been. The result of this is evident. We are living through the greatest crisis in the history of man; and this crisis is centered precisely in the country that has made a fetish out of action and has lost (or perhaps never had) the sense of contemplation. Far from being irrelevant, prayer, meditation, and contemplation are of the utmost important in America today. . . .

. . . prayer and meditation have an important part to play in the opening up of new ways and new horizons. . . .

"THE INNER EXPERIENCE: KINDS OF CONTEMPLATION (IV)"[6]
Union with God in Activity

. . . There are many Christians who serve God with great purity of soul and perfect self-sacrifice in the active life. Their vocation does not allow them to find the solitude and silence and leisure in which to empty their minds entirely of created things and to lose themselves in God alone. They are too busy serving Him in His children on earth. At the same time, their minds and temperaments do not fit them for a purely contemplative life: They would know no peace without exterior activity. They would not know what to do with themselves. They would vegetate and their interior life would grow cold. Nevertheless, they know how to find God by devoting themselves to Him in self-sacrificing labors in which they are able to remain in His presence all day long. They live and work in His company. They realize that He is deep within them, and they taste deep, peaceful joy in being with Him. They lead lives of great simplicity in which they do not need to rise above the ordinary levels of vocal and affective prayer. Without realizing it, their extremely simple prayer is, for them, so deep and interior that it brings them to the threshold of contemplation. They never enter deeply into the contemplative life, but they are not unfamiliar with graces akin to contemplation. Although they are active laborers, they are also hidden contemplatives because of the great purity of heart maintained in them by obedience, fraternal charity, self-sacrifice, and perfect abandonment to God's will in all that they do and suffer. They are much closer to God than they realize.They enjoy a kind of "masked" contemplation. . . .

It might be well to point out here that "masked contemplation" has its advantages. Since contemplation is communion with a hidden God in His own hiddenness, it tends to be pure in proportion as it is itself hidden. Obscurity and sincerity seem to go together in the spiritual life. The "masked contemplative" is one whose contemplation is hidden from no one so much as from himself. This may seem like a contradiction in terms. Yet it is a strange and deep truth that the grace of contemplation is most secure and efficacious when it is no longer sought or cherished or desired. It is, in a sense, most pure when it is barely known. Of course, for it to be contemplation at all, there must be some awareness of it. If there is absolutely no awareness, then there is no contemplation.

Here we speak of an awareness that is present but utterly unselfconscious. It is a kind of negative awareness, an "unknowing." According to the classical expression of Pseudo-Dionysius, one knows God by "not knowing" Him. One reaches Him "apophatically" in the darkness beyond concepts. And one contemplates, so to speak, by forgetting that one is able to contemplate. As soon as one is aware of himself contemplating, the gift is spoiled. This was long observed by St. Anthony of the Desert who said: "That prayer is most pure in which the monk is no longer aware of himself or of the fact that he is praying."

Often people think that this remark of St. Anthony refers to some curious state of psychological absorption, a kind of mystical sleep. In point of fact, it refers to a state of selfless awareness, a spiritual liberty and a lightness and freedom which transcends all special psychological states and is "no state" at all. Would-be contemplatives must be on their guard against a kind of heavy, inert stupor in which the mind becomes swallowed up in itself. To remain immersed in one's own darkness is not contemplation, and no one should attempt to "stop" the functioning of his mind and remain fixed on his own nothingness. Rather, we must go out in hope and faith from our own nothingness and seek liberation in God.

The masked contemplative is liberated from temporal concern by his own purity of intention. He no longer seeks himself in action or in prayer, and he achieves a kind of holy indifference, abandoning himself to the will of God and seeking only to keep in touch with the realities of the present moment. By this of course I mean the inner and spiritual realities, not the surface emotions and excitements which are not reality but illusion.

The life of contemplation in action and purity of heart is then a life of great simplicity and inner liberty. One is not seeking anything special or demanding any particular satisfaction. One is content with what is. One does what is to be done, and the more concrete, the better. One is not worried about the results of what is done. One is content to have good motives and not too anxious about making mistakes. In this way, one can swim with the living stream of life and remain at every moment in contact with God, in the hiddenness and ordinariness of the present moment with its obvious tasks.

At such times, walking down a street, sweeping a floor, washing dishes, hoeing beans, reading a book, taking a stroll in the woods— all can be enriched with contemplation and with the obscure sense of the presence of God. This contemplation is all the more pure in that one does not "look" to see if it is there. Such "walking with God" is one of the simplest and most secure ways of living a life of prayer, and one of the safest. It never attracts anybody's attention, least of all the attention of him who lives it. And he soon learns not to want to see anything special in himself. This is the price of his liberty.

Whether in active or passive contemplation, purity of heart is always the guardian of contemplative truth. . . .

NEW SEEDS OF CONTEMPLATION[7]

37. SHARING THE FRUITS OF CONTEMPLATION
We do not see God in contemplation—we know Him by love: for

He is pure Love, and when we taste the experience of loving God for His own sake alone, we know by experience Who and what He is. . . .

We experience God in proportion as we are stripped and emptied of attachment to His creatures. And when we have been delivered from every other desire, we shall taste the perfection of an incorruptible joy.

God does not give His joy to us for ourselves alone, and if we could possess Him for ourselves alone, we would not possess Him at all. Any joy that does not overflow from our souls and help other men to rejoice in God does not come to us from God. (But do not think that you have to see how it overflows into the souls of others. In the economy of His grace, you may be sharing His gifts with someone you will never know until you get to heaven.)

If we experience God in contemplation, we experience Him not for ourselves alone but also for others. Yet if your experience of God comes from God, one of the signs may be a great diffidence in telling others about it. . . . No one is more shy than a contemplative to speak about his contemplation. . . .

At the same time, he most earnestly wants everybody else to share his peace and his joy. His contemplation gives him a new outlook on the world of men. He looks about him with a secret and tranquil surmise which he perhaps admits to no one, hoping to find in the faces of other men or to hear in their voices some sign of vocation and potentiality for the same deep happiness and wisdom. . . .

The highest vocation in the Kingdom of God is that of sharing one's contemplation with others and bringing other men to the experimental knowledge of God that is given to those who love Him perfectly. But the possibility of mistake and error is just as great as the vocation itself.

In the first place, the mere fact that you have discovered something of contemplation does not yet mean that you are supposed to pass it on to somebody else. The sharing of contemplation with others implies two vocations: one to be a contemplative and another still to teach contemplation. Both of them have to be verified.

But then, as soon as you think of yourself as teaching contemplation to others, you make another mistake. No one teaches contemplation except God, Who gives it. The best you can do is write something or say something that will serve as an occasion for someone else to realize what God wants of him.

The French priest, Henri le Saux, lived most of his Benedictine life in India. He synthesized in his own person Christianity and Hindu advaitic (non-dualistic) mysticism. So profound was his enlightenment that toward the end of his life, he attained the distinction of being a guru for both Christian and Hindu disciples.

HENRI LE SAUX or ABHISHIKTANANDA

Just as Greek culture enriched nascent Christianity's life and development, contemporary Christianity's "Eastern turn" seems to be producing similar fruits. Arnold Toynbee once predicted that when future historians write about the 20th century, they will consider the meeting of East and West on the level of religious experience as the most significant event of the century. To some extent, the Second Vatican Council has facilitated Christianity's Eastern awakening through its openness to the holiness, wisdom, and truth found among the great non-Christian religions.

Long before Christianity's fascination with Eastern religions was in vogue, Henri le Saux was a builder of bridges between Indian and Christian spirituality and mysticism, between the oldest Indian monastic tradition and the Christian Desert Fathers. He desired to make Indian Christians aware of the rich cultural heritage that the Church must integrate into its life for the good of all Christianity. Because he understood India from within, he succeeded in "Indianizing" Christianity by incarnating it into India's culture, way of life, prayer, contemplation, and liturgy.

Even more significant is the synthesis he achieved in his own person of Benedictine Christianity and Hindu advaitic mysticism, that is, the non-dualistic mysticism at the heart of the Hindu Upanishads. Although Le Saux never denied his Christianity, Hindus acknowledged him as an authentic Hindu *sannyasi* (wandering monk) and as one who had attained true advaitic enlightenment. So profound was his enlightenment that toward the end of his life, le Saux attained the distinction of being a guru for both Christian and Hindu disciples.

The eldest of eight children, Henri le Saux was born in Brittany, France on August 30, 1910. Attracted to the priesthood when 10 years old, he studied at a local minor seminary, at the major seminary at Rennes, and at the Benedictine monastery of St. Anne de Kergonan in 1929. He was solemnly professed and ordained priest in 1935 and remained at Anne de Kergonan teaching Church history and patristics until 1948. It must be emphasized that his Benedictine affection for liturgy and Gregorian chant indelibly stamped his life.

A love of India and a desire to "incarnate" Christian monasticism in the land of the gurus and seers motivated le Saux to obtain permission to join Abbé Jules Monchanin in founding the ashram of Shantivanam ("Woods of Peace") in Kulittali, southern India. Here he took the name Abhishikleshvarananda ("the joy of the anointed one"), shortened to Abhishiktananda.

Shortly upon arriving in India, he met Sri Ramana Maharishi, a man whom le Saux was convinced embodied the fullness of self-denial, self-actualization, and the wisdom of India. So powerful was the effect of this great Hindu sage upon le Saux that he became convinced that Christianity could enrich India spiritually only if and when it could produce mystics like Ramana. Le Saux would later write that Ramana's advaitic mysticism was his own birthplace, a mysticism that he sensed to be in continuity with his own Benedictine monasticism, while being something new.

This led him to discover the sacred mountain of Arunachala, where Ramana had lived, and where, for several long periods between 1952 and 1955, he lived as a hermit in several of its caves.[1] With the obscurity, silence, and self-renunciation characteristic of a Hindu sannyasi, le Saux penetrated the mystery of the advaitic experience of India's rishis (sages) and saints. About this experience, he says:

In my own innermost center, in the most secret
mirror of my heart, I tried to discover the
image of him whose I am, of him who lives and
reigns in the infinite space (*akasa*) of my
heart. But the reflected image gradually grew
faint, and soon it was swallowed up in the
radiance of its Original. Step by step, I
descended into what seemed to me to be
successive depths of my true self—my being,
my awareness of being, my joy in being.
Finally, nothing was left but he himself, the
Only One, infinitely alone, Being, Awareness,
and Bliss, Saccidananda. In the heart of
Saccidananda, I had returned to my Source.[2]

This experience brought le Saux a severe problem of conscience, for it seemed to conflict deeply with his own Christian experience. In his diary, he wrote: "I have already tasted too much from Advaita to return to the 'Gregorian' peace of a Christian monk. Earlier in my life, however, I had tasted too much 'Gregorian' peace not to be unsettled by my advaitic experience."

Convinced that he could achieve a synthesis in his person, le Saux placed himself under the direction of Sri Gnanananda to listen to "the Spirit who never ceases to call within" and to receive "the knowledge of the All."[3] In 1959, he and an Indian priest pilgrimaged to the source of the Ganges in the Himalayas, an Indian symbol for the inner journey to the source of Being. After taking a ritual bath in the Ganges with Hindu pilgrims and singing verses from the Upanishads, he celebrated what may well be the first Mass at that Hindu sacred site.[4]

In 1962, le Saux built a small hermitage in Uttarkashi, not far from the sources of the Ganges in the Himalayas. There he wrote his chief works, undertook many journeys to and from Shantivanam, and participated vigorously in numerous Hindu-Christian ecumenical meetings. With the arrival of Dom Bede Griffiths, O.S.B., in 1968, le Saux was free to spend the rest of his life in silent contemplation in the solitude of the Himalayas as the only Christian among the Hindu sannyasis. On July 14, 1973, he suffered a heart attack, and though he temporarily recovered—to even greater spiritual enlightenment—he succumbed the following December 7, his faculties and clarity undiminished. He was buried in the cemetery of the Fathers of the Divine Word in Dolda, near Indore.

Dom le Saux's main contribution to mysticism is not to be found in his books, but in the advaitic and Christian experiences he plumbed and made accessible to others. His view was that the monk has the duty to free his inner Mystery, thereby freeing the self. This is the monk's gift to the world. Because of a powerful desire to give the Hindus Christ, he went to India as a giver. However, through the interiority at the heart of the Hindu Upanishads, he discovered that India enabled him to come to know Christ more deeply. In fact, he contended that India plunged him more deeply into life's and Christ's mystery than anything from his Christian background.

Le Saux's inner partner in dialogue was the advaitic, or non-dualistic, *experience* of Ramana and Gnanananda. Advaita is essentially a mysticism and a derived theology. It maintains that the ultimate experience is one of undifferentiated unity and that the person's deepest self (*atman*) and the all-embracing absolute Reality (*Brahman*) cannot be two. In short, because *atman is Brahman*, one experiences that the self is the Absolute.

The advaitic mystic strives for the experience of the Absolute in a pure consciousness totally beyond all feelings, desires, images, thoughts, and multiplicity. Nothing less than experiencing the absoluteness of being satisfies the advaitic mystic. "It is the pure *silence*," le Saux wrote, "of the unnameable, unpersonifiable God discerned in the loss of one's own self at the profoundest depth of one's being."[5]

Le Saux's mysticism is a lovely, eastern-flavored, image-of-God mysticism. "If I am the image of God," he wrote, "this is true not only because I can discover in myself some analogies to the divine processions; it is primarily true because the Son reveals himself in me and lives in me, because the divine generation and the divine life are operative in me to my very depths."[6] India calls the image of God in the cave of the heart "Saccidananda," a compound of the Sanskrit words *sat* (being), *cit* (awareness), and *ananda* (bliss). Saccidananda signifies not only God's inmost mystery but also God's presence in the person's deepest core.

The text printed here was selected from le Saux's most important book, *Saccidananda*, to illustrate that by experiencing the "Gospel of the Absolute in the cave of his heart," he brought his advaitic experience into harmony with his Christian experience. Not only did he fathom the cosmic dimension of Christ's mystery, but he also discovered that the trinitarian and the advaitic experiences enrich each other and actually indwell each other.

The text was also chosen to underscore le Saux's view that the experience of the triune God is Christianity's central experience. To him, the Trinity is not an abstract idea, but a *community* of being that contains the pulse of life—God's and every person's. To savor the trinitarian mystery is also to savor one's own human mystery and vice versa. Moreover, the Trinity is the key to authentic relationships with other persons and with everything created.

In the Trinity's womb, one finds true being. One can and must say to this discovery, "Abba, Father." In the advaitic experience of saccidananda, le Saux experienced the Absolute as being (sat), awareness (*cit*), and bliss (*ananda*). In *sat*, the Christian experiences the Father as the source of being; in *cit*, the Son as the Father's self-consciousness and Word; in *ananda*, the Spirit of love as the nondual bliss of Father and the Son.

The text was furthermore selected to illustrate le Saux's tremendous gratitude for India's gift to him: an interiority that allowed him to experience himself as a son in the Son, face to face with the Father, and to rest silently in the Father's bosom in the nonduality of spirit. As he says, "Silence and Presence, silence that is presence and presence that is silence, such is essentially the call of the Spirit to the Christian in prayer, through the agency of India."[7]

Le Saux's radical apophatic mysticism led him beyond all feelings, desires, images, and thoughts to the self's very center, or "cave of the heart." The advaitic experience is *en*static, immerses the self into the self, and brings about a state of such silence and stillness that it is depicted as a dreamless sleep devoid of any self-consciousness. But then God's grace awakened le Saux to the mystery of being, awareness, and bliss. Through this experience of pure consciousness, one experiences, in his words, the "bliss of simple being; and I am this very bliss, this *ananda,* since I *am* . . . . It draws me irresistibly into its own infinitude, to my own deepest center, to the very heart of Being and of Being's Presence to itself."[8] In summary, "by awakening to self, man has awakened to God. By awakening to God, he has awakened himself to self, beyond God and self, in this eternal mystery of the Father, at a point where the Spirit leads this Spirit whom the word of God become man has come to spread all over the world."[9] And to le Saux, this is nothing less than "the experience of the Lord Jesus, the face to face of the Father and the Son in the nonduality of the Spirit."[10]

THE TEXTS

SACCIDANANDA[11]

AT THE HEART OF THE TRINITY
The night is far spent, and the day is at hand
It is time for you to wake from sleep (Romans 13:12).
I am going to awaken him (John 11:11).
Awaken, you who are sleeping,
and rise from the dead;
and Christ will give you light (Ephesians 5:14).

The experience of Saccidananda, which has been transmitted by Hindu tradition, is undoubtedly one of the loftiest peaks of spirituality to which man can aspire. When, however, it is considered in the light of Christian experience of the Trinity, it may give the impression of being essentially monistic and of terminating in unbroken silence. This would also appear to be the case with the OM, or *pranava,* which is its perfect symbol.

When all man's faculties are stilled and even thought ceases, he passes into a kind of death, of which the sign is the silent fourth part of OM, where every conceivable sound is left behind. But what appears in human eyes to be the stillness of death is not a real death. Even if, in a sense, it is a void, it is also a fullness. However, within this silent immobility, it may be difficult to recognize the presence of Life; and for the Christian, God has revealed himself in the Bible as "the living God"—first in the Old Testament showing himself as ceaselessly concerned with man and in communication with him, and then in Jesus laying bare his inner mystery as an infinite overflow and exchange of life and love. In contrast, OM is "enstatic" and seems to draw all things into an eternal silence and stillness that is forever shut in upon itself.

PASCHAL AWAKENING
But Being is essentially a call to life; in its inward stillness, it is a surging energy!

When the Christian awakes from the advaitic experience and from the apparent sleep in which all consciousness of himself has faded away in the overwhelming awareness of Saccidananda, he finds himself contemplating Saccidananda as if from within and at the same time rediscovers himself and all things. Hitherto he had tried to penetrate the mystery of being, awareness, and bliss as from outside, but the mystery withstood him like an adamantine wall. He was caught in a dilemma: Either he clung to an impossible dualism, imagining himself as an "other"; or, when he experienced the incomprehensible but inevitable nonduality, his individual self vanished and was lost in an apparent fusion of identity. This meant that he could only sink into a profound sleep, *susupti* [the state of dreamless sleep], in which he was no longer conscious of anything whatever: "I laid me down and slept. . ." (*ego dormivi et soporatus sum. . . .*), according to the mysterious vision of the Psalmist (3:5).

However, the Psalmist also prophesied an awakening from this slumber, from all slumber: ". . .and (I) rose up again, for the Lord sustained me" (*et exsurrexi quia Dominus suscepit me*).

Only the Lord, in fact, is capable of raising man from this slumber. This he does through his Word, which calls nothingness to be (Romans 4:17) and the dead to live (John 5:25) in that mighty "shaking" which marks the birth of the new creation (Haggai 2:6). This awakening however takes place in the very heart of Saccidananda, which is its source. Then the heavens behind which God had hitherto seemed to hide himself, the veil of emptiness and unknowing which enveloped the man who had direct experience of the Absolute, these at last are torn wide open (Mark 1:10)—as happened at the Lord's baptism, again at his transfiguration, and finally and forever in the glory of his ascension.

The Lord's chosen one then advances from depth to depth, to inner center after inner center, in the mystery of Being, in the mystery of his being himself, for in this unfathomable abyss there is no last level. Gregory of Nyssa refers to this drawing of the soul ever onward as "*epektasis*" and says that it will continue without end through an eternity of ages: "He who ascends never stops, as he passes from one beginning to another, in an endless series of beginnings." But it is a real progress from inwardness to inwardness to which he is called. From the bosom of Being itself he will contemplate Being and Truth, Wisdom and the Word, beholding what he is with an ineffable *awareness* of being in the *bliss* of the Spirit, *sat-cit-ananda*.

The "cave of the heart" in which he now dwells is the Son's own abode. It is as a son himself that he receives in the Son an entirely new gift of grace—the Christian experience of Saccidananda. In the rising again of the Risen Lord he awakes to himself and recovers himself. With the Lord's own life he lives, and in his bliss he shares [cf. John 15:11] . . . . Now that the Christian jñani [enlightened one] has penetrated to the heart of Saccidananda and experiences his "connaturality" with God, the Spirit of Wisdom makes known to him his last secrets. He now knows—

that Being, *sat*, opens itself at its very source to give birth eternally to the Son and in him to countless creatures, each of which in its own way will forever manifest and celebrate the infinite love and mercy of God;

that being is essentially "being with," communion, koinonia, the free gift of the self and the mutual communication of love;

that self-awareness, *cit*, only comes to be when there is mutual giving and receiving, for the I only awakes to itself in a Thou; that the

supreme and ultimate felicity, *ananda,* is fullness and perfect fulfillment only because it is the fruit of love, for being is love. There cannot be a solitary bliss anymore than there can be solitary being or
solitary self-awareness. There is no joy, as there is no being, except
in communication, in giving and receiving.

All this is not merely a matter of knowledge to the jñani; he lives by
it, he lives it, he is it. In the heart of Saccidananda there is no divi-
siveness, nothing withheld or concealed from the whole.

However, while abiding in the heart of Saccidananda, the jñani has
not been swallowed up "like a drop of water in the ocean," to quote
a much overworked simile. The richness of Saccidananda consists
precisely in the communication of its richness; its glory is the communication of glory. The glory is given to each one and also given
by each one. The very fact of receiving and giving is what consti-
tutes each of God's chosen ones as a personal center within the one
center of Saccidananda and enables him to recognize himself
within the boundless ocean of Being, Awareness, and Bliss. He
knows himself as one who receives from the Father in the Son, and
from the Son in the Spirit, born in eternity and in each moment of
time; and again, both in eternity and in each moment of time, he is
the one who, in return, gives himself to all and thereby in the Spirit
returns to the Father.

The jñani is the acceptance of the gift of God—the God who in his
infinite freedom has drawn him out of nothingness and in his infinite mercy has rescued him from sin and death. In accepting God's
gift of being and forgiveness, he, in his turn, is the gift of himself to
God, pure availability to his Lord. In every fiber of his being and to
the very core of his being, he is all communion—communion with
the Father, the Son, and the Spirit, communion with each of God's
creatures. At the same time, in the distinction which allows him to
have communion with the only Son, he is the son who hears the
loving address: "You are my beloved child." In the distinction
through which he has communion with his fellowmen, he represents the entire world in its longing to see the face of the Lord and
represents the whole Church, the koinonia of love, which in him as-
pires to its final perfection and fullness at the Parousia [the second
coming of Christ at the end of history]. In the distinction which

brings him, in the Son, face to face with the Father, he rests silently
in the bosom of the Father in the nonduality of the Spirit.

THE FATHER AND THE SON

If the Christian experience of the Trinity opens up to man new vis-
tas of meaning in the intuition of Saccidananda, it is equally true
that the terms *sat, cit, and ananda,* in their turn, greatly assist the
Christian in his own meditation on that central mystery of his faith.
No single theological language will ever be able to express all that
the Gospel has revealed to us concerning God who is Father, Son,
and Holy Spirit. It is therefore to be expected that just as Judaism
and Hellenism have made their contributions, so the divine preparation of India in its turn will serve to lead believers to contemplate
the mystery in a new depth. In particular, the intuition of
Saccidananda will be an aid in penetrating the mystery of the
Spirit, which, according to St. John's Gospel, relates chiefly to God's
presence to men in their hearts. And if anyone comes to the Gospel
with personal experience of Vedanta, it can be said with assurance
that the Gospel words will elicit profound echoes from the intuition
which he already had of Saccidananda; and that in turn this previous experience will cause marvelous harmonics to sound in his
present faith in the Holy Trinity. This is because all things are the
work of the one Spirit, who has been preparing for this man's awakening and resurrection ever since long ago he first revealed himself
to the heart of the rishis [seers] as the infinite presence.

Here there is no question of theological theorizing or of academic
comparison between the terms of the Christian revelation and those
in which India has expressed its own unique mystical experience. It
is rather a matter of an awakening, an awareness far beyond the
reach of the intellect, an experience which springs up and erupts in
the deepest recesses of the soul.

The experience of Saccidananda carries the soul beyond all merely
intellectual knowledge to her very center, to the source of her being.
Only there is she able to hear the Word which reveals within the undivided unity and advaita of Saccidananda the mystery of the Three
divine Persons: in sat, the Father, the absolute Beginning and Source of
being; in cit, the Son, the divine Word, the Father's Self-knowledge; in
ananda, the Spirit of love, Fullness and Bliss without end.

In *sat*, then, the Christian will adore especially the mystery of the First Person, the Father. The Father indeed is in himself un-originated Being, the unmanifested Source from which his self-manifestation proceeds. But if the Father alone is contemplated, then adoration must remain forever silent. For in himself, the Father is the One who has not yet spoken, who is essentially unmanifest, unknown. He is the Abyss of Silence. The Word alone makes him known, and it is only in his Word, his Son, that he is present to himself.

It is from the *sat*, the Simply Being, *san-matra* in Vedantic terms, that *cit* comes. *Cit* is the presence to itself, the consciousness of itself, the opening to itself, of *sat*. St. John says of the Word that he was "in the beginning." Of *sat*, the Father, nothing can conceivably be said to place him anywhere at all, whether in time or in eternity. The Father is origin, source, absolutely. The spring is not the stream of water that flows from it, and yet the spring is only known by this flowing stream. So what is the spring in itself, the pure source? What is Being, *sat*, in itself? What is the Father?

Cit is the self-awakening of Being, its coming to manifestation within itself. It is not merely an aspect or mode of Brahman, the Absolute. In Christian terms, it is a real procession, a real birth, first in eternity and subsequently in time. The Son is the consubstantial Word through whom the Father expresses himself within himself. And in that Word whereby the Father expresses himself, in his own self-awareness and presence to himself in the Son, everything that is has come to be.

At the heart of every thinking being, of every consciousness that awakens to itself, the eternal Presence is shining and making itself known—the Light that enlightens every consciousness that awakens in the world (John 1:9).

The seers in old time had an intuition of this very pure self-awareness lying at the very source of their beings as well as at the ultimate horizon of their thought, an intuition of that which unfailingly escapes the grasps of the devas, that is, of man's intellect and will (*Kena Upanishad* 3). What they thus obscurely recognized (1 Corinthians 13:12), the Christian by faith discovers in the eternal gaze of the Son. Being indeed in his deepest self the image of God, he recognizes himself in the perfect reflection of the Father's glory which the Son is.

There is but *one* Presence—so say the seers, those who have contemplated the truth. It is the presence of the Self to itself which, wherever it manifests itself, is identical.

For Christian faith, there is but one Son, divinely and eternally begotten. Jesus is the only Son of the Father, as—at another level, which is a sign of the first—he is also Mary's only child. In beholding his Son, the Father sees all things; in loving him, he loves all things. In the delight which he has in his Son, the Father delights in all things, finding them indeed to be "good, very good" (Genesis 1:10). Similarly, every "see-er" of God beholds the Father only through the eyes of the Son; every lover of God loves him in the Son's love; every worshipper glorifies the Father through the praises of his Son. Anything that does not pass through the Son really is *not*; it belongs to the sphere of nonreality, *a-sat*, the sphere of meaningless chaos.

In the world of men, there are countless faces which reflect the Son. Yet all are one, as the Son is. *Cit* is essentially nondual, *a-dvaita*. This may be baffling to our minds, but we have no right to empty the words of Christ of their meaning: whatever anyone does—or fails to do—for any of the brethren of Jesus, is done—or not done—to Jesus himself (Matthew 25:34f.) The apostle Paul, after an experience which pierced him to the heart and transformed his life, became a uniquely qualified witness and a tireless preacher of this truth. In eternity, it is the Son alone whom the Father contemplates and with whom he is well pleased. Each one of the elect is the manifestation by grace of the eternal awakening of the Father to himself in the Son.

For the Christian whom the Spirit has led to true awareness of his self, the Son is all and in all (Colossians 3:11). Everywhere, the Father's gaze rests on the Son and likewise the Son's rests on the Father; everywhere, there is only the manifestation of God to himself and in himself in the blessed Trinity of Persons. Thus no man can be a stranger to any other. As the Father awakens to himself in me and in me contemplates his only Son, so he does in every one of my brethren, however humble or insignificant he may seem. There is no man with whom I do not have communion in the mysterious circumincession (mutual penetration) and circuminsession (coinherence) which is characteristic of the one undivided life of the Holy Trinity.

Being only attains to itself in its self-awareness, *sat*, through *cit*, the Father through the Son. Self-awareness is only attained in Being itself, *cit* in *sat*, the Son in the Father. Only the Father knows the Son, apart from those who come to the Son, drawn by the Father (John 6:44); nor does anyone know the Father except the Son and those to whom he chooses to reveal him (Matthew 11:27). But it is precisely in order to reveal the Father (John 1:18) that the Son has come into the world and dwelt among us (John 1:14), living as a man among men, full of grace and truth.

In the land of Israel, the Word of Yahweh was heard by the prophets who faithfully communicated it to their people. For their part, the scholars and sages of Israel meditated upon the secret of the divine Wisdom which orders the universe. Thus God prepared his chosen people for the crowning revelation of the Son, who eternally abides "in the bosom of the Father," being the Word through whom he created the world and the Wisdom by which he directs it.

India was prepared by the Spirit in an even more interior manner, so that in the fullness of time she might hear that same Word. He led her into the depth of the mystery of Being, into that self-awareness in which being awakes to itself, to the point where all thought is annihilated. But that is the very place where he who abides in the bosom of the Father, being the Father's own Presence to himself and his own Self-awareness, is waiting for her to come to meet him.

In the Word, the Silence of Being comes to utterance. Apart from the Word, that Silence would remain for ever unbroken. But how could Being have remained eternally unmanifested to itself?

Only in the Glory rendered to him by his Son can we say that the Father *is*.

The German Jesuit priest, Karl Rahner, is the most significant mystical theologian of the 20th-century. No one has written as profoundly and convincingly of the "mysticism of daily life" and of the experience of God as the mystery who haunts every human heart.

KARL RAHNER

Rahner wrote about every significant theological topic in the Christian tradition and in our age. His critical respect for this tradition and his unusual sensitivity to the questions and problems of contemporary life prodded him to creative—although often controversial—reinterpretations of the Christian faith and criticism of much in the Church's practical life. In fact, his unanswered questions have provided fresh points of departure for a host of lesser thinkers.

Born the middle of seven children of a teachers' college professor and a "courageous" (Rahner's word) mother in Freiburg, West Germany, Karl Rahner was a Jesuit for 62 years, and a priest for 52. He led a "theological life" for almost 45 years. He taught theology at Innsbruck, Munich, and Münster and lectured throughout the world. Four thousand written works (paperback sales in excess of 1 million copies) and three volumes of television, radio, and newspaper interviews, make up his bibliography. In addition, he engaged in backbreaking editorial work on theological encyclopedias and reference books.

Rahner's ecumenical skills prompted him to enter into serious dialogue with Protestant, Jewish, Muslim, Buddhist, Marxist, atheistic, and scientific thinkers the world over. His impact upon the Second Vatican Council and his theological influence were so significant that he has been aptly called "the quiet mover of the Roman Catholic Church" and the "Father of the Catholic Church in the 20th century." Yet Rahner said of himself: "All I want to be, even in this work [of theology], is a human being, a Christian, and, as well as I can, a priest of the Church."

The countless ways in which he brought meaning, comfort, light, relief, and healing to so many persons compelled one distinguished German author to call Rahner "a most effective psychotherapist." And he was most priestly and generous with his time to young Jesuit friends who were leaving the priesthood. Students who understood very little of his lectures would state that they attended because they "felt better" about themselves in his presence. "This is a professor to whom I can confess," one said. Not many years before his death, Rahner often spent several hours of his intensely busy day helping a young German psychiatrist to recover some of the memory he had lost in a serious auto accident.

It is in this sense that one should understand Rahner's statement that his biography is his theology and that his personal life essentially—but not only—took place in his theological work.

Thus, it is understandable why this simple Jesuit priest is well-known as a profound and prolific speculative theologian. Nonetheless, Rahner is the 20th century's most important mystical theologian. Central to his thinking is the view that at the core of every person's deepest experience, what haunts every human heart, is a God whose mystery, light, and love have embraced the total person. God works in every person's life as the One to whom everyone must freely say his or her inmost yes or no. We may deny this, ignore it, or repress it, but deep down we know that God is in love with us and that we are all, at least secretly, in love with each other.

Thus, Rahner understands the human person as *homo mysticus*, as a mystic in the world, as an ecstatic being created to surrender freely and lovingly to the holy mystery that gives its own self to all and embraces all. As he says, "In *every* [emphasis added] human being. .there is something like an anonymous, unthematic, perhaps repressed, basic experience of being orientated to God, which is constitutive of man in his concrete makeup (of nature and grace), which can be repressed but not destroyed, which is 'mystical' or (if you prefer a more cautious terminology) has its climax in what the older teachers called infused contemplation."[1]

Thus, as Rahner explains it, the experience of God forms the ambience, the undertow, or the basal spiritual metabolism, of daily life. Because of God's *universal* self-communication, a communication that the human person must freely accept or reject, anyone—even the agnostic or atheist—who lives moderately, selflessly, honestly, courageously, and in silent service to others experiences the mysticism of daily life. The courageous, total acceptance of life and of oneself, even when everything tangible seems to be collapsing, is perhaps the primary mystical experience of everyday life. Anyone who does so accepts implicitly the holy mystery that fills the emptiness both of oneself and of life. And because Christ's grace supports this hope against hope, the experience is, at least anonymously, Christian, that is, Christian in fact if not in name. Thus, self-surrender to the depths of one's humanity, to the depths of life, to mystery itself, fostered either with or without introversion, meditation, or contemplative techniques is the key to Rahner's notion of mysticism.

Rahner's theology can be called mystical for three reasons: 1) It takes seriously the experience, although often hidden or repressed, of God's self-communication; 2) it leads persons into their own deepest mystery by awakening, deepening, and explicating what every person already lives; and 3) it attempts to compress, to simplify, and to concentrate all Christian beliefs by indicating how they evoke the experience of God's loving self-communication to us in the crucified and risen Christ.

In Rahner's view, Christ is the perfectly enfleshed mystical word. Christ's humanity is the prime exemplar of all authentic mysticism, because it surrendered so perfectly to God that it is God's humanity in the world. Christ's cross symbolizes that we must eventually die to all created things to belong totally to loving mystery. Christ's resurrection symbolizes that mystery accepts and confirms total self-surrender; that dying to self and to all created things is not ultimately absurd but the beginning of eternal life.

Impelled by his "Ignatian mysticism of joy in the world" and of finding God in all things and all things in God, Rahner's mystical theology contains a movement of "unfolding" the mystery of God's suffering and victorious love in Christ into every dimension of human life. No other contemporary theologian has written a "theology of everyday things"—a theology of work, of getting about, sitting down, seeing, laughing, eating, sleeping, and working. And as the first of the following text selections illustrates, no other contemporary theologian has written so cogently about the "mysticism of everyday life."

Rahner's appreciation of the sacramental and incarnational dimension of Christian mysticism must be underscored. As he says, "It must be realized that in earthly man this emptying of self will not be accomplished by practicing pure inwardness but by real activity which is called humility, service, love of our neighbor, the cross and death. One must descend into hell together with Christ; lose one's soul, not directly to the God who is above all names but in the service of one's brethren."[2] There is a mystical dimension to human love, according to Rahner, because love of neighbor is love of God. Moreover, by underscoring both the individual and social aspects of the human person, Rahner contends, human love also contains a sociopolitical dimension. Thus, he wrote cogently not only about a person's solitary relationship with God but also of the mystics' relationship to liberation and political theology.

Rahner viewed the mysticism of the Christian saints as the extraordinarily dramatic psychological or parapsychological manifestation of the experienced faith, hope, and love that must exist in *any* Christian life. In fact, "mystical experience," Rahner wrote, "is not specifically different from the ordinary life of grace as such."[3]

In addition to the mysticism of the great Christian saints, he spoke of charismatic experiences as a "mysticism of the masses," as "mysticism in ordinary dress." Charismatic mysticism occurs more commonly than the extraordinary mysticism of the saints and more ostentatiously than the mysticism of everyday life. Thus, speaking in tongues, healings, conversion experiences, prophecy, slayings in the Spirit, and other charismatic gifts have an extraordinary power to intensify a person's ever-present experience of God and to deepen Christian lives of faith, hope, and love.

Rahner did not consider all mysticisms the same. He distinguished carefully God-mysticism from self-, nature-, and psychic-mysticisms. In God-mysticism, the ever-present experience of God is purified, intensified, and brought to a higher level of explicitness. In self-mysticism, the person plunges into the mysterious depths of the self's spiritual quality *without* explicitly experiencing God. Nature-mysticism fosters the experience of one's "pancosmic" unity with all creation. Finally, psychic-mysticism aims at an intensified experience of one's id, psychological levels, and archetypes.

Perhaps the secret of Rahner's appeal is his synthesis of two elements: critical respect for the Christian tradition and unusual sensitivity to the questions and problems of contemporary life. He never overlooked how difficult Christian faith is for a 20th-century person. But he could and did say to his contemporaries not only, "I am also someone who has been tempted by atheism," but also, "There is nothing more self-evident to me than God's existence." Therefore, while breathing the air of unbelief, Rahner would accept nothing less from theology than speaking about God and God's offer of his very own eternal life to us—not just so-called God-talk.

As stated before, the first text illustrates Rahner's conviction that intense experiences of God occur in the depths of one's daily, humdrum existence. What is implicit, hidden, anonymous, repressed, or bursting forth from the center of all we do? In Rahner's eyes, there is nothing profane in the depths of ordinary life. Wherever there is a self-forgetting for the sake of the other, an absolute yielding of everything to the mystery that embraces all life—there is the spirit of the crucified and risen Christ, the "mysticism of everyday life."

The second text was chosen to illustrate why Rahner has been called the teacher of prayer for the 20th century. It was also included as a summary of his mystical theology. To him, God is the incomprehensible mystery that embraces everything. The goal of life is to lose oneself in mystery by surrendering one's entire being. Only self-surrendering love grasps the incomprehensible.

Both texts serve to indicate why Rahner has earned the title, *Doctor Mysticus*, the teacher of 20th-century mystical theology.[4]

THE TEXTS

I can now refer to actual life experiences which, whether we come to know them reflectively or not, are experiences of the Spirit. It is important that we experience them in the right way. In the case of these indications of the actual experience of the Spirit in the midst of banal everyday life, it can no longer be a question of analyzing them individually right down to their ultimate depth—which is the Spirit. And no attempt can be made to make a systematic tabular summary of such experiences. Only arbitrarily and unsystematically selected examples are possible. . . .

Let us take, for instance, someone who is dissatisfied with his life, who cannot make the goodwill, errors, guilt, and fatalities of his life fit together, even when, as often seems impossible, he adds remorse to this accounting. He cannot see how he is to include God as an entry in the accounting, as one that makes the debit and credit, the notional and the actual values, come out right. This person surrenders himself to God or— both more imprecisely and more precisely—to the hope of an incalculable ultimate reconciliation of his existence in which he whom we call God dwells; he releases his unresolved and uncalculated existence, he lets go in trust and hope and does not know how this miracle occurs that he cannot himself enjoy and possess as his own self-actuated possession.

Here is someone who discovers that he can forgive though he receives no reward for it, and silent forgiveness from the other side is taken as self-evident.

Here is someone who tries to love God although no response of love seems to come from God's silent inconceivability, although no wave of emotive wonder any longer supports him, although he can no longer confuse himself and his life-force with God; although he thinks he will die from such a love because it seems like death and absolute denial; because with such a love one appears to fall into the void and the completely unheard-of; because this love seems like a ghastly leap into groundless space; because everything seems untenable and apparently meaningless.

Here is someone who does his duty where it can apparently only be done with the terrible feeling that he is denying himself and doing something ludicrous, which no one will thank him for. Here is a person who is really good to someone from whom no echo of understanding and thankfulness is heard in return, whose goodness is not even repaid by the feeling of having been selfless, noble, and so on.

Here is someone who is silent although he could defend himself, although he is unjustly treated; who keeps silent without feeling that his silence is his sovereign unimpeachability.

Here is someone who obeys not because he must and would otherwise find it inconvenient to disobey, but purely on account of that mysterious, silent, and inconceivable thing we call God and the will of God.

Here is a person who renounces something without thanks or recognition and even without a feeling of inner satisfaction. Here is someone who is absolutely lonely, who finds all the right elements of life pale shadows; for whom all trustworthy handholds take him into the infinite distance and who does not run away from this loneliness but treats it with ultimate hope.

Here is someone who discovers that his most acute concepts and most intellectually refined operations of the mind do not fit; that the unity of consciousness and that of which one is conscious in the destruction of all systems is now to be found only in pain; that he cannot resolve the immeasurable multitude of questions and yet cannot keep to the clearly known content of individual experiences and to the sciences.

Here is someone who suddenly notices how the tiny trickle of his life wanders through the wilderness of the banality of existence, apparently without aim and with the heartfelt fear of complete exhaustion. And yet he hopes, he knows not how, that this trickle will find the infinite expanse of the ocean, even though it may still be covered by the gray sands which seem to extend forever before him.

One could go on like this forever, perhaps even without coming to that experience which for this or that man is the experience of the Spirit, freedom, and grace in his life. For every man makes that experience in accordance with the particular historical and individual situation of his specific life. Every man! But he has, so to speak, to dig it out from under the rubbish of everyday experience and must not run away from it where it begins to become legible, as though it were only an undermining and disturbance of the self-evidence of his everyday life and his scientific assurance.

Let me repeat, though I may say it in almost the same words: where the one and entire hope is given beyond all individual hopes, which comprehends all impulses in silent promise,

—where a responsibility in freedom is still accepted and borne where it has no apparent offer of success and advantage,

—where a man experiences and accepts his ultimate freedom which no earthly compulsions can take away from him,

—where the leap into the darkness of death is accepted as the beginning of everlasting promise,

—where the sum of all accounts of life, which no one can calculate alone, is understood by the inconceivable Other as good, though it still cannot be "proven,"

—where the fragmentary experience of love, beauty, and joy is experienced and accepted purely and simply as the promise of love, beauty, and joy, without their being understood in ultimate cynical skepticism as a cheap form of consolation for some final deception,

—where the bitter, deceptive, and vanishing everyday world is withstood until the accepted end and accepted out of a force whose ultimate source is still unknown to us but can be tapped by us,

—where one dares to pray into a silent darkness and knows that one is heard, although no answer seems to come back about which one might argue and rationalize,

—where one lets oneself go unconditionally and experiences this capitulation as true victory,

—where falling becomes true uprightness,

—where desperation is accepted and is still secretly accepted as trustworthy without cheap trust,

—where a man entrusts all his knowledge and all his questions to the silent and all-inclusive mystery which is loved more than all our individual knowledge which makes us such small people,

—where we rehearse our own deaths in everyday life and try to live in such a way as we would like to die, peaceful and composed,

—where . . . (as I have said, we could go on and on):

—*there* is God and his liberating grace. There we find what we Christians call the Holy Spirit of God. Then we experience something which is inescapable (even when suppressed) in life and which is offered to our freedom with the question whether we want to accept it or whether we want to shut ourselves up in a hell of freedom by trying to barricade ourselves against it. There is the mysticism of everyday life, the discovery of God in all things; there is the sober intoxication of the Spirit, of which the Fathers and the liturgy speak, which we cannot reject or despise because it is real. Let us look for that experience in our own lives. Let us seek the specific experiences in which something like that happens to us. If we find them, we have made the experience of the Spirit which we are talking about.

GOD OF MY LIFE[6]

I should like to speak with You, my God, and yet what else can I speak of but You? Indeed, could anything at all exist which had not been present with You from all eternity, which didn't have its true home and most intimate explanation in Your mind and heart? Isn't everything I ever say really a statement about You?

On the other hand, if I try, shyly and hesitantly, to speak to You about Yourself, You will still be hearing about me. For what could I say about You except that You are my God, the God of my beginning and end, God of my joy and my need, God of my life? Of course, You are endlessly more than merely the God of my life—if that's all You were, You wouldn't really be God at all. But even when I think of your towering majesty, even when I acknowledge You as someone Who has no need of me, Who is infinitely far exalted above the lowly valleys through which I drag out the paths of my life—even then I have called you once again by the same name, God of my life. . . .

Without You, I should founder helplessly in my own dull and groping narrowness. I could never feel the pain of longing, not even deliberately resign myself to being content with this world, had not my mind again and again soared over its own limitations into the hushed reaches which are filled by You alone, the Silent Infinite. Where should I flee before You, when all my yearning for the unbounded, even my bold trust in my littleness, is really a confession of You?. . .

What a poor creature You have made me, O God! All I know about You and about myself is that You are the eternal mystery of my life. Lord, what a frightful puzzle man is! He belongs to You and You are the Incomprehensible—Incomprehensible in Your Being and even more so in Your ways and judgments. For if all Your dealings with me are acts of Your freedom, quite unmerited gifts of Your grace which knows no "why," if my creation and my whole life hang absolutely on Your free decision, if all my paths are, after all, Your paths and, therefore, unsearchable, then, Lord, no amount of questioning will ever fathom Your depths—You will still be the Incomprehensible, even when I see You face to face.

But if You were not incomprehensible, You would be inferior to me, for my mind could grasp and assimilate You. You would belong to me, instead of I to You. And that would truly be hell, if I should belong only to myself! It would be the fate of the damned, to be doomed to pace up and down for all eternity in the cramped and confining prison of my own finiteness.

But can it be that You are my true home? Are You the One who will release me from my narrow little dungeon? Or are You merely adding another torment to my life, when you throw open the gates leading out upon Your broad and endless plain? Are You anything more than my own great insufficiency, if all my knowledge leads only to Your Incomprehensibility? Are You merely eternal unrest for the restless soul? Must every question fall dumb before You, unanswered? Is Your only response the mute "I will have it so" that so coldly smothers my burning desire to understand?

But I am rambling on like a fool—excuse me, O God. You have told me through Your Son that You are the God of my love, and You have commanded me to love You. Your commands are often hard because they enjoin the opposite of what my own inclinations would lead me to do, but when You bid me love You, You are ordering something that my own inclinations would never even dare to suggest: to love You, to come intimately close to You, to love Your very life. You ask me to lose myself in You, knowing that You will take me to Your Heart, where I may speak on loving, familiar terms with You, the incomprehensible mystery of my life. And all this because You are Love Itself.

Only in love can I find You, my God. In love, the gates of my soul spring open, allowing me to breathe a new air of freedom and forget my own petty self. In love, my whole being streams forth out of the rigid confines of narrowness and anxious self-assertion, which make me a prisoner of my own poverty and emptiness. In love, all the powers of my soul flow out toward You, wanting never more to return but to lose themselves completely in You, since by Your love You are the inmost center of my heart, closer to me than I am to myself.

But when I love You, when I manage to break out of the narrow circle of self and leave behind the restless agony of unanswered questions, when my blinded eyes no longer look merely from afar and from the outside upon Your unapproachable brightness, and much more when You Yourself, O Incomprehensible One, have become through love the inmost center of my life, then I can bury myself entirely in You, O mysterious God, and with myself all my questions.

Love such as this wills to possess You as You are . . . . Love wants You as You are . . . .

When I abandon myself in love, then You are my very life, and Your Incomprehensibility is swallowed up in love's unity. When I am allowed to love You, the grasp of Your very mystery becomes a positive source of bliss. Then the farther Your Infinity is removed from my nothingness, the greater is the challenge to my love. The more complete the dependence of my fragile existence upon Your unsearchable counsels, the more unconditional must be the surrender of my whole being to You, beloved God. The more annihilating the incomprehensibility of Your ways and judgments, the greater must be the holy defiance of my love. And my love is all the greater and more blessed, the less my poor spirit understands of You.

God of my life, Incomprehensible, be my life. God of my faith, who leads me into Your darkness—God of my love, who turn Your darkness into the sweet light of my life, be now the God of my hope, so that You will one day be the God of my life, the life of eternal love.

SELECTED BIBLIOGRAPHY

Baker, Eve *The Mystical Journey*. A Western Alternative. London: Wildwood, 1977.

Bancroft, Anne *Six Medieval Mystics and Their Teaching*. Boston: Allen & Unwin, 1982.

Bastige, Roger *The Mystical Life*, trans. H. F. Kynaston-Snell and David Waring. London: Jonathan Cape, 1934.

Bataille, Georges *Inner Experience*, trans. Leslie Ann Boldt. Albany: State University of New York Press, 1988.

Baumgardt, David *Great Western Mystics: Their Lasting Significance*. New York: Columbia University Press, 1961.

Bell, Randolph M. *Holy Anorexia*. Chicago: University of Chicago Press, 1985.

Bouyer, Louis *The Christian Mystery. From Pagan Myth to Christian Mysticism*. Edinburgh: T. & T. Clark, 1989.

___. *Orthodox Spirituality and Protestant and Anglican Spirituality*, trans. Barbara Wall. New York: Seabury, 1982.

___. *The Spirituality of the New Testament and The Fathers*, trans. Mary P. Ryan. New York: Descle, 1960.

___. *The Cistercian Heritage*. London: A. R. Mowbray, 1956.

___. François Vandenbroucke, and Jean Leclercq. *The Spirituality of the Middle Ages*. New York: Seabury, 1982.

Bridges, Hal *American Mysticism. From James to Zen*. San Francisco: Harper & Row, 1970.

Brown, Peter *Augustine of Hippo*. Berkeley: University of California Press, 1967.

Buber, Martin *Ecstatic Confessions*, ed. Paul Mendes-Flohr, trans. Esther Cameron. San Francisco: Harper & Row, 1985.

Butler, Dom Cuthbert *Western Mysticism*. San Francisco: Harper & Row, 1966.

Capps, Walter H., and Wendy M. Wright *Silent Fire. An Invitation to Western Mysticism.* San Francisco: Harper & Row, 1978.

Clark, James M. *The Great German Mystics: Eckhart, Tauler and Suso.* Folcroft, Pa.: Folcroft Press, 1969.

The Classics of Western Spirituality. A Library of the Great Spiritual Masters, ed. Richard J. Payne. Mahwah, N.J.: Paulist Press, 1978—.

College, Eric, ed. *The Mediaeval Mystics of England.* New York: Schribner's, 1961.

Dupré, Louis *The Deeper Life. An Introduction to Christian Mysticism.* New York: Crossroad, 1981.

___. *The Other Dimension: A Search for the Meaning of Religious Attitudes.* New York: Doubleday, 1973.

___ and James A. Wiseman, *Light from Light: An Anthology of Christian Mysticism.* Mahwah, N.J.: Paulist Press, 1988.

Egan, Harvey D. *Ignatius Loyola the Mystic.* Wilmington, Del.: Michael Glazier, 1987.

___. *Christian Mysticism: The Future of a Tradition.* New York: Pueblo, 1984.

___. *What Are They Saying About Mysticism?.* Mahway, N.J.: Paulist Press, 1982.

Elder, E. Rozanne, ed. *The Spirituality of Western Christendom.* Kalamazoo, Mich.: Cistercian Publications, 1976.

Ellwood, Robert S. *Mysticism and Religion.* Englewood Cliffs, N.J.: Prentice-Hall, 1980.

Fletcher, Frank T. H. *Pascal and the Mystical Tradition.* Oxford: Blackwell, 1954)

Fox, Matthew *The Coming of the Cosmic Christ. The Healing of Mother Earth and the Birth of Global Renaissance.* San Francisco: Harper & Row, 1988.

Fremantle, Anne J. *The Protestant Mystics.* Boston: Little Brown, 1964.

Gilson, Etienne *The Mystical Theology of St. Bernard*. New York: Sheed and Ward, 1940.

Graef, Hilda C. *The Story of Mysticism*. Garden City, N.Y.: Doubleday, 1965.

___. *Mystics of Our Times*. Garden City, N.Y.: Hanover House, 1962.

___. *The Way of the Mystics*. Westminster, Md.: Newman Bookshop, 1948.

Grant, Patrick, ed *A Dazzling Darkness. An Anthology of Western Mysticism*. Grand Rapids, Mich.: Wm. B. Eerdmans, 1985.

___. *The Literature of Mysticism in the Western Tradition*. New York: St. Martin's Press, 1983.

Happold, F. C. *Mysticism, A Study and an Anthology*. London: Penguin, 1963.

Harkness, Georgia E. *The Dark Night of the Soul. A Modern Interpretation*. London: E. Melrose, 1966.

___. *Mysticism: Its Meaning and Message*. Nashville: Abingdon Press, 1973.

Inge, William R. *Christian Mysticism*. London: Methuen, 1948.

___. *Mysticism in Religion*. Chicago: University of Chicago Press, 1948.

James, William *The Varieties of Religious Experience. A Study in Human Nature*. New York: New American Library, 1958.

Johnston, William *Being in Love: The Practice of Christian Prayer*. San Francisco: Harper & Row, 1989.

___. *Christian Mysticism Today*. San Francisco: Harper & Row, 1984.

___. *The Mirror Mind. Spirituality and Transformation*. San Francisco: Harper & Row, 1981.

___. *The Inner Eye of Love. Mysticism and Religion*. San Francisco: Harper & Row, 1978.

___. *Silent Music. The Science of Meditation*. San Francisco: Harper &

Row, 1974.

___. *The Still Point. Reflections on Zen and Christian Mysticism*. San Francisco: Harper & Row, 1970.

Jones, Rufus *The Flowering of Mysticism*. New York: Macmillan, 1939.

___. *New Studies in Mystical Religion*. New York: Macmillan, 1927.

___. *Studies in Mystical Religion*. New York: Macmillan, 1909.

Katz, Steven T., ed. *Mysticism and Religious Tradition*. New York: Oxford University Press, 1983.

___, ed. *Mysticism and Philosophical Analysis*. New York: Oxford University Press, 1978.

Knowles, David *The Nature of Mysticism*. New York: Hawthorn Books, 1966.

___. *Cistercians and Cluniacs. The Controversy Between St. Bernard and Peter the Venerable*. London: Oxford University Press, 1955.

Leclercq, Jean *Bernard of Clairvaux and the Cistercian Spirit*, trans. Claire Lavoie. Kalamazoo, Mich.: Cistercian Publications, 1976.

Lossky, Vladimir *The Mystical Theology of the Eastern Church*. Westminster, Md.: Christian Classics, 1957.

Louth, Andrew *The Origins of the Christian Mystical Tradition: From Plato to Denys*. Oxford: Oxford University Press, 1981.

Maes, B. *Franciscan Mysticism*. London: Sheed & Ward, 1928.

Marchal Joseph *Studies in the Psychology of the Mystics*, trans. Algar Thorold. Albany: Magi Books, 1964.

Naranjo, Claudio, and Robert Ornstein *On the Psychology of Meditation*. New York: Viking Press, 1971.

Nieli, Russell *Wittgenstein: From Mysticism to Ordinary Language*. Albany: State University of New York Press, 1987.

O'Brien, Elmer *The Varieties of Mystic Experience*. New York: New American Library, 1965.

Otto, Rudolf *The Idea of the Holy*. New York: Oxford University Press, 1958.

Ozment, Stephen E *Mysticism and Dissent. Religious Ideology and Social Protest in the Sixteenth Century*. New Haven, Conn.: Yale University Press, 1973.

Parrinder, Geoffrey *Mysticism in World Religions*. New York: Oxford University Press, 1976.

Peers, E. Allison *Mystics of Spain*. New York: Fernhill Press, 1951.

___. *Studies of the Spanish Mystics*. New York: Macmillan, 1951.

Plé, A., and others *Mystery and Mysticism*. New York: Philosophical Library, 1956.

Poulain, Auguste F. *The Graces of Interior Prayer. A Treatise on Mystical Theology*. St. Louis: Herder, 1950.

Rahner, Karl *The Dynamic Element in the Church*, trans. W. J. O'Hara. New York: Herder & Herder, 1964.

___. *Visions and Prophecies*. New York: Herder & Herder, 1963.

Reinhold, H. A. *The Soul Afire. Revelations of the Mystics*. Garden City, N.Y.: Doubleday, 1973.

Schakle, Emma *Christian Mysticism*. Butler, Wis.: Clergy Book Service, 1978.

Scharfstein, Ben-Ami *Mystical Experience*. Baltimore, Md.: Penguin, 1973.

Smith, Margaret *An Introduction to Mysticism*. New York: Oxford University Press, 1977.

Stace, Walter T. *The Teachings of the Mystics*. New York: New American Library, 1960.

___. *Mysticism and Philosophy*. Philadelphia: J. B. Lippincott, 1960.

Szarmach, Paul E., ed. *An Introduction to the Medieval Mystics of Europe*. Albany: State University of New York Press, 1984.

Tart, Charles *Altered States of Consciousness. A Book of Readings*.

New York: John Wiley & Sons, 1969.

Underhill, Evelyn *Essentials of Mysticism and Other Essays*. New York: E. P. Dutton, 1972.

___. *The Mystics of the Church*. New York: Schocken Books, 1964.

___. *Mysticism. A Study in the Nature and Development of Man's Spiritual Consciousness*. New York: E. P. Dutton, 1955.

___. *The Mystic Way*. London: Dent, 1913.

Von Hügel, Baron Friedrich *The Mystical Element of Religion as Studied in Saint Catherine of Genoa and Her Friends*. London: Dent, 1923.

Waddell, Helen. *The Desert Fathers*. Ann Arbor: University of Michigan Press, 1957.

Wainwright, William J *Mysticism. A Study of Its Nature, Cognative Value, and Moral Implications*. Madison: University of Wisconsin Press, 1981.

Walsh, James *Spirituality through the Centuries. Ascetics and Mystics of the Western Church*. New York: P. J. Kenedy, 1964.

Wikenhauser, Alfred *Pauline Mysticism. Christ in the Mystical Teaching of St. Paul*, trans. Joseph Cunningham. New York: Herder & Herder, 1960.

Woods, Richard, ed. *Understanding Mysticism*. Garden City, N.Y.: Image-Doubleday, 1980.

Zaehner, Robert C. *Zen, Drugs and Mysticism*. New York: Pantheon, 1973.

___. *Mysticism, Sacred and Profane. An Inquiry into Some Varieties of Praeter-Natural Experience*. Oxford: Clarendon Press, 1957.

NOTES

PREFACE

[1]Trans. William J. Young, S.J., and ed. George E. Ganss, S.J. (St. Louis: Institute of Jesuit Sources, 1964).

[2]New York: New American Library, 1964.

[3]St. Louis: Institute of Jesuit Sources, 1976.

[4]Wilmington, Delaware: Michael Glazier, Inc.

[5]*The Teachings of the Mystics* (New York: New American Library, 1960).

[6]Walter H. Capps & Wendy M. Wright. *Silent Fire. An Invitation to Western Mysticism* (San Francisco: Harper & Row, 1978).

[7]Mahwah, N.J.: Paulist Press, 1982.

[8]New York: Pueblo Publishing Company, 1984.

INTRODUCTION

[1]As quoted in *The Teaching of the Catholic Church*, prepared by Josef Neuner, S.J., and Heinrich Roos, S.J., ed. Karl Rahner, S.J., trans. Geoffrey Stevens (Staten Island, N.Y.: Alba House, 1967), p. 110.

[2]On this point, see my "The Mysticism of Everyday Life," *Studies in Formative Spirituality* X,1 (February, 1989), pp. 7-26.

[3]Karl Rahner, S.J., "Teresa of Avila: Doctor of the Church," in *Opportunities for Faith*, trans. Edward Quinn (New York: Seabury, 1974), p. 125.

[4]Louis Bouyer, Cong. Orat., "'Mysticism': An Essay on the History of the Word," in *Mystery and Mysticism: A Symposium* (London: Blackfriars, 1956), p. 136.

[5]Walter T. Stace, *The Teachings of the Mystics* (New York: New American Library, 1960), p. 20.

[6]Karl Barth, *The Epistle to the Romans* (New York: Oxford University Press, 1968), pp. 109-110.

[7]See: Evelyn Underhill, "Mysticism in the Bible," *The Mystics of the Church* (New York: Schocken Books, 1964), pp. 29-51; William Ralph Inge, "The Mystical Element in the Bible," *Christian Mysticism* (New York: Schribner's, 1899), pp. 39-74; Sister Sylvia Mary, C.S.M.V., *Pauline and Johannine Mysticism* (London: Darton, Longman & Todd, 1964); Alfred Wikenhauser, *Pauline Mysticism* (New York: Herder and Herder, 1960); L. Cerfaux, "St. Paul's Mysticism," *Mystery and Mysticism* (London: Blackfriars, 1956), pp. 33-46; F. Vandenbroucke, O.S.B., "Die Ursprünglichkeit der biblischen Mystik," *Gott in Welt. Festgabe für Karl Rahner* I, hrsg. H. Vorgrimler (Freiburg i. Br.: Herder, 1964), pp. 463-91; and Joseph Huby, S.J., *Mystiques Paulinienne et Johannique* (Paris: Desclée de Brouwer, 1946). For a discussion of the difficult problem concerning the first-hand experiences of significant biblical figures and how the bibli-

cal writers interpreted and formulated these experiences, see Gerald O'Collins, S.J., *Fundamental Theology* (Mahwah, N.J.: Paulist Press, 1981), pp. 53-113.

BIBLICAL MYSTICISM

[1] "Dogmatic Constitution on Divine Revelation," *The Documents of Vatican II*, ed. Walter M. Abbott, S.J. (New York: American Press, 1966), no. 15, p. 122.

[2] Quoted by Sister Sylvia Mary, *Pauline and Johannine Mysticism*, p. x.

[3] Gershom Scholem, *Major Trends in Jewish Mysticism* (New York: Schocken, 1954, pp. 6-7), writes: "It would be absurd to call Moses, the man of God, a mystic, or to apply this term to the Prophets, on the strength of their immediate religious experience." With other commentators, I disagree with Scholem's tacit acceptance of undifferentiated unity, or the fusion experience of monism, as the hallmark of all mysticism.

[4] See: Rudolf Otto, *The Idea of the Holy* (New York: Oxford University Press, 1958).

[5] On this point, see: Claus Westermann, *The Praise of God in the Psalms* (Richmond, Va.: John Knox Press, 1965).

[6] See: Karl Rahner, S.J., "Dogmatic Reflections on the Knowledge and Self-Consciousness of Christ,"*Theological Investigations V,* trans. Karl H. Kruger (Baltimore: Helicon, 1966), pp. 193-215.

[7] See: Joachim Jeremias, *New Testament Theology* (New York: Scribner's, 1971), pp. 61-68; James G. D. Dunn, *Christology in the Making* (Philadelphia: Westminster Press, 1980), pp. 22-33; Bruce Vawter, *This Man Jesus* (Garden City, N.Y.: Doubleday, 1973), pp. 135-39.

[8] See: Hans Küng, *On Being a Christian* (Garden City, N.Y.: Doubleday, 1976), pp. 119-49.

[9] One finds a similar Cross-centered mysticism in Mark's Gospel. Mark wrote essentially for Gentile Christians who were overly interested in miracles and a glorious, divine man. Therefore, Mark shifted the emphasis away from Jesus' miracles to his sufferings and death. It is Markan irony and mysticism that has the pagan centurion recognize Jesus' true identity—not by way of his miracles—but in his torturous death on the Cross ("Truly this man was the Son of God!" [Mk 15:39]).

[10] The Pauline triadic formulae underscore the depths of his trinitarian mysticism. See: 1 Cor 6:11; 12:4f.; 2 Cor 1:21-22; 13:14.

[11] See, Andrew Louth, *The Origins of the Christian Mystical Tradition: From Plato to Denys* (New York: Oxford University Press, 1981). The title of Louth's exceptionally perceptive book is somewhat misleading, because he actually focuses upon the origins of the theology of the Christian mystical tradition.

[12] Karl Rahner, S.J. & Herbert Vorgrimler, "Mysticism," *Dictionary of Theology* (New York: Crossroad, 1981), p. 326.

ORIGEN

[1] See, *Origen—An Exhortation to Martyrdom, Prayer, On First Principles: Book IV, The Prologue to the Commentary on the Song of Songs, Homily XXVII on Numbers*, trans. and intro. Rowan A. Greer (Mahwah, N.J.: Paulist Press, 1979), pp. 41-79.

[2] For further study, see Jean Daniélou, *Origen*, trans. Walter Mitchell (New York: Sheed & Ward, 1955).

[3] *Ibid.*, pp. 48-51.

[4] *Ibid.*, pp. 55-56.

[5] *Ibid.*, pp. 217-219.

[6] *Ibid.*, p. 223.

[7] *Ibid.*, pp. 230-231.

[8] *Ibid.*, p. 232.

[9] *Ibid.*, pp. 236-239.

[10] Reprinted from *Origen—Spirit and Fire: A Thematic Study of His Writings*, by Hans Urs von Balthasar, trans. Robert J. Daly, S.J. (Washington, D.C.: The Catholic University of America Press, 1984), pp. 220-221.

GREGORY OF NYSSA

[1] *Gregory of Nyssa: The Life of Moses*, trans., intro., and notes by Everett Ferguson and Abraham J. Malherbe (Mahwah, N.J.: Paulist Press, 1978), p. 96.

[2] *Commentary on the Song of Songs*, sermon 12, quoted in *Gregory of Nyssa: The Life of Moses*, p.22.

[3] For further information, see Jean Daniélou's excellent introduction to, *From Glory to Glory: Texts from Gregory of Nyssa's Mystical Writings*, ed. and intro. Jean Daniélou, S.J., trans. and ed. Herbert Musurillo, S.J. (New York: Charles Scribner's Sons, 1961), pp. 3-78.

[4] *Ibid.*, pp. 246-250.

[5] *Ibid.*, pp. 245-246.

[6] *Ibid.*, pp. 270-271.

[7] *Ibid.*, pp. 163-165.

[8] *Ibid.*, pp. 156-157.

[9] *Ibid.*, pp. 174-175.

[10] *Ibid.*, pp. 238-240.

[11] *Ibid.*, pp. 240-242.

EVAGRIUS PONTICUS

[1]*Chapters on Prayer*, supplement 4, quoted by F. Refoulé, "Evagrius Ponticus," *New Catholic Encyclopedia* V., pp. 644-645.

[2]PG 40:1244A, quoted by John Eudes Bamberger, O.C.S.O., *Evagrius Ponticus—The Praktikos and Chapters on Prayer*, trans, intro., and notes by John Eudes Bamberger, O.C.S.O. (Spencer, Mass. & Kalamazoo, Mich: Cistercian Publications, 1970), p. xci.

[3]For an excellent theological solution to this problem, see William Johnston, S.J., *The Still Point* (San Francisco: Harper and Row, 1970), chapter 9, "Incarnation," pp. 151-170 and *The Mysticism of the Cloud of Unknowing* (St. Meinrad, Ind.: Abbey Press, 1965), pp. 67-79. For more information about Evagrius, see the excellent introduction by John Eudes Bamberger, *Evagrius Ponticus—Praktikos and the Chapters on Prayer*, pp. xxiii-xciv.

[4]*Ibid.*, pp. 14-39.

[5]*Ibid.*, pp. 56-80.

AUGUSTINE OF HIPPO

[1]Dour Cuthert Butler, *Western Mysticism* (New York: Gordon Press, 1975, 3rd ed.), pp. 24, 26.

[2]*Augustine of Hippo—Selected Writings*, trans. & intro. Mary T. Clark (Mahwah, N.J.: Paulist Press, 1984), *The Confessions*, VII, c. 17, p. 75.

[3]Reprinted from Louis Bouyer, *The Spirituality of the New Testament and the Fathers*, trans. Mary P. Ryan (New York: Desclée, 1963), p. 475, and from Dom Cuthbert Butler, *Western Mysticism*, pp. 21-24.

[4]Reprinted from *Augustine of Hippo—Selected Writings*, trans. and intro. Mary T. Clark (Mahway, N.J.: Paulist, 1984), pp. 114-115, 125-127, 144, 342, 347.

[5]*Ibid.*, pp. 125-127, 144.

[6]*Ibid.*, pp. 342 , 347.

JOHN CASSIAN

[1]Owen Chadwick, in the introduction to *John Cassian—Conferences*, trans. Colm Luibheid (Mahwah, N.J.: Paulist, 1985), p. 13.

[2]For additional information, see Owen Chadwick, *John Cassian*, 2nd ed. (Cambridge: Cambridge University Press, 1968).

[3]Reprinted from *John Cassian—Conferences*, trans. Colm Luibheid (Mahwah, N.J.: Paulist Press, 1985), pp. 85-86.

[4] *Ibid.*, pp. 132-138.

[5] *Ibid.*, p. 116.

PSEUDO-MACARIUS

[1] *Fifty Spiritual Homilies of St. Macarius the Great*, trans. A. J. Mason (Willits, Calif.: Eastern Orthodox Books, 1974), Homily XI, no. 11, p. 86.

[2] For more information, see *Intoxicated with God—The Fifty Homilies of Macarius*, trans. and intro. George A. Maloney, S. J. (Denville, N. J. : Dimension Books, 1978), pp. 5-21.

[3] Reprinted from *Fifty Spiritual Homilies of St. Macarius the Great*, pp. 1-2 & 10-11.

[4] *Ibid.*, pp. 65-66, 68.

[5] *Ibid.*, pp. 112-113, 115-116.

[6] *Ibid.*, pp. 56-57.

[7] *Ibid.*, p. 216.

[8] *Ibid.*, pp. 224-225.

[9] *Ibid.*, p. 240.

[10] *Ibid.*, pp. 261-262.

[11] *Ibid.*, pp. 265-266.

[12] *Ibid.*, pp. 287-288.

PSEUDO-DIONYSIUS

[1] *The Ecclesiastical Hierarchy*, in *Pseudo-Dionysius—The Complete Works*, trans. Colm Luibheid; foreword, notes, and translation collaboration by Paul Rorem; preface by René Roques; introductions by Jaroslav Pelikan, Jean Leclercq, and Karlfried Froehlich (Mahwah, N.J.: Paulist Press, 1987), V, 2, 501D, p. 234.

[2] *The Celestial Hierarchy*, in *Pseudo-Dionysius—The Complete Works*, III, 1, 424D, p. 209.

[3] *The Divine Names*, *Pseudo-Dionysius—The Complete Works*, VII, 3, 872A, p. 108.

[4] *The Divine Names*, *Pseudo-Dionysius—The Complete Works*, V, 8, 842B, p. 101.

[5] *The Celestial Hierarchy*, *Pseudo-Dionysius—The Complete Works*, III, 1-2, 164D-165A, pp. 153-154, my emphasis.

[6] *The Celestial Hierarchy*, *Pseudo-Dionysius—The Complete Works*, I, 1, 376A, p. 198.

[7] For further information, see the introductions by Jaroslav Pelikan, Jean Leclerq, and Karlfried Froehlich in *Pseudo-Dionysius—The Complete Works*.

[8] Reprinted from Elmer O'Brien, *Varieties of Mystic Experience* (New York: New American Library, 1965), pp. 69-76. O'Brien arranged the translation from the Greek colometrically "because the text seems to demand it and the impression—wholly justified—of an incantation is better conveyed" (p. 69).

GREGORY THE GREAT

[1] For further information, see, Dom Cuthbert Butler, *Western Mysticism*, (New York: Gordon Press, 1975, 3rd ed.), pp. 65-92, 171-188.

[2] *Ibid.*, p. 68.

[3] *Ibid.*, p. 69-71.

[4] *Ibid.*, p. 82.

[5] *Ibid.*, p. 68.

[6] *Ibid.*, pp. 73-74.

[7] *Ibid.*, p. 74.

[8] *Ibid.*, pp. 78-79.

[9] *Ibid.*, p. 79.

[10] *Ibid.*, p. 85.

[11] *Ibid.*, p. 88.

[12] *Ibid.*, p. 89.

[13] *Ibid.*, p. 84.

[14] *Ibid.*, pp. 86-87.

JOHN CLIMACUS

[1] *John Climacus: The Ladder of Divine Ascent,* intro. Kallistos Ware, trans. Colm Luibheid and Norman V. Russell (Mahwah, N.J.: Paulist Press, 1982), Step 30, p. 286.

[2] In Kallistos Ware's introduction to *John Climacus: The Ladder of Divine Ascent,* p. 1.

[3] For further information, see Colm Luibheid's preface and Kallistos Ware's introduction to *John Climacus: The Ladder of Divine Ascent,* pp. xi-xxviii and 1-68. Although the selections are taken from the Luibheid and Russell translation, the translation by Archimandrite Lazarus Moore (Willits, California: Eastern Orthodox Books, 1959) is also very good.

[4] Reprinted from *John Climacus: The Ladder of Divine Ascent,* pp. 185-186.

[5] *Ibid.*, p. 170.

[6] *Ibid.*, p. 79.

[7] *Ibid.*, p. 234.

[8] *Ibid.*, pp. 95-97.

[9] *Ibid.*, pp. 123-125.

[10] *Ibid.*, p. 128.

[11] *Ibid.*, p. 262.

[12] *Ibid.*, p. 266.

[13] *Ibid.*, p. 103.

[14] *Ibid.*, pp. 274-276.

[15] *Ibid.*, pp. 278-279, 239, 286, 290.

[16] *Ibid.*, p. 197.

[17] *Ibid.*, pp. 242, 255.

[18] *Ibid.*, pp. 249, 223.

[19] *Ibid.*, p. 137.

[20] *Ibid.*, p. 273.

[21] *Ibid.*, pp. 139-140, 259.

[22] *Ibid.*, p. 220.

[23] *Ibid.*, pp. 89-90.

MAXIMUS CONFESSOR

[1] For further information, see, Jaroslav Pelikan's introduction to *The Four Hundred Chapters on Love*, in *Maximus Confessor—Selected Writings*, trans. George C. Berthold, intro. Jaroslav Pelikan (Mahwah, N.J.: Paulist Press, 1985), pp. 1-13. Also see, Hans Urs von Balthasar, *Liturgie cosmique—Maxime le Confessor* (Paris, 1947).

[2] Reprinted from *Maximus Confessor—Selected Writings*, pp. 36-84,

[3] *Ibid.*, pp. 150-156, 163-164.

[4] *Ibid*, p. 203.

ISAAC THE SYRIAN

[1] See, *The Ascetical Homilies of Saint Isaac the Syrian*, trans. by The Holy Transfiguration Monastery (Brookline, Mass.: Holy Transfiguration Monastery, 1984).

[2] For further information, see the introductory material to the *Ascetical Homilies*, pp. xxv-cxii. Also see, Élie Khalifé Hachem, "Isaac de Ninive," *Dictionnaire de Spiritualité Ascétique et Mystique* VII, cols. 2041-2054.

[3] Reprinted from *The Ascetical Homilies of Saint Isaac the Syrian*, pp. 238-240.

[4] *Ibid.*, pp. 115-122.

SYMEON THE NEW THEOLOGIAN

[1] *Symeon the New Theologian—The Discourses*, trans. C.J. de Catanzario and intro. George Maloney, S.J. (Mahwah, N.J.: Paulist Press, 1980).

[2] *Hymns of Divine Love by Symeon the New Theologian*, trans. and intro. George A. Maloney, S.J. (Denville, N.J.: Dimension Books, 1976).

[3] For more information, see: George A. Maloney, S.J., *The Mystic of Light and Fire: St. Symeon, the New Theologian* (Denville, N.J.: Dimension Books, 1975).

[4] Reprinted from *Hymns of Divine Love by Symeon the New Theologian*, trans. and intro. George A. Maloney, S.J. (Denville, N.J.: Dimension Books, 1976) pp. 135-138.

WILLIAM OF ST. THIERRY

[1]*William of St. Thierry—The Enigma of Faith,* trans. John D. Anderson (Kalamazoo, Mich.: Cistercian Publications, 1974), no. 41, p. 73.

[2]*Ibid.*

[3]*William of St. Thierry—On Contemplating God, Prayer, Meditations,* trans. Sister Penelope, C.S.M.V. (Kalamazoo, Mich.: Cistercian Publications, 1977), *Meditation* 3:8, p. 106.

[4]*Meditations* 7:7, p. 137.

[5]*On Contemplating God,* no. 11, p. 57.

[6]*William of St. Thierry—The Mirror of Faith,* trans. Thomas X. Davis (Kalamazoo, Mich.: Cistercian Publications, 1979), chapter 4, no. 6, p. 18.

[7]*On Contemplating God,* no. 3, p. 38.

[8]For further information, see Jean-Marie Déchanet, *William of St. Thierry, the Man and his Works,* trans. Richard Strachan (Kalamazoo, Mich.: Cistercian Publications, 1972).

[9]Reprinted from *William of St. Thierry—The Golden Epistle,* trans. Theodore Berkeley, OCSO (Kalamazoo, Mich.: Cistercian Publications, Inc., 1971), pp. 92-105.

BERNARD OF CLAIRVAUX

[1]*Bernard of Clairvaux—On the Song of Songs I,* trans. Kilian Walsh, O.C.S.O. (Kalamazoo, Mich.: Cistercian Publications, 1971), Sermon 15, no. 6, p. 110. References to Bernard's 86 sermons in the four-volume Cistercian Publication series will be given according to volume, sermon, paragraph, and page number.

[2]*On the Song of Songs,* I, Sermon 20, no. 4, p. 150.

[3]*Ibid.,* no. 6, p. 152.

[4]*On the Song of Songs,* II, Sermon 43, no. 4, pp. 222-223.

[5]"Bernard, St.," *The Oxford Dictionary of the Christian Church,* ed. F.L. Cross, (New York: Oxford University Press, 1984, 2nd revised ed.), p. 162.

[6]*On the Song of Songs,* I, Sermon 4, no. 1, p. 21.

[7]*On the Song of Songs,* II, Sermon 32, no. 3, pp. 135-136.

[8]*On the Song of Songs,* I, Sermon 8, no. 5, pp. 47-48.

[9]For further information, read the excellent introduction to Bernard by Jean Le-Clercq., O.S.B., in *Bernard of Clairvaux—Selected Works,* trans. and foreword G. R. Evans (Mahwah, N.J.: Paulist Press, 1987), pp. 13-57. Also see, Etienne Gilson, *The Mystical Theology of Saint Bernard of Clairvaux* (New York: Sheed & Ward, 1955).

[10]Reprinted from *Bernard of Clairvaux—On the Song of Songs,* trans. Kilian Walsh, OCSO (Kalamazoo, Michigan: Cistercian Publications, 1971), I, pp. 7-9; I, pp. 7-9.

[11]Reprinted from *Bernard of Clairvaux—On the Song of Songs* II, trans. Kilian Walsh, O.C.S.O. (Kalamazoo, Mich.: Cistercian Publications, 1976), pp. 206-207.

[12] Reprinted from *Bernard of Clairvaux—On the Song of Songs III*, trans. Kilian Walsh, O.C.S.O. (Kalamazoo, Mich.: Cistercian Publications, 1979), pp. 51-54.

[13] Reprinted from *Bernard of Clairvaux—On the Songs of Songs IV*, trans. Kilian Walsh, O.C.S.O. (Kalamazoo, Mich.: Cistercian Publications, 1980), pp. 89-92.

[14] *Ibid.*, pp. 182-186.

[15] *Ibid.*, pp. 209-210

AELRED OF RIEVAULX

[1] *Aelred of Rievaulx—On Spiritual Friendship*, trans. Mary Eugenia Laker, S.S.N.D. (Washington, D.C.: Cistercian Publications, 1974), 2:10-11, pp. 71-72.

[2] *On Spiritual Friendship*, Prolgue, no. 5, p. 46

[3] For further information, see Douglas Roby's introduction and M. Basil Pennington, O.C.S.O.'s preface in *On Spiritual Friendship*, pp. 3-35 and 36-41.

[4] Reprinted from *Aelred of Rievaulx—On Spiritual Friendship*, pp. 111-112

[5] *Ibid.*, pp. 74-77.

[6] *Ibid.*, pp. 65-66, 73.

[7] *Ibid.*, p. 65.

RICHARD OF ST. VICTOR

[1] For further information, see Grover Zinn's excellent introduction to Richard of St. Victor in, *Richard of St. Victor—The Twelve Patriarchs, The Mystical Ark, Book Three of the Trinity*, trans. and intro. Grover A. Zinn (Mahwah, N.J.: Paulist Press, 1979), pp. 1-49.

[2] Reprinted from *Richard of Saint Victor: Selected Writings on Contemplation*, trans., intro., and notes by Clare Kirchberger (New York: Harper & Brothers, 1957), pp. 213-233.

HILDEGARD OF BINGEN

[1] Some of her music is available on records and tapes.

[2] *Hildegard of Bingen—Scivias*, trans. Mother Columba Hart and Jane Bishop (Mahwah, N.J.: Paulist Press, 1990), p. 59.

[3] See *Illuminations of Hildegard of Bingen* with a commentary by Matthew Fox, O.P. (Santa Fe, N. M.: Bear & Co., 1985).

[4] *Scivias*, p. 60.

[5] For further information, see Barbara J. Newman's introduction to *Hildegard of Bingen—Scivias*, pp. 9-53; Francesca Maria Steele, *The Life and Visions of St. Hildegard* (St. Louis: B. Herder, 1915); Valerie M. Lagorio, "The Medieval Continental Women Mystics: An Introduction," in *An Introduction to the Medieval Mystics of Europe*, ed. Paul E. Szarmach (Albany: State University of New York, 1984), pp. 161-193.

[6] Reprinted from *Hildegard of Bingen—Scivias*, pp. 161-165.

GUIGO II

[1] For further information, see the introduction by Edmund College, O.S.A. and James Walsh, S.J., in *Guigo II: The Ladder of Monks. A Letter on the Contemplative Life and Twelve Meditations*, trans. and intro. Edmund College, O.S.A. and James Walsh, S.J. (Kalamazoo, Mich.: Cistercian Publications, 1981), pp. 3-63.

[2] Reprinted from *Guigo II: The Ladder of Monks. A Letter on the Contemplative Life and Twelve Meditations*, pp. 67-82.

[3] *Ibid.*, pp. 89-90.

[4] *Ibid.*, pp. 100-101.

[5] *Ibid.*, pp. 118, 122, 124.

FRANCIS OF ASSISI

[1] For further information, see Raphael Brown's introduction to *The Little Flowers of St. Francis*, trans., ed., and intro. Raphael Brown (Garden City, N.Y.: Doubleday, 1958), pp. 13-37.

[2] Reprinted from *The Little Flowers of St. Francis*, pp. 190-193.

[3] *Ibid.*, pp. 317-318.

GILES OF ASSISI

[1] *The Golden Sayings of the Blessed Giles of Assisi*, newly ed. and trans. Paschal Robinson (Philadelphia: Dolphin Press, 1907). See also, *Golden Words*, trans. I. O'Sullivan (Chicago: Franciscan Herald, 1966).

[2] For more information, see Raphael Brown's introduction to *The Little Flowers of St. Francis*, trans. and intro. Raphael Brown (Garden City, N.Y.: Doubleday, 1958), pp. 13-37.

[3] Reprinted from *The Little Flowers of St. Francis*, p. 245.

[4] Reprinted from *Actus Beati Francisci et Sociorum Ejus*, quoted by Martin Buber, in *Ecstatic Confessions*, ed. Paul Mendes-Flohr and trans. Esther Cameron (San Francisco: Harper and Row, 1985), pp. 48-50.

[5] *Ibid.*

HADEWIJCH OF ANTWERP

[1] *Hadewijch—The Complete Works*, trans. and intro. Mother Columba Hart, O.S.B. (Mahwah, N.J.: Paulist Press, 1980), vision 13, no. 97, p. 299.

[2] *Hadewijch—The Complete Works, Poems in Stanzas*, 10:4, p. 153.

[3] *Hadewijch—The Complete Works*, vision 1, no. 138, p. 266.

[4]*Hadewijch—The Complete Works*, letter 6:227, p. 61.

[5]For further information, see Paul Mommaers's preface and Mother Columba Hart's introduction to *Hadewijch—The Complete Works*, pp. xiii-xxiv and 1-42.

[6]Reprinted from *Hadewijch—The Complete Works*, p. 86.

[7]*Ibid.*, pp. 88-89.

[8]*Ibid.*, pp. 280-282.

BONAVENTURE

[1]*The Life of St. Francis*, in *Bonaventure—The Soul's Journey into God, The Tree of Life, The Life of St. Francis*, trans. and intro. Ewert Cousins (Mahwah, N.J.: Paulist Press, 1978), p. 182.

[2]*The Soul's Journey into God*, VI, no. 7, pp. 107-8.

[3]*The Tree of Life*, no. 29, p. 154.

[4]For further information, see Ewert Cousins's excellent introduction to *Bonaventure—The Soul's Journey into God, The Tree of Life, The Life of St. Francis*, pp. 1-48. Also see, Etienne Gilson, *The Philosophy of St. Bonaventure*, trans. Dom Illtyd Trethowan and Frank Sheed (Paterson, N.J.: St. Anthony Guild Press, 1965).

[5]Reprinted from *Bonaventure—The Soul's Journey into God, The Tree of Life, The Life of St. Francis*, 54-55.

[6]*Ibid.*, pp. 60-63 & 67-69.

[7]*Ibid.*, pp. 69 & 75-77.

[8]*Ibid.*, pp. 79-80.

[9]*Ibid.*, pp. 87-89.

[10]*Ibid.*, pp. 94-97.

[11]*Ibid.*, pp. 102-103 and 107-108.

[12]*Ibid.*, pp. 110-113 and 115-116.

MECHTILD OF MAGDEBURG

[1]*The Revelations of Mechtild of Magdeburg* or *The Flowing Light of the Godhead*, trans. Lucy Menzies (London: Longmans, Green and Co., 1953), IV/13, p. 108 & VI/43, p. 203.

[2]*The Flowing Light of the Godhead*, IV/12, p. 105.

[3]*Ibid.*, III/3, pp. 69-71.

[4]*Ibid.*, IV/12, p. 108.

[5]*Ibid.*, VII/47, p. 244.

[6]*Ibid.*, VII/2, p. 211.

[7]For further information, see "Mechtild of Magdeburg: The Flowing Light of God," in *Cistercians in the Late Middle Ages*, ed. E. Rozanne Elder (Kalamazoo, Mich.: Cistercian Publications, 1981), pp. 19- 37; "Mechtild of Magdeburg," in José de Vinck, *Revelations of Women Mysticism: From the Middle Ages to Modern Times* (Staten Island, N.Y.: Alba House, 1985).

[8]Reprinted from *The Revelations of Mechtild of Magdeburg: The Flowing Light of the Godhead*, I/44, pp. 20-25.

GERTRUDE THE GREAT

[1]For further information, see Mary F. Robinson, *The End of the Middle Ages: Essays and Questions in History* (London: T. F. Unwin, 1889).

[2]Reprinted from *The Life and Revelations of Saint Gertrude, Virgin and Abbess of the Order of St. Benedict*, trans. M. F. C. Cusak (Westminster, Md.: Christian Classics, 1983), pp. 79-81.

[3]*Ibid.*, pp. 85-86.

[4]*Ibid.*, p. 87.

[5]*Ibid.*, p. 89.

[6]*Ibid.*, p. 91.

JACOPONE DA TODI

[1]*Jacopone da Todi—The Lauds*, trans. Serge and Elizabeth Hughes, intro. Elizabeth Hughes (Mahwah, N.J.: Paulist Press, 1982).

[2]*Ibid.*, Laud 65, p. 198.

[3]*Ibid.*, Laud 65, p. 200.

[4]*Ibid.*, Laud 91, pp. 271 and 266.

[5]*Ibid.*, pp. 272 and 269.

[6]*Ibid.*, Laud 57, p. 178.

[7]For additional information, see George T. Peck, *Fool of God—Jacopone da Todi* (University, Ala.: Alabama University Press, 1980).

[8]Reprinted from *Jacopone da Todi—The Lauds*, pp. 257-265.

[9]*Ibid.*, pp. 187-189.

[10]*Ibid.*, p. 183.

[11]*Ibid.*, pp. 184-186.

[12]*Ibid.*, pp. 164-165.

ANGELA OF FOLIGNO

[1]*The Book of Divine Consolation of the Blessed Angela of Foligno*, trans. Mary G. Steegmann (New York: Duffield and Windus, 1909), p. 166.

[2]*Ibid.*

[3]*Ibid.*, pp. 24-31.

[4]*Ibid.*, p. 185.

[5]For further information, see Algar Thorold, *An Essay in Aid of a Better Understanding to Catholic Mysticism: Illustrated From the Writings of Blessed Angela of Foligno* (London: Kegan & Trench & Trubner, 1900).

[6]Reprinted from *The Book of Divine Consolation of the Blessed Angela of Foligno*, pp. 186-194.

RAMON LULL

[1]Ramon Lull, *Blanquerna: A Thirteenth Century Romance*, trans. E. Allison Peers (London: Jarrolds Publishers, 1926), Book V, chap. XCIX, pp. 411-468, 532-533.

[2]For further information, see J. N. Hillgarth, *Ramon Lull and Lullism in Fourteenth Century France* (Oxford Warburg Studies, 1971).

[3]Reprinted from *Ramon Lull, The Book of the Lover and Beloved*, ed. Kenneth Leech, trans. E. Allison Peers (Mahwah, N.J.: Paulist Press, 1978).

MEISTER ECKHART

[1]The *Defense* may be found in *Meister Eckhart: A Modern Translation*, trans. Raymond B. Blakney (San Francisco: Harper & Row, 1941), pp. 258-305.

[2]*Meister Eckhart—Teacher and Preacher*, ed. Bernard McGinn with the collaboration of Frank Tobin and Elvira Borgstädt (Mahwah, N.J.: Paulist Press, 1986), p. 270.

[3]For further information, see Edmund Colledge, "Historical Data," and Bernard McGinn, "Theological Summary," *Meister Eckhart—The Essential Sermons, Commentaries, Treatises, and Defense*, trans. and intro. Edmund Colledge, O.S.A. and Bernard McGinn (Mahwah, N.J.: Paulist Press, 1981), pp. 5-23 and 24-61.

[4]Reprinted from *Meister Eckhart: A Modern Translation*, pp. 227- 232.

[5]Reprinted from *Meister Eckhart—The Essential Sermons, Commentaries, Treatises, and Defense*, pp. 186-189.

[6]Ibid., pp. 197-198.

[7]Reprinted from *Meister Eckhart—Teacher and Preacher*, pp. 340- 341.

RICHARD ROLLE

[1] *Richard Rolle—The Fire of Love*, trans. Clifton Wolters (Harmondsworth, England: Penguin, 1972), p. 83.

[2] *Rolle—The Fire of Love*, p. 60.

[3] For further information, see Rosamund S. Allen's introduction to *Richard Rolle—The English Writings*, trans., ed., and intro. Rosamund Allen (Mahwah, N.J.: Paulist Press, 1988), pp. 9-63; M. L. del Mastro's introduction to *Richard Rolle: The Fire of Love and The Mending of Life*, trans. and intro. M. L. del Mastro (Garden City, N.Y.: Doubleday, 1981), pp. 11-41.

[4] Reprinted from *Richard Rolle: The Fire of Love and The Mending of Life*, pp. 91-95.

[5] Reprinted from *Richard Rolle—The English Writings*, p. 173.

GREGORY PALAMAS

[1] For additional information, see John Meyendorff, *St. Gregory Palamas and Orthodox Spirituality* (Crestwood, N.Y.: St. Vladimir's Seminary Press, 1974).

[2] Reprinted from *Gregory Palamas—The Triads*, trans. Nicholas Gendle, ed. and intro. John Meyendorff (Mahwah, N.J.: Paulist Press, 1983), pp. 31-36.

[3] *Ibid.*, pp. 41-55.

JOHANNES TAULER

[1] For further information, see Josef's Schmidt's introduction to *Johannes Tauler: Sermons*, trans. Maria Shrady and intro. Josef Schmidt (Mahwah, N.J.: Paulist Press, 1985), pp. 1-34.

[2] Reprinted from *Johannes Tauler: Sermons*, pp. 103-108.

HENRY SUSO

[1] Henry Suso's Life, in *The Exemplar—Life and Writings of Blessed Henry Suso*, O.P., critical intro. and explanatory notes by Nicholas Heller, trans. Sister M. Ann Edward, O.P. (Dubuque, Iowa: Priory Press, 1962), vol. I, p. 3.

[2] *Little Book of Eternal Wisdom and Little Book of Truth*, trans. James M. Clark (London: Faber & Faber, 1953).

[3] See, *The Exemplar—Life and Writings*, vol. II.

[4] For further information, see Bernard McGinn's preface and Frank Tobin's introduction to *Henry Suso—The Exemplar, With Two German Sermons* (Mahwah, N.J.: Paulist Press, 1989), pp. 3-7 and 13-59.

[5] Reprinted from *Henry Suso's Life*, in *The Exemplar—Life and Writings of Blessed Henry Suso*, O.P., vol. I., pp. 7-12.

[6] *Ibid.*

[7]*Ibid.*, vol. II, pp. 28-31.

[8]Reprinted from *Little Book of Eternal Wisdom and Little Book of Truth*, pp. 52-56.

JOHN RUUSBROEC

[1]*The Spiritual Espousals*, in *John Ruusbroec—The Spiritual Espousals and Other Works*, trans. and intro. James A. Wiseman, O.S.B. (Mahwah, N.J.: Paulist Press, 1985), p. 152. For further study, see Louis Dupré, *The Common Life: The Origins of Trinitarian Mysticism and Its Development by John Ruusbroec* (New York: Crossroad, 1984).

[2]Reprinted from *John Ruusbroec—The Spiritual Espousals and Other Works*, pp. 253-256, 115, 262-267.

CATHERINE OF SIENA

[1]*Catherine of Siena—The Dialogue*, trans. Suzanne Noffke, O.P. (Mahwah, N.J.: Paulist Press, 1980), pp. 64-65.

[2]For further information, see Suzanne Noffke's introduction to *Catherine of Siena— The Dialogue*, pp. 1-22; *The Letters of St. Catherine of Siena* I, trans. Suzanne Noffke, O.P. (Binghamton, N.Y.: Medieval and Renaissance Texts and Studies, 1988), pp. 1-31; and Noffke's introduction to *The Prayers of Catherine of Siena*, ed. and trans. Suzanne Noffke, O.P.(Mahwah, N.J.: Paulist Press, 1983), pp. 1-11.

[3]Reprinted from *Catherine of Siena—The Dialogue*, pp. 147-148.

[4]*Ibid.*, p. 161.

[5]*Ibid.*

[6]*Ibid.*, pp. 168-169.

[7]*Ibid.*, pp. 179-181.

[8]Reprinted from *The Letters of St. Catherine of Siena* I, pp. 107-111.

CLOUD OF UNKNOWING

[1]For further information, see William Johnston, S.J., *The Mysticism of the Cloud of Unknowing* (St. Meinrad, Ind.: Abbey Press, 1975).

[2]Reprinted from *The Cloud of Unknowing and the Book of Privy Counselling*, ed. William Johnston, S.J. (Garden City, N.Y.: Doubleday, 1973), pp. 48-49.

[3]*Ibid.*, pp. 53-54.

[4]*Ibid.*, p. 56.

[5]*Ibid.*, pp. 162-163.

[6]*Ibid.*, pp. 181-183.

[7]Reprinted from *The Assessment of Inward Stirrings*, in *The Pursuit of Wisdom and Other Works, By The Author Of the Cloud of Unknowing*, trans., ed., and annotated James A. Walsh, S.J. (Mahwah, N.J.: Paulist Press, 1988), pp. 142-143, 111.

[8]Reprinted from *The Cloud of Unknowing and the Book of Privy Counselling*, pp. 105-106, 115-116.

WALTER HILTON

[1]For further information, see M. L. del Mastro's introduction to *The Stairway to Perfection*, trans. and intro. M. L. del Mastro (Garden City, N.J.: Doubleday, 1979), pp. 5-47; Dom Gerald Sitwell's introduction to *The Scale of Perfection*, trans. and intro. Dom Gerald Sitwell, O.S.B. (London: Burns Oates, 1953), pp. v-xviii.

[2]Reprinted from *The Scale of Perfection*, by Walter Hilton, abridged and presented by Dom Illytd Trethowan, trans. Leo Sherley-Price (St. Meinrad, Ind.: Abbey Press, 1975), pp. 71-76, 78-83.

JULIAN OF NORWICH

[1]*Julian of Norwich—Showings*, trans. and intro. Edmund Walsh, O.S.A. and James Walsh, S.J. (Mahwah, N.J.: Paulist Press, 1978), *Long text*, pp. 183-184.

[2]For further information, see Brant Pelphrey, *Julian of Norwich* (Wilmington, Del.: Michael Glazier, 1989).

[3]Reprinted from *Julian of Norwich—Showings*, trans. and intro. Edmund Walsh, O.S.A. and James Walsh, S.J. (Mahwah, N.J.: Paulist Press, 1978), pp. 183-184.

[4]*Ibid.*, p. 229.

[5]*Ibid.*, pp. 267-276.

[6]*Ibid.*, pp. 292-298.

[7]*Ibid.*, pp. 342-343.

THOMAS À KEMPIS

[1]For further information, see J. E. G. de Montmorency, *Thomas à Kempis: His Age and Book* (London: Methuen, 1906).

[2]Reprinted from *My Imitation of Christ*, trans. Msgr. John J. Gorman (Brooklyn, N.Y.: Confraternity of the Precious Blood, 1982), pp. 437-439 and 441.

[3]*Ibid.*, p. 157.

[4]*Ibid.*, p. 103.

[5]*Ibid.*, pp. 105-106.

[6]*Ibid.*, p. 213.

[7]*Ibid.*, p. 232.

[8]*Ibid.*, p. 67.

[9]*Ibid.*, pp. 267-268 and 192.

[10]*Ibid.*, pp. 277-278.

[11] *Ibid.*, pp. 304-305.

[12] *Ibid.*, p. 327.

[13] *Ibid.*, pp. 11-12.

[14] *Ibid.*, p. 353.

[15] *Ibid.*, pp. 172-174.

CATHERINE OF GENOA

[1] For further information, see Friedrich von Hügel, *The Mystical Element of Religion as Studied in Saint Catherine of Genoa and Her Friends* (London: J. M. Dent & Sons, 1923).

[2] Reprinted from *Catherine of Genoa: Purgation and Purgatory, The Spiritual Dialogue,* trans. Serge Hughes (Mahwah, N.J.: Paulist Press, 1979), pp. 109-110, 118-120, 122-123.

[3] *Ibid.*, pp. 77-81 and 86.

FRANCISCO DE OSUNA

[1] *Francisco de Osuna—The Third Spiritual Alphabet,* trans. and intro. Mary E. Giles (Mahwah, N.J.: Paulist Press, 1981), p. 45.

[2] *Third Spiritual Alphabet,* p. 40.

[3] For further information, see Mary E. Giles' introduction to *Francisco de Osuna—The Third Spiritual Alphabet,* pp. 1-34.

[4] Reprinted from *Francisco de Osuna—Third Spiritual Alphabet,* pp. 494-496 & 512-513.

[5] *Ibid.*, pp. 463-466.

[6] *Ibid.*, pp. 338, 343, 345-346, 349-350.

[7] *Ibid.*, pp. 387-388.

[8] *Ibid.*, pp. 475-480.

[9] *Ibid.*, pp. 480-481.

[10] *Ibid.*, pp. 484-487.

[11] This paragraph is from *ibid.*, p. 566.

[12] *Ibid.*, pp. 559-562.

IGNATIUS OF LOYOLA

[1] For further information, see Harvey D. Egan, S.J., *Ignatius Loyola the Mystic* (Wilmington, Del.: Michael Glazier, 1987).

[2] Reprinted from *A Pilgrim's Journey: The Autobiography of Ignatius of Loyola,* intro., trans., and commentary by Joseph N. Tylenda, S.J. (Wilmington, Del.: Michael Glazier, 1985), pp. 14- 16, 35-39.

[3] Reprinted from *Iñigo: Discernment Log-Book—The Spiritual Diary of Saint Ignatius of*

Loyola, ed. and trans. Joseph A. Munitiz, S.J. (London: Iñigo Enterprises, 1987), pp. 29-30, 35-41, 43-44, 47, 52, 56-57. The marginal numbers are correct. Ignatius wrote 25 instead of 35, hence the seeming disorder.

[4]Reprinted from *Letters of St. Ignatius of Loyola*, selected and trans. by William J. Young, S.J. (Chicago: Loyola University Press, 1959), pp. 18-24.

TERESA OF AVILA

[1]*The Interior Castle*, in *The Collected Works of St. Teresa of Avila*, II, trans. Kieran Kavanaugh, O.C.D. and Otilio Rodriguez, O.C.D. (Washington, D.C.: Institute of Carmelite Studies, 1980), p. 284.

[2]*The Book of Her Life*, in *The Collected Works of St. Teresa of Avila*, I, trans. Kieran Kavanaugh, O.C.D. and Otilio Rodriguez, O.C.D. (Washington, D.C.: Institute of Carmelite Studies, 1976), p. 67.

[3]*The Book of Her Life*, p. 144.

[4]*The Book of Her Life*, p. 177.

[5]*The Way of Perfection*, Collected Works II, p. 40.

[6]For further information, see: Mary Luti, *The Way of Teresa of Avila* (Collegeville, Minn.: The Liturgical Press, 1991).

[7]Reprinted from *The Collected Works of St. Teresa of Avila*, II, pp. 341-346.

[8]*Ibid.*, pp. 429-435.

JOHN OF THE CROSS

[1]*The Living Flame of Love*, in *The Collected Works of St. John of the Cross*, trans. Kieran Kavanaugh, O.C.D. and Otilio Rodriguez, O.C.D. (Washington, D.C.: Institute of Carmelite Studies, 1976), p. 578.

[2]*Ibid.*

[3]*The Ascent of Mount Carmel*, in *Collected Works*, pp. 103-104.

[4]*The Ascent of Mount Carmel*, p. 69.

[5]*Spiritual Canticle*, in *Collected Works*, p. 408.

[6]For further information, see Kieran Kavanaugh's introduction to *The Collected Works*, pp. 15-37.

[7]Reprinted from *The Collected Works of St. John of the Cross*, pp. 311-318 and 335-350.

[8]*Ibid.*, pp. 578-579.

FRANCIS DE SALES

[1]*Francis de Sales, Treatise on the Love of God*, trans. John K. Ryan (Rockford, Ill.: Tan Books, 1975), Vol. I, p. 40.

[2]*Ibid.*, p. 43.

[3]*Ibid.*, p. 272.

[4]*Ibid.*, pp. 273-274.

[5]*Ibid.*, p. 275.

[6]*Ibid.*

[7]*Ibid.*, p. 276.

[8]*Ibid.*, p.299.

[9]For further information, see E. M. Lajeunie, *Saint Francis de Sales, The Man, The Thinker, His Influence*, 2 vols., trans. Rory O'Sullivan, O.S.F.S. (Bangalore, India: S.F.S. Publications, 1986-1987). Also see Wendy M. Wright and Joseph F. Power, O.S.F.S.'s introduction to *Francis de Sales, Jane de Chantal—Letters of Spiritual Direction*, trans. Péronne Marie Thibert, V.H.M., sel. and intro. Wendy M. Wright and Joseph F. Power, O.S.F.S. (Mahwah, N.J.: Paulist Press, 1988), pp. 9-90.

[10]Reprinted from *Francis de Sales, Treatise on the Love of God*, Vol. II, pp. 13-18.

[11]The above *paragraph* is taken from *ibid.*, p. 292.

[12]The above *two paragraphs* are taken from *ibid.*, pp. 286-287, 293-294.

[13]*Ibid.*, pp. 21-25.

[14]*Ibid.*, pp. 25-26.

[15]*Ibid.*, pp. 27-29.

[16]*Ibid.*, pp. 29-31.

[17]*Ibid.*, p. 33.

[18]*Ibid.*, p. 37.

BLAISE PASCAL

[1]For further information, see Francis X. J. Coleman, *Neither Angel Nor Beast: The Life and Work of Blaise Pascal* (New York: Routledge & Kegan Paul, 1986).

[2]Reprinted from *The Essential Pascal*, sel. and ed. Robert W. Gleason, S.J., and trans. G. F. Pullen (New York: New American Library, 1966), pp. 205-206.

[3]Reprinted from *Blaise Pascal—Pensées*, trans. A.J. Krailsheimer (New York: Penguin Classics, 1966), pp. 312-316.

[4]Reprinted from *The Essential Pascal*, 195, 200-201, and 107.

[5]*Ibid.*, pp. 69 and 53-66.

MARIE OF THE INCARNATION

[1]*Marie of the Incarnation—Selected Writings*, ed. Irene Mahoney, O.S.U. (Mahwah, N.J.: Paulist Press, 1989), p. 150.

[2]*Marie of the Incarnation—Selected Writings*, p. 130.

[3]For further information, see Irene Mahoney, O.S.U.'s introduction to *Marie of the Incarnation—Selected Writings*, pp. 5-40. Also see, Fernand Jetté, *The Spiritual Teaching of Mary of the Incarnation* (New York: Sheed & Ward, 1963).

[4]Reprinted from *Marie of the Incarnation—Selected Writings*, ed. Irene Mahoney, O.S.U. (Mahwah, N.J.: Paulist Press, 1989), pp. 81-83.

[5]*Ibid.*, pp. 99-100.

[6]*Ibid.*, pp. 103 and 105.

[7]*Ibid.*, pp. 112-114.

[8]*Ibid.*, p. 115.

[9]*Ibid.*, p. 116.

[10]*Ibid.*, pp. 142-143.

[11]*Ibid.*, pp. 169-170.

ANGELUS SILESIUS

[1]For further information, see Josef Schmidt's introduction to *Angelus Silesius—The Cherubinic Wanderer.* trans. and foreword by Maria Shrady, intro. and notes by Josef Schmidt (Mahwah, N.J.: Paulist Press, 1986), pp. 3-33.

[2]Reprinted from *Angelus Silesius—The Cherubinic Wanderer,* Chapter,. epigram, and page numbers given in parentheses.

THÉRÈSE OF LISIEUX

[1]*Story of a Soul: The Autobiography of St. Thérèse of Lisieux*, trans. John Clark, O.C.D. (Washington, D.C.: Institute of Carmelite Studies, 1976), p. 210, my emphases.

[2]*Saint Thérèse of Lisieux: General Correspondence I*, trans. John Clarke, O.C.D. (Washington, D.C.: Institute of Carmelite Studies, 1973), LT 85, p. 546. In her letter to her sister Céline (LT 65, p. 467), she writes: "What a grace when, in the morning, we feel no courage, no strength to practice virtue; that is the moment to put the axe to the root of the tree. . . in one act of love, even unfelt love, all is repaired. . . ."

[3]*St. Thérèse of Lisieux: Her Last Conversations*, trans. John Clarke, O.C.D. (Washington, D.C.: Institute of Carmelite Studies, 1977), p. 217.

[4]*Story of a Soul*, p. 72.

[5]*Ibid.*

[6]*Novissima Verba: The Last Conversations of St. Thérèse of the Child Jesus, May—September, 1897* (New York: P.J. Kenedy and Sons, 1929), p. 44.

[7]*Her Last Conversations*, p. 77.

[8]*Ibid.*, p. 135.

[9]*Ibid.*, p. 205.

[10]For further information, see: Guy Gaucher, *The Story of a Life: St. Thérèse of Lisieux*, trans. Sister Anee Marie Brennan, O.C.D. (San Francisco: Harper and Row, 1987).

[11]Reprinted from *Story of a Soul: The Autobiography of St. Thérèse of Lisieux*, pp. 192-200 and 276-277.

GEMMA GALGANI

[1]For further information, see Benedict Williamson, *Gemma of Lucca* (St. Louis: B. Herder, 1932).

[2]Reprinted from *The Life of the Servant of God Gemma Galgani: An Italian Maiden of Lucca*, by Father Germanicus, CP, trans. A. M. O'Sullivan, O.S.B. (St. Louis: B. Herder, 1913), p. 187.

[3]*Ibid.*, p. 189.

[4]*Ibid.*, pp. 301-305.

[5]*Ibid.*, pp. 240-242.

[6]*Ibid.*, pp. 244-245.

[7]*Ibid.*, pp. 282-283, 287, 289, and 290.

[8]*Ibid.*, pp. 58-60.

[9]*Ibid.*, pp. 64-65.

[10]*Ibid.*, p. 71.

[11]*Ibid.*, pp. 67-68.

[12]*Ibid.*, pp. 97-99.

[13]*Ibid.*, p. 187.

[14]*Ibid.*, pp. 224-225.

[15]*Ibid.*, p. 227.

[16]*Ibid.*

[17]*Ibid.*, pp. 208, 213, 216.

[18]*Ibid.*, pp. 197, 198, 199, 203-204, 205 and 206.

ELIZABETH OF THE TRINITY

[1]From her letter of August 2, 1902 (L 131), quoted by Conrad de Meester, O.C.D., *Light Love Life: A Look at a Face and A Heart*, trans. Sr. Aletheia Kane, O.C.D. (Washington, D.C.: Institute of Carmelite Studies, 1987), p. 88.

[2]From her letter of October 28, 1906 (L 335), quoted by Conrad de Meester, O.C.D., *Light Love Life: A Look at a Face and A Heart*, p. 140.

[3]For further information, see Hans Urs von Balthasar, *Elizabeth of Dijon. An Interpretation of Her Spiritual Mission*, trans. and adapted by A. V. Littledale (New York: Pan-

theon, 1956).

[4] Reprinted from the French, poem 93, trans. Sr. Mary Magdalen, O.C.D., Darlington Carmelite Convent, Durham, England.

[5] Reprinted from the French, letter 177, trans. Sr. Mary Magdalen, O.C.D.

[6] Reprinted from Conrad de Meester, O.C.D., *Light Love Life: A Look at a Face and A Heart*, L 169, pp. 94, 97, 101.

[7] Reprinted from *Elizabeth of the Trinity. Complete Works*, vol. II, ed. Conrad de Meester, O.C.D., trans. Sister Elizabeth, O.C.D. (Washington, D.C.: Institute of Carmelite Studies, 1990), L 309.

[8] *Ibid.*, L 314.

[9] *Ibid.*, L 314.

[10] *Ibid.*, L 158.

[11] Reprinted from the French, letter 294, trans. Sr. Mary Magdalen, O.C.D.

[12] *Ibid.*

[13] *Light Love Face*, PN 13.

[14] Reprinted from *Elizabeth of the Trinity. Complete Works*, vol. I, ed. Conrad de Meester, O.C.D., trans. Sister Aletheia Kane, O.C.D. (Washington, D.C.: Institute of Carmelite Studies, 1984), pp. 183-184.

M. FAUSTINA KOWALSKA

[1] Stockbridge, Mass.: Marian Press, 1987.

[2] For further information, see Sr. Sophia Michalenko, *Mercy My Mission: The Life of Sister M. Faustina Kowalska* (Stockbridge, Mass.: Marian Press, 1987).

[3] Reprinted from *Divine Mercy in my Soul: The Diary of the Servant of God Sister M. Faustina Kowalska, Perpetually Professed Member of the Congregation of Sisters of Our Lady of Mercy*, pp. 24-25, 74-76, 86-87, 185, 193-195, 207-208, 307-310, 353, 417, 470, 600- 601, 627-629.

PIERRE TEILHARD DE CHARDIN

[1] Pierre Teilhard de Chardin, *Science and Christ*, trans. René Hague (San Francisco: Harper & Row, 1968), pp. 24-27.

[2] Pierre Teilhard de Chardin, *Christianity and Evolution*, trans. René Hague (New York: Harcourt Brace Jovanovich, 1971), p. 234.

[3] Pierre Teilhard de Chardin, *Toward the Future*, trans. René Hague (New York: Harcourt Brace Jovanovich, 1975), p. 16.

[4]Pierre Teilhard de Chardin, *The Phenomenon of Man*, trans. Bernard Wall (San Francisco: Harper & Row, 1959), pp. 284-285.

[5]Pierre Teilhard de Chardin, *Letters from a Traveler*, trans. unidentified (San Francisco: Harper & Row, 1962), p. 86.

[6]Pierre Teilhard de Chardin, *How I Believe*, trans. René Hague (San Francisco: Harper & Row, 1969), p. 3.

[7]For further information, see Ursula King, *Towards a New Mysticism: Teilhard de Chardin and Eastern Religions* (New York: Seabury, 1980).

[8]Reprinted from "The Mystical Milieu," in *Writings in Time of War*, by Pierre Teilhard de Chardin,trans. René Hague (San Francisco: Harper & Row, 1968), pp. 117-121, 123-125, 127-134, 136-139, 142-148.

THOMAS MERTON

[1]Raymond Bailey, *Thomas Merton on Mysticism*, (Garden City, N.Y.: Doubleday, 1975), p. 12.

[2]*The Asian Journal of Thomas Merton*, eds. Naomi Burton, Brother Patrick Hart, and James Laughlin (New York: New Directions, 1973), pp. 332-333.

[3]For further information, see Michael Mott, *The Seven Mountains of Thomas Merton* (Boston: Houghton Mifflin, 1984) and Elena Malits, *The Solitary Explorer* (San Francisco: Harper & Row, 1980).

[4]Reprinted from Thomas Merton, *The Climate of Monastic Prayer* (Spencer, Mass. & Kalamazoo, Mich.: Cistercian Publications, 1969), pp. 121-123. The last paragraph is from, Thomas Merton, "First Christmas at Gethsemani," Catholic World (December 1979), p. 30.

[5]Reprinted from Thomas Merton, *Contemplation in a World of Action* (Garden City, N.Y.: Doubleday, 1973), pp. 172, 178-179.

[6]Reprinted from "The Inner Experience: Kinds of Contemplation (IV)," *Cistercian Studies* XVIII,4 (1983), pp. 294-297.

[7]Reprinted from Thomas Merton, *New Seeds of Contemplation* (New York, N.Y.: New Directions, 1962), pp. 268-271.

HENRY LE SAUX

[1]Abhishiktananda, *The Secret of Arunachala: A Christian Hermit on Shiva's Holy Mountain* (Delhi: I.S.P.C.K., 1979).

[2]Abhishiktananda, *Saccidananda: A Christian Approach to Advaitic Experience* (Dehli: I.S.P.C.K., 1984 [revised]), p. 172.

[3]See Abhishiktananda, "A Sage from the East," in *Guru and Disciple* (London: SPCK, 1974), pp. 5-131.

[4]For an excellent account of this pilgrimage, see le Saux's "The Mountain of the

Lord," in *Guru and Disciple,* pp. 135-174.

[5]Henri le Saux, *The Eyes of Light* (Denville, N.J.: Dimension, 1983), p. 24.

[6]*Saccidananda,* p. 165.

[7]*Ibid.,* p. 45.

[8]*Ibid.,* p. 171.

[9]*The Eyes of Light,* p. 32.

[10]*Ibid.,* p. 118. For further information, see Emmanuel Vattakuzhy, *Indian Christian Sannyasa and Swami Abhishiktananda* (Bangalore: Theological Publications in India, 1981); *Swami Abhishiktananda: The Man and His Teaching, ed.* Vandana (Delhi: I.S.P.C.K., 1986).

[11]Reprinted from *Saccidananda: A Christian Approach to Advaitic Experience,* pp. 174-181.

KARL RAHNER

[1]"Teresa of Avila: Doctor of the Church," in Karl Rahner, *Opportunities for Faith,* trans. Edward Quinn (New York: Seabury, 1970), p. 125.

[2]Karl Rahner, *Visions and Prophecies,* trans. Charles Henkey and Richard Strachan (New York: Herder & Herder, 1964), p. 14, n. 12.

[3]"Mysticism," in Karl Rahner (ed.), *Encyclopedia of Theology* (New York: Seabury, 1975), pp. 1010-1011.

[4]For further information, see Harvey D. Egan, S.J., *What Are They Saying About Mysticism?* (Mahwah, N.J.: Paulist Press, 1982), pp. 98-108 and Harvey D. Egan, S.J., "The Mysticism of Everyday Life," *Studies in Formative Spirituality* X,1 (February 1989), pp. 8-26.

[5]Reprinted from "Experiencing the Spirit," in Karl Rahner, *The Practice of Faith: A Handbook of Contemporary Spirituality* (New York: Crossroad, 1983), pp. 81-84.

[6]Reprinted from "God of my Life," in Karl Rahner, *Encounters with Silence,* trans. James M. Demske, S.J. (Westminster, Md.: Newman, 1966), pp. 3-10.

ACKNOWLEDGMENTS

ABHISHIKTANANDA SOCIETY
Texts from Saccidananda: *A Christian Approach to Advaitic Experience*, (Delhi: I.S.P.C.K., 1984, rev. ed.), reprinted with permission of the Abhishiktananda Society, Delhi, India.

CASSELL PLC
Texts from *The Scale of Perfection*, by Walter Hilton, abridged and presented by Dom Illytd Trethowan, trans. Leo Sherley-Price (St. Meinrad, Ind.: Abbey Press, 1975). Copyright 1975 by Geoffrey Chapman Publishers. Reprinted by permission of Cassell PLC, Artillery House, Artillery Row, London SW1P 1RT England.

THE CATHOLIC UNIVERSITY OF AMERICA PRESS
Texts from *Origen—Spirit and Fire: A Thematic Study of His Writings*, by Hans Urs von Balthasar, trans. Robert J. Daly, S.J., Reprinted with permission of The Catholic University of America Press.

CENTER FOR MEDIEVAL AND EARLY RENAISSANCE STUDIES
Texts from *The Letters of St. Catherine of Siena* I, trans. Suzanne Noffke, O.P. (Binghamton, N.Y.: Medieval and Renaissance Texts and Studies, 1988). Copyright 1988 by the Center for Medieval and Early Renaissance Studies, Binghamton, New York, vol. 52 of Medieval & Renaissance Texts & Studies. Reprinted with permission of the Center for Medieval and Early Renaissance Studies.

CHRISTIAN CLASSICS
Texts from "God of my Life," in *Karl Rahner, Encounters with Silence*, trans. James M. Demske, S. J. (Westminster, Md.: Newman, 1966). Reprinted by permission of Christian Classics, Westminster, Maryland.

Texts from "Experiencing the Spirit," in *Karl Rahner, The Practice of Faith: A Handbook of Contemporary Spirituality* (New York: Crossroad, 1983). Reprinted by permission of The Crossroad Publishing Company.

CISTERCIAN PUBLICATIONS
Texts from *Evagrius Ponticus—The Praktikos* and *Chapters on Prayer*, trans., intro., and notes by John Eudes Bamberger, O.C.S.O. (Spencer, Mass. & Kalamazoo, Mich: Cistercian Publications, 1970). Copyright 1972 by Cistercian Publications. Reprinted by permission of Cistercian Publications, Western Michigan University Station, Kalamazoo, Michigan 49008.

Texts from *William of St. Thierry—The Golden Epistle*, trans. Theodore Berkeley, O.C.S.O. (Kalamazoo, Mich.: Cistercian Publications, Inc., 1971). Copyright 1971 by Cistercian Publications. Reprinted with permission of Cistercian Publications, Western Michigan University Station, Kalamazoo, Michigan 49008.

Texts from *Bernard of Clairvaux—On the Song of Songs*, vols. IIV, trans. Kilian Walsh, OCSO (Kalamazoo, Mich.: Cistercian Publications, 1971, 1976, 1979, 1980). Copyright 1971 (vol. I), 1976 (vol. II), 1979 (vol. III), 1980 (vol. IV) by Cistercian Publications. Reprinted by permission of Cistercian Publications, Western Michigan University Station, Kalamazoo, Michigan 49008.

Texts from *Aelred of Rievaulx—On Spiritual Friendship*, trans. Mary Eugenia Laker, S.S.N.D. (Washington, D.C. & Kalamazoo, Mich.: Cistercian Publications, 1974). Copyright 1974 by Cistercian Publications. Reprinted by permission of Cistercian Publications, Western Michigan University Station, Kalamazoo, Michigan 49008.

Texts from *Thomas Merton, The Climate of Monastic Prayer* (Spencer, Mass. & Kalamazoo: Cistercian Publications, 1969). Reprinted by permission of Cistercian Publications, Western Michigan University Station, Kalamazoo, Michigan 49008.

CISTERCIAN STUDIES
Texts from Thomas Merton, "The Inner Experience: Kinds of Contemplation (IV)," Cistercian Studies XVIII,4 (1983), pp. 294-297. Reprinted by permission of Cistercian Studies.

CONFRATERNITY OF THE PRECIOUS BLOOD
Texts from *My Imitation of Christ*, trans. Msgr. John J. Gorman (Brooklyn, N.Y.: Confraternity of the Precious Blood, 1982). Reprinted by permission of the Confraternity of the Precious Blood, 5300 Fort Hamilton Parkway, Brooklyn, New York, New York 11219.

CONGREGATION OF MARIANS
Texts from *Divine Mercy in my Soul: The Diary of the Servant of God Sister M. Faustina Kowalska, Perpetually Professed Member of the Congregation of Sisters of Our Lady of Mercy* (Stockbridge, Mass.: Marian Press, 1987). Copyright 1987 by the Congregation of Marians, Eden Hill, Stockbridge, Mass. 01263. Reprinted with permission of the Congregation of Marians.

CROSSROAD PUBLISHING
Texts from "Experiencing the Spirit," in *Karl Rahner, The Practice of Faith: A Handbook of Contemporary Spirituality* (New York: Crossroad, 1983). Reprinted by permission of The Crossroad Publishing Company.

CURTIS BROWN
Texts from Elmer O'Brien, *Varieties of Mystic Experience* (New York: New American Library, 1965). Copyright 1964 by Elmer O'Brien. Reprinted by permission of Curtis Brown, Ltd., 10 Astor lace, New York, New York 10003.

DIMENSION BOOKS
Texts from *Hymns of Divine Love by Symeon the New Theologian*, trans. and intro. George A. Maloney, S.J. (Denville, N.J.: Dimension Books, 1976). Reprinted by permission of Dimension Books, Inc., Denville, N.J. 07834.

DOUBLEDAY
Texts from *Guigo II: The Ladder of Monks. A Letter on the Contemplative Life and Twelve Meditations*, trans. and intro. Edmund College, O.S.A. and James Walsh, S.J. (Kalamazoo, Mich.: Cistercian Publications, 1981). Translation copyright 1978 by Edmund College and James Walsh. Used by permission of Doubleday, a division of Bantam, Doubleday, Dell Publishing Group, Inc.

Texts from *The Little Flowers of St. Francis*, trans. Raphael Brown (Garden City, N.Y.: Doubleday, 1958). Translation copyright 1958 by Beverly Brown. Reprinted by permission of Doubleday, a division of Bantam, Doubleday, Dell Publishing Group, Inc.

Texts from *Richard Rolle: The Fire of Love and The Mending of Life*, trans. and intro. M. L. del Mastro (Garden City, N.Y.: Doubleday, 1981). Translation copyright 1981 by M.

L. del Mastro. Reprinted by permission of Doubleday, a division of Bantam, Doubleday, Dell Publishing Group, Inc.

Texts from *The Cloud of Unknowing* and the *Book of Privy Counselling*, ed. William Johnston, S.J. (Garden City, N.Y.: Doubleday, 1973). Copyright 1973 by William Johnston. Reprinted by permission of Doubleday, a division of Bantam, Doubleday, Dell Publishing Group, Inc.

Texts from *Thomas Merton, Contemplation in a World of Action* (Garden City, N.Y.: Doubleday, 1973). Copyright 1965, 1969, 1970, 1971 by the Trustees of the Merton Legacy Trust. Reprinted by permission of Doubleday, a division of Bantam, Doubleday, Dell Publishing Group, Inc.

DITIONS BERNARD GRASSET
Texts from "The Mystical Milieu," in *Writings in Time of War*, by Pierre Teilhard de Chardin, trans. Ren Hague (San Francisco: Harper & Row, 1968). Copyright 1965 by ditions Bernard Grasset. Reprinted by permission of Éditions Bernard Grasset, 61 rue des Saint-Prés, 75006 Paris.

FABER AND FABER LTD.
Texts from *Richard of Saint Victor: Selected Writings on Contemplation*, trans. with an intro. and notes by Clare Kirchberger (New York: Harper & Brothers, 1957). Reprinted by permission of Faber and Faber Ltd.

Texts from *Little Book of Eternal Wisdom* and *Little Book of Truth*, trans. James M. Clark (London: Faber & Faber, 1953). Reprinted by permission of Faber & Faber Ltd.

MICHAEL GLAZIER, INC.
Texts from *A Pilgrim's Journey: The Autobiography of Ignatius of Loyola*, intro., trans., and commentary by Joseph N. Tylenda, S.J. (Wilmington, Del.: Michael Glazier, 1985). Reprinted by permission of Michael Glazier, Inc., 1935 West Fourth St., Wilmington, Delaware 19805.

GORDON PRESS
Dom Cuthbert Butler, *Western Mysticism* (New York: Gordon Press, 1975, 3rd ed.). Copyright 1922 by Dom Cuthbert Butler. Reprinted by permission of Gordon Press, P.O. Box 459, Bowling Green Station, New York, New York 10004.

HARPER AND ROW
Texts from *Actus Beati Francisci et Sociorum Ejus*, quoted by *Martin Buber, Ecstatic Confessions*, ed. Paul Mendes-Flohr and trans. Esther Cameron (San Francisco: Harper and Row, 1985). Copyright 1985 by Harper & Row, Publishers, Inc. Reprinted by permission of the publisher.

Texts from *Meister Eckhart: A Modern Translation*, trans. Raymond B. Blakney (New York: Harper & Row, 1941). Copyrighted 1941 by Harper & Row, Publishers, Inc. Reprinted by permission of the publisher.

HOLY TRANSFIGURATION MONASTERY
Texts from *The Ascetical Homilies of Saint Isaac the Syrian*, trans. by The Holy Transfiguration Monastery (Brookline, Mass.: Holy Transfiguration Monastery, 1984). Copyrighted 1984 by The Holy Transfiguration Monastery. Reprinted by permission of The Holy Transfiguration Monastery, 278 Warren Street, Brookline, Mass. 02146.

INIGO ENTERPRISES

Texts from *Inigo: Discernment Log-Book—The Spiritual Diary of Saint Ignatius of Loyola,* ed. and trans. Joseph A. Munitiz, S.J. (London: Inigo Enterprises, 1987). Copyright 1988 by William Hewett. Reprinted by permission of Inigo Enterprises, 120 West Heath Road, London NW3 7TY.

INSTITUTE OF CARMELITE STUDIES

Texts from *The Collected Works of St. Teresa of Avila,* II, trans. Kieran Kavanaugh, O.C.D. and Otilio Rodriguez, O.C.D. (Washington, D.C.: Institute of Carmelite Studies, 1980). Copyright 1980 by the Washington Province of Discalced Carmelites. Reprinted by permission of ICS Publications, 2131 Lincoln Road, N.E., Washington, D.C. 20002.

Texts from *The Collected Works of St. John of the Cross,* trans. Kieran Kavanaugh, O.C.D. and Otilio Rodriguez, O.C.D. (Washington, D.C.: Institute of Carmelite Studies, 1976). Copyright 1979 by the Washington Province of Discalced Carmelites. Reprinted by permission of ICS Publications, 2131 Lincoln Road, N.E., Washington, D.C. 20002 U.S.A.

Texts from *Story of a Soul: The Autobiography of St. Thérèse of Lisieux,* trans. John Clark, O.C.D. (Washington, D.C.: Institute of Carmelite Studies, 1976). Copyright 1976 by the Washington Province of Discalced Carmelites. Reprinted by permission of ICS Publications, 2131 Lincoln Road, N.E., Washington, D.C. 20002.

Texts from Conrad de Meester, O.C.D., *Light Love Life: A Look at a Face and A Heart,* trans. Sr. Aletheia Kane, O.C.D. (Washington, D.C.: Institute of Carmelite Studies, 1987). Copyright 1987 by the Washington Province of Discalced Carmelites. Reprinted by permission of ICS Publications, 2131 Lincoln Road, N.E., Washington, D.C. 20002.

Texts from *Elizabeth of the Trinity. Complete Works,* vol. I, ed. Conrad de Meester, O.C.D., trans. Sister Aletheia Kane, O.C.D. (Washington, D.C.: Institute of Carmelite Studies, 1984). Copyright 1984 by the Washington Province of Discalced Carmelites. Reprinted by permission of ICS Publications, 2131 Lincoln Road, N.E., Washington, D.C. 20002.

Texts from *Elizabeth of the Trinity. Complete Works,* vol. II, ed. Conrad de Meester, O.C.D., trans. Sister Elizabeth, O.C.D. (Washington, D.C.: Institute of Carmelite Studies, 1990). Copyright 1990 by the Washington Province of Discalced Carmelites, Inc. Reprinted by permission of ICS Publications, 2131 Lincoln Road, N.E., Washington, D.C. 20002.

IONA COMMUNITY

Texts from *The Revelations of Mechtild of Magdeburg: The Flowing Light of the Godhead,* trans. Lucy Menzies (London: Longmans, Green and Co., 1953). Copyright 1953 Iona Community/Wild Goose Publications. Reprinted by permission of Iona Community/Wild Goose Publications, Pearce Institute, Govan, Glasgow G51 3UT, Scotland.

LOYOLA UNIVERSITY PRESS

Texts from *Letters of St. Ignatius of Loyola,* selected and trans. by William J. Young, S.J. (Chicago: Loyola University Press, 1959). Copyright 1959 by Loyola University Press. Reprinted by permission of the publisher.

Apostle in the State of New York. Reprinted by permission of Paulist Press.

Texts from *Meister Eckhart—The Essential Sermons,* Commentaries, Treatises, and Defense, trans. and intro. Edmund College, O.S.A. and Bernard McGinn (Mahwah, N.J.: Paulist Press, 1981). Copyright 1981 by The Missionary Society of St. Paul the Apostle in the State of New York. Reprinted by permission of Paulist Press.

Texts from *Meister Eckhart—Teacher and Preacher,* ed. Bernard McGinn with the collaboration of Frank Tobin and Elvira Borgstdt (Mahwah, N.J.: Paulist Press, 1986). Copyright 1986 by Bernard McGinn. Reprinted by permission of Paulist Press.

Texts from *Richard Rolle—The English Writings,* trans., ed., and intro. Rosamund Allen (Mahwah, N.J.: Paulist Press, 1988). Copyright 1988 by Rosamund S. Allen. Reprinted with permission of Paulist Press.

Texts from *Gregory Palamas—The Triads,* trans. Nicholas Gendle, ed. and intro. John Meyendorff (Mahwah, N.J.: Paulist Press, 1983). Copyright 1983 by The Missionary Society of St. Paul the Apostle in the State of New York. Reprinted by permission of Paulist Press.

Texts from *Johannes Tauler: Sermons,* trans. Maria Shrady (Mahwah, N.J.: Paulist Press, 1985). Copyright 1985 by Maria Shrady. Reprinted by permission of Paulist Press.

Texts from *John Ruusbroec—The Spiritual Espousals and Other Works,* trans. and intro. James A. Wiseman, O.S.B. (Mahwah, N.J.: Paulist Press, 1985). Copyright 1985 by James B. Wiseman, O.S.B.. Reprinted by permission of Paulist Press.

Texts from *Catherine of Siena—The Dialogue,* trans. Suzanne Noffke, O.P. (Mahwah, N.J.: Paulist Press, 1980). Copyright 1980 by The Missionary Society of St. Paul the Apostle in the State of New York. Reprinted by permission of Paulist Press.

Texts from *The Assessment of Inward Stirrings,* in *The Pursuit of Wisdom and Other Works,* By The Author Of the Cloud of Unknowing, trans., ed., and annotated James A. Walsh, S.J. (Mahwah, N.J.: Paulist Press, 1988). Copyright 1988 by The British Province of the Society of Jesus. Reprinted by permission of Paulist Press.

Texts from *Julian of Norwich—Showings,* trans. and intro. Edmund Walsh, O.S.A. and James Walsh, S.J. (Mahwah, N.J.: Paulist Press, 1978). Copyright 1978 by The Missionary Society of St. Paul the Apostle in the State of New York. Reprinted by permission of Paulist Press.

Texts from *Catherine of Genoa: Purgation and Purgatory, The Spiritual Dialogue,* trans. Serge Hughes (Mahwah, N.J.: Paulist Press, 1979). Copyright 1979 by The Missionary Society of St. Paul the Apostle in the State of New York. Reprinted by permission of Paulist Press.

Texts from *Francisco de Osuna—Third Spiritual Alphabet,* trans. Mary E. Giles (Mahwah, N.J.: Paulist Press , 1981). Copyright 1981 by The Missionary Society of St. Paul the Apostle in the State of New York. Reprinted by permission of Paulist Press.

Texts from *Marie of the Incarnation—Selected Writings,* ed. Irene Mahoney, O.S.U. (Mahwah, N.J.: Paulist Press, 1989). Copyright 1989 by The Ursuline Community of St. Teresa. Reprinted by permission of Paulist Press.

Texts from *Angelus Silesius—The Cherubinic Wanderer*, trans. Maria Shrady (Mahwah, N.J.: Paulist Press, 1986). Copyright 1986 by Maria Shrady. Reprinted by permission of Paulist Press.

PENGUIN BOOKS
Texts from *Blaise Pascal—Pensées*, trans. A.J. Krailsheimer (New York: Penguin Classics, 1966). Copyright A. J. Krailsheimer, 1966. Reprinted by permission of Penguin Books Ltd.

PRIORY PRESS
Texts from Henry Suso's Life, in *The Exemplar—Life and Writings of Blessed Henry Suso*, O.P., vols 1 & 2, critical intro. and explanatory notes by Nicholas Heller, trans. Sister M. Ann Edward, O.P. (Dubuque, Iowa: Priory Press, 1962). Copyright 1962 by Dominican Province of St. Albert the Great, 7200 West Division Street, River Forest, Illinois 60305. Reprinted by permission of the Dominican Province of St. Albert the Great.

CHARLES SCRIBNER'S SONS
Texts from *From Glory to Glory: Texts from Gregory of Nyssa's Mystical Writings*, ed. and intro. Jean Daniélou, S.J., trans. and ed. Herbert Musurillo, S.J. (New York: Charles Scribner's Sons, 1961). Copyright 1961 by Charles Scribner's Sons. Reprinted with permission of Charles Scribner's Sons, an imprint of Macmillan Publishing Company.

SPCK
Texts from *Ramon Lull, The Book of the Lover and Beloved*, ed. Kenneth Leech, trans. E. Allison Peers. Copyright 1978 by SPCK. Reprinted by permission of SPCK, London.

TAN BOOKS
Texts from *Francis de Sales, Treatise on the Love of God*, trans. John K. Ryan (Rockford, Ill.: Tan Books, 1975). Reprinted with permission of TAN Books and Publishers, Inc., P.O. Box 424, Rockford, Illinois 61105.

A

B

Baptism, 19, 20, 57
  in the Spirit, 82, 147

Barlaam, 312

Barth, Karl, xxiii

Basil the Elder, St., 31, 44, 92

Basil the Great, St., 31, 80, 92

Bègue, Lambert le, 225

Beguines, 225-226, 247

Benedict XI, Pope, 265

Benedict, St., 70, 106
  Rule of, 167

Benjamin Major (Richard of St. Victor), 187, 188, 365

Benjamin Minor (Richard of St. Victor), 187, 188, 365

Bernard of Clairvaux, 153, 154, 166-170, 365

Bernard of the North. *See* Aelred of Rievaulx

Black Death, 386

Blanquerna (Lull), 285

Bliss, state of (*ananda*), 590

Bloemardinne, 343

Blood mysticism, 357

Blood, tears of, 521

Boehme, Jacob, 500

Bonaventure, 221, 234-238

Boniface VIII, Pope, 264-265, 266

Book of Divine Consolation (Angela of Foligno), 278

Council of Constantinople, 18, 32, 41, 47

Council of Sens, 168

Counterculture, American, 574

Counter-Reformation, 423, 464, 466

D

Dame Poverty, 264, 266

Dance, mystical, 249, 250

Dante, 186, 264

Darkness
   cloud of knowing, 367
   divine, 94
   glowing, 377
   superluminous, 235
   without God, 481

Dark night of the soul, xvi, 490, 511, 523

Dark night of the spirit, 453, 546

Death, 536-537
   mysticism xvi, 353, 536-537
   sickness unto, 384
   temporary, 59

Decius, Emperor, 18

Deeds of St. Francis and his Companions, 217

Defense (Eckhart), 292

Dejamiento, 412, 413

Demetrius of Alexandria, 17-18

Demons, 45, 46, 125

De Operatione Dei (Hildegard), 198

Desert Fathers, 44, 45, 72, 92, 115-116, 125, 585

Devil, 46, 81, 82, 424, 524

satanic attacks, 521, 522, 523, 546

Exposition of the Gospels (Hildegard), 198

F

Faith, and love, 157

Fecundity, spiritual, 170, 437

Ferdinand of Aragon, 411

Fifty Homilies (Pseudo-Macarius), 80

Fire
   God as, 190, 481
   inner, 304, 305
   prayer of, 71
   tears of, 356

Fire of Love (Rolle), 303, 304

Flowing Light of the Godhead, The (Mechtild of Magdeburg), 247

Fool of Love (Lull), 285

Four Hundred Chapters on Love (Maximus Confessor), 125

Francis of Assisi, 215-217, 235, 236, 266, 274
   prayer of, 220

Franciscans
   Conventuals, 235, 265
   Dominican controversy, 293
   mysticism, 235, 264, 274-275, 277, 293, 413, 501-502
   Spirituals, 235, 264, 277
   Third Order, 274-275, 284

Francisco de Osuna, 411-414

Franckenberg, Abraham von, 500

Frankl, Viktor, 115

Friends of God, 321-322, 334

Friendship
   love of friends, 182
   mystical, 221-222

spiritual, 181-182

Future of Man (Teilhard de Chardin), 558

G

Gaetani, Cardinal Benedetto, 264

Galgani, Gemma, 521-526

Germaine of Jesus, Mother, 535

German romanticism, 405

German visionary mystics, 321, 322

Gertrude the Great, 249, 257-259

Giannini, Cecilia, 522

Giles of Assisi, 217, 221-222

Gilson, Etienne, 234

Gluttony, 45, 115

Gnanananda, Sri, 587

Goad of Love (Hilton), 376

God
    abandonment to will of, 412, 413, 467
    abyss, 332, 333
    ascent to, 45, 58, 72, 92, 95, 107, 125, 136, 167, 208, 305, 323, 356
        "breakthrough," 332
    as burning fire, 190, 481
    communion with, 546
    Darkness, 94
    of evolution, 557, 558, 559
    feminine side of, 387
    as friendship, 182
    grace of, 156
    image of, 588-589
    immanence, 94
    as ineffable, 501
    as interior, 59

Greed, spiritual, 440

Gregory X, Pope, 235

Gregory XI, Pope, 354

Gregory XV, Pope, 423

Gregory the Great, 105-108

Gregory of Nazianzus, 144

Gregory of Nyssa, 31-34, 80, 92

Griffiths, Dom Bede, 587

Groote, Geert de, 396

Guérin, Zélie, 509

Guigo II, 207-208

Guyart, Marie. *See* Marie of the Incarnation

H

Hadewijch of Antwerp, 225-229

Hagioritic Tome, 312

Harnack, Adolf von, xxiii

Hazelnut vision, 386

Heart
   care of, 589
   has its reasons, 481
   mystical, 258, 356
   prayer of, 311
   purity of, 72
   seat of thoughts, 81
   seeking God in, 354

Heart of Matter (Teilhard de Chardin), 558

Heiler, Friedrich, xxiii

Helfta mystics, 257, 258, 259

experience of Sonship, 6
Father-centered mysticism, 5-6
humanity, 47-48, 249, 285-286, 438-439, 440, 441, 600
indwelling mysticism and, 59
as light and love, 13, 377
madness of love, 265
marital union with, 198, 259
mystical, 236-237, 285-286, 377, 398, 481
new commandment, 12-13
Passion, 384, 406, 481
prayer, 118, 310, 311
resurrection of, 14
sacred heart of, 258
trinitarian consciousness, 5, 7-8, 12
viewed from within and without, 333
wounds of, 217, 323, 523, 545

Lull, Ramon, 284-286, 413

M

Madelaine de la Peltrie, 489

Maharishi, Sri Ramama, 586

Making of Man (Teilhard de Chardin), 558

Mandela, Nelson, 115

Manichaeism, 56-57

Marabotta, Cataneo, 405

Marie of the Incarnation, 488-491

Marriage
    mysticism/mystical, 169, 170, 437, 452, 490
    spiritual, 169, 170, 441

Martin I, Pope, 125

Martin, Dom Claude, 489

Martin, Joseph Claude, 488

Martin, Louis, 509

Martin, Marie Françoise Thérèse. *See* Thérèse of Lisieux

Martyrdom
    bloodless, 32, 44
    of love, 217, 512, 513
    secret, 19-20
    wedding, 357
    white, 44

Marxist ideology, 574

Mary (Virgin Mary), 523, 536

Masked contemplation, 577

Masseo, Brother, 217

Master of the Sacred Page, 19

as God's fiery love, 404, 406

Rolle, Richard, 303-306

Ruoppolo, Fr. Germano San Stanislao, 522

Ruusbroec, John 228, 294, 342-345

S

Saccidananda: A Christian Approach to Advaitic Experience (Henri le Saux), 589

Sacramental mysticism, 356

Sacred Heart of Jesus, 523

Sales, Francis de, 222, 464-467

Sannyasi, 586, 587, 588

Satan, 46, 81, 82, 424, 524
  Satanic assaults, 521, 522, 523, 546

Scale of Perfection (Hilton), 376

Scheffler, Johannes. *See* Angelus Silesius

Schism, Great, 354, 386

Scholasticism, 167, 186, 293

Science and Christ (Teilhard de Chardin), 558

Scivias (Hildegard), 199

Scripture, xviii-xix, 1-2, 18, 21, 166, 209, 490-491

Secondary pheonomena
  mysticism/mystical, 521-522
  as God's self-communication, 524-525
  illuminations, 523
  locutions, 522, 545
  pathology of, 525
  role in mystical life, 524, 525-526
  satanic assaults, 522, 523, 546
  stigmata, 216, 217, 267, 353, 521, 523
  wounds of Christ, 523
  See also Visions

Spiritual marriage, 169, 170, 441

Spiritual person, 156

Spiritual poverty, 295, 490

Stace, Walter, xxii

Standard of the Cross (Francis de Sales), 465

Stephen of Nicomedia, Archbishop, 145

Stigmata, 216, 217, 267, 353, 521, 523

Suffering Servant mysticism, 513

Suso, Henry, 294, 321, 331-334

Sweetness, divine, 304

Symeon the New Theologian, 144-147

Symeon the Studite, 144, 145

Symphonia Aermoie Coelestium Revelationum (Hildegard), 197

T

Tabor-light mysticism, 82, 118, 311, 313

Tauler, Johannes, 294, 321-324

Tears
of blood, 521
of fire, 156
mystical, 137, 147
of the soul, 118
unitive, 356

Teilhard de Chardin, Pierre, 557-561

Teresa of Avila, 48, 222, 411-413, 436-441, 450, 467

Teresa de Adhumada. *See* Teresa of Avila

Teutonic prophetess. *See* Hildegard of Bingen

"Theodidact", 145

Theodore the Studite, St., 145